lonely planet

New Zealand's South Island
(Te Waipounamu)

D0011362

Marlborough
& Nelson
(p56)

The
West
Coast
(p99)

Christchurch
& Canterbury
(p131)

Queenstown
& Wanaka
(p214)

Dunedin
& Otago
(p182)

Fiordland &
Southland
(p249)

THIS EDITION WRITTEN AND RESEARCHED BY
Charles Rawlings-Way,
Sarah Bennett, Peter Dragicevich, Lee Slater

Contents

ON THE ROAD

SKATER AT TREBLE CONE
P221

Contents

RAILWAY STATION, DUNEDIN P192

MICHAEL RUNKEL / ROBERTHARDING / GETTY IMAGES ©

Welcome to the South Island

Welcome to one of the world's ultimate outdoor playgrounds, bursting with opportunities for adventure amid diverse and inspiring landscapes.

Walk on the Wild Side

With just a million people scattered across 151,215 sq km, the South Island has a population density even lower than Tasmania in Australia. Filling the gaps are the sublime forests, mountains, lakes, beaches and fiords that have made New Zealand's 'Mainland' one of the best hiking destinations on the planet. Tackle one of the South Island's six Great Walks, such as the world-famous Heaphy, Routeburn or Milford Tracks, or choose from one of countless other options ranging from 15-minute nature trails to multiday, backcountry epics. The Department of Conservation's track and hut network makes it easy to find a way in.

Action Aplenty

Hiking (known as 'tramping' here) may be the South Island's classic adventure, but there are far racier ways to immerse yourself in its landscapes. Raft down the tumbling Buller or Rangitata Rivers, or kayak around the coves of the Marlborough Sounds, Abel Tasman National Park or Fiordland. Scare yourself silly with Queenstown's gravity-defying menu of bungy, paragliding or skydiving, or mount a mountain bike to wheel through the stunning scenery along the Alps 2 Ocean Cycle Trail. During winter, go snow crazy on the ski fields around Wanaka, Queenstown or Mt Hutt.

Food, Wine & Beer

Travellers with an appetite for great food and drink are in for a treat. A seasonal parade of produce includes luscious Nelson berries and Central Otago stone fruit, Canterbury asparagus and Southland's earthy root vegetables. Roadside kiosks sell everything from farm eggs to grandma's tomato relish; local seafood, game and other meats are easy to find, as are artisan dairy foods from cheese to ice cream. This can be washed down with some of the world's best cool-climate wines, such as Otago's superb pinot noir. Nelson's hop farms fuel exciting craft breweries from Nelson to Invercargill.

Meet the Locals

Prepare to meet the South Island's idiosyncratic wildlife: whales, fur seals, dolphins and penguins all frequent the coastal waters around Kaikoura, partnered by an armada of pelagic bird species including petrels and albatrosses. Endangered Hector's dolphins cavort in Akaroa Harbour and the Catlins, while the Otago Peninsula has penguins, royal albatrosses and sea lions. Further south, remote and wild Stewart Island boasts a healthy population of NZ's iconic but shy kiwi. The kaka and the kea parrots are unmistakable, with the latter inclined to chew car aerials and unattended hiking boots.

THPSTOCK / GETTY IMAGES ©

Why I Love the South Island

By Sarah Bennett, Writer

My childhood was spent at the top of the South Island, but with most holidays featuring a sandfly-infested awning and a gold pan for fun, the beauty of my home island was somewhat lost on me. Not so now. Obsessed with all things outdoors including hiking, mountain biking and wildlife-watching, I now realise that New Zealand's South Island is a truly special place to be. Its coastline, mountain ranges, valleys and plains present endless adventure regardless of your interests or ability, enriched by unique natural history and colourful stories from both Māori and colonial times.

For more about our writers, see p352

Above: Mackay Falls, Milford Track (p256)

New Zealand – South Island

ELEVATION

2000m
1500m
1250m
1000m
750m
500m
250m
0m

TASMAN SEA

Marlborough Sounds
Scenic waterways, bush trails and winding drives (p62)

Abel Tasman National Park
Tramping, kayaking and hidden coves (p88)

Buller Region
Day hikes beckon in this history-rich area (p101)

TranzAlpine
The great coast-to-coast train journey (p112)

Kaikoura
Crayfish and wildlife in this appealing little town (p72)

WELLINGTON

Cape Palliser

Cook Strait

Marlborough Sounds

Picton

Blenheim

Nelson

Tasman Bay

Golden Bay

Farewell Spit

Cape Farewell

Takaka

Collingwood

Motueka

Richmond

Abel Tasman National Park

St Arnaud

Nelson Lakes National Park

Hanmer Springs

Kaikoura Peninsula

Kaikoura

Pegasus Bay

Karamea

Murchison

Lewis Pass

Westport

Reefton

Paparoa National Park

Punakaiki

Greymouth

Arthur's Pass

Arthur's Pass National Park

Hokitika

Ross

Whataroa

To Chatham Islands

100 miles
200 km

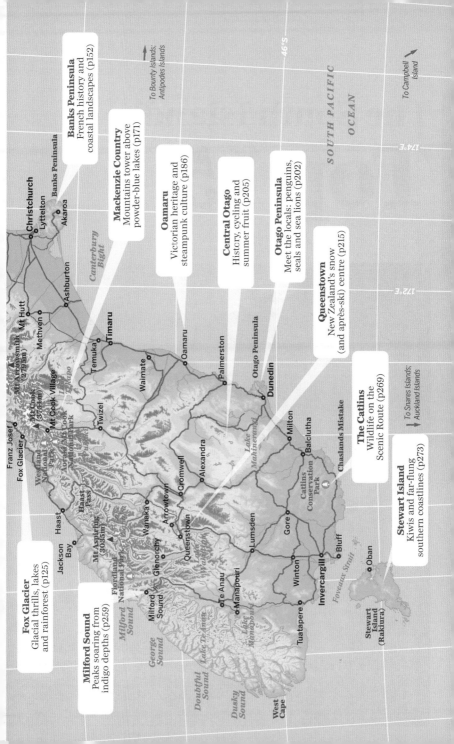

Fox Glacier
Glacial thrills, lakes and rainforest (p125)

Milford Sound
Peaks soaring from indigo depths (p259)

Banks Peninsula
French history and coastal landscapes (p152)

Mackenzie Country
Mountains tower above powder-blue lakes (p171)

Oamaru
Victorian heritage and steampunk culture (p186)

Central Otago
History, cycling and summer fruit (p205)

Otago Peninsula
Meet the locals: penguins, seals and sea lions (p202)

Queenstown
New Zealand's snow (and après-ski) centre (p215)

The Catlins
Wildlife on the Scenic Route (p269)

Stewart Island
Kiwis and far-flung southern coastlines (p273)

To Bounty Islands;
Antipodes Islands

46°S

SOUTH PACIFIC

OCEAN

To Campbell
Island

174°E

172°E

Christchurch
Lyttelton
Akaroa
Banks Peninsula

Canterbury
Bight

Ashburton

Franz Josef
Fox Glacier

Mt Hutt
Mt Arrowsmith
(2795m)

Methven

Westland
National
Park

Mt Cook/
Aoraki (3754m)

Mt Cook Village

Aoraki/Mt Cook
National Park

Lake Tekapo

Timaru

Temuka

Haast

Jackson
Bay

Haast
Pass

Twizel

Waimate

Oamaru

Palmerston

Otago Peninsula

Mt Aspiring
(3033m)

Wanaka

Cromwell

Alexandra

Lake
Mahinerangi

Dunedin

Fiordland
National Park

Arrowtown

Glenorchy

Queenstown

Milford
Sound

Milford Sound

Lake Wakatipu

Te Anau

Manapouri

Lumsden

Gore

Milton

Balclutha

Chaslands Mistake

Catlins
Conservation
Park

George Sound

Lake Te Anau

Lake Manapouri

Doubtful
Sound

Dusky Sound

West
Cape

Tuatapere

Winton

Invercargill

Bluff

Foveaux Strait

To Snares Islands;
Auckland Islands

Stewart
Island
(Rakiura)

Oban

The South Island's
Top 15

Abel Tasman National Park

1 This is New Zealand nature at its most glorious and seductive: lush green hills fringed with golden sandy coves, slipping gently into warm shallows before meeting a crystal-clear sea of cerulean blue. Abel Tasman National Park (p88) is the quintessential postcard paradise, where you can put yourself in the picture, assuming an endless number of poses: tramping, kayaking, swimming, sunbathing or even makin' whoopee in the woods. This sweet-as corner of NZ's South Island raises the bar and effortlessly keeps it there.

Kaikoura

2 First settled by Māori with their keen nose for seafood, Kaikoura (p72) – meaning 'eat crayfish' – is NZ's best spot for both consuming and communing with marine life. While whales are definitely off the menu, you're almost guaranteed a good gander at Moby's mates on a whale-watching tour. There's also swimming with seals and dolphins, or spotting albatrosses, petrels and other pelagic birds. When it comes to 'sea food and eat it', crayfish is king, but on fishing tours you can hook into other edible wonders of the unique Kaikoura deep. Bottom right: Fur seal, Kaikoura coast.

JASON FRIEND PHOTOGRAPHY LTD / GETTY IMAGES ©

ERIC MIDDELKOOP / GETTY IMAGES ©

Queenstown

3 Queenstown (p215) may be known as the birthplace of bungy jumping, but there's way more to New Zealand's adventure hub than leaping off a bridge tied to a giant rubber band. Amid ridiculously beautiful scenes such as Lake Wakatipu, the Shotover River and the Remarkables mountain range, travellers can spend their days hiking, mountain biking, paragliding, rafting or heading cross-country on a 4WD tour. The fun hospitality hubs of Queenstown and Arrowtown are a stimulating place to relive the adventures over a drink or dinner.

Akaroa & Banks Peninsula

4 Infused with a healthy dash of Gallic ambience, French-themed Akaroa village sits within one of the prettiest harbours on Banks Peninsula (p152). Sleek dolphins and plump penguins inhabit clear waters that are perfect for sailing and exploring. Elsewhere on the peninsula, the spidery Summit Rd lines the rim of an ancient volcano, while winding roads descend to hidden bays and coves. Spend your days tramping and kayaking amid the improbably beautiful land- and sea-scapes, while relaxing at night in cosy bistros and atmospheric town or rural accommodation. Top right: Akaroa

TERRY LEE / 500PX ©

WILLCA0911 / GETTY IMAGES ©

RADIUS IMAGES / GETTY IMAGES ©

Central Otago

5 Central Otago (p205) presents a chance to balance virtue and vice, all with a background of some of NZ's most starkly beautiful landscapes. Hire a bike to cycle the easy-going Otago Central Rail Trail or the unexpected wonderland of Roxburgh Gorge. Slake your thirst with a cold beer in laid-back country pubs, or linger for a classy lunch in the vineyard restaurants of Bannockburn and Gibbston Valley. Other foodie diversions include Cromwell's weekly farmers market, and the summer fruit harvest starring sweet nectarines, peaches, plums and cherries.

Bottom right: Bannockburn region in autumn

Milford Sound

6 Fingers crossed you'll be lucky enough to see Milford Sound (p259) on a clear, sunny day, when the world-renowned collage of waterfalls, verdant cliffs and peaks, and dark cobalt waters is at its best. More likely though is the classic Fiordland scenario of rain, with the landscape an arguably more dramatic scene of gushing waterfalls and Mitre Peak revealed slowly through swirling mist. It's awesome either way, particularly when special inhabitants such as seals, dolphins and birds reveal themselves on a boat cruise or kayak trip.

Marlborough Sounds

7 Way more than just a ferry docking point, Picton is a vibrant hang-out and hub for adventure trips into the serpentine Marlborough Sounds (p62), which is made up of four different waterways linked by bush trails and winding drives. Boat trips allow the deepest penetration into the area's countless nooks and crannies. Hike or bike the Queen Charlotte Track, or paddle a kayak between back-to-nature campsites. A host of cruise trips offer everything from adventure-activity combos to lunch cruises and trips to Motuara Island to meet precious rare birds.

MATTEO COLOMBO / GETTY IMAGES ©

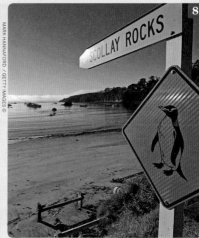

Stewart Island

8 Stewart Island (p273), the country's rugged southern addendum, is paradise for trampers, birdwatchers and travellers seeking an authentic NZ travel experience. Test yourself on the challenging North West Circuit Track or spend three days on the easier, but still spectacular, Rakiura Track. Join the friendly locals at NZ's southernmost pub quiz at the South Sea Hotel in Oban, before making plans to explore the abundant birdlife on nearby Ulva Island, or join a kiwi-spotting tour to see NZ's shy feathered icon mooching around at twilight on isolated beaches.

Mackenzie Country

9 Canterbury's Mackenzie Country (p171) is the star of scenic Highway 8 between Christchurch and Queenstown, serving up such icons as Lake Tekapo and Aoraki/Mt Cook. However this unique basin – ringed by mountain ranges and infilled with golden tussock, brightly coloured lupins, surreal blue hydro lakes and canals – offers plenty more for those with time to explore. The mostly gentle Alps 2 Ocean Cycle Trail is an unparalleled way to take in the scenery, but horse-trekking, scenic flights, hiking and star-gazing tours all jostle for position.
Bottom right: Lupins by Lake Tekapo (p172)

ANNA GORIN / GETTY IMAGES ©

KEVIN WELLS NATURE PHOTOGRAPHY / GETTY IMAGES ©

DAVID WALL / GETTY IMAGES ©

12

Buller Region

10 Avoid the common mistake of most West Coast travellers by heading north when you hit the town of Westport. Beyond it, the Buller Region (p101) boasts an incredible array of sights and experiences, starting with a walk around ghostly Denniston Plateau. Rich human and natural history abounds in other highlights such as Charming Creek – one of NZ's best day walks – and the sublime limestone arches of Oparara Basin. Beyond the relaxed, estuaryside town of Karamea is the Kohaihai end of the Heaphy Track, where there's a memorable half-day hike to raw, empty Scotts Beach. Top left: Moria Gate Arch (p108)

Fox Glacier

11 Unusually close to both the Tasman Sea and the loftiest peaks of the Southern Alps, the twin glaciers of Franz Josef and Fox (p125) are a must-see for their crazy valleys and spectacular ice flows. Hiking on the ice is a great way to view them, as are scenic flights soaring over them up to Aoraki/Mt Cook. Fox Glacier's amazing extras are Lake Matheson, the famous 'mirror' lake fringed with beautiful rainforest, and wild Gillespies Beach; where there are rusting mining relics and a walkway to a remote seal colony. Bottom left: Fox Glacier

TranzAlpine

12 New Zealand's most scenic train journey is the TranzAlpine (p112), a five-hour island crossing from the Pacific Ocean to the Tasman Sea. Having left Christchurch and sped across the bucolic Canterbury Plains, it heads into the foothills of the Southern Alps, negotiating tunnels and viaducts to reach the broad Waimakariri Valley. A stop within Arthur's Pass National Park is followed by the 8.5km-long Otira tunnel, burrowing right through the bedrock of NZ's alpine spine. Then it's all downhill: through the Taramakau River Valley, past Lake Brunner and finally into sleepy Greymouth. Unforgettable.

The Catlins

13 Even for many Kiwis, the rugged Catlins (p269) coast is unknown territory. Avoid the fast but functional inland route linking Dunedin and Invercargill; traverse instead through the Catlins' diverse and interesting procession of isolated bays and coves, dramatic landforms such as waterfalls and caves, and opportunities to chinwag with friendly locals and spot local wildlife. Highlights include the quirky Lost Gypsy Gallery at Papatowai, swimming (or surfing) with dolphins at Curio Bay, and the walk to windswept Slope Point, the southernmost tip of the South Island. Bottom left: Nugget Point (p273)

Otago Peninsula

14 Few cities in the world can lay claim to such remarkable wildlife on their doorstep as Dunedin. Within 15 minutes' drive of downtown, Otago Peninsula (p202) is a rugged thumb lined with peaceful beaches, craggy coves and cliffs. It's a haven for seals and sea lions, but its seabirds are what make it so special. Among numerous notable residents are rare yellow-eyed penguins (hoiho). Another is the royal albatross, which nests at Taiaroa Head, the world's only mainland colony. Visit in January or February to see them soaring and making clumsy landings. Top right: Taiaroa Head (p202)

13

Oamaru

15 Whether it's the wonderfully restored Victorian townscape, the quirky celebration of steampunk culture, or the nightly arrival of hundreds of little blue penguins, surprising Oamaru (p186) has plenty of reasons for a mandatory inclusion on your South Island itinerary. Explore the town's harbourside historic precinct on a penny-farthing bicycle before adjourning for high tea or a homemade pie in charming cafes or the bakery. At dusk grab a grandstand seat to say g'day to penguins returning home after a day's fishing, before toasting their ocean-going bravery with a beer at the nearby brewery.

Need to Know

For more information, see Survival Guide (p313)

Currency
New Zealand dollar ($)

Language
English, Māori and New Zealand Sign Language

Visas
Citizens of Australia, the UK and 58 other countries don't need visas for NZ (length-of-stay allowances vary). See www.immigration.govt.nz.

Money
ATMs widely available in cities and larger towns. Credit cards accepted in most hotels and restaurants.

Mobile Phones
European phones will work on NZ's network, but most American or Japanese phones will not. Use global roaming or a local SIM card and pre-paid account.

Time
New Zealand time is GMT/UTC plus 12 hours (two hours ahead of Australian Eastern Standard Time).

When to Go

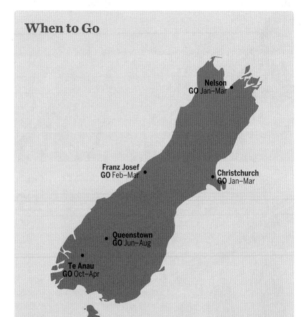

Nelson
GO Jan–Mar

Franz Josef
GO Feb–Mar

Christchurch
GO Jan–Mar

Queenstown
GO Jun–Aug

Te Anau
GO Oct–Apr

High Season
(Dec–Feb)

➡ Best weather and conditions for beach-time and outdoor adventures.

➡ Domestic holidaymakers fill up hot spots and keep roads busy.

➡ Major international tourist influx fills all available gaps.

Shoulder
(Mar–Apr & Sep–Nov)

➡ Generally settled weather; a great time to travel.

➡ New Zealanders in school and work so lighter traveller volumes.

➡ Temperatures during September to November may be cool in the south, especially at night.

Low Season
(May–Aug)

➡ Unpredictable weather: from glorious to ghastly.

➡ No crowds, easy bookings, but quiet towns go into hibernation.

➡ Skiiing and other snow sports abound, especially around Queenstown.

Useful Websites

100% Pure New Zealand
(www.newzealand.com) Official tourism site.

Department of Conservation
(www.doc.govt.nz) DOC parks and camping info.

Lonely Planet (www.lonely planet.com/new-zealand) Destination information, hotel bookings, traveller forum and more.

Destination New Zealand
(www.destination-nz.com) Resourceful tourism site.

DineOut (www.dineout.co.nz) Restaurant reviews.

Te Ara (www.teara.govt.nz) Online encyclopedia of NZ.

Important Numbers

Regular NZ phone numbers have a two-digit area code followed by a seven-digit number. When dialling within a region, the area code is still required. Drop the initial 0 if dialling from abroad.

NZ country code	64
International access code from NZ	00
Emergency (fire, ambulance, police)	111
Directory assistance	018
International directory assistance	0172

Exchange Rates

Australia	A$1	NZ$1.10
Canada	C$1	NZ$1.15
China	Y10	NZ$2.40
Euro zone	€1	NZ$1.62
Japan	¥100	NZ$1.25
Singapore	S$1	NZ$1.08
UK	UK£1	NZ$2.31
US	US$1	NZ$1.53

For current exchange rates see www.xe.com.

Daily Costs

**Budget:
Less than $150**

➡ Dorm beds or campsites: $25–38 per night

➡ Main course in a budget eatery: less than $15

➡ Explore NZ with a Naked Bus or InterCity bus pass: five trips from $151

Midrange: $150–250

➡ Double room in a midrange hotel/motel: $120–200

➡ Main course in a midrange restaurant: $15–32

➡ Hire a car and explore further: from $30 per day

**Top End:
More than $250**

➡ Double room in a top-end hotel: from $200

➡ Three-course meal in a classy restaurant: $80

➡ Domestic flight Auckland to Christchurch: from $100

Opening Hours

Opening hours vary seasonally (eg Dunedin is quiet during winter), but use the following as a general guide. Note that most places close on Christmas Day and Good Friday.

Banks 9.30am–4.30pm Monday to Friday; some also 9am–noon Saturday

Cafes 7am–4pm

Post Offices 8.30am–5pm Monday to Friday; larger branches also 9.30am–1pm Saturday

Pubs & Bars noon–late ('late' varies by region and day)

Restaurants noon–2.30pm and 6.30–9pm

Shops & Businesses 9am–5.30pm Monday to Friday and 9am to noon or 5pm Saturday

Supermarkets 8am–7pm often 9pm or later in cities.

Arriving on the South Island

Christchurch Airport (p326) Christchurch Metro Purple Line runs into the city regularly from 6.45am to 11pm. Door-to-door shuttles run 24 hours. A taxi into the city costs around $50 (20 minutes).

Queenstown Airport (p326) Connectabus buses run every 15 minutes from 6.50am to 11pm. The pre-booked shuttle bus provides a 24-hour door-to-door service. Taxis into the city cost $40 to $45 (15 minutes).

Getting Around

The South Island is long and skinny, and many roads are two-lane country byways: getting from A to B requires some thought.

Car Travel at your own tempo, explore remote areas and visit regions with no public transport. Hire cars in major towns. Drive on the left; the steering wheel is on the right (in case you can't find it).

Bus Reliable, frequent services around the country (usually cheaper than flying).

Plane Fast-track your holiday with affordable, frequent, fast internal flights. Carbon offset your flights if you're feeling guilty.

Train Reliable, regular services (if not fast or cheap) along specific South Island routes.

PLAN YOUR TRIP NEED TO KNOW

For much more on **getting around**, see p327

What's New

Old Ghost Road

One of the most ambitious of NZ's new cycle trails, the 85km Old Ghost Road is a true backcountry experience retracing two historic gold-mining routes through untouched mountain landscapes. (p104)

Christchurch Art Gallery

The city's premier art institution, closed since the 2011 earthquake, has finally reopened better and brighter, and displays some of NZ's finest works. (p136)

Christchurch CBD

In the midst of its major rebuild, downtown Christchurch is cranking out new bars, restaurants and accommodation at a rapid rate of knots. (p134)

Hydro Attack

What's that leaping out of the waters of placid Lake Wakatipu? Yep, it's a giant shark. Or at least a jet-propelled, torpedo-like vessel painted to look like one. (p219)

Bill Richardson Transport World

This vast new automotive museum in Invercargill is home to an astonishing collection of beautifully restored historic trucks. (p264)

Omaka Aviation Heritage Centre

A new wing at this astounding Blenheim museum houses 'Dangerous Skies', a collection of WWII planes to compliment the WWI collection next door. (p67)

Cardrona Distillery & Museum

Nose your way into some single-malt whisky, vodka, gin and orange liqueur on a tour of this new distillery near Wanaka. (p247)

Geraldine Museum

Inside Geraldine's vintage Town Board Office building, this wee southern museum has a new side wing to house yet more historic knick-knackery. (p170)

For more recommendations and reviews, see lonelyplanet.com/new-zealand

CLAVER CARROLL / GETTY IMAGES ©

Christchurch Art Gallery (p136)

If You Like...

Cities

Christchurch Old, new, emerging, exciting – postquake Christchurch is surprising and rewarding. (p134)

Dunedin Gothic architecture, edgy arts, student culture and wildlife on the doorstep. (p192)

Nelson Art, culture, cuisine and beaches – it's no wonder this town is touted as NZ's lifestyle capital. (p77)

Invercargill It ain't rock 'n' roll, but it's gloriously retro, friendly and full of neat old buildings. (p264)

Beaches

Wharariki No ice-cream van, no swimsuits. Just an enthralling, empty beach for wanderers and ponderers. (p95)

Abel Tasman Coast Track Forget Photoshop, these surreal golden sands, blue waters and verdant green hills are for real. (p88)

Kaka Point A sweeping surf beach on a coast home to seals, sea lions and myriad seabirds. (p273)

Colac Bay A top spot for surfing, but this far south be sure to pack a decent wetsuit. (p263)

Māori Culture

Te Ana Māori Rock Art Centre Learn about traditional Māori rock art in the museum and at hidden sites. (p168)

Okains Bay Māori & Colonial Museum View an outstanding array of heritage treasures including *waka taua* (war canoes). (p152)

Hokitika Watch the masters carve stone, bone, paua and genuine *pounamu* (greenstone) in traditional Māori designs. (p115)

Ko Tane See a replica Māori village and an evening cultural show at Willowbank Wildlife Reserve. (p143)

Museums & Galleries

Otago Museum Enlightening human stories and an introduction to the area's unique wildlife. (p193)

Canterbury Museum A wide-ranging collection of exhibits presented in a splendid earthquake survivor. (p137)

World of WearableArt Museum Home to the world-famous, wonderfully weird and wacky art show. (p80)

Eastern Southland Gallery Houses impressive works by iconic NZ artists Ralph Hotere and Rita Angus. (p266)

Shantytown Delve into the West Coast's flinty gold- and coal-mining past at this replica pioneer village. (p112)

Tramping

Milford Track Touted as the greatest of the Great Walks – 54km of fiords, sounds, peaks and a lofty pass. (p256)

Routeburn Track The Great Walk competing with the Milford as the best of the bunch. (p233)

Mt Robert Circuit Track Nelson Lakes' premier day walk with stupendous views earned via the Pinchgut Track. (p97)

Old Ghost Road Built for bikers, this new multiday wilderness epic is also a hiker's delight. (p104)

Pubs, Bars & Beer

Nelson Tour pubs and breweries on a craft-beer trail throughout NZ's original home of hops. (p82)

Christchurch Pubs such as Pomeroy's and the Brewery show commitment to the craft cause. (p148)

Dunedin Lively bars are a speciality of this university city. (p199)

Queenstown Quench your thirst after a day's mountain biking, bungy jumping or skiing. (p230)

Invercargill Brewery Meet the workhorse with its own range that also brews drops for some of NZ's best. (p264)

Snowsport

Treble Cone Challenging downhill terrain within a stone's throw of Wanaka. (p221)

Canterbury Mt Hutt's the hero, but there are stacks of smaller fields like Ohau, Roundhill, Porters and Broken River. (p162)

Coronet Peak Ski or snowboard Queenstown's oldest field then get in on the resort town's legendary après-ski scene. (p221)

Wine Regions

Marlborough Superb sauvignon blanc and pretty winery restaurants are just the start of story. (p70)

Nelson Marlborough's near neighbour is smaller-scale but super-fine and equally scenic. (p77)

Waitaki Valley Truly boutique producers wrangling tricky terroir – NZ's edgiest wine region. (p185)

Central Otago Scores of cellar doors nestled amid schist landscapes producing sublime pinot noir. (p205)

Extreme Activities

Queenstown Bungy jump with the world's originals at AJ Hackett's Kawarau Bridge or Nevis sites. (p217)

Skydive Franz If you're going to do it, go for the highest – 19,000ft above the alps and glaciers. (p124)

Abel Tasman Canyons Paddle, swim, slide and leap through a hidden gorge in the national park. (p91)

Raft the Buller Bounce through the thrilling rapids on this mighty West Coast river. (p101)

Top: A vineyard in the Marlborough wine region (p70)
Bottom: Watering Cove, Abel Tasman National Park (p88)

Month by Month

January

New Zealand peels its eyes open after New Year's Eve, gathers its wits and gets set for another year. Great weather, the cricket season in full swing, and it's happy holidays for the locals.

🎭 World Buskers Festival

Christchurch throngs with jugglers, musos, tricksters, puppeteers, mime artists and dancers... Shoulder into the crowd, watch the performances, and leave a few dollars. Avoid if you're scared of audience participation. (p144)

☆ Nelson Jazz Festival

Get your jazz 'n' blues groove on at rockin' venues and ad hoc street corners. Acts range from Kiwi funkateers through to local hipsters, and Nelson's reputation for great wine and beer makes it very easy to enjoy the diverse beats. (p80)

February

The sun is shining, the nights are long and the drinks are chillin' in the fridge: this is prime party time across NZ. Book your festival tickets (and beds) in advance.

🍷 Marlborough Wine Festival

Revel in mandatory over-indulgence at NZ's biggest and best wine festival, featuring tastings from over 40 Marlborough wineries, plus fine food and entertainment. We hope you like sauvignon blanc. (p68)

🎭 Rippon Festival

Wanaka's super-relaxed alternative-music festival – held in a gently sloping lakeside vineyard – features a well-curated selection of NZ sounds with a dance, reggae, rock and electronica spin. (p243)

March

March brings a hint of autumn, and it's harvest time in the vineyards of Marlborough and orchards of Central Otago. Expect long dusky evenings and plenty of festivals plumping out the calendar.

🍴 Hokitika Wildfoods Festival

Eat worms, hare testicles or venison pies at Hokitika's comfort-zone-challenging food fest. Not for the mild-mannered or weak-stomached... But even if you are, it's still fun to watch! There are plenty of fine-quality NZ brews to cleanse the palate. (p118)

🍷 Gibbston Wine & Food Festival

Head to the Queenstown Gardens in mid-March to sample the products from the rugged and meandering river valley to the east of Queenstown. Look forward to fine wines from 10 vineyards, cheese and chocolate, and cooking masterclasses from celebrated NZ chefs (www.gibbstonwine andfood.co.nz).

April

April is when canny travellers hit NZ: the ocean is swimmable and the weather still mild, with nary a tourist or queue in sight. Easter equals pricey accommodation everywhere.

�֍ Warbirds Over Wanaka

Held every second Easter in even-numbered years, Warbirds Over Wanaka is an internationally renowned airshow set against rugged Central Otago scenery. Heritage and iconic aircraft pull crazy manoeuvres for up to 50,000 spectators. (p243)

🍷 Clyde Wine & Food Festival

Sleepy Clyde is well known as the northern terminus of the Otago Central Rail Trail, but the cool-climate pinot noir and riesling of local vineyards are also damn fine. Held annually on Easter Sunday. (p211)

May

Party nights are long gone and a chilly NZ winter beckons. Thank goodness for the Comedy Festival. It's also your last chance to explore Fiordland and Southland in reasonable weather.

☆ New Zealand International Comedy Festival

This three-week laugh-fest (www.comedyfestival. co.nz) in May kicks off in the North Island, but then hits the South Island with the on-the-road Comedy Convoy. International gag-merchants line up next to home-grown talent.

🔪 Bluff Oyster & Food Festival

Bluff and oysters go together like, well, like a bivalve. Truck down to the deep south for some slippery, salty specimens (www.bluff oysterfest.co.nz). It's chilly down here in May, but the live music and oyster eating/opening competitions warm everybody up.

June

Time to head south: it's ski season. Queenstown and Wanaka hit their strides, and international legions of skiers and snowboarders hit Coronet Peak, the Remarkables, Treble Cone and Cardrona.

✖֍ New Zealand Golden Guitar Awards

We like both kinds of music: country *and* western! These awards (www. goldguitars.co.nz) in Gore cap off a week of everlovin' country twang and boot-scootin' good times, with plenty of concerts and buskers.

July

Queenstown gets more than a little crazy with the annual winter festival. Expect increases in accommodation prices while it's happening. If you're feeling less active, combine cinema, chocolate and craft beer in Dunedin.

✖֍ Queenstown Winter Festival

Running since 1975, this snow-fest attracts around 45,000 snowbunnies. It's a 10-day party, studded with fireworks, jazz, street parades, comedy, a Mardi Gras, a masquerade ball and lots of snow-centric activities on the slopes. (p225)

☆ New Zealand International Film Festival

After seasons (www.nziff. co.nz) in Dunedin (July–August) and Christchurch (August), this festival hits the road for screenings in regional towns from July to November. Film buffs in Greymouth and Invercargill get very excited at the prospect.

August

Land a good deal on accommodation pretty much anywhere except the ski towns. Winter is almost spent, but there's still not much happening outside: music, art and rugby games are your saviours.

✖֍ Christchurch Arts Festival

The South Island's biggest arts festival takes place in odd-numbered years. Celebrate with cultured Cantabrians at a wide array of venues right across the city. Music, theatre and dance all feature. (p144)

September

Spring has sprung, and baby lambs are running amok. There are accommodation bargains to be had, but definitely be ready for four seasons in one day. The snow season often lingers.

🏃 Snowsports

Forget Europe or South America. Here's your chance to experience the widest range of snow-sports activities in the southern hemisphere. Focus on your downhill at Coronet Peak, achieve snowboarding nirvana at Cardrona, or go Nordic at Snow Farm New Zealand.

October

Post-rugby and pre-cricket sees sports fans twiddling their thumbs: a trip to Kaikoura, Akaroa or Nelson perhaps? October is 'shoulder season', with reasonable accommodation rates and smaller crowds.

🍴 Kaikoura Seafest

Kaikoura is a town built on crayfish. Well, not literally, but there sure are plenty of crustaceans, many of which find themselves on plates at Seafest (www.seafest.co.nz), which is also a great excuse to drink a lot and dance around.

✨ French Fest

Allez à toute vitesse to Akaroa's French Fest – held in odd-numbered years in early October to celebrate the harbour peninsula's Gallic heritage. Quirky events include a waiters'

Top: Venison pie, Wildfoods Festival (p118)
Bottom: Aerial display at Warbirds Over Wanaka (p243)

race and a French cricket tournament. (p155)

 Wanaka Fest

Outdoorsy Wanaka showcases its emerging gourmet side at the annual Wanaka Fest. Come along and tuck into lots of local cuisine. (p243)

November

Another NZ summer threatens as days get longer following the introduction of daylight saving. Now's a good time to hike the Great Walks, but you'll need to book ahead.

Oamaru Victorian Heritage Celebrations

Hark back to the good old days when Queen Vic sat on the throne, hems were low, collars high, and civic decency was *de rigueur*. Oamaru pays tongue-in-cheek homage (www.vhc. co.nz) with dress-ups, penny-farthing races, choirs, guided tours etc.

NZ Cup & Show Week

Christchurch's iconic, annual NZ Cup & Show Week is a great opportunity for the good people of Christchurch to celebrate with fashion shows, horse racing and the country-comes-to-town appeal of the A&P (agricultural and pastoral) Show. (p144)

Highlands 101

Get your motor running for Highlands 101 (www. highlands.co.nz), a supercharged rev-fest in Cromwell featuring 40-odd race cars doing 101 laps of a 4.1km circuit. Three hours of power.

December

Summertime! The crack of leather on willow resounds across the nation's cricket pitches and office workers surge towards the finish line. Everyone gears up for Christmas: avoid shopping centres like the plague.

Queen Charlotte Track

Beat the summer rush on the popular Queen Charlotte Track (www.qctrack. co.nz), either on two legs or two wheels, or even integrate a spot of sea kayaking into your journey.

Itineraries

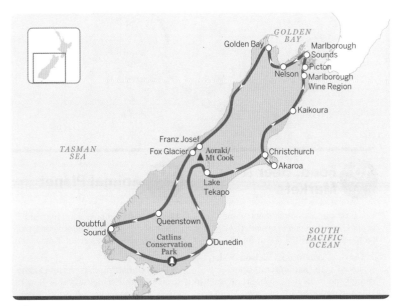

3 WEEKS Southern Circuit

This comprehensive tour of the South Island's highlights takes in a remarkable range of landscapes and diverse experiences from wine tasting and whale-watching to hiking on ice.

Head to **Christchurch** to immerse yourself in the exciting post-earthquake scene. Get the caffeine buzz at Supreme Supreme, then visit Canterbury Museum and the Transitional Cathedral. Wander along the Avon River in the Botanic Gardens, and tour the city on the historic tram before heading up the Gondola for excellent views.

City saturated? Drive out to Banks Peninsula and French-flavoured Akaroa village, then head north for whale-watching in **Kaikoura**. Continue to the Marlborough wine region and pretty harbour town of Picton to spend a day or two in the **Marlborough Sounds**.

Detour west past artsy Nelson to ecofriendly **Golden Bay** before heading down the West Coast where Punakaiki and the glaciers – **Franz Josef** and **Fox** – are the tip of the iceberg. Go crazy in adventurous **Queenstown**, be mesmerised by **Doubtful Sound** and chill out around the sleepy **Catlins**. Back up the East Coast, drop in to Scottish-flavoured **Dunedin**, then detour through the Waitaki Valley to the snowy heights of **Aoraki/Mt Cook** and Lake Tekapo, before rolling back into Christchurch.

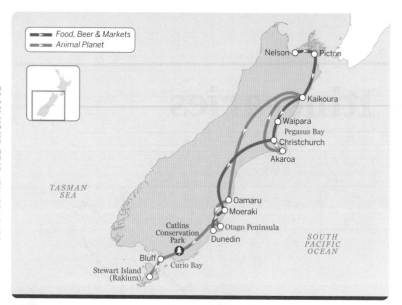

Food, Beer & Markets
Animal Planet

Food, Beer & Markets
10 DAYS

Fresh produce, seafood, dairy, game, grapes, hops – if you're obsessed with your stomach, have we got a tour for you...

Hop into gear around **Nelson**, widely regarded as the nation's craft-brewing capital and home to microbreweries such as Hop Federation and Townshend. Head over to **Marlborough,** the country's best wine-touring territory, then down the South Island's rugged East Coast to **Kaikoura** for delicious seafood. Graduate from Kaikoura's rustic seafood eateries to classier dining at vineyard restaurants in the wine region around **Waipara**, north of Christchurch.

Journey into **Christchurch** to sample the restaurant scenes around Victoria and New Regent Sts, and Lyttelton, and don't miss the excellent Christchurch Farmers Market on Saturday mornings.

Continue south to North Otago and award-winning eateries such as Riverstone Kitchen in **Oamaru** and Fleur's Place in **Moeraki**. Emerson's and Green Man are the breweries to check out further south in **Dunedin** before loading up the car with organic, free-range and locavore goodies at Dunedin's Otago Farmers Market.

Animal Planet
10 DAYS

The South Island boasts a remarkable range of unique and unusual creatures. This tour presents a veritable menagerie on land and in sea.

From Christchurch travel to **Akaroa** to swim with Hector's dolphins, New Zealand's smallest and rarest. Squeeze in a return trip up the coast to **Kaikoura** for whale-watching and swimming with NZ fur seals, before travelling south to **Oamaru**. There's a fascination with steampunk culture and a wonderful historic precinct, but nature buffs should beeline for the little blue penguin colony that awakes at dusk.

From Oamaru travel to the **Otago Peninsula** for more little blues and their extremely rare cousin, the yellow-eyed penguin (hoiho). Join a tour to meet seals and sea lions before admiring the royal albatross colony on nearby Taiaroa Head.

Continue south to the rugged and isolated **Catlins**. Penguins, Hector's dolphins and sea lions are all regular visitors to **Curio Bay**. Head further south and leave the South Island at Bluff for kiwi-spotting on wild and idiosyncratic **Stewart Island**. Now you can really say you've met a kiwi.

Plan Your Trip
Hiking on the South Island

Hiking (aka bushwalking, trekking or tramping, as Kiwis call it) is the perfect activity for a close encounter with the South Island's natural beauty. There are thousands of kilometres of tracks here – some well marked (including the six South Island Great Walks), some barely a line on a map – plus an excellent network of huts and campgrounds.

Planning

When to Go

Mid-December–late January Tramping high season is during the school summer holidays, starting a couple of weeks before Christmas – avoid it if you can.

January–March The summer weather lingers into March: wait until February if you can, when tracks are (marginally) less crowded. Most non-alpine tracks can be walked enjoyably at any time from about October through to April.

June–August Winter is not the time to be out in the wild, especially at altitude – some paths close in winter because of avalanche danger and reduced facilities and services.

What to Bring

Primary considerations: your feet and your back. Make sure your footwear is tough and comfortable, and your pack fits well and isn't too heavy. Warm clothing and wet-weather gear are essential wherever you hike, as well as a hat to keep you warm and protect you from NZ's harsh sun. If you're camping or staying in huts without cooking facilities, bring a camping stove. Also pack insect repellent to keep sandflies away (although covering up is best), and don't forget your scroggin – a mixture of dried fruit and nuts (and sometimes chocolate) for munching en route.

Top Multiday Hikes
Abel Tasman Coast Track, Abel Tasman National Park

Heaphy Track, Kahurangi National Park

Milford Track, Fiordland National Park

Top Day Hikes
Mt Robert Circuit, Nelson Lakes National Park

Avalanche Peak, Canterbury

Key Summit, Fiordland National Park

Top Wildlife Encounters
Bird life, St Arnaud Range Track, Nelson Lakes

Seals, Cape Foulwind Walkway, West Coast

Kiwi, Rakiura Track, Stewart Island

Best Hikes for Beginners
Queen Charlotte Track, Marlborough Sounds

Abel Tasman Coast Track, Abel Tasman National Park

Rob Roy Track, Mt Aspiring National Park

Books & Resources

Before heading into the bush, get up-to-date information from the appropriate authority – usually the DOC (Department of Conservation, www.doc.govt.nz) or regional i-SITE visitor information centres. As well as current track condition and weather info, the DOC supplies detailed books on the flora, fauna, geology and history of NZ's national parks, plus leaflets (mostly $2 or less) detailing hundreds of South Island walking tracks.

➡ Lonely Planet's *Hiking & Tramping in New Zealand* describes over 50 walks of various lengths and degrees of difficulty.

➡ *101 Great Tramps* by Mark Pickering and Rodney Smith has suggestions for two- to six-day tramps around the country. The companion guide, *202 Great Walks: The Best Day Walks in New Zealand,* by Mark Pickering, is handy for shorter, family-friendly excursions.

➡ *A Walking Guide To New Zealand's Long Trail: Te Araroa* by Geoff Chapple is the definitive book for NZ's continuous trail that runs the length of the country.

➡ The Mountain Safety Council's *Bushcraft Manual* will help keep you safe on the trails and bring out your inner Bear Grylls.

➡ *Tramping* by Shaun Barnett and Chris Maclean is a meticulously researched history of NZ's favourite outdoor pastime.

➡ Bird's Eye Tramping Guides from Potton & Burton Publishing have fab topographical maps, and there are countless books covering tramps and short urban walks around NZ – scan the bookshops.

Maps

The NZ Topo50 topographical map series produced by Land Information New Zealand (www.linz.govt.nz) is the most commonly used. Bookshops don't often have a good se-

---

RESPONSIBLE TRAMPING

If you went straight from the cradle into a pair of hiking boots, some of these tramping tips will seem ridiculously obvious; others you mightn't have considered. Online, www.lnt.org is a great resource for low-impact hiking, and the DOC site www.camping.org.nz has plenty more responsible camping tips. When in doubt, ask DOC or i-SITE staff.

The ridiculously obvious:

➡ Time your tramp to avoid peak season: less people equals less stress on the environment and fewer snorers in the huts.

➡ Carry out *all* your rubbish. Burying rubbish disturbs soil and vegetation, encourages erosion, and animals will probably dig it up anyway.

➡ Don't use detergents, shampoo or toothpaste in or near lakes and waterways (even if they're biodegradable).

➡ Use lightweight kerosene, alcohol or Shellite (white gas) stoves for cooking; avoid disposable butane gas canisters.

➡ Where there's a toilet, use it. Where there isn't one, dig a hole and bury your by-product (at least 15cm deep, 100m from any waterway).

➡ If track pass through muddy patches, just plough straight on through – skirting around the outside increases the size of the quagmire.

You mightn't have considered:

➡ Wash your dishes 50m from watercourses; use a scourer, sand or snow instead of detergent.

➡ If you *really* need to scrub your bod, use biodegradable soap and a bucket, at least 50m from any watercourse. Spread the waste water around widely to help the soil filter it.

➡ If open fires are allowed, use only dead, fallen wood in existing fireplaces. Leave any extra wood for the next happy camper.

➡ Keep food-storage bags out of reach of scavengers by tying them to rafters or trees.

➡ Feeding wildlife can lead to unbalanced populations, diseases and animals becoming dependent on handouts. Keep your dried apricots to yourself.

TRACK SAFETY

Thousands of people tramp across NZ without incident, but every year too many folks meet their maker in the mountains. Some trails are only for the experienced, fit and well equipped – don't attempt these if you don't fit the bill. Ensure you are healthy and used to walking for sustained periods.

The South Island's volatile climate subjects high-altitude walks to snow and ice, even in summer, and rivers can rise rapidly: always check weather and track conditions before setting off, and be prepared to change your plans or sit out bad weather. Resources include:

www.doc.govt.nz DOC's track info, alerts and a lot more.

www.adventuresmart.org.nz Log your walk intentions online (and tell a friend or local!).

www.mountainsafety.org.nz Tramping safety tips.

www.metservice.co.nz Weather forecasts.

lection of these maps, but the LINZ website has a list of retailers, and DOC offices often sell the latest maps for local tracks. Outdoor stores also stock them. NZ Topo Map (www.topomap.co.nz) has an interactive topographic map, useful for planning.

Websites

www.doc.govt.nz Descriptions, alerts, and exhaustive flora and fauna information for all tracks in the conservation estate.

www.tramper.co.nz Articles, photos, forums, and excellent track and hut information.

www.teararoa.org.nz The official website for NZ's 3000km trail from Cape Reinga to Bluff.

www.topomap.co.nz Online topographic map of the whole country.

www.mountainsafety.org.nz Safety tips, gear advice and courses.

www.freewalks.co.nz Descriptions, maps and photos of long and short tramps all over NZ.

www.trampingnz.com Region-by-region track info with readable trip reports.

Track Classifications

Tracks in NZ are classified according to various features, including level of difficulty. The widely used track classification system is as follows:

Short Walk (Easiest) Well formed; possibly allows for wheelchair access or is constructed to 'walking shoe' standard (ie walking boots not required). Suitable for people of all ages and fitness levels.

Walking Track (Easy) Well-formed longer walks; walking shoes or boots recommended. Suitable for people of most ages and fitness levels.

Great Walk or Easier Tramping Track (Intermediate) Well formed; major water crossings have bridges and track junctions have signs. Light hiking boots and average fitness required.

Tramping Track (Advanced) Requires skill and experience; hiking boots essential. Suitable for people of moderate physical fitness. Water crossings may not have bridges.

Route (Expert) Requires a high degree of skill, experience and navigation skills. Sturdy hiking boots essential. Well-equipped, fit trampers only.

The Great Walks

NZ's nine official Great Walks are the country's most popular tracks: six of them are on the South Island. Natural beauty abounds, but prepare yourself for crowds, especially over summer.

All of the South Island's Great Walks are described in Lonely Planet's *Hiking & Tramping in New Zealand,* and are detailed in pamphlets provided by DOC visitor centres and online at www.greatwalks.co.nz.

Tickets & Bookings

To tramp these tracks you'll need to book online or at DOC visitor centres and some i-SITES before setting out. These track-specific tickets cover you for hut accommodation (from $22 to $54 per adult per night, depending on the track) and/or camping ($6 to $18 per adult per night). You can camp

Great Walks

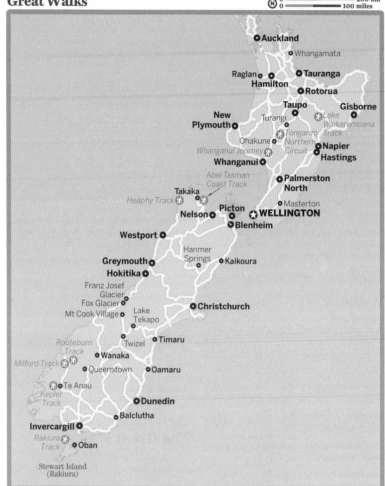

only at designated camping grounds; note there's no camping on the Milford Track.

In the off-peak season (May to September) you can use Backcountry Hut Passes or pay-as-you-go Hut Tickets on all South Island Great Walks except for the Heaphy Track, Abel Tasman Coast Track and Rakiura Track (advance bookings required year-round). Kids under 17 stay in huts and camp for free on all Great Walks.

For bookings see www.greatwalks.co.nz, email greatwalksbookings@doc.govt.nz, phone 0800 694 732, or visit DOC visitor centres. Book as far in advance as possible, especially if planning to walk in summer.

Other Tracks

Banks Peninsula Track A 35km, two-day (medium) or four-day (easy) walk over the hills and along the coast of Banks Peninsula.

Hollyford Track A typically hair-brained scheme of the era, the settlement of Jamestown was always a long shot. Cue: colourful characters and a dash of drama. A four- to five-day, 57km low-level tramping track in Fiordland.

Welcome Flat Follow the Karangarua River in the shadow of some of NZ's loftiest peaks, then reward yourself with a soak in natural hot pools. A

THE SOUTH ISLAND'S SIX GREAT WALKS

WALK	DISTANCE	DURATION	DIFFICULTY	DESCRIPTION
Abel Tasman Coast Track *	60km	3-5 days	Easy to intermediate	NZ's most popular walk (or sea kayak); beaches and bays in Abel Tasman National Park (p88)
Heaphy Track *	78km	4-6 days	Intermediate	Forests, beaches and karst landscapes in Kahurangi National Park (p96)
Kepler Track **	60km	3-4 days	Intermediate	Lakes, rivers, gorges, glacial valleys and beech forest in Fiordland National Park (p254)
Milford Track **	53.5km	4 days	Easy to intermediate	Rainforest, sheer valleys and peaks, and 580m-high Sutherland Falls in Fiordland National Park (p256)
Rakiura Track *	39km	3 days	Intermediate	Bird life (kiwi!), beaches and lush bush on remote Stewart Island (Rakiura; p276)
Routeburn Track **	32km	2-4 days	Intermediate	Eye-popping alpine scenery around Mt Aspiring and Fiordland National Parks (p233)

* Bookings required year-round

** Booking required peak season only (end April to end Oct)

two- to three-day moderate tramp over 50km in Westland Tai Poutini National Park.

Mueller Hut Route Yes, it involves a hard-core 1040m climb up the Sealy Range near Aoraki/ Mount Cook, but this is a quintessential alpine experience: geological wonders, fascinating plant life and an amazing hut.

Lake Angelus Track A startling alpine ridge leads to a flash DOC hut beside a pristine cirque lake in Nelson Lakes National Park. A 22km-return, two-day moderate hike.

Queen Charlotte Track A 71km, three- to five-day moderate walk in the Marlborough Sounds, affording great watery views. Top-notch accommodation and water transport available.

Rees-Dart Track A 70km, four- to five-day hard tramping track in Mt Aspiring National Park, through glacier-fed valleys and over an alpine pass.

St James Walkway This tramping track passes through a significant conservation area, home to some 430 species of flora from lowland grasses to mountain beech and alpine herbs. Five days over 66km around Lewis Pass.

Tuatapere Hump Ridge Track An excellent three-day, 58km alpine and coastal circuit beginning and ending at Te Waewae Bay, 20km from Tuatapere.

Backcountry Huts

In addition to Great Walk huts, DOC maintains more than 950 Backcountry Huts in NZ's national and forest parks. Hut categories are as follows:

Basic Huts Very basic enclosed shelters with little or no facilities. Free.

Standard Huts No cooking equipment and sometimes no heating, but mattresses, water supply and toilets. Fees are $5 per adult per night.

Serviced Huts Mattress-equipped bunks or sleeping platforms, water supply, heating, toilets and sometimes cooking facilities. Fees are $15 per adult per night.

Note that bookings are required for some huts (see the website for listings): book online at https://booking.doc.govt.nz or at DOC visitor centres. Kids aged 11 to 17 stay for half-price; kids 10 and under stay free. For comprehensive hut details see www.doc.govt.nz/parks-and-recreation/places-to-stay.

If you do a lot of tramping, a six-month **Backcountry Hut Pass** ($92 per adult) might be a good idea; otherwise use pay-as-you-go **Hut Tickets** ($5: you'll need to

AMOS CHAPPLE / GETTY IMAGES ©

DPEL23 / GETTY IMAGES ©

Top: Te Araroa walking trail at Ninety Mile Beach

Bottom: Cape Foulwind (p105), south of Westport

use three of these for a Serviced Hut). Date your tickets and put them in the boxes provided at huts. Accommodation is on a first-come, first-served basis. In the low season (May to September), Backcountry Hut Tickets and Passes can also be used to procure a bunk or campsite on some Great Walks.

Backcountry Campsites are often nearby the huts, and usually have toilets and fresh water; possibly also picnic tables, fireplaces and/or cooking shelters. Prices vary from free to $8 per person per night.

Conservation Campsites

Aside from Great Walk campsites, DOC also manages 220-plus Conservation Campsites (often vehicle-accessible), with categories as follows:

Basic Campsites Basic toilets and fresh water; free on a first-come, first-served basis.

Standard Campsites Toilets and water supply, and perhaps barbecues and picnic tables; from $6 on a first-come, first-served basis.

Scenic Campsites High-use sites with toilets and tap water, and sometimes barbecues, fireplaces, cooking shelters, cold showers, picnic tables and rubbish bins. Fees are $10 per night.

Serviced Campsites Full facilities: flush toilets, tap water, hot showers and picnic tables. They may also have barbecues, a kitchen and a laundry; around $15 per night.

Note that bookings are necessary for all Serviced Campsites, plus some Scenic and Standard Campsites in peak season (October to April). Book online – https://booking.doc.govt.nz – or at DOC visitor centres.

DOC publishes free brochures with descriptions, and instructions to find every campsite (even GPS coordinates). Pick up copies from DOC offices before you hit the road, or download them from their website.

Guided Walks

If you're new to tramping or just want a more comfortable experience than the DIY alternative, several companies can escort

TE ARAROA
Epic! Te Araroa (www.teararoa.org.nz) is a 3000km tramping trail from Cape Reinga in NZ's north to Bluff in the south (or the other way around). The route links up existing tracks with new sections. Built over almost 20 years, mostly by volunteers, it's one of the longest hikes in the world: check the website for maps and track notes, plus blogs and videos from hardy types who have completed the end-to-end epic.

you through the wilds, usually staying in comfortable huts (showers!), with meals cooked and equipment carried for you.

Walks on the South Island where you can sign up for some guided assistance include the Abel Tasman Coast Track, Queen Charlotte Track, Heaphy Track, Routeburn Track, Milford Track or Hollyford Track. Prices for multiday guided walks start at around $1500, and rise towards $2200 for more deluxe experiences.

Getting To & From Trailheads

Getting to and from trailheads can be problematic, except for popular trails serviced by public and dedicated trampers' transport. Having a vehicle only helps with getting to one end of the track (you still have to collect your car afterwards). If the track starts or ends down a dead-end road, hitching will be difficult.

Of course, tracks accessible by public transport or shuttle bus services (eg Abel Tasman Coast Track) are also the most crowded. An alternative is to arrange private transport, either with a friend or by chartering a vehicle to drop you at one end then pick you up at the other. If you intend to leave a vehicle at a trailhead, don't leave anything valuable inside – theft from cars in isolated areas is a significant problem.

Plan Your Trip
Skiing & Snowboarding on the South Island

New Zealand's South Island is an essential southern-hemisphere destination for snow bunnies, with downhill skiing, cross-country (Nordic) skiing and snowboarding all passionately pursued. The South Island ski season is generally June through September, though it varies considerably from one ski area to another, and can run as late as October.

Best Skiing & Snowboarding

Best for Beginners or with Kids

Mt Hutt, Central Canterbury

Mt Dobson, South Canterbury

Coronet Peak, Queenstown

The Remarkables, Queenstown

Best Snowboarding

Mt Hutt, Central Canterbury

Treble Cone, Wanaka

Cardrona, Wanaka

Ohau, South Canterbury

Best Après-Ski Watering Holes

Dubliner, Methven

Cardrona Hotel, Cardrona

Lalaland, Wanaka

Rhino's Ski Shack, Queenstown

Planning
Where to Go

The variety of locations and conditions makes it difficult to rate NZ's ski fields in any particular order. Some people like to be near Queenstown's party scene; others prefer the quality high-altitude runs on Mt Hutt, uncrowded Rainbow or less-stressed club skiing areas. Club areas are publicly accessible and usually less crowded and cheaper than commercial fields, even though nonmembers pay a higher fee.

Practicalities

The South Island's commercial ski areas aren't generally set up as 'resorts' with chalets, lodges or hotels. Rather, accommodation and après-ski carousing are often in surrounding towns, connected with the slopes via daily shuttles. Many club areas have lodges where you can stay, subject to availability.

Visitor information centres in NZ, and Tourism New Zealand (www.newzealand.com) internationally, have info on the various ski areas and can make bookings

and organise packages. Lift passes usually cost between $70 and $110 per adult per day (half-price for kids). Lesson-and-lift packages are available at most areas. Ski and snowboard equipment rental starts at around $50 a day (cheaper for multiday hire). Private/group lessons start at around $120/60 per hour.

Websites

www.snow.co.nz Reports, cams and ski info across the country.

www.nzski.com Reports, employment, passes and webcams for Mt Hutt, Coronet Peak and the Remarkables.

www.newzealandski.co.nz Good all-round online portal for South Island ski areas.

www.chillout.co.nz Info on Mt Lyford, Awakino, Hanmer Springs, Cheeseman, Roundhill, Rainbow, Temple Basin, Treble Cone, Fox Peak, Mt Dobson, Mt Olympus, Porters, Craigieburn Valley and Broken River ski areas.

South Island Ski Regions
Queenstown & Wanaka

Coronet Peak (p221) At the Queenstown region's oldest ski field, snow-making systems and treeless slopes provide excellent skiing and snowboarding for all levels. There's night skiing Friday and Saturday from July to September. Shuttles run from Queenstown, 16km away.

The Remarkables (p221) Visually remarkable, this ski field is also near Queenstown (24km away) – shuttle buses run during ski season. It has a good smattering of intermediate, advanced and beginner runs (kids under 10 ski free). Look for the sweeping 'Homeward Bound' run.

Treble Cone (p221) The highest and largest of the southern lakes ski areas is in a spectacular location 26km from Wanaka, with steep slopes suitable for intermediate to advanced skiers

PLAN YOUR TRIP SKIING & SNOWBOARDING ON THE SOUTH ISLAND

Ski Areas

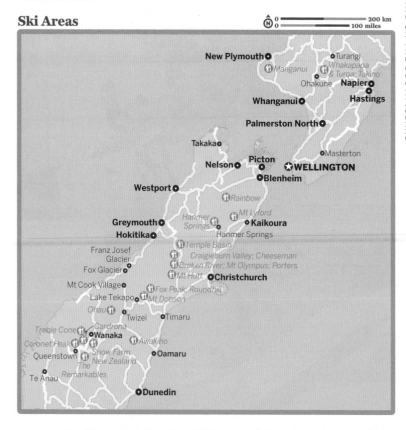

SIMON FERGUSSON / STRINGER / GETTY IMAGES ©

WILL SALTER / GETTY IMAGES ©

Top: Mt Hutt (p165) near Methvan

Bottom: Coronet Peak (p221) near Queenstown

(a rather professional vibe). There are also half-pipes and a terrain park for boarders.

Cardrona (p247) Around 34km from Wanaka, with several high-capacity chairlifts, beginners tows and Parks 'n' Pipes for the freestylers. Buses run from Wanaka and Queenstown during ski season. A friendly scene with good services for skiers with disabilities, plus an on-mountain crèche.

Snow Farm New Zealand (p247) NZ's only commercial Nordic (cross-country) ski area is 33km from Wanaka on the Pisa Range, high above the Cardrona Valley. There are 55km of groomed trails, huts with facilities, and thousands of hectares of open snow.

South Canterbury

Ohau (p175) This commercial ski area is on Mt Sutton, 42km from Twizel. There are plenty of intermediate and advanced runs, excellent snowboarding, two terrain parks and Lake Ohau Lodge.

Mt Dobson (p172) The 3km-wide basin here, 26km from Fairlie, caters for learners and intermediates, and has a terrain park and famously dry powder. On a clear day you can see Aoraki/Mt Cook and the Pacific Ocean from the summit.

Fox Peak (p172) An affordable club ski area 40km from Fairlie in the Two Thumb Range. Expect rope tows, good cross-country skiing and dorm-style accommodation.

Roundhill (p173) A small field with wide, gentle slopes, perfect for beginners and intermediates. It's 32km from Lake Tekapo village. 'Ski Tekapo!'.

Central Canterbury

Mt Hutt (p165) One of the highest ski areas in the southern hemisphere, as well as one of NZ's best. It's close to Methven; Christchurch is 118km to the west – ski shuttles service both towns. Road access is steep – be extremely cautious in lousy weather. Plenty of beginner, intermediate and advanced slopes, with chairlifts, heliskiing and wide-open faces that are good for learning to snowboard.

Porters (p162) The closest commercial ski area to Christchurch (96km away on the Arthur's Pass road). 'Big Mama', at 620m, is one of the steepest runs in NZ, but there are wider, gentler slopes, too. There's also a terrain park, good cross-country runs along the ridge, and lodge accommodation.

HELISKIING

NZ's remote heights are tailor-made for heliskiing, with operators covering a wide off-piste area along the pristine slopes of the Southern Alps, including extreme skiing for the hard core. Costs range from around $825 to $1450 for three to eight runs. Heliskiing is available at Coronet Peak, Treble Cone, Cardrona, Mt Hutt, Mt Lyford, Ohau and Hanmer Springs. Independent operators include the following:

Alpine Heliski (p222)

Harris Mountains Heli-Ski (p222)

Methven Heliski (p165)

Over The Top (p223)

Southern Lakes Heliski (p222)

Temple Basin (p162) A club field 4km from the Arthur's Pass township. It's a 50-minute walk uphill from the car park to the ski-area lodges. There's floodlit skiing at night and excellent backcountry runs for snowboarders.

Craigieburn Valley (p162) Centred on Hamilton Peak, Craigieburn Valley is 40km from Arthur's Pass. It's one of NZ's most challenging club areas, with intermediate and advanced runs (no beginners). Accommmodation in please-do-a-chore lodges.

Broken River (p162) Not far from Craigieburn Valley, this club field is a 15- to 20-minute walk from the car park and has a real sense of isolation. Reliable snow and a laid-back vibe. Catered or self-catered lodge accommodation available.

Cheeseman (p162) Another cool club area in the Craigieburn Range, this family-friendly operation is around 100km from Christchurch. Based on Mt Cockayne, it's a wide, sheltered basin with drive-to-the-snow road access. Lodge accommodation available.

Mt Olympus (p162) Difficult to find (but worth the search), 2096m Mt Olympus is 58km from Methven and 12km from Lake Ida. This club area has intermediate and advanced runs, and there are solid cross-country trails to other areas. Access is sometimes 4WD-only, depending on conditions. Lodge accommodation available.

DOUG PEARSON / GETTY IMAGES ©

The Remarkables (p221) ski field near Queenstown

Northern South Island

Hanmer Springs (p159) A commercial field based on Mt St Patrick, 17km from Hanmer Springs township, with mostly intermediate and advanced runs. The Adventure Centre provides shuttles during the season.

Mt Lyford (p159) Around 60km from both Hanmer Springs and Kaikoura, and 4km from Mt Lyford village, this is more of a 'resort' than most NZ ski fields, with accommodation and eating options. There's a good mix of runs and a terrain park.

Rainbow (p98) Borders Nelson Lakes National Park (100km from Nelson and a similar distance from Blenheim), has varied terrain, minimal crowds and good cross-country skiing. Chains are often required. St Arnaud is the closest town (32km).

Otago

Awakino (p186) A small player in North Otago, but worth a visit for intermediate skiers. Oamaru is 45km away and Omarama is 66km inland. Weekend lodge-and-ski packages available.

Plan Your Trip

Extreme Sports on the South Island

An abundance of adventure activities tempt even the meekest and mildest to push their limits, but it's not all about the adrenaline buzz. Pants-wetting, often illogical escapades such as skydiving, bungy jumping, mountain biking and jetboating may be thrilling, but they also immerse you in the South Island's amazing landscapes in inspiring new ways.

On the Land

Bungy Jumping

Bungy jumping was made famous by Kiwi AJ Hackett's 1986 plunge from the Eiffel Tower, after which he teamed up with champion NZ skier Henry van Asch to turn the endeavour into an everyday pursuit.

Today their original home base of Queenstown is a spiderweb of bungy cords, including the AJ Hackett's triad: the 134m Nevis Bungy (the highest); the 43m Kawarau Bungy (the original); and the Ledge Bungy (at the highest altitude – diving off a 400m-high platform). There's another scenic jump at Thrillseekers Canyon near Hanmer Springs. Huge rope swings offer variation on the theme; head to Queenstown's Shotover Canyon or Nevis Swings for that swooshy buzz.

Caving

Caving (aka spelunking) opportunities abound in NZ's honeycombed karst (limestone) regions. On the South Island you'll find local clubs and organised tours around Westport and Karamea. Golden Bay also has some mammoth caves.

Top Extreme Experiences

Top White-Water Rafting Trips
Buller Gorge, Murchison

Rangitata, Geraldine

Shotover Canyon, Queenstown

Top Mountain-Biking Tracks
Queen Charlotte Track, Marlborough

West Coast Wilderness Trail, Hokitika

Alps 2 Ocean, South Canterbury

Top Anti-Gravity Activities
Nevis Swing, Queenstown

Ledge Bungy, Queenstown

Tandem hang gliding, Wanaka

Best Skydive Drop Zones
Queenstown

Motueka

Fox & Franz Josef Glaciers

Top Surf Spots
St Clair Beach, Dunedin

Kaikoura Peninsula, Marlborough

Punakaiki, West Coast

For comprehensive information including details of specific areas and clubs, see the website of the New Zealand Speleological Society (www.caves.org.nz).

Paragliding & Hang Gliding

A surprisingly gentle but still thrilling way to take to the skies, paragliding involves setting sail from a hillside or clifftop under a parachute-like wing. Hang gliding is similar but with a smaller, rigid wing. Most flights are conducted in tandem with a master pilot, although it's also possible to get lessons to go it alone. To give it a whirl on the South Island, try a tandem flight in Queenstown, Wanaka, Nelson or Motueka. The New Zealand Hang Gliding and Paragliding Association (www.nzhgpa.org.nz) rules the roost.

Horse Trekking

New Zealanders are pretty keen horse-people, and unlike some other parts of the world where beginners' horses get led by the nose around a paddock, treks in NZ offer a chance to explore some remarkable landscapes – from farms to forests and along rivers and beaches. Rides range from one-hour jaunts (from around $60) to week-long, fully supported treks.

On the South Island, options range from beachy trips in western Golden Bay to adventures around mountain foothills near Mt Cook, Lake Tekapo, Queenstown and Glenorchy. Spectacular treks are offered from Punakaiki into Paparoa National Park. For info and operator listings, check out True NZ Horse Trekking (www.truenz.co.nz/horsetrekking).

Mountain Biking

NZ has gone mountain-bike mad. Referred to as 'the new golf' for its popularity among people of a certain age, it has actually emerged as an obsession for all ages. The New Zealand Cycle Trail has certainly propelled this off-road juggernaut, but there are a seemingly endless number of other trails all over the country.

Mountain-bike parks, most with various trail grades and skills areas (and handy bike hire, usually), are great for trying mountain biking NZ style. On the South Island, head for Queenstown's downhill park, fed by the Skyline Gondola.

Classic South Island trails include the Rameka on Takaka Hill and the trails around Christchurch's Port Hills – but this is just the tip of the iceberg. An increasing number of DOC hiking trails are being converted to dual use – such as the tricky but epic Heaphy Track – but mountain biking is often restricted to low season due to hiker numbers. Track damage is also an issue, so assume nothing.

Your clue that there's some great biking around is the presence of bike-hire outfits. Bowl on up and pick their brains. Most likely cycle-obsessed themselves, they'll soon point you in the direction of an appropriate ride. The go-to book is *Classic New Zealand Mountain Bike Rides* (from bookshops, bike shops and www.kennett.co.nz).

But what, you may ask, about cycle touring? Often perceived as uncomfortable and dangerous due to changeable weather and road conditions, there are some remarkable road journeys such as the Southern Scenic Route in the deep south. To find out

NGA HAERENGA, THE NEW ZEALAND CYCLE TRAIL

The New Zealand Cycle Trail (www.nzcycletrail.com) – known in Māori as Nga Haerenga, 'the journeys' – is a 23-strong series of off-road trails known as Great Rides, 13 of which are on the South Island. Spread from north to south they are of diverse length, terrain and difficulty, with many following history-rich old railway lines and pioneer trails, while others are freshly cut, flowing and big fun. Almost all penetrate into remarkable landscapes.

There are plenty of options for beginner to intermediate cyclists, with several hard-core exceptions including the Old Ghost Road on the South Island, which is set to be an internationally renowned classic. The majority are also well supported by handy bike hire, shuttles, and dining and accommodation options, making them a mighty desirable way to explore New Zealand. Most trails have their own websites with comprehensive details, but see the umbrella site listed here for an overview and links.

Top: Surfers at a beach near Dunedin (p192)

Bottom: Rock climbers at Lovers Leap (p203) on the Otago Peninsula

Top: Rafting on Shotover river (p219)

Bottom: Alps 2 Ocean cycle trail (p175) near Twizel

more about this pursuit, check out the *Pedallers' Paradise* booklets by Nigel Rushton (www.paradise-press.co.nz).

Mountaineering

NZ has a proud mountaineering history – this was, after all, the home of Sir Edmund Hillary (1919–2008), who, along with Tenzing Norgay, was the first to summit Mt Everest. When he came back down, Sir Ed famously uttered to friend George Lowe, 'Well, George, we knocked the bastard off!'

The Southern Alps are studded with amazing climbs. The Aoraki/Mt Cook region is outstanding, but there are other zones extending throughout the spine of the South Island from the Kaikoura Ranges and the Nelson Lakes peaks all the way through to the hotbeds of Mt Aspiring National Park and Fiordland. Be warned, though: this is rugged and often remote stuff, and climber deaths are a regular occurrence.

The Christchurch-based New Zealand Alpine Club (www.alpineclub.org.nz) has background, news and useful links, and produces the annual *NZAC Alpine Journal* and the quarterly *The Climber* magazine. It also has details on upcoming climbing courses.

Rock Climbing

Time to chalk-up your fingers and don some natty little rubber shoes. On the South Island, popular rock-climbing areas include the Port Hills area above Christchurch and Castle Hill on the road to Arthur's Pass. West of Nelson, the marble and limestone mountains of Golden Bay and Takaka Hill provide prime climbing. Other options are Long Beach (north of Dunedin), and Mihiwaka and Lovers Leap on the Otago Peninsula.

Raining? You'll find indoor climbing walls all around the country, including Christchurch.

Climb New Zealand (www.climb.co.nz) has the low-down on the gnarliest overhangs around NZ, plus access and instruction info.

Skydiving

With some of the most scenic jump-zones in the world, New Zealand is a fantastic place to make the leap. First-time skydivers can knock off this bucket-list item with a tandem jump, strapped to a qualified instructor, experiencing up to 75 seconds of free fall before the chute opens. The thrill is worth every dollar (from $250 for a 9000ft jump to $560 from a whopping

SURFING THE SOUTH ISLAND

As a surfer I feel particularly guilty in letting the reader in on a local secret – NZ has a sensational mix of quality waves perfect for beginners and experienced surfers. As long as you're willing to travel off the beaten track, you can score some great, uncrowded waves. The islands of NZ are hit with swells from all points of the compass, so with a little weather knowledge and a little effort, numerous options present themselves. Point breaks, reefs, rocky shelves and hollow sandy beach breaks can all be found – take your pick!

Surfing New Zealand (www.surfingnz.co.nz) recommends a number of surf schools on its website. Most NZ beaches hold good rideable breaks. Some South Island spots I particularly enjoy:

Marlborough & Nelson Kaikoura Peninsula, Mangamaunu and Meatworks.

Canterbury Taylors Mistake and Sumner Bar.

Otago Dunedin is a good base for surfing on the South Island, with access to a number of superb breaks, such as St Clair Beach.

West Coast Punakaiki and Tauranga Bay.

Southland Porridge and Centre Island.

NZ water temperatures and climate vary greatly from north to south. For comfort while surfing, wear a wetsuit. On the South Island in summer go for a 2mm–3mm steamer; in winter 3mm–5mm with all the extras.

Josh Kronfeld, surfer and former All Black

19,000ft; extra for a DVD/photographs).
Check out the New Zealand Parachute
Federation (www.nzpf.org) for more info.

On the Water

Jetboating

The jetboat was invented in NZ by an engineer from Fairlie – Bill Hamilton – who wanted a boat that could navigate shallow, local rivers. He credited his eventual success to Archimedes, but as most jetboat drivers will inevitably tell you, Kiwi Bill is the hero of the jetboat story.

River jetboat tours can be found throughout NZ, and while much is made of the hair-raising 360-degree spins that see passengers drenched and grinning from ear to ear, they are really just a sideshow. Just as Bill would have it, jetboat journeys take you deep into wilderness you could otherwise never see, and as such they offer one of NZ's most rewarding tour experiences.

Big ticket South Island river trips such as Queenstown's Shotover, Kawarau and Dart all live up to the hype. But the quieter achievers will blow your skirt up just as high: check out the Buller, Waiatoto (Haast) and Wilkin in Mt Aspiring National Park.

Parasailing & Kiteboarding

Parasailing (dangling from a modified parachute over the water while being pulled along by a speedboat or jet ski) is perhaps the easiest way for humans to achieve assisted flight. On the South Island there are operators in Wanaka and Queenstown.

Kiteboarding (aka kitesurfing), where a mini parachute drags you across the ocean on a mini surfboard. On the South Island you can try it in Nelson.

You will also note that the stand-up paddleboard (SUP) is most definitely on the up, but this activity is less extreme and more knackering.

Sea Kayaking

Sea kayaking offers a wonderful perspective of the coastline and gets you close to marine wildlife you may otherwise never see. It's also lots of fun and thrilling at times. There is a potential pitfall, and it's to do with tandem kayaks...let's just say that they don't call them 'divorce boats' for nothing!

As you'd expect for a seafaring nation, there are ample places to get paddling. South Island hot spots include the Marlborough Sounds (from Picton) and Abel Tasman National Park. Kaikoura is exceptional for wildlife spotting, and Fiordland for jaw-dropping scenery. The Kiwi Association of Sea Kayakers (www.kask.org.nz) has useful information.

Scuba Diving

NZ has some rewarding scuba territory, with warm waters in the north, interesting sea life all over and the odd wreck for good measure. In the Marlborough Sounds, the *Mikhail Lermontov* is the largest diveable cruise-ship wreck in the world. In Fiordland head for Dusky Sound, Milford Sound and Doubtful Sound, which offer amazingly clear conditions.

Expect to pay anywhere from $180 for a short, introductory, pool-based scuba course, and around $600 for a four-day, PADI-approved, ocean-dive course. One-off organised boat- and land-based dives start at around $170. Resources include:

New Zealand Underwater Association (www.nzu.org.nz)

Dive New Zealand (www.divenewzealand.com)

White-Water Rafting, Kayaking & Canoeing

Epic mountain ranges and associated rainfall mean there's no shortage of great rivers to raft, nor any shortage of operators ready to get you into the rapids. Rivers are graded from I to VI (VI meaning 'unraftable'), with operators often running a couple of different trips to suit ability and age (rougher stretches are usually limited to rafters aged 13 or above).

On the South Island, Queenstown's Shotover and Kawarau Rivers are deservedly popular, but the Rangitata (Geraldine), Buller (Murchison) and the Arnold and Waiho rate just as highly. For a multiday epic, check out the Landsborough.

Kayaking and canoeing are rampant, particularly on friendly lake waters, although there are still plenty of places to paddle the rapids. Resources include:

New Zealand Rafting Association (www.nz-rafting.co.nz)

Whitewater NZ (www.rivers.org.nz)

New Zealand Kayak (www.kayaknz.co.nz)

Vineyard at Blenheim (p67)

Plan Your Trip
Food & Drink

Travellers, start your appetites! Eating on the South Island is
a highlight of any visit. You can be utilitarian if money is tight,
or embrace NZ's full culinary bounty, from fresh seafood and
gourmet burgers to farmers market fruit-and-veg and crisp-linen
fine dining. Eateries range from fish and chip shops and pub
bistros to retro cafes and ritzy dining rooms. Drinking here, too,
presents boundless opportunities to have a good time, with Kiwi
coffee, craft beer and wine at the fore.

Best South Island Restaurants

Roots (p151) One of NZ's most stylish and lauded restaurants: local and seasonal degustation in little Lyttelton.

Arbour (p71) Arguably the best winery restaurant in NZ (argue over a glass of sav blanc...).

Blue Kanu (p229) This surprising Queenstown eatery presents some of the best Māori, Pasifika and Asian flavours in NZ.

Twenty Seven Steps (p147) Upstairs (count 'em – 27?) in Christchurch is this elegant Mod NZ operator.

Pegasus Bay (p161) The pick of the Waipara Valley winery restaurants.

Bracken (p199) Tasting menus at the top of Dunedin's dining scene.

La Rumbla (p239) Bringing bold Spanish flavours and late-night dining to Arrowtown.

Riverstone Kitchen (p191) Homegrown goodness in superior rustic style near Oamaru.

Modern NZ

Once upon a time in a decade not so far away, New Zealand subsisted on a modest diet of 'meat and three veg'. Fine fare was a Sunday roast boiled into submission, and lasagne was considered exotic. Fortunately the country's culinary sophistication has evolved: kitchens now thrive on bending conventions and absorbing multicultural influences from around the planet. The resultant cuisine is dynamic and surprising.

Immigration has been key to this culinary rise – particularly the post-WWII influx of migrants from Europe, Asia and the Middle East – as has an adventurous breed of local restaurant-goers and the elevation of Māori and Pacific Islander flavours and ingredients to the mainstream.

In order to wow the socks off increasingly demanding diners, restaurants must now succeed in fusing contrasting ingredients and traditions into ever more innovative fare. The phrase 'Modern NZ' has been coined to classify this unclassifiable technique: a melange of East and West, a swirl of Atlantic and Pacific Rim, and a dash of authentic French and Italian.

If this all sounds overwhelming, fear not. Traditional staples still hold sway (lamb, beef, venison, green-lipped mussels), but dishes are characterised by interesting flavours and fresh ingredients rather than fuss, clutter or snobbery. Spicing ranges from gentle to extreme, seafood is plentiful and meats are tender and full flavoured. Enjoy!

Vegetarians & Vegans

Most large urban centres have at least one dedicated vegetarian cafe or restaurant: see the Vegetarians New Zealand website (www.vegetarians.co.nz) for listings. Beyond this, almost all restaurants and cafes offer some vegetarian menu choices (although sometimes only one or two). Many eateries also provide gluten-free and vegan options. Always check that house-made stocks and sauces are vegetarian, too!

Lonely Planet uses a vegetarian icon in Eating listings to indicate either a good vegetarian selection, or an entirely vegetarian menu.

Farmers Markets

There are more than 50 farmers markets held around NZ. Most happen on weekends and are upbeat local affairs, where visitors can meet local producers and find fresh regional produce. Mobile coffee is usually present, and tastings are offered by enterprising and innovative stall holders. Bring a carry bag, and get there early for

LOCAL DELICACIES

Touring the South Island menus, keep an eye out for these local delights: kina (sea urchin), paua (abalone), kumara (sweet potato, often served as chips), whitebait (tiny fish, often cooked into fritters or omelettes) and the humble kiwifruit.

the best stuff! Check out www.farmers-markets.org.nz for South Island market locations, dates and times.

Cafes & Coffee

Somewhere between the early 2000s and today, New Zealand cottoned on to coffee culture in a big way. Caffeine has become a nationwide addiction: there are Italian-style espresso machines in virtually every cafe, boutique roasters are de rigueur and, in urban areas, the qualified barista (coffee maker) is the norm. On the South Island, Christchurch and student-filled Dunedin have produced generations of coffee aficionados. The cafe scenes here are vibrant, inclusive and family friendly: join the arty local crew and dunk yourself into it over a late-night conversation or an early-morning recovery.

Pubs, Bars & Beer

Gone are the days when Kiwi pubs were male bastions with dim lighting, smoky air and sticky beer-soaked carpets – these days locals go to the pub with their kids for brunch or to meet friends for some tapas as much as anything else. Food has become integral to the NZ pub experience, along with the inexorable rise of craft beer in the national drinking consciousness.

Craft beer – small-batch beers brewed independently of big-label brewers with local ingredients, flavours and enthusiasm – is New Zealand's most recent obsession. Myriad small breweries have popped up around the country in the last several years, paralleled by a boom in small bars in which to sample the product, with revolving beers on tap and passionate bar staff who know all there is to know about where the beers have come from, who made them and what's in them. A night on the tiles here has become less about volume and capacity, and more about selectivity and virtue.

But aside from the food and the fancy beer, the NZ pub remains a place where all Kiwis can unite with a common purpose: to watch their beloved All Blacks play rugby on the big screen. Try to catch an AB's

An espresso in the making

game at a pub or a bar while you're here – a raucous experience to say the least!

Wine Regions

Like the wine industry in neighbouring Australia, the New Zealand version has European migrants to thank for its status and success – visionary visitors who knew good soils and a good climate when they saw it, and planted the first vines. NZ's oldest vineyard – **Mission Estate Winery** (06-845 9354; www.missionestate.co.nz; 198 Church Rd, Taradale; 9am-5pm Mon-Sat,

> ### YOUR SHOUT!
> At the bar, 'shouting' is a revered custom, where people take turns to pay for a round of drinks. Disappearing before it's your shout won't win you many friends. Once the drinks are distributed, a toast of 'Cheers!' is standard practice: look each other in the eye and clink glasses.

Whitebait fritters, a local delicacy

10am-4.30pm Sun) in Hawke's Bay on the North Island – was established by French Catholic missionaries in 1851 and is still producing top-flight wines today.

But it wasn't until the 1970s that things really got going, with traditional agricultural exports dwindling, Kiwis travelling more and the introduction of BYO ('Bring Your Own' wine) restaurant licensing conspiring to raise interest and demand for local wines.

Since then, New Zealand cool-climate wines have conquered the world, with a clutch of key regions producing the lion's share of bottles. Organised day tours via minivan or bicycle are a great way to visit a few select wineries.

On the South Island, the key regions are:

Marlborough NZ's biggest and most widely known wine region sits at the top of the South Island, where a microclimate of warm days and cool nights is perfect for growing sauvignon blanc. You could spend many days touring the many cellar doors here (why not?). (p70)

Central Otago Reaching from Cromwell in the north to Alexandra in the south and Gibbston near Queenstown in the west, the South Island's Central Otago region produces sublime riesling and pinot noir. (p205)

Waipara Valley Not to be left out of proceedings, Christchurch has its own nearby wine region – the Waipara Valley just north of the city – where divine riesling and pinot gris comes to fruition. (p161)

Plan Your Trip
Travel with Children

The South Island is a terrific place to travel with kids: safe and affordable, with loads of playgrounds, kid-centric activities, a moderate climate and chilli-free cuisine. And it never takes too long to get from A to B here – helpful when the backseat drivers (or those in the front) are running thin on patience.

South Island for Kids

Fabulous wildlife parks, beaches, parks, snowy slopes, interactive museums and kids' playgrounds (with slides, swings, see-saws etc) proliferate across the South Island. This is a place where things happen on a manageable scale for kids.

Accommodation

Many motels and holiday parks have playgrounds, games rooms and kids' DVDs, and often fenced swimming pools, trampolines and acres of grass. Cots and high chairs aren't always available at budget and midrange accommodation, but top-end hotels supply them and often provide child-minding services. Many B&Bs promote themselves as blissfully kid-free, and hostels tend to focus on the backpacker demographic. But there are plenty of hostels (including YHA) that do allow kids.

For large families, book ahead if you all want to sleep in the same room: many motels and hotels have adjoining rooms that can be opened up to form large family suites.

Admission Fees & Discounts

Kids' and family rates are often available for accommodation, tours, attraction entry

Best Regions for Kids

Queenstown & Wanaka
The NZ snow scene can be very 'adult' if you want it to be. But it's just as easy to enjoy with kids (actually, it's more fun). Head for the kid-friendly resorts and go snow-crazy.

Christchurch & Canterbury
Nature parks, rowboats and botanic gardens in the big city, and the amazing Banks Peninsula not far away (wildlife aplenty). Or cross the entire country in a train!

The West Coast
Kooky rock formations, glaciers, wild beaches, mirror-flat lakes, whitebait fritters and cheeky keas: the West Coast is a wild wonderland for kids (or anyone, really) with a curious spirit.

Marlborough & Nelson
Paddle a kayak, swim at a golden-sand beach, check out some sea mammals or tackle an easy-going trail in the Marlborough Sounds on two feet or two wheels.

fees, and air, bus and train transport, with discounts of as much as 50% off the adult rate. Note that the definition of 'child' can vary from under 12 to under 18 years; toddlers (under four years old) usually get free admission and transport.

Babysitting

For specialised child care, try www.rockmybaby.co.nz, or look under 'babysitters' and 'child care centres' in the Yellow Pages (www.yellow.co.nz).

Breastfeeding & Nappy Changing

Most Kiwis are relaxed about public breastfeeding and nappy changing: wrestling with a nappy (diaper) in the open boot of a car is a common sight! Alternatively, most major towns have public rooms where parents can go to feed their baby or change a nappy. Infant formula and disposable nappies are widely available.

Eating Out with Children

If you sidestep the flashier restaurants, children are generally welcome in South Island eateries. Cafes are kid-friendly, and you'll see families getting in early for dinner in pub dining rooms. Most places can supply high chairs. Dedicated kids' menus are common, but selections are usually uninspiring (ham-and-pineapple pizza, fish fingers, chicken nuggets etc). If a restaurant doesn't have a kids' menu, find something on the regular menu and ask the kitchen to downsize it. It's usually fine to bring toddler food in with you. If the sun is shining, hit the farmers markets and find yourself a picnic spot.

Children's Highlights

Getting Active

Queenstown (p217) Everything from kids' rafting trips to paragliding, bungy jumping, ziplines, iceskating and (of course) skiing.

Queen Charlotte Track (p64) Accessible tramping for families.

Marahau (p88) Saddle up a horse (or a pony) and head out along the beach.

Beaches

St Kilda Beach (p195) It's a chilly swim in Dunedin, but the kids don't seem to mind.

Wharariki Beach (p95) Dunes, seals, islets and wild waves (just don't think about swimming).

Pohara (p94) A beach as wide as London Heathrow Airport's runway!

Wildlife Encounters

Kiwi Birdlife Park (p216) Spot a Kiwi in Queenstown.

West Coast Wildlife Centre (p122) Meet a rowi – the rarest kiwi in the world at Franz Josef.

Farewell Spit (p95) Say hello to the godwits, terns and Australasian gannets on the South Island's far northwestern tip.

Amazing Museums

Canterbury Museum (p137) A mummy, dinosaur bones and a cool Discovery Centre in Christchurch.

Omaka Aviation Heritage Centre (p67) Peter Jackson's awesome collection of big birds from WWI and WWII.

Southland Museum & Art Gallery (p264) Check out Henry, the 115-year-old tuatara!

Mum, Dad, We're Hungry

Whitebait Fritters The classic West Coast snack.

Nelson Farmers' Market (p82) Wednesday afternoon edible delights for all ages.

Kiwifruit (p85) Pick up a ripe bag at harvest time around Motueka.

Planning

Lonely Planet's *Travel with Children* contains buckets of useful information for travel with little 'uns. To aid your planning once you get to NZ, look for the free *Kidz Go!* (www.kidzgo.co.nz) and *LetsGoKids* (www.letsgokids.com.au) magazines at visitor information centres.. Handy family websites include:

➡ www.kidspot.co.nz

➡ www.kidsnewzealand.com

➡ www.kidsfriendlytravel.com

Regions at a Glance

Get ready for an oft-changing selection of some of the planet's most surprising scenery. From the marine labyrinth of the Marlborough Sounds to the craggy volcanic legacy of Banks Peninsula, the South Island packs a stunning scenic punch. Along the way, taste test the best of the country's emerging gourmet scene, balancing enjoyment of excellent wine and craft beer with active adventure amid the great outdoors. Kayak through the mist of Doubtful Sound or test yourself on the Milford or Routeburn Tracks – often in the company of New Zealand's quirky wildlife – before experiencing colonial history around the heritage streets of Dunedin and Oamaru.

Marlborough & Nelson

Wilderness
Food & Wine
Wildlife

National Parks

Not satisfied with just one national park, the Nelson region has three – Nelson Lakes, Kahurangi and the Abel Tasman. You could tramp in all three over a week.

Marlborough Wine Touring

Bobbing in Marlborough's sea of sauvignon blanc, riesling, pinot noir and bubbly are barrel-loads of quality cellar-door experiences and some fine regional food.

Kaikoura

The top of the South Island is home to myriad creatures, both in the water and on the wing. Kaikoura is a great one-stop shop for spotting a whale or swimming with dolphins and seals.

p56

The West Coast

Natural Wonders
Outdoor Activities
History

Crazy Rock Formations

Don't miss Oparara's famous arches, Punakaiki's Pancake Rocks and the sublime Hokitika Gorge.

Hiking

The West Coast offers tracks from an easy hour through to hard-core epics. Old mining and milling routes like Charming Creek Walkway and Mahinapua Tramline entice beginners and history buffs.

Pioneer Tales

The West Coast's pioneering history comes vividly to life at places such as Denniston, Shantytown, Reefton and Jackson Bay.

p99

Christchurch & Canterbury

Architecture
Outdoor Activities
Scenery

Christchurch & Akaroa

Earthquakes have damaged Christchurch's architectural heritage but the Canterbury Museum, Botanic Gardens and New Regent St still showcase the city's proud history. Nearby, Akaroa celebrates its French heritage.

Hiking & Kayaking

Tramp the alpine valleys around Arthur's Pass; kayak with dolphins on pristine Akaroa Harbour; or tramp and kayak amid the glacial lakes of Aoraki/Mt Cook National Park.

Banks Peninsula & the Southern Alps

Descend Banks Peninsula's Summit Rd to explore hidden bays and coves, and experience nature's grand scale: river valleys, soaring peaks and glaciers.

p131

Dunedin & Otago

Wildlife
Wine Regions
History

Birds, Seals & Sea Lions

Otago Peninsula's wild menagerie – seals, sea lions and penguins – patrol the rugged coastline, while rocky Taiaroa Head is the planet's only mainland breeding location for the magnificent royal albatross.

Bannockburn & Waitaki Valley

Barrel into the craggy valleys of Bannockburn for excellent vineyard restaurants and the world's best pinot noir, or delve into the up-and-coming Waitaki Valley wine scene for riesling and pinot gris.

Victoriana

Explore the arty and storied streets of Dunedin, or escape by foot or penny-farthing bicycle into the heritage ambience of Oamaru's restored Victorian Precinct.

p182

Queenstown & Wanaka

Outdoor Activities
Scenery
Wine Regions

Queenstown Adrenaline

Nowhere else offers so many adventurous activities: bungy jumping, river rafting and mountain biking only scratch the adrenaline-fuelled surface. Could this be the world's ultimate skydiving drop zone?

Mountains & Lakes

Queenstown's combo of Lake Wakatipu and the soaring Remarkables is a real jawdropper. Venture into prime NZ wilderness around Glenorchy and Mt Aspiring National Park.

Central Otago Wineries

Lunch at Amisfield Winery's award-winning restaurant near Arrowtown; explore the Gibbston Valley; and finish with a riesling tasting at Rippon, overlooking gorgeous Lake Wanaka.

p214

Fiordland & Southland

Scenery
Wilderness
Outdoor Activities

Epic Landscapes

The star of the show is remarkable Milford Sound, but take time to explore the peculiar landforms around the rugged Catlins coast or experience the remote, end-of-the-world appeal of Stewart Island.

National Parks

Fiordland National Park comprises much of New Zealand's precious Southwest New Zealand (Te Wahipounamu) World Heritage Area. Further south, Rakiura National Park showcases Stewart Island's beauty.

Hiking & Sea Kayaking

Test yourself by tramping a Great Walk such as the Milford or Kepler Tracks, or by negotiating a sea kayak around gloriously isolated Doubtful Sound.

p249

On the
Road

Marlborough & Nelson

Best Places to Eat

➡ Arbour (p71)

➡ Hopgood's (p82)

➡ Green Dolphin (p76)

➡ Sans Souci Inn (p94)

➡ DeVille (p81)

Best Places to Sleep

➡ Hopewell (p66)

➡ Bay of Many Coves Resort (p65)

➡ Kaikoura Cottage Motels (p75)

➡ Adrift (p93)

➡ St Leonards (p69)

Why Go?

For many travellers, Marlborough and Nelson will be their introduction to what South Islanders refer to as the 'Mainland'. Having left windy Wellington, and made a white-knuckled crossing of Cook Strait, folk are often surprised to find the sun shining and the temperature 10°C warmer.

These top-of-the-South neighbours have much in common beyond an amenable climate: both boast renowned coastal holiday spots, particularly the Marlborough Sounds, Abel Tasman National Park and Kaikoura. There are two other national parks (Kahurangi and Nelson Lakes) amid more mountain ranges than you can poke a Leki-stick at.

And so it follows that these two regions have an abundance of produce, from game and seafood to summer fruits, and most famously the grapes that work their way into the wine glasses of the world's finest restaurants. Keep your penknife and picnic set at the ready.

When to Go

➡ The forecast is good: Marlborough and Nelson soak up some of New Zealand's sunniest weather, with January and February the warmest months when daytime temperatures average 22°C.

➡ July is the coldest, averaging 12°C. However, the top of the South sees some wonderful winter weather, with frosty mornings often giving way to sparklingly clear skies and T-shirt temperatures.

➡ The rumours are true: it *is* wetter and more windswept the closer you get to the West Coast.

➡ From around Christmas to mid-February, the top of the South teems with Kiwi holidaymakers, so plan ahead during this time and be prepared to jostle for position with a load of jandal-wearing families.

ℹ️ Getting There & Away

Cook Strait can be crossed slowly and scenically on the ferries between Wellington and Picton, and swiftly on flights servicing key destinations.

InterCity is the major bus operator, but there are also local shuttles. From October to May, KiwiRail's Coastal Pacific train takes the scenic route from Picton to Christchurch, via Blenheim and Kaikoura.

Renting a car is easy, with a slew of car-hire offices in Picton and depots throughout the region.

Popular coastal areas such as the Marlborough Sounds and Abel Tasman National Park are best navigated on foot or by kayak, with water-taxi services readily available to join the dots.

MARLBOROUGH REGION

Picton is the gateway to the South Island and the launching point for Marlborough Sounds exploration. A cork's pop south of Picton is Blenheim and its world-famous wineries, and further south still is Kaikoura, the whale-watching mecca.

History

Long before Abel Tasman sheltered on the east coast of D'Urville Island in 1642 (more than 100 years before James Cook blew through in 1770), Māori knew the Marlborough area as Te Tau Ihu o Te Waka a Māui (the prow of Māui's canoe). It was Cook who named Queen Charlotte Sound; his reports made the area the best-known sheltered anchorage in the southern hemisphere. In 1827 French navigator Jules Dumont d'Urville discovered the narrow strait now known as French Pass. His officers named the island just to the north in his honour. In the same year a whaling station was established at Te Awaiti in Tory Channel, which brought about the first permanent European settlement in the district.

ℹ️ Getting There & Away

Air New Zealand (☏ 0800 747 000; www.airnewzealand.co.nz) has direct flights between Blenheim airport and Wellington, Auckland, and Christchurch, with onward connections. **Soundsair** (☏ 0800 505 005, 03-520 3080; www.soundsair.co.nz; 3 Auckland St) connects Blenheim with Wellington, Paraparaumu and Napier. **KiwiRail Scenic** (☏ 0800 872 467; www.kiwirailscenic.co.nz) runs the Coastal Pacific service daily (October to May) each way between Picton and Christchurch via Blenheim and Kaikoura.

Buses serving Picton depart from the **Interislander terminal** (p61) or nearby **i-SITE** (p61).

ESSENTIAL MARLBOROUGH & NELSON

Eat Doris' bratwurst at the weekend markets in Nelson and Motueka (p87).

Drink A pint of Captain Cooker at Golden Bay's Mussel Inn (p93).

Read How to Drink a Glass of Wine by John Saker.

Listen to the dawn chorus in Nelson Lakes National Park (p97).

Watch The tide roll in, and then watch it roll away again...

Festival Marlborough Wine Festival (p68)

Go Green On the Heaphy Track (p96), a hotbed of ecological wonderment.

Online www.marlboroughnz.com, www.nelsonnz.com, www.kaikoura.co.nz

Area code ☏ 03

InterCity (☏ 03-365 1113; www.intercity.co.nz) runs buses between Picton and Christchurch via Blenheim and Kaikoura, with connections to Dunedin, Queenstown and Invercargill. Services also run between Nelson and Picton, with connections to Motueka and the West Coast. At least one bus daily on each of these routes connects with a Wellington ferry service. **Naked Bus** (☏ 0900 625 33; www.nakedbus.com) runs south to Christchurch, Dunedin and Queenstown.

Picton

POP 2950

Half asleep in winter, but hyperactive in summer (with up to eight fully laden ferry arrivals per day), boaty Picton clusters around a deep gulch at the head of Queen Charlotte Sound. It's the main traveller port for the South Island, and the best base for tackling the Marlborough Sounds and Queen Charlotte Track. Over the last few years this little town has really bloomed, and offers visitors plenty of reason to linger even after the obvious attractions are knocked off the list.

⊙ Sights

Edwin Fox Maritime Museum MUSEUM (www.edwinfoxsociety.co.nz; Dunbar Wharf; adult/child $15/5; ⊙9am-5pm) Purportedly the world's ninth-oldest surviving wooden ship, the *Edwin Fox* was built near Calcutta and

Marlborough & Nelson Highlights

1 Kaikoura (p72) Getting up close to wildlife, including whale, seals, dolphins and albatrosses.

2 Marlborough Wine Region (p57) Nosing your way through the wineries.

3 Queen Charlotte Track (p64) Tramping or biking in the Marlborough Sounds.

4 Great Taste Trail (p83) Eating and drinking your way along this popular cycle trail.

5 Abel Tasman National Park (p88) Kayaking or tramping in this postcard-perfect park.

6 Omaka Aviation Heritage Centre (p67)

Getting blown away at one of NZ's best museums.

7 Farewell Spit (p95) Driving through a dunescape with gannets and godwits for company.

8 Heaphy Track (p96) Reaching the wild West Coast on foot, crossing through Kahurangi National Park.

launched in 1853. During its chequered career it carried troops to the Crimean War, convicts to Australia and immigrants to NZ. This museum has maritime exhibits, including the venerable old dear herself.

Picton Museum   MUSEUM
(London Quay; adult/child $5/1; ⊙10am-4pm) If you dig local history – whaling, sailing and the 1964 Roller Skating Champs – this will float your boat. The photo displays are well worth a look, especially for five bucks.

🏃 Activities

The majority of activity happens around the Marlborough Sounds, but landlubbers will still find enough to occupy themselves.

The town has some very pleasant walks. A free i-SITE map details many of these, including an easy 1km track to Bob's Bay. The Snout Track (three hours return) continues along the ridge offering superb water views. Climbing a hill behind the town, the Tirohanga Track is a two-hour leg-stretching loop offering the best view in the house. For town explorations, hire bikes for the whole family from Wilderness Guides (p62).

Nine Dives   DIVING
(☑0800 934 837, 03-573 7199; www.ninedives. co.nz; trips $195-350) Offers dive trips around the Sounds taking in marine reserves and various wrecks including the *Mikhail Lermontov*, plus diver training. Snorkelling seal-swims also available ($150).

👉 Tours

Marlborough Tour Company   TOUR
(☑0800 990 800, 03-577 9997; www. marlboroughtourcompany.co.nz; Town Wharf; adult/child $145/59; ⊙departs 1.30pm) Runs the 3½-hour 'Seafood Odyssea' cruise to a salmon farm, complete with an ocean bounty and sauvignon blanc tasting.

🛏 Sleeping

★ Jugglers Rest   HOSTEL $
(☑03-573 5570; www.jugglersrest.com; 8 Canterbury St; sites from $20, dm $33, d $75-85; ⊙closed Jun-Sep; @ 🛜) 🏄 Jocular hosts keep all their balls in the air at this well-run, ecofriendly, bunk-free backpackers. Peacefully located a 10-minute walk from town, or even less on a free bike. Cheery gardens are a good place to socialise with fellow travellers, especially during the occasional circus-skills shows.

Buccaneer Lodge   LODGE $
(☑03-573 5002; www.buccaneerlodge.co.nz; 314 Waikawa Rd, Waikawa; s $90, d $99-124; 🛜) This Waikawa Bay lodge offers tidy, basic en suite rooms, many with expansive views of the Sounds from the 1st-floor balcony. Town transfers, bike hire and home-baked bread come courtesy of the kindly owners.

Tombstone Backpackers   HOSTEL $
(☑03-573 7116; www.tombstonebp.co.nz; 16 Gravesend Pl; dm $30-34, d with/without bathroom $87/80; @ 🛜) Rest in peace in a smart dorm, double room, or self-contained apartment ($118). Also on offer are a spa overlooking the harbour, free breakfast, a sunny reading room, table tennis, free internet, ferry pickup and drop-off... The list goes on.

Sequoia Lodge Backpackers   HOSTEL $
(☑0800 222 257, 03-573 8399; www.sequoialodge. co.nz; 3a Nelson Sq; dm $29-31, d with/without bathroom $84/74; 🛜) A well-managed backpackers in a colourful, high-ceilinged Victorian house. It's a little out of the centre, but has bonuses including free wi-fi, hammocks, barbecues, a hot tub and nightly chocolate pudding. Complimentary breakfast May to October.

Picton Top 10 Holiday Park   HOLIDAY PARK $
(☑0800 277 444, 03-573 7212; www.pictontop10. co.nz; 70 Waikawa Rd; sites from $36, units $75-185; @ 🛜 🏊) About 500m from town, this compact, well-kept park has plenty of lawn and picnic benches, plus crowd-pleasing facilities including a playground, barbecue area and swimming pool.

★ Whatamonga Homestay   HOMESTAY $$
(☑03-573 7192; www.whsl.co.nz; 425 Port Underwood Rd; d incl breakfast $180; @ 🛜) Follow Waikawa Rd, which becomes Port Underwood Rd, for 8km and you'll bump into this classy waterside option – two self-contained units with king-sized beds and balconies with magic views. Two other rooms under the main house share a bathroom. Free kayaks, dinghies and fishing gear are available. Minimum two-night stay.

Harbour View Motel   MOTEL $$
(☑03-573 6259, 0800 101 133; www.harbour viewpicton.co.nz; 30 Waikawa Rd; d $145-185; 🛜) Its elevated position means this motel commands good views of Picton's mast-filled harbour from its smart, self-contained studios with timber decks.

Picton

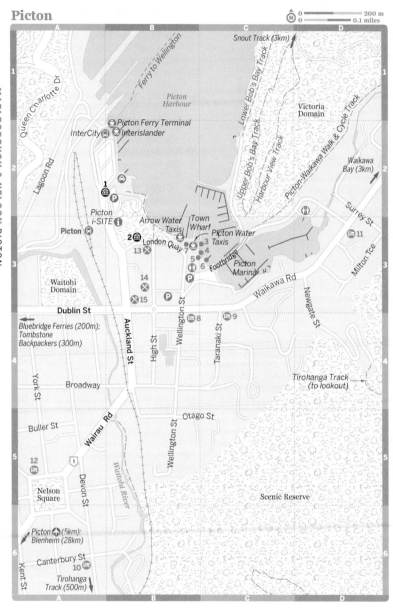

Gables B&B B&B **$$**
(☎ 03-573 6772; www.thegables.co.nz; 20 Waikawa Rd; s $100, d $140-170, units $155-175; @ 🛜) This historic B&B (once home to Picton's mayor) has three individually styled rooms in the main house and two homely self-contained units out the back. Lovely hosts show good humour (ask about the Muffin Club) and provide excellent local advice.

Picton

✗ Eating

Gusto   CAFE $
(33 High St; meals $11-21; ⊙7.30am-2.30pm; 🖉) This friendly and hard-working joint does beaut breakfasts including first-class salmon-scrambled eggs and a 'Morning Glory' fry-up worth the calories. Lunch options may include local mussels or a steak sandwich.

Picton Village Bakkerij   BAKERY $
(cnr Auckland & Dublin Sts; bakery items $2-8; ⊙6am-4pm Mon-Fri, to 3.30pm Sat; 🖉) Dutch owners bake trays of European goodies here, including interesting breads, filled rolls, cakes and custardy, tarty treats. An excellent stop before or after the ferry, or to stock a packed lunch.

Café Cortado   CAFE $$
(www.cortado.co.nz; cnr High St & London Quay; mains $16-34; ⊙8am-late) A pleasant corner cafe and bar with sneaky views of the harbour through the foreshore's pohutukawa and palms. This consistent performer turns out fish dishes, homemade cheeseburgers and decent pizza.

ℹ Information

Picton i-SITE (🖉03-520 3113; www.marlboroughnz.com; Foreshore; ⊙8am-5pm Mon-Fri, to 4pm Sat & Sun) All vital tourist guff including maps, Queen Charlotte Track information, lockers and transport bookings. Dedicated Department of Conservation (DOC) counter.

ℹ Getting There & Away

AIR

Soundsair (p57) flies between Picton and Wellington (adult/child from $99/89); a shuttle bus to/from the airstrip at Koromiko is available.

BOAT

There are two operators crossing Cook Strait between Picton and Wellington, and although all ferries leave from more or less the same place, each has its own terminal. The main transport hub (with car-rental depots) is at the Interislander Terminal, which also has a cafe and internet facilities.

Bluebridge Ferries (🖉0800 844 844, 04-471 6188; www.bluebridge.co.nz; adult/child from $51/26; 🖳) Crossings take 3½ hours, and the company runs up to four sailings in each direction daily. Cars and campervans from $120, motorbikes $51, bicycles $10. The sleeper service arrives in Picton at 6am.

Interislander (🖉0800 802 802; www.interislander.co.nz; Interislander Ferry Terminal, Auckland St; adult/child $55/28) Crossings take at least three hours 10 minutes; up to four sailings in each direction daily. Cars are priced from $121, campervans (up to 5.5m) from $153, motorbikes $56, bicycles $15.

BUS

Buses serving Picton depart from the Interislander ferry terminal or the nearby i-SITE.

InterCity (🖉03-365 1113; www.intercity.co.nz; outside Interislander Ferry Terminal, Auckland St) runs south to Christchurch twice daily (5½ hours) via Blenheim (30 minutes) and Kaikoura (2½ hours), with connections to Dunedin, Queenstown and Invercargill. Services also run to/from Nelson (2¼ hours), with connections to Motueka and the West Coast. At least one bus daily on each of these routes connects with a Wellington ferry service.

Smaller shuttles running to Christchurch and Nelson include **Atomic Shuttles** (🖉03-349 0697, 0508 108 359; www.atomictravel.co.nz).

TRAIN

KiwiRail Scenic (p57) runs the Coastal Pacific service daily (October to May) each way between Picton and Christchurch via Blenheim and Kaikoura (and via 22 tunnels and 175 bridges!), departing Picton at 1.15pm and Christchurch at 7am. Adult one-way Picton–Christchurch fares start at $79. The service connects with the Interislander ferry (p61).

ℹ Getting Around

Shuttle services around town and beyond are offered by **A1 Picton Shuttles** (🖉022 018 8472; www.a1pictonshuttles.co.nz).

Renting a car in Picton is easy and competitively priced (as low as $40 per day), with numerous

MĀORI NZ: MARLBOROUGH & NELSON

While Māori culture on the South Island is much less evident than in the north, it can still be found in pockets, particularly around Kaikoura, which is rich in Māori history. Maori Tours Kaikoura (p73) provide an illuminating historical and contemporary insight into Māoridom.

rental companies based at the Interislander ferry terminal and many others within a short walk. **Ace** (☑ 03-573 8939; www.acerentalcars. co.nz; Interislander Ferry Terminal) and **Omega** (☑ 03-573 5580; www.omegarentalcars.com; 1 Lagoon Rd) are reliable local operators. Most agencies allow drop-offs in Christchurch; if you're planning to drive to the North Island, most companies suggest you leave your car at Picton and pick up another one in Wellington after crossing Cook Strait.

Marlborough Sounds

The Marlborough Sounds are a maze of peaks, bays, beaches and watery reaches, formed when the sea flooded deep river valleys after the last ice age. They are very convoluted: Pelorus Sound, for example, is 42km long but has 379km of shoreline.

Many spectacular locations can be reached by car. The wiggly 35km drive along Queen Charlotte Drive from Picton to Havelock is a great Sounds snapshot, but if you have a spare day, head out to French Pass (or even D'Urville Island) for some big-picture framing of the Outer Sounds. Roads are predominantly narrow and occasionally unsealed; allow plenty of driving time and keep your wits about you.

Sounds travel is invariably quicker by boat (for example, Punga Cove from Picton by car takes two to three hours, but just 45 minutes by boat). Fortunately, an armada of vessels offer scheduled and on-demand boat services, with the bulk operating out of Picton for the Queen Charlotte Sound, and some from Havelock for Kenepuru and Pelorus Sounds.

There are loads of walking, kayaking and biking opportunities, but there's diving as well – notably the wreck of the *Mikhail Lermontov*, a Russian cruise ship that sank in Port Gore in 1986.

◎ Sights

Motuara Island WILDLIFE RESERVE
(www.doc.govt.nz; Queen Charlotte Sound) ⬤
This DOC-managed, predator-free island reserve is chock-full of rare NZ birds including Okarito kiwi (rowi), native pigeons (kereru), saddleback (tieke) and King Shags. You can get here with water taxi and tour operators working out of Picton.

☞ Tours

From Picton

★**Wilderness Guides** TOUR
(☑ 0800 266 266, 03-573 5432; www.wilderness guidesnz.com; Town Wharf; 1-day guided trips from $130, kayak/bike hire per day $60) Host of the popular and flexible one- to three-day 'multisport' trips (kayak/walk/cycle) plus many other guided and independent biking, tramping and kayaking tours, including a remote Ship Cove paddle. Mountain bikes and kayaks for hire, too.

Cougar Line TOUR
(☑ 0800 504 090, 03-573 7925; www.cougarline. co.nz; Town Wharf; track round-trips $105, full-day tours from $85) Queen Charlotte Track transport, plus various half- and full-day cruise/ walk trips, including the rather special (and flexible) eco-cruise to Motuara Island and a day walk from Resolution Bay to Furneaux Lodge.

Beachcomber Cruises TOUR
(☑ 0800 624 526, 03-573 6175; www.beachcomber cruises.co.nz; Town Wharf, Picton; mail runs $97, cruises from $69, track round-trips $99) Two- to eight-hour cruise adventures, including the classic 'Magic Mail Run', plus walking, biking and resort lunch options and round-trip track transport.

Marlborough Sounds Adventure Company TOUR
(☑ 0800 283 283, 03-573 6078; www.marlborough sounds.co.nz; Town Wharf; half- to 3-day guided packages $95-595, kayak hire per half-day from $40) Bike-walk-kayak trips, with options to suit every inclination and duration. A top day option is the kayak and hike ($175). Bikes, kayaks, stand-up paddle boards and camping equipment also available.

From Anakiwa

Sea Kayak Adventures KAYAKING, BIKING
(☑ 03-574 2765, 0800 262 5492; www.nzseakay aking.com; cnr Queen Charlotte Dr & Anakiwa Rd; half-/1-day guided paddles $85/125) Guided and

Marlborough Sounds

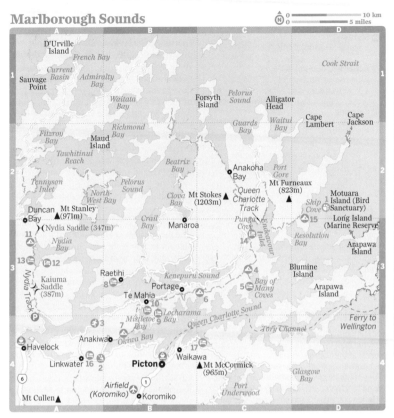

'guided then go' kayaking with bike/hike options around Queen Charlotte, Kenepuru and Pelorus Sounds. Also offers kayak and mountain-bike rental (half-/full-day $40/60).

From Havelock

Pelorus Mail Boat CRUISE
(☑ 03-574 1088; www.themailboat.co.nz; Jetty 1, Havelock Marina; adult/child $128/free; ⊙ departs 9.30am Tue, Thu & Fri) Popular full-day boat cruise through the far reaches of Pelorus Sound on a genuine NZ Post delivery run. Bookings essential; BYO lunch. Picton and Blenheim pick-up and drop-off available.

Waterways Boating Safaris BOATING
(☑ 03-574 1372; www.waterways.co.nz; 745 Kenepuru Rd; half-/full-day $110/150) Be guided around Kenepuru Sound while piloting your own zippy boat. A fun way to get out on the water, see the scenery and learn about the area's ecology and history. BYO lunch.

Greenshell Mussel Cruise CRUISE
(☑ 03-577 9997, 0800 990 800; www.marlborough tourcompany.co.nz; Havelock Marina; adult/child $125/45; ⊙ departs 1.30pm) Three-hour cruise to mussel in on Kenepuru's aquaculture. Includes a tasting of steamed mussels and a glass of wine. Bookings essential.

🛏 Sleeping

Some Sounds sleeping options are accessible only by boat and are deliciously isolated, but the most popular are those on (or just off) the Queen Charlotte Track. Some places close over winter; call ahead to check.

There are over 30 DOC camping grounds throughout the Sounds (many accessible only by boat), providing water and toilet facilities but not much else.

Ask at Picton i-SITE (p61) about local bachs for rent, of which there are many.

Marlborough Sounds

◎ **Sights**

⊕ **Activities, Courses & Tours**

⊜ **Sleeping**

❶ Getting There & Away

The Marlborough Sounds are most commonly explored from Picton, where boat operators congregate at the centrally located Town Wharf. They offer everything from lodge transfers to cruises taking in sites such as **Ship Cove** and **Motuara Island** bird sanctuary, to round-trip **Queen Charlotte Track** transport and pack transfers that allow trampers to walk without a heavy burden. Bikes and kayaks can also be transported.

Arrow Water Taxis (✆ 027 444 4689, 03-573 8229; www.arrowwatertaxis.co.nz; Town Wharf, Picton) Pretty much anywhere, on demand, for groups of four or more.

Float Plane (✆ 021 704 248, 03-573 9012; www.nz-scenic-flights.co.nz; Ferry Terminal, Picton; flights from $110) Offers Queen Charlotte Track and Sounds accommodation transfers and scenic flights, plus flights and trips to Nelson, Abel Tasman National Park and across to Wellington.

Kenepuru Water Taxi (✆ 021 132 3261, 03-573 4344; www.kenepuru.co.nz; 7170 Kenepuru Rd, Raetihi) Taxi and sightseeing trips around Kenepuru Sound, on demand.

Pelorus Sound Water Taxi (✆ 0508 4283 5625, 027 444 2852; www.pelorussoundwatertaxis.co.nz; Pier C, Havelock Marina) Taxi and sightseeing trips from Havelock, around Pelorus and Kenepuru Sounds, on demand.

Picton Water Taxis (✆ 03-573 7853, 027 227 0284; www.pictonwatertaxis.co.nz; The Waterfront, cnr London Quay & Wellington St, Picton) Water taxi and sightseeing trips around Queen Charlotte, on demand.

Queen Charlotte Track

One of NZ's classic walks – and now one of its Great Rides, too – the meandering, 70km Queen Charlotte Track offers gorgeous coastal scenery on its way from historic Ship Cove to Anakiwa, passing through a mixture of privately owned land and DOC reserves. Access depends on the cooperation of local landowners; respect their property by utilising designated campsites and toilets, and carrying out your rubbish. Your purchase of the **Track Pass** ($10 to $18), available from the i-SITE and track-related businesses, provides the co-op with the means to maintain and enhance the experience for all.

🏃 Activities

Queen Charlotte is a well-defined track, suitable for people of average fitness. Numerous boat and tour operators service the track, allowing you to tramp the whole three- to five-day journey, or to start and finish where you like, on foot or by kayak or bike. We're talking mountain biking here, and a whole lot of fun for fit, competent off-roaders. Part of the track is off-limits to cyclists from 1 December to the end of February, but there is still good riding to be had during this time.

Ship Cove is the usual (and recommended) starting point – mainly because it's easier to arrange a boat from Picton to Ship Cove than vice versa – but the track can be started from Anakiwa. There's a public phone at Anakiwa but not at Ship Cove.

Estimated walk times:

TRACK SECTION	DISTANCE (KM)	DURATION (HR)
Ship Cove to Resolution Bay	4.5	1½-2
Resolution Bay to head of Endeavour Inlet	10.5	2½-3
Endeavour Inlet to Camp Bay/Punga Cove	12	3-4
Camp Bay/Punga Cove to Torea Saddle/Portage	24	6-8
Torea Saddle/ Portage to Te Mahia Saddle	7.5	3-4
Te Mahia Saddle to Anakiwa	12.5	3-4

🛏 Sleeping

The beauty of the Queen Charlotte Track is that there are plenty of great day-trip options, allowing you to base yourself in Picton. However, there is also plenty of accommodation nicely spaced along the way, and boat operators will transport your luggage along the track for you.

At the self-sufficient end of the scale are six DOC campsites: **Schoolhouse Bay** (www.doc.govt.nz; adult/child $6/3), **Camp Bay** (www.doc.govt.nz; adult/child $6/3), **Bay of Many Coves** (www.doc.govt.nz; adult/child $6/3), **Black Rock** (www.doc.govt.nz; adult/child $6/3), **Cowshed Bay** (www.doc.govt.nz; adult/child $10/5) and **Davies Bay** (www.doc.govt.nz; adult/child $6/3). All have toilets and a water supply but no cooking facilities. There's also a variety of resorts, lodges, backpackers and guesthouses. Unless you're camping, it pays to book your accommodation waaay in advance, especially in summer.

Smiths Farm Holiday Park   HOLIDAY PARK $
(☑ 03-574 2806; www.smithsfarm.co.nz; 1419 Queen Charlotte Dr, Linkwater; campsites from $16 per person, cabins $60, units $110-130; @ 🛜) 🏊 Located on the aptly named Linkwater flat between Queen Charlotte and Pelorus, friendly Smiths makes a handy base camp for the track and beyond. Well-kept cabins and motel units face out onto the bushy hillside, while livestock nibble around the lush camping lawns. Short walks extend to a waterfall and magical glowworm dell.

Mistletoe Bay   HOLIDAY PARK $
(☑ 03-573 4048; www.mistletoebay.co.nz; Onahau Bay; campsites adult/child $16/10, dm/d $30/70, linen $7.50; 🛜) 🏊 Surrounded by bushy hills, Mistletoe Bay offers attractive camping with no-frills facilities. There are eight modern cabins ($140) sleeping up to six, plus a bunkhouse. Environmental sustainability abounds, as does the opportunity to jump off the jetty, kayak in the bay, or tramp the Queen Charlotte Track.

★ Te Mahia Bay Resort   RESORT $$
(☑ 03-573 4089; www.temahia.co.nz; 63 Te Mahia Rd; d $160-258; 🛜) This lovely low-key resort is within cooee of the Queen Charlotte Track in a picturesque bay on Kenepuru Sound. It has a range of delightful rooms-with-a-view, our pick of which are the great-value heritage units. The on-site shop has precooked meals, pizza, cakes, coffee and camping supplies (wine!), plus there is kayak hire and massage.

Lochmara Lodge   RESORT $$
(☑ 0800 562 462, 03-573 4554; www.lochmaralodge.co.nz; Lochmara Bay; units $99-300; 🛜) 🏊 This arty, eco-retreat can be reached via the Queen Charlotte Track or direct from Picton aboard the lodge's water taxi ($30 one-way). There are en suite doubles, units and chalets, all set in lush surroundings, a fully licensed cafe and restaurant, plus a bathhouse where you can indulge in a spa or massage.

Anakiwa 401   HOSTEL $$
(☑ 03-574 1388; www.anakiwa401.co.nz; 401 Anakiwa Rd; s/q $75/180, d $100-140; 🛜) At the southern end of the track, this former schoolhouse is a soothing spot to rest and reflect. There are two doubles (one with en suite), one twin and a beachy self-contained bunk. Jocular owners will have you jumping off the jetty for joy and imbibing espresso and ice cream (hallelujah) from their little green caravan (open summer afternoons). Free bikes and kayaks.

★ Bay of Many Coves Resort   RESORT $$$
(☑ 0800 579 9771, 03-579 9771; www.bayofmanycoves.co.nz; Bay of Many Coves; 1-/2-/3-bedroom apt $710/930/1100; 🛜 🏊) These schmick and secluded apartments feature all mod cons and private balconies overlooking the water. As well as upmarket cuisine, there are various indulgences such as massage, a spa and a hot tub. Kayaking and bush walks are also on the cards, as are adventures in the Sounds organised by the charming, hands-on owners and staff.

Mahana Lodge   LODGE $$$
(☑ 03-579 8373; www.mahanalodge.co.nz; Camp Bay, Endeavour Inlet; d $210; ⊙ closed Jun-Aug) 🏊 This beautiful property features a pretty waterside lawn and purpose-built lodge with four en suite doubles. Ecofriendly initiatives include bush regeneration, pest trapping and an organic veggie garden. In fact, feel-good factors abound: free kayaks, home baking and a blooming conservatory where prearranged evening meals are served (three courses $55).

Punga Cove Resort   RESORT $$$
(☑ 03-579 8561; www.pungacove.co.nz; Endeavour Inlet; units $275-450; @ 🛜 🏊) A rustic, charming resort offering self-contained studios, A-frame chalets and a lodge (sleeping up to seven), most with sweeping sea views. The backpackers is basic (single/double $58/116) but Punga's location atones. Ample activities (pool, spa, games and kayaks), plus a restaurant and boat-shed bar/cafe serving decent local beers and $26 pizza.

ℹ️ Information

The best place to get track information and advice is Picton **i-SITE** (p61), which also handles bookings for transport and accommodation. Also see the Queen Charlotte Track website (www.qctrack.co.nz).

ℹ️ Getting There & Away

Picton water taxis can drop you off and pick you up at numerous locations along the track.

Kenepuru & Pelorus Sounds

Kenepuru and Pelorus Sounds, to the west of Queen Charlotte Sound, are less populous and therefore offer fewer traveller services, including transport. There's some cracking scenery, however, and those with time to spare will be well rewarded by their explorations.

Havelock is the hub of this area, the western bookend of the 35km Queen Charlotte Drive (Picton being the eastern one) and the self-proclaimed 'Greenshell Mussel Capital of the World'. While hardly the most rock-and-roll of NZ towns, Havelock offers most necessities, including accommodation, fuel and food.

⊙ Sights

If a stroll through the streets of Havelock leaves you thinking that there *must* be more to this area, you're right – and to get a taste of it you need go no further than the **Cullen Point Lookout**, a 10-minute drive from Havelock along the Queen Charlotte Drive. A short walk leads up and around a headland overlooking Havelock, the surrounding valleys and Pelorus Sound.

Information on local sites and activities can be found at the Havelock i-SITE (p67), which shares its home with the Eyes On Nature museum, chock-full of frighteningly lifelike, full-size replicas of birds, fish and other critters.

And of course, there's plenty to see and do exploring the Marlborough Sounds (p62) themselves.

🏃 Activities

Pelorus Eco Adventures   KAYAKING
(☑ 0800 252 663, 03-574 2212; www.kayaknewzealand.com; Blue Moon Lodge, 48 Main Rd, Havelock; per person $175) Float in an inflatable kayak on scenic Pelorus River, star of the barrel scene in *The Hobbit*. Wend your

way down exhilarating rapids, through crystal-clear pools and past native forest and waterfalls. No experience required. Minimum two people.

Nydia Track   TRAMPING
(www.doc.govt.nz) The Nydia Track (27km, 10 hours) starts at Kaiuma Bay and ends at Duncan Bay (or vice versa). You'll need water and road transport to complete the journey; Havelock's Blue Moon Lodge runs a shuttle to Duncan Bay.

Around halfway along is beautiful **Nydia Bay**, where there's a **DOC campsite** (www.doc.govt.nz; adult/child $6/3) and **Nydia Lodge** (☑ 03-520 3002; www.doc.govt.nz; Nydia Bay; dm $15, minimum charge $60), an unhosted 50-bed lodge. Also in Nydia Bay, **On the Track Lodge** (☑ 03-579 8411; www.nydiatrack.org.nz; Nydia Bay; dm $40, s $80-100, d $130-160) 🍃 is a tranquil, eco-focused affair offering everything from packed lunches to evening meals and a hot tub.

🛏️ Sleeping

There's plenty of accommodation around Kenepuru and Pelorus, much of which is accessible off the Queen Charlotte Track. There are also some picturesque DOC campgrounds (most full to bursting in January), a few remote lodges and the very handy Smiths Farm (p65) holiday park at Linkwater, the crossroads for Queen Charlotte and Kenepuru, where you'll find a petrol station with snacks. Havelock also has a couple of decent offerings.

★ Hopewell   LODGE $
(☑ 03-573 4341; www.hopewell.co.nz; 7204 Kenepuru Rd, Double Bay; dm/cottages from $40/195, d with/without bathroom from $140/105; @ 🛜) Beloved of travellers from near and far, remote Hopewell sits waterside surrounded by native bush. Savour the long, winding drive to get there, or take a water taxi from Te Mahia ($20). Stay at least a couple of days, so you can chill out or enjoy the roll-call of activities: mountain biking, kayaking, sailing, fishing, eating gourmet pizza, soaking in the outdoor hot tub, and more.

Blue Moon Lodge   HOSTEL $
(☑ 03-574 2212, 0800 252 663; www.bluemoonhavelock.co.nz; 48 Main Rd, Havelock; dm $33, r with/without bathroom from $96/82; @ 🛜) 🍃 This pleasant and relaxed lodge has homely rooms in the main house, a spa family unit ($160), and cabins and a bunkhouse in the

yard. Notable features include a sunny barbecue deck, inflatable kayak trips on the Pelorus River, and Nydia Track transport.

Havelock Garden Motels　MOTEL $$
(☑03-574 2387; www.gardenmotels.com; 71 Main Rd, Havelock; d $125-160; ☏) Set in a large, graceful garden complete with dear old trees and blooms galore, these 1960s units have been tastefully revamped to offer homely comforts. Local activities are happily booked for you.

❶ Information

Havelock i-SITE (☑03-577 8080; www. pelorusnz.co.nz; 61 Main Rd, Havelock; ⊙9am-5pm summer only) This helpful wee visitor centre shares its home with the Eyes On Nature museum, chock-full of frighteningly lifelike, full-size replicas of birds, fish and other critters.

❶ Getting There & Away

InterCity (p57) runs daily from Picton to Havelock via Blenheim (one hour), and from Havelock to Nelson (1¼ hours). **Atomic Shuttles** (p61) plies the same run. Buses depart from near the **Havelock i-SITE**.

Blenheim

POP 30,600

Blenheim is an agricultural town 29km south of Picton on the pretty Wairau Plains between the Wither Hills and the Richmond Ranges. The last decade or so has seen town beautification projects, the maturation of the wine industry and the addition of a landmark museum significantly increase the town's appeal to visitors.

◉ Sights

★Omaka Aviation Heritage Centre　MUSEUM
(☑03-579 1305; www.omaka.org.nz; 79 Aerodrome Rd; adult/child $30/12, family from $45; ⊙9am-5pm Dec-Mar, 10am-4pm Apr-Nov) This exceptionally brilliant museum houses film-director Peter Jackson's collection of original and replica Great War aircraft, brought to life in a series of dioramas that depict dramatic wartime scenes, such as the death of the Red Baron. A new wing houses Dangerous Skies, a WW2 collection. Vintage biplane flights are available (20 minutes, $390 for two people).

A cafe and shop are on-site, and next door is **Omaka Classic Cars** (☑03-577 9419;

DON'T MISS

PELORUS BRIDGE

A peaky pocket of deep, green forest tucked between paddocks of bog-standard pasture, 18km west of Havelock, this scenic reserve contains one of the last stands of river-flat forest in Marlborough. It survived only because a town planned in 1865 didn't get off the ground by 1912, by which time obliterative logging made this little remnant look precious. Visitors can explore its many tracks, admire the historic bridge, take a dip in the limpid Pelorus River (alluring enough to star in Peter Jackson's *The Hobbit*), and partake in some home baking at the cafe. The fortunate few can stay overnight in DOC's small but perfectly formed **Pelorus Bridge Campground** (☑03-571 6019; www.doc.govt.nz; Pelorus Bridge, SH6; unpowered/powered sites per person $15/7.50), with its snazzy facilities building. Come sundown keep an eye out for long-tailed bats – the reserve is home to one of the last remaining populations in Marlborough.

---

www.omakaclassiccars.co.nz; adult/child $10/free; ⊙10am-4pm), which houses more than 100 vehicles dating from the '50s to the '80s.

Pollard Park　PARK
(Parker St) Ten minutes' walk from town, this 25-hectare park boasts beautiful blooming and scented gardens, a playground, tennis courts, croquet and a nine-hole golf course. It's pretty as a picture when lit up on summer evenings. Five minutes away, on the way to or from town, is the extensive **Taylor River Reserve**, a lovely place for a stroll.

Marlborough Museum　MUSEUM
(☑03-578 1712; www.marlboroughmuseum.org. nz; 26 Arthur Baker Pl, off New Renwick Rd; adult/child $10/5; ⊙10am-4pm) Besides a replica street-scene, vintage mechanicals and well-presented historical displays, there's the *Wine Exhibition*, for those looking to cap off their vineyard experiences.

🏃 Activities

★Driftwood Eco-Tours　KAYAKING, ECOTOUR
(☑03-577 7651; www.driftwoodecotours.co.nz; 749 Dillons Point Rd; kayak tours $70-180, 4WD tours for 2/3 people from $440/550) Go on a kayak or 4WD tour with passionate locals Will and

Rose for fascinating tours on and around the ecologically and historically significant Wairau Lagoon, just 10 minute' drive from Blenheim. Rare birds and the muppetty Royal Spoonbill may well be spotted. The self-contained 'retreat' offers accommodation for up to four people (double/quad $190/310; breakfast extra $15 per person) next to the Opawa River.

Wither Hills Farm Park WALKING
In a town as flat as a pancake, this hilly 11-sq-km park provides welcome relief, offering over 60km of walking and mountain-biking trails with grand views across the Wairau Valley and out to Cloudy Bay. Pick up a map from the i-SITE or check the information panels at the many entrances including Redwood St and Taylor Pass Rd.

High Country Horse Treks HORSE RIDING
(✈03-577 9424; www.high-horse.co.nz; 961 Taylor Pass Rd; 1-2hr treks $60-100) These animal-mad folks run horse treks for all abilities from their base 11km southwest of town (call for directions).

☞ Tours

Wine tours are generally conducted in a minibus, last between four and seven hours, take in four to seven wineries and range in price from $65 to $95 (with a few grand tours up to around $200 for the day, including a winery lunch).

Highlight Wine Tours TOUR
(✈03-577 9046, 027 434 6451; www.highlightwine tours.co.nz) Visit a chocolate factory, too. Custom tours available.

Bubbly Grape Wine Tours TOUR
(✈027 672 2195, 0800 228 2253; www.bubbly grape.co.nz) Three different tours including a gourmet lunch option.

Sounds Connection TOUR
(✈03-573 8843, 0800 742 866; www.sounds connection.co.nz) This operator partners up with **Herzog Winery** (✈03-572 8770; www. herzog.co.nz; 81 Jefferies Rd; mains $24-36; ⊙12-3pm & 6-9pm Wed-Sun) for a wine-and-food-matched lunch.

Bike2Wine TOUR
(✈03-572 8458, 0800 653 262; www.bike2wine. co.nz; 9 Wilson St, Renwick; standard/tandem per day $30/60, pick ups from $10) An alternative to the usual minibus tours – get around the grapes on two wheels. This operator offers self-guided, fully geared and supported tours.

⭐ Festivals & Events

Marlborough Wine Festival FOOD, WINE
(www.wine-marlborough-festival.co.nz; tickets $57; ⊙mid-Feb) Held at Brancott Vineyard (p70), this is an extravaganza of local wine, fine food and entertainment. Book accommodation well in advance.

🛏 Sleeping

Blenheim's budget beds fill with long-stay seasonal workers; hostels will help find work and offer weekly rates. Numerous mid-range motels can be found on Middle Renwick Rd west of the town centre, and SH1 towards Christchurch.

🛏 Central Blenheim

Grapevine Backpackers HOSTEL $
(✈03-578 6062; www.thegrapevine.co.nz; 29 Park Tce; dm $25-26, d $60-70, tr $84-90; ☎) Located inside an old maternity home a 10-minute walk from the town centre, Grapevine has respectable rooms set aside for travellers. The kitchen is tight, but offset by free canoes and a peaceful barbecue deck by the Opawa River. Bike hire is $25 per day.

Blenheim Top 10 Holiday Park HOLIDAY PARK $
(✈03-578 3667, 0800 268 666; www.blenheim top10.co.nz; 78 Grove Rd; sites $45, cabins $80-92, units & motel $135-145; @☎☎) Ten minutes' walk to town, this holiday park spreads out under and alongside the main road bridge over the Opawa River. Ask for the quietest spot available. Cabins and units are tidy but plain-Jane, set in a sea of asphalt. Funtime diversions include a spa, a pool, a playground and bike hire.

171 on High MOTEL $$
(✈0800 587 856, 03-579 5098; www.171onhighmo-tel.co.nz; 171 High St; d $145-185; ☎) A welcoming option close to town, these tasteful, splash-o colour studios and apartments are bright and breezy in the daytime, warm and shimmery in the evening. Expect a wide complement of facilities and 'extra mile' service.

Lugano Motorlodge MOTEL $$
(✈03-577 8808, 0800 584 266; www.lugano.co.nz; 91 High St; d $140-155; ☎) In a prime location opposite pretty Seymour Sq and a two-minute walk to the centre of town, this is a beige but smart and upmarket motel complex with modern conveniences. Ask about the end unit with two balconies, or at least plump for upstairs. Hush glass mutes the main-road traffic noise.

🛏 Wine Region

Watson's Way Lodge   LODGE $

(☑03-572 8228; www.watsonswaylodge.com; 56 High St, Renwick; campervans per person $18, d & tw $98; ⊘closed Aug-Sep; @🖥) This traveller-focused lodge has spick-and-span en suite rooms in a sweetly converted bungalow with a full kitchen and comfy lounge. There are also spacious leafy gardens dotted with fruit trees and hammocks, an outdoor claw-foot bath, bikes for hire (guest/public rate $18/28 per day) and local information aplenty.

★St Leonards   COTTAGES $$

(☑03-577 8328; www.stleonards.co.nz; 18 St Leonards Rd, Blenheim; d incl breakfast $125-320; 🖥🖳) Tucked into the 4.5-acre grounds of an 1886 homestead, these five stylish and rustic cottages offer privacy and a reason to stay put. Each is unique in its layout and perspective on the gardens and vines. Our pick is the capacious and cosy Woolshed, exuding agricultural chic. Resident sheep, chickens and deer await your attention.

Olde Mill House   B&B $$

(☑03-572 8458; www.oldemillhouse.co.nz; 9 Wilson St, Renwick; d $160; 🖥) On an elevated section in otherwise flat Renwick, this charming old house is a treat. Dyed-in-the-wool local hosts run a welcoming B&B, with stately decor, and home-grown fruit and homemade goodies for breakfast.

Free bikes, an outdoor spa and gardens make this a tip-top choice in the heart of the wine country.

Marlborough Wine Region

Marlborough Wine Region

MARLBOROUGH WINERIES

Marlborough is NZ's vinous colossus, producing around three-quarters of the country's wine. At last count, there were 229 sq km of vines planted – that's approximately 26,500 rugby pitches! Sunny days and cool nights create the perfect conditions for cool-climate grapes: world-famous sauvignon blanc, top-notch pinot noir, and notable chardonnay, riesling, gewürztraminer, pinot gris and bubbly. Drifting between tasting rooms and dining amongst the vines is a quintessential South Island experience.

A Taste of the Tastings

Around 35 wineries are open to the public. Our picks of the bunch provide a range of high-quality cellar-door experiences, with most being open from around 10.30am till 4.30pm (some scale back operations in winter). Wineries may charge a small fee for tasting, normally refunded if you purchase a bottle. Pick up a copy of the *Marlborough Wine Trail* map from **Blenheim i-SITE** (p71), also available online at www.wine-marlborough.co.nz. If your time is limited, pop into **Wino's** (www.winos.co.nz; 49 Grove Rd; ☉10am-7pm Sun-Thu, to 8pm Fri & Sat) in Blenheim, a sterling one-stop shop for some of Marlborough's finer and less common drops.

Auntsfield Estate (☑03-578 0622; www.auntsfield.co.nz; 270 Paynters Rd; ☉11am-4.30pm Mon-Fri summer only)

Bladen (www.bladen.co.nz; 83 Conders Bend Rd; ☉11am-4.30pm)

Brancott Estate Heritage Centre (www.brancottestate.com; 180 Brancott Rd; ☉10am-4.30pm)

Clos Henri Vineyard (www.clos-henri.com; 639 State Hwy 63, RD1; ☉10am-4pm Mon-Fri summer only)

Cloudy Bay (www.cloudybay.co.nz; 230 Jacksons Rd, Blenheim; ☉10am-4pm) 🖉

Forrest (www.forrest.co.nz; 19 Blicks Rd; ☉10am-4.30pm)

Framingham (www.framingham.co.nz; 19 Conders Bend Rd, Renwick; ☉10.30am-4.30pm) 🖉

Huia (www.huia.net.nz; 22 Boyces Rd, Blenheim; ☉10am–5pm Oct-May) 🖉

Saint Clair Estate (www.saintclair.co.nz; 13 Selmes Rd, Rapaura; ☉9am-5pm)

Marlborough Vintners Hotel HOTEL $$$
(☑0800 684 190, 03-572 5094; www.mvh.co.nz; 190 Rapaura Rd, Blenheim; d $190-325; 🖗) 🖉 Sixteen architecturally designed suites make the most of valley views and boast wet-room bathrooms and abstract art. The stylish reception building has a bar and restaurant opening out on to a cherry orchard and organic veggie garden.

✖ Eating & Drinking

★ **Burleigh** DELI $
(☑03-579 2531; 72 New Renwick Rd, Burleigh; pies $6; ☉7.30am-3pm Mon-Fri, 9am-1pm Sat) The humble pie rises to stratospheric heights at this fabulous deli; try the sweet pork-belly or savoury steak and blue cheese, or perhaps both. Fresh-filled baguettes, local sausage, French cheeses and great coffee also make tempting appearances. Avoid the lunchtime rush.

Gramado's BRAZILIAN
(☑03-579 1192; www.gramadosrestaurant.com; 74 Main St, Blenheim; mains $26-38; ☉4pm-late Tue-Sat) Injecting a little Latin American flair into the Blenheim dining scene, Gramado's is a fun place to tuck into unashamedly hearty meals such as lamb *assado*, feijoada (smoky pork and bean stew) and Brazilian-spiced fish. Kick things off with a caipirinha, of course.

Dodson Street CRAFT BEER
(☑03-577 8348; www.dodsonstreet.co.nz; 1 Dodson St, Mayfield; ☉11am-11pm) Pub and garden with a beer-hall ambience and suitably Teutonic menu (mains $17 to $27) featuring pork knuckle, bratwurst and schnitzel. The stars of the show are the 24 taps pouring quality, ever-changing craft beer, including award-winning brewer and neighbour, Renaissance.

Spy Valley Wines (www.spyvalleywine.co.nz; 37 Lake Timara Rd, Waihopai Valley; ⊙10.30am-4.30pm daily summer, 10.30am-4.30pm Mon-Fri winter) ✐

Te Whare Ra (www.twrwines.co.nz; 56 Anglesea St, Renwick; ⊙11am-4.30pm Mon-Fri, 12pm-4pm Sat & Sun Nov-Mar) ✐

Vines Village (www.thevinesvillage.co.nz; 193 Rapaura Rd; ⊙10am-5pm)

Wairau River (www.wairauriverwines.com; 11 Rapaura Rd; ⊙10am-5pm) ✐

Yealands Estate (☑03-575 7618; www.yealandsestate.co.nz; cnr Seaview & Reserve Rds, Seddon; ⊙10am-4.30pm) ✐

Wining & Dining

Arbour (☑03-572 7989; www.arbour.co.nz; 36 Godfrey Rd, Renwick; mains $31-38; ⊙3pm-late Tue-Sat year-round, 6pm-late Mon Jan-Mar; ✐) Located in the thick of Renwick wine country, this elegant restaurant offers 'a taste of Marlborough' by focusing on local produce fashioned into contemporary yet crowd-pleasing dishes. Settle in for a three-, four- or multiple-course à la carte offering ($73/85/98), or an end-of-the-day nibble and glass or two from the mesmerising wine list.

Wairau River Restaurant (☑03-572 9800; www.wairauriverwines.com; cnr Rapaura Rd & SH6, Renwick; mains $21-27; ⊙noon-3pm) Modishly modified mud-brick bistro with wide veranda and beautiful gardens with plenty of shade. Order the mussel chowder, or the double-baked blue-cheese soufflé. Relaxing and thoroughly enjoyable.

Rock Ferry (☑03-579 6431; www.rockferry.co.nz; 80 Hammerichs Rd, Blenheim; mains $23-27; ⊙11.30am-3pm) Pleasant environment inside and out, with a slightly groovy edge. The compact summery menu – think roasted salmon and peppers or organic open steak sandwich – is accompanied by wines from Marlborough and Otago.

Wither Hills (☑03-520 8284; www.witherhills.co.nz; 211 New Renwick Rd, Blenheim; mains $24-33, platters $38-68; ⊙11am-4pm) Simple, well-executed food in a stylish space. Pull up a beanbag on the Hockneyesque lawns and enjoy smoked lamb, Asian pork belly or a platter, before climbing the ziggurat for impressive views across the Wairau.

☆ Entertainment

Marlborough Civic Theatre   THEATRE
(☑03-520 8558; www.mctt.co.nz; 42a Alfred St, Blenheim) Brand-spanking new theatre presenting a wide program of concerts and performances. Check out www.follow-me.co.nz to see what's on here and beyond.

ℹ Information

Blenheim i-SITE (☑03-577 8080; www.marlboroughnz.com; 8 Sinclair St, Blenheim Railway Station; ⊙9am-5pm Mon-Fri, 9am-3pm Sat, 10am-3pm Sun) Has information on Marlborough and beyond, wine-trail maps and can manage bookings for everything under the sun.

Wairau Hospital (☑03-520 9999; www.nmdhb.govt.nz; Hospital Rd, Blenheim)

Post Office (cnr Scott & Main Sts, Blenheim)

ℹ Getting There & Away

AIR

Marlborough Airport (www.marlboroughairport.co.nz; Tancred Cres, Woodbourne) is 6km west of town on Middle Renwick Rd.

Air New Zealand (p57) has direct flights to/from Wellington, Auckland and Christchurch with onward connections. **Soundsair** (p57) connects Blenheim with Wellington, Paraparaumu and Napier.

BUS

InterCity (p57) Buses run daily from the Blenheim i-SITE to Picton (30 minutes) and Nelson (1¾ hours). Buses also head down south to Christchurch (two daily) via Kaikoura.

Naked Bus (p57) Tickets bargain seats on some of the same services, and on its own buses on major routes.

TRAIN

KiwiRail Scenic (p57) runs the daily Coastal Pacific service (October to May), stopping at

Blenheim en route to Picton (from $29) heading north, and Christchurch (from $79) via Kaikoura (from $59) heading south.

ℹ Getting Around

Avantiplus (☑ 03-578 0433; www.bike marlborough.co.nz; 61 Queen St; hire per half-/full day from $25/40) rents bikes; extended hire and delivery by arrangement.

Blenheim Shuttles (☑ 03-577 5277, 0800 577 527; www.blenheimshuttles.co.nz) Offer shuttles around Blenheim and the wider Marlborough region.

Marlborough Taxis (☑ 03-577 5511) Four-wheeled rescue is offered by Marlborough Taxis.

Kaikoura

POP 1971

Take SH1 129km southeast from Blenheim (or 180km north from Christchurch) and you'll encounter Kaikoura, a pretty peninsula town backed by the snow-capped Seaward Kaikoura Range. Few places in the world are home to such a variety of easily spottable wildlife: whale, dolphins, NZ fur seals, penguins, shearwaters, petrels and several species of albatross all live in or pass by the area.

Marine animals are abundant here due to ocean-current and continental-shelf conditions: the seabed gradually slopes away from the land before plunging to more than 800m where the southerly current hits the continental shelf. This creates an upwelling of nutrients from the ocean floor into the feeding zone.

◉ Sights

Point Kean Seal Colony   WILDLIFE RESERVE

At the end of the peninsula seals laze around in the grass and on the rocks, lapping up all the attention. Give them a wide berth (10m), and never get between them and the sea – they will attack if they feel cornered and can move surprisingly fast.

Kaikoura Museum   MUSEUM

(www.kaikoura.govt.nz; 14 Ludstone Rd; adult/child $5/1; ◷ 10am-4.30pm Mon-Fri, 2-4pm Sat & Sun) This provincial museum displays historical photographs, Māori and colonial artefacts, a huge sperm-whale jaw and the fossilised remains of a plesiosaur.

Fyffe House   HISTORIC BUILDING

(www.heritage.org.nz; 62 Avoca St; adult/child $10/free; ◷ 10am-5pm daily Oct-Apr, to 4pm Thu-Mon May-Sep) Kaikoura's oldest surviving building, Fyffe House's whale-bone foundations were laid in 1844. Proudly positioned and fronted with a colourful garden, the little two-storey cottage offers a fascinating insight into the lives of colonial settlers. Interpretive displays are complemented by historic objects, while peeling wallpaper and the odd cobweb lend authenticity. Cute maritime-themed shop.

🏃 Activities

There's a safe swimming **beach** in front of the Esplanade, alongside which is the **Lion's Swimming Pool** (191 Esplanade; adult/child $3/2; ◷ 10am-6pm Mon-Fri, 11am-5pm Sat & Sun) for those with a salt aversion.

Decent **surfing** can be found in the area, too, particularly at **Mangamaunu Beach** (15km north of town), where there's a 500m point break, which is fun in good conditions. Water-sports gear hire and advice are available from **Board Silly Surf & SUP Adventures** (☑ 027 418 8900, 0800 787 352; www.boardsilly.co.nz; 1 Kiwa Rd, Mangamaunu; 3hr lessons $80, board & suit from $40) and **Coastal Sports** (☑ 03-319 5028; www.coastalsports.co.nz; 24 West End; ◷ 9am-5.30pm Mon-Sat, 10am-5pm Sun, extended hours summer).

★ **Kaikoura Peninsula Walkway**   WALKING

A foray along this walkway is a must-do. Starting from the town, the three- to four-hour loop heads out to Point Kean, along the cliffs to South Bay, then back to town over the isthmus (or in reverse, of course). En route you'll see fur seals and red-billed seagull and shearwater colonies. Lookouts and interesting interpretive panels abound. Collect a map at the i-SITE or follow your nose.

Kaikoura Coast Track   TRAMPING

(☑ 03-319 2715; www.kaikouratrack.co.nz; 356 Conway Flat Rd, Ngaroma; $190) This easy two-day, 26km, self-guided walk across private farmland combines coastal and alpine views. The price includes two nights' farm-cottage accommodation and pack transport; BYO sleeping bag and food. Starts 45km south of Kaikoura.

Clarence River Rafting   RAFTING

(☑ 03-319 6993; www.clarenceriverrafting.co.nz; 1/3802 SH1, at Clarence Bridge; half-day trips adult/child $120/80) Raft the bouncy Grade II rapids of the scenic Clarence River on a half-day trip (2½ hours on the water), or on longer journeys including a five-day adventure with wilderness camping (adult/child $1400/900). Based on SH1, 40km north of Kaikoura near Clarence Bridge.

⌐⃗ Tours

Marine Mammal-Watching

Whale Watch Kaikoura　　　ECOTOUR
(🖉 0800 655 121, 03-319 6767; www.whalewatch. co.nz; Railway Station; 3½hr tours adult/child $150/60) 🖋 With knowledgeable guides and fascinating 'world of whales' on-board animation, Kaikoura's biggest operator heads out on boat trips (with admirable frequency) to introduce you to some of the big fellas. It'll refund 80% of your fare if no whales are sighted (success rate: 95%). If this trip is a must for you, allow a few days flexibility in case the weather turns to custard.

Dolphin Encounter　　　ECOTOUR
(🖉 03-319 6777, 0800 733 365; www.encounter-kaikoura.co.nz; 96 Esplanade; swim adult/child $175/160, observation $95/50; ⊘ tours 8.30am & 12.30pm year-round, plus 5.30am Nov-Apr) 🖋 Claiming NZ's highest success rate (90%) for both locating and swimming with dolphins, this operator runs feel-good three-hour tours, which often encounter sizeable pods of sociable duskies – the classic Kaikoura treat.

Seal Swim Kaikoura　　　ECOTOUR
(🖉 0800 732 579, 03-319 6182; www.seal swimkaikoura.co.nz; 58 West End; tours $70-110, viewing adult/child $55/35; ⊘ Oct-May) Take a (warmly wet-suited) swim with Kaikoura's healthy population of playful seals – including very cute pups – on two-hour guided snorkelling tours (by boat) run by the Chambers family.

Birdwatching

★ Albatross Encounter　　　BIRDWATCHING
(🖉 0800 733 365, 03-319 6777; www.encounter kaikoura.co.nz; 96 Esplanade; adult/child $125/60; ⊘ tours 9am & 1pm year-round, plus 6am Nov-Apr) 🖋 Even if you don't consider yourself a bird-nerd, you'll love this close encounter with pelagic species such as shearwaters, shags, mollymawks and petrels. It's the various albatross species, however, that steal the show. Just awesome.

Fishing

Kaikoura Fishing Charters　　　FISHING
(🖉 03-319 6888; www.kaikourafishing.co.nz) Dangle a line from the 12m *Takapu*, then take your filleted, bagged catch home to eat.

CRAY CRAZY

Among all of Kaikoura's munificent marine life, the one species you just can't avoid is the crayfish, whose delicate flesh dominates local menus. Unfortunately (some say unnecessarily), it's pricey – at a restaurant you'll (pardon the pun) shell out around $50 for half a cray or up to $100 for the whole beast. You can also buy fresh cooked or uncooked crays from **Cods & Crayfish** (81 Beach Rd; ⊘ 8am-6pm), or from the iconic **Nins Bin** (SH1) and **Cay's Crays** (SH1), surf-side caravans around a 20-minute drive north of town. Upwards of $50 should get you a decent specimen. Alternatively, go out on a fishing tour, or simply head to the **Kaikoura Seafood BBQ** (p76) near the peninsula seal colony where cooked crays can be gobbled in the sunshine, by the sea.

Fishing at Kaikoura　　　FISHING
(🖉 03-319 3003; gerard.diedrichs@xtra.co.nz) Fishing, crayfishing, scenic tours and water-skiing, on the 6m *Sophie-Rose*.

Other Tours

Kaikoura Kayaks　　　KAYAKING
(🖉 0800 452 456, 03-319 7118; www.kaikourakay-aks.nz; 19 Killarney St; 3hr tours adult/child $95/70; ⊘ tours 8.30am, 12.30pm & 4.30pm Nov-Apr, 9am & 1pm May-Oct) Excellent guided sea-kayak tours to view fur seals and explore the peninsula's coastline. Family-friendly; kayak fishing and other on-demand trips available; plus freedom kayak and paddle board hire.

Kaikoura Wilderness Walks　　　TRAMPING
(🖉 0800 945 337, 03-319 6966; www.kaikoura wilderness.co.nz; 2-night packages adult/child $1895/1595) 🖋 Three-day guided walks through the privately owned Puhi Peaks Nature Reserve high in the Seaward Kaikoura range. Packages include accommodation and sumptuous meals at the luxurious Shearwater Lodge.

Maori Tours Kaikoura　　　CULTURAL TOUR
(🖉 0800 866 267, 03-319 5567; www.maoritours. co.nz; 3½hr tours adult/child $134/74; ⊘ tours 9am & 1.30pm) 🖋 Fascinating half-day, small-group tours laced with Māori hospitality and local lore. Visit historic sites, hear legends and learn about indigenous use of trees and plants. Advance bookings required.

Kaikoura

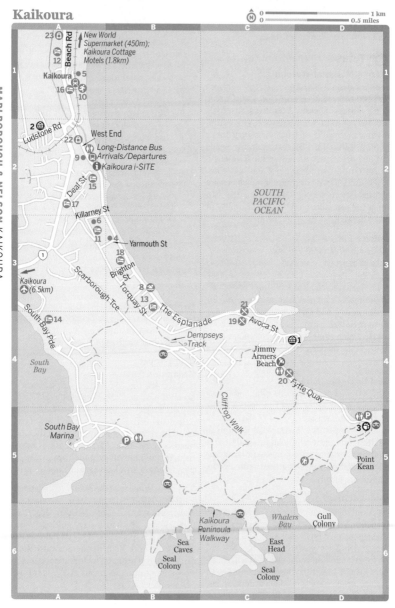

New World
Supermarket (450m);
Kaikoura Cottage
Motels (1.8km)

Beach Rd

Kaikoura

Ludstone Rd

West End

Long-Distance Bus
Arrivals/Departures
Kaikoura i-SITE

Deal St

Killarney St

Yarmouth St

Brighton St

Torquay St

Scarborough Tce

Kaikoura
(6.5km)

The Esplanade

Avoca St

SOUTH
PACIFIC
OCEAN

South Bay Pde

South
Bay

Dempseys
Track

Jimmy
Armers
Beach

Fyffe Quay

South Bay
Marina

Clifftop Walk

Point
Kean

Kaikoura
Peninsula
Walkway

Whalers
Bay

Gull
Colony

Sea
Caves

East
Head

Seal
Colony

Seal
Colony

Kaikoura Helicopters SCENIC FLIGHTS
(☏03-319 6609; www.worldofwhales.co.nz; Railway Station; 15-60min flights $100-490) Reliable whale-spotting flights (standard tour 30 minutes, $220 each for three or more people), plus jaunts around the peninsula, Mt Fyffe and peaks beyond.

Wings over Whales SCENIC FLIGHTS
(☏03-319 6580, 0800 226 629; www.whales.co.nz; 30min flights adult/child $180/75) Light-plane

Kaikoura

flights departing from Kaikoura Airport, 8km south of town on SH1. Spotting success rate: 95%.

⊨ Sleeping

Albatross Backpacker Inn　　　　HOSTEL $
(☑0800 222 247, 03-319 6090; www.albatross-kaikoura.co.nz; 1 Torquay St; dm $29-32, tw/d $69/74; 🐾) 🐾 This arty backpackers resides in three sweet buildings, one a former post office. It's colourful and close to the beach but sheltered from the breeze. As well as a laid-back lounge with musical instruments for jamming, there are decks and verandas to chill out on.

Dolphin Lodge　　　　　　　　HOSTEL $
(☑03-319 5842; www.dolphinlodge.co.nz; 15 Deal St; dm $29, d with/without bathroom $74/66; @🐾) This small home-away-from-home has a lovely scented garden, sweet ocean views and a kindly owner. When the sun's shining most of the action is out on the fantastic deck, around the barbecue, or in the spa pool.

Alpine Pacific Holiday Park　　HOLIDAY PARK $
(☑0800 692 322, 03-319 6275; www.alpine-pacific.co.nz; 69 Beach Rd; sites from $46, cabins $78, units & motels $137-200; @🐾🏊) This compact and proudly trimmed park copes well with its many visitors and offers excellent facilities, including a pool, hot tubs and a barbecue pavilion. Rows of cabins and units are a tad more stylish than the average, and mountain views can be enjoyed from many angles.

Kaikoura Top 10 Holiday Park　HOLIDAY PARK $
(☑0800 363 638, 03-319 5362; www.kaikouratop10.co.nz; 34 Beach Rd; sites $52, cabins $70-95, units & motels $110-185; @🐾🏊) Hiding from the highway behind a massive hedge, this busy, shipshape holiday park offers family-friendly facilities (heated pool, hot tub, jumping pillow) and cabins and units to the usual Top 10 standard.

★**Kaikoura Cottage Motels**　　MOTEL $$
(☑0800 526 882, 03-319 5599; www.kaikouracottagemotels.co.nz; cnr Old Beach & Mill Rds; d $140-160; 🐾) This enclave of eight modern tourist flats looks mighty fine, surrounded by attractive native plantings. Oriented for mountain views, spick-n-span self-contained units sleep four between an open plan studio-style living room and one private bedroom. Proud, lovely hosts seal the deal.

Bay Cottages　　　　　　　　　MOTEL $$
(☑03-319 5506; www.baycottages.co.nz; 29 South Bay Pde; cottages/motel r $120/140; 🐾) Here's a great-value option on South Bay, a few kilometres south of town: five tourist cottages with kitchenette and bathroom that sleep up to four, and two slick motel rooms with stainless-steel benches, a warm feel and clean lines. The cheery owner may even take you crayfishing in good weather.

Sails Motel　　　　　　　　　　MOTEL $$
(☑03-319 6145; www.sailsmotel.co.nz; 134 Esplanade; d/apt $125/150; 🐾) There are no sea views (nor sails) at this motel, so the cherubic owner has to impress with quality. The four secluded, tastefully appointed

self-contained units are down a driveway in a garden setting (private outdoor areas abound).

Nikau Lodge B&B $$$
(☑ 03-319 6973; www.nikaulodge.com; 53 Deal St; d $190-290; @ 🗟) A waggly tailed welcome awaits at this beautiful B&B high on the hill with grand-scale vistas. Five en suite rooms are plush and comfy, with additional satisfaction arriving in the form of cafe-quality breakfasts accompanied by fresh local coffee. Good humour, home baking, free wi-fi, complimentary drinks, a hot tub and blooming gardens: you may want to move in.

Anchor Inn Motel MOTEL $$$
(☑ 03-319 5426; www.anchorinn.co.nz; 208 Esplanade; d $185-255; 🗟) The Aussie owners liked this Kaikoura motel so much they bought it and moved here. The sharp and spacious units are a pleasant 15-minute walk from town and about 10 seconds from the ocean.

✖ Eating

Reserve Hutt CAFE $
(72 West End; meals $10-20; ⊙ 8.30am-3pm; 🗷) The best coffee in town, roasted on-site and espressoed by cheery baristas in Kaikoura's grooviest cafe. Puttin' out that rootsy retro-Kiwiana vibe we love so much, this is a neat place to linger over a couple of flatties and down a chocolate brownie, delicious ham croissant or the full eggy brunch.

Cafe Encounter CAFE $
(96 Esplanade; meals $8-23; ⊙ 7am-5pm; 🗟🗷) This cafe in the Encounter Kaikoura complex is more than just somewhere to wait for your tour. The cabinet houses respectable sandwiches, pastries and cakes, plus there's a tasteful range of daily specials such as homemade soup and pulled-pork rolls. A sunny patio provides sea views.

Kaikoura Seafood BBQ SEAFOOD $
(Fyffe Quay; items from $5; ⊙ 10.30am-6pm) Conveniently located on the way to the Point Kean seal colony, this long-standing roadside barbecue is a great spot to sample local seafood, including crayfish (half/full from $25/50) and scallops, at an affordable price.

Pier Hotel PUB FOOD $$
(☑ 03-319 5037; www.thepierhotel.co.nz; 1 Avoca St; lunch $16-25, dinner $25-38; ⊙ 11am-late) Situated in the town's primo seaside spot, with panoramic views, the historic Pier Hotel is a friendly and inviting place for a drink and respectable pub grub, including crayfish (half/whole $45/90). Great outside area for sundowners.

★ Green Dolphin MODERN NZ $$$
(☑ 03-319 6666; www.greendolphinkaikoura. com; 12 Avoca St; mains $26-39; ⊙ 5pm-late) Kaikoura's consistent top-ender dishes up high-quality local produce including seafood, beef, lamb and venison, as well as seasonal flavours such as fresh tomato soup. There are lovely homemade pasta dishes, too. The hefty drinks list demands attention, featuring exciting aperitifs, craft beer, interesting wines and more. Booking ahead is advisable, especially if you want to secure a table by the window and watch the daylight fade.

ℹ Information

Kaikoura i-SITE (☑ 03-319 5641; www.kaikoura. co.nz; West End; ⊙ 9am-5pm Mon-Fri, to 4pm Sat & Sun, extended hours Dec-Mar) Helpful staff make tour, accommodation and transport bookings, and help with DOC-related matters.

ℹ Getting There & Away

BUS

InterCity (p57) buses run between Kaikoura and Nelson once daily (3¾ hours), and Picton (2¼ hours) and Christchurch (2¼ hours) twice daily. The **bus stop** is next to the i-SITE (tickets and info inside).

Atomic Shuttles (p61) also services Kaikoura on its Christchurch to Picton run, which links with destinations as far afield as Nelson, Queenstown and Invercargill.

Naked Bus (p57) tickets bargain seats on its own buses on major routes, and on other services depending on capacity.

TRAIN

KiwiRail Scenic (p57) runs the daily Coastal Pacific service (October to May), stopping at Kaikoura en route to Picton (from $59, 2¼ hours), and Christchurch (from $59, 2¾ hours). The northbound train departs Kaikoura at 9.59am; the southbound at 3.50pm.

ℹ Getting Around

Kaikoura Shuttles (☑ 03-319 6166; www. kaikourashuttles.co.nz) will run you around the local sights as well as to and from the airport. For local car hire, contact **Kaikoura Rentals** (☑ 03-319 3311; www.kaikourarentals.co.nz; 94 Churchill St).

NELSON REGION

The Nelson region is centred upon Tasman Bay. It stretches north to Golden Bay and Farewell Spit, and south to Nelson Lakes. It's not hard to see why it's such a popular travel destination for international and domestic travellers alike: not only does it boast three national parks (Kahurangi, Nelson Lakes and Abel Tasman), it can also satisfy nearly every other whim, from food, wine and beer, art, craft and festivals, to that most precious of pastimes for which the region is well known: lazing about in the sunshine.

ℹ️ Getting There & Away

Nelson is the region's primary gateway, with competitive domestic airline connections, and comprehensive bus services linking it with all major South Island towns.

Abel Tasman Coachlines (☑ 03-548 0285; www.abeltasmantravel.co.nz)

Golden Bay Coachlines (☑ 03-525 8352; www.gbcoachlines.co.nz)

Trek Express (☑ 027 222 1872, 0800 128 735; www.trekexpress.co.nz)

Nelson

POP 46,440

Dishing up a winning combination of beautiful surroundings, sophisticated art and culinary scenes, and lashings of sunshine, Nelson is hailed as one of NZ's most 'liveable' cities. In summer it fills up with local and international visitors, who lap up its diverse offerings.

◉ Sights

Nelson has an inordinate number of galleries, most of which are listed in the *Art & Crafts Nelson City* brochure (with walking-trail map) available from the i-SITE (p82). A fruitful wander can be had by starting at the woolly **Fibre Spectrum** (☑ 03-548 1939; www.fibrespectrum.co.nz; 280 Trafalgar St), before moving on to *The Lord of the Rings* jeweller **Jens Hansen** (☑ 03-548 0640; www.jenshansen.com; 320 Trafalgar Sq), glass-blower **Flamedaisy** (☑ 03-548 4475; www.flamedaisy.co.nz; 324 Trafalgar Sq), then around the corner to the home of Nelson pottery, **South Street Gallery** (☑ 03-548 8117; www.nelsonpottery.co.nz; 10 Nile St W). Other interesting local creations can be found at the Nelson Market (p82) on Saturday.

★**Tahuna Beach** BEACH

Nelson's primo playground takes the form of an epic sandy beach (with lifeguards in summer) backed by dunes, and a large grassy parkland with a playground, an espresso cart, a hydroslide, bumper boats, a roller-skating rink, a model railway, and an adjacent restaurant strip. Weekends can get veerrrrry busy!

Suter Art Gallery GALLERY

(www.thesuter.org.nz; 208 Bridge St; ⊙9.30am-4.30pm) FREE Adjacent to Queen's Gardens, Nelson's public art gallery presents changing exhibitions, floor talks, musical and theatrical performances, and films. The Suter's long-awaited reopening after a fabulous redevelopment is scheduled for late 2016. Check the website to confirm it's open, and to find out what's on.

NZ Classic Motorcycles MUSEUM

(☑ 03-546 7699; www.nzclassicmotorcycles.co.nz; 75 Haven Rd; adult/child $20/10; ⊙9am-4pm Mon-Fri, 10am-3pm Sat & Sun) Motorcycle enthusiasts should race round to this exceptional 300+ collection of classic bikes, including a clutch of super-rare Brough Superiors and a tribe of Indians. Well-considered displays across two floors and a handy mobile app allow close inspection from multiple perspectives.

McCashin's Brewery BREWERY

(☑ 03-547 5357; www.mccashins.co.nz; 660 Main Rd, Stoke; ⊙7am-6pm Mon & Tue, 7am-9.30pm Wed-Sat, 9am-6pm) A groundbreaker in the new era of craft brewing in NZ, which started way back in the 1980s. Visit the historic cider factory for a tasting, cafe meal or tour.

Nelson Provincial Museum MUSEUM

(☑ 03-548 9588; www.nelsonmuseum.co.nz; cnr Trafalgar St and Hardy St; adult/child $5/3; ⊙10am-5pm Mon-Fri, to 4.30pm Sat & Sun) This modern museum space is filled with cultural heritage and natural history exhibits which have a regional bias, as well as regular touring exhibitions (for which admission fees vary). It also features a great rooftop garden.

Christ Church Cathedral CHURCH

(www.nelsoncathedral.org; Trafalgar Sq; ⊙9am-6pm) FREE The enduring symbol of Nelson, the art-deco Christ Church Cathedral lords it over the city from the top of Trafalgar St. The best time to visit is during the 10am and 7pm Sunday services when you can hear the organist and the choir in song.

Central Nelson

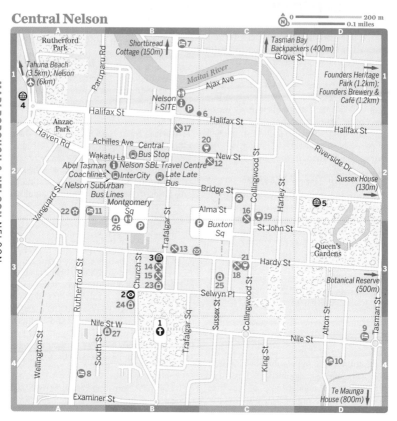

Central Nelson

◎ Sights
1 Christ Church Cathedral....................B4
2 Jens Hansen B3
3 Nelson Provincial Museum...................B3
4 NZ Classic Motorcycles A1
5 Suter Art Gallery D2

✪ Activities, Courses & Tours
6 Trail Journeys..B1

🛏 Sleeping
7 Cedar Grove Motor Lodge......................B1
8 Palazzo Motor Lodge A4
9 Prince Albert..D4
10 Trampers Rest D4
11 YHA Nelson by Accents A2

✕ Eating
12 DeVille C2
13 Falafel Gourmet B3

14 Ford's B3
15 Hopgood's...B3
16 Indian Café C2
17 Stefano's...B2
18 Urban Oyster C3

🍸 Drinking & Nightlife
19 Free House C2
20 Rhythm and Brown C2
21 Sprig & Fern C3

✪ Entertainment
22 Theatre Royal...A2

🛍 Shopping
23 Fibre Spectrum..B3
24 Flamedaisy Glass Design B3
25 Nelson Farmers' Market........................C3
26 Nelson Market...B2
27 South Street Gallery B4

Botanical Reserve PARK

(Milton St) Walking tracks ascend Botanical Hill, where a spire proclaims the **Centre of New Zealand**. NZ's first-ever rugby match was played at the foot of the hill on 14 May 1870: Nelson Rugby Football Club trounced the lily-livered players from Nelson College 2-0.

Founders Heritage Park MUSEUM

(⌨ 03-548 2649; www.founderspark.co.nz; 87 Atawhai Dr; adult/child/family $7/5/15; ⊙ 10am-4.30pm) Two kilometres from the city centre, this park comprises a replica historic village with a museum, gallery displays, and artisan products such as chocolate and clothing. It makes for a fascinating wander, which you can augment with a visit to the on-site **Founders Brewery & Café** (⌨ 03-548 4638; www.foundersbrewery.co.nz; 87 Atawhai Dr; ⊙ 9am-4.30pm, later in summer).

🏃 Activities

Walking & Cycling

There's plenty of walking and cycling to be enjoyed in and around the town, for which the i-SITE has maps. The classic walk from town is up the **Centre of NZ** atop the Botanical Reserve; if you enjoy that then ask about the **Grampians**.

Nelson has two of the New Zealand Cycle Trail's 23 Great Rides: **Dun Mountain Trail** (www.heartofbiking.org.nz), an awesome but challenging one-day ride ranging over the hills to the south of the city; and the Great Taste Trail (p83) offering a blissfully flat meander through beautiful countryside dotted with wine, food and art stops.

Gentle Cycling Company BICYCLE TOUR

(⌨ 0800 932 453, 03-929 5652; www.gentlecycling.co.nz; day tours $95-105) Self-guided cycle tours along the Great Taste Trail, with drop-ins (and tastings) at wineries, breweries, cafes and occasional galleries. Bike hire (per day $45) and shuttles also available.

Trail Journeys BICYCLE TOUR

(⌨ 0800 292 538, 03-540 3095; www.trailjourneysnelson.co.nz; MD Outdoors, 1/37 Halifax St; full-day tours from $89) Trail Journeys offers a range of self-guided cycle tours around Nelson city, and beyond along the Great Taste Trail, based at three conveniently located depots in central Nelson, Mapua Wharf and Kaiteriteri.

Nelson Cycle Hire & Tours BICYCLE TOUR

(⌨ 03-539 4193; www.nelsoncyclehire.co.nz; Nelson Airport; bike hire per day $45) Provides comfortable bikes for independent riding, plus guided or supported tours around the Great Taste Trail and beyond. Pick-up and delivery service, region-wide.

Paragliding, Hang Gliding & Kiteboarding

Nelson is a great place for adrenaline activities, with plenty of action in summer, particularly around the rather divine Tahuna Beach (p77). Tandem paragliding costs around $180, introductory kitesurfing starts at $150, and paddle board hire is around $20 per hour.

Nelson Paragliding PARAGLIDING

(⌨ 03-544 1182; www.nelsonparagliding.co.nz) Get high in the sky over Tahunanui with Nelson Paragliding.

Kite Surf Nelson KITESURFING

(⌨ 0800 548 363; www.kitesurfnelson.co.nz) Learn to kite surf at Tahunanui, or hire a stand-up paddle board.

Other Activities

Cable Bay Kayaks KAYAKING

(⌨ 03-545 0332; www.cablebaykayaks.co.nz; Cable Bay Rd, Hira; half-/full day guided trips $85/145) Fifteen minutes' drive from Nelson city, Nick and Jenny offer richly rewarding guided sea-kayaking trips exploring the local coastline, where you'll likely meet local marine life (snorkelling gear on board helps) and may even enter a cave.

Moana SUP WATER SPORTS

(⌨ 027 656 0268; www.moananzsup.co.nz) Learn what SUP with the guys at Moana, or hire a board if you're already enlightened.

Happy Valley Adventures ADVENTURE SPORTS

(⌨ 03-545 0304, 0800 157 300; www.happyvalleyadventures.co.nz; 194 Cable Bay Rd; Skywire adult/child $85/55, quad-bike tours from $100, horse treks $75) Dangle 150m above the forest in the 'Skywire' (a chairlift/flying-fox hybrid), then soar through the air for its 1.65km length. If that ain't enough, take a quad-bike tour; or if it's too much, try a horse trek instead. Located a 15-minute drive northeast of Nelson along SH6; on-site cafe.

👉 Tours

Nelson Tours & Travel TOUR

(⌨ 027 237 5007, 0800 222 373; www.nelsontoursandtravel.co.nz) CJ and crew run various

THE WONDROUS WORLD OF WEARABLE ART

Nelson is the birthplace of New Zealand's most inspiring fashion show, the annual World of WearableArt Awards Show. You can see 70 or so current and past entries in the sensory-overloading galleries of the **World of WearableArt & Classic Cars Museum** (WOW; ✆ 03-547 4573; www.wowcars.co.nz; 1 Cadillac Way; adult/child $24/10; ⊙10am-5pm), which include a glow-in-the-dark room. Look out for the 'Bizarre Bras'.

More car than bra? Under the same roof are more than 100 mint-condition classic cars and motorbikes. Exhibits change, but may include a 1959 pink Cadillac, a yellow 1950 Bullet Nose Studebaker convertible and a BMW bubble car.

The World of WearableArt Awards Show began humbly in 1987 when Suzie Moncrieff held an off-beat event featuring art that could be worn and modelled. Folks quickly cottoned on to the show's creative (and competitive) possibilities. You name it, they've shown that a garment can be made from it; wood, metal, shells, cable ties, dried leaves, ping-pong balls... The festival now has a new home in Wellington.

Between the galleries, cafe and art shop, allow a couple of hours if you can.

---

small-group, flexible tours honing in on Nelson's wine, craft beer, art and scenic highlights. The five-hour 'Best of Both Worlds' combines indulgence with your special interest, be it galleries or a trip to Rabbit Island ($105). Day tours of Marlborough wineries also available ($195).

★☆ Festivals & Events

Nelson Jazz Festival   MUSIC
(www.nelsonjazzfest.co.nz; ⊙Jan) More scoobee-doo-bop events over a week in January than you can shake a leg at. Features local and national acts.

Nelson Arts Festival   PERFORMING ARTS
(www.nelsonartsfestival.co.nz; ⊙Oct) Over two weeks in October; events include a street carnival, exhibitions, cabaret, writers, theatre and music.

🛏 Sleeping

Trampers Rest   HOSTEL $
(✆03-545 7477; 31 Alton St; dm/s/d $30/52/64; ⊙closed Jun-Sep; @🛜) With just seven beds (no bunks), the tiny, much-loved Trampers is hard to beat for a homely environment. The enthusiastic owner is a keen tramper and cyclist, and provides comprehensive local information and free bikes. It has a small kitchen, a book exchange, and a piano for evening singalongs.

Shortbread Cottage   HOSTEL $
(✆03-546 6681; www.shortbreadcottage.co.nz; 33 Trafalgar St; dm $29, s & d $65; @🛜) This renovated 102-year-old villa has room for only a dozen or so beds, but it's packed with charm and hospitality. It offers free internet, fresh-baked

bread, and shortbread on arrival. It's also only a stone's throw from the town centre.

Prince Albert   HOSTEL $
(✆0800 867 3529, 03-548 8477; www.theprince albert.co.nz; 113 Nile St; dm $29 s/tw/d $50/75/85; 🛜) A five-minute walk from the city centre, this lively, well-run backpackers has roomy en suite dorms surrounding a sunny courtyard. Private rooms are upstairs in the main building, which also houses an English-style pub where guests can meet the locals and refuel with a good-value meal.

Tasman Bay Backpackers   HOSTEL $
(✆0800 222 572, 03-548 7950; www.tasmanbay backpackers.co.nz; 10 Weka St; sites from $19, dm $27-30, d $74-87; @🛜) This well-designed, friendly hostel has airy communal spaces with a Kiwi soundtrack, hypercoloured rooms, a sunny outdoor deck and a well-used hammock. Good freebies: wi-fi, decent bikes, breakfast during winter, and chocolate pudding and ice cream year-round.

Tahuna Beach
Kiwi Holiday Park   HOLIDAY PARK $
(✆03-548 5159, 0800 500 501; www.tahunabeach holidaypark.co.nz; 70 Beach Rd, Tahunanui; sites/cabins/units from $20/65/120; @🛜) Close to Tahuna Beach, 5km from the city, this mammoth park is home to thousands in high summer, which you'll either find hellish or bloody brilliant, depending on your mood. Off season, you'll have the cafe and minigolf mostly to yourself.

YHA Nelson by Accents   HOSTEL $
(✆03-545 9988, 0800 888 335; www.accentshostel.nz; 59 Rutherford St; dm/s $30/69, d with/

without bathroom $119/89; @ 🖥) A tidy, well-run, central hostel with spacious communal areas including well-equipped kitchens, a sunny terrace, a TV room and bike storage. Great local knowledge for tours and activities from new managers injecting some personality into this YHA-affiliated establishment.

Palazzo Motor Lodge   MOTEL $$
(📞 03-545 8171, 0800 472 5293; www.palazzo motorlodge.co.nz; 159 Rutherford St; studios $130-249, apt $230-390; 🖥) This modern, Italian-tinged motor lodge offers stylish studios and one- and two-room apartments featuring enviable kitchens with decent cooking equipment, classy glassware and a dishwasher. Its comfort and convenient location easily atone for the odd bit of dubious art.

Te Maunga House   B&B $$
(📞 03-548 8605; www.nelsoncityaccommodation. co.nz; 15 Dorothy Annie Way; s $90, d $125-145; 🖥) Aptly named ('the mountain'), this grand old family home has exceptional views and a well-travelled host. Two doubles and a twin have a homely feel with comfy beds and their own bathrooms. Your hearty breakfast can be walked off up and down *that* hill, a 10-minute climb with an extra five minutes to town. Closed May to October.

Sussex House   B&B $$
(📞 03-548 9972; www.sussex.co.nz; 238 Bridge St; d $170-190, tr $175; 🖥) In a relatively quiet riverside spot, only a five-minute walk to town, this creaky old lady dates back to around 1880. The five tastefully decorated rooms feature upmarket bedding, period-piece furniture and en suite bathrooms, except one room that has a private bathroom down the hall. Enjoy local fruit at breakfast in the grand dining room.

Cedar Grove Motor Lodge   MOTEL $$
(📞 03-545 1133; www.cedargrove.co.nz; cnr Trafalgar & Grove Sts; d $155-210; 🖥) A big old cedar landmark, this smart, modern block of spacious apartments is just a three-minute walk to town. Its range of studios and doubles are plush and elegant, with full cooking facilities.

🍴 Eating

Falafel Gourmet   MIDDLE EASTERN $
(📞 03-545 6220; 195 Hardy St; meals $11-19; ⊙9.30am-5.30pm Mon-Sat, to 8pm Fri; 🖊) A cranking joint dishing out the best kebabs for miles around. They're healthy, too!

Stefano's   PIZZA $
(📞 03-546 7530; www.pizzeria.co.nz; 91 Trafalgar St; pizzas $6-29; ⊙noon-2pm & 4.30pm-9pm; 🖊) Located upstairs in the State Cinema complex, this Italian-run joint turns out the town's best pizza. Thin, crispy, authentic and delicious, with some variations a veritable bargain. Wash it down with a beer and chase it with a creamy dessert.

★DeVille   CAFE $$
(📞 03-545 6911; www.devillecafe.co.nz; 22 New St; ⊙8am-4pm Mon-Sat, 8.30am-2.30pm Sun; 🖊) Most of DeVille's tables lie in its sweet walled courtyard, a hidden boho oasis in the inner city and the perfect place for a meal or morning tea. The food's good and local – from fresh baking to a chorizo-burrito brunch, Caesar salad and proper burgers, washed down with regional wines and beers. Open late for live music Fridays in summer.

Urban Oyster   MODERN NZ $$$
(📞 03-546 7861; www.urbaneatery.co.nz; 278 Hardy St; dishes $13-27; ⊙4pm-late Mon, 11am-late Tue-Sat) Slurp oysters from the shell, or revitalise with sashimi and ceviche, then sate your cravings with street-food dishes such as Korean fried chicken, or popcorn prawn tacos and a side of devilish poutine chips. Black butchery tiles, edgy artwork and fine drinks bolster this metropolitan experience.

Ford's   MODERN NZ $$
(📞 03-546 9400; www.fordsnelson.co.nz; 276 Trafalgar St; lunch $17-22; ⊙8am-late Mon-Fri, 9am-late Sat & Sun) Sunny pavement tables at the top of Trafalgar St make this a popular lunchtime spot, as does a menu of modern classics such as the excellent seafood chowder, steak sandwich, and house-smoked salmon niçoise. Pop in for coffee and a scone, or linger over dinner, for which prices leap up a tenner or so.

Indian Café   INDIAN $$
(📞 03-548 4089; www.theindiancafe.com; 94 Collingwood St; mains $13-23; ⊙12-2pm Mon-Fri, 5pm-late daily; 🖊) This saffron-coloured Edwardian villa houses an Indian restaurant that keeps the bhajis raised with impressive interpretations of Anglo-Indian standards such as chicken tandoori, rogan josh and beef madras. Share the mixed platter to start, then mop up your mains with one of 10 different breads.

★ **Hopgood's**   MODERN NZ **$$$**
(☑03-545 7191; www.hopgoods.co.nz; 284 Trafalgar St; mains $27-40; ☉5.30pm-late Mon-Sat) Tongue-and-groove-lined Hopgood's is perfect for a romantic dinner or holiday treat. The food is decadent and skilfully prepared but unfussy, allowing quality local ingredients to shine. Try confit duck with sour cherries, or pork belly and pine-nut butter. Desirable, predominantly Kiwi wine list. Bookings advisable.

Drinking & Nightlife

★ **Free House**   CRAFT BEER
(☑03-548 9391; www.freehouse.co.nz; 95 Collingwood St; ☉3pm-late Mon-Fri, noon-late Sat, 10.30am-late Sun) Come rejoice at this church of ales. Tastefully converted from its original, more reverent purpose, it's now home to an excellent, oft-changing selection of NZ craft beers. You can imbibe inside, out, or even in a yurt, where there's regular entertainment. Hallelujah.

Rhythm and Brown   BAR
(☑03-546 56319; www.facebook.com/rhythmandbrown; 19 New St; ☉4pm-late Tue-Sat) Nelson's slinkiest late-night drinking den, where classy cocktails, fine wines and craft beer flow from behind the bar and sweet vinyl tunes drift from the speakers. Regular Saturday-night microgigs in a compact, groovy space.

Sprig & Fern   CRAFT BEER
(☑03-548 1154; www.sprigandfern.co.nz; 280 Hardy St; ☉11am-late) This outpost of Richmond's Sprig & Fern brewery offers 18 brews on tap, from lager through to doppelbock and berry cider. No pokies, no TV, just decent beer, occasional live music and a pleasant outdoor area. Pizzas can be ordered in. Look for a second Sprig at 143 Milton St, handy to Founders Park.

☆ Entertainment

Theatre Royal   THEATRE
(☑03-548 3840; www.theatreroyalnelson.co.nz; 78 Rutherford St) State-of-the-art theatre in a charmingly restored heritage building. This 'grand old lady of Nelson' (aged nearly 140) boasts a full program of local and touring drama, dance and musical productions. Visit the website for the current program and bookings, or visit the box office (10am to 4pm Monday to Friday). Also check out website (or www.itson.co.nz) for what's on and book online at www.ticketdirect.co.nz, or in the foyer.

🛍 Shopping

Nelson Farmers' Market   MARKET
(☑022 010 2776; www.nelsonfarmersmarket.org.nz; Morrison Sq, cnr Morrison & Hardy Sts; ☉11pm-4pm Wed) Weekly market full to bursting with local produce to fill your picnic hamper.

Nelson Market   MARKET
(☑03-546 6454; www.nelsonmarket.co.nz; Montgomery Sq; ☉8am-1pm Sat) Don't miss Nelson Market, a big, busy weekly market featuring fresh produce, food stalls, fashion, local arts, crafts and buskers.

ℹ Information

After Hours & Duty Doctors (☑03-546 8881; 96 Waimea Rd; ☉8am-10pm)
Nelson Hospital (☑03-546 1800; www.nmdhb.govt.nz; Waimea Rd)
Nelson i-SITE (☑03-548 2304; www.nelsonnz.com; cnr Trafalgar & Halifax Sts; ☉8.30am-5pm Mon-Fri, 9am-4pm Sat & Sun) A slick centre complete with DOC information desk for the low-down on national parks and walks (including Abel Tasman and Heaphy tracks). Pick up a copy of the *Nelson Tasman Visitor Guide*.
Post Office (www.nzpost.co.nz; 209 Hardy St)

ℹ Getting There & Away

Book Abel Tasman Coachlines, InterCity, KiwiRail Scenic and Interisland ferry services at the **Nelson SBL Travel Centre** (☑03-548 1539; www.nelsoncoachlines.co.nz; 27 Bridge St) or the i-SITE.

AIR
Airline competition has hotted up in recent years: Nelson has never been so accessible.

IN PURSUIT OF HOPPINESS
. . . .

The Nelson region lays claim to the title of craft-brewing capital of New Zealand. World-class hops have been grown here since the 1840s, and a dozen breweries are spread between Nelson and Golden Bay.

Pick up a copy of the *Nelson Craft Beer Trail* map (available from the i-SITE and other outlets, and online at www.craftbrewingcapital.co.nz) and wind your way between brewers and pubs. Top picks for a tipple include the **Free House**, **McCashin's** (p77), the **Moutere Inn** (p85), **Golden Bear** (p84), and the **Mussel Inn** (p93).

> **WORTH A TRIP**
>
> ## GREAT TASTE TRAIL
>
> In a stroke of genius inspired by great weather and easy topography, the Tasman region has developed one of NZ's most popular cycle trails. Why is it so popular? Because no other is so frequently punctuated by stops for food, wine, craft beer and art, as it passes through a range of landscapes from bucolic countryside to estuary boardwalk.
>
> The 174km **Great Taste Trail** (www.heartofbiking.org.nz) stretches from Nelson to Kaiteriteri, with plans afoot to propel it further inland. While it can certainly be ridden in full in a few days, stopping at accommodation en route, it is even more easily ridden as day trips of various lengths. Mapua is a great place to set off from, with bike hire from **Wheelie Fantastic** (p84) and **Trail Journeys** (p79) at the wharf, and a ferry ride over to the trails of Rabbit Island. The trail also passes through thrilling **Kaiteriteri Mountain Bike Park** (p87).
>
> Nelson's many other cycle-tour and bike-hire companies can get you out on the trail, with bike drops and pick-ups.

Nelson Airport is 5km southwest of town, near Tahunanui Beach. A taxi from there to town will cost around $25, or **Super Shuttle** (☏ 03-547 5782, 0800 748 885; www.supershuttle.co.nz) offers door-to-door service for around $20.

Air New Zealand (☏ 0800 737 000; www.airnewzealand.co.nz) Direct flights to/from Wellington, Auckland and Christchurch.

Air2There (☏ 04-904 5133, 0800 777 000; www.air2there.com) Flies/to from Paraparaumu.

Jetstar (☏ 09-975 9426, 0800 800 995; www.jetstar.com) Flies to/from Auckland and Wellington.

Kiwi Regional Airlines (☏ 07-444 5020; www.flykiwiair.co.nz) Flies to/from Dunedin and Hamilton.

Originair (☏ 0800 380 380; www.originair.co.nz) Based in Nelson; flies to/from Wellington and Palmerston North.

Soundsair (☏ 03-520 3080, 0800 505 005; www.soundsair.com) Loyal and long-standing provider; flies to/from Wellington and Paraparaumu.

BUS

Abel Tasman Coachlines (☏ 03-548 0285; www.abeltasmantravel.co.nz) operates bus services to Motueka (one hour), Takaka (two hours), Kaiteriteri and Marahau (both two hours). These services also connect with **Golden Bay Coachlines** (p77) services for Takaka and around. Transport to/from the three national parks is provided by **Trek Express** (p77).

Atomic Shuttles (☏ 0508 108 359, 03-349 0697; www.atomictravel.co.nz) runs from Nelson to Blenheim (2 hours), Picton (2¼ hours), and Christchurch (7¾ hours) with a Greymouth connection, plus other southern destinations as far as Queenstown, Dunedin and Invercargill. Services can be booked at (and depart from) Nelson i-SITE.

InterCity (☏ 03-548 1538; www.intercity.co.nz; Bridge St, departs SLB Travel Centre) runs from Nelson to most key South Island destinations including Picton (two hours), Kaikoura (3½ hours), Christchurch (seven hours) and Greymouth (six hours).

❶ Getting Around

BICYCLE

Bikes are available for hire from **Nelson Cycle Hire & Tours** (p79), among many other cycle tour companies.

BUS

Nelson Suburban Bus Lines (SBL; ☏ 03-548 3290; www.nbus.co.nz; 27 Bridge St) Nelson Suburban Bus Lines operates NBUS, the local service between Nelson, Richmond via Tahunanui and Stoke until about 7pm weekdays, 4.30pm on weekends. It also runs the Late Late Bus (www.nbus.co.nz; ⊗ hourly 10pm-3am Fri & Sat) from Nelson to Richmond via Tahunanui, departing the Westpac Bank on Trafalgar St. Maximum fare for these services is $4.

TAXI

Nelson City Taxis (☏ 03-548 8225; www.nelsontaxis.co.nz)

Sun City Taxis (☏ 03-548 2666; www.suncitytaxis.co.nz)

Ruby Coast & Moutere Hills

From Richmond, south of Nelson, there are two routes to Motueka: the quicker, busier route along the Ruby Coast, and the inland route through the Moutere Hills. If you're making a round-trip from Nelson, drive one route out, and the other on the way back.

The Ruby Coast route begins on SH60 and skirts around Waimea Inlet before diverting along the well signposted **Ruby Coast Scenic Route**. Although this is the quickest way to get from Nelson to Motueka (around a 45-minute drive), there are various distractions waiting to slow you down. Major attractions include Rabbit Island (p84) recreation reserve, and **Mapua**, near the mouth of the Waimea River, home to arty shops and eateries.

The inland **Moutere Highway** (signposted at Appleby on SH60) is a pleasant alternative traversing gently rolling countryside dotted with farms, orchards and lifestyle blocks. Visitor attractions are fewer and further between, but it's a scenic and fruitful drive, particularly in high summer when roadside stalls are laden with fresh produce. The main settlement along the way is **Upper Moutere**. First settled by German immigrants and originally named Sarau, today it's a sleepy hamlet with a couple of notable stops. Look for the *Moutere Artisans* trail guide (www.moutereartisans.co.nz).

The two highways aren't particularly far apart, and the whole area can be explored by bicycle on the Great Taste Trail (p83), so named for the many wineries and other culinary (and art) stops along the way. The *Nelson Wine Guide* pamphlet (www.winenelson.co.nz) will help you find them. Other useful resources for this area are the *Nelson Art Guide* or *Nelson's Creative Pathways* pamphlets.

○ Sights

Golden Bear Brewing Company   BREWERY
(www.goldenbearbrewing.com; Mapua Wharf, Mapua; meals $10-16) In Mapua village it won't be hard to sniff out the Golden Bear – a microbrewery with tons of stainless steel out back, and a dozen or so brews out front. Authentic Mexican food (burritos, quesadillas and huevos rancheros; meals $10 to $16) will stop you from getting a sore head, and there's regular live music on Friday nights and Sunday afternoons.

★ **Waimea**   WINERY
(☑ 03-544 6385; www.waimeaestates.co.nz; 59 Appleby Hwy, Richmond; ☉ 10am-5pm Mon-Wed, to 9pm Thu-Sun) Just 2km from Richmond you'll hit Waimea winery, where a diverse range of interesting wines is available to taste. On-site is the deservedly popular **Cellar Door** (www.thecellardoor.net.nz; mains $18-30; ☉ 10am-5pm Mon-Wed, to 9pm Thu-Sun).

Rabbit Island/Moturoa   BEACH, FOREST
Around 9km from Richmond on SH60 is the signposted turn-off to Rabbit Island/Moturoa, a recreation reserve offering estuary views from many angles, sandy beaches and quiet pine forest trails forming part of the Great Taste Trail (p83). The bridge to the island closes at sunset; overnight stays are not allowed.

Höglund Art Glass   GALLERY
(☑ 03-544 6500; www.hoglundartglass.com; 52 Lansdowne Rd, Appleby; ☉ 10am-5pm) Ola, Marie and their associates work the furnace to produce internationally acclaimed glass art. The process is amazing to watch, and the results beautiful to view in the gallery. Their jewellery and penguins make memorable souvenirs if their signature vases are too heavy to take home.

⚡ Activities

Wheelie Fantastic   BICYCLE TOUR
(☑ 03-543 2245; www.wheeliefantastic.co.nz; Mapua Wharf, Mapua; self-guided tours from $95, bike hire per day from $30) Conveniently located at Mapua Wharf, this operator offers several different self-guided and fully guided day tours around the Great Taste Trail, with shuttle pick-ups available.

✕ Eating & Drinking

★ **Jester House**   CAFE $
(☑ 03-526 6742; www.jesterhouse.co.nz; 320 Aporo Rd, Tasman; meals $15-22; ☉ 9am-5pm) Long-standing Jester House is reason alone to take this coastal detour, as much for its tame eels as for the peaceful sculpture gardens that encourage you to linger over lunch. A short, simple menu puts a few twists into staples (venison burger, lavender shortbread), and there is local beer and wines. It's 8km to Mapua or Motueka.

Smokehouse   FISH & CHIPS $
(www.smokehouse.co.nz; Mapua Wharf, Mapua; fish & chips $8-12; ☉ 11am-8pm) Visit this Mapua institution to order fish and chips and eat them on the wharf while the gulls eye up your crispy bits. Get some delicious wood-smoked fish and pâté to go.

Jellyfish   MODERN NZ $$
(☑ 03-540 2028; www.jellyfishmapua.co.nz; Mapua Wharf, Mapua; lunch $16-24, dinner $24-34; ☉ 9am-late; ✎) Between the waterside location, sunny patio and inspired East–West menu you've got an A-grade all-day cafe.

Local fish and other produce feature heavily as do fine wines and craft beer.

Moutere Inn PUB
(☑ 03-543 2759; www.moutereinn.co.nz; 1406 Moutere Hwy, Upper Moutere) Reputedly NZ's oldest pub, complete with genuine retro interior, the Moutere Inn is a welcoming establishment serving thoughtful meals ($13 to $20; homemade burgers, falafel salad) and predominantly local craft beer. Sit in the sunshine with a beer-tasting platter, or settle in on music nights with a folksy bent. Rooms are on offer if you need to rest your head.

❶ Getting There & Away

InterCity (p83) buses service Nelson and Motueka, but to access the Ruby Coast and Moutere Hills you'll need your own transport. Biking the **Great Taste Trail** (p83) is a good way of exploring.

Motueka

POP 7600

Motueka (pronounced mott-oo-ecka, meaning 'Island of Weka') is a bustling agricultural hub, and a great base from which to explore the region. It has vital amenities, ample accommodation, cafes and roadside fruit stalls, all in a beautiful river and estuary setting. Stock up here if you're en route to Golden Bay or the Abel Tasman and Kahurangi National Parks.

◉ Sights

While most of Mot's drawcards are out of town, there are a few attractions worth checking out, the buzziest of which is the active aerodrome, home to several air-raising activities. It's a good place to soak up some sun and views, and watch a few folks drop in.

While you might not realise it from the high street, Motueka is just a stone's throw from the sea. Eyeball the waters (with birds and saltwater baths) along the **estuary walkway** (which can also be cycled; hire bikes from the **Bike Shed** (☑ 03-929 8607; www.motuekabikeshed.co.nz; 145b High St; half-/full-day hire from $25/40)). Follow your nose or obtain a town map from the i-SITE (p87), where you can also get the *Motueka Art Walk* pamphlet detailing sculptures, murals and occasional peculiarities around town.

Hop Federation BREWERY
(☑ 03-528 0486; www.hopfederation.co.nz; 483 Main Rd, Riwaka; ⊙11am-6pm) Pop in for tast-

ings ($3) and fill a flagon to go at this teeny-weeny but terrific craft brewery 5km from Mot. Our pick of the ales is the Red IPA. (And note the cherry stall across the road.)

Motueka District Museum MUSEUM
(☑ 03-528 7660; www.motuekadistrictmuseum. org.nz; 140 High St; admission by donation; ⊙10am-4pm Mon-Fri Dec-Mar, to 3pm Tue-Fri Apr-Nov) An interesting collection of regional artefacts, housed in a dear old school building.

🏃 Activities

⭐**Skydive Abel Tasman** ADVENTURE SPORTS
(☑ 03-528 4091, 0800 422 899; www.skydive. co.nz; Motueka Aerodrome, 60 College St; jumps 13,000ft/16,500ft $299/399) Move over, Taupo: we've jumped both and think Mot takes the cake. Presumably so do the many sports jumpers who favour this drop zone, some of whom you may see rocketing in. Photo and video packages are extra. Excellent spectating from the front lawn.

U-fly Extreme ADVENTURE SPORTS
(☑ 03-528 8290, 0800 360 180; www.uflyextreme. co.nz; Motueka Aerodrome, 60 College St; 15min $395, 20min $495, plus flight lesson $200) You handle the controls in an open-cockpit Pitts Special stunt bi-plane. No experience necessary, just a stomach for loops and barrel rolls. Roger wilco!

Tasman Sky Adventures SCENIC FLIGHTS
(☑ 0800 114 386, 027 223 3513; www.skyadventures.co.nz; Motueka Aerodrome, 60 College St; 15/30min flights $105/205) A rare opportunity to fly in a microlight. Keep your eyes open and blow your mind on a scenic flight above Abel Tasman National Park. Wow. And there's tandem hang gliding for the brave (15/30 minutes, 2500ft/5280ft $195/330).

🛌 Sleeping

⭐**Motueka Top 10 Holiday Park** HOLIDAY PARK **$**
(☑ 03-528 7189; www.motuekatop10.co.nz; 10 Fearon St; sites from $48, cabins $69-160, units & motels $113-457; @ 🛜 🌊) 🚲 Close to town and the Great Taste Trail, this place is packed with grassy, green charm – check out those lofty kahikatea trees! Shipshape communal amenities include a swimming pool, spa and jumping pillow, and there are ample accommodation options from smart new cabins to an apartment sleeping up to 11. On-site bike hire, plus local advice and bookings freely offered.

Motueka

0 ——— 200 m
0 ——— 0.1 miles

Eden's Edge Lodge   HOSTEL $
(☏ 03-528 4242; www.edensedge.co.nz; 137 Lodder Lane, Riwaka; sites from $18, dm $31, d/tr with bathroom $99/86; ☎) ✿ Surrounded by farmland, 4km from the bustle of Motueka, this purpose-built lodge comes pretty close to backpacker heaven. Well-designed facilities include a gleaming kitchen and inviting

communal areas including a grassy garden. There's bike hire for tackling the Great Taste Trail, but it's also within walking distance of beer, ice cream and coffee.

Laughing Kiwi   HOSTEL $
(☏ 03-528 9229; www.laughingkiwi.co.nz; 310 High St; dm $29, d with/without bathroom $76/68; ☎) Compact, low-key YHA hostel with rooms spread between an old villa and a purpose-built backpacker lodge with a smart kitchen/lounge. The self-contained bach is a good option for groups of up to four ($180).

★ **Equestrian Lodge Motel**   MOTEL $$
(☏ 0800 668 782, 03-528 9369; www.equestrian lodge.co.nz; Avalon Ct; d $125-158, q $175-215; ☎☀) No horses, no lodge, but no matter. This excellent motel complex is close to town (off Tudor St) and features expansive lawns, rose gardens, and a heated pool and spa alongside a series of continually refreshed units. Cheerful owners will hook you up with local activities.

Resurgence   LODGE $$$
(☏ 03-528 4664; www.resurgence.co.nz; 574 Riwaka Valley Rd; d lodge from $695, chalets from $575; @☎☀) ✿ Choose a luxurious en suite lodge room or a self-contained chalet at this magical green retreat. It's a 15-minute drive from Abel Tasman National Park, and a 30-minute walk from the picturesque source of the Riwaka River. Lodge rates include aperitifs and a four-course dinner as well as breakfast; chalet rates are for B&B, with dinner an extra $120.

✕ Eating

Patisserie Royale   BAKERY $
(152 High St; baked goods $2-8; ⊘5am-5pm Mon-Fri, to 3pm Sat & Sun; ✿) The best of several Mot bakeries and worth every delectable calorie. Lots of French fancies, delicious pies and bread with bite.

★ **Toad Hall**   CAFE $$
(☏ 03-528 6456; www.toadhallmotueka.co.nz; 502 High St; breakfast $10-20, lunch $10-23; ⊘8am-6pm, to 9pm summer) This fantastic cafe serves smashing breakfasts, such as smoked salmon rösti, and wholesome yet decadent lunches including pork-belly burgers. The sweet outdoor space is home to live music and pizza on Friday and Saturday nights in summer. Inside is a fine selection of smoothies, juices, baked goods, pies and selected groceries.

Motueka Sunday Market MARKET
(Wallace St; ⊙8am-1pm Sun) On Sundays the car park behind the i-SITE fills up with trestle tables for the Motueka Sunday Market: produce, jewellery, buskers, arts, crafts and Doris' divine bratwurst.

Drinking & Nightlife

Sprig & Fern CRAFT BEER
(☑03-528 4684; www.sprigandfern.co.nz; Wallace St; ⊙2pm-late) A member of the local Sprig & Fern brewery family, this backstreet tavern is the pick of Motueka's drinking holes. Small and pleasant, with two courtyards, it offers 20 hand-pulled brews, simple food (pizza, platters and an awesome burger; meals $15 to $23) and occasional live music.

☆ Entertainment

Gecko Theatre CINEMA
(☑03-528 9996; www.geckotheatre.co.nz; 23b Wallace St; tickets $9-13) Pull up an easy chair at this wee, independent theatre and see interesting art-house flicks.

ⓘ Information

Motueka i-SITE (☑03-528 6543; www.motuekaisite.co.nz; 20 Wallace St; ⊙8.30am-5pm Mon-Fri, 9am-4pm Sat & Sun) A endlessly busy info centre with helpful staff handling bookings from Kaitaia to Bluff and provide local national-park expertise and necessaries.

ⓘ Getting There & Away

Bus services depart from Motueka i-SITE.
Abel Tasman Coachlines (☑03-548 0285; www.abeltasmantravel.co.nz) runs daily from Nelson (where you can connect to other South Island Destinations via **InterCity** (p57)) to Motueka (one hour), Kaiteriteri (25 minutes) and Marahau (30 minutes). These services connect with **Golden Bay Coachlines** (p77) services to Takaka (1¼ hours) and other Golden Bay destinations including Totaranui in Abel Tasman National Park, Collingwood, and on to the Heaphy Track trailhead. Note that from May to September all buses run less frequently.

Kaiteriteri

POP 790

Known simply as 'Kaiteri', this seaside hamlet 13km from Motueka is the most popular resort town in the area. During the summer holidays its golden swimming beach feels more like Noumea than NZ, with more towels than sand. Consider yourself warned.

Kaiteri is also a major departure point for Abel Tasman National Park transport, although Marahau is the main base.

🏃 Activities

Kaiteriteri

Mountain Bike Park MOUNTAIN BIKING
(www.kaiteriterimtbpark.org.nz) Extensive MTB park with tracks to suit all levels of rider.

🛏 Sleeping & Eating

Kaiteri Lodge LODGE $
(☑03-527 8281; www.kaiterilodge.co.nz; Inlet Rd; dm $35, d $80-160; @☎) Modern, purpose-built lodge with small, simple dorms and en suite doubles. The nautical decor adds some cheer to the somewhat lazily maintained communal areas. The sociable **Beached Whale** (dinner $18-28; ⊙4pm-late, reduced hours in winter) bar is on-site.

Torlesse Coastal Motels MOTEL $$
(☑03-527 8063; www.torlessemotels.co.nz; 8 Kotare Pl, Little Kaiteriteri Beach; d $190-210, q $300-350; ☎) Just 200m from Little Kaiteriteri Beach (around the corner from the main beach) is this congregation of roomy hillside units with pitched ceilings, full kitchens and laundries. Most have water views, and there's a ferny barbecue area and spa.

Bellbird Lodge B&B $$$
(☑03-527 8555; www.bellbirdlodge.co.nz; 160 Kaiteriteri-Sandy Bay Rd; d $275-350; @☎) An upmarket B&B 1.5km up the hill from Kaiteri Beach, offering two en suite rooms, bush and sea views, extensive gardens, spectacular breakfasts (featuring homemade muesli and fruit compote), and gracious hosts. Dinner by arrangement in winter, when local restaurant hours are irregular.

Shoreline RESTAURANT $$
(☑03-527 8507; www.shorelinekaiteriteri.co.nz; cnr Inlet & Sandy Bay Rds; meals $18-22; ⊙7.30am-9pm, reduced hours Apr-Nov) A modern, beige cafe-bar-restaurant right on the beach. Punters chill out on the sunny deck, lingering over sandwiches, pizzas, burgers and other predictable fare, or pop in for coffee and cake. Erratic winter hours; burger booth out the back.

ⓘ Getting There & Away

Kaiteriteri is serviced by **Abel Tasman Coachlines** (☑03-548 0285; www.abeltasmantravel.co.nz).

MARLBOROUGH & NELSON KAITERITERI

Marahau

POP 120

Just up the coast from Kaiteriteri and 18km north of Motueka, Marahau is the main gateway to Abel Tasman National Park. It's less of a town, more of a procession of holiday homes and tourist businesses.

🏃 Activities

Marahau Horse Treks HORSE RIDING

(📞 03-527 8425; Marahau-Sandy Bay Rd; children's pony rides $35, 2hr horse rides $90) If you're in an equine state of mind, Marahau Horse Treks offers you a chance to belt along the beach on a horse, your hair streaming out behind you.

🛏 Sleeping

Barn HOSTEL $

(📞 03-527 8043; www.barn.co.nz; 14 Harvey Rd; unpowered/powered sites per person $20/22, dm $32, d $68-85; @ 🛜) This backpackers has hit its straps with comfortable new dorms, a toilet block and a grassy camping field added to a mix of microcabins, alfresco kitchens and barbecue areas. The barn itself is the hub – the communal kitchen and lounge area are good for socialising, as is the central deck, which has a fireplace. Activity bookings and secure parking available.

Abel Tasman Marahau Lodge MOTEL $$

(📞 03-527 8250; www.abeltasmanlodge.co.nz; 295 Sandy Bay-Marahau Rd; d $145-175, q $200-260; @ 🛜) 🍃 Enjoy halcyon days in this arc of 15 studios and self-contained units with groovy styling and cathedral ceilings, opening out on to landscaped gardens. There's also a fully equipped communal kitchen for self-caterers, plus spa and sauna. Cuckoos, tui and bellbirds squawk and warble in the bushy surrounds.

Ocean View Chalets CHALET $$

(📞 03-527 8232; www.accommodationabeltasman. co.nz; 305 Sandy Bay-Marahau Rd; d $145-235, q $290; 🛜) On a leafy hillside affording plenty of privacy, these cheerful, cypress-lined chalets are 300m from the Coast Track with views out to Fisherman Island. All except the cheapest studios are self-contained; breakfast and packed lunches available.

🍴 Eating

Fat Tui BURGERS $

(cnr Marahau-Sandy Bay & Marahau Valley Rds; burgers $13-18; ⊙noon-8pm daily summer, Wed-Sun winter) Everyone's heard about this bird, based in a caravan that ain't rollin' anywhere fast. Thank goodness. Superlative burgers, such as the Cowpat (beef), the Ewe Beaut (lamb) and Roots, Shoots & Leaves (vege). Fish and chips, and coffee, too.

Hooked CAFE $$

(📞 03-527 8576; www.hookedonmarahau.co.nz; 229 Marahau-Sandy Bay Rd; lunch $11-20, dinner $26-32; ⊙8am-10pm Dec-Mar, 8am-11am & 3pm-10pm Oct-Nov & Apr) This popular place certainly reels them in, so reservations are advisable for dinner. The art-bedecked interior opens on to an outdoor terrace with distracting views. Lunch centres on salads and seafood, while the dinner menu boasts fresh fish of the day, green-lipped mussels and NZ lamb shanks.

Park Cafe CAFE $$

(📞 03-527 8270; www.parkcafe.co.nz; Harvey Rd; lunch $10-22, dinner $17-36; ⊙8am-late mid-Sep–May; 🍴) Sitting at the Coast Track trailhead, this breezy cafe is perfectly placed for fuelling up or restoring the waistline. High-calorie options include the big breakfast, burgers and cakes, but there are also seafood and salad options plus wood-fired pizza Thursday through Saturday evenings. Enjoy in the room with a view or the sunny courtyard garden. Live music on occasion.

ℹ Getting There & Away

Marahau is serviced by **Abel Tasman Coachlines** (📞 03-548 0285; www.abeltasmantravel. co.nz).

Abel Tasman National Park

Coastal Abel Tasman National Park blankets the northern end of a range of marble and limestone hills that extend from Kahurangi National Park. Various tracks in the park include an inland route, although the Coast Track is what everyone is here for – it's NZ's most popular Great Walk.

🏃 Activities

Abel Tasman Coast Track

This is arguably NZ's most beautiful Great Walk – 60km of sparkling seas, golden sand, quintessential coastal forest, and hidden surprises such as Cleopatra's Pool. Such pulling power attracts around 30,000

Abel Tasman National Park

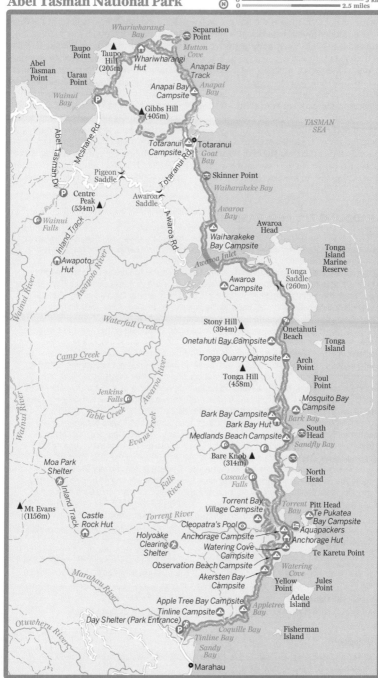

overnight trampers and kayakers per year, each of whom stay at least one night in the park. A major attraction is the terrain: well cut, well graded and well marked. It's almost impossible to get lost here and the track can be tramped in sneakers.

You will, however, probably get your feet wet, as this track features long stretches of beach and crazy tides. In fact the tidal differences in the park are among the greatest in the country, up to a staggering 6m. At Torrent and Bark Bays, it's much easier and more fun to doff the shoes and cross the soggy sands, rather than take the high-tide track. At Awaroa Bay you have no choice but to plan on crossing close to low tide. Tide tables are posted along the track and on the DOC website; regional i-SITEs also have them.

It's a commonly held belief that the Coast Track ends at Totaranui, but it actually extends to a car park near Wainui Bay. The entire tramp takes only three to five days, although with water taxi transport you can convert it into an almost endless array of options, particularly if you combine it with a kayak leg. If you can only spare a couple of days, a rewarding option is to loop around the northern end of the park, tramping the Coast Track from Totaranui, passing Anapai Bay and Mutton Cove, overnighting at Whariwharangi Hut, then returning to Totaranui via the Gibbs Hill Track. This will give you

PADDLING THE ABEL TASMAN

The Abel Tasman Coast Track has long been tramping territory, but its coastal beauty makes it an equally seductive spot for sea kayaking, which can easily be combined with walking and camping.

A variety of professional outfits are able to float you out on the water, and the possibilities and permutations for guided or freedom trips are vast. You can kayak from half a day up to three days, camping, or staying in DOC huts, bachs, even a floating backpackers, either fully catered or self-catering. You can kayak one day, camp overnight then walk back, or walk further into the park and catch a water taxi back.

Most operators offer similar trips at similar prices. Marahau is the main base, but trips also depart from Kaiteriteri. There are numerous day-trip options, including guided trips often departing Marahau and taking in bird-filled Adele Island (around $200). There are also various multiday guided trips, with three days a common option, costing anything from $260 to $750 depending on accommodation and other inclusions.

Freedom rentals (double-kayak and equipment hire) are around $70/110 per person for one/two days; all depart from Marahau with the exception of Golden Bay Kayaks (p94), which is based at Tata Beach in Golden Bay.

Instruction is given to everyone, and most tour companies have a minimum age of either eight or 14 depending on the trip. None allow solo hires. Camping gear is usually provided on overnight trips; if you're disappearing into the park for a few days, most operators provide free car parking.

November to Easter is the busiest time, with December to February the absolute peak. You can, however, paddle all year round, with winter offering its own rewards; the weather is surprisingly amenable, the seals are more playful, and there's more birdlife and less haze.

Following are the main players in this competitive market (shop around):

Abel Tasman Kayaks (☎ 0800 732 529, 03-527 8022; www.abeltasmankayaks.co.nz; Main Rd, Marahau)

Kahu Kayaks (☎ 0800 300 101, 03-527 8300; www.kahukayaks.co.nz; 11 Marahau Valley Rd)

Kaiteriteri Kayaks (☎ 0800 252 925, 03-527 8383; www.seakayak.co.nz; Kaiteriteri Beach)

Marahau Sea Kayaks (☎ 0800 529 257, 03-527 8176; www.msk.co.nz; Abel Tasman Centre, Franklin St, Marahau)

R&R Kayaks (☎ 0508 223 224; www.rrkayaks.co.nz; 279 Sandy Bay-Marahau Rd)

Sea Kayak Company (☎ 0508 252 925, 03-528 7251; www.seakayaknz.co.nz; 506 High St, Motueka)

Wilsons Abel Tasman (☎ 03-528 2027, 0800 223 582; www.abeltasman.co.nz; 409 High St, Motueka) See p91.

a slice of the park's best features (beaches, seals, coastal scenery) while being far less crowded than other segments.

The track operates on DOC's Great Walks Pass. Children are free but bookings are still required. Book online (www.doc.govt.nz), contact the **Nelson Marlborough Bookings Helpdesk** (☏03-546 8210), or book in person at the Nelson, Motueka or Takaka i-SITES or DOC offices, where staff can offer suggestions to tailor the track to your needs and organise transport at each end. Book your trip well ahead of time, especially huts between December and March.

This track is so well trodden that a topographical map isn't essential for navigation. The map within DOC's *Abel Tasman Coast Track* brochure provides sufficient detail, and you can readily buy more illuminating maps at local visitor centres.

Other Activities

★ **Abel Tasman Canyons**   ADVENTURE SPORTS
(☏0800 863 472, 03-528 9800; www.abeltasmancanyons.co.nz; full-day trips $259) Few Abel Tasman visitors see the Torrent River; here's your chance to journey down its staggeringly beautiful granite-lined canyon, via a fun-filled combination of swimming, sliding, abseiling and big leaps into jewel-like pools.

☞ Tours

Tour companies usually offer free Motueka pick-up/drop-off, with Nelson pick-up available at extra cost.

★ **Wilsons Abel Tasman**   TOUR
(☏03-528 2027, 0800 223 582; www.abeltasman.co.nz; 409 High St, Motueka) This long-standing, family-owned operator offers an impressive array of cruises, walking, kayaking and combo tours, including a $36 day-walk special. Overnight stays are available at Wilsons' lodges in pretty Awaroa and Torrent Bay for guided-tour guests.

Offers an Explorer Pass for unlimited boat travel on three days over a seven-day period (adult/child $150/75).

Abel Tasman Eco Tours   TOUR
(☏0800 223 538, 03-528 0946; www.abeltasmanecotours.co.nz; day tours adult/child $159/99) Take an ecology-focused day trip with marine scientist Stew Robertson, either cruising around the coast in a boat, or on a five-hour tramping trip in the Wainui Valley.

Abel Tasman Tours & Guided Walks   WALKING TOUR
(☏03-528 9602; www.abeltasmantours.co.nz; tours from $245) Small-group, day-long walking tours (minimum two people) that include a packed lunch and water taxis.

Abel Tasman Charters   BOAT TOUR
(☏027 441 8588, 0800 223 522; www.abeltasmancharters.com; 6hr tours $265) Offers a six-hour trip combining walking, kayaking, swimming and cruising into the park from Stephen's Bay (near Kaiteriteri).

Abel Tasman Sailing Adventures   SAILING
(☏0800 467 245, 03-527 8375; www.sailingadventures.co.nz; Kaiteriteri; day trips $185) Scheduled and on-demand catamaran trips, with sail/walk/kayak combos available. The popular day trip includes lunch on Anchorage Beach.

🛏 Sleeping

Along the Abel Tasman Coast Track are four Great Walk huts ($32) with bunks, heating, flush toilets and limited lighting, but no cooking facilities. There are also 19 designated Great Walk campsites ($14). As the Coast Track is a Great Walk, all huts and campsites must be booked in advance year-round, either online through **Great Walks Bookings** (☏0800 694 732; www.doc.govt.nz) or at DOC visitor centres nationwide. Hut tickets and annual passes cannot be used on the track, and there is a two-night limit on stays in each hut or campsite, except for Totaranui campsite which has a one-night limit. Penalty fees apply to those who do not have a valid booking, and you may be required to leave the park if caught.

Aquapackers   HOSTEL
(☏0800 430 744; www.aquapackers.co.nz; Anchorage; dm/d incl breakfast $75/225; ⊘closed May-Sep) The specially converted 13m *Catarac* (catamaran), moored permanently in Anchorage Bay, provides unusual but buoyant backpacker accommodation for 22. Facilities are basic but decent; prices include bedding, dinner and breakfast. Bookings essential.

Totaranui Campsite   CAMPGROUND
(☏03-528 8083; www.doc.govt.nz; summer/winter $15/10) An extremely popular facility with a whopping capacity (850 campers) and a splendid setting next to the beach backed by some of the best bush in the park. A staffed DOC office has interpretive displays, flush toilets, cold showers and a public phone.

ⓘ Getting There & Away

The closest big town to Abel Tasman is Motueka, with nearby Marahau the southern gateway. Although Wainui is the official northern trailhead, it is more common to finish in Totaranui, either skipping the northernmost section or looping back to Totaranui over Gibbs Hill Track. All gateways are serviced by either **Abel Tasman Coachlines** (p77) and **Golden Bay Coachlines** (p77).

ⓘ Getting Around

Once you hit the park, it is easy to get to/from any point on the track via numerous tour companies and water taxi operators offering scheduled and on-demand services, either from Kaiteriteri or Marahau. Typical one-way prices from either Marahau or Kaiteriteri: Anchorage and Torrent Bay ($35), Bark Bay ($40), Awaroa ($45) and Totaranui ($47).

Abel Tasman Aqua Taxi (☑ 0800 278 282, 03-527 8083; www.aquataxi.co.nz; Marahau-Sandy Bay Rd, Marahau) Scheduled and on-demand services as well as boat/walk options.

Marahau Water Taxis (☑ 0800 808 018, 03-527 8176; www.marahauwatertaxis.co.nz; Abel Tasman Centre, Franklin St, Marahau) Scheduled services plus boat/walk options.

Golden Bay

From Motueka, SH60 takes a stomach-churning meander over Takaka Hill to Golden Bay, a small region mixing rural charm, artistic endeavour, alternative lifestyles and a fair share of transient folk spending time off the grid.

For the visitor its main attractions are access to both the Abel Tasman and Kahurangi National Parks, along with other natural wonders including Farewell Spit and a swathe of beautiful beaches. Look out for (or download) DOC's *Walks in Golden Bay* brochure to kick-start your adventures.

ⓘ Getting There & Away

Golden Bay is well serviced by **Golden Bay Coachlines** (☑ 03-525 8352; www.gbcoachlines.co.nz), with daily runs between Nelson and the Heaphy Track via Motueka and Takaka, but to get to quiet corners you'll need to be wily or have your own wheels.

Takaka Hill

Takaka Hill (791m) butts in between Tasman Bay and Golden Bay. It looks pretty bushy but closer inspection reveals a remarkable marble landscape formed by millions of years of erosion. Its smooth beauty is revealed on the one-hour drive over the hill road (SH60), a steep, winding route punctuated by spectacular lookout points and a smattering of other interesting stops.

Just before the summit is the turn-off to **Canaan Downs Scenic Reserve**, reached at the end of an 11km gravel road. This area stars in both the *The Lord of the Rings* and *The Hobbit* movies, but **Harwoods Hole** is the most famous feature here. It's one of the largest *tomo* (caves) in the country at 357m deep and 70m wide, with a 176m vertical drop. It's a 30-minute walk from the car park. Allow us to state the obvious: the cave is off-limits to all but the most experienced cavers.

Mountain-bikers with intermediate-level skills can venture along a couple of loop tracks, or head all the way down to Takaka via the titillating **Rameka Track**. There's a basic DOC Campsite (adult/child $6/$3) here, too.

Also close to the top, the **Takaka Hill Walkway** is a three-hour loop through marble karst rock formations, native forest and farmland. Further along the road **Harwood Lookout** affords tantalising views down the Takaka River Valley to Takaka and Golden Bay. For more walks on the sunny side of the hill, see DOC's brochure *Walks in Golden Bay*.

◎ Sights

Ngarua Caves CAVES
(SH60; adult/child $17/7; ⊙45min tours hourly 10am-4pm Sep-May, open Sat & Sun only Jun-Aug) Just below the summit of Takaka Hill (literally) are the Ngarua Caves, a rock-solid attraction karst in stone, where you can see myriad subterranean delights including moa bones. Access is restricted to tours – you can't go solo spelunking.

Takaka
POP 1240

Boasting NZ's highest concentration of yoga pants, dreadlocks and bare feet in the high street, Takaka is a lovable little town and the last 'big' centre before the road west ends at Farewell Spit. You'll find most things you need here, and a few things you don't, but we all have an unworn tie-dyed tank top in our wardrobe, don't we?

◎ Sights

Many of Takaka's sights can readily be reached via bicycle. Cycle hire and maps are both available from the time-warped **Quiet**

Revolution Cycle Shop ([📞] 03-525 9555; www.
quietrevolution.co.nz; 11 Commercial St; bike hire per
day $25-65) on the main street. Shopping is
also a highlight if you enjoy festival chic and
homespun art and craft. To extend your arty
ambles, look for the free *Arts in Golden Bay*
and *Arts Trail* pamphlets.

Rawhiti Cave   CAVE
(www.doc.govt.nz) The ultimate in geological
eye-candy around these parts are the phyto-
karst features of Rawhiti Cave, a 15-minute
drive from Takaka (reached via Motupipi,
turning right into Glenview Rd, then left
into Packard Rd and following the signs).
The rugged two-hour-return walk (steep in
places; dangerous in the wet) may well leave
you speechless (although we managed 'mon-
ster', 'fangs', and even 'Sarlacc').

Grove Scenic Reserve   VIEWPOINT
(www.doc.govt.nz) Around a 10-minute drive
from Takaka (signposted down Clifton Rd),
you will find this crazy limestone maze
punctuated by gnarled old rata trees. The
walkway takes around 10 minutes and passes an impressive lookout.

Te Waikoropupū Springs   SPRING
(www.doc.govt.nz) The largest freshwater
springs in the southern hemisphere and
some of the clearest in the world, 'Pupū
Springs' is a colourful little lake refreshed
with around 14,000L of water per second
surging from underground vents. From
Takaka, head 4km northwest on SH60 and
follow the signs inland for 3km from Waita-
pu Bridge. There are illuminating information panels at the car park and a 30-minute
forest loop taking in the waters, which are
sacred and therefore off limits.

🏃 Activities

Pupu Hydro Walkway   TRAMPING
(www.doc.govt.nz; Pupu Valley Rd) This enjoyable two-hour circuit follows an old water
race through beech forest, past engineering
and gold-mining relics to the restored (and
operational) Pupu Hydro Powerhouse, built
in 1929. It's 9km from Takaka at the end of
Pupu Valley Rd; just follow the signs at the
Te Waikoropupū Springs junction.

👉 Tours

Golden Bay Air   SCENIC FLIGHTS
([📞] 0800 588 885, 03-525 8725; www.goldenbayair.
co.nz; Takaka Airfield, SH60) Scenic and charter
flights around Golden Bay and surrounds;
from $35.

🛏 Sleeping

Kiwiana   HOSTEL $
([📞] 0800 805 494, 03-525 7676; www.kiwianaback
packers.co.nz; 73 Motupipi St; tent sites per person
$18, dm $29-31, s/d $54/68; @ 🛜) Beyond the
welcoming garden is a cute cottage where
rooms are named after classic Kiwiana (the
jandal, Buzzy Bee...). The garage has been
converted into a convivial lounge, with wood-
fired stove, table tennis, pool table, music,
books and games; free bikes for guest use.

Takaka Campground   CAMPGROUND $
([📞] 03-525 7300; www.takakacampingandcabins.
co.nz; 53 Motupipi St; sites per person $18, cab-
ins s/d/tr $35/65/75; 🛜) This low-key and
convenient campground, within walking
distance of the Takaka high street, sports a
splendid rural outlook.

Golden Bay Kiwi Holiday Park   HOLIDAY PARK $
([📞] 03-525 9742; www.goldenbayholidaypark.co.nz;
99 Tukurua Rd, Tukurua; unpowered/powered sites
$43/47, cabins d $85; @ 🛜) Eighteen kilometres north of Takaka with a quiet beach
right out front, this gem of a park has acres
of grass, graceful shade trees and hedge-
rows, easily atoning for tight communal facilities. There are tidy, family-friendly cabins
for budget travellers, and luxury beach houses sleeping up to four ($180 to $270).

★ Adrift   COTTAGES $$$
([📞] 03-525 8353; www.adrift.co.nz; 53 Tukurua Rd,
Tukurua; d $250-540; 🛜) 🖉 Adrift on a heav-
enly bed of beachside bliss is what you'll be
in one of these five cottages dotted within
beautifully landscaped grounds, right on
the beach. Tuck into your breakfast hamper,
then self-cater in the fully equipped kitchen,
dine on the sunny deck, or soak in the spa
bath.

🍴 Eating & Drinking

Dangerous Kitchen   CAFE $$
([📞] 03-525 8686; 46a Commercial St; meals $13-
28; ⏰9am-8pm Mon-Sat; 🖉) 🖉 Dedicated
to Frank Zappa, DK serves largely healthy,
good-value fare such as falafel, pizza, bean
burritos, pasta, great baking and juices as
well as local wines and craft beer. It's mel-
low and musical, with a sunny courtyard out
back and people-watching out front.

★ Mussel Inn   PUB
([📞] 03-525 9241; www.musselinn.co.nz; 1259 SH60,
Onekaka; all-day snacks $5-17, dinner $13-30;
⏰11am-late, closed Jul-Aug) You will find one

of NZ's most beloved brewery-taverns halfway between Takaka and Collingwood. The Mussel Inn is rustic NZ at its most genuine, complete with creaking timbers, a rambling beer garden with a brazier, regular music and other events, and hearty, homemade food. Try the signature 'Captain Cooker', a brown beer brewed naturally with manuka.

☆ Entertainment

Village Theatre   CINEMA
(☑03-525 8453; www.villagetheatre.org.nz; 32 Commercial St; adult/child $14/8) Demonstrating, yet again, provincial NZ's commitment to quality viewing.

❶ Information

Golden Bay Visitor Centre (☑03-525 9136; www.goldenbaynz.co.nz; Willow St; ⊗9am-4pm Mon-Fri, to 1pm Sat) A friendly little centre with all the necessary information, including the indispensable official tourist map. Bookings and DOC passes.

Golden Bay Area DOC Office (☑03-525 8026; www.doc.govt.nz; 62 Commercial St; ⊗1-3pm Mon-Fri) Information on Abel Tasman and Kahurangi National Parks, the Heaphy Track, Farewell Spit and Cobb Valley. Sells hut passes.

❶ Getting There & Away

Golden Bay Air (p93) flies at least once and up to four times daily between Wellington and Takaka.

Golden Bay Coachlines (p77) departs from Takaka on Golden Bay and runs through to Collingwood (25 minutes), the Heaphy Track (one hour), Totaranui (one hour), and over the hill to Motueka (1¼ hours) and Nelson (2¼ hours).

Pohara

POP 550

About 10km northeast of Takaka is pint-sized Pohara, a beachy village with a population that quadruples over summer. It has more flash holiday homes than other parts of Golden Bay, but an agreeable air persists nonetheless, aided by decent food and lodging, and a beach that at low tide is as big as Heathrow's runway.

Pohara lies close to the northern gateway of Abel Tasman National Park. The largely unsealed road into the park passes **Tarakohe Harbour** (Pohara's working port), followed by **Ligar Bay**. It's worth climbing to the Abel Tasman lookout as you pass by.

The next settlement along is **Tata Beach**, where **Golden Bay Kayaks** (☑03-525 9095;

www.goldenbaykayaks.co.nz; Tata Beach; half-day guided tours adult/child from $85/40, freedom hire half-/full day $90/120) offers freedom rental of kayaks and stand-up paddle boards, as well as guided trips (including multiday) into Abel Tasman National Park.

Signposted from the Totaranui Rd at **Wainui Bay** is a leafy walk to the best cascade in the bay: **Wainui Falls**. It's a one-hour return trip, but you could easily take longer by dipping a toe or two in the river.

🛏 Sleeping & Eating

Pohara Beach

Top 10 Holiday Park   HOLIDAY PARK $
(☑0800 764 272, 03-525 9500; www.poharabeach.com; 809 Abel Tasman Dr; sites per person from $22, cabins & units $65-169; @🐾) Lining grassy parkland between the dunes and the main road, this place is in prime position for some beach time. Sites are nice and there are some beaut cabins, but be warned – this is a favourite spot for NZ holidaymakers so it goes a bit mental in high summer. General store and takeaway on-site.

★Sans Souci Inn   LODGE $$
(☑03-525 8663; www.sanssouciinn.co.nz; 11 Richmond Rd; s/d $95/120, units from $160; ⊗closed Jul–mid-Sep; 🐾) 🍴 Sans Souci means 'no worries' in French, and this will be your mantra too after staying in one of the seven Mediterranean-flavoured, mud-brick rooms. Guests share a plant-filled, mosaic bathroom that has composting toilets, and an airy lounge and kitchen which open out on to the semitropical courtyard. Dinner in the on-site restaurant (bookings essential; mains $35 to $37) is highly recommended; breakfast by request.

Ratanui   LODGE $$$
(☑03-525 7998; www.ratanuilodge.com; 818 Abel Tasman Dr; d $155-359; @🐾🏊) A romantic haven close to the beach, this boutique lodge is styled with Victorian panache. It features myriad sensual stimulants such as perfumed rose gardens, a swimming pool, a spa, a massage service, cocktails, and a candelabra-lit restaurant showcasing local produce (open to the public; bookings required). Free bikes, too.

Penguin Café & Bar   PUB FOOD $$
(☑03-525 6126; www.penguincafe.co.nz; 822 Abel Tasman Dr; bar snacks $6-15, meals $16-31; ⊗11am-late Nov-Apr, 4pm-late Mon-Wed & 11am-late Thu-Sun May-Oct) A popular locals' hangout, this well-run spot sports a large garden suited to sundowners and thirst-quenchers

DON'T MISS

FAREWELL SPIT

Bleak, exposed and positively sci-fi, Farewell Spit is a wetland of international importance and a renowned bird sanctuary – the summer home of thousands of migratory waders, notably the godwit (which flies all the way from the Arctic tundra), Caspian tern and Australasian gannet. Walkers can explore the first 4km of the spit via a network of tracks (see DOC's *Farewell Spit & Puponga Farm Park* brochure; $2 or downloadable from www.doc.govt.nz). Beyond that point access is limited to trips with the brilliant Farewell Spit Eco Tours, scheduled according to the tide.

The spit's 35km beach features colossal, crescent-shaped dunes, from where panoramic views extend across Golden Bay and a vast low-tide salt marsh.

At the foot of the spit is a hilltop visitor-centre-cum-cafe – a convenient spot to write a postcard over a coffee, especially on an inclement day.

Farewell Spit Eco Tours (☑ 0800 808 257, 03-524 8257; www.farewellspit.com; 6 Tasman St, Collingwood; tours $125-165) has been operating for more than 70 years. Led by the inimitable Paddy and his expert guides, this company runs memorable tours ranging from two to 6½ hours. Departing from Collingwood, tours take in the spit, the lighthouse, and up to 20 species of bird which may include gannets and godwits. Expect ripping yarns aplenty.

Befitting a frontier, this is the place to saddle up: **Cape Farewell Horse Treks** (☑ 03-524 8031; www.horsetreksnz.com; McGowan St, Puponga; treks from $80) is en route to Wharariki Beach. Treks in this wind-blown country range from 1½ hours (to Pillar Point) to three hours (to Wharariki Beach), with longer (including overnight) trips by arrangement.

---

on sunny days. There's an open fire inside for the odd inclement day. Chow down on belly-filling bar-snacks, and look out for local seafood specials come dinner time.

ⓘ Getting There & Away

Golden Bay Coachlines (☑ 03-525 8352; www.gbcoachlines.co.nz) runs daily from Takaka to Pohara (15 minutes) on the way to Totaranui.

Collingwood & Around

POP 240

Far-flung Collingwood (population 240) is the last town in Golden Bay, and has a real end-of-the-line vibe. It's busy in summer, though for most people it's simply a launch pad for the Heaphy Track or Farewell Spit.

◉ Sights

Wharariki Beach   BEACH

Remote, desolate Wharariki Beach is along an unsealed road, then a 20-minute walk from the car park over farmland (part of the DOC-administered Puponga Farm Park). It's a wild introduction to the West Coast, with mighty dune formations, looming rock islets just offshore and a seal colony at its eastern end (keep an eye out for seals in the stream on the walk here). As inviting as a swim here may seem, there are strong undertows – what the sea wants, the sea shall have...

Collingwood Museum   MUSEUM

(Tasman St, Collingwood; admission by donation; ☺ 9am-6pm) The Collingwood Museum fills a tiny, unstaffed corridor with a quirky collection of saddlery, Māori artefacts, moa bones, shells and old typewriters.

Next door, the **Aorere Centre** has an on-rotation slide show featuring the works of the wonderful pioneer photographer, Fred Tyree.

🛏 Sleeping & Eating

★**Innlet Backpackers & Cottages** HOSTEL $
(☑ 03-524 8040, 027 970 8397; www.theinnlet.co.nz; 839 Collingwood-Puponga Rd, Pakawau; dm/d $34/80, cabins from $90; ☺ closed Jun-Aug; ☏) 🖋 This flower-filled charmer is 10km from Collingwood on the way to Farewell Spit. The main house has elegant backpacker rooms, and there are self-contained options including a cottage sleeping six; campers can enquire about sites. Enjoy the garden, explore the local area on a bike or in a kayak, or venture out for a tramp on the property.

Somerset House   HOSTEL $
(☑ 03-524 8624; www.backpackerscollingwood.co.nz; 10 Gibbs Rd, Collingwood; dm/s/d incl breakfast $32/50/78; ☺ closed May-Oct; @☏) A small, low-key hostel in a bright, historic building on a hill with views from the deck. Get tramping advice from the charming

owners, who offer track transport, free bikes and kayaks, freshly baked bread for breakfast, and your fourth night's stay free.

Old School Cafe CAFE $$
(1115 Collingwood-Puponga Rd, Pakawau; mains $14-31; ⊙4pm-late Thu-Fri, 11am-late Sat & Sun) These folks get an A for effort by providing honest food to an unpredictable flow of passing trade. What it lacks in imagination (steak, pizza and even a shrimp cocktail), it more than makes up for with arty ambience, a garden bar and a welcoming disposition.

ⓘ Getting There & Away

Golden Bay Coachlines (⌾03-525 8352; www.gbcoachlines.co.nz) runs twice daily from Takaka to Collingwood (25 minutes).

Kahurangi National Park

Kahurangi – 'blue skies' in one of several translations – is the second largest of NZ's national parks, and also one of its most diverse. Its most eye-catching features are geological, ranging from windswept beaches and sea cliffs to earthquake-shattered slopes and moraine-dammed lakes, and the smooth, strange karst forms of the interior tableland.

Around 85% of the 4520 sq km park is forested, with beech prevalent, along with rimu and other podocarps. In all, more than 50% of all NZ's plant species can be found in the park, including more than 80% of its alpine plant species. Among the park's 60 birds species are great spotted kiwi, kea, kaka and whio (blue duck). There are creepy cave weta, weird beetles and a huge, leggy spider, but there's also a majestic and ancient snail known as Powelliphanta – something of a (slow) flag bearer for the park's animal kingdom. If you like a field trip filled with plenty that's new and strange, Kahurangi National Park will certainly satisfy.

🏃 Activities

The best-known walk in Kahurangi is the Heaphy Track. The more challenging **Wangapeka** is not as well known as the Heaphy, but many consider it a more enjoyable walk. Taking about five days, the track starts 25km south of Karamea at Little Wanganui and runs 52km east to Rolling River near Tapawera. There's a chain of huts along the track.

The Heaphy and Wangapeka, however, are just part of a 650km network of tracks which includes excellent full-day and overnight walks such as those in the **Cobb Valley** and **Mt Arthur/Tablelands**. See www.doc.govt.nz for detailed information on all Kahurangi tracks.

Heaphy Track

The Heaphy Track is one of the most popular tracks in the country. A Great Walk in every sense, it traverses diverse terrain – dense native forest, the mystical Gouland Downs, secluded river valleys, and beaches dusted in salt spray and fringed by nikau palms.

Although quite long, the Heaphy is well cut and benched, making it easier than any other extended tramp found in Kahurangi National Park. That said, it may still be found arduous, particularly in unfavourable weather.

Walking from east to west most of the climbing is done on the first day, and the scenic beach walk is saved for the end, a fitting and invigorating grand finale.

The track is open to mountain bikers between May and October. Factoring in distance, remoteness and the possibility of bad weather, this epic journey is only suited to well-equipped cyclists with advanced riding skills. A good port of call for more information is the Quiet Revolution Cycle Shop (p92) in Takaka.

A strong tramper could walk the Heaphy in three days, but most people take four or five days. For a detailed track description, see DOC's *Heaphy Track* brochure. Estimated walking times:

ROUTE	TIME (HR)
Brown Hut to Perry Saddle Hut	5
Perry Saddle Hut to Gouland Downs Hut	2
Gouland Downs Hut to Saxon Hut	1½
Saxon Hut to James Mackay Hut	3
James Mackay Hut to Lewis Hut	3½
Lewis Hut to Heaphy Hut	2½
Heaphy Hut to Kohaihai River	5

⤳ Tours

Kahurangi Guided Walks TRAMPING
(⌾03-391 4120; www.kahurangiwalks.co.nz) Offers all-inclusive, week-long Heaphy hikes ($1750), plus one- to five-day trips in Abel Tasman National Park ($250 to $1400).

Bush & Beyond TRAMPING
(☑03-543 3742; www.bushandbeyond.co.nz)
Natural-history-orientated hikes around Kahurangi, ranging from Mt Arthur or Cobb Valley day walks ($250) through to a guided six-day Heaphy Track package ($1795).

🛏 Sleeping

Seven designated Great Walk huts ($32) lie along the Heaphy Track, which have bunks and a kitchen area, heating, flush toilets and washbasins with cold water. Most but not all have gas rings; a couple have lighting. There are also nine Great Walk campsites ($14), plus the beachside **Kohaihai Campsite** (www.doc.govt.nz; $6) at the West Coast trailhead. The two day shelters are just that; overnight stays are not permitted.

As the Heaphy is a Great Walk, all huts and campsites must be booked in advance year-round. Bookings can be made online through **Great Walks Bookings** (☑0800 694 732; www.doc.govt.nz) or at DOC visitor centres nationwide.

❶ Getting There & Away

The two road ends of the Heaphy Track are an almost unfathomable distance apart: 463km to be precise. From Takaka, you can get to the Heaphy Track (via Collingwood) with **Golden Bay Coachlines** (p77) ($35, one hour).

The Kohaihai trailhead is 15km from the small town of Karamea. **Karamea Express** (☑03-782 6757; info@karamea-express.co.nz) departs from the shelter at 1pm and 2pm for Karamea from October to the end of April ($15). **Karamea Connections** (☑03-782 6767; www.karamea connections.co.nz) offers on-demand pick-ups.

Heaphy Bus (☑0272 221 872, 0800 128 735; www.theheaphybus.co.nz) offers a round-trip shuttle service – drop off at Brown Hut and pick up from Kohaihai ($150) – and other on-demand local track transport.

Heaphy Track Help (☑03-525 9576; www. heaphytrackhelp.co.nz) offers car relocations (around $300, depending on the direction and time), food drops, shuttles and advice.

Adventure Flights Golden Bay (☑03-525 6167, 0800 150 338; www.adventureflights goldenbay.co.nz; Takaka Airfield, SH60) will fly you back to Takaka from Karamea (or vice versa) for $185 to $200 per person (up to five people). **Golden Bay Air** (☑0800 588 885; www.goldenbayair.co.nz) flies the same route for $149 to $169 per person, as does **Helicopter Charter Karamea** (p97), which will take up to three/six passengers $750/1350.

Nelson Lakes National Park

Nelson Lakes National Park surrounds two lakes – Rotoiti and Rotoroa – fringed by sweet-smelling beech forest with a backdrop of greywacke mountains. Located at the northern end of the Southern Alps, and with a dramatic glacier-carved landscape, it's an awe-inspiring place to get up on high.

Part of the park, east of Lake Rotoiti, is classed as a 'mainland island' where a conservation scheme aims to eradicate introduced pests (rats, possums and stoats), and regenerate native flora and fauna. It offers excellent tramping, including short walks, lake scenery and one or two sandflies... The park is flush with birdlife, and famous for brown-trout fishing.

The human hub of the Nelson Lakes region is the small, low-key village of **St Arnaud**.

🏃 Activities

Many spectacular walks allow you to appreciate this rugged landscape, but before you tackle them, stop by the DOC Nelson Lakes Visitor Centre (p98) for maps, track/weather updates and to pay your hut or camping fees.

There are two fantastic day hikes to be had. The five-hour **Mt Robert Circuit Track** starts at Mt Robert car park (a short drive away from St Arnaud, serviced by Nelson Lakes Shuttles, p98) and circumnavigates the mountain. The optional side trip along Robert Ridge offers staggering views into the heart of the national park. Alternatively, the **St Arnaud Range Track** (five hours return), on the east side of the lake, climbs steadily to the ridgeline adjacent to Parachute Rocks. Both tracks are strenuous, but reward with jaw-dropping vistas of glaciated valleys, arête peaks and Lake Rotoiti. Only attempt these tramps in fine weather. At other times they are both pointless (no views) and dangerous.

There are also plenty of shorter (and flatter) walks from Lake Rotoiti's Kerr Bay and the road end at Lake Rotoroa. These and the longer day tramps are described in DOC's *Walks in Nelson Lakes National Park* pamphlet ($2).

The fit and well-equipped can embark upon longer hikes such as the **Lake Angelus Track**. This magnificent two-to-three day tramp follows Robert Ridge to Lake Angelus, where you can stay at the fine Angelus Hut (adult/child $20/10, bookings essential late November to April; backcountry pass/tickets valid the rest of the year) for a night or two before returning to St Arnaud via one of three routes. Pick up or download DOC's *Angelus Hut Tracks & Routes* pamphlet ($2) for more details. And if you've heard about Blue Lake, seek advice from the visitor centre before you even so much as contemplate it.

Rainbow SKIING, SNOWBOARDING
(☑ 03-521 1861, snow-phone 0832 226 05; www.skirainbow.co.nz; daily lift pass adult/child $75/35) The sunny Nelson region has a ski area, just 100km away (a similar distance from Blenheim). Rainbow borders the Nelson Lakes National Park, with varied terrain, minimal crowds and good cross-country skiing. Chains are often required. St Arnaud is the closest town (32km).

🛏 Sleeping

Kerr Bay DOC Campsite CAMPGROUND $
(www.doc.govt.nz; unpowered/powered sites per person $10/15) Near the Lake Rotoiti shore, the hugely popular Kerr Bay campsite has powered sites, toilets, hot showers, a laundry and a kitchen shelter. It's an inspiring base for your adventures, but do book in advance. Overflow camping is available around at DOC's West Bay Campsite (☑ 03-521 1806; www.doc.govt.nz; $6; ☉ summer), which is more basic.

Travers-Sabine Lodge HOSTEL $
(☑ 03-521 1887; www.nelsonlakes.co.nz; Main Rd; dm/d $28/65; ☎) This hostel is a great base for outdoor adventure, being a short walk to Lake Rotoiti, inexpensive, clean and comfortable. It also has particularly cheerful Technicolor linen in the dorms, doubles and family room. The owners are experienced adventurers themselves, so tips come as standard; tramping equipment available for hire.

★ Alpine Lodge LODGE $$
(☑ 03-521 1869; www.alpinelodge.co.nz; Main Rd, St Arnaud; d $155-210; @☎) Family owned and a consistent performer, this large lodge complex offers a range of accommodation,

the pick of which are the split-level doubles with mezzanine bedroom and spa. If nothing else, go for the inviting in-house restaurant – a snug affair sporting an open fire, mountain views, good food (meals $10 to $32; takeaway pizza $20) and local beer.

The restaurant serves lunch and dinner November to April; dinner only May and July through October; and closes for June.

The adjacent backpacker lodge (dorm/double $29/69) is spartan but warm and tidy. There's on-site bike hire, too.

Nelson Lakes Motels MOTEL $$
(☑ 03-521 1887; www.nelsonlakes.co.nz; Main Rd, St Arnaud; d $125-140, q $135-180; ☎) These log cabins and newer board-and-batten units offer all the creature comforts, including kitchenettes and Sky TV. Bigger units have full kitchens and sleep up to six.

ℹ Information

DOC Nelson Lakes Visitor Centre (☑ 03-521 1806; www.doc.govt.nz; View Rd; ☉ 8am-4.30pm, to 5pm in summer) The Nelson Lakes Visitor Centre proffers park-wide information (weather, activities) and hut passes, plus displays on park ecology and history.

ℹ Getting There & Around

Nelson Lakes Shuttles (☑ 027 547 6896, 03-547 6896; www.nelsonlakesshuttles.co.nz) runs thrice-weekly scheduled services between Nelson and the national park from December to April (Monday, Wednesday and Friday; $45), and on-demand the rest of the year. It will also collect/drop off at Kawatiri Junction on SH63 to meet other bus services heading between Nelson and the West Coast, and offers services from St Arnaud through to Picton, Kaikoura, Hanmer Springs and other top-of-the-South destinations on demand. Try also Trek Express (p77), which regularly plies such routes.

Rotoiti Water Taxis (☑ 021 702 278; www.rotoitiwatertaxis.co.nz) Runs to/from Kerr Bay and West Bay to southern end of Lake Rotoiti (3/4 passengers $100/120). Kayaks, canoes and rowing boats can be hired from $50 per half-day; fishing trips and scenic lake cruises by arrangement.

The West Coast

Why Go?

Hemmed in by the wild Tasman Sea and the Southern Alps, the West Coast is like nowhere else in New Zealand.

The far extremities of the coast have a remote, end-of-the-road feel, from sleepy Karamea surrounded by farms butting up against Kahurangi National Park, to the southern end of State Hwy 6, gateway to NZ's World Heritage areas. In between is an alluring combination of wild coastline, rich wilderness, and history in spades.

Built on the wavering fortunes of gold, coal and timber, the stories of Coast settlers are hair-raising. A hardy and individual breed, they make up less than 1% of NZ's population, scattered around almost 9% of its land area.

Travellers tend to tick off the 'must see' sights of Punakaiki, and Franz Josef and Fox Glaciers, but sights such as Oparara Basin, Okarito Lagoon and the Coast's many lakes will amaze in equal measure.

Best Short Walks

➡ Scotts Beach (p107)

➡ Charming Creek Walkway (p105)

➡ Lake Matheson (p125)

➡ Ship Creek (p129)

Best Places to Sleep

➡ Old Slaughterhouse (p106)

➡ Breakers (p111)

➡ Drifting Sands (p118)

➡ Okarito Campground (p120)

When to Go

➡ December through February is peak season, so book accommodation ahead during this period.

➡ The shoulder months of October/November and March/April are increasingly busy, particularly around Punakaiki, Hokitika and the Glaciers.

➡ May to September can be warm and clear, with fewer crowds and cheaper accommodation.

➡ The West Coast has serious rainfall (around 5m annually) but still sees as much sunshine as Christchurch.

➡ No matter what time of year, backcountry trampers should check conditions with local DOC office staff. Rivers can prove seriously treacherous.

West Coast Highlights

1 Oparara Basin
(p108) Exploring the limestone forms and forest.

2 Buller River
(p101) Getting wet 'n' wild on this mighty river.

3 Reefton (p102) Delving into the West Coast's glittering past.

4 Punakaiki (p110) Marvelling at nature's beautiful fury at the 'Pancake Rocks'.

5 West Coast Wilderness Trail
(p113) Getting back to nature by bike or on foot.

6 Hokitika (p115) Hunting out authentic local greenstone in working studios.

7 Hokitika Gorge
(p116) Admiring surreal turquoise waters from a lofty swing bridge.

8 Okarito (p120) Kayaking through bird-filled, rainforest channels.

9 Fox Glacier
(p125) & **Franz Josef Glacier** (p121) Flying high over the ice, up into the Southern Alps.

10 Waiatoto River
(p130) Jetboating deep into Haast's World Heritage wilderness.

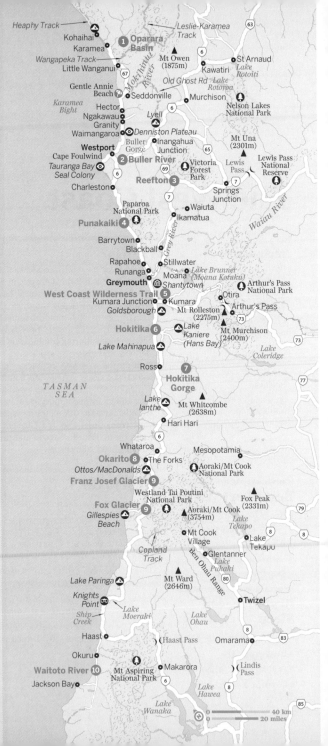

ℹ Getting There & Away

Air New Zealand (📞 0800 737 000; www.airnz.co.nz) flies between Hokitika and Christchurch; **Sounds Air** (📞 03-520 3080, 0800 505 005; www.soundsair.com) flies between Westport and Wellington.

Coaches and shuttle transport – while not exceptionally frequent – are at least reliable, and reach pretty much everywhere you might like to go including Nelson, Christchurch and Queenstown. Major and extensive networks are operated by **Atomic Travel** (p114), **InterCity** (📞 03-365 1113; www.intercity.co.nz) and **Naked Bus** (www.nakedbus.com), while **West Coast Shuttle** (p114) runs a daily service between Greymouth and Christchurch. Local shuttle operators go here and there.

The **TranzAlpine** (p112), one of the world's great train journeys, links Greymouth and Christchurch.

BULLER REGION

Arriving from the east, Murchison is the gateway to the Buller region. Your big decision is which way to head when you reach the forks at Inangahua. Continuing west along SH6 through the Lower Buller Gorge will lead you to Westport, the gateway to the far north, and the northern end of the Great Coast Road leading to Punakaiki. Head south from Inangahua on SH69 and you skip Punakaiki but reach Reefton, where you can either head west to the coast at Greymouth, or east over the Lewis Pass to Hanmer Springs. You can also cut directly through to the Lewis Pass via SH65, 10km west of Murchison.

Murchison & Buller Gorge

POP 492

Murchison, 125km southwest of Nelson and 95km east of Westport, lies on the 'Four Rivers Plain'. In fact there aren't just four but multitudinous rivers, the mightiest being the Buller, which runs alongside the town. Whitewater sports and trout fishing are popular here, while the surrounding forested hills dish up adventure for intrepid adventurers.

From Murchison, SH6 snakes through Buller Gorge to the coast at Westport, a journey that could easily take a day or two by the time you've taken a rafting or jetboating trip and stopped at other interesting sites along the way.

◎ Sights

Murchison Museum MUSEUM
(60 Fairfax St; admission by donation; ⏱10am-4pm) This museum showcases all sorts

ESSENTIAL WEST COAST

Eat Fish and chips, sitting near the beach at sunset.

Drink The only roast on the coast, organic and fair trade Kawatiri Coffee.

Read Eleanor Catton's 2013 Man Booker Prize–winning novel, *The Luminaries*, set around Hokitika.

Listen to Karamea's laid-back community radio station on 107.5FM; you can even spin your own tunes.

Watch *Denniston Incline* on YouTube, then imagine sitting in the wagon on the way down.

Festival Go bush-food crazy at Hokitika's Wildfoods Festival (p118).

Go Green At West Coast Wildlife Centre (p122) – fluffy kiwi chicks! Too cute!

Online www.westcoastnz.com, www.buller.co.nz, www.glaciercountry.co.nz

Area code 📞 03

of local memorabilia, the most interesting of which relates to the 1929 and 1968 earthquakes.

🏃 Activities

Ask at the Murchison Information Centre (p102) for a copy of the *Murchison District Map*, which features local walks, such as the Skyline, Six Mile and Johnson Creek Tracks, plus mountain-bike rides. Staff can also hook you up with excellent trout-fishing guides.

★ Wild Rivers Rafting RAFTING
(📞 050 846 7238; www.wildriversrafting.co.nz; 2hr rafting adult/child $160/85) White-water rafting with Bruce and Marty on the particularly exciting Earthquake Rapids section of the beautiful Buller River (good luck with 'gunslinger' and the 'pop-up toaster'!).

Buller Canyon Jet JETBOATING
(📞 03-523 9883; www.bullercanyonjet.co.nz; SH6; adult/child $105/60; ⏱Sep-Apr) Launching from Buller Gorge Swingbridge is one of NZ's most scenic and best-value jetboat trips – 40 minutes of ripping through the beautiful Buller with a good-humoured captain.

Ultimate Descents RAFTING
(📞 0800 748 377, 03-523 9899; www.rivers.co.nz; 38 Waller St) Offers white-water rafting and

MĀORI NZ: THE WEST COAST

Early Māori forged paths through to the alps' mountains and river valleys to the West Coast in search of highly prized *pounamu* (greenstone), carved into tools, weapons and adornments. View the *pounamu* exhibit at **Hokitika Museum** (p116) to polish your knowledge of the precious rock before admiring the classy carvings created by the town's artists.

kayaking trips on the Buller, including the classic grade III-IV gorge trip ($160), and gentler family excursions (adult/child $130/100); plus helirafting trips by arrangement. Based in Murchison.

Buller Gorge Swingbridge   ADVENTURE SPORTS
(☑0800 285 537; www.bullergorge.co.nz; SH6; bridge crossing adult/child $10/5; ☉8am-7pm Dec-Apr, 9am-5.30pm May-Nov) About 15km west of Murchison is NZ's longest swingbridge (110m), across which lie short walks taking in the White Creek Faultline, epicentre of the 1929 earthquake. Coming back, ride the 160m Cometline Flying Fox, either seated (adult/child $30/15) or 'Supaman' ($60).

☞ Tours

Natural Flames Experience   TOUR
(☑0800 687 244; www.naturalflames.co.nz; adult/child $85/65) An enjoyable, informative half-day 4WD and bushwalking tour through remote valleys and beech forest to a hot spot among the trees and ferns, where natural gas seeping out of the ground has been burning since 1922. Boil a billy on the flames and cook pancakes before returning to civilisation.

☰ Sleeping & Eating

**Kiwi Park Motels
& Holiday Park**   MOTEL, HOLIDAY PARK $
(☑0800 228 080, 03-523 9248; www.kiwipark.co.nz; 170 Fairfax St; sites unpowered/powered from $20/25, cabins $65-85, motels $140-225; @ ☎) This leafy park on the edge of town has plenty of accommodation options, from a campervan and tent area graced with mature trees, through to basic cabins, and roomy motel units nestled among the blooms. Cheery hosts and a menagerie of friendly farm animals make this one happy family.

Lazy Cow   HOSTEL $
(☑03-523 9451; www.lazycow.co.nz; 37 Waller St; dm $30-32, d $84-96; ☎) It's easy to be a lazy cow here, with all the comforts of home, including cosy bedrooms and a sunny backyard. Guests are welcomed with free muffins or cake, and freshly cooked evening meals are sometimes available when the hosts aren't running their popular on-site Cow Shed restaurant.

Murchison Lodge   B&B $$
(☑0800 523 9196, 03-523 9196; www.murchisonlodge.co.nz; 15 Grey St; s $150-210, d $175-235; ☎) This quality B&B surrounded by extensive gardens and paddocks is a short walk from the Buller River. Attractive timber features and charming hosts add to the comfortable feel. A hearty breakfast, home baking and plenty of local information are complimentary.

Cow Shed   PIZZA
(☉5pm-9pm Wed-Sat) In the garage of the Lazy Cow backpackers, the cute Cow Shed restaurant is a deservedly popular option for its homey, good-value meals served in intimate surrounds. There's takeaway pizza for those who can't get a table.

❶ Information

Murchison has no ATM; the postal agency is on Fairfax St.

The **Murchison Information Centre** (☑03-523 9350; www.nelsonnz.com; 47 Waller St; ☉10am-6pm Nov-Mar, to 4pm Apr & Oct, closed May-Sep) has info on local activities and transport.

❶ Getting There & Away

Buses passing through Murchison between the West Coast and Nelson/Picton are **InterCity** (☑03-365 1113; www.intercity.co.nz) and **Naked Bus** (www.nakedbus.com), both of which stop at Beechwoods Cafe on Waller St, as does **Trek Express** (p107), which runs frequently between Nelson and the Wangapeka/Heaphy Tracks during the peak tramping season.

Reefton

POP 1026

For generations, Reefton's claims to fame have been mining and its early adoption of the electricity grid and street lighting. Hence the tagline, 'the city of light'. Today, however, it's a different story, one which starts – improbably – with the building of the world-class Roller Park, which attracts stunt lovers from all corners of NZ. To quote a local, 'it's more than we deserve'. We disagree. If this many volunteers and sponsors are prepared to build such an edgy civic amenity in a town that still looks like the set of *Bonanza,* we suggest there's something a bit special about this crazy little town.

◎ Sights

With loads of crusty old buildings situated within a 200m radius, Reefton is a fascinating town for a stroll. To find out who lived where and why, undertake the short **Heritage Walk** outlined in the *Historic Reefton* leaflet ($1), available from the Reefton i-SITE (p104).

Waiuta HISTORIC SITE
(www.waiuta.org.nz; off SH7) A once-burgeoning gold town abandoned in 1951 after the mineshaft collapsed, remote Waiuta is one of the West Coast's most famous ghost towns, complete with a big old rusty boiler, an overgrown swimming pool, stranded brick chimneys and the odd intact cottage, which face off against Mother Nature who has sent in the strangleweed. Spread over a square kilometre or so of plateau, surrounded by lowland forest and looking out towards the Southern Alps, Waiuta is a very satisfying place for an amble.

To get to there, drive 23km south of Reefton on SH7 to the signposted turn-off from where it's another 17km, the last half of which is unsealed, winding and narrow in places. Ask at local information centres for more information and maps.

Blacks Point Museum MUSEUM
(☑03-732 8391; blksptmus@hotmail.co.nz; Franklyn St, Blacks Point, SH7; adult/child/family $5/3/15; ☺9am-noon & 1-4pm Wed-Fri & Sun, 1-4pm Sat Oct-Apr, plus school holidays during winter) Housed in an old church 2km east of Reefton on the Christchurch road, this museum is crammed with prospecting paraphernalia. Just up the driveway is the still-functional **Golden Fleece Battery** (☑03-732 8391; blksptmus@hotmail.co.nz; Franklyn St, Blacks Point, SH7; adult/child $1/free; ☺1pm-4pm Wed & Sun Oct-Apr), used for crushing gold-flecked quartz. The Blacks Point walks also start from here.

Bearded Mining Company HISTORIC BUILDING
(☑03-732 8377; Broadway; admission by donation; ☺9am-2pm) Looking like a ZZ Top tribute

band, the fellas hangin' at this high-street mining hut are champing at the bit to rollick your socks off with tales tall and true. If you're lucky, you'll get a cuppa from the billy.

⭑ Activities

Look out for a copy of the free *Reefton* leaflet detailing short walks, including the **Bottled Lightning Powerhouse Walk** (40 minutes) that has its own mobile app.

Surrounding Reefton is the 206,000-hectare **Victoria Forest Park** (NZ's largest forest park), which sports diverse flora and fauna as well as hidden historic sites, such as the old goldfields around Blacks Point. Starting at Blacks Point, the enjoyable **Murray Creek Track** is a five-hour return trip.

Other tramps in the Forest Park include the three-day **Kirwans** or two-day **Big River Track**, both of which can be traversed on a mountain bike. Pick up the free *Reefton Mountain Biking* ('the best riding in history') leaflet for more information; bikes can be hired from **Reefton Sports Centre** (☑03-732 8593; 56 Broadway; bike rental per day $30; ☺9am-5pm Mon-Sat), where you can also inquire about legendary trout fishing in the environs.

Inland Adventures RAFTING
(☑0508 723 846; www.inlandadventures.co.nz) Runs day-long rafting trips on the grade III Upper Grey River (adult/child $190/160), and gentler half-day trips on the Arnold River, better suited to smaller children (adult/child $130/100). Based in Reefton.

⛺ Sleeping & Eating

Old Nurses Home Guesthouse GUESTHOUSE $
(☑03-732 8881; www.reeftonaccommodation.co.nz; 104 Shiel St; s/d $60/80; ☜) This stately old building is warm and comfortable, with noteworthy communal areas, including a pretty garden and patio. Bedrooms (shared bathrooms) are clean and airy with comfy beds.

Reef Cottage B&B B&B $$
(☑03-732 8440; www.reefcottage.co.nz; 51-55 Broadway; d 135-170; ☜) This converted 1887 barrister's office has compact rooms furnished in period style with modern touches, including swish bathrooms and a guest kitchen and lounge. Full breakfasts at the cafe next door are included in the price.

Broadway Tearooms & Bakery BAKERY $$
(☑03-732 8497; 31 Broadway; snacks $3-8, meals $13-20; ☺8am-5pm) This joint gets by far the

THE WEST COAST REEFTON

most day-time traffic, being a civilised place for a spot of lunch, and to pick up a fresh loaf or a packet of shortbread. Middle-of-the-road meals range from egg breakfasts to a whitebait lunch. Survey Reefton's high-street bustle from tables out the front.

☆ Entertainment

Reefton Cinema   CINEMA
(🗹 03-732 8391; www.reefton.co.nz; cnr Smith & Shiels Sts; adult/child $13.50/8.50) Reefton has gone digital and 3D at this cutesy cinema! Tickets and enquiries at the i-SITE.

ℹ Information

Reefton i-SITE (🗹 03-732 8391; www.reefton. co.nz; 67 Broadway; ⊙ 9am-4.30pm Mon-Fri, 9.30am-2pm Sat, 9.30am-1pm Sun) This i-SITE has helpful staff, and a compact recreation of the Quartzopolis Mine (gold coin entry). There's internet at the library, which doubles as the postal agency.

ℹ Getting There & Away

East West Coaches (🗹 03-789 6251; www. eastwestcoaches.co.nz) East West Coaches stops in Reefton every day except Saturday on the run between Westport (1¼ hours) and Christchurch (four hours).

Westport & Around

POP 4035

The 'capital' of the northern West Coast is Westport. The town's fortunes have waxed and waned on coal mining, but in the current climate it sits quietly stoked up on various industries, including dairy and, increasingly, tourism. It boasts respectable hospitality and visitor services, and makes a good base for exploring the fascinating coast north to Denniston, Charming Creek, Karamea and the Heaphy Track.

◎ Sights

The most riveting sights are beyond Westport's city walls, particularly heading north on SH67, which passes **Granity**, **Ngakawau** (home to the utterly Charming Creek) and **Hector**, where stands a monument to Hector's dolphins, NZ's smallest, although you'll be lucky to see them unless your timing is impeccable. It's also worth poking around **Seddonville**, a small bush town on the Mokihinui River where **Seddonville Holiday Park** (🗹 03-782 1314; 108 Gladstone St; sites per person $10) offers respectable camping in

the grounds of the old school. This small dot on the map is about to get slightly bigger, being the northern trailhead for the spectacular new Old Ghost Road (p104).

Denniston Plateau   HISTORIC SITE
(www.doc.govt.nz) Six hundred metres above sea level, Denniston was once NZ's largest coal town, with 1500 residents in 1911. By 1981 there were eight. Its claim to fame was the fantastically steep Denniston Incline, which hurtled laden wagons down a 45-degree hillside.

Excellent interpretive displays bring the plateau's history to life. **Denniston Experience** (🗹 0800 881 880; www.denniston.co.nz; Denniston) guided tours ride the 'gorge express' train into Banbury mine for an intriguing two-hour adventure (adult/child $99/40). A one-hour option (adult/child $45/20) rides the train to the mine entrance.

The *Denniston Rose Walking Tour* brochure ($2 from DOC and Westport Library; also available as an app) may lead the eager to read Jenny Pattrick's evocative novels set in these parts.The turn-off to Denniston is 16km north of Westport at Waimangaroa, with a shop with a stop for a homemade pie and ice cream. Denniston is another nine winding kilometres inland from there.

Coaltown Museum   MUSEUM
(www.coaltown.co.nz; 123 Palmerston St; adult/child $10/2; ⊙ 9am-5pm Mon-Fri, 10am-4pm Sat & Sun) This modern museum retells the same old yarns of hard times, but with well-scripted display panels alongside an excellent selection of photographs, surrounding relics of local industries and general pioneer ephemera. The Denniston displays are a highlight.

🏃 Activities

Westport is good for a stroll – the i-SITE (p107) can direct you to the **Millennium Walkway** and **North Beach Reserve**. The most thrilling adventure in the area is cave rafting with Underworld Adventures (p105), although mountain biking is gaining momentum as a popular pastime among local and visiting backcountry adventurers. The folk at Habitat Sports (p107) offer bike rental, maps and advice.

Old Ghost Road   TRAMPING, CYCLING
(www.oldghostroad.org.nz) One of the gnarliest of NZ's new cycle trails, the 85km Old Ghost Road follows a historic miners' track that was started in the in 1870s but never

finished as the gold rush petered out. Finally completed after an epic build, the spectacular track traverses native forests, tussock tops, river flats and valleys.

The southern trailhead is at Lyell, 50 minutes' drive (62km) east of Westport along the scenic Buller Gorge (SH6). The DOC campsite and day walks here have long been popular, with visitors drawn in by readily accessible historic sites, including a graveyard secreted in the bush. The northern trailhead is at Seddonville, 45 minutes' drive (50km) north of Westport off SH67, from where the track sidles along the steep-sided and utterly stunning Mokihinui River. Joining the two ends is a spectacular alpine section, with views from sunrise to sunset.

The track is dual use, but favours walkers (allow five days). For advanced mountain bikers, however, it is pretty much the Holy Grail, completed in two to four days, preferably from Lyell to Seddonville. The four huts along the way need to be booked in advance on the Old Ghost Road website, which also details a range of other ways to experience the track other than an end-to-end ride or hike. Day trips from either end are a rewarding, flexible way in, particularly from the West Coast end via the inimitable Rough & Tumble Lodge (p106).

Being a long and remote track through wild terrain, conditions can change quickly, so check the trail website for status. Westport's Buller Adventure Tours, Habitat Sports (p107) and **Hike n Bike Shuttle** (🗷 027 446 7876; www.hikenbikeshuttle.co.nz) provide bike and equipment hire, shuttles and other related services.

Cape Foulwind Walkway   WALKING
(www.doc.govt.nz) On a good day, Cape Foulwind Walkway (1½ hours return) is a wonderful amble, traversing coastal hills between Omau and Tauranga Bay, south of Westport. Towards the southern end is the **seal colony** where – depending on the season – up to 200 NZ fur seals loll on the rocks. Further north the walkway passes a replica astrolabe (a navigational aid) and lighthouse.

Abel Tasman was the first European to sight the Cape, in 1642, naming it Clyppygen Hoek (Rocky Point). However, his name was eclipsed by James Cook in 1770, who clearly found it less than pleasing.

Cape Foulwind is well signposted from Westport. It's 13km to Lighthouse Rd at Omau, where the welcoming Star Tavern (p106) signals the walkway's northern end.

The southern end is 16km from town at Tauranga Bay, popular with surfers who dodge its rocky edges.

Charming Creek Walkway   WALKING
(www.doc.govt.nz) Starting from either Ngakawau (30km north of Westport), or near Seddonville, a few kilometres further on, this is one of the best day walks on the coast, taking around six hours return. Following an old coal line through the Ngakawau River Gorge, it features rusty relics galore, tunnels, a suspension bridge and waterfall, and lots of interesting plants and geological formations.

Ask a local about transport if you don't want to walk it both ways.

Underworld Adventures   CAVING
(☑ 03-788 8168, 0800 116 686; www.caverafting. com; SH6, Charleston) From its monolithic new base at Charleston, 26km south of Westport, this friendly bunch runs unforgettable 'Underworld' cave-rafting trips ($175, four hours) into the glowworm-filled Nile River Caves. Glow without the flow (no rafting) is $110 per person. Tours begin with a fun rainforest railway ride, available separately (adult/child $20/15, 1½ hours). The on-site cafe provides simple food during the day.

The Adventure Caving trip ($340, five hours) includes a 40m abseil into Te Tahi tomo (hole) with rock squeezes, waterfalls, prehistoric fossils and trippy cave formations.

Buller Adventure Tours   JETBOATING, HORSE RIDING
(☑ 03-789 7286, 0800 697 286; www.adventure tours.co.nz; SH6) Located 5km from Westport, Barry and crew run jetboating trips through the lower Buller Gorge (adult/child $89/69); two-hour riverbank horse treks (adult/youth $89/69); and runs provides bike and transport packages for the Old Ghost Road.

🛏 Sleeping

⭐ **Bazil's Hostel**   HOSTEL $
(☑ 03-789 6410; www.bazils.com; 54 Russell St, Westport; dm $30, d $100, without bathroom $72; 🛜) Mural-painted Bazil's is managed by worldly, sporty types who run their own surf school (three-hour lesson $70; board and suit hire per day $40) and rainforest SUP trips, as well as offering mountain-bike hire, free kayaks and hook-ups with other activities. Their tour-bus clientele are considerately corralled into a separate zone, leaving indy travellers in peace.

THE WEST COAST WESTPORT & AROUND

★ **Old Slaughterhouse** HOSTEL $
(⌨ 027 529 7640, 03-782 8333; www.oldslaughter house.co.nz; SH67, Hector; dm $34-38, d $84; ⊙ sometimes closed Jun-Oct) ✎ Around 1km north of Hector, this is a rather special hostel nestled high on the hill among native bush with epic views of the Tasman Sea. Built mainly from recycled timbers and dotted with interesting art and eclectic furniture, it also offers tranquil communal areas ideal for contemplation. The steep, 10-minute walk up the hill is well worth it and bolsters the off-the-grid charm.

Carters Beach
Top 10 Holiday Park HOLIDAY PARK, MOTEL $
(⌨ 03-789 8002, 050 893 7876; www.top10 westport.co.nz; 57 Marine Pde, Carters Beach; sites from $38, units $70-205; @⑤) Right on Carters Beach and conveniently located 4km from Westport and 12km to Tauranga Bay, this tidy complex has pleasant sites as well as comfortable cabins and motel units. It's a good option for tourers seeking a peaceful stop-off, and perhaps even a swim.

Trip Inn HOSTEL $
(⌨ 03-789 7367, 0800 737 773; www.tripinn.co.nz; 72 Queen St, Westport; dm $29-34, d & tw $96, without bathroom $75; ⑤) This stately option is a grand 150-year-old villa with mature gardens. There's a variety of tidy rooms within, plus more in an annexe, and voluminous communal areas.

★ **Rough & Tumble Lodge** LODGE $$
(⌨ 03-782 1337; www.roughandtumble.co.nz; Mokihi nui Rd, Seddonville; d incl continental breakfast $160, extra person $20; ⑤) This hidden treasure sits at the West Coast end of the Old Ghost Road at a bend in the Mokihinui River recently saved from decimation by hydro-dam. Invigorated and inspiring, it offers five atmospheric quad rooms in a virgin wilderness setting, with a homey lodge feel complete with honest meals (dinner $60) in the dining room.

Enquire about self-catering in the quieter low season.

Archer House B&B $$
(⌨ 0800 789 877, 03-789 8778; www.archerhouse. co.nz; 75 Queen St, Westport; d incl breakfast $190; @⑤) This beautiful 1890 heritage home sleeps up to eight in three rooms with private bathrooms, all sharing no fewer than three lounges, plus peaceful gardens. Lovely hosts, complimentary sherry and generous continental breakfast make this Westport's most refined accommodation option.

Omau Settlers Lodge LODGE $$
(⌨ 03-789 5200; www.omausettlerslodge.co.nz; 1054 Cape Rd, Cape Foulwind; r incl breakfast $165; ⑤) Close to Cape Foulwind and across the road from the excellent Star Tavern, these contemporary and stylish units offer rest, relaxation and satisfying continental breakfasts. Rooms have kitchenettes, but a shared kitchen and dining room offer a chance to socialise. A hot tub surrounded by bush maximises the take-it-easy quotient.

Charming Creek B&B B&B $$
(⌨ 03-782 8007; www.bullerbeachstay.co.nz; Nga kawau; d incl breakfast $149-179; ⑤) This lovely little B&B has homey rooms and a driftwood-fired hot tub right by the sea, where the self-contained 'Beach Nest' bach sleeps three to four people ($100 to $149, minimum two-night stay). Ask about the two-night walking package that includes dinners and a picnic lunch.

✕ Eating

Whanake Gallery & Espresso Bar CAFE $
(⌨ 03-789 5076; www.whanake.co.nz; 173 Palmerston St, Westport; snacks $3-8; ⊙ 7.30am-5.30pm Mon-Fri, 8.30am-4.30pm Sat & Sun) Cranking out the town's best espresso and delicious biscuits, this neat little cafe was expanding to provide a greater range of food when last we visited. Pop in for a shot and check out the owners' inspiring photography and local souvenirs.

PR's Cafe CAFE $
(⌨ 03-789 7779; 124 Palmerston St, Westport; meals $10-20; ⊙ 7am-4.30pm Mon-Fri, 7am-3pm Sat & Sun; ⑤) Westport's sharpest cafe has a cabinet full of sandwiches and pastries, and a counter groaning under the weight of cakes (Dutch apple, banoffee pie) and cookies. An all-day menu delivers carefully composed meals such as salmon omelette with dill aioli, spanakopita, and fish and chips.

Star Tavern PUB FOOD $$
(⌨ 03-789 6923; 6 Lighthouse Rd, Omau; meals $9-30; ⊙ 4pm-late Mon-Fri, noon-late Sat & Sun) A motto of 'arrive as strangers, leave as friends' is backed up at this rural tavern handily positioned near Cape Foulwind. It dishes up generously proportioned grub in its old-fashioned dining room, a warm welcome, a pool table and a jukebox in its unprepossessing public bar, and relaxation in the garden. Proper hospitality, that's what this is.

ℹ Information

DOC Westport Office (☑ 03-788 8008; www. doc.govt.nz; 72 Russell St, Westport; ⊙ 8-11am & 2-4.30pm Mon-Fri) DOC bookings and information can be obtained from the i-SITE. For curly questions, visit this field office.

Westport i-SITE (☑ 03-789 6658; www. buller.co.nz; 123 Palmerston St, Westport; ⊙ 9am-5pm Mon-Fri, 10am-4pm Sat & Sun; ☎) Information on local tracks, walkways, tours, accommodation and transport. Self-help terminal for DOC information and hut and track bookings. See also www.westcoastnz.com.

ℹ Getting There & Away

AIR

Sounds Air (p101) has two to three flights daily to/from Wellington.

BUS

Westport is a stop on the daily Nelson to Fox Glacier runs of **InterCity** (☑ 03-365 1113; www. intercity.co.nz). Travel time to Nelson is 3½ hours, to Greymouth 2¼ hours, and to Franz Josef six hours. **Naked Bus** (www.nakedbus. com) runs the same route three times per week. Buses leave from the i-SITE.

East West Coaches (p104) Operates a service through to Christchurch, via Reefton and the Lewis Pass, every day except Saturday, departing from the Caltex petrol station.

Karamea Express (☑ 03-782 6757; info@ karamea-express.co.nz) Links Westport and Karamea (two hours) Monday to Friday May to September, plus Saturday from October to April, departing from the i-SITE.

Trek Express (☑ 0800 128 735, 027 221 872; www.trekexpress.co.nz) Passes through Westport on its frequent high-season tramper transport link between Nelson and the Wangapeka/Heaphy Tracks.

ℹ Getting Around

BICYCLE

Hire bikes and obtain advice from **Habitat Sports** (☑ 03-788 8002; www.habitatsports. co.nz; 234 Palmerston St, Westport; bike rental from $35; ⊙ 9am-5pm Mon-Fri, 9am-1pm Sat).

CAR

Hire some wheels at **Westport Hire** (☑ 03-789 5038; wesporthire@xtra.co.nz; 294 Palmerston St, Westport).

TAXI

Buller Taxis (☑ 03-789 6900) can take you to/ from the airport (around $25).

Karamea & Around

POP 375

North from Westport, SH67 winds along the coast and over the view-filled Karamea Bluff to Karamea and the northern coast. If you're driving, fill your tank in Westport as it's 98km to the next petrol station. As you head over the bluff, it's worth stopping to do the **Lake Hanlon** walk (30 minutes return) on the Karamea side of the hill.

The relaxed town of Karamea (population 375) considers itself the West Coast's 'best kept secret', but those who've visited tend to boast about its merits far and wide. An end-of-the-road town it may well be, but it still has a bit of the 'hub' about it, servicing the end (or start) of the Heaphy and Wangapeka Tracks, and the magical Oparara Basin. With a friendly climate, and a take-it-easy mix of locals and chilled-out imports, the Karamea area is a great place to jump off the well-trodden tourist trail for a few lazy days.

◉ Sights

★**Scotts Beach**   BEACH
It's a 45-minute walk each way from Kohaihai over the hill to Scotts Beach – a wild, empty shoreline shrouded in mist, awash in foamy waves, strewn with driftwood and backed by nikau palm forest. Watch and wander in wonder, but don't even think about dipping a toe in – there are dangerous currents at work here.

⚐ Activities

Hats off to the Karamea community who have established the very pleasant **Karamea Estuary Walkway**, a long-as-you-like stroll bordering the estuary and Karemea River. The adjacent beach can be reached via Flagstaff Rd, north of town. Both features plenty of birdlife and are best walked at sunset. The Karamea Information & Resource Centre (p109) has various maps, including the free *Karamea* brochure which details other walks such as **Big Rimu** (45 minutes return), **Flagstaff** (one hour return) and the **Zig Zag** (one hour return).

Longer walks around Karamea include the **Fenian Track** (four hours return) leading to **Cavern Creek Caves** and **Adams Flat**, where there's a replica gold-miner's hut; and the first leg of the **Wangapeka Track** to Belltown Hut. The Wangapeka Track is a four-to-six-day backcountry trip suitable for experienced trampers only.

THE WEST COAST KARAMEA & AROUND

DON'T MISS

OPARARA BASIN

To quote a local: 'if this were anywhere else, there'd be hordes streaming in'. Too true. Lying within Kahurangi National Park, the Oparara Basin is a natural spectacle of the highest order – a hidden valley concealing wonders such as limestone arches and strange caves within a thick forest of massive, moss-laden trees that tower over an undergrowth of Dr Seuss-esque form in every imaginable hue of green. Excellent information panels can be perused at the main car park and picnic area.

The valley's signature sight is the 200m-long, 37m-high Oparara Arch, spanning the picturesque Oparara River – home to the super-cute, rare blue duck (whio) – which wends alongside the easy walkway (45 minutes return). The smaller but no less stunning Moria Gate Arch (43m long, 19m high) is reached via a simply divine forest loop walk (1½ hours), which also passes the Mirror Tarn.

Just a 10-minute walk from the second car park are the Crazy Paving and Box Canyon Caves. Take your torch to enter a world of weird subterranean shapes and rare, leggy spiders. Spiders, caves, darkness...sound like fun?

Beyond this point are the superb Honeycomb Hill Caves and Arch, accessible only by guided tours (3-/5-/8-hour tours $95/150/240) run by the Karamea Information & Resource Centre (p109). Ask about other guided tours of the area, and also about transport for the Oparara Valley Track, a rewarding five-hour independent walk through ancient forest, along the river, popping out at the Fenian Walk car park.

To drive to the valley from Karamea, travel 10km along the main north road north and turn off at McCallum's Mill Rd, where signposts will direct you a further 14km up and over into the valley along a road that is winding, gravel, rough in places and sometimes steep.

Other local activities include swimming, fishing, whitebaiting, kayaking and mountain biking. Your best bet for advice on these is to ask a local and always use common sense – especially when it comes to the watery stuff. Flexible and friendly **Karamea Outdoor Adventures** (☑ 03-782 6181; www.karameaadventures.co.nz; Bridge St; guided kayak/riverbug trips from $80, kayak/bike hire per 2hr $40/30) offers guided and freedom kayaking and riverbug trips, plus mountain-bike hire and advice on other adventures, including horse treks.

Heaphy Track

The West Coast road ends 14km from Karamea at Kohaihai, the western trailhead (and most commonly, the finish point) of the Heaphy Track (p96), where there's also a DOC campsite (www.doc.govt.nz; sites per adult/child $6). A day walk or overnight stay can readily be had from here. Walk to Scotts Beach (p107) (1½ hours return), or go as far as the fabulous new Heaphy Hut (www.doc.govt.nz; huts/campsites $32/14) (five hours) and stay a night or two before returning.

This section can also be mountain-biked, as can the whole track (two to three days) from May to September; ask at Westport's Habitat Sports (p107) for bike hire and details.

Helicopter Charter Karamea (p109) offers flights through to the northern trailhead

in Golden Bay: up to three/six passengers $750/1350; up to three/six passengers with mountain bikes $900/1550.

🛏 Sleeping

Rongo Backpackers   HOSTEL $
(☑ 03-782 6667; www.rongobackpackers.com; 130 Waverley St, Karamea; sites from $20, dm $32-35, s/tw/d $75/80/90; @ 🛜) 🐾 Part neo-hippie artists' haven and part organic vegie garden, this rainbow-coloured, carbon-negative hostel also runs the community radio station (107.5 FM, www.karamearadio.com). Popular with long-term guests who often end up tending the garden and spinning a few tunes. Every fourth night is free.

Karamea Farm Baches   CABIN $
(☑ 03-782 6838; www.karameafarmbaches.com; 17 Wharf Rd, Karamea; d/tr/q $95/120/145; 🛜) 🐾 Pushing reuse/recycle to the limit, these seven 1960s self-contained bachs are the real McCoy, right down to period wallpaper and grandma's carpet. If you dig organic gardening, friendly dogs and colourful hosts, this place will win you over.

Karamea Holiday Park   HOLIDAY PARK $
(☑ 03-782 6758; www.karamea.com; Maori Point Rd, Karamea; sites d powered/unpowered $33/30, units s $30-45, d $40-95; @ 🛜) A simple,

old-fashioned camp alongside the estuary in bush surrounds, 3km south of Karamea village. The retro weatherboard cabins are clean and well maintained.

Last Resort LODGE $$
(☑03-782 6617, 0800 505 042; www.lastresort. co.nz; 71 Waverley St, Karamea; s $50, d $97-155, q $195; ☎) This iconic, rambling and rustic resort has entered an era of friendly welcomes and good management, and has had a general tidy up. Scope the joint with espresso and cake or a beer in the cafe or bar (meals $11 to $30) then consider the plunge into rooms ranging from simple doubles to family suites, all handcrafted using local timbers.

Karamea River Motels MOTEL $$
(☑03-782 6955; www.karameamotels.co.nz; 31 Bridge St, Karamea; r $125-169; ☎) The smart rooms at this comfortable motel, five minutes' walk from Market Cross, range from studios to two-bedroom units. Features include relaxing blue hues, long-range views, a barbecue and lush gardens.

✖ Eating

Karamea Village Hotel PUB FOOD $$
(☑03-782 6800; www.karameahotel.co.nz; cnr Waverley & Wharf Sts, Karamea; meals $11-34; ☺11am-11pm) Here lies simple pleasures and proper hospitality: a game of pool, a pint of ale, and a tasty roast dinner followed by old-fashioned pudding.

ⓘ Information

Karamea Information & Resource Centre
(☑03-782 6652; www.karameainfo.co.nz; Market Cross; ☺9am-5pm Mon-Fri, 10am-1pm Sat & Sun, shorter hours May-Dec) This excellent, community-owned centre has the local low-down, internet access, maps and DOC hut tickets. It also doubles as the petrol station.

ⓘ Getting There & Away

Karamea Express (p107) links Karamea and Westport ($35, two hours, Monday to Friday May to September, plus Saturdays from October to April). It also services Kohaihai twice daily during peak summer, and other times on demand. Wangapeka transport is also available.

Heaphy Bus (☑0800 128 735, 03-540 2042; www.theheaphybus.co.nz), based in Nelson, services both ends of the Heaphy Track, as well as the Wangapeka.

Fly from Karamea to Takaka with **Helicopter Charter Karamea** (☑03-782 6111; www. karameahelicharter.co.nz; 79 Waverley St, Karamea), **Golden Bay Air** (☑0800 588 885;

www.goldenbayair.co.nz) or **Adventure Flights Golden Bay** (☑0800 150 338, 03-525 6167; www.adventureflightsgoldenbay.co.nz) starting from $150 per person, then walk back on the Heaphy Track; contact the Karamea Information & Resource Centre for details.

Based at Rongo Backpackers, **Karamea Connections** (☑03-782 6767; www.karameaconnections.co.nz) runs track and town transport, including services to Heaphy, Wangapeka, Oparara Basin and Westport on demand.

THE GREAT COAST ROAD

There are fine views all the way along this beautiful stretch of SH6, although its most famous attractions are the geologically fascinating Pancake Rocks at Punakaiki. Fill up in Westport if you're low on petrol and cash – there's no fuel until Runanga, 92km away, and the next ATM is in Greymouth.

Westport to Punakaiki

Set on 42 serene hectares, 17km south of Westport, the solar-powered, energy-efficient **Beaconstone Eco Lodge** (☑027 431 0491; www.beaconstoneecolodge.co.nz; Birds Ferry Rd; dm $34, d/tw $80-88; ☺Oct-May; ☎) ⍝ is a bushy retreat with touches of Americana cool. Inside are cosy beds and a laid-back communal area, while beyond the doorstep are bush walks leading to peaceful river swimming holes. There's only room for 14 people, so booking is recommended.

Jack's Gasthof (☑03-789 6501; www.jacks gasthof.co.nz; SH6; mains $12-28; ☺from 11am Oct-Apr) is 21km south of Westport on the Little Totara River, where Berliners Jack and Petra run their eternally popular pizzeria with an adjacent bar improbably bejewelled with a disco ball. Avail yourself of campsites (from $8) and a basic room ($50) if you require a sleepover.

For a true taste of the region's gold-mining past (with the odd trap-door spider), swing into **Mitchell's Gully Gold Mine** (☑03-789 6257; SH6; adult/child $10/free; ☺9am-5pm), 22km south of Westport, where you'll meet a pioneer's descendants and explore the family mine. There are interesting tales, tunnels, railway tracks, a waterwheel and the last working stamping battery in the village.

The next stop is **Charleston**, 26km south of Westport. It's hard to believe it now, but this place boomed during the 1860s gold rush, with 80 hotels, three breweries and hundreds of thirsty gold-diggers staking claims along the Nile River. There's not much left now except a motel, camping ground, a clutch of local houses, and the brilliant Underworld Adventures (p105), with which you can explore some utterly amazing hidden treasures.

From here to Punakaiki is a staggeringly beautiful panorama of lowland pakihi scrub and lush green forest alongside a series of bays dramatically sculpted by relentless ocean fury. Drive as slowly as the traffic behind you will allow.

Punakaiki & Paparoa National Park

POP 70

Located midway between Westport and Greymouth is Punakaiki, a small settlement beside the rugged 38,000-hectare Paparoa National Park. Most visitors come for a quick squiz at the Pancake Rocks, which is a shame because there's excellent tramping and other wild adventures, and plenty of accommodation.

○ Sights

Paparoa National Park is blessed with high cliffs and empty beaches, a dramatic mountain range, crazy limestone river valleys, diverse flora, and a profusion of birdlife, including weka and the Westland petrel, a rare sea bird that nests only here.

★ **Pancake Rocks**   NATURAL FEATURE
(www.doc.govt.nz) Punakaiki's claim to fame is Dolomite Point, where a layering-weathering process called stylobedding has carved the limestone into what looks like piles of thick pancakes. Aim for high tide (tide timetables are posted in town; hope that it coincides with sunset) when the sea surges into caverns and booms menacingly through blowholes. See it on a wild day and be reminded that Mother Nature really is the boss. An easy 15-minute walk loops from the highway out to the rocks and blowholes.

🏃 Activities

Tramps around Punakaiki include the **Truman Track** (30 minutes return) and the **Punakaiki–Porari Loop** (3½ hours), which goes up the spectacular limestone Pororari River gorge before popping over a hill and coming down the bouldery Punakaiki River to rejoin the highway.

Surefooted types can embark on the **Fox River Cave Walk** (three hours return), 12km north of Punakaiki and open to amateur explorers. BYO torch and sturdy shoes.

Other tramps in the national park are detailed in the DOC *Paparoa National Park* pamphlet ($1). Note that many of Paparoa's inland walks are susceptible to river flooding so it is vital that you obtain updates from the Paparoa National Park Visitor Centre (p111) in Punakaiki before you depart.

Punakaiki Horse Treks   HORSE RIDING
(☑ 03-731 1839; www.pancake-rocks.co.nz; SH6; 2½hr ride $170; ⊗ Nov-May) Punakaiki Horse Treks, based at Hydrangea Cottages, conducts treks in the beautiful Punakaiki Valley, with river crossings, finishing at the beach.

Punakaiki Canoes   KAYAKING
(☑ 03-731 1870; www.riverkayaking.co.nz; SH6; canoe hire 2hr/full day $40/60, family rates available) This outfit rents canoes near the Pororari River bridge, for gentle, super-scenic paddling for all abilities.

🛏 Sleeping & Eating

★ **Punakaiki Beach Hostel**   HOSTEL $
(☑ 03-731 1852; www.punakaikibeachhostel.co.nz; 4 Webb St; sites per person $21, dm/s/d $29/65/77; @🛜) A laid-back hostel with a sea-view veranda, a short walk from Pancake Rocks, with savvy owners who know what makes a good hostel: good beds and great communal facilities, and staff who smile because they mean it. Cutesy Sunset Cottage ($130) and the en suite house bus ($115) are both well worth the splurge.

Te Nikau Retreat   HOSTEL $
(☑ 03-731 1111; www.tenikauretreat.co.nz; 19 Hartmount Pl; dm $28, d $75-90, cabins from $96; @🛜) 🍃 Relax, restore and explore at this clutch of accommodation offerings nestled into shady, rainforest nooks, just a short walk to the beach. There are rooms in the main building, several cute cabins, and the larger Nikau and Rata lodges sleeping up to five and 10 people respectively.

Punakaiki Beach Camp   HOLIDAY PARK $
(☑ 03-731 1894; www.punakaikibeachcamp.co.nz; 5 Owen St; sites per person powered/unpowered $20/17, d $68-98; 🛜) With a dramatic backdrop of sheer cliffs, this salty, beachside park with good grass is studded with clean, old-style cabins and amenities. A classic Kiwi coastal camping ground five to 10 minutes' walk from Pancake Rocks.

Hydrangea Cottages COTTAGES $$
(☑ 03-731 1839; www.pancake-rocks.co.nz; SH6; d $165-320; ☎) On a hillside overlooking the Tasman, these six standalone and mostly self-contained cottages (largest sleeping up to six) are built from salvaged timber and stone. It's a classy but relaxed enclave, with splashes of colourful mosaic tile, some outdoor baths, and pretty cottage gardens. The owners also run Punakaiki Horse Treks.

Punakaiki Tavern PUB FOOD $$
(☑ 03-731 1188; www.punakaikitavern.co.nz; SH6; mains $20-40; ⊘ 8am-late; ☎) Whether it's breakfast, lunch or dinner, this pub serves decent-size portions, and chips with pretty much everything, in comfortable surrounds featuring a pool table and out-of-tune piano. Beverage highlights include Benger nectarine juice.

❶ Information

Paparoa National Park Visitor Centre (☑ 03-731 1895; www.doc.govt.nz; SH6; ⊘ 9am-5pm Oct-Nov, to 6pm Dec-Mar, to 4.30pm Apr-Sep) The Paparoa National Park Visitor Centre has information on the park and track conditions, and handles bookings for some local attractions and accommodation, including hut tickets.

❶ Getting There & Away

InterCity (☑ 03-365 1113; www.intercity.co.nz) travels daily north to Westport (45 minutes), and south to Greymouth (45 minutes) and Fox Glacier (five hours). **Naked Bus** (www.nakedbus.com) runs to the same destinations three days a week. Both companies stop long enough for passengers to admire the Pancake Rocks.

Punakaiki to Greymouth

The highway between Punakaiki and Greymouth is flanked by white-capped waves and rocky bays on one side, and the steep, bushy Paparoa Ranges on the other.

At **Barrytown**, 17km south of Punakaiki, Steve and Robyn run **Barrytown Knifemaking** (☑ 0800 256 433, 03-731 1053; www.barrytownknifemaking.com; 2662 SH6, Barrytown; classes $150; ⊘ closed Mon), where you can make your own knife – from hand-forging the blade to crafting a handle from native rimu timber. The day-long course features lunch, archery, axe-throwing and a stream of entertainingly bad jokes from Steve. Bookings essential, and transport from Punakaiki can be arranged.

With a rainforest backdrop and coastal views, **Ti Kouka House** (☑ 03-731 1460; www.tikoukahouse.co.nz; 2522 SH6, Barrytown; d incl breakfast $295; ☎) boasts splendid architectural design, recycled building materials, and sculptural artwork both inside and out. You'll want to move in permanently, but you'll have to settle for a B&B stay in one of its three luxurious rooms.

Breakers (☑ 03-762 7743; www.breakers.co.nz; 1367 SH6, Nine Mile Creek; d incl breakfast $255-385; ☎), 14km north of Greymouth, is one of the best-kept secrets on the coast. Beautifully appointed en suite rooms overlook the sea, with fine surfing opportunities at hand for the intrepid. The hosts are sporty, friendly and have a nice dog.

Two kilometres south is **Rapahoe**, 12km shy of Greymouth. This tiny seaside settlement is the northern trailhead for the enjoyable Point Elizabeth Walkway (p113). Should you require refreshment before or after your walk, call in to the **Rapahoe Hotel** (☑ 03-762 7701; 1 Beach Rd, Rapahoe; mains $14-30), a simple country pub offering warm hospitality and a good feed of fish and chips in a picturesque location.

GREYMOUTH REGION

Bookending NZ's most famous alpine highway – Arthur's Pass – and sitting more or less halfway along the West Coast road, the Greymouth area provides easy access to the attractions north and south as well as offering a decent smattering of diversions within its boundaries.

Greymouth

POP 10,000

Welcome to the 'Big Smoke', crouched at the mouth of the imaginatively named Grey River. Known to Māori as Mawhera, the West Coast's largest town has gold in its veins, and today its fortunes still ebb and flow with the tide of mining. Tourism and dairy farming, however, are increasingly vital to the economy. The town is well geared for travellers, offering all the necessary services and the odd tourist attraction, the most famous of which is Shantytown.

◉ Sights

★ **Left Bank Art Gallery** GALLERY
(www.leftbankarts.org.nz; 1 Tainui St; admission by donation; ⊘ 11am-4.30pm Tue-Fri, 11am-2pm Sat) This 95-year old former bank houses

THE WEST COAST PUNAKAIKI TO GREYMOUTH

Greymouth

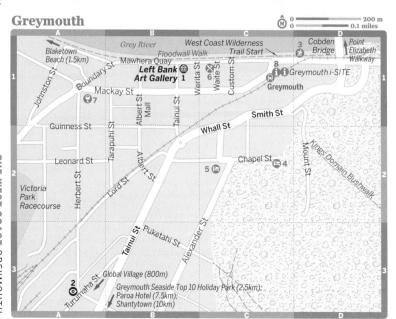

contemporary NZ jade carvings, prints, paintings, photographs and ceramics. The gallery also fosters and supports a wide society of West Coast artists.

Monteith's Brewing Co   BREWERY
(☑ 03-768 4149; www.monteiths.co.nz; cnr Turumaha & Herbert Sts; guided tour $22; ⊙ 11am-8pm)

The original Monteith's brewhouse may simply be brand HQ for mainstream product largely brewed elsewhere, but it still delivers heritage in spades through its excellent-value guided tour (25 minutes, includes generous samples; four tours daily). The flash tasting room-cum-bar is now Greymouth's most exciting watering hole (tasty snacks $9 to $22) – shame it shuts up shop so early.

Shantytown   MUSEUM
(www.shantytown.co.nz; Rutherglen Rd, Paroa; adult/child/family $33/16/78; ⊙ 8.30am-5pm)

Eight kilometres south of Greymouth and 2km inland from SH6, Shantytown evocatively presents and preserves local history through a recreated 1860s gold-mining town, complete with steam-train rides, pub and Rosie's House of Ill Repute. There's also gold panning, a sawmill, a gory hospital, and short holographic movies in the Princess Theatre.

🏃 Activities

TranzAlpine   TRAIN TOUR
(☑ 0800 872 467, 03-341 2588; www.kiwirailscenic.co.nz; one way adult/child from $99/69; ⊙ departs Christchurch 8.15am, Greymouth 1.45pm) The TranzAlpine is one of the world's great train journeys, traversing the Southern Alps be-

WORTH A TRIP

WEST COAST WILDERNESS TRAIL

The 136km **West Coast Wilderness Trail** (www.westcoastwildernesstrail.co.nz) is one of 23 NZ Cycle Trails (www.nzcycletrail.com). Stretching from Greymouth to Ross, the mostly gently graded track follows gold-rush trails, water races, logging tramways and old railway lines, as well as forging new routes cross-country. Along the way it reveals outstanding landscapes of dense rainforest, glacial rivers, lakes and wetlands, with views all the way from the snow-capped mountains of the Southern Alps to the wild Tasman Sea. It's a great way to immerse yourself in this special place.

The full shebang is a good four days of riding but can easily be sliced up into sections of various lengths, catering to every ability and area of interest. Ask about the 'Big Day Out' from Kawhaka to Kaniere, which takes in major highlights, or a ride taking in the track's historic pubs at Paroa, Kumara and Ross.

Bike hire, transport and advice is available from the major setting-off points. In Hokitika, contact **Wilderness Trail Shuttle** (☑03-755 5042, 021 263 3299; www.wildernesstrailshuttle.co.nz) and in Greymouth **Trail Transport** (☑03-768 6618; www.trailtransport.co.nz).

tween Christchurch and Greymouth, from the Pacific Ocean to the Tasman Sea, passing through Arthur's Pass National Park. En route is a sequence of dramatic landscapes, from the flat, alluvial Canterbury Plains, through narrow alpine gorges, an 8.5km tunnel, beech-forested river valleys and alongside a lake fringed with cabbage trees.

The 4½-hour journey is unforgettable, even in bad weather (if it's raining on one coast, it's probably fine on the other).

Point Elizabeth Walkway   WALKING
(www.doc.govt.nz) Accessible from Dommett Esplanade in Cobden, 6km north of Greymouth, this enjoyable walkway (three hours return) skirts around a richly forested headland in the shadow of the Rapahoe Range to an impressive ocean lookout, before continuing on to the northern trailhead at Rapahoe (11km from Greymouth) – small town, big beach, friendly local pub.

Floodwall Walk   WALKING
Take a 10-minute riverside stroll along Mawhera Quay (the start of the West Coast Wilderness Trail (p113)), or keep going for an hour or so, taking in the fishing boat harbour, Blaketown Beach and breakwater – a great place to experience the power of the ocean and savour a famous West Coast sunset.

🛏 Sleeping

★**Global Village**   HOSTEL **$**
(☑03-768 7272; www.globalvillagebackpackers.co.nz; 42 Cowper St; sites per person $18, dm/d/tr $30/76/102; @🛜) A collage of African and Asian art is infused with a passionate trav-

ellers' vibe here. Free kayaks – the Lake Karoro wetlands reserve is just metres away – and mountain bikes are on tap, and relaxation comes easy with a spa, sauna, barbecue and fire pit.

Ardwyn House   B&B **$**
(☑03-768 6107; ardwynhouse@hotmail.com; 48 Chapel St; s/d incl breakfast from $65/100; 🛜) This old-fashioned, homey B&B nestles amid steep gardens on a quiet dead-end street. Mary, the well-travelled host, cooks a splendid breakfast.

Greymouth Seaside
Top 10 Holiday Park   HOLIDAY PARK, MOTEL **$**
(☑03-768 6618, 0800 867 104; www.top10greymouth.co.nz; 2 Chesterfield St; sites $40-46, cabins $60-125, motel r $110-374; @🛜) Well positioned for sunset walks on the adjacent beach and 2.5km south of the town centre, this large park has various tent and campervan sites as well as accommodation ranging from simple cabins to deluxe sea-view motels – arguably the flashest units in town. A shipshape stop for every budget.

Noah's Ark Backpackers   HOSTEL **$**
(☑0800 662 472, 03-768 4868; www.noahs.co.nz; 16 Chapel St; sites per person $18, dm/s/d $30/74/74; @🛜) Originally a monastery, colourful Noah's has eccentric animal-themed rooms, a sunset-worthy balcony and a pretty back garden with a spa pool. Bikes and fishing rods are provided free of charge.

Paroa Hotel   HOTEL **$$**
(☑0800 762 6860, 03-762 6860; www.paroa.co.nz; 508 Main South Rd, Paroa; d $128-140; 🛜) Opposite the Shantytown turn-off, this

family-owned hotel (62 years and counting) has spacious units sharing a large lawned garden next to the beach. The notable bar and restaurant (mains $18 to $35) dishes up warm hospitality in the form of roast dinners, whitebait, pavlova and beer, amid local clientele.

🍴 Eating & Drinking

DP1 Cafe
CAFE $

(104 Mawhera Quay; meals $7-23; ☺ 8am-5pm Mon-Fri, 9am-5pm Sat & Sun; 🛜) A stalwart of the Greymouth cafe scene, this hip joint serves great espresso, along with good-value grub. Groovy tunes, wi-fi, local art and quayside tables make this a welcoming spot to linger. Swing in for the $6 morning muffin and coffee special.

Ferrari's
BAR

(☑ 03-768 4008; www.ferraris.co.nz; 6 Mackay St; ☺ 5pm-late Thur-Sat, 12-6pm Sun) Valiantly trying to capture the sophistication and glamour of golden-era Hollywood in good old Greymouth, this bar inside the Regent Cinema is an atmospheric and comfortable place to plonk yourself down in a leather sofa for a drink or two.

ℹ Information

Grey Base Hospital (☑ 03-768 0499; High St)

Greymouth i-SITE (☑ 03-768 5101, 0800 473 966; www.westcoasttravel.co.nz; 164 Mackay St, Greymouth Train Station; ☺ 9am-5pm Mon-Fri, 9.30am-4pm Sat & Sun; 🛜) The helpful crew at the train station can assist with all manner of advice and bookings, including those for DOC huts and walks. See also www.westcoastnz.com.

ℹ Getting There & Away

Combined with the i-SITE in the train station, the **West Coast Travel Centre** (☑ 03-768 7080; www.westcoasttravel.co.nz; 164 Mackay St, Greymouth Train Station; ☺ 9am-5pm Mon-Fri, 10am-4pm Sat & Sun; 🛜) books local and national transport, and offers luggage storage.

BUS

All buses stop outside the train station.

InterCity (p101) has daily buses north to Westport (two hours) and Nelson (six hours), and south to Franz Josef Glacier (3½ hours).

Naked Bus (p101) runs the same route three days a week. Both companies offer connections to destinations further afield.

Atomic Travel (☑ 03-349 0697, 0508 108 359; www.atomictravel.co.nz) runs daily between Greymouth and Christchurch, as does **West Coast Shuttle** (☑ 03-768 0028, 0274 927 000; www.westcoastshuttle.co.nz).

TRAIN

KiwiRail Scenic (☑ 0800 872 467; www.kiwirailscenic.co.nz)

ℹ Getting Around

Several car-hire company desks are located within the train station. Local companies include **Alpine West** (☑ 0800 257 736, 03-768 4002; www.alpinerentals.co.nz; 11 Shelley St) and **NZ Rent-a-Car** (☑ 03-768 0379; www.nzrentacar.co.nz; 170 Tainui St).

Greymouth Taxis (☑ 03-768 7078)

Blackball

POP 291

Around 25km upriver of Greymouth sits the ramshackle town of Blackball – established in 1866 to service gold diggers; coal mining kicked in between 1890 and 1964. The National Federation of Labour (a trade union) was conceived here, born from influential strikes in 1908 and 1931. This story is retold in historical displays on the main road.

Alongside you will find the hub of the town, **Formerly the Blackball Hilton** (☑ 03-732 4705, 0800 425 225; www.blackballhilton.co.nz; 26 Hart St; s/d incl breakfast $55/110; 🛜), where you can collect a copy of the helpful 'Historic Blackball' map. This official historic place has memorabilia galore, hot meals ($15 to $34), cold beer, heaps of afternoon sun and a host of rooms oozing the charm of yesteryear; it was named so after a certain global hotel chain got antsy when its name was appropriated.

Competing with the Hilton in the fame stakes is the **Blackball Salami Co** (☑ 03-732 4111; www.blackballsalami.co.nz; 11 Hilton St; ☺ 8am-4pm Mon-Fri, 9am-2pm Sat), manufacturer of tasty salami and sausages ranging from chorizo to black pudding.

Blackball's other claim to fame is as the southern end of the historic **Croesus Track** (www.doc.govt.nz), a one- to two-day hike (or bike ride) clambering over to Barrytown. In the next few years it will form part of the new **Pike River Great Walk**. Watch this space.

ℹ Getting There & Away

From the West Coast Hwy it's half an hour's drive or so to Blackball; you'll need your own wheels.

Lake Brunner

POP 270

Lying inland from Greymouth, Lake Brunner (www.golakebrunner.co.nz) can be reached via the SH7 turn-off at Stillwater, a journey of 39km. It can also be reached from the south via Kumara Junction.

One of many lakes in the area, Brunner is a tranquil spot for bushwalks, bird-spotting and various watersports, including boating and fishing. Indeed, the local boast is that the lake and Arnold River are 'where the trout die of old age', which implies that the local fish are particularly clever or the fisherfolk are somewhat hopeless. Greymouth i-SITE can hook you up with a guide. Head to the marina to undertake one or all of several pretty short walks.

Moana is the main settlement, home to numerous accommodation options of which the best is Lake Brunner Country Motel (☑03-738 0144; www.lakebrunnermotel.co.nz; 2014 Arnold Valley Rd; sites from $34, cabins $62-72, cottages d $135-150; ☏), 2km from the lake. It features cabins, cottages and campervan sites tucked into native plantings through extensive parklike grounds, while tenters can enjoy the lush grassy camping field. This is proper peace and quiet, unless you count birdsong and the bubbling of the spa pool.

Moana also has a couple of places to eat, including a cafe opposite the train station where the *TranzAlpine* pulls in. There's also food at the local pub, which is trending upward, and groceries at the petrol station.

ⓘ Getting There & Away

The *TranzAlpine* pulls into Moana train station twice daily on its way between Christchurch and Greymouth. **Atomic Travel** (p114) shuttles also pass through on on the same journey.

Kumara

POP 309

Thirty kilometres south of Greymouth, near the western end of Arthur's Pass (SH73), Kumara was yet another busy gold-rush town that ground to a halt, leaving behind a thin posse of flinty citizens. In recent times its claim to fame has been as stellar supporter of the Coast to Coast (www.coasttocoast. co.nz), NZ's most famous multisport race. Held each February, the strong, the brave and the totally knackered run, cycle and kayak a total of 243km all the way across the mountains to Christchurch, with top competitors dusting it off in just under 11 hours.

Nowadays Kumarians extend their hospitality to highway travellers and an increasing number of cyclists following the West Coast Wilderness Trail (p113), which passes through the town. Anticipating their arrival is the show-stopping **Theatre Royal Hotel** (☑03-736 9277; www.theatreroyalhotel. co.nz; 81 Seddon St, SH73, Kumara; d $100-290; ☏10am-late; ☏), a fully restored beauty that has kicked Kumara well and truly into the 21st century with its classy restaurant and sumptuous accommodation options styled with full historic honours. The attention to detail in furnishings and heritage displays is simply wonderful. Stop in to enjoy some of the best food on the coast (fish and chips, game, pizza and cakes) or just pull in for a drink and a yarn with the locals.

Should you be to-ing or fro-ing over Arthur's Pass, consider staying at **Jacksons Retreat** (☑03-738 0474; www.jacksonsretreat. co.nz; Jacksons, SH73, Kumara; sites from $40; @☏; ☏, 33km west of Arthur's Pass Village. Set upon 15 sloping acres with exceptional views over the Taramakau River, it offers stacks of excellent amenities for campervanner and tenter alike.

ⓘ Getting There & Away

West Coast Shuttle (p114) passes through Kumara (not to be confused with Kumara Junction, close to the coast) on its daily service between Greymouth and Christchurch.

WESTLAND

The bottom third or so of the West Coast is known as Westland, a mix of farmland and rainforest backed by the Southern Alps, which pop straight up in a neck-cricking fashion. This region is most famous for its glaciers, currently in retreat but fortunately surrounded by equally spectacular sights ready to steal the show.

Hokitika

POP 3078

Popular with history buffs and the setting for numerous NZ novels, including the 2013 Man Booker Prize–winning *The Luminaries* by Eleanor Catton, Hokitika's riches come in many forms. Founded on gold, today

Hokitika

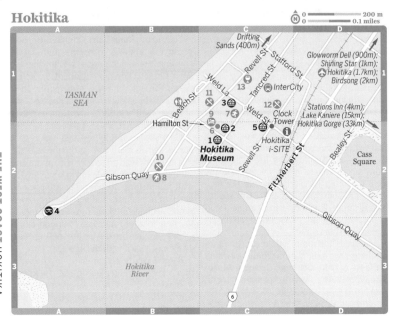

the town is the stronghold of indigenous *pounamu* (greenstone), which jostles for attention amid many other arts and crafts, drawing rafts of visitors to its wide open streets.

◉ Sights

★ Hokitika Museum
MUSEUM

(www.hokitikamuseum.co.nz; 17 Hamilton St; adult/child $6/3; ⊙ 10am-5pm Nov-Mar, 10am-2pm Apr-Oct) Housed in the imposing Carnegie Building (1908), this is an exemplary provincial museum, with intelligently curated exhibitions presented in a clear, modern style. Highlights include the fascinating *Whitebait!* exhibition, and the Pounamu room – the ideal primer before you hit the galleries looking for greenstone treasures.

★ Lake Kaniere
LAKE

(www.doc.govt.nz) Lying at the heart of a 7000-hectare scenic reserve, beautiful Lake Kaniere is 8km long, 2km wide, 195m deep, and freezing cold as you'll discover if you swim. You may, however, prefer simply to camp or picnic at Hans Bay (p118), or undertake one of numerous walks in the surrounds, ranging from the 15-minute Canoe Cove Walk to the seven-hour return gut-buster up Mt Tuhua. The historic Kaniere Water Race Walkway (3½ hours one way) forms part of the West Coast Wilderness Trail (p113).

Hokitika Gorge
GORGE

(www.doc.govt.nz) A picturesque 35km drive leads to Hokitika Gorge, a ravishing ravine with unbelievably turquoise waters coloured by glacial 'flour'. Photograph the scene from every angle via the short forest walkway and swingbridge. The gorge is well signposted from Stafford St (past the dairy factory). En route, you will pass **Kowhitirangi**, the site of one of NZ's deadliest mass murders (immortalised in the 1982 classic film *Bad Blood*). A poignant roadside monument lines up the farmstead site through a stone shaft.

Sunset Point   VIEWPOINT
(Gibson Quay) A spectacular vantage point at any time of day, this is – as the name suggests – the primo place to watch the day's light fade away. Surfers, seagulls, longshore drift, and fish and chips: *this* is New Zealand.

Glowworm Dell   NATURAL FEATURE
On the northern edge of town, a short stroll from SH6 leads to this glowworm dell, an easy opportunity to enter the other-worldly home of NZ's native fungus gnat larvae (so not even a worm at all). An information panel at the entrance will further illuminate your way.

Galleries
Art and craft galleries are a strong spoke in Hoki's wheel, and you could easily spend a day spinning around the lot. There are plenty of opportunities to meet the artists, and in some studios you can watch them at work. Be aware that some galleries sell jade imported from Europe and Asia, as precious local *pounamu* (greenstone) is not surrendered lightly by the wilds.

Hokitika Craft Gallery   GALLERY
(www.hokitikacraftgallery.co.nz; 25 Tancred St; ⊙8.30am-5pm) The town's best one-stop shop, this co-op showcases a wide range of local work, including *pounamu*, jewellery, textiles, ceramics and woodwork.

Waewae Pounamu   GALLERY
(www.waewaepounamu.co.nz; 39 Weld St; 8am-5pm) This stronghold of NZ *pounamu* displays traditional and contemporary designs in its main-road gallery.

Hokitika Glass Studio   GALLERY
(www.hokitikaglass.co.nz; 9 Weld St; ⊙8.30am-5pm) Glass art covering a continuum from garish to glorious; watch the blowers at the furnace on weekdays.

🏃 Activities
Hokitika is a great base for walking and cycling. Download or collect a copy of DOC's

WHITEBAIT FEVER

On even the swiftest of visits to the West Coast you are sure to come across a little whitebait or two, whether sold from a backdoor in Harihari or served at a local cafe or restaurant.

These tiny, transparent fish are the young of some of New Zealand's precious native fish, including inanga, kokopu, smelt and even eels. Commanding around $80 a kilo on the Coast (and much more elsewhere), competition is tough to net the elusive critters during the season, August to November, when riverbanks bustle with baiters from Karamea to Haast. Conservationists, however, say they shouldn't be eaten at all. And on the balance of evidence, it sounds like they're right. Back to the bacon sandwich, then.

To see what all the fuss is about, check out the excellent *Whitebait!* exhibition at Hokitika Museum (p116).

brochure *Walks in the Hokitika Area* ($1), and visit **Hokitika Cycles & Sports World** (📞03-755 8662; www.hokitikasportsworld.co.nz; 33 Tancred St; bike rental per day $55) for bike rental and advice on tracks, including the West Coast Wilderness Trail (p113).

Bonz 'N' Stonz   CARVING
(www.bonz-n-stonz.co.nz; 16 Hamilton St; full-day workshop $85-180) Design, carve and polish your own *pounamu*, bone or paua (shellfish) masterpiece, with tutelage from Steve. Prices vary with materials and design complexity. Bookings recommended.

Hokitika Heritage Walk   WALKING
Ask staff at the i-SITE for the worthy 50c leaflet before wandering the old wharf precinct, or ask them about a guided walk with Mr Verrall. Another map details the **Hokitika Heritage Trail**, an 11km (two- to three-hour) loop taking in historic sites and interesting town views.

Wilderness Wings   SCENIC FLIGHTS
(📞0800 755 8118; www.wildernesswings.co.nz; Hokitika Airport; flights from $285) A highly regarded operator running scenic flights over Hokitika and further afield to Aoraki/Mt Cook and the glaciers.

✿ Festivals & Events

Driftwood & Sand · ART
(www.driftwoodandsand.co.nz; ⊘ Jan) During three days in January, flotsam and jetsam is fashioned into a surprising array of arty, crafty and daft sculpture on Hokitika beach.

Wildfoods Festival · FOOD
(www.wildfoods.co.nz; ⊘ Mar) Held in early March, this fun festival attracts swarms of curious and brave gourmands who eat a whole lot of things they would usually flee from or flick from their hair. Book early.

🛏 Sleeping

★ Drifting Sands · HOSTEL $
(☎ 03-755 7654; www.driftingsands.co.nz; 197 Revell St; dm $36, d & tr $109; 🖥) If only all hostels were this stylish. Natural tones and textures, upcycled furniture, chic furnishings and hip vibes make this beachside pad a winner, as does quality bedding, a cosy lounge and hot bread in the morning. Fab!

Hans Bay DOC Campground · CAMPGROUND $
(www.doc.govt.nz; sites per adult/child $6/3) This basic DOC campsite occupies a prime site on grassy terraces with grandstand views of the lake and bushy surrounding hills.

Birdsong · HOSTEL $
(☎ 03-755 7179; www.birdsong.co.nz; SH6; dm/s $34/67, d $119, without bathroom $85; 🖥) Located 2.5km north of town, this bird-themed hostel has sea views and a homey atmosphere. Free bikes, handy beach access and hidden extras will entice you into extending your stay.

Shining Star · HOLIDAY PARK, MOTEL $$
(☎ 03-755 8921; 16 Richards Dr; sites unpowered/powered $32/40, d $115-199; 🖥) Attractive and versatile beachside spot with everything from camping to classy self-contained seafront units. Kids will love the menagerie, including pigs and alpacas straight from Dr Doolittle's appointment book. Parents might prefer the spa or sauna.

Stations Inn · MOTEL $$
(☎ 03-755 5499; www.stationsinnhokitika.co.nz; Blue Spur Rd; d $170-300; 🖥) Five minutes' drive from town on rolling hills overlooking the distant ocean, this smart, modern motel complex has plush units featuring king-sized beds and spa bath. With a patio, pond and waterwheel out the front, the on-site restaurant (mains $30 to $45; open from 5pm Tuesday to Saturday) specialises in meaty fare.

Teichelmann's B&B · B&B $$$
(☎ 03-755 8232; www.teichelmanns.co.nz; 20 Hamilton St; d $235-260; 🖥) Once home to surgeon, mountaineer and professional beard-cultivator Ebenezer Teichelmann, this old gem is now a charming B&B with amicable hosts. All rooms have an airy, restorative ambience along with their own bathrooms, including the more private Teichy's Cottage in the garden.

🍴 Eating & Drinking

Dulcie's Takeaways · FISH & CHIPS $
(cnr Gibson Quay & Wharf St; fish & chips $6-12; ⊘ 11am-9pm Tue-Sun) Net yourself some excellent fish and chips (try the turbot or blue cod), then scoff them down the road at Sunset Point for an extra sprinkle of sea salt.

★ Fat Pipi Pizza · PIZZA $$
(89 Revell St; pizzas $20-30; ⊘ 12-2.30pm Wed-Sun, 5-9pm daily; 🍴) Vegetarians, carnivores and everyone in between will be salivating for the pizza (including a whitebait version) made with love right before your eyes. Lovely cakes, honey buns and Benger juices, too. Best enjoyed in the garden bar – one of the town's (in fact the West Coast's) best dining spots.

Ramble + Ritual · CAFE
(☎ 03-755 6347; 51 Sewell St; snacks $3-8, meals $8-15; ⊘ 8am-4pm Mon-Fri, 9am-1pm Sat; 🍴) Tucked away near the Clock Tower, this gallery-cum-cafe is a stylish little spot to linger over great espresso, delicious fresh baking and simple, healthy salads made to order. The ginger oaty may well be the best in the land.

West Coast Wine Bar · WINE BAR
(www.westcoastwine.co.nz; 108 Revell St; ⊘ 8am-late Tue-Sat, 8am-2pm Mon) Upping Hoki's sophistication factor, this weeny joint with a cute garden bar packs a fridge full of fine wine and craft beer, with the option of ordering up pizza from Fat Pipi Pizza, down the road.

ℹ Information

Hokitika i-SITE (☎ 03-755 6166; www.hokitika.org; 36 Weld St; ⊘ 8.30am-6pm Mon-Fri, 9am-5pm Sat & Sun) One of NZ's best i-SITEs offers extensive bookings, including all bus services. Also holds DOC info, although you'll need to book online or at DOC visitor centres further afield. See also www.westcoastnz.com.

Westland Medical Centre (☎ 03-755 8180; 54a Sewell St; ⊘ 8am-4.45pm Mon-Fri) Ring after hours.

ℹ Getting There & Away

AIR
Hokitika Airport (www.hokitikaairport.co.nz; Airport Dr, off Tudor St) is 1.5km east of the town centre. **Air New Zealand** (p101) has three flights most days to/from Christchurch.

BUS
InterCity (☑ 03-365 1113; www.intercity.co.nz) buses leave from the Kiwi Centre on Tancred St, then outside the i-SITE, daily for Greymouth (45 minutes), Nelson (seven hours) and Franz Josef Glacier (two hours). **Naked Bus** (www.nakedbus.com) services the same destinations three times a week, with both companies offering connections to destinations further afield.

ℹ Getting Around

Car hire is available from **NZ Rent A Car** (☑ 027 294 8986, 03-755 6353; www.nzrentacar.co.nz) in town; there are a couple of other options at Hokitika Airport.

Hokitika Taxis (☑ 03-755 5075)

Hokitika to Westland Tai Poutini National Park

From Hokitika it's 140km south to Franz Josef Glacier. Most travellers fast-forward without stopping, but there are some satisfying stopping points for those inclined. Bus services with InterCity and Naked Bus stops along this stretch of SH6.

Lake Mahinapua

Mahinapua Walkway follows an old logging tramway with relics and a diverse range of forest. It's a lovely four-hour return walk and now part of the West Coast Wilderness Trail (p113). The walkway car park is located 8km south of Hokitika on SH6.

Two kilometres south of the Mahinapua Walkway car park is the entrance to tranquil **Lake Mahinapua Scenic Reserve**, with a picnic area, DOC campsite and several short walks.

Five kilometres further on is a signposted turn-off to the **West Coast Treetops Walkway** (☑ 03-755 5052, 050 887 3386; www.treetopsnz.com; 1128 Woodstock-Rimu Rd; adult/child $38/15; ⊗ 9am-5pm), a further 2km away. This steel walkway – 450m long and 20m off the ground – offers an unusual perspective on the rainforest canopy, featuring many old rimu and kamahi. The highlight is the 40m-high tower, from where there are extensive views across Lake Mahinapua, the Southern Alps and Tasman Sea. There's a cafe and souvenir shop in the information centre.

Ross
POP 297

Ross, 30km south of Hokitika, is where the unearthing of NZ's largest gold nugget (the 2.772kg 'Honourable Roddy') caused a kerfuffle in 1907. The **Ross Goldfields Heritage Centre** (www.ross.org.nz; 4 Aylmer St; ⊗ 9am-4pm Dec-Mar, to 2pm Apr-Nov) displays a replica Roddy, along with a scale model ($2) of the town in its shiny years. The town now bookends the new West Coast Wilderness Trail (p113).

The **Water Race Walk** (one hour return) starts near the museum, passing old gold-diggings, caves, tunnels and a cemetery. Try **gold panning** by hiring a pan from the information centre ($10) and head to Jones Creek to look for Roddy's great, great grandnuggets.

Established in 1866, the **Empire Hotel** (☑ 03-755 4005; 19 Aylmer St) is one of the West Coast's hidden gems, the bar (and many of its patrons) are testament to a bygone era. Breathe in the authenticity, along with a whiff of woodsmoke, over a pint and an honest meal.

Hari Hari
POP 330

About 22km south of Lake Ianthe, Hari Hari is where swashbuckling Australian aviator Guy Menzies crash-landed his trusty biplane into a swamp after completing the first solo trans-Tasman flight from Sydney, in 1931. Read all about it and view a replica of his plane at a commemorative park at the southern end of town.

The 2¾-hour **Hari Hari Coastal Walk** (www.doc.govt.nz) is a low-tide loop along the Poerua and Wanganui Rivers through bogs, estuaries and a swamp forest. The walk starts 20km from SH6, the last 8km unsealed; follow the signs from Wanganui Flats Rd. Tide times are posted at the Pukeko Store, which serves tearoom food and coffee.

Should you need a sleepover, **Flaxbush Motels** (☑ 03-753 3116; www.flaxbushmotels.co.nz; SH6; d $65-120; 🐾) has characterful cabins and units covering a wide range of budgets. It also has a friendly disposition towards birds (ducks and peacocks in particular), and a willingness to negotiate room rates for longer stays. Ask about glowworms.

Whataroa

POP 288

A dot of a town strung out along SH6, Whataroa is the departure point for tours to the **Kotuku Sanctuary**, NZ's only nesting site for the kotuku (white heron), which roosts here between November and February. The only way to visit the nesting site is with **White Heron Sanctuary Tours** (☑0800 523 456, 03-753 4120; www.whiteheron tours.co.nz; SH6, Whataroa; adult/child $120/55; ☺4 tours daily late Aug-Mar) on an enjoyable 2½-hour tour involving a gentle jetboat ride and short boardwalk to a viewing hide. Seeing the scores of birds perched in the bushes is a magical experience. A scenic rainforest tour without the herons is available year-round for the same price.

White Heron Sanctuary Tours also runs the **Sanctuary Tours Motel** (☑0800 523 456, 03-753 4120; www.whiteherontours.co.nz; SH6; cabins $65-75, d $110-135), with basic cabins with shared bathrooms ($10 extra for bedlinen), and enthusiastically painted motel units.

Glacier Country Scenic Flights (☑03-753 4096, 0800 423 463; www.glacieradventures.co.nz; SH6, Whataroa; flights $195-435) offers a range of scenic flights and helihikes, lifting off from Whataroa Valley. These guys give you more mountain-gawping for your buck than many of the operators flying from the glacier townships.

If it's open, call in to the **Peter Hlavacek Gallery** (☑03-753 4199; www.nzicescapes.com; SH6, Whataroa; ☺9am-5pm Mon-Fri) on the highway. Many regard him as one of NZ's finest landscape photographers.

Okarito

POP 30

The magical seaside hamlet of Okarito sits alongside **Okarito Lagoon**, the largest unmodified wetland in NZ and a superb place for spotting birds, including rare kiwi and the majestic kotuku. Okarito has no shops and limited visitor facilities, so stock up and book before you arrive. Travelling by car, 15km south of Whataroa is the turn-off to the Forks, which branches west for 13km to Okarito.

🏃 Activities

From a car park on the Strand you can begin the easy **Wetland Walk** (20 minutes), a longer mission along the **Three Mile Pack Track** (three hours, with the coastal return route tide dependent, so check in with the

locals for tide times), and a jolly good puff up to **Okarito Trig** (1½ hours return), which rewards the effort with spectacular Southern Alps and Okarito Lagoon views (weather contingent).

★**Okarito Nature Tours** KAYAKING
(☑03-753 4014, 0800 652 748; www.okarito.co.nz; kayaking half-/full day $65/75) Hires out kayaks for paddles across the lagoon into luxuriant rainforest channels where all sorts of birds hang out. Guided tours are available (from $100), while overnight rentals ($100) allow experienced paddlers to explore further afield. There's espresso, smoothies, snacks and wi-fi in the office-lounge.

Okarito Boat Tours WILDLIFE TOUR
(☑03-753 4223; www.okaritoboattours.co.nz) Okarito Boat Tours runs bird-spotting lagoon tours, the most fruitful of which is the 'early bird' ($80, 1½ hrs, 7.30am). The popular two-hour 'ecotour' offers deeper insight into this remarkable natural area ($90, 9am and 11.30am). Cheery, long-time Okaritians Paula and Swade can also fix you up with accommodation in the village.

Okarito Kiwi Tours WILDLIFE TOUR
(☑03-753 4330; www.okaritokiwitours.co.nz; 3hr tours $75) Runs nightly expeditions to spot the rare bird (95% success rate) with an interesting education along the way. Numbers are limited to eight, so booking is recommended.

🛏 Sleeping

Okarito Campground CAMPGROUND $
(off Russell St; sites adult/child $12.50/free) Okarito Campground is a breezy patch of community-managed greenery complete with kitchen, barbecue area and hot showers ($1). Gather driftwood from the beach for the firepit, or build your bonfire on the beach while the sun goes down. No reservations necessary.

Okarito Beach House LODGE $
(☑03-753 4080; www.okaritobeachhouse.com; The Strand; d & tw $85-105; 🐾) The Okarito Beach House has a variety of accommodation. The weathered, self-contained 'Hutel' ($120, sleeping two people) is worth every cent. The Summit Lodge has commanding views and the best dining-room table you've ever seen.

ℹ Getting There & Away

To reach Okarito you'll need your own wheels.

WESTLAND TAI POUTINI NATIONAL PARK

The biggest drawcards of Westland Tai Poutini National Park are the Franz Josef and Fox Glaciers. Nowhere else at this latitude do glaciers come so close to the ocean. The glaciers' existence is largely due to the West Coast's ample rain, with snow falling in the glaciers' broad accumulation zones that fuses into clear ice at 20m depth, and then creeps down the steep valleys.

During the last ice age (15,000 to 20,000 years ago) Westland's twin glaciers reached the sea. In the ensuing thaw they may have crawled back even further than their current positions, but in the 14th century a mini ice age caused them to advance to their greatest modern-era extent around 1750, and the terminal moraines from this time are still visible.

Climate change, however, has seen a consistent retreat over recent years, reducing opportunities for viewing these glaciers on foot. Both glacier terminal faces are roped off to prevent people being caught in icefalls and river surges, and the only way to get close to or on to the ice safely is with a guided tour. Check in with DOC and the locals to get the latest information on the best viewpoints.

Beyond the glaciers, the park's lower reaches harbour deserted Tasman Sea beaches, rising up through rich podocarp forests to NZ's highest peaks. Diverse and often unique habitats huddle next to each other in interdependent ecological sequence. Seals frolic in the surf as deer sneak through the forests. The resident endangered bird species include kakariki, kaka and rowi (the Okarito brown kiwi), as well as kea, the South Island's native parrot. Kea are inquisitive and endearing, but feeding them can kill them.

Heavy tourist traffic often swamps the twin towns of Franz and Fox, 23km apart. Franz is the more action-packed of the two, while Fox has a subdued alpine charm. From November through March visitor numbers can get a little crazy in both towns, so consider visiting in either April or October.

Franz Josef Glacier

POP 444

The early Māori knew Franz Josef as Ka Roimata o Hine Hukatere (Tears of the Avalanche Girl). Legend tells of a girl losing her lover who fell from the local peaks, and her

---

GLACIERS FOR DUMMIES

Hashtag a few of these suckers into your social media posts and make yourself look like a #geologist #geek.

Ablation zone Where the glacier melts.

Accumulation zone Where the ice and snow collects.

Bergschrund A large *crevasse* in the ice near the glacier's starting point.

Blue ice As the accumulation zone (*névé*) snow is compressed by subsequent snowfalls, it becomes *firn* and then blue ice.

Calving The process of ice breaking away from the glacier terminal face.

Crevasse A crack in the glacial ice formed as it crosses obstacles while descending.

Firn Partly compressed snow en route to becoming *blue ice*.

Glacial flour Finely ground rock particles in the milky rivers flowing off glaciers.

Icefall When a glacier descends so steeply that the upper ice breaks into a jumble of ice blocks.

Kettle lake A lake formed by the melt of an area of isolated dead ice.

Moraine Walls of debris formed at the glacier's sides (lateral moraine) or end (terminal moraine).

Névé Snowfield area where *firn* is formed.

Seracs Ice pinnacles formed, like *crevasses*, by the glacier rolling over obstacles.

Terminal The final ice face at the bottom of the glacier.

Franz Josef Glacier & Village

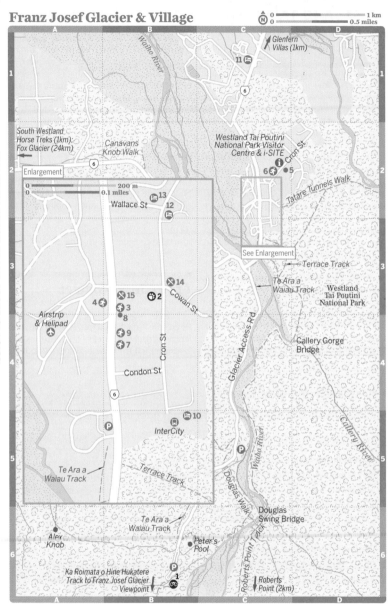

flood of tears freezing into the glacier. The glacier was first explored by Europeans in 1865, with Austrian Julius Haast naming it after the Austrian emperor. The car park for various glacier valley walks is 5km from Franz Josef Village.

◉ Sights

West Coast Wildlife Centre　　　WILDLIFE
(www.wildkiwi.co.nz; cnr Cron & Cowan Sts; day pass adult/child/family $35/20/85, incl backstage pass $55/35/145) ✈ The purpose of this feel-good attraction is breeding two of the

Franz Josef Glacier & Village

world's rarest kiwi – the rowi and the Haast tokoeka. The entry fee is well worthwhile by the time you've viewed the conservation, glacier and heritage displays, and hung out with real, live kiwi in their ferny enclosure. The additional backstage pass into the incubating and rearing area is a rare opportunity to learn how a species can be brought back from the brink of extinction.

Cafe and shop on-site.

Activities

Independent Walks

A series of walks start from the glacier car park, all rewarding way beyond a view of the ice. A nice, short option is **Sentinel Rock** (20 minutes return), while **Ka Roimata o Hine Hukatere Track** (1½ hours return), the main glacier valley walk, leads you to the best permissible view of the terminal face.

Other walks include the **Douglas Walk** (one hour return), off the Glacier Access Rd, which passes moraine piled up by the glacier's advance in 1750, and **Peter's Pool**, a small kettle lake. The **Terrace Track** (30 minutes return) is an easy amble over bushy terraces behind the village, with Waiho River views. Two good rainforest walks, **Tatare Tunnels** and **Callery Gorge Walk** (both around 1½ hours return), start from Cowan St.

Much more challenging walks, such as the five-hour **Roberts Point Track** and eight-hour **Alex Knob Track**, are detailed, along with all the others, in DOC's excellent *Glacier Region Walks* booklet ($2), which provides maps and illuminating background reading.

A rewarding alternative to driving to the glacier car park is the richly rainforested **Te Ara a Waiau Walkway/Cycleway**, starting from near the fire station at the south end of town. It's a one-hour walk (each way) or half that by bicycle (available for hire from

Across Country Quad Bikes (☑ 0800 234 288, 03-752 0123; www.acrosscountryquadbikes. co.nz; Air Safaris Bldg, Main Rd) or the YHA; p124). Leave your bikes at the car park – you can't cycle on the glacier walkways.

Guided Walks & Helihikes

Small group walks with experienced guides (boots, jackets and equipment supplied) are offered by **Franz Josef Glacier Guides** (☑ 0800 484 337, 03-752 0763; www.franzjosefglacier.com; 63 Cron St). Both standard tours require helicopter transfers on to the ice: the 'Ice Explorer' ($339) is bookended by a four-minute flight, with around three hours on the ice; the easier 'Heli Hike' ($435) explores higher reaches of the glacier, requiring a 10-minute flight with around two hours on the ice. Taking around three hours, the 'Glacier Valley Walk' ($75) follows the Waiho River up to the moraine, offering a chance to get beyond the public barriers for close-up views of the ice. All trips are $10 to $30 cheaper for children.

Glacier Valley Eco Tours   GUIDED TOUR
(☑ 0800 999 739, 03-752 0699; www.glaciervalley. co.nz) Offers leisurely three- to eight-hour walking tours around local sights ($75 to $170), packed with local knowledge; plus regular shuttle services to the glacier car park ($12.50 return).

Skydiving & Aerial Sightseeing

Forget sandflies and mozzies. The buzzing you're hearing is a swarm of aircraft in the skies around the glaciers and just beyond in the realm of Aoraki/Mt Cook. A common heliflight ($220 to $240) is 20 minutes' long, and goes to the head of Franz Josef Glacier with a snow landing up top. A 'twin glacier' flight – taking in Fox as well as Franz in around 30 minutes – costs in the region of $300, with a 40-minute trip (swooping around Aoraki/Mt Cook) from $420. Fares for children under 12 years cost between 50% and 70% of the adult price. Shop around: most operators are situated on the main road in Franz Josef Village.

Skydive Franz   SKYDIVING
(☑03-752 0714, 0800 458 677; www.skydivefranz. co.nz; Main Rd) Claiming NZ's highest jump (19,000ft, 80 to 90 seconds freefall; $559), this company also offers 16,000ft for $419, and 13,000ft for $319. With Aoraki/Mt Cook in your sights, this could be the most scenic jump you ever do.

Air Safaris   SCENIC FLIGHTS
(☑0800 723 274, 03-752 0716; www.airsafaris. co.nz; Main Rd) Franz' only fixed-wing flyer offers 30-minute 'twin glacier' ($270) and 50-minute 'grand traverse' ($360) flights.

Fox & Franz Josef Heliservices   SCENIC FLIGHTS
(☑03-752 0793, 0800 800 793; www.scenic-flights. co.nz; Main Rd; 20-40min flights $210-420) Operator based in Franz Josef with over 30 years' experience zipping sightseers up and down the glaciers, and around Aoraki/Mt Cook on longer flights. It also has an office in Fox Glacier (p127).

Glacier Country Helicopters   SCENIC FLIGHTS
(☑0800 359 37269, 03-752 0203; www.glacier countryhelicopters.co.nz; 25-45min flights $235-440) Based in Franz Josef, this family-owned and operated company offers five different scenic options, including an affordable 12-minute flight ($165).

Glacier Helicopters   SCENIC FLIGHTS
(☑0800 800 732, 03-752 0755; www.glacier helicopters.co.nz; 20-40min flights $235-450) Scenic flights around the glaciers and Aoraki/ Mt Cook, all with a snow landing. The helihike option ($399) gets you out on the ice for at least a couple of hours.

Helicopter Line   SCENIC FLIGHTS
(☑03-752 0767, 0800 807 767; www.helicop ter.co.nz; Main Rd; 20-40min flights $235-450) Long-standing operator offering multiple scenic flight options, including a majestic 40-minute flight taking in Aoraki/Mt Cook and Tasman Glacier – NZ's longest glacier.

Mountain Helicopters   SCENIC FLIGHTS
(☑0800 369 423, 03 -751 0045; www.mountainheli copters.co.nz; Main Rd; 20-40min flights $220-420) Privately owned company offering flights over Fox and Franz Josef Glaciers, including a short but affordable 10-minute trip ($99 to $119).

Other Activities

★ Glacier Hot Pools   HOT SPRING
(☑03-752 0099; www.glacierhotpools.co.nz; 63 Cron St; adult/child $26/22; ☺1-9pm, last entry 8pm) Cleverly set into a pretty rainforest setting on the edge of town, this stylish and well-maintained outdoor hot-pool complex is perfect après-hike or on a rainy day. Massage and private pools also available.

Glacier Country Kayaks   KAYAKING
(☑0800 423 262, 03-752 0230; www.glacier kayaks.com; 64 Cron St; 3hr kayak $115) Take a guided kayak trip on Lake Mapourika (7km north of Franz), with fascinating commentary, birdlife, mountain views, a serene channel detour and an additional bushwalk on offer. Go in the morning for better conditions. Ask about family trips and the new small-boat cruises.

Eco-Rafting   RAFTING
(☑03-755 4254, 021 523 426; www.ecorafting. co.nz; family trip adult/child $135/110, 7hr trip $450) Rafting adventures throughout the coast, from gentle, family trips, to the seven-hour 'Grand Canyon' trip on the Whataroa River with its towering granite walls, which includes a 15-minute helicopter ride.

South Westland Horse Treks   HORSE RIDING
(☑0800 187 357, 03-752 0223; www.horsetreknz. com; Waiho Flats Rd; 1/2/3hr trek $70/110/165) Located 5km west of town, this trekking company runs equine excursions across farmland and remote beaches, with spectacular views aplenty.

🛏 Sleeping

Franz Josef
Top 10 Holiday Park   HOLIDAY PARK $
(☑0800 467 8975, 03-752 073; www.franzjosef top10.co.nz; 2902 Franz Josef Hwy; sites $42-48, d $65-165; @🛜) This spacious holiday park, 1.5km from the township, has more sleeping options than you can shake a stick at. Tenters are well catered for with sunny, free-draining grassy sites away from the road, looking out over farm paddocks.

Franz Josef Glacier YHA   HOSTEL $
(☑03-752 0754; www.yha.co.nz; 2-4 Cron St; dm $26-33, s $85, d $107-135; 🛜) This tidy hostel has warm, spacious communal areas, family rooms, free sauna, on-site bike hire, and a booking desk for transport and activities. It has 87 beds, but you'll still need to book ahead.

Rainforest Retreat HOSTEL, HOLIDAY PARK $$
(☑0800 873 346, 03-752 0220; www.rainforest retreat.co.nz; 46 Cron St; sites $39-44, dm $30-34, d $69-220; @ 🛜) This capacious enterprise packs plenty of options into its forested grounds. The pick are the tree huts and self-contained options nestled in the bush. Campervans enjoy similar privacy but lose out on tight, manky facilities, while the backpacker lodge brims with tour-bus custom. The on-site Monsoon Bar has a low top shelf, lively atmosphere and decent meals ($20 to $32).

⭐**Glenfern Villas** APARTMENT $$$
(☑0800 453 633, 03-752 0054; www.glenfern. co.nz; SH6; d $217-239; 🛜) A desirable 3km from the tourist hubbub, these delightful one- and two-bedroom villas sit amid groomed grounds with private decks surveying mountain scenery. Top-notch beds, full kitchens, bike hire and family-friendly facilities strongly suggest 'holiday', not 'stop-off'.

Te Waonui Forest Retreat HOTEL $$$
(☑0800 696 963, 03-752 0555; www.tewaonui. co.nz; 3 Wallace St; s/d from $579/699; @ 🛜) 🌿 Franz' top-end hotel appears earthy and unflashy, with the inside following suit in natural, textured tones brightened by bold, zippy carpet. It offers a classy package of porter service, degustation dinners (included, with breakfast, in the price) and a snazzy bar, along with luxurious rooms in which you'll sleep like a log. All have a deck facing into the forest.

🍴 Eating

Alice May MODERN NZ $$
(☑03-752 0740; www.alicemay.co.nz; cnr Cowan & Cron Sts; mains $20-32; ⊙4pm-late) A faux Tudor corner pub with pastoral chic, mellow vibe and family-friendly attitude, Alice May serves up meaty meals with $20 options, including a daily roast, pasta, and venison burger, with sirloin steak and fish at the upper end. Sticky toffee pudding also features, as does happy hour and mountain views from outdoor tables.

Landing Bar & Restaurant PUB FOOD $$
(☑03-752 0229; www.thelandingbar.co.nz; Main Rd; mains $20-42; ⊙7.30am-late; 🛜) This busy but well-run pub offers an inordinately huge menu of crowd-pleasing food such as burgers, steaks and pizza. The patio – complete with sunshine and gas heaters – is a good place to warm up after a day on the ice.

ℹ️ Information

Franz Josef Health Centre (☑03-752 0700, 0800 7943 2584; 97 Cron St; ⊙9am-4pm Mon-Fri) South Westland's main medical centre.

Franz Josef i-SITE (www.glaciercountry.co.nz; 63 Cron St) Helpful local centre offering advice and booking service for activities, accommodation and transport in the local area and beyond.

Westland Tai Poutini National Park Visitor Centre (☑03-752 0360; www.doc.govt.nz; 69 Cron St; ⊙8.30am-6pm summer, to 5pm winter) Housed in its flash new quarters, the national park visitor centre has insightful exhibits, weather information, maps, and all-important track updates and weather forecasts.

ℹ️ Getting There & Away

The bus stop is opposite the Fern Grove Four Square supermarket.

InterCity (☑03-365 1113; www.intercity.co.nz) has daily buses south to Fox Glacier (35 minutes) and Queenstown (eight hours); and north to Nelson (10 hours). Book at the DOC office or YHA. **Naked Bus** (www.nakedbus.com) services the same routes three times a week. Both provide connections to destinations further afield.

ℹ️ Getting Around

Glacier Valley Eco Tours (p123) runs scheduled shuttle services to the glacier car park (return trip $12.50).

Fox Glacier

POP 306

Fox Glacier is relatively small and quiet, with a farmy feel and open aspect. Beautiful Lake Matheson is a highlight, as are the salty walks down at Gillespies Beach.

🔵 Sights

Fox Glacier Lookout LOOKOUT
This is one of the best land-based positions from which to see Fox Glacier, although its retreat may mean you see just a snippet.

🏃 Activities

Independent Walks

⭐**Lake Matheson** TRAMPING
(www.doc.govt.nz) The famous 'mirror lake' can be found about 6km down Cook Flat Rd. Wandering slowly (as you should), it will take 1½ hours to complete the circuit. The best time to visit is early morning, or when the sun is low in the late afternoon, although the presence of the Matheson Cafe (p128) means that any time is a good time.

Fox Glacier & Village

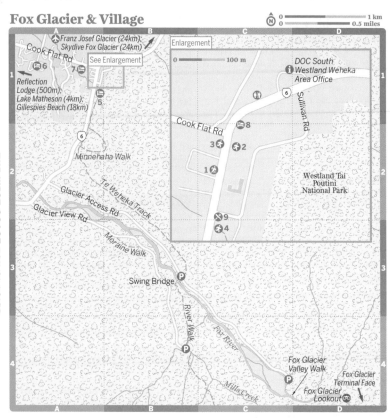

Fox Glacier & Village

At the far end of the circuit – on a clear day – you may, just may, get the money shot, but failing that you can buy a postcard at the excellent gift store by the car park.

Copland Track
TRAMPING

(www.doc.govt.nz) About 26km south of Fox Glacier, along SH6, is the trailhead for the Copland Track, a six-to-seven-hour tramp to legendary Welcome Flat, where thermal springs bubble up next to DOC's **Welcome Flat Hut** (www.doc.govt.nz; adult/child $15/7.50). Unsurprisingly, the hut and adjacent camping ground are extremely popular, with wardens in attendance, so book in advance either online or in person at DOC visitor centres.

Gillespies Beach
TRAMPING

(www.doc.govt.nz) Follow Cook Flat Rd for its full 21km (unsealed for the final 12km) to the remote black-sand Gillespies Beach, site of an old mining settlement (and basic campsite). Interesting walks from here include a five-minute zip to the old miners' cemetery, and the 3½-hour return walk to **Galway Beach**, a seal haul-out. Don't disturb them.

Along the road to Gillespie's Beach is **Peak View Picnic Area**, which offers a faraway but fine perspective of Fox Glacier. You can also spin the dial to identify which mountain you're looking at.

Glacier Walks & Helihikes

The only way on to the ice is by taking a helihiking trip, run by Fox Glacier Guiding (p127). Independent walks, however, offer a chance to explore the valley – raw and staggeringly beautiful even in its ice-less lower reaches – and get as close to the glacier's terminal face as safety allows.

It's 1.5km from Fox Village to the glacier turn-off, and a further 2km to the car park, which you can reach under your own steam via **Te Weheka Walkway/Cycleway**, a pleasant rainforest trail starting just south of the Bella Vista motel. It's just over an hour each way to walk, or 30 minutes to cycle (leave your bikes at the car park – you can't cycle on the glacier walkways). Hire bikes from Westhaven (p127).

From the car park, the terminal-face viewpoint is around 40 minutes' walk, depending on current conditions. Obey all signs: this place is dangerously dynamic.

Short walks near the glacier include the **Moraine Walk** (over a major 18th-century advance) and **Minnehaha Walk**. The fully accessible **River Walk Lookout Track** (20 minutes return) starts from the Glacier View Rd car park and allows people of all abilities the chance to view the glacier.

Pick up a copy of DOC's excellent *Glacier Region Walks* booklet ($2), which provides maps and illuminating background reading.

Fox Glacier Guiding　　　　GUIDED WALK
(☑03-751 0825, 0800 111 600; www.foxguides. co.nz; 44 Main Rd) Guided helihikes (equipment provided) are organised by Fox Glacier Guiding. The standard trip (up to three hours on the ice) is $399/369 per adult/ child, but there are other options, including an easygoing two-hour interpretive walk to the glacier (adult/child $59/45). Note that age restrictions vary depending on the trip.

Skydiving & Aerial Sightseeing

A common heliflight ($220 to $240) is 20 minutes' long, and goes to the head of Fox Glacier with a snow landing up top. A 'twin glacier' flight – taking in Franz as well as Fox in around 30 minutes – costs in the region of $300, with a 40-minute trip (swooping around Aoraki/Mt Cook) from $420. Fares for children under 12 years cost between 50% and 70% of the adult price. Shop around: most operators are situated on the main road in Fox Glacier Village.

Skydive Fox Glacier　　　　SKYDIVING
(☑0800 751 0080, 03-751 0080; www.skydivefox. co.nz; Fox Glacier Airfield, SH6) Eye-popping scenery abounds on leaps from 16,500ft ($399) or 13,000ft ($299). The airfield is conveniently located three minutes' walk from village centre.

Fox & Franz Josef Heliservices　SCENIC FLIGHTS
(☑03-751 0866, 0800 800 793; www.scenic-flights. co.nz; 44 Main Rd; 20-40min flights $210-420) Operator with over 30 years' experience zipping sightseers up and down the glaciers, and around Aoraki/Mt Cook on longer flights. It also has an office in Franz Josef (p124).

Glacier Helicopters　　　　SCENIC FLIGHTS
(☑0800 800 732, 03-751 0803; www.glacier helicopters.co.nz; SH6; 20-40min flights $235-450) Scenic flights around the glaciers and Aoraki/Mt Cook, all with a snow landing. The helihike option ($399) gets you out on the ice for at least a couple of hours.

Helicopter Line　　　　　SCENIC FLIGHTS
(☑0800 807 767, 03-752 0767; www.helicopter. co.nz; SH6; 20-40min flights $235-450) Long-standing operator offering multiple scenic flight options, including a majestic 40-minute flight taking in Aoraki/Mt Cook and Tasman Glacier – NZ's longest glacier.

Mountain Helicopters　　　SCENIC FLIGHTS
(☑03-751 0045, 0800 369 423; www.mountain helicopters.co.nz; 43 Main Rd; 20-40min flights $220-420) Privately owned company offering flights over Fox and Franz Josef Glaciers, including a short but affordable 10-minute trip ($99 to $119).

🛏 Sleeping

⭐**Fox Glacier**

Top 10 Holiday Park　　　HOLIDAY PARK $
(☑0800 154 366, 03-751 0821; www.fghp.co.nz; Kerrs Rd; sites $42-45, cabins & units $73-255; @🛜) This park has options to suit all budgets, from grassy and hard campervan sites, to lodge rooms and upscale motel units. Excellent amenities include a modern communal kitchen and dining room, playground and spa pool, but it's the mountain views that give it the X-factor.

Westhaven　　　　　　　MOTEL $$
(☑0800 369 452, 03-751 0084; www.thewest haven.co.nz; SH6; d $145-185; 🛜) These smart suites are a classy combo of corrugated steel and local stone amid burnt-red and ivory walls. The deluxe king rooms have spa baths, and there are bikes to hire for the energetic (half-/full day $20/40).

Rainforest Motel
MOTEL $$

(✆0800 724 636, 03-751 0140; www.rainforest motel.co.nz; 15 Cook Flat Rd; d $125-160; 🛜) Rustic log cabins on the outside with neutral decor on the inside. Epic lawns for running around on or simply enjoying the mountain views. A tidy, good-value option.

Reflection Lodge
B&B $$$

(✆03-751 0707; www.reflectionlodge.co.nz; 141 Cook Flat Rd; d $210; 🛜) The gregarious hosts of this ski-lodge-style B&B go the extra mile to make your stay a memorable one. Blooming gardens complete with alpine views and a Monet-like pond seal the deal.

Fox Glacier Lodge
B&B, MOTEL $$$

(✆0800 369 800, 03-751 0888; www.foxglacier lodge.com; 41 Sullivan Rd; d $175-225; 🛜) Beautiful timber adorns the exterior and interior of this attractive property, imparting a mountain-chalet vibe. Similarly woody self-contained mezzanine units with spa baths and gas fires are also available.

Eating

★ Matheson Cafe
MODERN NZ $$

(✆03-751 0878; www.lakematheson.com; Lake Matheson Rd; breakfast & lunch $10-21, dinner $17-33; ⊙8am-late Nov-Mar, to 4pm Apr-Oct) Next to Lake Matheson, this cafe does everything right: sharp architecture that maximises inspiring mountain views, strong coffee, craft beers and upmarket fare from a smoked-salmon breakfast bagel, to slow-cooked lamb followed by berry crumble. Part of the complex is the ReflectioNZ Gallery next door, stocking quality, primarily NZ-made art and souvenirs.

Last Kitchen
CAFE $$

(✆03-751 0058; cnr Sullivan Rd & SH6; lunch $10-20, dinner $24-32; ⊙11.30am-late) Making the most of its sunny corner location with outside tables, the Last Kitchen is a good option, serving contemporary fare, such as haloumi salad, pistachio crusted lamb and genuinely gourmet burgers. It also satisfies for coffee and a wine later in the day.

ℹ Information

Activity operators and accommodation providers are well-oiled at providing information on local services (and usually a booking service, too), but you can also find info online at www.glaciercountry.co.nz. Note that there's no ATM in Fox (which means no cash out south until Wanaka), and that **Fox Glacier Motors** (✆03-751 0823; SH6) is your last chance for fuel before Haast, 120km away.

DOC South Westland Weheka Area Office

(✆03-751 0807; SH6; ⊙10am-2pm Mon-Fri) This is no longer a general visitor-information centre, but has the usual DOC information, hut tickets, and weather and track updates.

Fox Glacier Health Centre (✆0800 7943 2584, 03-751 0836; SH6) Clinic opening hours are displayed at the centre, or ring the 0800 number for assistance from the **Franz Josef Health Centre** (p125).

ℹ Getting There & Away

Most buses stop outside the Fox Glacier Guiding building.

InterCity (✆03-365 1113; www.intercity.co.nz) runs two buses a day north to Franz Josef (40 minutes), the morning bus continuing to Nelson (11 hours). Daily southbound services run to Queenstown (7½ hours).

Naked Bus (www.nakedbus.com) runs three times a week north along the coast all way through to Nelson, and south to Queenstown.

ℹ Getting Around

Fox Glacier Shuttles, staffed by the inimitable Murray, will drive you around the area from Franz Josef to the Copland Valley, and including Lake Matheson, Gillespies Beach and the glaciers. Look for him parked opposite **Fox Glacier Motors** (p128).

HAAST REGION

Between Fox Glacier and Haast it's a 120km (two-hour) drive along a scenic stretch of highway chopped through lowland forest and occasional pasture, with views inland to sheer-sided valleys and intermittent but grand views seaward. This section of highway only opened in 1965, as commemorated in the roadside monument at Knights Point (p129), 5km south of Lake Moeraki. Stop there if humanly possible – it's an utterly cracking viewpoint.

The Haast region bookends the West Coast road. It's a vast and rich wilderness of kahikatea and rata forests, wetlands, sand dunes, seal and penguin colonies, birdlife and sweeping beaches, hence its inclusion in the Southwest New Zealand (Te Wahipounamu) World Heritage Area.

Haast

POP 240

Haast crouches around the mouth of the wide Haast River in three distinct pockets: Haast Junction, Haast Village and Haast Beach. As well as being a handy stop for filling the tank and tummy, it's also the gateway to some spectacular scenery along the road to the end of the line at Jackson Bay. Explore with the help of the free Haast Visitor Map (www. haastnz.com) or DOC's brochure *Walks and Activities in the Haast Area* ($2, or downloadable online), but also seriously consider a trip with Waiatoto River Safaris (p130) – it's up there with NZ's best jetboat adventures.

If you're heading north, check your fuel gauge as Haast petrol station is the last one before Fox Glacier.

◉ Sights & Activities

Knights Point   LOOKOUT
A monument at this spectacular roadside lookout commemorates the opening of this section of coastal highway, in 1965. It's an easy pull-over off the highway, 5km south of Lake Moeraki.

Lake Moeraki   LAKE
Alongside the highway and within the bounds of the World Heritage wilderness, Lake Moeraki is an undeveloped and tranquil spot to contemplate the forested, mountainous surroundings. There's a car park at the southeastern end.

★ Ship Creek   WALKING
(www.doc.govt.nz) Ship Creek, 15km north of Haast, is a terrific place to stretch the legs, boasting two fascinating walks with interesting interpretive panels: the Dune Lake Walk (30 minutes return), which is all sand dunes and stunted forest, leading to a surprising view, and the unsurprisingly swampy Kahikatea Swamp Forest Walk (20 minutes return).

🛏 Sleeping & Eating

Haast Beach Holiday Park   HOLIDAY PARK **$**
(☑ 0800 843 226, 03-750 0860; www.haastpark.com; 1348 Jackson Bay Rd, Haast Beach; sites from $34, dm $25, d $50-110) Well worth the 14km drive south of Haast Junction, this old dear dishes up just enough charm, with its clean and tidy facilities that range from basic cabins to self-contained units, and a pleasant campers' block with a comfortable lounge and views from the deck. The Hapuka Estuary Walk is across the road, and it's 20 minutes' walk to an epic beach.

Haast Lodge   LODGE **$**
(☑ 03-750 0703, 0800 500 703; www.haastlodge. com; Marks Rd, Haast Village; sites from $16, dm $25, d & tw $55-65, units d $98-130; 🛜) Covering all accommodation bases, Haast Lodge offers clean, well-maintained facilities that include a pleasant communal area for lodge

users and campervanners, and tidy motel units at the Aspiring Court next door.

Collyer House   B&B **$$**
(☑ 03-750 0022; www.collyerhouse.co.nz; Cuttance Rd, Okuru; d $180-250; @ 🛜) This gem of a B&B has thick bathrobes, quality linen, beach views and a sparkling host who cooks a terrific breakfast. This all adds up to make Collyer House a comfortable, upmarket choice. Follow the signs off SH6 for 12km down Jackson Bay Rd.

Wilderness Lodge Lake Moeraki   LODGE **$$$**
(☑ 03-750 0881; www.wildernesslodge.co.nz; SH6; d incl breakfast & dinner $790-1150; 🛜) ⌀ At the southern end of Lake Moeraki, 31km north of Haast, you will find one of NZ's best nature lodges. Set in a verdant setting on the edge of the Moeraki River, it offers comfortable rooms and four-course dinners, but the real delights here are the outdoor activities, such as kayak trips and coastal walks, guided by people with conservation in their blood.

Hard Antler   PUB FOOD **$$**
(☑ 03-750 0034; Marks Rd, Haast Village; dinner mains $20-30; ⊙ 11am-late, dinner 5-9pm) This display of deer antlers confirms that you're in manly territory, as does the general ambience of this bold but welcoming and well-run pub. Plain, meaty food on offer with bain-marie action on the side.

ℹ Information

DOC Haast Visitor Centre (☑ 03-750 0809; www.doc.govt.nz; cnr SH6 & Jackson Bay Rd; ⊙ 9am-6pm Nov-Mar, to 4.30pm Apr-Oct) Located near Haast Junction, the Visitor Centre has wall-to-wall regional information and screens the all-too-brief but free Haast landscape film *Edge of Wilderness*.

Haast Promotions (www.haastnz.com)

ℹ Transport

InterCity (☑ 03-365 1113; www.intercity.co.nz) buses stop on Marks Rd (opposite Wilderness Backpackers) on their daily runs between the West Coast and Queenstown. **Naked Bus** (www.nakedbus.com) also passes through three times a week.

Haast Pass Highway

Early Māori travelled this route between Central Otago and the West Coast in their quest for *pounamu*, naming it Tioripatea, meaning 'Clear Path'. The first party of Europeans to

WORTH A TRIP

JACKSON BAY ROAD

From Haast Junction, the road most travelled is SH6, upwards or across. But there is another option, heading south to the end of the line along the quiet and intensely scenic Jackson Bay Rd.

Towered over by the Southern Alps, the farms on the flat and the settlements dotted between them stand testament to some of the hardiest souls who ever attempted settlement in New Zealand. Up until the 1950s, the only way to reach Haast overland was via bush tracks from Hokitika and Wanaka. Supplies came by a coastal shipping service that called every couple of months or so.

Besides the ghosts and former glories, which make an appearance here and there, there's plenty to warrant a foray down to Jackson Bay.

Near Okuru is the **Hapuka Estuary Walk** (www.doc.govt.nz) (20 minutes return), a winding boardwalk that loops through a sleepy wildlife sanctuary with good interpretation panels en route.

Five kilometres further south (19km south of Haast Junction) is where you'll find the base for **Waiatoto River Safaris** (☏ 03-750 0780, 0800 538 723; www.riversafaris.co.nz; 1975 Haast-Jackson Bay Rd, Hannahs Clearing; adult/child $199/139; ◷ trips 10am, 1pm & 4pm), which offers a memorable two-hour jetboat trip up river and down, through distinct landscapes from deep-mountain World Heritage forest to the salt-misted river mouth. Operators Wayne and Ruth, and the Waiatoto's remote wilderness atmosphere make this one of NZ's best boat tours.

The road continues west to **Arawhata Bridge**, where a turn-off leads to the **Lake Ellery Track** (www.doc.govt.nz), 3.5km away. This pleasant amble through mossy beech forest (1½ hours return) leads to **Ellery Lake**, where a picnic bench encourages lunch with perhaps a skinny dip for afters.

It's less than an hour's drive from Haast town to the fishing hamlet of **Jackson Bay**, the only natural harbour on the West Coast. Migrants arrived here in 1875 under a doomed settlement scheme, their farming and timber-milling aspirations mercilessly shattered by never-ending rain and the lack of a wharf, not built until 1938. Those families who stayed turned their hands to largely subsistence living.

With good timing you will arrive when the **Cray Pot** (fish & chips $17-29; ◷ 12-4pm, hours may vary) is open. This place is just as much about the dining room (a caravan) and location (looking out over the bay) as it is about the honest seafood, including a good feed of fish and chips, crayfish, chowder or whitebait. Ask a local to confirm current opening times.

Walk off your fries on the **Wharekai Te Kou Walk** (www.doc.govt.nz), 40 minutes return, to Ocean Beach, a tiny bay that hosts pounding waves and some interesting rock formations, or the longer, three- to four-hour **Smoothwater Bay Track**, nearby.

make the crossing may well have been led by the German geologist Julius von Haast, in 1863 – hence the name of the pass, river and township – but evidence suggests that Scottish prospector Charles Cameron may have pipped Haast at the post. It was clearly no mean feat, for such is the terrain that the Haast Pass Hwy wasn't opened until 1965.

Heading inland from Haast towards Wanaka (145km, 2½ hours), the highway (SH6) snakes alongside the Haast River, crossing the boundary into Mt Aspiring National Park shortly after you hit fourth gear. The further you go, the narrower the river valley becomes, until the road clambers around sheer-sided valley walls streaked with waterfalls and scarred by rock slips. Princely sums are involved in keeping this

highway clear, and even so it sets plenty of traps for unwary drivers.

Stop to admire the scenery, availing yourself of the many signposted lookouts and short walkways, such as those to **Fantail** and **Thunder Creek** falls. These are detailed in DOC's booklet *Walks along the Haast Highway* ($2), but sufficient detail is provided at the trailheads.

The highway tops out at the 563m pass mark, shortly after which you will reach food and fuel at Makarora. Oh, hello Otago!

❶ Getting There & Away

InterCity (p129; daily) and **Naked Bus** (thrice weekly) travel over Haast Pass between the West Coast and Wanaka/Queenstown.

Christchurch & Canterbury

Best Places to Eat

➜ Pegasus Bay (p161)

➜ Twenty Seven Steps (p147)

➜ Supreme Supreme (p146)

➜ Bodhi Tree (p148)

➜ Oxford (p170)

Best Places to Sleep

➜ Onuku Farm Hostel (p154)

➜ Halfmoon Cottage (p154)

➜ Peel Forest (p167)

➜ Lake Ohau Lodge (p175)

➜ Lake Tekapo Lodge (p174)

Why Go?

Nowhere in New Zealand is changing and developing as fast as post-2016-earthquake Christchurch. Visiting the country's second-largest city as it's being rebuilt and reborn is both interesting and inspiring.

A short drive from Christchurch's dynamic re-emergence, Banks Peninsula conceals hidden bays and beaches – a backdrop for wildlife cruises with a sunset return to the attractions of Akaroa. To the north are the vineyards of the Waipara Valley and the family-holiday ambience of Hanmer Springs. Westwards, the chequerboard farms of the Canterbury Plains morph quickly into the dramatic wilderness of the Southern Alps.

Canterbury's summertime attractions include tramping along alpine valleys and over passes around Arthur's Pass, and mountain biking around the turquoise lakes of Mackenzie Country. During winter, the attention switches to the ski fields. Throughout the seasons, Aoraki/Mt Cook, the country's tallest peak, stands sentinel over this diverse region.

When to Go

➜ Canterbury is one of NZ's driest regions, as moisture-laden westerlies from the Tasman Sea dump their rainfall on the West Coast before hitting the eastern side of the South Island. Visit from January to March for hot and settled summer weather, and plenty of opportunities to get active amid the region's spectacular landscapes.

➜ The shoulder seasons of October to November and March to May can be cool and dry, and blissfully uncrowded.

➜ Hit the winter slopes from July to October at Mt Hutt or on one of Canterbury's smaller club ski fields.

Christchurch & Canterbury Highlights

1 Christchurch (p134) Experiencing the dynamic rebuilding and re-emergence of the city's earthquake.

2 Christchurch Botanic Gardens (p136) Meandering through the city's beautiful green heart.

3 Mt John (p173) Marvelling at the otherworldly views of Mackenzie Country and the surreal azure blue of Lake Tekapo from the top.

4 Hanmer Springs Thermal Pools (p158) Taking a soothing soak at this famous hot spring.

5 Banks Peninsula (p152) Admiring the surf-bitten edges from Summit Rd before descending to the quaint and Francophilic village of Akaroa (p154).

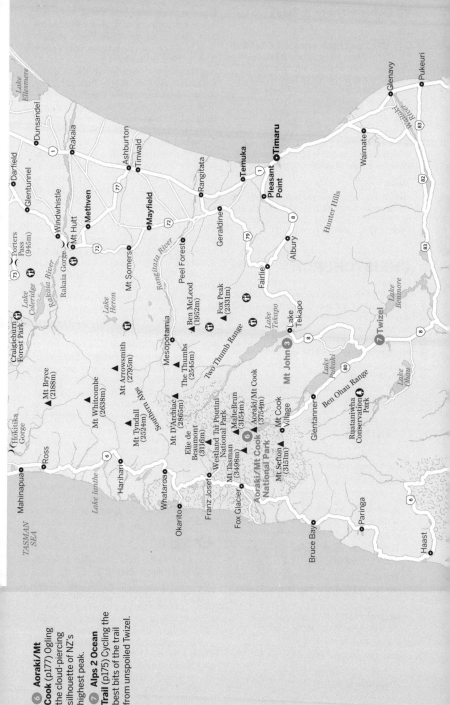

6 Aoraki/Mt Cook (p177) Ogling the cloud-piercing silhouette of NZ's highest peak.

7 Alps 2 Ocean Trail (p175) Cycling the best bits of the trail from unspoiled Twizel.

❶ Getting There & Away

AIR

Christchurch's international airport is the South Island's main hub. Air New Zealand flies here from 15 domestic destinations, while Jetstar has flights from Auckland and Wellington. Air New Zealand also flies between Timaru and Wellington.

BUS

Christchurch is the hub for coaches and shuttles heading up the coast as far as Picton, down the coast to Dunedin (and on to Te Anau), over the Alps to Greymouth and inland down to Queenstown.

TRAIN

The TranzAlpine service connects Christchurch and Greymouth, and the Coastal Pacific chugs north to Picton, with ferry connections across Cook Strait to the North Island.

CHRISTCHURCH

POP 342,000

Welcome to a vibrant city in transition, coping creatively with the aftermath of NZ's second-worst natural disaster. Traditionally the most English of NZ cities, Christchurch's heritage heart was all but hollowed out following the 2010 and 2011 earthquakes that left 186 people dead.

Today Christchurch boasts more road cones and repurposed shipping containers

---

ESSENTIAL CHRISTCHURCH & CANTERBURY
....

Eat Salmon spawned in the shadow of NZ's tallest mountains.

Drink Some of NZ's finest pinot noir and riesling from the Waipara Valley.

Read *Old Bucky & Me*, a poignant account of the 2011 earthquake by Christchurch journalist Jane Bowron.

Listen To the soulful tones and uplifting beats of Christchurch's Ladi6.

Watch Accounts of bravery and resilience at Christchurch's Quake City (p137).

Go green At the ecofriendly Okuti Garden (p154) on Banks Peninsula.

Online www.christchurchnz.com, www.mtcooknz.com, www.midcanterburynz.com, www.visithurunui.co.nz

Area code ☏03

---

than anywhere else in the world, waypoints in an epic rebuild that sees construction sites throughout the CBD. There is dust, noise, and heavy traffic at times. But don't be deterred. The city centre is graced by numerous notable arts institutions, the stunning Botanic Gardens and Hagley Park. Inner-city streets conceal art projects and pocket gardens, dotted among a thinned-out cityscape featuring remnant stone buildings and the sharp, shiny architecture of the new.

Curious travellers will revel in this chaotic, crazy and colourful mix, full of surprises and inspiring in ways you can't even imagine. And despite all the hard work and heartache, the locals will be only too pleased to see you.

History

The first people to live in what is now Christchurch were moa hunters, who arrived around 1250. Immediately prior to colonisation, the Ngāi Tahu tribe had a small seasonal village on the banks of the Avon called Otautahi.

When British settlers arrived in 1880 it was an ordered Church of England project; the passengers on the 'First Four Ships' were dubbed 'the Canterbury Pilgrims' by the British press. Christchurch was meant to be a model of class-structured England in the South Pacific, not just another scruffy colonial outpost. Churches were built rather than pubs, the fertile farming land was deliberately placed in the hands of the gentry, and wool made the elite of Christchurch wealthy.

In 1856 Christchurch officially became NZ's first city, and a very English one at that. Town planning and architecture assumed a close affinity with the 'Mother Country' and English-style gardens were planted, earning it the nickname, the 'Garden City'. To this day, Christchurch in spring is a glorious place to be.

◉ Sights

Starting from the ground up after the earthquakes, the Gap Filler folks fill the city's empty spaces with creativity and colour. Projects range from temporary art installations, performance spaces and gardens, to a minigolf course scattered through empty building sites and the 'Grandstandium' – a mobile grandstand that's a total fun-magnet. Gaps open up and get filled, so check out the Gap Map on the website (www.gapfiller.org.nz), or simply wander the streets and see what you can find.

Christchurch

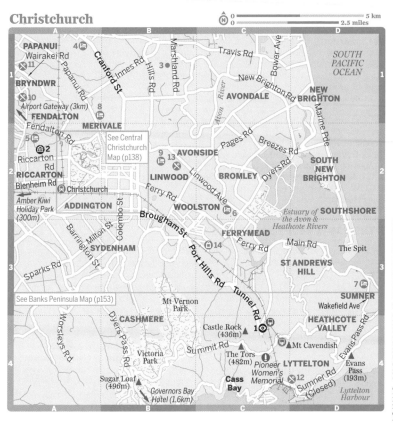

N 0 ——— 5 km
0 ——— 2.5 miles

Christchurch

⊙ City Centre

★ **Christchurch Botanic Gardens** GARDENS
(Map p138; www.ccc.govt.nz; Rolleston Ave; ⊘ 7am-
8.30pm Oct-Mar, to 6.30pm Apr-Sep) FREE Stroll-
ing through these blissful 30 riverside hectares of arboreal and floral splendour is a
consummate Christchurch experience. Gorgeous at any time of the year, the gardens
are particularly impressive in spring when
the rhododendrons, azaleas and daffodil
woodland are in riotous bloom. There are
thematic gardens to explore, lawns to sprawl
on, and a playground adjacent to the **Botanic Gardens Information Centre** (Map p138;
☑ 03-941 8999; ⊘ 9am-4pm Mon-Fri, 10.15am-
4pm Sat & Sun).

Guided walks ($10) depart at 1.30pm
(mid-September to mid-May) from the Canterbury Museum (p137), or you can chug
around the gardens on the **Caterpillar train**
(☑ 0800 88 22 23; www.welcomeaboard.co.nz;
adult/child $20/9; ⊘ 11am-3pm).

★ **Christchurch Art Gallery** GALLERY
(Map p138; ☑ 03-941 7300; www.christchurchart-
gallery.org.nz; cnr Montreal St & Worcester Blvd;
⊘ 10am-5pm Thu-Tue, to 9pm Wed) FREE Damaged in the earthquakes, Christchurch's
fantastic art gallery has reopened brighter
and bolder, presenting a stimulating mix of
primarily NZ exhibitions.

THE CANTERBURY EARTHQUAKES

Christchurch's seismic nightmare began at 4.35am on 4 September 2010. Centred
40km west of the city, a 40-second, 7.1-magnitude earthquake jolted Cantabrians from
their sleep, and caused widespread damage to older buildings in the central city. Close to
the quake's epicentre in rural Darfield, huge gashes erupted amid grassy pastures, and
the South Island's main railway line was bent and buckled. Because the tremor struck in
the early hours of the morning when most people were home in bed, there were no fatali-
ties, and many Christchurch residents felt that the city had dodged a bullet.

Fast forward to 12.51pm on 22 February 2011, when central Christchurch was busy with
shoppers and workers enjoying their lunch break. This time the 6.3-magnitude quake was
much closer, centred just 10km southeast of the city and only 5km deep. The tremor was
significantly greater, and many locals report being flung violently and almost vertically into
the air. The peak ground acceleration exceeded 1.8, almost twice the acceleration of gravity.

When the dust settled after 24 traumatic seconds, NZ's second-largest city had
changed forever. The towering spire of the iconic ChristChurch Cathedral lay in ruins;
walls and verandas had cascaded down on shopping strips; and two multistorey buildings had pancaked. Of the 185 deaths (across 20 nationalities), 115 occurred in the
six-storey Canterbury TV building, where many international students at a language
school were killed. Elsewhere, the historic port town of Lyttelton was badly damaged;
roads and bridges were crumpled; and residential suburbs in the east were inundated as
a process of rapid liquefaction saw tons of oozy silt rise from the ground.

In the months that followed literally hundreds of aftershocks rattled the city's trauma-
tised residents (and claimed one more life), but the resilience and bravery of Cantabrians
quickly became evident. From the region's rural heartland, the 'Farmy Army' descended
on the city, armed with shovels and food hampers. Social media mobilised 10,000 students, and the Student Volunteer Army became a vital force for residential clean-ups in
the city's beleaguered eastern suburbs. Heartfelt aid and support arrived from across NZ,
and seven other nations sent specialised urban-search-and-rescue teams.

The impact of the events of a warm summer's day in early 2011 will take longer than
a generation to resolve. Entire streets and neighbourhoods in the eastern suburbs have
had to be abandoned, and Christchurch's heritage architecture is irrevocably damaged.
Families in some parts of the city have been forced to live in substandard accommodation, waiting for insurance claims to be settled. Around 80% of the buildings within the
city centre's famed four avenues have been or are still due to be demolished. Amid the
doomed, the saved, and the shiny new builds are countless construction sites and empty
plots still strewn with rubble.

Plans for the next 20 years of the city's rebuild include a compact, low-rise city centre,
large green spaces, and parks and cycleways along the Avon River. It's estimated that the
total rebuild and repair bill could reach $40 or even $50 billion.

Hagley Park   PARK

(Map p138; Riccarton Ave) Wrapping itself around the Botanic Gardens, Hagley Park is Christchurch's biggest green space, stretching for 165 hectares. Riccarton Ave splits it in two and the Avon River snakes through the north half. It's a great place to stroll, whether on a foggy autumn morning, or a warm spring day when the cherry trees lining Harper Ave are in flower. Joggers make the most of the tree-lined avenues, year-round.

Canterbury Museum   MUSEUM

(Map p138; ☑03-366 5000; www.canterbury museum.com; Rolleston Ave; ☺9am-5pm) FREE
Yes, there's a mummy and dinosaur bones, but the highlights of this museum are more local and more recent. The Māori galleries contain some beautiful *pounamu* (greenstone) pieces, while Christchurch Street is an atmospheric walk through the colonial past. The reproduction of Fred & Myrtle's gloriously kitsch Paua Shell House embraces Kiwiana at its best, and kids will enjoy the interactive displays in the Discovery Centre (admission $2). Hour-long guided tours commence at 3.30pm on Tuesday and Thursday.

Quake City   MUSEUM

(Map p138; www.quakecity.co.nz; 99 Cashel St; adult/child $20/free; ☺10am-5pm) A must-visit for anyone interested in the Canterbury earthquakes and conveniently located in the Re:START Mall, this compact museum tells stories through photography, video footage and various artefacts, including bits that have fallen off the Cathedral. Most affecting of all is the film featuring locals recounting their own experiences.

Transitional Cathedral   CHURCH

(Map p138; www.cardboardcathedral.org.nz; 234 Hereford St; entry by donation; ☺9am-5pm, to 7pm summer) Universally known as the Cardboard Cathedral due to the 98 cardboard tubes used in its construction, this interesting structure serves as both the city's temporary Anglican cathedral and as a concert venue. Designed by Japanese 'disaster architect' Shigeru Ban, the entire building was up in 11 months.

Gondola   CABLE CAR

(Map p135; www.gondola.co.nz; 10 Bridle Path Rd; return adult/child $28/12; ☺10am-5pm) Take a ride to the top of Mt Cavendish (500m) on this 945m cable car for wonderful views over the city, Lyttelton, Banks Peninsula and the Canterbury Plains. At the top there's a cafe and the child-focused *Time Tunnel* ride through historical scenes. You can also walk

ⓘ WELCOME ABOARD COMBOS

Welcome Aboard (☑03-366 7830; www.welcomeaboard.co.nz) is the company that runs the punting (p141), tram (p143), gondola (p137) and Botanic Gardens Caterpillar Train (p136), as well as Thrillseekers Adventures (p159) in Hanmer Springs. A baffling array of combo tickets is available, which will save you some money if you're considering doing more than one activity. It also operates the six-hour Grand Tour (adult/child $129/69), which includes all four Christchurch-based activities and a stop in Sumner.

to Cavendish Bluff Lookout (30 minutes return) or the **Pioneer Women's Memorial** (Map p135), one hour return.

Arts Centre   HISTORIC BUILDING

(Map p138; www.artscentre.org.nz; 2 Worcester Blvd) Dating from 1877, this enclave of Gothic Revival buildings was originally Canterbury College, the forerunner of Canterbury University. The college's most famous alumnus was the father of nuclear physics Lord Ernest Rutherford, the NZ physicist who first split the atom in 1917 (that's him on the $100 bill).

You'll have to be content to admire the architecture from the street, as the complex was badly damaged in the earthquakes. Some parts are due to reopen during 2016, with the whole project due for completion in 2019.

Cathedral Square   SQUARE

(Map p138) Christchurch's city square stands largely flattened and forlorn amid the surrounding rebuild, with the remains of ChristChurch Cathedral emblematic of the loss. The February 2011 earthquake brought down the 63m-high spire, while subsequent earthquakes in June 2011 and December 2011 destroyed the prized stained-glass rose window. Other heritage buildings around the square were also badly damaged, but one modern landmark left unscathed is the 18m-high metal sculpture *Chalice*, designed by Neil Dawson. It was erected in 2001 to commemorate the new millennium.

The much-loved Gothic ChristChurch Cathedral lies at the centre of a battle between those who seek to preserve what remains of Christchurch's heritage, the fiscal pragmatists, and those ideologically inclined

CHRISTCHURCH & CANTERBURY CHRISTCHURCH

Central Christchurch

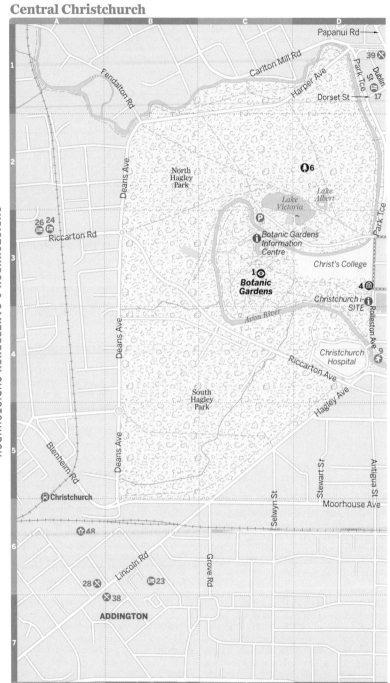

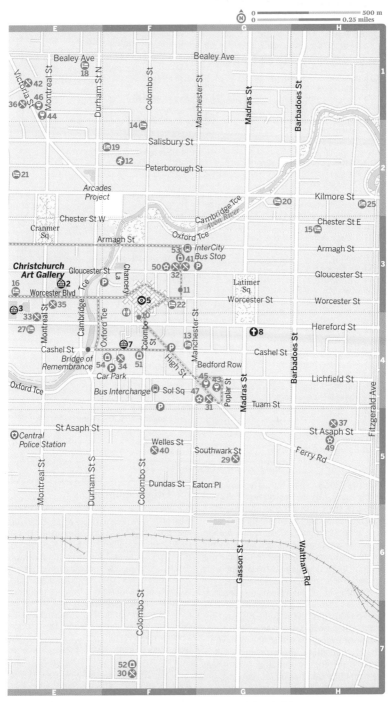

0 ——————————— 500 m
0 ——————————— 0.25 miles

Bealey Ave
Bealey Ave
18
42
46
36
44
Montreal St
Durham St N
Colombo St
Manchester St
Madras St
Barbadoes St
14
Salisbury St
19
12
Peterborough St
21
Arcades
Project
20
Kilmore St
25
Chester St W
Cambridge Tce
Avon River
Chester St E
Cranmer
Sq
Oxford Tce
15
Armagh St
Armagh St
Christchurch
Art Gallery
2
Gloucester St
Chancery La
53
41
InterCity
Bus Stop
Gloucester St
50
32
Latimer
Sq
16
Worcester Blvd
Cambridge Tce
Oxford Tce
Colombo St
11
Worcester St
Worcester St
3
33
35
5
22
8
27
13
Hereford St
7
Cashel St
Manchester St
Cashel St
Barbadoes St
Bridge of
Remembrance
54
34
51
High St
Bedford Row
Lichfield St
Fitzgerald Ave
Oxford Tce
Car Park
Bus Interchange
Sol Sq
47
45
43
Poplar St
Madras St
Tuam St
31
Central
Police Station
St Asaph St
37
St Asaph St
49
Welles St
40
Southwark St
29
Ferry Rd
Montreal St
Durham St S
Colombo St
Dundas St
Eaton Pl
Gasson St
Waltham Rd
Colombo St
52
30

CHRISTCHURCH & CANTERBURY CHRISTCHURCH

Central Christchurch

to things new. Despite the nave remaining largely intact, the deconstruction and demolition of the cathedral was announced in March 2012 by the Anglican Diocese. Heritage advocates launched court proceedings to prevent the demolition, and an independent, Government-appointed consultant was brought in to negotiate between opposing parties. Their report concluded that 're- placing the cathedral presents no particular challenges from an engineering perspective'. In effect this has just muddied the waters, and at time of writing no concrete decisions had been made regarding the cathedral's rebuild, demolition, replacement or 'adaptation'. A plethora of opposing views means the wrangling could go on for years.

◎ Other Suburbs

Riccarton House & Bush   HISTORIC BUILDING
(Map p135; www.riccartonhouse.co.nz; 16 Kahu Rd, Riccarton) **FREE** Historic Riccarton House (1856) sits proudly amid 12 hectares of pretty parkland and forest beside the Avon River, and hosts the popular Christchurch Farmers' Market (p147) on Saturdays. Guided tours of the house run from 2pm Sunday to Friday (adult/child $18/5).

Even more venerable is the small patch of predator-free bush behind the cottage. Enclosed by a vermin-proof fence, this is the last stand of kahikatea floodplain forest in Canterbury.

Kahikatea is NZ's tallest native tree, growing to heights of 60m; the tallest trees here are a mere 30m and around 300 to 600 years old. A short loop track heads through the heart of the forest.

Orana Wildlife Park   ZOO
(☑03-359 7109; www.oranawildlifepark.co.nz; McLeans Island Rd, McLeans Island; adult/child $34.50/9.50; ☉10am-5pm) Orana describes itself as an 'open range zoo' and you'll know what they mean if you opt to jump in the cage for the lion encounter (an additional $45). There's an excellent, walk-through native-bird aviary, a nocturnal kiwi house, and a reptile exhibit featuring tuatara. Most of the 80-hectare grounds are devoted to Africana, including rhino, giraffe, zebras, cheetahs and even gorillas.

Willowbank Wildlife Reserve   ZOO
(☑03-359 6226; www.willowbank.co.nz; 60 Hussey Rd, Northwood; adult/child $28/11; ☉9.30am-7pm Oct-Apr, to 5pm May-Sep) 🏊 About 10km north of the central city, Willowbank focuses on native NZ critters (including kiwi), heritage farmyard animals and hands-on enclosures with wallabies, deer and lemurs. There's also a recreated Māori village, the setting for the evening Ko Tane (p143).

International Antarctic Centre   MUSEUM
(☑0508 736 4846; www.iceberg.co.nz; 38 Orchard Rd, Christchurch Airport; adult/child $39/19; ☉9am-5.30pm) Part of a huge complex built for the administration of the NZ, US and Italian Antarctic programs, this centre gives visitors the opportunity to see penguins and learn about the icy continent. Attractions include the Antarctic Storm chamber, where you can get a taste of -18°C wind chill.

A free shuttle departs from outside the Canterbury Museum (p137) on the hour from 10am to 4pm, and from the Antarctic Centre on the half-hour.

The 'Xtreme Pass' (adult/child $59/29) includes the '4D theatre' (a 3D film with moving seats and a water spray) and rides on a Hägglund all-terrain amphibious Antarctic vehicle. An optional extra is the Penguin Backstage Pass (adult/child $25/15), which allows visitors behind the scenes of the Penguin Encounter.

🏃 Activities
Boating
Antigua Boat Sheds   BOATING, KAYAKING
(Map p138; ☑03-366 6768; www.boatsheds.co.nz; 2 Cambridge Tce; ☉9am-5pm) Dating from 1882, the photogenic green-and-white Antigua Boat Sheds hires out rowing boats ($35), kayaks ($12), Canadian canoes ($35) and bikes (adult/child $10/5); all prices are per hour. There's also a good cafe.

Punting on the Avon   BOATING
(Map p138; www.punting.co.nz; 2 Cambridge Tce; adult/child $28/20; ☉9am-6pm Oct-Mar, 10am-4pm Apr-Sep) 🏊 The Antigua Boat Sheds are the starting point for half-hour punting trips through the Botanic Gardens. Relax in a flat-bottomed boat while a strapping lad in Edwardian clobber with a long pole does all the work. An alternative trip departs from the Worcester St Bridge and punts through the city's regenerating centre.

CHRISTCHURCH IN...
Two Days
After breakfast at **Supreme Supreme** (p146), take some time to walk around the ruined and regenerating city centre, visit **Quake City** (p137) and wander through **Cathedral Square** (p137). Make your way to **Christchurch Art Gallery** (p136) then gather picnic supplies at **Canterbury Cheesemongers** (p147). After lunch, visit the excellent **Canterbury Museum** (p137) and take a walk through the lovely **Botanic Gardens** (p136). That evening, explore the Victoria St restaurant strip or head to **Smash Palace** (p148) for beer and a burger amid the hipster-bogans.

Start day two at the **Addington Coffee Co-op** (p147) and then head up Mt Cavendish on the gondola for views and a walk at the top. Continue on to Lyttelton for lunch before returning through the tunnel and around to Sumner for a late-afternoon swim or stroll, then stop for dinner and catch a flick at the **Hollywood Cinema** (Map p135; www.hollywoodcinema.co.nz; 28 Marriner St; adult/child $17/12).

Four Days
Follow the two-day itinerary, then head to Akaroa to explore its wildlife-rich harbour and walk its pretty streets, enjoying stupendous views on the way there and back again. On day four, visit **Orana Wildlife Park** (p141) and finish the day with shopping, beer and pizza at the **Tannery** (p149) in Woolston.

Swimming & Surfing

Despite having separate names for different sections, it's one solid stretch of sandy beach that spreads north from the estuary of the Avon and Heathcote rivers. Closest to the city centre is **New Brighton**, with a distinctive pier reaching 300m out to sea. On either side, **South New Brighton** and **North Beach** are quieter options. **Waimairi**, a little further north, is our personal pick.

The superstar is **Sumner**, 12km from the city centre on the south side of the estuary. Its beachy vibe, eateries and art-house cinema make it a satisfying place for a day trip.

Further east around the headland, isolated **Taylors Mistake** has the cleanest water of any Christchurch beach and some good surf breaks. Beginners should stick to Sumner or New Brighton.

Walking

The i-SITE provides information on walking tours as well as independent town and country options including the rewarding **Avon River Walk**, which takes in major city sights. At the time of writing a new map was due out detailing the popular **Port Hills** trails; you can also search www.ccc.govt.nz with the keywords 'Port Hills'.

For long-range city views, take the walkway from the **Sign of the Takahe** on Dyers Pass Rd. The various 'Sign of the...' places in this area were originally roadhouses built during the Depression as rest stops. This walk leads up to the **Sign of the Kiwi**, through Victoria Park and then along the view-filled Summit Rd to Scotts Reserve.

You can walk to Lyttelton on the **Bridle Path** (1½ hours), which starts at Heathcote Valley (take bus 28). The **Godley Head Walkway** (two hours return) begins at Taylors Mistake, crossing and recrossing Summit Rd, and offers beautiful views on a clear day.

Walks in Christchurch and throughout Canterbury are well detailed at www.christchurchnz.com.

Cycling

Being mostly flat and boasting more than 300km of cycle trails, Christchurch is a brilliant place to explore on two wheels. For evidence, look no further than the free *Christchurch City Cycle Guide* pamphlet or the city council's website (www.ccc.govt.nz). The i-SITE can advise on bicycle hire and guided tours.

There's some great off-road riding around the Port Hills; look out for the new trails map. Towards Banks Peninsula you'll find the best section of the Little River Trail (p153), one of New Zealand's Great Rides.

Vintage Peddler Bike Hire Co   BICYCLE RENTAL
(Map p138; ☑ 03-365 6530; www.thevintagepeddler.co.nz; 7/75 Peterborough St; per hour/day from $15/30) Take to two retro wheels on these funky vintage bicycles. Helmets, locks and local knowledge are all supplied.

City Cycle Hire   BICYCLE RENTAL
(☑ 03-377 5952; www.cyclehire-tours.co.nz; bike hire half-/full day from $25/35) Offers door-to-door delivery of on- and off-road city bikes and touring bikes. Will also meet you with a bike at the top of the gondola if you fancy a 16km descent ($70 including gondola ride; 1½ hours).

🎓 Courses

Bone Dude   COURSE
(Map p135; ☑ 03-385 4509; www.thebonedude.co.nz; 153 Marshland Rd, Shirley; from $60; ☉ 1-4pm Fri, 10am-1pm Sat) Creative types should consider booking a session with the Bone Dude, who'll show you how to carve your own bone pendant (allow three hours). Sessions are limited to eight participants, so book ahead.

CHRISTCHURCH FOR CHILDREN

There's no shortage of kid-friendly sights and activities in Christchurch. If family fun is a priority, consider planning your travels around NZ's biggest children's festival, **KidsFest** (p144). It's held every July and is chock-full of shows, workshops and parties. The annual **World Buskers Festival** (p144) is also bound to be a hit.

For picnics and open-air frolicking, visit the **Botanic Gardens** (p136); there's a playground beside the cafe, and little kids will love riding on the Caterpillar train. Extend your nature-based experience with a wildlife encounter at **Orana Wildlife Park** (p141) or the **Willowbank Wildlife Reserve** (p141), or get them burning off excess energy in a rowing boat or kayak from the **Antigua Boat Sheds** (p141). Fun can be stealthily combined with education at the **International Antarctic Centre** (p141) and the Discovery Centre at **Canterbury Museum** (p137).

If the weather's good, hit the beaches at Sumner or New Brighton.

MĀORI NZ: CHRISTCHURCH & CANTERBURY

Only 14% of NZ's Māori live on the South Island: of those, half live in Canterbury. The first major tribe to become established here were Waitaha, who were subsequently conquered and assimilated into the Ngāti Māmoe tribe in the 16th century. In the following century, they in turn were conquered and subsumed by Ngāi Tahu (www.ngaitahu.iwi. nz), a tribe that has its origins in the East Coast of the North Island.

In 1848 most of Canterbury was sold to the crown under an agreement which stipulated that an area of 10 acres per person would be reserved for the tribe; less than half of that actually was. With so little land left to them, Ngāi Tahu were no longer able to be self-sufficient and suffered great financial hardship. It wasn't until 1997 that this injustice was addressed, with the tribe receiving an apology from the crown and a settlement valued at $170 million. Part of the deal was the official inclusion of the Māori name for the most spiritually significant part of the tribe's ancestral land: Aoraki/Mt Cook.

Today, Ngāi Tahu is considered to be one of Māoridom's great success stories, with a reputation for good financial management, sound cultural advice and a portfolio including property, forestry, fisheries and many high-profile tourism operations.

There are many ways to engage in Māori culture in Canterbury. Artefacts can be seen at **Canterbury Museum** (p137), **Akaroa Museum** (p155), **Okains Bay Māori & Colonial Museum** (p152) and **South Canterbury Museum** (p168). **Willowbank Wildlife Reserve** (p141) has a replica Māori village and an evening cultural show. Further south in Timaru, the **Te Ana Māori Rock Art Centre** (p168) has interactive displays and arranges tours to see centuries-old work in situ.

⌖ Tours

★ Tram TRAM
(Map p138; ☑03-377 4790; www.tram.co.nz; adult/child $20/free; ☺9am-6pm Oct-Mar, 10am-5pm Apr-Sep) Excellent driver commentary makes this so much more than a tram ride. The beautifully restored old dears trundle around a 17-stop loop, leaving every 15 minutes, taking in a host of city highlights including Cathedral Sq and New Regent St. The full circuit takes just under an hour, and you can hop-on and hop-off all day.

TranzAlpine TRAIN TOUR
(☑0800 872 467, 03-341 2588; www.kiwirailscenic. co.nz) The TranzAlpine is one of the world's great train journeys, traversing the Southern Alps between Christchurch and Greymouth, from the Pacific Ocean to the Tasman Sea, passing through Arthur's Pass National Park. En route is a sequence of dramatic landscapes, from the flat, alluvial Canterbury Plains to narrow alpine gorges, an 8.5km tunnel, beech-forested river valleys, and a lake fringed with cabbage trees.

The 4½-hour journey is unforgettable, even in bad weather (if it's raining on one coast, it's probably fine on the other). Departs Christchurch at 8.15am, Greymouth at 1.45pm.

Christchurch Free Tours WALKING TOUR
(Map p138; www.freetours.co.nz; Cathedral Sq; ☺11am) FREE Yes, a free tour. Just turn up

at the *Chalice* sculpture in Cathedral Sq and look for the red-T-shirted person. If you enjoy your two-hour amble, tip your guide. Nice!

Red Bus Rebuild Tour BUS TOUR
(☑0800 500 929; www.redbus.co.nz; adult/child $35/17) Commentaries focus on the past, present and future of earthquake-damaged sites in the city centre. Tours take 90 minutes and include video footage of the old streetscapes.

Hassle Free Tours BUS TOUR
(☑03-385 5775; www.hasslefree.co.nz) Explore Christchurch on an open-top double-decker bus (adult/child $35/19). Regional options include a 4WD alpine safari, Kaikoura whale-watching, and visiting the location of Edoras from the *Lord of the Rings* trilogy.

Christchurch Bike & Walking Tours CYCLING, WALKING
(Map p138; ☑0800 733 257; www.chchbiketours. co.nz; 2 Cambridge Tce) See the city's highlights on an informative, two-hour bicycle tour (adult/child $50/30) or two-hour walking tour (adult/child $35/20). Tours leave from the Antigua Boat Sheds at 10am and 2pm daily; bookings are essential.

Ko Tane CULTURAL TOUR
(www.kotane.co.nz; 60 Hussey Rd, Northwood; adult/child $135/68; ☺5.30pm) Rousing Māori cultural performance by members of the

Ngāi Tahu tribe comprising a *powhiri* (welcome), the famous *haka*, a buffet *hangi* (earth-oven) meal, and plenty of *waiata ā ringa* (singing and dancing). At Willowbank Wildlife Reserve (p141).

Christchurch Sightseeing Tours BUS TOUR
(☑03-377 5300; www.christchurchtours.co.nz; tours from $75) City tours, plus further-afield options to Akaroa, Hanmer Springs and the Waipara wine region.

Garden City Helicopters SCENIC FLIGHT
(☑03-358 4360; www.helicopters.net.nz; 515 Memorial Ave; 20min $199) Flights above the city and Lyttelton let you observe the impact of the earthquake and the rebuilding efforts.

Discovery Tours BUS TOUR
(☑0800 372 879; www.discoverytravel.co.nz; tours from $155) Excursions to Akaroa, Aoraki/Mt Cook, Hanmer Springs, Kaikoura and the Waipara Valley wine region. The Arthur's Pass tour ($315) packs the *TranzAlpine* train, jetboating and a farm tour into one action-packed day.

⭐ Festivals & Events

World Buskers Festival PERFORMING ARTS
(www.worldbuskersfestival.com; ☉Jan) National and international talent entertains passers-by for 10 days in mid-January. Check the website for locations – and don't forget to throw money in the hat.

Festival of Flowers FLORAL
(www.festivalofflowers.co.nz; ☉Feb) A three-week blooming spectacle around Christchurch's heritage gardens.

KidsFest CHILDREN
(www.kidsfest.org.nz; ☉Jul) If family fun is a priority, consider planning your travels around NZ's biggest children's festival, KidsFest. It's chock-full of shows, workshops and parties.

Christchurch Arts Festival PERFORMING ARTS
(www.artsfestival.co.nz; ☉mid-Aug–mid-Sep) Month-long biennial (2017, 2019 etc) arts extravaganza, celebrating music, theatre and dance.

NZ Cup & Show Week SPORTS
(www.nzcupandshow.co.nz; ☉Nov) Various horse races, fashion shows, fireworks and the centrepiece A&P Show, where the country comes to town. Held over a week.

Garden City SummerTimes MUSIC
(www.summertimes.co.nz; ☉Dec-Mar) Say g'day to summer at a huge array of outdoor events.

🛏 Sleeping

🛏 City Centre

Chester Street Backpackers HOSTEL $
(Map p138; ☑03-377 1897; www.chesterst.co.nz; 148 Chester St E; dm/d $34/74; @🖥) This relaxed wooden villa is painted in bright colours and has a sunny front room for reading. Vinnie the house cat is a regular guest at hostel barbecues in the peaceful wee garden.

YHA Christchurch HOSTEL $
(Map p138; ☑03-379 9536; www.yha.co.nz; 36 Hereford St; dm/d from $40/100; @🖥) Smart, well-run 100-plus-bed hostel conveniently located near the museum and botanical gardens. Dorms and doubles include many with en suite bathrooms. If it's full here, Christchurch's other YHA is one street away (5 Worcester Blvd).

Dorset House Backpackers HOSTEL $
(Map p138; ☑03-366 8268; www.dorset.co.nz; 1 Dorset St; dm $38, d $99-119; P@🖥) 🏃 Built in 1871, this tranquil wooden villa has a sunny deck, a large regal lounge with a pool table, and beds instead of bunks. It's a short stroll to Hagley Park.

Foley Towers HOSTEL $
(Map p138; ☑03-366 9720; www.backpack.co.nz/foley.html; 208 Kilmore St; dm $31-34, d with/without bathroom $80/74; P@🖥) Sheltered by well-established trees, Foley Towers provides a wide range of well-maintained rooms and dorms encircling quiet garden-trimmed courtyards. Friendly, helpful staff will provide the latest local info.

Pomeroy's on Kilmore B&B $$
(Map p138; ☑03-374 3532; www.pomeroysonkilmore.co.nz; 282 Kilmore St; r $145-195; P🖥) Even if this cute wooden house wasn't the sister and neighbour of Christchurch's best craft-beer pub, it would still be one of our favourites. Three of the five elegantly furnished, en suite rooms open on to a sunny garden. Rates include breakfast at Little Pom's (p148) cafe.

Focus Motel MOTEL $$
(Map p138; ☑03-943 0800; www.focusmotel.com; 344 Durham St N; r $160-250; P🖥) Sleek and centrally located, this friendly motel offers studio and one-bedroom units with big-screen TVs, iPod docks, kitchenettes and super-modern decor. There's a guest barbecue and laundry, and pillow-top chocolates sweeten the deal.

BreakFree on Cashel HOTEL **$$**
(Map p138; ☑ 03-360 1064; www.breakfreecashel.co.nz; 165 Cashel St; d $90-220; ⓟ🅢) ☝ This new, large hotel in the heart of the city's rejuvenating CBD has options to suit all budgets. Rooms are compact and sharply designed, with high-tech features such as smart TVs and sci-fi pod bathrooms.

CentrePoint on Colombo MOTEL **$$**
(Map p138; ☑ 03-377 0859; www.centrepointoncolombo.co.nz; 859 Colombo St; r/apt from $165/195; ⓟ🅢) The friendly Kiwi-Japanese management has imbued this centrally located motel with style and comfort. Little extras such as stereos, blackout curtains and spa baths (in the deluxe rooms) take it to the next level.

★George HOTEL **$$$**
(Map p138; ☑ 03-379 4560; www.thegeorge.com; 50 Park Tce; r $356-379, ste $574-761; ⓟ@🅢) ☝ The George has 53 handsomely decorated rooms within a defiantly 1970s-looking building on the fringe of Hagley Park. Discreet staff attend to every whim, and ritzy features include huge TVs, luxury toiletries, glossy magazines and two highly rated in-house restaurants – Pescatore and 50 Bistro.

Classic Villa B&B **$$$**
(Map p138; ☑ 03-377 7905; www.theclassicvilla.co.nz; 17 Worcester Blvd; s $199, d $299-409, ste $499; ⓟ🅢) ☝ Pretty in pink, this 1897 house is one of Christchurch's most elegant accommodation options. Rooms are trimmed with antiques and Turkish rugs, and the Mediterranean-style breakfast is a shared social occasion.

Eliza's Manor HOTEL **$$$**
(Map p138; ☑ 03-366 8584, 0800 366 859; www.elizas.co.nz; 82 Bealey Ave; r $245-345; ⓟ🅢) ☝ An infestation of teddy bears has done little to dint the heritage appeal of this large 1861 mansion. Wisteria curls around weatherboards, while inside the rooms are spacious and frilly.

Heritage Christchurch HOTEL **$$$**
(Map p138; ☑ 03-983 4800; www.heritagehotels.co.nz; 28-30 Cathedral Sq; ste $235-440; 🅢) ☝ Standing grandly on Cathedral Sq while all around it is in ruins, the 1909 Old Government Building owes its survival to a thorough strengthening when it was converted to a hotel in the 1990s. After a three-year postearthquake restoration its spacious suites are more elegant than ever. All have full kitchens.

🛏 Merivale

Merivale Manor MOTEL **$$**
(Map p135; ☑ 03-355 7731; www.merivalemanor.co.nz; 122 Papanui Rd; d $165-229; ⓟ🅢) A gracious 19th-century Victorian mansion is the hub of this elegant motel, with units both in the main house and in the more typically motel-style blocks lining the drive. Accommodation ranges from studios to two-bedroom apartments, and there's a bonus complimentary continental breakfast.

🛏 Fendalton

Fendalton House B&B **$$**
(Map p135; ☑ 03-343 1661; www.fendaltonhouse.co.nz; 28a Kotare St; r $185; ⓟ⊖🅢) There's only one guest room available at this friendly, homestay-style B&B amid the pleasant streets of leafy Fendalton. Rates include a cooked breakfast and free wi-fi.

🛏 Riccarton

Amber Kiwi Holiday Park HOLIDAY PARK **$**
(☑ 03-348 3327, 0800 348 308; www.amberpark.co.nz; 308 Blenheim Rd, Riccarton; sites $42-50, units $82-200; @🅢) Blooming lovely gardens and close proximity to the city centre make this urban holiday park a great option for campervaners and tenters. Tidy cabins and more-spacious motel units are also available.

Lorenzo Motor Inn MOTEL **$$**
(Map p138; ☑ 03-348 8074; www.lorenzomotorlodge.co.nz; 36 Riccarton Rd; units $169-239; ⓟ🅢) There's a Mediterranean vibe to this trim two-storey motel – the best of many on the busy Riccarton Rd strip. Units range from studio to two-bedroom apartments; some have spa baths and little balconies.

Roma on Riccarton MOTEL **$$**
(Map p138; ☑ 03-341 2100; www.romaonriccarton.co.nz; 38 Riccarton Rd; d $158-235; ⓟ🅢) It may be the mirror image of neighbouring Lorenzo Motor Inn, but they are completely separate businesses. Like its twin, the units are all thoroughly modern, ranging from studios to two-bedroom apartments.

🛏 Addington

★Jailhouse HOSTEL **$**
(Map p138; ☑ 03-982 7777, 0800 524 546; www.jail.co.nz; 338 Lincoln Rd, Addington; dm $35-38, tw/d $90/95; @🅢) From 1874 to 1999 this was Addington Prison; it's now one of

Christchurch's most appealing and friendly hostels. Private rooms are a bit on the small side – they don't call them cells for nothing. Bikes for hire (half-day/full day $10/15).

Sumner

Le Petit Hotel
B&B $$

(Map p135; ☑03-326 6675; www.lepetithotel. co.nz; 16 Marriner St, Sumner; d $159-175; [P] [@] [🖥]) Relaxed coffee-and-croissant breakfasts, friendly owners, Francophilic furnishings and close proximity to Sumner beach make this a definite 'oui' from us. Get in early and request an upstairs room with a view.

Other Suburbs

Haka Lodge
HOSTEL $

(Map p135; ☑03-980 4252; www.hakalodge.com; 518 Linwood Ave, Woolston; dm/d/apt $33/84/170; [🖥]) ⚑ Sprawled across three floors of a modern suburban house, Haka Lodge is one of Christchurch's newest hostels. Bunk-free dorms and rooms are clean and colourful. Bonuses include a comfy lounge and bird-filled garden with barbecue.

Old Countryhouse
HOSTEL $

(Map p135; ☑03-381 5504; www.oldcountry housenz.com; 437 Gloucester St, Linwood; dm $42-45, d with/without bathroom $145/120; [P] [@] [🖥]) Spread between three separate villas, 2km east of Cathedral Sq, this chilled-out hostel has handmade wooden furniture, a reading lounge and a lovely garden with native ferns and lavender. A spa pool and sauna heat things up.

Christchurch Top 10
HOLIDAY PARK $

(Map p135; ☑03-352 9176; www.christchurch top10.co.nz; 39 Meadow St, Papanui; sites $35-52, units with/without bathroom from $94/76; [P] [@] [🖥] [🏊]) ⚑ Family owned and operated for nearly 50 years, this large holiday park has a wide range of accommodation along with various campervan nooks and grassy tent sites. It has a raft of facilities and bike hire, too. Of particular interest is travel advice and bookings provided by enthusiastic staff.

Airport Gateway
MOTEL $$

(☑03-358 7093; www.airportgateway.co.nz; 45 Roydvale Ave, Burnside; d $140-199; [P] [@] [🖥]) Handy for those early flights, this large motel has a variety of rooms with good facilities. Airport transfer is available 24-hours a day, at no extra charge. The newer block is very comfortable and good value.

 Eating

While many cafes and restaurants still occupy the suburban premises they were forced into after the earthquakes – particularly around Addington, Riccarton, Merivale and Sumner – many new places are springing up in the midst of the CBD rebuild. Expect plenty of high-quality, exciting surprises.

City Centre

★Supreme Supreme
CAFE $

(Map p138; ☑03-365 0445; www.supreme supreme.co.nz; 10 Welles St; breakfast $7-18, lunch $10-20; ⊙7am-4pm Mon-Fri, 8am-4pm Sat & Sun; [🚲]) With so much to love, where to start? Perhaps with a kimchi Bloody Mary, a chocolate-fish milkshake, or maybe just an exceptional espresso alongside ancient-grain muesli or pulled corn-beef hash. One of NZ's original and best coffee roasters comes to the party with a right-now cafe of splendid style, form and function.

Caffeine Laboratory
CAFE $

(Map p138; www.caffeinelab.co.nz; 1 New Regent St; snacks $4-12, meals $14-26; ⊙8am-late Wed-Sat, to 4pm Tue & Sun; [🚲]) The small-scale, corner C-lab is hooked on coffee, but also cooks up addictive deliciousness such as house-smoked salmon, smashed broad beans, and burgers with homemade patties. In the evening, eschew the espresso for craft beer and tapas.

Dimitris
GREEK $

(Map p138; ☑03-377 7110; Re:START Mall, Cashel St; souvlaki $11-16; ⊙11am-4pm; [🚲]) Amid a cluster of food trucks in the Re:START Mall, Dimitris rules the roost with souvlaki full of tasty chicken, lamb or falafel, wrapped up with heaps of fresh salad in a light, puffy bread. Sooooo good.

Vic's Cafe
CAFE $

(Map p138; www.vics.co.nz; 132 Victoria St; mains $10-22; ⊙7.30am-4.30pm; [🚲]) Pop in for a robust breakfast on the big shared tables or linger over lunch on the front terrace. Otherwise grab baked goodies and still-warm artisanal bread for a DIY riverside picnic.

Black Betty
CAFE $

(Map p138; ☑03-365 8522; www.blackbetty. co.nz; 165 Madras St; mains $9-20; ⊙8am-4pm; [🖥]) Infused with aromas from Switch Espresso's roastery, Black Betty's industrial-chic warehouse is a popular destination for students from the nearby college. Attractions include avocado smash on the all-day breakfast menu, excellent counter food, fine wine and craft beer.

C1 Espresso
CAFE **$**

(Map p138; www.c1espresso.co.nz; 185 High St; mains $10-21; ⊙7am-10pm; 🛜) 🥐 C1 sits pretty in a grand former post office that somehow escaped the cataclysm. Recycled materials fill the interior (Victorian oak panelling, bulbous 1970s light fixtures) and tables spill onto a little square. Eggy brekkies and bagels are available all day, while sliders slip onto the afternoon/evening menu.

Canterbury Cheesemongers
DELI **$**

(Map p138; ✓ 03-379 0075; www.cheesemongers. co.nz; rear, 301 Montreal St; ⊙9am-5pm Tue-Fri, to 4pm Sat) Pop in to gather up artisanal cheese, bread and accompaniments such as pickles and smoked salmon, then get your espresso to go and head down the road to the Botanic Gardens for your picnic.

Fiddlesticks
MODERN NZ **$$**

(Map p138; ✓ 03-365 0533; www.fiddlesticksbar. co.nz; 48 Worcester Blvd; lunch $25-40, dinner $24-48; ⊙8am-late Mon-Fri, 9am-late Sat & Sun) Sidle into slick Fiddlesticks and seat yourself in either the more formal dining room or the glassed-in patio attached to the curvy cocktail bar. Food ranges from soups and beautifully presented salads to fluffy gnocchi and Angus steaks.

Lotus Heart
VEGETARIAN **$$**

(Map p138; ✓ 03-377 2727; www.thelotusheart.co.nz; 363 St Asaph St; mains $13-25; ⊙7.30am-3pm Tue-Sun & 5-9pm Fri & Sat; 🖍) 🥐 Run by students of Sri Chinmoy, this vegetarian eatery serves curry, pizza, wraps, burgers and freshly squeezed organic juices. Organic, vegan and gluten-free options abound, and there's an interesting gift and music shop on-site.

★ Twenty Seven Steps
MODERN NZ **$$$**

(Map p138; ✓ 03-366 2727; www.twentyseven steps.co.nz; 16 New Regent St; mains $30-40; ⊙5pm-late Tue-Sat) Upstairs on the Edwardian New Regent St strip, the pared-back interior of this elegant restaurant puts the focus firmly on a menu showcasing local produce. Mainstays include modern renditions of lamb, beef, venison and seafood, but there's also outstanding risotto and desserts such as caramelised lemon tart.

Saggio di Vino
EUROPEAN **$$$**

(Map p138; ✓ 03-379 4006; www.saggiodivino. co.nz; 179 Victoria St; mains $40-43; ⊙5pm-late) Elegant Italo-French restaurant that's up there with Christchurch's best. Expect delicious, modern takes on terrine, rack of lamb and *Café de Paris* steak, plus a well-laden cheese trolley to finish you off. The wine list makes long, interesting reading.

King of Snake
ASIAN **$$$**

(Map p138; ✓ 03-365 7363; www.kingofsnake. co.nz; 145 Victoria St; mains $27-43; ⊙11am-late Mon-Fri, 4pm-late Sat & Sun) Dark wood, gold tiles and purple skull-patterned wallpaper fill this hip restaurant and cocktail bar with just the right amount of sinister opulence. The exciting menu gainfully plunders the cuisines of Asia – from India to Korea – to delicious, if pricey, effect.

🍴 Riccarton

Christchurch Farmers Market
MARKET **$**

(Map p135; www.christchurchfarmersmarket.co.nz; 16 Kahu Rd, Riccarton; ⊙9am-1pm Sat) Held in the pretty grounds of Riccarton House (p140), this excellent farmers market offers a tasty array of organic fruit and vegies, South Island cheeses and salmon, local craft beer and ethnic treats.

🍴 Addington

Addington Coffee Co-op
CAFE **$**

(Map p138; ✓ 03-943 1662; www.addingtoncoffee. org.nz; 297 Lincoln Rd; meals $8-21; ⊙7.30am-4pm Mon-Fri, 9am-4pm Sat & Sun; 🛜🖍) You will find one of Christchurch's biggest and best cafes packed to the rafters most days. A compact shop selling fair-trade gifts jostles for attention with delicious cakes, gourmet pies and the legendary house breakfasts (until 2pm). An on-site launderette completes the deal for busy travellers.

Mosaic by Simo
MOROCCAN **$**

(Map p138; www.mosaicbysimo.co.nz; 300 Lincoln Rd, Addington; tapas & mains $8-20; ⊙9am-9pm Mon-Sat; 🖍) This deli-cafe is popular for its takeaway *bocadillos* (grilled wraps filled with a huge selection of Middle Eastern– and African-inspired fillings, sauces and toppings). Other tasty offerings include super-generous platters, merguez sausages and tagines.

🍴 Sumner

Cornershop Bistro
FRENCH **$$**

(Map p135; ✓ 03-326 6720; www.cornershop bistro.co.nz; 32 Nayland St, Sumner; lunch $17-35, dinner $29-38; ⊙10am-3pm Fri-Sun, 5.30pm-10pm Wed-Sun) Classic dishes such as *coq au vin* are expertly executed at this superior French-style bistro which never forgets it's in a relaxed beachside suburb. Spend longer than you planned to lingering over brunch.

✖ Other Suburbs

★ Bodhi Tree BURMESE $$
(Map p135; ☑ 03-377 6808; www.bodhitree.co.nz; 399 Ilam Rd, Bryndwr; dishes $13-21; ☺ 6-10pm Tue-Sat;) Bodhi Tree has been wowing locals with the nuanced flavours of Burmese cuisine for more than a decade. Its feel-good food comes in sharing-sized dishes and sings with zing. Standouts include *le pet thoke* (pickled tea-leaf salad) and *ameyda nut* (slow-cooked beef curry).

Kinji JAPANESE $$
(Map p135; ☑ 03-359 4697; www.kinjirestaurant. com; 279b Greers Rd, Bishopdale; mains $16-24; ☺ 5.30-10pm Mon-Sat) Despite being hidden away in suburbia this acclaimed Japanese restaurant has a loyal following, so it's wise to book. Tuck into the likes of sashimi, grilled ginger squid and venison tataki, but save room for the green tea tiramisu, a surprising highlight.

Under the Red Verandah CAFE $$
(Map p135; www.utrv.co.nz; 29 Tancred St, Linwood; mains $14-25; ☺ 7.30am-4pm Mon-Fri, 8.30am-4pm Sat & Sun;) This lucky suburban backstreet boasts a cafe beloved by locals and travellers alike. Take a seat under said veranda and tuck into baked goodies, oaty pancakes, homemade pies and eggs multiple ways.

Burgers & Beers Inc BURGERS $$
(Map p138; www.burgersandbeersinc.co.nz; 355 Colombo St, Sydenham; burgers $14-18; ☺ 11am-late) Quirkily named gourmet burgers – try the Woolly Sahara Sand Hopper (Moroccan-spiced lamb with lemon yogurt) or the Shagged Stag (venison with tamarillo and plum chutney) – and an ever-changing selection of Kiwi craft beers give you reason to head south.

🍷 Drinking & Nightlife

🍸 City Centre

★ Smash Palace BAR
(Map p138; ☑ 03-366 5369; www.thesmashpalace. co.nz; 172 High St; ☺ 4pm-late Mon-Fri, 12pm-late Sat & Sun) Epitomising the spirit of transience, tenacity and number-eight wire that Christchurch is now known for, this deliberately downcycled and ramshackle beer garden is an intoxicating mix of grease-monkey garage, trailer-trash park, and proto-hipster hang-out complete with a psychedelic school bus, edible garden and blooming roses. There's craft beer, chips and cereal, and burgers made from scratch ($11 to $15).

★ Pomeroy's Old Brewery Inn PUB
(Map p138; ☑ 03-365 1523; www.pomspub.co.nz; 292 Kilmore St; ☺ 3-11pm Tue-Thu, noon-11pm Fri-Sun) For fans of great beer, there's no better place than Pomeroy's for supping a drop or two alongside a plate of proper pork crackling. Among this British-style pub's many other endearing features are regular live music, a snug, sunny courtyard and Victoria's Kitchen, serving comforting pub food (mains $24 to $30). The newest addition, pretty Little Pom's cafe, serves super-fine fare (meals $14 to $22) until mid-afternoon.

Dux Central BAR
(Map p138; ☑ 03-943 7830; www.duxcentral.co.nz; 6 Poplar St; ☺ 11am-late) Pumping a whole lot of heart back into the flattened High St precinct, the epic new Dux comprises a brew bar serving its own and other crafty drops, the Emerald Room wine bar, Upper Dux restaurant and the Poplar Social Club cocktail bar, all within the confines of a lovingly restored old building.

Boo Radley's BAR
(Map p138; ☑ 03-366 9906; www.booradleys.co.nz; 98 Victoria St; ☺ 4pm-late) Above Tequila Mockingbird, this companion bar is decked out in fine fashion: Southern style with bourbons galore and dude food such as sliders, fried chicken and mac-and-cheese croquettes (snacks $8 to $20). An intimate, speakeasy vibe makes Boo's an alluring late-night hang-out.

Tequila Mockingbird BAR
(Map p138; www.tequilamockingbird.co.nz; 98 Victoria St; shared plates $8-30; ☺ 5pm-late Mon-Fri, 9.30am-late Sat & Sun) If the awesome name's not enough to lure you through the door of this upmarket Latin bar-restaurant, then perhaps the Caribbean-inflected cocktails, nifty decor and late-night DJs will. The food's excellent, too.

Revival BAR
(Map p138; ☑ 03-379 9559; www.revivalbar. co.nz; 92-96 Victoria St; ☺ 3pm-late Mon-Thu, 12pm-late Fri-Sun) Revival is the hippest of Christchurch's shipping container bars. Expect regular DJs and a funky lounge area dotted with a quirky collection of automotive rear ends and vintage steamer trunks.

🍸 Other Suburbs

The Brewery CRAFT BEER
(Map p135; www.casselsbrewery.co.nz; 3 Garlands Rd, Woolston; ☺ 7am-late) An essential destination for beer-loving travellers, the Cassels & Sons' brewery crafts beers using a wood-

fired brew kettle, resulting in big, bold ales. Tasting trays are available for the curious and the indecisive, live bands perform regularly, and the food – including wood-fired pizzas ($20 to $24) – is top-notch, too.

☆ Entertainment

For live music and club listings, see www.undertheradar.co.nz, www.mukuna.co.nz and www.christchurchmusic.org.nz. Also look out for the *Groove Guide* magazine in cafes.

Isaac Theatre Royal   THEATRE
(Map p138; ☑ 03-366 6326; www.isaactheatreroyal.co.nz; 145 Gloucester St) This century-old dear survived the quakes and emerged restored to full glory in 2014. Its heritage features are a decided bonus for those venturing in for shows ranging from opera and ballet to concerts of virtually every persuasion.

Alice Cinematheque   CINEMA
(Map p138; ☑ 03-365 0615; www.aliceinvideoland.co.nz; 209 Tuam St; adult/child $17/12) This small Egyptian-themed art-house cinema can be found within the long-standing and excellent Alice In Videoland speciality video and DVD shop.

darkroom   LIVE MUSIC
(Map p138; www.darkroom.bar; 336 St Asaph St; ⊙7pm-late Wed-Sun) A hip combination of live-music venue and bar, darkroom has lots of Kiwi beers and great cocktails. Live gigs are frequent – and frequently free.

Court Theatre   THEATRE
(Map p138; ☑ 03-963 0870; www.courttheatre.org.nz; Bernard St, Addington) Christchurch's original Court Theatre was an integral part of the city's Arts Centre, but it was forced to relocate to this warehouse after the earthquakes. The new premises are much more spacious; it's a great venue to see popular international plays and works by NZ playwrights.

🛍 Shopping

★ Tannery   SHOPPING CENTRE
(Map p135; www.thetannery.co.nz; 3 Garlands Rd, Woolston; ⊙10am-5pm Mon-Wed, Fri & Sat, to 8pm Thu) In a city mourning the loss of its heritage, this postearthquake conversion of a 19th-century tannery couldn't be more welcome. The Victorian buildings have been jooshed up in period style, and filled with boutique shops selling everything from books to fashion to surfboards. Don't miss the woolly hats. Nonshoppers can slink off to The Brewery (p148) or catch a movie in the brand-new cinemas.

Re:START Mall   MALL
(Map p138; www.restart.org.nz; Cashel St; ⊙10am-5pm; 🛜) This labyrinth of shipping containers was the first retail 'mall' to reopen in the CBD postquakes. With cafes, food trucks, shops and people-watching opportunities, it remains a pleasant place to hang out, particularly on a sunny day. At the time of writing, there were no plans for the Re:START to disappear any time soon.

New Regent St   MALL
(Map p138; www.newregentstreet.co.nz) A forerunner to the modern mall, this pretty little stretch of pastel Spanish Mission–style shops was described as NZ's most beautiful street when it was completed in 1932. Fully restored postearthquake, it's once again a delightful place to stroll and peruse the tiny galleries, gift shops and cafes.

Ballantynes   DEPARTMENT STORE
(Map p138; www.ballantynes.com; cnr Colombo & Cashel Sts; ⊙9am-5pm) A venerable Christchurch department store selling men's and women's fashions, cosmetics, travel goods and speciality NZ gifts. Fashionistas should check out the Contemporary Lounge upstairs.

Colombo Mall   MALL
(Map p138; www.thecolombo.co.nz; 363 Colombo St; ⊙ 9am-5.30pm Mon-Sat, 10am-5pm Sun) Within walking distance of the CBD, this neat little mall sports interesting, independent shops with an emphasis on gorgeous and groovy, plus respectable food outlets proffering dumplings, French fancies and picnic supplies.

ℹ Information

EMERGENCY & IMPORTANT NUMBERS

Ambulance, fire service & police (111)

CERA (www.cera.govt.nz) The Canterbury Earthquake Recovery Authority has the lowdown on rebuild plans and status updates.

Christchurch City Council (www.ccc.govt.nz) The city council's official website.

MEDICAL SERVICES

24-Hour Surgery (☑ 03-365 7777; www.24hoursurgery.co.nz; cnr Bealey Ave & Colombo St) No appointment necessary.

Christchurch Hospital (☑ 03-364 0640, emergency dept 03-364 0270; www.cdhb.govt.nz; 2 Riccarton Ave) Has a 24-hour emergency department.

Urgent Pharmacy (☑ 03-366 4439; cnr Bealey Ave & Colombo St; ⊙6-11pm Mon-Fri, 9am-11pm Sat & Sun) Located beside the 24 Hour Surgery.

TOURIST INFORMATION

Christchurch Airport i-SITE (☑ 03-353 7774; www.christchurchnz.com; ☺8am-6pm)

Christchurch DOC Visitor Centre (Map p138; ☑ 03-379 4082; www.doc.govt.nz; Cashel St, Re:START Mall; ☺10am-5pm) Offers country-wide information and Great Walk bookings. A change in premises was on the cards at the time of writing; ring or check the website for dates.

Christchurch i-SITE (Map p138; ☑ 03-379 9629; www.christchurchnz.com; Botanic Gardens, Rolleston Ave; ☺8.30am-5pm, extended hours summer) This ever-helpful and eternally busy i-SITE also now has an outpost in the Re:START Mall, open daily from November to March.

Visitor Kiosk (Map p138; ☑ 03-379 9629; www.christchurchnz.com; Cashel Mall, Re:START Mall; ☺8.30am-5pm Nov-Apr) Outpost of the ever-helpful and eternally busy **i-SITE** (p150) located in the Botanic Gardens.

ⓘ Getting There & Away

AIR

Christchurch Airport (CHC; ☑ 03-358 5029; www.christchurchairport.co.nz; 30 Durey Rd) is the South Island's main international gateway, with excellent facilities including baggage storage, hire-car counters, ATMs, foreign-exchange offices and an i-SITE visitor information centre.

Air New Zealand (☑ 0800 737 000; www.airnewzealand.co.nz) Flies to/from Auckland, Wellington, Dunedin and Queenstown. Code-share flights with smaller regional airlines head to/from Blenheim, Hamilton, Hokitika, Invercargill, Napier, Nelson, New Plymouth, Palmerston North, Paraparaumu, Rotorua and Tauranga.

Jetstar (☑ 0800 800 995; www.jetstar.com) Flies to/from Auckland and Wellington.

BUS

The following services stop outside the Canterbury Museum on Rolleston Ave, unless otherwise stated. Enquire at the i-SITE about seasonal ski shuttles.

Akaroa French Connection (☑ 0800 800 575; www.akaroabus.co.nz; one way/return $25/45) Daily service to Akaroa.

Akaroa Shuttle (☑ 0800 500 929; www.akaroashuttle.co.nz; one way/return $35/50) Heads to Akaroa daily, increasing to twice daily from November to April.

Atomic Shuttles (☑ 03-349 0697; www.atomictravel.co.nz) Destinations include Picton ($35, 5¼ hours), Greymouth ($45, 3¾ hours), Timaru ($25, 2½ hours), Dunedin ($30 to $35, 5¾ hours) and Queenstown ($50, 7 hours).

Budget Buses & Shuttles (☑ 03-615 5119; www.budgetshuttles.co.nz; ☺Mon-Sat) Offers a door-to-door shuttle to Geraldine ($57) and Timaru ($50), along with cheaper scheduled runs (from $27).

Hanmer Connection (☑ 0800 242 663; www.hanmerconnection.co.nz; one way/return $30/50) Daily bus to/from Hanmer Springs via Amberley and Waipara.

InterCity (☑ 03-365 1113; www.intercity.co.nz) New Zealand's widest and most reliable coach network. The **main bus stop** (Map p138; www.intercity.co.nz) is on Armagh St, between New Regent and Manchester Sts. Coaches head to Picton (from $26, 5¼ hours), Timaru (from $28, 2½ hours), Dunedin (from $40, six hours) and Queenstown (from $55, eight to 11 hours) twice daily; and to Te Anau (from $61, 10¾ hours) daily.

Naked Bus (www.nakedbus.com) Destinations include Picton (4½ to 5¾ hours), Kaikoura (1½ hours), Dunedin (six hours), Wanaka (7½ hours) and Queenstown (eight hours).

West Coast Shuttle (☑ 03-768 0028; www.westcoastshuttle.co.nz) Bus stop is at the **Bus Interchange** (Map p138) on Lichfield St, heading to/from Springfield ($32, 1¼ hours), Arthur's Pass ($42, 2¾ hours) and Greymouth ($55, four hours).

TRAIN

Christchurch Railway Station (www.kiwirailscenic.co.nz; Troup Dr, Addington; ☺ticket office 6.30am-3pm) is the terminus for two highly scenic train journeys, the hero of which is the **TranzAlpine** (p143). The other, the *Coastal Pacific*, runs daily from September to April, departing from Christchurch at 7am and arriving at Picton at 12.20pm ($79 to $179). Other stops include Waipara ($59, 56 minutes), Kaikoura ($49 to $69, three hours) and Blenheim ($79 to $159, 4¾ hours). It then departs Picton at 1.15pm, returning to Christchurch at 6.23pm.

ⓘ Getting Around

TO/FROM THE AIRPORT

Christchurch Airport is only 10km from the city centre but a **taxi** between the two can cost a hefty $45 to $65. Alternatively, the airport is well served by **public buses** (www.metroinfo.co.nz). The purple line bus heads through Riccarton (25 minutes) to the central bus station (35 minutes) and on to Sumner (80 minutes). Bus 29 heads through Fendalton (10 minutes) to the bus station (30 minutes). Both services cost $8 and run every half-hour from roughly 7am to 11pm.

Shuttle services include the following:

Steve's Shuttle (☑ 0800 101 021; www.steveshuttle.co.nz; city centre fares $23, each additional passenger $5; ☺3.30am-6pm)

Super Shuttle (☑ 0800 748 885; www.supershuttle.co.nz; city centre fares $24, each additional passenger $5; ☺24hr)

CAR & MOTORCYCLE

Most major car- and campervan-rental companies have offices in Christchurch, as do numerous smaller local companies. Operators with national networks often want cars from Christchurch to be returned to Auckland because most renters travel in the opposite direction, so you may find a cheaper price on a northbound route.

Local options include the following:

Ace Rental Cars (☑ 03-360 3270; www.ace rentalcars.co.nz; 20 Abros Pl, Burnside)

First Choice (www.firstchoice.co.nz)

New Zealand Motorcycle Rentals & Tours (☑ 09-486 2472; www.nzbike.com)

Omega Rental Cars (☑ 03-377 4558; www. omegarentalcars.com; 252 Lichfield St)

Pegasus Rental Cars (☑ 03-358 5890; www. rentalcars.co.nz; 34b Sheffield Cres, Burnside)

PUBLIC TRANSPORT

Christchurch's **Metro** (☑ 03-366 8855; www. metroinfo.co.nz) bus network is inexpensive and efficient. Most buses run from the **Bus Interchange** (p150). Get timetables from the i-SITE or the station's information kiosk. Tickets (adult/child $3.50/1.80) can be purchased on board and include one free transfer within two hours. Metrocards allow unlimited two-hour/full-day travel for $2.50/5; cards cost $10 and must be loaded up with a minimum of $10 additional credit.

TAXI

Blue Star (☑ 03-379 9799; www.bluestartaxis. org.nz)

First Direct (☑ 03-377 5555; www.firstdirect. net.nz)

Gold Band (☑ 03-379 5795; www.goldband taxis.co.nz)

AROUND CHRISTCHURCH

Lyttelton

POP 2859

Southeast of Christchurch are the prominent Port Hills, which slope down to the city's port on Lyttelton Harbour. Christchurch's first European settlers landed here in 1850 to embark on their historic trek over the hills. Nowadays a 2km road tunnel makes the journey considerably quicker.

Lyttelton was badly damaged during the 2010 and 2011 earthquakes, and many of the town's heritage buildings along London St were subsequently demolished. However, Lyttelton has re-emerged as one of Christchurch's most interesting communi-

ties. The town's arty, independent and bohemian vibe is stronger than ever, and it's once again a hub for good bars, cafes and restaurants. It's well worth catching the bus from Christchurch and getting immersed in the local scene, especially on a Saturday morning when the market's buzzing.

 Eating

Lyttelton Farmers' Market   MARKET $

(Map p135; www.lyttelton.net.nz; London St; ⊙10am-1pm Sat) Every Saturday morning, food stalls take the place of cars on Lyttelton's main street. As well as being a great place to stock up on local produce, there's always plenty of excellent baked goods and hot food to snack on at the market.

Lyttelton Coffee Company   CAFE $$

(Map p135; ☑ 03-328 8096; www.lytteltoncoffee. co.nz; 29 London St; meals $11-23; ⊙7am-4pm Mon-Fri, 8am-4pm Sat & Sun; 🖉 ♿) Local institution Lyttelton Coffee Company has risen from the rubble and continued its role as a supergroovy, family-friendly cafe serving wholesome food, including great salads and soothing smoothies. Cool artwork, occasional music and harbour views from the back deck further its appeal.

Freemans   ITALIAN $$

(Map p135; ☑ 03-328 7517; www.freemansdining room.co.nz; 47 London St; breakfast $16-18, lunch $20-27, dinner $22-38; ⊙3pm-late Wed & Thu, 11.30am-late Fri, 10am-late Sat & Sun; 🖉) Freemans consistently pleases with fresh pasta, top-notch pizzas and craft beers from Christchurch's Three Boys. Grab a spot on the deck for great harbour views and Sunday afternoon jazz from 3pm.

★**Roots**   MODERN NZ $$$

(Map p135; ☑ 03-328 7658; www.rootsrestaurant. co.nz; 8 London St; 5-/8-/12-course degustation excl wine $90/125/185; ⊙11.30am-2pm Fri & Sat, 5.30pm-late Tue-Sat) 🖉 Let chef/owner Giulio Sturla take you on a magical mystery tour via degustation menus championing all things local and seasonal. Individual dishes are revealed and described as they arrive at the table, and can be accompanied by carefully curated wine matches, should you choose to splurge.

Drinking & Nightlife

Wunderbar   BAR

(Map p135; ☑ 03-328 8818; www.wunderbar.co.nz; 19 London St; ⊙5pm-late Mon-Fri, 1pm-late Sat & Sun) Wunderbar is a top spot to get down, with regular live music covering all spectra, and clientele to match. The kooky decor and decapitated dolls' heads alone are worth the trip to Lyttelton. Enter via the rear car park.

Civil and Naval   BAR
(Map p135; ☑ 03-328 7206; www.civilandnaval. co.nz; 16 London St; ⊙ 10am-11pm Mon-Thu & Sun, to 1am Fri & Sat) Steadfast staff at this compact, bijou bar serve up a quality selection of cocktails, fine wines and craft beers, while the kitchen keeps patrons civil with an eclectic range of tapas ($6 to $18).

Governors Bay Hotel   PUB
(☑ 03-329 9433; www.governorsbayhotel.co.nz; 52 Main Rd, Governors Bay; ⊙ 11am-late; 🛜) Take a scenic 9km drive from Lyttelton to one of NZ's oldest still-operating pubs (1870). You couldn't want for a more inviting deck and garden in which to quaff an afternoon tipple. The food is good, too, covering all of the classic pub-grub bases (mains $23 to $35).

Upstairs is accommodation in chicly renovated rooms with shared bathrooms (double rooms $119 to $169).

ℹ Information

Lyttelton Visitor Information Centre (Map p135; ☑ 03-328 9093; www.lytteltonharbour. info; 20 Oxford St; ⊙ 10am-4pm)

ℹ Getting There & Away

Buses 28 and 535 run from Christchurch to Lyttelton (adult/child $3.50/1.80, 25 minutes). At the time of writing, Summit Rd between Christchurch and Lyttelton (via Sumner) was still closed.

From Lyttelton, **Black Cat** (Map p135; ☑ 03-328 9078; www.blackcat.co.nz; 5 Norwich Quay) provides ferries to sheltered Quail Island (adult/child return $30/15, October to April only), as well as to sleepy Diamond Harbour (adult/child one way $6.20/3.10).

Banks Peninsula

POP 3050

Gorgeous Banks Peninsula (Horomaka) was formed by two giant volcanic eruptions about eight million years ago. Harbours and bays radiate out from the peninsula's centre, giving it an unusual cogwheel shape. The historic town of Akaroa, 80km from Christchurch, is a highlight, as is the absurdly beautiful drive along Summit Rd around the edge of one of the original craters. It's also worth exploring the little bays that dot the peninsula's perimeter.

The waters around Banks Peninsula are home to the smallest and one of the rarest dolphin species, the Hector's dolphin, found only in NZ waters. A range of tours depart from Akaroa to spot these and other critters, including white-flippered penguins, orcas and seals.

History

James Cook sighted the peninsula in 1770. Thinking it was an island, he named it after the naturalist Sir Joseph Banks.

In 1831 Onawe *pa* (fortified village) was attacked by the Ngāti Toa chief Te Rauparaha and in the massacres that followed, the local Ngāi Tahu population was dramatically reduced. Seven years later, whaling captain Jean Langlois negotiated the purchase of Banks Peninsula from the survivors and returned to France to form a trading company. With French government backing, 63 settlers headed for the peninsula in 1840, but only days before they arrived, panicked British officials sent their own warship to raise the flag at Akaroa, claiming British sovereignty under the Treaty of Waitangi. Had the settlers arrived two years earlier, the entire South Island could have become a French colony, and NZ's future might have been quite different.

The French did settle at Akaroa, but in 1849 their land claim was sold to the New Zealand Company, and in 1850 a large group of British settlers arrived. The heavily forested land was cleared and soon farming became the peninsula's main industry.

◉ Sights

Hinewai Reserve   FOREST
(Long Bay Rd) 🚶 FREE Get a glimpse of what the peninsula once looked like in this privately owned 1050-hectare nature reserve which has been replanted with native forest. Pick up a map outlining the walking tracks at the visitor centre.

**Okains Bay
Māori & Colonial Museum**   MUSEUM
(www.okainsbaymuseum.co.nz; 1146 Okains Bay Rd; adult/child $10/2; ⊙ 10am-5pm) Northeast of Akaroa, this museum has a respectable array of European pioneer artefacts, but it is the nationally significant Māori collection, featuring a replica *wharenui* (meeting house), *waka* (canoes), stone tools and personal adornments, that makes this a mustsee. Note the cute shop down the road.

Banks Peninsula

N 0 ——— 10 km
0 ——— 5 miles

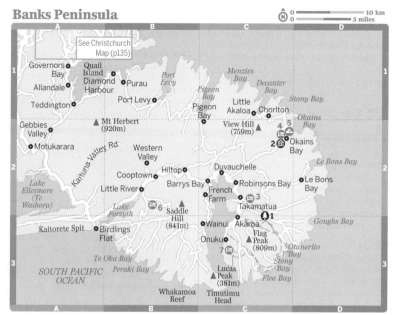

🏃 Activities

Tramping

Banks Peninsula Track TRAMPING

(☑06-304 7612; www.bankstrack.co.nz; 2-/4-days from $185/295; ☺Oct-Apr) This privately owned and maintained 35km four-day walk traverses farmland and forest along the dramatic coast east of Akaroa. Fees include transport from Akaroa and hut accommodation. The two-day option covers the same ground at twice the pace.

Cycling

One of the new Great Rides of the NZ Cycle Trail, this easy-graded, 49-km cycle trail (www.littleriverrailtrail.co.nz) runs from Hornby, on the outskirts of Christchurch, to **Little River** at the base of the Banks Peninsula. Along the way it rolls across rural plains, past weathered peaks, and along the shores of Lake Ellesmere, home to NZ's most diverse bird population, and its smaller twin Lake Forsyth. The best section of track can be enjoyed as a return-ride from Little River where there is a cafe and bike hire.

👉 Tours

Pohatu Plunge WILDLIFE TOUR

(☑03-304 8542; www.pohatu.co.nz) Runs evening tours from Akaroa to the Pohatu

Banks Peninsula

◎ Sights
1 Hinewai Reserve C3
2 Okains Bay Māori & Colonial
   Museum C2

◎ Sleeping
3 Coombe Farm C2
4 Double Dutch.. C2
5 Okains Bay Camping Ground.............. C2
6 Okuti Garden B2
7 Onuku Farm Hostel C3

white-flippered penguin colony (adult/child $75/55), with a self-drive option available (adult /child $25/12). Viewing is best during breeding season, August to January, but is possible throughout the year. Sea kayaking and 4WD nature tours are also available, as is the option of staying overnight in a secluded cottage.

Akaroa Farm Tours TOUR

(☑03-304 8511; www.akaroafarmtours.com; adult/child $80/50) Tours depart from Akaroa iSITE and head to a hill-country farm near Paua Bay for shearing demonstrations, sheepdog shenanigans, garden strolls and homemade scones; allow 2¾ hours.

Tuatara Tours WALKING TOUR

(📞 03-962 3280; www.tuataratours.co.nz; per person $1695; ☉ Nov-Apr) You'll need to carry only your day-pack on the guided *Akaroa Walk*, a leisurely 39km, three-day guided stroll from Christchurch to Akaroa via the gorgeous Summit Ridge. Good accommodation and gourmet food included.

🛏️ Sleeping

⭐ **Halfmoon Cottage** HOSTEL $

(📞 03-304 5050; www.halfmoon.co.nz; SH75, Barrys Bay; dm/s/d $33/55/80; ☉ closed Jul-Aug; @🛜) This pretty 1896 cottage, 12km from Akaroa, is a blissful place to spend a few days lazing on the big verandas or in the hammocks dotting the gardens. It offers proper home comforts and style, with the bonus of bicycles and kayaks to take exploring.

⭐ **Onuku Farm Hostel** HOSTEL $

(📞 03-304 7066; www.onuku.co.nz; Hamiltons Rd, Onuku; sites from $15, dm/d from $29/68; ☉ Oct-Apr; @🛜) Set on a working farm 6km south of Akaroa, this blissfully isolated backpackers has a grassy camping area, simple, tidy rooms in a farmhouse and 'stargazer' cabins ($40 for two, BYO linen). Tonga Hut affords more privacy and breathtaking sea views ($80). Ask about the swimming-with-dolphins tours (from $100), kayaking trips (from $50) and the Skytrack walk.

Okuti Garden HOSTEL $

(📞 03-325 1913; www.okuti.co.nz; 216 Okuti Valley Rd; per adult/child $50/25; ☉ closed May-Sep; @🛜) 🌿 Ecologically sound creds are just part of this delightfully eccentric package which features a house truck and a series of romantic yurts dotted throughout colourful potager gardens. Freshly picked herbs, a pizza oven, a fire-warmed bath, hammocks and free-roaming chickens give this place some serious *Good Life* vibe.

Double Dutch HOSTEL $

(📞 03-304 7229; www.doubledutch.co.nz; 32 Chorlton Rd; dm/s $32/64, d with/without bathroom $86/78; @🛜) Posh enough to be a B&B, yet budget-friendly, this relaxed hostel is perched in 20 acres of farmland on a secluded river estuary. There's a general store (and a beach) just a short walk away, but it's best to bring your own ingredients for the flash kitchen.

Okains Bay Camping Ground CAMPGROUND $

(📞 03-304 8789; www.okainsbaycamp.co.nz; 1357 Okains Bay Rd; sites adult/child $12/6) This up-and-coming camp sits on a pine-tree-peppered swathe of land right by a lovely beach and estuary. Tidy facilities are limited to kitchens, toilets and coin-operated hot showers, but the locale wins the day.

Coombe Farm B&B $$

(📞 03-304 7239; www.coombefarm.co.nz; 18 Old Le Bons Track, Takamatua Valley; d $170-190; 🛜) Choose between the private and romantic Shepherd's Hut – complete with an outdoor bath – and the historic farmhouse lovingly restored in shades of Laura Ashley. After breakfast you can take a walk to the waterfall with Ned, the friendly dog.

🍴 Eating

Little River Cafe & Gallery CAFE $

(www.littlerivergallery.com; SH75, Little River; mains $9-20; ☉ 9am-5pm) On SH75 between Christchurch and Akaroa, the flourishing settlement of Little River is home to this fantastic combo of contemporary art gallery, store and cafe. It's top-notch in all departments, with some particularly delectable home-baking on offer as well as yummy deli goods to go.

⭐ **Hilltop Tavern** PUB FOOD $$

(📞 03-325 1005; www.thehilltop.co.nz; 5207 Christchurch-Akaroa Rd; pizzas $24-26, mains $23-30; ☉ 10am-late, reduced hours in winter) Killer views, craft beer, proper wood-fired pizzas and a pool table. Occasional live music seals the deal for locals and visitors alike at this historic pub. Enjoy grandstand views of Akaroa harbour backdropped by the peninsula.

ℹ️ Getting There & Away

From November to April the **Akaroa Shuttle** (📞 0800 500 929; www.akaroashuttle.co.nz; one way/return $35/50) runs daily services from Christchurch to Akaroa (departs 8.30am), returning to Christchurch at 3.45pm. Check the website for Christchurch pick-up options. Scenic tours from Christchurch exploring Banks Peninsula are also available.

French Connection (📞 0800 800 575; www. akaroabus.co.nz; return $45) has a year-round daily departure from Christchurch at 9am, returning from Akaroa at 4pm.

Akaroa

POP 624

Akaroa ('Long Harbour' in Māori) was the site of the country's first French settlement and descendants of the original French pioneers still reside here. It's a charming town that strives to recreate the feel of a French provincial village, down to the names of its streets and houses. Generally it's a sleepy place, but the peace is periodically shattered by hordes descending from gargantuan cruise ships. The ships used to dock in Lyttelton Harbour but since the earthquakes Akaroa has been a popular substitute. Even when Lyttelton's back on its feet, the ships will be reluctant to leave.

◉ Sights

★ Giant's House   GARDENS
(www.thegiantshouse.co.nz; 68 Rue Balguerie; adult/child $20/10; ⊙ 12-5pm Jan-Apr, 2-4pm May-Dec) An ongoing labour of love by local artist Josie Martin, this playful and whimsical combination of sculpture and mosaics cascades down a hillside garden above Akaroa. Echoes of Gaudí and Miró can be found in the intricate collages of mirrors, tiles and broken china, and there are many surprising nooks and crannies to discover. Martin also exhibits her paintings and sculpture in the lovely 1880 house, the former residence of Akaroa's first bank manager.

★ Akaroa Museum   MUSEUM
(www.akaroamuseum.org.nz; cnr Rues Lavaud & Balguerie; ⊙ 10.30am-4.30pm) FREE An arduous postquake revamp has rewarded Akaroa with one of the smartest regional museums in the land. Learn about the various phases of the peninsula's settlement and its fascinating natural and industrial history, and hear stories of old characters including Pompey the penguin. A 20-minute film fills in some gaps while several adjacent historic buildings keep it real. Note the donation box.

St Peter's Anglican Church   CHURCH
(46 Rue Balguerie) Graciously restored in 2015, this 1864 Anglican gem features extensive exposed timbers, stained glass and an historic organ, and it has a few stories to tell. Well worth a look whether you're godly or not.

Old French Cemetery   CEMETERY
The first consecrated burial ground in Canterbury, this hillside cemetery makes for a poignant wander. Follow the trail off Rue Brittan.

🏃 Activities

Akaroa Guided
Sea Kayaking Safari   KAYAKING
(☑ 021 156 4591; www.akaroakayaks.com; 3hr/half-day $125/159) Paddle out at 7.30am on a three-hour guided Sunrise Nature Safari, or if early starts aren't your thing, try the 11.30am Bays & Nature Paddle. The half-day Try Sea Kayaking Experience is a more challenging option.

Akaroa Sailing Cruises   SAILING
(☑ 0800 724 528; www.aclasssailing.co.nz; Main Wharf; adult/child $75/37.50) Set sail for a 2½-hour hands-on cruise on a gorgeous 1946 A-Class yacht.

Akaroa Adventure Centre   OUTDOORS
(☑ 03-304 7784; www.akaroa.com; 74a Rue Lavaud; ⊙ 9am-6pm) Rents out sea kayaks and stand-up paddle boards (per hour/day $20/60), paddle boats (per hour $30), bikes (per hour/day $15/65), and fishing rods (per day $10). Based at the i-SITE.

👉 Tours

Black Cat Cruises   BOAT TOUR
(☑ 03-304 7641; www.blackcat.co.nz; Main Wharf; nature cruises adult/child $74/30, dolphin swims adult/child $155/120) As well as a two-hour nature cruise, Black Cat offers a three-hour 'swimming with dolphins' experience. Wet suits and snorkelling gear are provided, plus hot showers back on dry land. Observers can tag along (adult/child $80/40) but only 12 people can swim per trip, so book ahead.

Cruises have a 98% success rate in seeing dolphins, and an 81% success rate in actually swimming with them (there's a $50 refund if there's no swim).

Akaroa Dolphins   BOAT TOUR
(☑ 03-304 7866; www.akaroadolphins.co.nz; 65 Beach Rd; adult/child $75/35; ⊙ 12.45pm year-round, plus 10.15am & 3.15pm Oct-Apr) Two-hour wildlife cruises on a comfortable 50ft catamaran, complete with a complimentary drink, home baking and, most importantly, the company of Sydney, wildlife-spotting dog extraordinaire.

Coast Up Close   BOAT TOUR
(☑ 0800 126 278; www.coastupclose.co.nz; Main Wharf; adult/child from $75/25; ⊙ departs 10.15am & 1.45pm Oct-Apr) Scenic boat trips with an emphasis on wildlife watching. Fishing trips can be arranged.

Eastern Bays Scenic Mail Run   DRIVING TOUR
(☑ 03-304 8526; tours $80; ⊙ 9am Mon-Fri) Travel along with the ex-conservation-ranger postie to visit isolated communities and bays on this 120km, five-hour mail delivery service. Departs from the i-SITE (p158); bookings are essential as there are only eight seats available.

🎊 Festivals & Events

French Fest   FOOD
(www.ccc.govt.nz; ⊙ Oct) This Gallic-inspired, two-day get together has an emphasis on

Akaroa

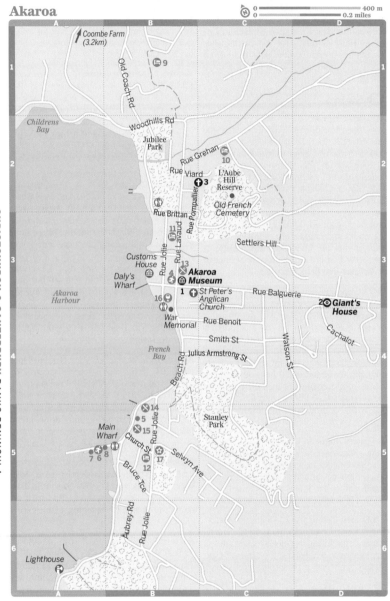

food, wine, music and art. Don't miss (or stand on) *Le Race D'Escargots,* where sleek, highly trained snails negotiate a compact course. It's held biennially (odd-numbered years).

🛌 Sleeping

Chez la Mer HOSTEL **$**
(☑ 03-304 7024; www.chezlamer.co.nz; 50 Rue Lavaud; dm $30, d with/without bathroom $86/76; 🛜) Pretty in pink, this historic building is home to a friendly backpackers with well-

Akaroa

kept rooms and a shaded garden, complete with fish pond, hammocks and barbecue. It's a TV-free zone but free bikes and fishing rods are available.

Akaroa Top 10 Holiday Park   HOLIDAY PARK **$**
(☑0800 727 525, 03-304 7471; www.akaroa-holidaypark.co.nz; 96 Morgans Rd; sites from $40-44, units $72-135; @🛜🖳) Grandstand views of the harbour and peninsula hills are the main drawcard for this holiday park. Cabins and motels are basic but tidy, while the facilities blocks could do with an overhaul.

Tresori Motor Lodge   MOTEL **$$**
(☑03-304 7500; www.tresori.co.nz; cnr Rue Jolie & Church St; d $160-205; 🛜) There are 12 clean and smart units at this modern motel. All have kitchenettes, but given its proximity to Akaroa's waterfront cafe and restaurant strip, you needn't worry about using them. Blooming flower boxes are a nice touch.

★**Beaufort House**   B&B **$$$**
(☑03-304 7517; www.beauforthouse.co.nz; 42 Rue Grehan; r $375; ⊙closed Jun-Aug; 🛜) Tucked away along a quiet street and behind gorgeous gardens, this lovely 1878 house is adorned with covetable artwork and antiques, and even has its own boutique vineyard. The only one of the five rooms without an en suite compensates with a large private bathroom with a claw-foot tub just across the hall.

✖ Eating & Drinking

Akaroa Butchery & Deli   DELI **$**
(67 Rue Lavaud; ⊙10am-5.30pm Mon-Fri, 9am-4pm Sat) A dream scenario for picnickers and self-caterers, this sharp butchery champions all manner of local produce from bread,

salmon, cheese and pickles, to delicious pies, smallgoods and meat for the barbecue.

Bully Hayes   CAFE **$$**
(www.bullyhayes.co.nz; 57 Beach Rd; breakfast $14-23, lunch $11-30, dinner $22-43; ⊙8am-9pm; 🛜) Named after a well-travelled American buccaneer, Bully Hayes is Akaroa's best breakfast option. A sunny spot overlooking the harbour draws the brunch-time crowd for the likes of eggs, burgers and fresh seafood, while a bar vibe keeps them lingering over a few cold ones later in the day.

Trading Rooms   FRENCH **$$$**
(☑03-304 7656; www.thetradingrooms.co.nz; 71 Beach Rd; lunch $18-35, dinner $28-43; ⊙10am-3pm Thu-Mon, 5-10pm Fri-Mon) Housed in Akaroa's most impressive waterside shopfront, decked out period-style in dark timbers and burgundy, this is an atmospheric spot to linger over a refined meal. French cuisine such as snails and cassoulet dominate, although at lunch its Gallic guard drops a little to reveal burgers and gourmet club sandwiches.

Harbar   BAR
(83 Rue Jolie; ⊙5pm-9.30pm) Sporadic opening hours, dictated by weather and demand, should not deter you from attempting a sundowner at Akaroa's favourite waterside bar. A crowd may gather, and a guitar may get strummed.

☆ Entertainment

Akaroa Cinema & Café   CINEMA
(☑03-304 8898; www.cinecafe.co.nz; cnr Rue Jolie & Selwyn Ave; adult/child $15/13; 🛜) Grab a beer and settle in to watch an art-house, classic or foreign flick with high-quality sound and projection.

ℹ Information

Akaroa i-SITE & Adventure Centre (☑ 03-304 8600; www.akaroa.com; 74a Rue Lavaud; ⊗ 9am-5pm) A helpful little hub offering info and bookings for local activities, transport, et al. Doubles as the post office.

NORTH CANTERBURY

Heading south from Kaikoura, SH1 crosses the Hundalee Hills and heads into Hurunui District, an area known for its wine and the thermal resort of Hanmer Springs. It's also the start of the Canterbury Plains, a vast, flat, richly agricultural area partitioned by distinctive braided rivers. The region is bounded to the west by the Southern Alps. If you're crossing into Canterbury from either Westport or Nelson, the most direct route cuts through the Alps on the beautiful Lewis Pass Hwy (SH7).

Lewis Pass

The northernmost of the three main mountain passes connecting the West Coast to the east, 864m-high Lewis Pass is not as steep as the others (Arthur's and Haast) and the forest isn't as dense either. However, the drive is arguably just as scenic. Vegetation comprises mainly beech (red and silver) and kowhai trees growing along river terraces.

From Lewis Pass the highway wiggles east for 62km before reaching the turn-off to Hanmer Springs.

🏃 Activities

The area has some interesting **tramps**, passing through beech forest with a backdrop of snow-capped mountains, lakes, and alpine tarns and rivers. Popular tracks include the **St James Walkway** (66km; four to five days) and those through **Lake Sumner Forest Park**; see the Department of Conservation (DOC) pamphlet *Lake Sumner & Lewis Pass* ($2). Subalpine conditions apply, so make sure you sign the intentions books at the huts.

Maruia Springs   SPA, HOT SPRING
(☑ 03-523 8840; www.maruiasprings.co.nz; SH7; adult/child $22/12, guests free; ⊗ pools 8am-7.30pm) Maruia Springs is a small Japanese-style hot spring resort on the banks of the Maruia River, 6km west of Lewis Pass, with fairly spartan accommodation (doubles $159 to $199), a cafe-bar and a Japanese restaurant (dinner only). Water with black mineral flakes, known as 'hot spring

flowers', is pumped into outdoor rock pools. It's a magical setting during a winter snowfall, but mind the sandflies in summer.

At the time of writing, new owners were about to take over. Changes (and hopefully upgrades) are afoot, but the hot water should keep flowing.

ℹ Transport

East West Coaches (☑ 03-789 6251; www.eastwestcoaches.co.nz) East West Coaches stop at Maruia Springs and the St James Walkway on their way between Westport and Christchurch, and back again.

Hanmer Springs

POP 843

Ringed by sculpted mountains, Hanmer Springs is the main thermal resort on the South Island. It's a pleasantly low-key spot to indulge yourself, whether by soaking in hot pools, dining out or being pampered in the spa complex. If that all sounds too soporific, fear not; there are plenty of family-friendly activities on offer, including a few to get the adrenaline pumping.

◉ Sights

Hanmer Springs Animal Park   FARM
(☑ 03-315 7772; www.hanmer-animal-park.nz; 108 Rippingale Rd; adult/child/family $12/6/35; ⊗ 10am-5pm Wed-Sun, daily during school holidays; 👪) With more animals than Dr Dolittle's Facebook page, this farm park is great for kids. Llamas, Tibetan yak, deer, goats, guinea pigs and chinchillas all feature, and many of the critters can be hand-fed; pony rides are also available. For mum and dad there's a licensed cafe and a craft gallery.

🏃 Activities

★**Hanmer Springs Thermal Pools**   HOT SPRING
(☑ 03-315 0000; www.hanmersprings.co.nz; 42 Amuri Ave; adult/child $22/11, locker $2; ⊗ 10am-9pm; 👪) 🍃 Māori legend has it that these hot springs are the result of embers from Mt Ngauruhoe in the North Island falling from the sky. The main complex consists of a series of large pools of various temperatures, along with smaller, adult-only landscaped rock pools, a freshwater 25m lap pool, private thermal pools ($30 per 30 minutes) and a cafe.

Kids of all ages will love the water slides and the whirl-down-the-plughole-thrill of the Superbowl ($10). There's also an adjacent spa (p159).

Hanmer Forest Park TRAMPING, MOUNTAIN BIKING
(www.visithurunui.co.nz) Trampers and mountain bikers will find plenty of room to move within the 130 sq km expanse of forest abutting the town. The easy Woodland Walk starts 1km up Jollies Pass Rd and goes through Douglas fir, poplar and redwood stands before joining Majuba Walk, which leads to Conical Hill Lookout and then back towards town (1½ hours). The Waterfall Track is an excellent half-day tramp starting at the end of McIntyre Rd. The i-SITE (p161) stocks a *Forest Park Walks* booklet and a mountain-biking map (both $3).

Hanmer Springs Spa SPA
(☑ 03-315 0029, 0800 873 529; www.hanmer-springs.co.nz; 42 Amuri Ave; ☺ 10am-7pm) Hanmer Springs Spa has massage and beauty treatments from $85. Recent refurbishments have lifted the spa to international standards.

Entry to the adjacent Hanmer Springs Thermal Pools (p158) is discounted to $15 if you partake of the spa's facilities.

Mt Lyford Alpine Resort SKIING
(☑ 0274 710 717, snow-phone 03-366 1220; www.mtlyford.co.nz; day passes $75/35) Around 60km from both Hanmer Springs and Kaikoura, and 4km from Mt Lyford Village, this is more of a 'resort' than most NZ ski fields, with accommodation and eating options. There's a good mix of runs and a terrain park.

Hanmer Springs Ski Area SKIING
(☑ 027 434 1806; www.skihanmer.co.nz; day passes adult/child/family $60/30/130) Only 17km from town via an unsealed road, this small complex has runs to suit all levels of ability. The **Adventure Centre** (☑ 0800 368 7386, 03-315 7233; www.hanmeradventure.co.nz; 20 Conical Hill Rd; ☺ 8.30am-5pm) provides shuttles during the season.

Thrillseekers Adventures ADVENTURE SPORTS
(☑ 03-315 7046, 0800 661 538; www.thrillseekers.co.nz; 839 Hanmer Springs Rd) Bungy off a 35m-high bridge ($169), jetboat the Waiau Gorge (adult/child $115/60), explore the Grade II Waiau River in a raft (adult/child $149/79) or inflatable kayak (five hours, adult/child $299/189), or get dirty on a quad bike (adult/child $149/99). The Thrillseekers Adventure centre is next to the bridge near the turn-off from SH7, and there's a **booking office** (☑ 03-315 7346, 0800 661 538; www.thrillseekers.co.nz; Conical Hill Rd; ☺ 9am-5pm) in town.

Hanmer Springs

Hanmer Springs

⊕ **Activities, Courses & Tours**
1 Hanmer Springs Adventure Centre...A2
Hanmer Springs Spa ....(see 2)
2 Hanmer Springs Thermal Pools A2
3 Thrillseekers Adventures Booking Office.....................................A2

⊜ **Sleeping**
4 Chalets Motel A2
5 Cheltenham House.............................B2
6 Hanmer Springs Top 10 ....A3
7 Kakapo Lodge A3
8 Rosie's A2
9 Scenic Views...A3
10 St James A2

⊗ **Eating**
11 Coriander's A2
12 Hanmer Springs Bakery A2
13 No. 31..A3
14 Powerhouse Cafe..................................A2

⊝ **Drinking & Nightlife**
15 Monteith's Brewery Bar A2

🛏 Sleeping

Jack in the Green HOSTEL $
(☑ 03-315 5111; www.jackinthegreen.co.nz; 3 Devon St; site per person $20, dm $32, d with/without bathroom $92/76; @ 🛜) This charming

CHRISTCHURCH & CANTERBURY HANMER SPRINGS

MOLESWORTH STATION

Filling up 1807 mountainous sq km between Hanmer Springs and Blenheim, Molesworth Station is NZ's largest farm, with the country's largest cattle herd (up to 10,000). It's also an area of national ecological significance and the entire farm is now administered by DOC (☑03-572 9100; www.doc.govt.nz).

Visits are usually only possible when the Acheron Rd through the station is open from November to early April (weather permitting; check with DOC or at the Hanmer Springs i-SITE). The 207km drive from Hanmer Springs north to Blenheim on this narrow, unsealed backcountry road takes around six hours. Note that the gates are only open from 7am to 7pm, and overnight camping (adult/child $6/3) is permitted in certain areas (no open fires allowed). Pick up DOC's *Molesworth Station* brochure from the i-SITE (p161) or download it from the website.

Molesworth Heritage Tours (☑027 201 4536, 03-315 7401; www.molesworth.co.nz; tours $198-750; ☉Oct-May) leads 4WD coach trips to the station from Hanmer Springs. Day tours include a picnic lunch, but there's also a five-hour 'no frills' option. From the Blenheim side, **Molesworth Tours** (☑03-572 8025; www.molesworthtours.co.nz) offers one- to four-day all-inclusive heritage and 4WD trips ($220 to $1487), as well as four-day fully supported (and catered) mountain-bike adventures ($1460).

converted old home is a 10-minute walk from the centre. Large rooms (no bunks), relaxing gardens and a lovely lounge area are the main drawcards. For extra privacy, book an en suite garden 'chalet'.

Kakapo Lodge HOSTEL $
(☑03-315 7472; www.kakapolodge.co.nz; 14 Amuri Ave; dm $28, d with/without bathroom $90/66; ☎) The YHA-affiliated Kakapo has a cheery owner, a roomy kitchen and lounge, chill-busting underfloor heating and a 1st-floor deck. Bunk-free dorms (some with bathrooms) are joined by two motel-style units ($95 to $100).

Hanmer Springs Top 10 HOLIDAY PARK $
(☑0800 904 545, 03-315 7113; www.hanmerspringstop10.co.nz; 5 Hanmer Springs Rd; sites $34-50, units with/without bathroom from $95/78; @☎) This family-friendly park is just a few minutes' walk from the town's eponymous pools. Kids will love the playground and jumping pillow. Take your pick from basic cabins (BYO everything) to attractive motel units with everything supplied.

★**Woodbank Park Cottages** COTTAGE $$
(☑03-315 5075; www.woodbankcottages.co.nz; 381 Woodbank Rd; d $190-210) These two plush cottages in a woodland setting are a six-minute drive from Hanmer, but feel a million miles away. Decor is crisp and modern, bathrooms and kitchens are well appointed, and wooden decks come equipped with gas barbecues and rural views. Log burners, and complimentary fresh juices and cheese platters, seal the deal.

Chalets Motel MOTEL $$
(☑03-315 7097; www.chaletsmotel.co.nz; 56 Jacks Pass Rd; d $140-180; ☎) Soak up the mountain views from these tidy, reasonably priced, free-standing wooden chalets, set on the slopes behind the town centre. All chalets have full kitchens, and one unit has a spa bath.

Scenic Views MOTEL $$
(☑03-315 7419, 0800 843 974; www.hanmerscenicviews.co.nz; 2 Amuri Ave; d $140-240; ☎) ✿ An attractive timber-and-stone complex with modern studios (one with an outdoor spa pool) and two- and three-bedroom apartments. Mountain views come standard, as do free wi-fi and plunger coffee.

Rosie's B&B $$
(☑03-315 7095; www.rosiesbandbhanmer.co.nz; 9 Cheltenham St; d $95-145; ☎) Rosie has left the building but the hospitality continues at this homely, good-value B&B. Half the rooms are en suite, and rates include a continental breakfast and scrummy toasted croissants.

St James APARTMENTS $$$
(☑03-315 5225; www.thestjames.co.nz; 20 Chisholm Cres; apt $190-365; ☎) Luxuriate in a schmick modern apartment with all mod cons, including iPod dock and fully equipped kitchen. Sizes range from studios to two-bedroom apartments, with balconies or patios. Most have mountain views.

Cheltenham House B&B $$$
(☑03-315 7545; www.cheltenham.co.nz; 13 Cheltenham St; r $235-280; ☎) This large 1930's house has room for both a billiard table

and a grand piano. There are four art-filled suites in the main house and two in cosy garden cottages. Cooked gourmet breakfasts are delivered to the rooms and wine is served in the evening.

✖️ Eating

Hanmer Springs Bakery   BAKERY $
(☑ 03-315 7714; www.hanmerbakery.co.nz; 16 Conical Hill Rd; ⏱ 6am-4pm) In peak season queues stretch out the door for this humble bakery's meat pies and salmon bagels.

Coriander's   INDIAN $$
(☑ 03-315 7616; www.corianders.co.nz; Chisholm Cres; mains $14-22; ⏱ 11.30am-2pm Mon-Fri, 5-10pm daily; 🖊) Spice up your life at this brightly painted North Indian restaurant complete with bhangra-beats soundtrack. It's a beef-free zone, but there are plenty of tasty lamb, chicken and seafood dishes to choose from, plus a fine vegetarian selection.

Powerhouse Cafe   CAFE $$
(☑ 03-315 5252; www.powerhousecafe.co.nz; 8 Jacks Pass Rd; brunch $15-24; ⏱ 7.30am-3pm; 🖊) Power up with a huge High Country breakfast, or a Highland Fling caramelised whisky-sodden porridge. Return for a burger, laksa or salmon salad for lunch, then finish with one of the lavishly iced friands.

No. 31   MODERN NZ $$$
(☑ 03-315 7031; www.restaurant-no31.nz; 31 Amuri Ave; mains $36-39; ⏱ 5.30-11pm Tue-Sun) Substantial servings of good-quality, albeit conservative, cuisine are on offer in this pretty wooden cottage. The upmarket ambience befits the prices; the paper napkins and chunky glasses don't. Good beer list, and solid wine selection.

🍷 Drinking & Nightlife

Monteith's Brewery Bar   PUB
(☑ 03-315 5133; www.mbbh.co.nz; 47 Amuri Ave; ⏱ 9am-11pm) This large, overlit and slightly worn brand-pub is the town's busiest. It serves food all day (breakfast $15 to $21, bar snacks $9 to $16, dinner $24 to $35). Live musicians kick off from 4pm Sundays.

ℹ️ Information

Hanmer Springs i-SITE (☑ 03-315 0020, 0800 442 663; www.visithanmersprings.co.nz; 40 Amuri Ave; ⏱ 10am-5pm) Books transport, accommodation and activities.

ℹ️ Getting There & Away

The **main bus stop** is near the corner of Amuri Ave and Jacks Pass Rd.

Hanmer Connection (☑ 03-382 2952, 0800 242 663; www.hanmerconnection.co.nz; one way/return $30/50) Runs daily bus to/from Christchurch via Waipara and Amberley.

Hanmer Tours & Shuttle (☑ 03-315 7418; www.hanmertours.co.nz) Runs shuttles to/from Waipara ($20), Amberley ($20), Christchurch city centre ($30) and Christchurch airport ($40).

Waipara Valley

Conveniently stretched along SH1 near the Hanmer Springs turn-off, this resolutely rural area makes for a tasty pit stop en route to Christchurch. The valley's warm dry summers followed by cool autumn nights have proved a winning formula for growing grapes, olives, hazelnuts and lavender. While it accounts for less than 3% of NZ's grapes, it produces some of the country's finest cool-climate wines including riesling, pinot noir and gewürztraminer.

Of the region's 30 or so wineries, around a dozen have cellar doors to visit, four with restaurants. To explore the valley's bounty fully, pick up a copy of the *Waipara Valley Map* (or download it from www.waiparavalleynz.com). Otherwise, you'll spot several of the big players from the highway. The area's two main towns are tiny Waipara and slightly larger Amberley, although the latter is just outside the main wine-growing area.

🄾 Sights

★**Pegasus Bay**   WINERY
(☑ 03-314 6869; www.pegasusbay.com; Stockgrove Rd; ⏱ tastings 10am-5pm) It's fitting that Waipara Valley's premier winery should have the loveliest setting and one of Canterbury's best restaurants (mains $36 to $44, serving noon to 4pm Thursday to Monday). Beautiful gardens set the scene but it's the contemporary NZ menu and luscious wines that steal the show. Pétanque available upon request.

Black Estate   WINERY
(☑ 03-314 6085; www.blackestate.co.nz; 614 Omihi Rd/SH1; ⏱ 10am-5pm Wed-Sun, daily Dec-Jan) 🖊 The sharpest of Waipara's wineries architecturally, this striking black barn overlooking the valley is home to some excellent wine, and food that champions local producers (mains $25 to $40). As well as the region's common cool-climate wines, look out for its interesting pinot/chardonnay rosé and seductive chenin blanc.

Brew Moon   BREWERY
(☑ 03-314 8036; www.brewmoon.co.nz; 12 Markham St, Amberley; ⏱ 3pm-late Wed-Fri, noon-late

Sat & Sun) The variety of craft beers available to taste at this wee brewery never wanes. Stop in to fill a rigger (flagon) to take away, or sup an ale with a platter or a pizza (food from 3pm).

Sleeping & Eating

Old Glenmark Vicarage   B&B **$$$**
(☑ 03-314 6775; www.glenmarkvicarage.co.nz; 161 Church Rd, Waipara; d $230, barn d $210; 🛜🆒) There are two divine options in this beautifully restored century-old vicarage: cosy up with bed and breakfast in the main house, or lounge around in the character-filled, converted barn that sleeps up to five. The beautiful gardens and swimming pool are a blessed bonus.

★ **Little Vintage Espresso**   CAFE **$**
(20 Markham St, Amberley; brunch $8-18; ⏱ 7.30am-4.30pm Mon-Sat) This little cracker of a cafe just off SH1 serves up the best coffee in town with food to match. High-quality, contemporary sandwiches, slices and cakes are gobbled up by locals and tourists alike.

Pukeko Junction   CAFE, DELI **$$**
(☑ 03-314 8834; www.pukekojunction.co.nz; 458 Ashworths Rd/SH1, Leithfield; mains $15-21; ⏱ 9am-4.30pm; 🚗) A deservedly popular roadside pit stop, this cafe in Leithfield (south of Amberley) serves delicious baked goods including gourmet sausage rolls and lamb shank pies. As well as arts and crafts, the shop next door stocks an excellent selection of local wine.

Waipara Springs   CAFE **$$**
(www.waiparasprings.co.nz; SH1; mains $24-28; ⏱ 11am-5pm; 🚸) Slightly north of Waipara township, one of the valley's oldest vineyards has a fine line in righteous rieslings. The casual cafe serves platters and bistro fare in the lovely family-friendly garden.

ℹ Getting There & Away

The *Coastal Pacific* train (October to May) from Christchurch to Picton stops at Waipara. Wine tours are available from a few Christchurch-based companies.

Hanmer Connection (☑ 0800 242 663; www.hanmerconnection.co.nz) Heads to Hanmer Springs ($20, 50 minutes) and Christchurch ($20, 1¼ hours).

Hanmer Tours & Shuttle (☑ 03-315 7418; www.hanmertours.co.nz) Runs shuttles to/from Hanmer Springs ($20), Christchurch city centre ($15) and Christchurch airport ($25).

InterCity (☑ 03-365 1113; www.intercity.co.nz) Coaches head to/from Picton (from $29, 4½

hours), Blenheim (from $27, four hours), Kaikoura (from $16, 1¾ hours) and Christchurch (from $12, one hour) at least twice daily.

CENTRAL CANTERBURY

While the dead-flat agricultural heartland of the Canterbury Plains blankets the majority of the region, there's plenty of interest for travellers in the west, where the Southern Alps soar to snowy peaks. Here you'll find numerous ski fields and some brilliant wilderness walks.

Unusually for NZ, the most scenic routes avoid the coast, and most items of interest can be accessed from one of two spectacular roads: the Great Alpine Highway (SH73), which wends from the Canterbury Plains deep into the mountains and over to the West Coat, and the Inland Scenic Route (SH72), which skirts the mountains foothills on its way south towards Tekapo.

Selwyn District

Named after NZ's first Anglican bishop, this largely rural district has swallowed an English map book and regurgitated place names such as Lincoln, Darfield and Sheffield to punctuate this green and pleasant land. Yet any illusions of Albion are quickly dispelled by the looming presence of the snow-capped Southern Alps, providing a rugged retort to 'England's mountains green'.

Selwyn's numerous ski fields may not be the country's most glamorous but they provide plenty of thrills for ski bunnies. **Porters** (☑ 03-318 4002, snow-phone 03-379 9931; www.skiporters.co.nz; daily lift passes adult/child $84/44) is the main commercial field; club fields include **Mt Olympus** (☑ 03-318 5840; www.mtolympus.co.nz; daily lift passes adult/child $70/35), **Cheeseman** (☑ 03-344 3247, snow-phone 03-318 8794; www.mtcheeseman.co.nz; daily lift passes adult/child $79/39), **Broken River** (☑ 03-318 8713; www.brokenriver.co.nz; daily lift passes adult/child $75/35), **Craigieburn Valley** (☑ 03-318 8711; www.craigieburn.co.nz; daily lift passes adult/child $75/35) and **Temple Basin** (☑ 03-377 7788; www.templebasin.co.nz; daily lift passes adult/child $70/39).

The highly scenic Great Alpine Hwy pierces the heart of the district on its journey between Christchurch and the West Coast. Before it leaves the Canterbury Plains, it passes through the little settlement of **Springfield** (population 300), which is distinguished by a monument to notable local Rewi Alley

(1897–1987) who became a great hero of the Chinese Communist Party. His life story is a tale indeed, retold well in the roadside information panels.

The town's other major monument is a giant pink-iced doughnut, originally erected to promote *The Simpsons Movie* but now a permanent feature. Is that an #InstaDonut I feel coming on?

The Southern Alps loom larger as SH73 heads west from Springfield into Arthur's Pass.

🏃 Activities

Rubicon Horse Treks HORSE RIDING
(📞 03-318 8886; www.rubiconvalley.co.nz; 534 Rubicon Rd) Operating from a sheep farm 6km from Springfield, Rubicon offers hour-long farm treks ($55), two-hour river or valley rides ($98), two-hour sunset rides ($120), and six-hour mountain trail rides ($285).

🛏️ Sleeping & Eating

Smylies Accommodation HOSTEL $
(📞 03-318 4740; www.smylies.co.nz; 5653 West Coast Rd, Springfield; dm/s/d $30/50/80; 🛜) 🅿 This well-seasoned, welcoming, YHA-associated hostel has a piano, manga comics galore, and a DVD library. There's also a handful of self-contained motel units ($85 to $160) and a three-bedroom cottage ($220). Winter packages including ski-equipment rental and ski-field transport available.

Famous Sheffield Pie Shop BAKERY $
(www.sheffieldpieshop.co.nz; 51 Main West Rd, Sheffield; pies $5-6; ⏰ 7.30am-4pm) Heaven forbid you should blink and miss this roadside bakery, a stellar purveyor of meat pies produced here in more than 20 varieties. While you're at it, snaffle a bag of its exemplary afghan biscuits – such cornflakey, chocolatey goodness!

ℹ️ Getting There & Away

Public transport is limited in the Selwyn District, so it's best to organise your own vehicle.

Arthur's Pass

POP 300

Having left the Canterbury Plains at Springfield, the Great Alpine Hwy heads over Porter's Pass into the mountainous folds of the Torlesse and **Craigieburn** Ranges and into Arthur's Pass.

Māori used this pass to cross the Southern Alps long before its 'discovery' by Arthur Dobson in 1864. The Westland gold rush created the need for a dependable crossing over

the Alps from Christchurch, and the coach road was completed within a year. Later, the coal and timber trade demanded a railway, duly completed in 1923.

Today it's an amazing journey. Successive valleys display their own character and special sights, not least the spectacular braided Waimakariri River Valley, encountered as you enter **Arthur's Pass National Park**.

Arthur's Pass village (population 62) is 4km from the actual pass. At 900m, it's NZ's highest-altitude settlement and a handy base for tramps, climbs and skiing. The weather, however, is a bit of a shocker. Come prepared for rain.

◎ Sights

★ **Castle Hill/Kura Tawhiti** LANDMARK
Scattered across lush paddocks around 33km from Springfield, these limestone formations are so odd they were named 'treasure from a distant land' by early Māori. A car park (with toilets) provides easy access on foot into the strange rock garden, favoured by rock climbers and photographers.

Arthur's Pass National Park NATIONAL PARK
(www.doc.govt.nz) Straddling the Southern Alps and known to Māori as Ka Tiriti o Te Moana (steep peak of glistening white), this vast alpine wilderness became the South Island's first national park in 1923. Of its 1148 sq km, two-thirds lies on the Canterbury side of the main divide; the rest is in Westland. It is a rugged, mountainous area, cut by deep valleys, and ranging in altitude from 245m at the Taramakau River to 2408m at Mt Murchison. There are plenty of well-marked day walks, especially around Arthur's Pass village.

Pick up a copy of DOC's *Discover Arthur's Pass* booklet to read about popular walks including: **Arthur's Pass Walkway**, a reasonably easy track from the village to the Dobson Memorial at the summit of the pass (2½ hours return); the one-hour return walk to **Devils Punchbowl** falls; and the steep walk to beautiful views at **Temple Basin** (three hours return). More challenging, full-day options include **Bealey Spur** track and the classic summit hike to **Avalanche Peak**.

The park's many multiday trails are mostly valley routes with saddle climbs in between, such as **Goat Pass** and **Cass-Lagoon Saddles Tracks**, both two-day options. These and the park's longer tracks require previous tramping experience as flooding can make the rivers dangerous and the weather is extremely changeable. Always seek advice from DOC before setting out.

Cave Stream Scenic Reserve　　CAVE
(www.doc.govt.nz) Near Broken River Bridge, 2km northeast of Castle Hill, a car park signals access to this 594m-long cave. As indicated by the information panels, the walk through it is an achievable adventure, even for beginners, but only with a foolproof torch and warm clothing, and definitely only if the water level is less than waist-deep where indicated. Heed all notices, take necessary precautions and revel in the spookiness. Failing that, just wander around the 10-minute loop track for a gander at the surrounds.

🛏 Sleeping

Camping is possible near the basic **Avalanche Creek Shelter** (adult/child $6/3) opposite the DOC centre, where there's running water, a sink, tables and a toilet. You can also camp for free at **Klondyke Corner** or **Hawdon Shelter**, 8km and 24km south of Arthur's Pass respectively, where facilities are limited to toilets and stream water for boiling.

Mountain House YHA　　HOSTEL $
(☑ 03-318 9258; www.trampers.co.nz; 83 Main Rd; dm $31-34, s/d/unit $74/86/155; 🗑) Spread around the village, this excellent suite of accommodation includes a well-kept hostel, two upmarket motel units and two three-bedroom cottages with log fires ($340, for up to eight people). The enthusiastic manager runs a tight ship and can provide extensive local tramping information.

Arthur's Pass Village B&B　　B&B $$
(☑ 021 394 776; www.arthurspass.org.nz; 72 School Tce; d $140-160; 🗑) This lovingly restored former railway cottage is now a cosy B&B, complete with two guest bedrooms (share bathroom), free-range bacon and eggs, and freshly baked bread for breakfast, and the company of interesting owners. Home-cooked dinners are also available ($35). Ask about the scorched floorboard.

Arthur's Pass Alpine Motel　　MOTEL $$
(☑ 03-318 9233; www.apam.co.nz; 52 Main Rd; d $125-150; 🗑) On the southern approach to the village, this cabin-style motel complex combines the homely charms of yesteryear with the beauty of double-glazing and the advice of active, enthusiastic hosts.

Wilderness Lodge　　LODGE $$$
(☑ 03-318 9246; www.wildernesslodge.co.nz; Cora Lynn Rd, Bealey; s $499-749, d $778-1178; 🗑) 🍃 For tranquillity and natural grandeur, this mid-size alpine lodge tucked into beech forest just off the highway takes some beating. It's a class act with a focus on immersive, nature-based experiences. Two daily guided activities (such as tramping and kayaking) are included in the tariff along with dinner and breakfast.

🍴 Eating

Arthur's Pass Store & Cafe　　CAFE $
(85 Main Rd; breakfast & lunch $7-24; ⊘ 8am-5pm; 🗑) You want it, this is your best chance, with odds-on for egg sandwiches, hot chips, good coffee, petrol and basic groceries.

ℹ Information

DOC Arthur's Pass Visitor Centre (☑ 03-318 9211; www.doc.govt.nz; 80 Main Rd; ⊘ 8.30pm-4.30pm) Displays include ecological information and the history of Arthur's Pass. Helpful staff provide advice on suitable tramps and the all-important weather forecast. Detailed route guides and topographical maps will further aid your safety, as will hire of a locator beacon and logging your trip details on AdventureSmart (www.adventuresmart.org.nz) via the on-site computer.

ℹ Getting There & Away

Fill your fuel tank before you leave Springfield (or Hokitika or Greymouth, if you're travelling in the other direction). There's a pump at Arthur's Pass Store but it's expensive and only operates from 8am until 5pm.

Atomic Shuttles (☑ 03-349 0697; www.atomic travel.co.nz) From Arthur's Pass a bus heads to/from Christchurch ($35, 2½ hours), Springfield ($35, one hour), Lake Brunner ($30, 50 minutes) and Greymouth ($35, 1¼ hours).

TranzAlpine (☑ 04-495 0775, 0800 872 467; www.kiwirailscenic.co.nz; all fares $89) One train daily in each direction stops in Arthur's Pass, heading to/from Springfield (1½ hours) and Christchurch (2½ hours), or Lake Brunner (one hour) and Greymouth (two hours).

West Coast Shuttle (☑ 03-768 0028; www.westcoastshuttle.co.nz) Buses stopping at Arthur's Pass head to/from Christchurch ($42, 2¾ hours) and Greymouth ($32, 1¾ hours).

Methven

POP 1707

Methven is busiest in winter, when it fills up with snow bunnies heading to nearby Mt Hutt. At other times tumbleweeds don't quite blow down the main street – much to the disappointment of the wannabe gunslingers arriving for the raucous October rodeo. Over summer it's a low-key and affordable base for fisherfolk, and for trampers and mountain bikers heading into the spectacular mountain foothills.

🏃 Activities

Ask at the i-SITE (p166) about local walks (including the town heritage trail and Methven Walk/Cycleway) and longer tramps, horse riding, mountain biking, fishing, clay-shooting, archery, golfing, scenic helicopter flights, and jetboating through the nearby Rakaia Gorge.

Black Diamond Safaris   SKIING
(📞 027 450 8283; www.blackdiamondsafaris.co.nz) Provides access to uncrowded club ski fields by 4WD. Prices start at $150 for transport, safety equipment and familiarisation, while $275 includes a lift pass, guiding and lunch.

Methven Heliski   SKIING
(📞 03-302 8108; www.methvenheli.co.nz; Main St; 5-run day trips $1045) Epic guided, all-inclusive backcountry ski trips, featuring five runs averaging drops of 750 to 1000 vertical metres.

Aoraki Balloon Safaris   BALLOONING
(📞 03-302 8172; www.nzballooning.com; flights $385) Early-morning combo of snow-capped peaks and a breakfast with bubbly.

Skydiving Kiwis   SKYDIVING
(📞 0800 359 549; www.skydivingkiwis.com; Ashburton Airport, Seafield Rd) Offers tandem jumps from 6,000ft ($235), 9,000ft ($285) and 12,000ft ($335), departing Ashburton airport.

🛏 Sleeping

Some accommodation is closed in summer; others open year-round. During the ski season, it pays to book well ahead, especially for budget accommodation. We've listed summer prices; expect them to rise in winter.

Alpenhorn Chalet   HOSTEL $
(📞 03-302 8779; www.alpenhorn.co.nz; 44 Allen St; dm $30, d $65-85; @ 📶) This small, inviting home has a leafy conservatory housing an indoor spa pool, a log fire, and complimentary espresso coffee. Bedrooms are spacious and brightly coloured, with lots of warm, natural wood; one double room has an en suite bathroom.

Rakaia Gorge
Camping Ground   CAMPGROUND $
(📞 03-302 9353; 6686 Arundel-Rakaia Gorge Rd; sites per adult/child under 12 $8.50/free) There are no powered sites and only toilets, showers and a small kitchen shelter, but don't let that put you off. This is the best camping ground for miles, perched handsomely above the ultra-blue Rakaia River, and a good base for exploring the area. Amenities closed May to October.

MT HUTT

Mt Hutt (📞 03-302 8811; www.nzski.com; day lift passes adult/child $98/56; ⊗ 9am-4pm) One of the highest ski areas in the southern hemisphere, and one of NZ's best, Mt Hutt has the largest skiable area of any of NZ's commercial fields (365 hectares). The ski field is only 26km from Methven but in wintry conditions the drive takes about 40 minutes; allow two hours from Christchurch. Road access is steep: be extremely cautious in lousy weather. **Methven Travel** (p166) runs shuttle buses from both towns in season ($20).

Half of the terrain is suitable for intermediate skiers, with a quarter each for beginning and advanced skiers. The longest run stretches for 2km. Other attractions include chairlifts, heliskiing and wide-open faces that are good for learning to snowboard. The season usually runs from mid-June to mid-October.

Mt Hutt Bunkhouse   HOSTEL $
(📞 03-302 8894; www.mthuttbunkhouse.co.nz; 8 Lampard St; dm $31, d $68-80, cottage $280-350; 📶) Enthusiastic on-site owners run this basic, well-equipped, bright and breezy hostel. There's a comfy lounge, and a large garden sporting a barbecue and a volleyball court. The cottage (sleeps up to 18) is economical for large groups.

Big Tree Lodge   HOSTEL $
(📞 03-302 9575; www.bigtreelodge.co.nz; 25 South Belt; dm $35-40, r $75-80, apt $110-160; 📶) Once a vicarage, this relaxed hostel has bunk-free dorms and wood-trimmed bathrooms. Tucked just behind is Little Tree Studio, a self-contained unit sleeping up to four people.

Redwood Lodge   HOSTEL, LODGE $$
(📞 03-302 8964; www.redwoodlodge.co.nz; 3 Wayne Pl; s $55-65, d $104-149; @ 📶) Expect a warm, woolly welcome and no dorms at this charming and peaceful family-friendly lodge. Most rooms are en suite, and bigger rooms can be reconfigured to accommodate families. The large shared lounge is ideal for resting ski-weary limbs.

Whitestone Cottages   RENTAL HOUSE $$$
(📞 03-928 8050; www.whitestonecottages.co.nz; 3016 Methven Hwy; cottages $175-255) When you just want to spread out, cook a meal, do your laundry and have your own space, these four large free-standing houses in leafy grounds

are just the ticket. Each sleeps six in two en suite bedrooms. Base rates are for two; each extra person is $35.

✕ Eating

Cafe 131 CAFE $
(131 Main St; meals $10-20; ⊘ 7.30am-5pm; 🛜) Polished timber and lead-light windows lend atmosphere to this conservative but reliable local favourite. Highlights include good coffee, tasty all-day breakfasts and admirable home-baking, with a tipple on offer should you fancy it. Free wi-fi makes this the town's de facto internet cafe.

★ Dubliner RESTAURANT $$
(www.dubliner.co.nz; 116 Main St; meals $26-34; ⊘ 4pm-late) This authentically Irish bar and restaurant is housed in Methven's lovingly restored old post office. Great food includes pizza, Irish stew and other hearty fare suitable for washing down with a pint of craft beer.

Aqua JAPANESE $$
(🗷 03-302 8335; 112 Main St; mains $13-21; ⊘ 5-9pm, closed Nov) A ski-season stalwart with unpredictable summer hours (so ring ahead), this tiny restaurant sports kimono-clad waitresses and traditional Japanese cuisine including yakisoba (fried noodles), ramen (noodle soup) and izakaya-style small plates to share with ice-cold beer or warming sake.

☆ Entertainment

Cinema Paradiso CINEMA
(🗷 03-302 1975; www.cinemaparadiso.co.nz; Main St; adult/child $17/12; ⊘ Wed-Mon) Quirky cinema with an art-house slant.

ℹ Information

Methven i-SITE (🗷 03-302 8955; www.methvenmthutt.co.nz; 160 Main St; ⊘ 9.30am-5pm daily Jul-Sep, 9am-5pm Mon-Fri, 10am-3pm Sat & Sun Oct-Jun; 🛜) Ask staff here about local walks and other activities, then enjoy the free art gallery and the hands-on NZ Alpine & Agriculture Encounter (adult/child $12.70/7.50).

Medical Centre (🗷 03-302 8105; The Square, Main St; ⊘ 8.30am-5.30pm)

ℹ Getting There & Away

Methven Travel (🗷 0800 684 888, 03-302 8106; www.methventravel.co.nz; 160 Main St) Runs shuttles between Methven and Christchurch airport ($45) three to four times a week October to June, increasing to three times daily during the ski season. Also runs shuttles up to Mt Hutt ski field in winter ($20 return).

Mt Somers

The small settlement of Mt Somers sits on the edge of the Southern Alps, beneath the mountain of the same name. The biggest drawcard to the area is the **Mt Somers track** (26km), a two-day tramp circling the mountain, linking the popular picnic spots of Sharplin Falls and Woolshed Creek. Trail highlights include volcanic formations, Māori rock drawings, deep river canyons and botanical diversity. The route is subject to sudden weather changes, so precautions should be taken.

There are two DOC huts on the track: **Pinnacles Hut** and **Woolshed Creek Hut** (adult/child $15/7.50). Hut tickets and information are available at the Mt Somers General Store and Staveley Store.

🛏 Sleeping & Eating

Mt Somers Holiday Park HOLIDAY PARK $
(🗷 03-303 9719; www.mountsomers.co.nz; 87 Hoods Rd; sites $18-32, cabin with/without bathroom $80/55) This small, friendly park offers pleasant sites in leafy grounds along with en suite, fully made-up cabins. You'll need to bring your own linen (or hire it) for the standard cabins. There's wi-fi at the tavern across the road.

Stronechrubie MOTEL $$
(🗷 03-303 9814; www.stronechrubie.co.nz; cnr Hoods Rd & SH72; d $120-160; 🛜) Comfortable chalets overlooking bird-filled gardens range in size from studio to two-bedroom, but it's the up-and-coming culinary hub that's the draw here. Enjoy a more formal meal in the lauded, long-standing restaurant (mains $34 to $38; serves dinner Wednesday through Sunday and lunch Sunday). Or head to the flash new bar and bistro (open 5.30pm to late Thursday to Saturday) for modern, tapas-style fare alongside lovely wines and craft beer.

Staveley Store CAFE
(🗷 03-303 0859; 2 Burgess Rd, Staveley; ⊘ 9am-4.30pm) Call into this cute little country store for a cheese roll, a sausage roll, a salad roll, ice cream or basic groceries. Also sells hut tickets for the Mt Somers track.

ℹ Information

Mt Somers General Store (🗷 03-303 9831; 61 Pattons Rd; ⊘ 8am-6pm) Hut tickets for the Mt Somers track, plus information.

SOUTH CANTERBURY

After crossing the Rangitata River into South Canterbury, SH1 and the Inland Scenic Route (SH72) narrow to within 8km of each other at the quaint town of Geraldine. Here you can choose to take the busy coastal highway through the port city of Timaru (and on to Oamaru and Dunedin), or continue inland on SH79 into Mackenzie Country, the expansive high ground from which NZ's tallest peaks rise above powder blue lakes. Most travellers pick the latter.

The Mackenzie Basin is a wild, tussock-strewn bowl at the foot of the Southern Alps, carved out by ancient glaciers. It takes its name from the legendary James 'Jock' McKenzie, who ran his stolen flocks in this then-uninhabited region in the 1840s. When he was finally caught, other settlers realised the potential for grazing in this seemingly inhospitable land and followed in his footsteps.

Director Sir Peter Jackson made the most of this rugged and untamed landscape while filming the *Lord of the Rings* films, choosing Mt Cook Village as the setting for Minas Tirith and a sheep station near Twizel as Gondor's Pelennor Fields.

❶ Getting There & Away

Atomic Shuttles (☑ 03-349 0697; www.atom-ictravel.co.nz) and **InterCity** (☑ 03-548 1538; www.intercity.co.nz) are the main transport players in South Canterbury, while **Cook Connection** (☑ 0800 266 526; www.cookconnect.co.nz) will get you up close to NZ's highest mountain.

Peel Forest

POP 180

Tucked away between the foothills of the Southern Alps and the Rangitata River (well signposted from SH72), Peel Forest is a small but important remnant of indigenous podocarp (conifer) forest. Many of the totara, kahikatea and matai trees here are hundreds of years old and are home to an abundance of birdlife including riflemen, kereru (wood pigeons), bellbirds, fantails and grey warblers.

A road from nearby Mt Peel sheep station leads to Mesopotamia, the run of English writer Samuel Butler in the 1860s. His experiences here partly inspired his famous satire *Erewhon* ('nowhere' backwards, almost; 1872).

◎ Sights

St Stephen's Church　　　　　　CHURCH
(1200 Peel Forest Rd) Sitting in a pretty glade right next to the general store, this gor-

geous little Anglican church (1885) has a warm wooden interior and some interesting stained glass. Look for St Francis of Assisi surrounded by NZ flora and fauna (get the kids to play spot-the-tuatara).

🏃 Activities

The magnificent podocarp forest consists of totara, kahikatea and matai. One fine example of totara on the **Big Tree Walk** (30 minutes return) is 31m tall, has a circumference of 9m and is over 1000 years old. There are also trails to **Emily Falls** (1½ hours return), **Rata Falls** (two hours return) and **Acland Falls** (one hour return); pick up the *Peel Forest Area* brochure from Peel Forest Store or download it from the DOC website (www.doc.govt.nz).

★Rangitata Rafts　　　　　　RAFTING
(☑ 0800 251 251; www.rafts.co.nz; Rangitata Gorge Rd; ⊙ Sep-May) Three-hour trips start in the stupendously beautiful braided Rangitata River valley before heading on an exhilarating ride through the gorge's Grade V rapids ($210, minimum age 15). The gentler two-hour journey downstream encounters only Grade II rapids ($170, minimum age six).

Peel Forest Horse Trekking　HORSE RIDING
(☑ 03-696 3703; www.peelforesthorsetrekking.co.nz; 1hr/2hr/half-day/full day $55/110/180/360) Ride through lush forest on short stints or multi-day treks ($950 to $1600, minimum four people). Accommodation packages are available in conjunction with Peel Forest Lodge.

🛏 Sleeping & Eating

★Peel Forest DOC Campsite　CAMPGROUND **$**
(☑ 03-696 3567; www.peelforest.co.nz; sites per adult/child $17/7.50, cabins $50-80) Near the Rangitata River, around 3km beyond Peel Forest Store, this lovely campground is equipped with basic two- to four-berth cabins (bring your own sleeping bag), hot showers and a kitchen. Check in at the store.

Peel Forest Lodge　　　　　　LODGE **$$$**
(☑ 03-696 3703; www.peelforestlodge.co.nz; 96 Brake Rd; d $380, additional adult/child $40/20; 🐾) This beautiful log cabin hidden in the forest has four rooms sleeping eight people. It only takes one booking at a time, so you and your posse will have the place to yourself. It's fully self-contained, but meals can be arranged, as can horse treks, rafting trips and other explorations of this fascinating area.

Peel Forest Store　　　　　　CAFE **$$**
(☑ 03-696 3567; www.peelforest.co.nz; 1202 Peel Forest Rd; lunch $13-19, dinner $20-29;

⊙ 9.30am-5.30pm Sun-Thu, to 9pm Fri & Sat; 🛜) Your one-stop-shop for groceries, hut tickets, internet access and DOC campsite (p167) bookings. The attached cafe-bar offers espresso and takeaways as well as burgers, pizza and suchlike to eat in.

ⓘ Getting There & Away

Atomic Shuttles (p171) and **InterCity** (p172) buses will get you as close as Geraldine, but you'll need your own transport or a lift to get to Peel Forest itself.

Timaru

POP 31,000

Trucking on along the SH1 through Timaru, travellers could be forgiven for thinking that this small port city is merely a handy place for food and fuel halfway between Christchurch and Dunedin. Drop the anchors, people! Straying into the CBD reveals a remarkably intact Edwardian precinct boasting some good dining and interesting shopping, not to mention a clutch of cultural attractions and lovely parks, all of which sustain at least a day's stopover.

The town's name comes from the Māori name Te Maru, meaning 'The Place of Shelter'. No permanent settlement existed here until 1839, when the Weller brothers set up a whaling station. The *Caroline,* a sailing ship that transported whale oil, gave the picturesque bay its name.

⦿ Sights

★ **Aigantighe Art Gallery**   GALLERY
(www.timaru.govt.nz/art-gallery; 49 Wai-iti Rd; ⊙ 10am-4pm Tue-Fri, noon-4pm Sat & Sun) FREE One of the South Island's largest public galleries, this 1908 mansion houses a notable collection of NZ and European art across various eras, alongside changing exhibitions staged by the gallery's ardent supporters. The Gaelic name means 'at home' and is pronounced 'egg-and-tie'. Should the gallery be closed, take a wander in the sculpture garden.

Caroline Bay Park   PARK, BEACH
(Marine Pde) Fronting the town, this expansive park ranges over an Edwardian-style garden under the Bay Hill cliff, then across broad lawns to low sand dunes and the beach itself. It has something for everyone between its playground, skate park, soundshell, ice cream kiosk, and myriad other attractions. Don't miss the Trevor Griffiths Rose Garden, a triumphant collection of heritage varieties, and consider an evening picnic making the most of the late sun. If you're lucky enough

to spot a seal or penguin on the beach, do keep your distance.

Te Ana Māori Rock Art Centre   MUSEUM
(📱 03-684 9141; www.teana.co.nz; 2 George St; adult/child admission $22/11, tours $130/65; ⊙ 10am-3pm) Passionate Ngāi Tahu guides bring this innovative multimedia exhibition about Māori rock paintings to life. You can also take a three-hour excursion (departing 2pm, November to April) to see isolated rock art in situ; prior booking is essential.

South Canterbury Museum   MUSEUM
(www.timaru.govt.nz/museum; Perth St; admission by donation; ⊙ 10am-4.30pm Tue-Fri, 1.30-4.30pm Sat & Sun) Historic and natural artefacts of the region are displayed here. Highlights include the Māori section and a replica of the aeroplane designed and flown by local pioneer aviator and inventor Richard Pearse. It's speculated that his mildly successful attempts at flight came before the Wright brothers' famous achievement in 1903.

Sacred Heart Basilica   CHURCH
(7 Craigie Ave, Parkside) Roman Catholic with a definite emphasis on the Roman, this beautiful neoclassical church (1911) impresses with multiple domes, Ionian columns and richly coloured stained glass. Its architect, Francis Petre, also designed the large basilicas in Christchurch (now in ruins) and Oamaru. Inside, there's an art-nouveau feel to the plasterwork, which includes intertwined floral and sacred-heart motifs. There are no set opening hours; try the side door.

Timaru Botanic Gardens   GARDENS
(cnr King & Queen Sts; ⊙ 8am-dusk) FREE Established in 1864, these gardens are a restful place to while away an hour or two, with a pond, lush lawns, shady trees, a playground and vibrant plant collections. With luck you'll arrive during rhododendron or rose bloom-time. Enter from Queen St, south of the city centre.

Trevor Griffiths Rose Garden   GARDENS
(Caroline Bay Park, Marine Pde) FREE Rose fans should visit the Trevor Griffiths Rose Garden, with almost 1200 romantic blooms set around arbours and water features. The finest displays are from December to February. It's a fragrant place to sit and contemplate on a balmy afternoon.

✷ Festivals & Events

Timaru Festival of Roses   CULTURAL
(www.festivalofroses.co.nz; ⊙ Nov) Featuring a market day, concerts and family fun, this week-long celebration capitalises on Tima-

Timaru

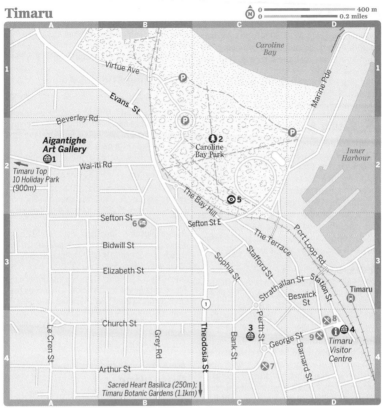

ru's obsession with all things rose-y. The festival is held annually for one week at the end of November.

🛏 Sleeping

Timaru Top 10 Holiday Park   HOLIDAY PARK $
(📞 03-684 7690; www.timaruholidaypark.co.nz; 154a Selwyn St, Marchwiel; sites $39-44, units with/without bathroom from $97/65; 🛜) 🅿 Tucked away in the suburbs, this excellent holiday park has clean, colourful amenities and a host of accommodation options throughout mature, leafy grounds. Helpful staff go out of their way to assist with local advice and bookings.

Glendeer Lodge   B&B $$
(📞 03-686 9274; www.glendeer.co.nz; 51 Scarborough Rd, Scarborough; d $170-260; 🛜) 🅿 Set on five acres, 4km from downtown, this purpose-built lodge is a peaceful option away from busy SH1. Walk to the lighthouse, relax in the garden watching fallow deer nibbling the paddock, then retire to the plush,

self-contained lodge offering three en suite rooms. The owners' fly-fishing guiding business lends a wilderness vibe.

Sefton Homestay
B&B $$

(☑ 03-688 0017; www.seftonhomestay.co.nz; 32 Sefton St, Seaview; s & d $130-140; ☎) Set back behind a pretty garden, this imposing heritage house has two guest rooms: one with an en suite, and a larger bedroom with an adjoining sun lounge and a bathroom across the hall. Swap travel stories over a glass of port in the guest sitting room.

✖ Eating & Drinking

Arthur Street Kitchen
CAFE $

(8 Arthur St; snacks $2-8, mains $9-19; ☺ 7am-5.30pm Mon-Fri, 9am-3pm Sat; ☑) Timaru's hippest coffee house follows the recipe for success: namely great coffee, contemporary cafe fare, good tunes and a mix of arty inside and sunny outside seating. Made with flair and care, the food offering includes grainy salads, refined sandwiches and pastry treats, plus an à la carte breakfast and lunch menu.

★ Oxford
MODERN NZ $$

(☑ 03-688 3297; www.theoxford.co.nz; 152 Stafford St; mains $26-32; ☺ 11am-late Mon & Wed-Fri, 9.30am-late Sat & Sun) This sophisticated corner restaurant honours its 1925 building with stylish monochrome decor and a feature wall commemorating the day Timaru went bust. The food is high-class comfort food starring local produce such as venison, beef and salmon, while an alluring drinks list encourages a pop in for wine and cheese, or a glass of sticky with golden syrup pudding.

Koji
JAPANESE $$

(☑ 03-686 9166; 7 George St; snacks $5-15, mains $23-36; ☺ 11am-2pm & 5-9pm Tue-Fri, 5pm-10pm Sat & Sun) Unassuming it may be from the exterior, but this split-level restaurant makes a jolly good job of creating a Japanese vibe. Sit in the downstairs dining room or at the cute bar, or better still head up to the upper level and watch flames rise from the teppanyaki grill. Delicious dishes include sashimi, tempura, gyoza and *takoyaki* complete with dancing bonito flakes.

Speight's Ale House
PUB

(www.timarualehouse.co.nz; 2 George St; ☺ 11.30am-late; ☎) The pub most likely to be registering a pulse of an evening, this enterprise redeems its dubious decor and over-branding with a sunny courtyard and the historic features of the 1870s stone warehouse it occupies.

❶ Information

Timaru Visitor Centre (☑ 03-687 9997; www.southcanterbury.org.nz; 2 George St; ☺ 10am-3pm; ☎) Across from the train station (trains in this area only carry freight, not passengers), the visitor centre shares its building with the Te Ana Māori Rock Art Centre. There's free wi-fi throughout Timaru's CBD and Caroline Bay Park.

❶ Getting There & Away

AIR

Air New Zealand (☑ 0800 737 000; www.airnewzealand.co.nz) Flies from Timaru's Richard Pearse Airport to Wellington and Auckland, and back, around twice daily.

BUS

Atomic Shuttles (☑ 03-349 0697; www.atomictravel.co.nz) Stops by the visitor centre twice daily, en route to Christchurch ($25, 2½ hours), Oamaru ($20, 1¼ hours) and Dunedin ($25, 2¾ hours).

Budget Buses & Shuttles (☑ 03-615 5119; www.budgetshuttles.co.nz; ☺ Mon-Sat) Offers a door-to-door shuttle to Christchurch ($47), along with scheduled runs ($27).

InterCity (☑ 03-365 1113; www.intercity.co.nz) Stops outside the train station, with buses to Christchurch (from $28, 2½ hours, two daily), Oamaru (from $14, one hour, two daily), Dunedin (from $32, three hours, two daily), Gore (from $47, six hours, daily) and Te Anau (from $51, eight hours, daily).

Geraldine

POP 2420

Consummately Canterbury in its dedication to English-style gardening, pretty Geraldine has a village vibe and an active arts scene. In spring, duck behind the war memorial on Talbot St to the River Garden Walk, where green-fingered locals have gone completely bonkers planting azaleas and rhododendrons. Ask visitor centre staff about the trails in Talbot Forest on the town fringe.

◎ Sights & Activities

Geraldine Museum
MUSEUM

(5 Cox St; ☺ 10am-3pm Mon-Sat, 12.30-3pm Sun) **FREE** Occupying the photogenic Town Board Office building (1885), and sporting a new side wing, this cute little museum tells the town's story with an eclectic mix of exhibits, including an extensive collection of photographs.

Vintage Car & Machinery Museum
MUSEUM

(☑ 03-693 8756; 178 Talbot St; adult/child $10/free; ☺ 9.30am-4pm Oct-May, 10am-4pm Sat & Sun Jun-Sep) You don't have to be a rev-head to enjoy this vintage car collection featuring a 1907 De Dion-Bouton and a gleaming 1926

Bentley. There's also a purpose-built Daimler used for the 1954 royal tour, plus some very nice Jags, 1970s muscle cars and all sorts of farm machinery.

Big Rock Canyons ADVENTURE SPORTS
(☑ 0800 244 762; www.bigrockcanyons.co.nz; ☉ Oct-Apr) Offers slippy, slidey day-long adventures in the Kaumira Canyon ($360) near Geraldine, as well as in five other canyons with varying degrees of difficulty.

🛏 Sleeping

Rawhiti Backpackers HOSTEL $
(☑ 03-693 8252; www.rawhitibackpackers.co.nz; 27 Hewlings St; dm/s/d $34/50/78; 🛜) On a hillside on the edge of town, this former maternity hospital is now a sunny and spacious hostel with good communal areas, comfortable rooms, a lemon tree and two cute cats. Bikes are available to borrow.

Geraldine Kiwi Holiday Park HOLIDAY PARK, MOTEL $
(☑ 03-693 8147; www.geraldineholidaypark.co.nz; 39 Hislop St; sites $34-39, d $52-135; @🛜) 🐾 This top-notch holiday park is set amid well-established parkland, two minutes' walk from the high street. Tidy accommodation ranges from budget cabins to plusher motel units, plus there's a TV room and playground.

Scenic Route Motor Lodge MOTEL $$
(☑ 03-693 9700; www.motelscenicroute.co.nz; 28 Waihi Tce; d $135-155; 🛜) There's a vaguely heritage feel to this stone and timber motel, but the modern units have double-glazing, flat-screen TVs and even stylish wallpaper. Larger studios have spa baths.

✕ Eating

Long overdue to be lauded 'Cheese & Pickle Capital of NZ', Geraldine is excellent for self-caterers. It boasts a terrific butchery and numerous artisan producers in the Four Peaks Plaza; seek out a bag of Heartland potato chips here, made down the road. Every Saturday during summer the town kicks into foodie gear with a **farmers' market** (St Mary's Church car park; ☉ 9am-12.30pm Sat Oct-Apr) 🐾.

★ Talbot Forest Cheese DELI $
(www.talbotforestcheese.co.nz; Four Peaks Plaza, Talbot Rd; cheeses $5-10; ☉ 9am-5pm; 🍴) This little shop not only showcases the cheeses made on-site (including fine Parmesan and Gruyère), it doubles as a deli with all you need for a tasty picnic.

MACKENZIE COUNTRY

Heading to Queenstown and the southern lakes from Christchurch means a turn off SH1 onto SH79, a scenic route towards the high country and the Aoraki/Mt Cook National Park's eastern foothills. The road passes through Geraldine and Fairlie before joining SH8, which heads over Burkes Pass to the blue intensity of Lake Tekapo.

The expansive high ground from which the scenic peaks of Aoraki/Mt Cook National Park escalate is known as Mackenzie Country, after the legendary James 'Jock' McKenzie, who ran his stolen flocks in this then-uninhabited region in the 1840s. When he was finally caught, other settlers realised the potential of the land and followed in his footsteps. The first people to traverse the Mackenzie were the Māori, trekking from Banks Peninsula to Otago hundreds of years ago.

Verde CAFE $
(☑ 03-693 9616; 45 Talbot St; mains $11-18; ☉ 9am-4pm; 🍴) Down the lane beside the old post office and set in beautiful gardens, this excellent cafe is easily the best of Geraldine's eateries. It's just a shame that it's not open for dinner.

☆ Entertainment

Geraldine Cinema CINEMA
(☑ 03-693 8118; www.geraldinecinema.co.nz; Talbot St; adult/child $12/8) Snuggle into an old sofa to watch a Hollywood favourite or an art-house surprise. There's also occasional live music, usually with a folk, blues or country spin.

ℹ Information

Geraldine Visitor Information Centre (☑ 03-693 1101; www.southcanterbury.org.nz; 38 Waihi Tce; ☉ 8am-5.30pm) The information centre is located inside the Kiwi Country visitor complex. See also www.gogeraldine.co.nz.

ℹ Getting There & Away

Atomic Shuttles (☑ 03-349 0697; www.atomictravel.co.nz) Daily buses to/from Christchurch ($30, two hours), Lake Tekapo (from $20, 1¼ hours), Twizel ($30, two hours), Cromwell (from $30, 4¼ hours) and Queenstown ($35, five hours).

Budget Buses & Shuttles (☑ 03-615 5119; www.budgetshuttles.co.nz; ☉ Mon-Sat) Offers a door-to-door shuttle to Christchurch ($57), along with a cheaper scheduled run ($47).

InterCity (☏ 03-365 1113; www.intercity.co.nz) Daily coaches head to/from Christchurch (from $32, 2¼ hours), Lake Tekapo (from $21, 1¼ hours), Cromwell (from $40, 4¾ hours) and Queenstown (from $42, 5¾ hours).

Fairlie

POP 693

Leafy Fairlie describes itself as 'the gateway to the Mackenzie', but in reality this wee, rural town feels a world away from tussocky Mackenzie Country over Burkes Pass, to the west. The bakery and picnic area make it a good lunchtime stop.

◎ Sights

Fairlie Heritage Museum   MUSEUM
(www.fairlieheritagemuseum.co.nz; 49 Mt Cook Rd; adult/child $6/free; ⊙9.30am-5pm) A somewhat dusty window on to rural NZ of old, this museum endears with its farm machinery, model aeroplanes, dodgy dioramas and the generally random. Highlights include the home-spun gyrocopter, historic cottage, and new automotive wing featuring mint-condition tractors. The little cafe attached bakes a good biscuit.

🏃 Activities

The information centre can provide information on nearby **tramping and mountain biking** tracks. The main ski resort, **Mt Dobson** (☏ 03-685 8039; www.mtdobson.co.nz; daily lift passes adult/child $78/44), lies in a 3km-wide treeless basin 26km northwest of Fairlie. There's also a club ski field 29km northwest at **Fox Peak** (☏ 03-685 8539, snow-phone 03-688 0044; www.foxpeak.co.nz; daily lift passes adult/child $60/10) in the Two Thumb Range.

🛏 Sleeping & Eating

Musterer's   MOTEL $$
(☏ 03-685 8284; www.musterers.co.nz; 9 Gordon St; d $150, extra adult/child $25/15; 🅿) On the western edge of Fairlie, these stylish self-contained cottages afford all mod cons with the bonus of a shared barbecue area and woolshed 'lounge', plus donkeys, goats and a pony. Plush, with tiled bathrooms, the three family units (sleeping up to six) and one double studio each have their own wood-fired hot tub ($40 extra) for a stargazing soak.

★Fairlie Bakehouse   BAKERY $
(www.liebers.co.nz; 74 Main St; pies $5-7; ⊙7.30am-4.30pm; 🅿) Famous for miles around and probably the top-ranking reason to stop in

Fairlie, this terrific little bakery turns out exceptional pies including the legendary salmon and bacon. American doughnuts and raspberry cheesecake elbow their way in among Kiwi classics such as custard squares and cream buns. Yum.

ℹ️ Information

Fairlie Heartland Resource & Information Centre (☏ 03-685 8496; www.fairlienz.com; 67 Main St; ⊙10am-4pm Mon-Fri) This helpful centre stocks the well-produced *Fairlie* brochure (free).

ℹ️ Getting There & Away

Atomic Shuttles (☏ 03-349 0697; www.atomic travel.co.nz) Daily buses to/from Christchurch ($30, 2½ hours), Geraldine ($20, 35 minutes), Lake Tekapo ($20, 40 minutes), Cromwell ($35, 3¾ hours) and Queenstown ($35, 4½ hours).

InterCity (☏ 03-365 1113; www.intercity.co.nz) Daily coaches head to/from Christchurch (from $34, 3¼ hours), Lake Tekapo (from $13, 35 minutes), Mt Cook (from $30, 2½ hours), Cromwell (from $39, four hours) and Queenstown (from $40, five hours).

Lake Tekapo

POP 369

Born of a hydropower scheme completed in 1953, today Tekapo is booming off the back of a holiday home explosion and tourism, although it has long been a popular tour-bus stop on the route between Christchurch and Queenstown. Its popularity is well deserved: the town faces out across the turquoise lake to a backdrop of snow-capped mountains.

Such splendid Mackenzie Country and Southern Alps views are reason enough to linger, but there's infinitely more to see if you wait till dark. In 2012 the Aoraki Mackenzie area was declared an International Dark Sky Reserve, one of only ten in the world, and Tekapo's Mt John – under pollution free skies – is the ultimate place to experience the region's glorious night sky.

◎ Sights

Church of the Good Shepherd   CHURCH
(Pioneer Dr; ⊙9am-5pm) The prime disgorging point for tour buses, this interdenominational lakeside church was built of stone and oak in 1935. A picture window behind the altar gives churchgoers a distractingly divine view of lake and mountain majesty; needless to say, it's a firm favourite for weddings. Come early in the morning or late afternoon to avoid the peace-shattering masses.

Nearby is a statue of a collie, a tribute to the sheepdogs that helped develop Mackenzie Country.

🏃 Activities

When the Mackenzie Basin was scoured out by glaciers, **Mt John** (1029m) remained as an island of tough bedrock in the centre of a vast river of ice. A road leads to the summit, or you can walk via a circuit track (2½ hours return). To extend it to an all-day tramp, continue on to Alexandrina and McGregor Lakes.

The free town map details this and other walks in the area, along with cycling tracks including **Cowan's Hill** and those in **Lake Tekapo Regional Park**. Mountain bikes (per hour/half-day $10/25) and kayaks (per hour $25) can be hired from the YHA Lake Tekapo (p174).

In winter, Lake Tekapo is a base for downhill skiing at Mt Dobson (p172) and **Roundhill** (☑ 021 680 694, snow-phone 03-680 6977; www.roundhill.co.nz; daily lift passes adult/child $78/39), and cross-country skiing on the Two Thumb Range.

Mackenzie Alpine Horse Trekking HORSE RIDING
(☑ 0800 628 269; www.maht.co.nz; Godley Peaks Rd; 1hr/2hr/day $70/110/310) Located on the road to Mt John, these folks run various treks taking in the area's amazing scenery.

Tekapo Springs SPA
(☑ 03-680 6550; www.tekaposprings.co.nz; 6 Lakeside Dr; adult/child pools $22/13, ice-skating $16/12; ◷ 10am-9pm) Turn up the heat from the 36°C pool, to the 38°C and 40°C pools, soaking in the thermal goodness in landscaped surrounds overlooking the lake. There's a steam room and sauna ($6 extra), along with a day spa offering various indulgences including massage (from $80). Cold pools and an 'aqua play' park were under development on our last visit.

Attached to the complex is a winter ice-skating rink and snow-tubing slide, while in summer there's the world's largest inflatable slide and slippery-slope tubing.

👉 Tours

Earth & Sky TOUR
(☑ 03-680 6960; www.earthandsky.co.nz; SH8) 🚶
If you've ever wanted to tour an observatory and survey the night sky, this is the place to do it. Nightly tours head up to the University of Canterbury's observatory on Mt John (adult/child $145/80). Day tours of the facility are given on demand in winter, while in summer there's usually a guide available at

---

LAKE PUKAKI LOOKOUT

The largest of the Mackenzie's three alpine lakes, Pukaki is a vast jewel of totally surreal colour. On its shore, just off SH8 between Twizel and Lake Tekapo, is a well-signed and perennially popular lookout affording picture-perfect views across the lake's waters all the way up to Aoraki/Mt Cook and its surrounding peaks.

Beside the lookout, the **Lake Pukaki Visitor Centre** (www.mtcookalpinesalmon.com; SH8; ◷ 8.30am-6pm) is actually an outpost of Mt Cook Alpine Salmon, the highest salmon farm on the planet, which operates in a hydroelectric canal system some distance away. The visitor centre offers the opportunity to pick up some sashimi ($10) or a smoked morsel for supper.

---

the observatory from around midday to 3pm (adult/child $20/10).

For those on a tighter budget or with small children in tow (the minimum age for Mt John tours is eight), there are hour-long night tours to the smaller Cowan Observatory (adult/child $90/50).

Air Safaris SCENIC FLIGHTS
(☑ 03-680 6880; www.airsafaris.co.nz; SH8) Awe-inspiring views of Aoraki/Mt Cook National Park's peaks and glaciers are offered on the 'Grand Traverse' fixed-wing flight (adult/child $360/230), and there are various other options including similar trips in a helicopter.

Tekapo Helicopters SCENIC FLIGHTS
(☑ 03-680 6229; www.tekapohelicopters.co.nz; SH8) Offers five options, from a 20-minute flight ($199) to an hour-long trip taking in Aoraki/Mt Cook, and Fox and Franz Josef Glaciers ($500). All flights include an alpine landing.

🛏 Sleeping

Tailor-Made-Tekapo Backpackers HOSTEL $
(☑ 03-680 6700; www.tailor-made-backpackers.co.nz; 11 Aorangi Cres; dm/s $32/62, d with/without bathroom $95/85; 🛜) Favouring beds rather than bunks, this sociable hostel is spread over three well-tended houses on a peaceful street 300m from town. There's also a large garden complete with barbecue, hammock, chickens and bunnies, plus tennis and basketball courts next door for the energetic.

Tekapo Motels & Holiday Park   HOLIDAY PARK, MOTEL **$**
(☑03-680 6825; www.laketekapo-accommodation.co.nz; 2 Lakeside Dr; sites $34-44, dm $30-32, d $90-110; 🛜) Supremely situated on terraced, lakefront grounds, this place has something for everyone. Backpackers get the cosy, log-cabin-style lodge, while others can enjoy cute Kiwi 'bachs', basic cabins, and smart en suite units with particularly good views. Campervaners and tenters are spoilt for choice, and share the fantastic new amenities block.

YHA Lake Tekapo   HOSTEL **$**
(☑03-680 6857; www.yha.co.nz; 3 Simpson Lane; sites per person $20, dm $33-38, d $99-104; @🛜) 🏵 Older-style, tidy, and well-maintained hostel with million-dollar views of Lake Tekapo. Snuggle around the fire in winter, or chill out by the lake in summer. Make the most of the local cycle trails with bikes for hire.

★**Lake Tekapo Lodge**   B&B **$$$**
(☑03-680 6566; www.laketekapolodge.co.nz; 24 Aorangi Cres; r $300-450; 🛜) This fabulously designed, luxurious B&B is filled to the brim with covetable contemporary Kiwi art, and boasts painterly views of the lake and mountains from the sumptuous rooms and lounge. Fine-dining evening meals by arrangement.

Chalet Boutique Motel   APARTMENTS **$$$**
(☑03-680 6774; www.thechalet.co.nz; 14 Pioneer Dr; units $190-310; 🛜) The 'boutique motel' tag doesn't do justice to this collection of attractive accommodation options in three adjacent properties beside the lake. The wonderfully private 'Henkel hut' is a stylish option for lovebirds. Charming hosts will happily provide all the local information you need.

🍴 Eating & Drinking

★**Astro Café**   CAFE **$**
(Mt John University Observatory; mains $7-12; ⏱9am-5pm) This glass-walled pavilion atop Mt John has spectacular 360-degree views across the entire Mackenzie Basin – quite possibly one of the planet's best locations for a cafe. Tuck into bagels with local salmon, or fresh ham-off-the-bone sandwiches; coffee and cake are good, too.

Kohan   JAPANESE **$$**
(☑03-680 6688; www.kohannz.com; SH8; dishes $8-20, mains $19-30; ⏱11am-2pm daily, 6-9pm Mon-Sat) With all the aesthetic charm of an office cafeteria, this is still one of Tekapo's best dining options, both for its distracting lake views, and its authentic Japanese food including

fresh-as-a-daisy salmon sashimi. Leave room for the handmade green-tea ice cream.

Mackenzie's Bar & Grill   BAR
(SH8; ⏱11.30am-late Mon-Fri, 10am-late Sat & Sun) While full immersion on the menu front is not necessarily advisable, this tidy gastro-pub-style establishment is a safe bet for a few cold ones and some bar snacks. The views are grand, particularly outside from the patio and garden in front.

ℹ Information

Kiwi Treasures & Information Centre (☑03-680 6686; SH8; ⏱8am-5.30pm Mon-Fri, to 6pm Sat & Sun) This little gift shop doubles as the post office and info centre with local maps and advice, plus bookings for local activities and national bus services. See also www.tekapotourism.co.nz.

ℹ Getting There & Away

Atomic Shuttles (☑03-349 0697; www.atomictravel.co.nz) Daily buses to/from Christchurch ($30, 3¼ hours), Geraldine ($20, 1¼ hours), Twizel ($20, 40 minutes), Cromwell ($30, three hours) and Queenstown ($30, 3¾ hours).

Cook Connection (☑0800 266 526; www.cookconnect.co.nz) Shuttle service to Mt Cook ($35, 1½ hours).

InterCity (☑03-365 1113; www.intercity.co.nz) Daily coaches head to/from Christchurch (from $36, 3¾ hours), Geraldine (from $21, 1¼ hours), Mt Cook (from $30, 1½ hours), Cromwell (from $36, 2¾ hours) and Queenstown (from $36, 4¾ hours).

Twizel

POP 1300

Pronounced 'twy-zel' but teased with 'Twizzel' and even 'Twizzelsticks' by outsiders, Twizel gets the last laugh. The town was built in 1968 to service construction of the nearby hydroelectric power station, and was due for obliteration in 1984 when the project was completed. But there was no way the locals were upping their twizzlesticks and relinquishing their relaxed, mountain country lifestyle.

Today the town is thriving with a modest boom in holiday home subdivisions and recognition from travellers that – as plain-Jane as it is – it's actually in the middle of everything and has almost everything one might need (within reason).

🏃 Activities

Twizel sits in the midst of some spectacular country offering all sorts of adventure. On

ALPS 2 OCEAN CYCLE TRAIL

One of the best Great Rides within the New Zealand Cycle Trail (www.nzcycletrail.com), the 'A2O' serves up epic vistas on its way from the foot of the Southern Alps all the way to the Pacific Ocean at Oamaru.

New Zealand's highest mountain – Aoraki/Mt Cook – is just one of many stunning sights. Others include braided rivers, glacier-carved valleys, turquoise hydro-lakes, tussock-covered highlands and lush farmland. Off-the-bike activities include wine tasting, penguin spotting, glider flights and soaking in alfresco hot tubs. Country hospitality, including food and accommodation, along with shuttles and other services, make the whole trip easy to organise and enjoy.

The trail is divided into nine easy-to-intermediate sections across terrain varying from canal paths, quiet country roads, old railway lines and expertly cut cross-country track, to some rougher, hilly stuff for the eager. The whole journey takes around four to six days, but it can easily be sliced into short sections.

Twizel is an excellent base for day rides. Options include taking a shuttle to Lake Tekapo for a five- to six-hour, big-sky ride back to Twizel, or riding from Twizel out to Lake Ohau Lodge for lunch or dinner. Both rides, sections of the Alps 2 Ocean, serve up the sublime lake and mountain scenery for which the Mackenzie is famous.

The trail is well supported by tour companies offering bike hire, shuttles, luggage transfers and accommodation. These include Twizel-based **Cycle Journeys** (☑ 03-435 0578, 0800 224 475; www.cyclejourneys.co.nz; 2a Wairepo Rd) and **Jollie Biker** (☑ 027 223 1761, 03-435 0517; www.thejolliebiker.co.nz; 193 Glen Lyon Rd). The Alps 2 Ocean website (www.alps2ocean.com) has comprehensive details.

the edge of town, **Lake Ruataniwha** is popular for rowing, boating and windsurfing. Pick up the excellent town map to find it, along with walking and cycle trails including a nice ramble along the river. Twizel is also the best hub for day rides on the Alps 2 Ocean Cycle Trail.

Fishing in local rivers, canals and lakes is also big business; ask at the information centre about local guides, and ask them about swimming in **Loch Cameron** while you're at it (but don't tell them we tipped you off!).

Ohau SKIING, SNOWBOARDING
(☑ 03-438 9885; www.ohau.co.nz; daily lift passes adult/child $83/34) This commercial ski area lines the flanks of Mt Sutton, 42km from Twizel. Expect a high percentage of intermediate and advanced runs, excellent terrain for snowboarding, two terrain parks, and Lake Ohau Lodge for après-ski.

☞ Tours

Helicopter Line SCENIC FLIGHTS
(☑ 03-435 0370; www.helicopter.co.nz; Pukaki Airport, Harry Wigley Dr) Flight options include the hour-long Aoraki/Mt Cook Discovery ($750), the 45-minute Southern Alps Experience ($540), the 35-minute Alpine Scenic Flight ($355) and the 25-minute Alpine Express ($295). All but the shortest guarantee snow landings.

OneRing Tours TOUR
(☑ 03-435 0073, 0800 213 868; www.lordoftheringstour.com; cnr Ostler & Wairepo Sts) How often do you get the opportunity to charge around like a mad thing wielding replica *LOTR* gear? Not often enough! Tours head onto the sheep station used for the location of the Battle of the Pelennor Fields and include lots of information about the filming. Choose between a two-hour version (adult/child $84/45) and a truncated one-hour option (adult/child $64/35).

There's also an adults-only twilight tour; enjoy beer, wine and nibbles as the sun sets over Gondor ($115).

🛏 Sleeping

Twizel Holiday Park HOLIDAY PARK $
(☑ 03-435 0507; www.twizelholidaypark.co.nz; 122 Mackenzie Dr; sites from $36, dm $32, units $95-215; 🖧) Offers green, flower-filled grounds, and accommodation in a refurbished maternity hospital. There are a few en suite cabins and a bunk room along with grassed sites and tight communal facilities. The modern, self-contained cottages are particularly good value. Bike hire is available for $35 per day.

★**Lake Ohau Lodge** LODGE $$
(☑ 03-438 9885; www.ohau.co.nz; Lake Ohau Rd; s $144-200, d $159-220) 🍃 Idyllically sited

OFF THE BEATEN TRACK

RUATANIWHA CONSERVATION PARK

Taking in a large chunk of the space between Lake Pukaki and Lake Ohau, the 368-sq-km protected area of **Ruataniwha Conservation Park** (www.doc.govt.nz) includes the rugged Ben Ohau Range along with the Dobson, Hopkins, Huxley, Temple and Maitland valleys. It offers plenty of tramping and mountain-biking opportunities, as detailed in DOC's *Ruataniwha Conservation Park* pamphlet (available online), with several day options close to Twizel.

DOC huts and camping areas are scattered throughout the park, and a more comfortable stay is available at Lake Ohau Lodge (p175). Passing through these parts is the Alps 2 Ocean Cycle Trail (p175), a great way to survey these grand surroundings.

on the western shore of remote Lake Ohau, 42km west of Twizel. Accommodation includes everything from budget rooms with shared facilities to upmarket rooms with decks and mountain views.

The lodge is the buzzy wintertime hub of the Ohau Ski Field; in summer it's a quieter retreat. DB&B packages are available.

Omahau Downs　　　　LODGE, COTTAGE **$$**
(☑ 03-435 0199; www.omahau.co.nz; SH8; s $115, d $135-165, cottages $125-225; ☉ closed Jun-Aug; ☜) This farmstead, 2km north of Twizel, has two cosy, self-contained cottages (one sleeping up to six), and a lodge with sparkling, modern rooms and a deck looking out at the Ben Ohau Range.

Heartland Lodge　　　B&B, APARTMENT **$$$**
(☑ 03-435 0008; www.heartland-lodge.co.nz; 19 North West Arch; apt $170, s $240-280, d $280-320; ☜) Built on the leafy outskirts of town, this elegant modern house offers spacious, en suite rooms upstairs and comfortable, convivial communal space on the ground floor. Friendly hosts prepare a cooked breakfast using organic, local produce where possible. The adjacent 'retreat' apartment (sleeping up to six) has its own kitchenette; breakfast not provided.

✗ Eating

★ Shawty's　　　　　　　CAFE **$$**
(☑ 03-435 3155; www.shawtys.co.nz; 4 Market Pl; brunch $12-20, dinner $29-34; ☉ 8.30am-3pm Mon & Tue, to late Wed-Sun Apr-Oct, to late daily Nov-Mar; ☜ ☜ ☜) The town centre's social hub and hottest meal ticket serves up big breakfasts, gourmet pizzas ($18 to $20) and fancy lamb racks as the sun goes down. A considerate kids' menu, cocktails, alfresco dining and live music make it all the more endearing.

High Country Salmon　　　　FISH **$$**
(☑ 0800 400 385; www.highcountrysalmonfarm.co.nz; SH8; ☉ 8.30am-6pm) The glacial waters of this floating fish farm, 3km from Twizel, produce mighty delicious fish, available as fresh whole fillets and smoked portions. Our pick is the hot-smoked, flaked into hot pasta, perhaps with a dash of cream. (The Lonely Planet Cookbook, coming to a bookshop near you...)

ℹ Information

Twizel Information Centre (☑ 03-435 3124; www.twizel.info; Market Pl; ☉ 8.30am-5pm Mon-Fri, 11am-3pm Sat & Sun)

ℹ Getting There & Away

Atomic Shuttles (☑ 03-349 0697; www.atomictravel.co.nz) Runs daily services to the following:

DESTINATION	FARE	DURATION
Christchurch	$35	3¾hr
Cromwell	$30	2¼hr
Geraldine	$25	2hr
Lake Tekapo	$20	40min
Queenstown	$30	3¼hr

Cook Connection (☑ 0800 266 526; www.cookconnect.co.nz) runs daily shuttle services to Mt Cook Village (one way/return $27/49, one hour).

InterCity (☑ 03-365 1113; www.intercity.co.nz) Runs daily services to the following:

DESTINATION	FARES FROM	DURATION
Christchurch	$40	5¼hr
Cromwell	$29	2hr
Lake Tekapo	$13	50mins
Mt Cook Village	$32	1hr
Queenstown	$35	3hr

Naked Bus (www.nakedbus.com) services Christchurch and Queenstown/Wanaka.

Aoraki/Mt Cook National Park

POP 120

The spectacular 700-sq-km Aoraki/Mt Cook National Park, along with Fiordland, Aspiring and Westland National Parks, is part of the Southwest New Zealand (Te Wahipounamu) World Heritage Area, which extends from Westland's Cook River down to Fiordland. Fenced in by the Southern Alps and the Two Thumb, Liebig and Ben Ohau Ranges, more than one-third of the park has a blanket of permanent snow and glacial ice.

Of the 23 NZ mountains over 3000m, 19 are in this park. The highest is mighty Aoraki/Mt Cook – at 3754m it's the tallest peak in Australasia. Among the region's other many great peaks are Sefton, Tasman, Silberhorn, Malte Brun, La Perouse, Hicks, De la Beche, Douglas and the Minarets. Many can be ascended from Westland National Park, and there are climbers' huts on both sides of the divide.

Aoraki/Mt Cook is a wonderful sight, assuming there's no cloud in the way. Most visitors arrive on tour buses, stop at the Hermitage hotel for photos, and then zoom off back down SH80. Hang around to soak up this awesome peak and the surrounding landscape, and to try the excellent short walks. On the trails, look for the thar, a Himalayan goat; the chamois, smaller and of lighter build than the thar, and originally hailing from Europe; and red deer, also European. Summertime brings into bloom the Mt Cook lily, a large mountain buttercup, and mountain daisies, gentians and edelweiss.

History

Known to Māori as Aoraki (Cloud Piercer), after an ancestral deity in Māori mythology, the mountain was given its English name in 1851, in honour of explorer Captain James Cook.

This region has always been the focus of climbing in NZ. On 2 March 1882 William Spotswood Green and two Swiss alpinists failed to reach the summit of Cook after an epic 62-hour ascent. Two years later a trio of local climbers – Tom Fyfe, George Graham and Jack Clarke – were spurred into action by the news that two well-known European alpinists were coming to attempt Cook, and set off to climb it before the visitors. On Christmas Day 1894 they ascended the Hooker Glacier and north ridge, a brilliant climb in those days, and stood on the summit.

In 1913 Australian climber Freda du Faur became the first woman to reach the summit. In 1948 Edmund Hillary's party climbed the south ridge; Hillary went on to become the first to reach the summit of Mt Everest. Since then, most of the daunting face routes have been climbed.

⊙ Sights

★ **Aoraki/Mt Cook National Park Visitor Centre** MUSEUM
(☑ 03-435 1186; www.doc.govt.nz; 1 Larch Grove; ⊙ 8.30am-4.30pm, to 5pm Oct-Apr) **FREE** Arguably the best DOC visitor centre in NZ. It not only dispatches all necessary information and advice on tramping routes and weather conditions, it also houses excellent displays on the park's natural and human history. It's a fabulous place to commune with the wilderness, even on a rainy day. Most activities can be booked here.

Sir Edmund Hillary Alpine Centre MUSEUM
(www.hermitage.co.nz; The Hermitage, Terrace Rd; adult/child $20/10; ⊙ 7am-8.30pm Oct-Mar, 8am-7pm Apr-Sep) This multimedia museum opened just three weeks before the January 2008 death of the man widely regarded as the greatest New Zealander of all time. Sir Ed's commentary tracks were recorded only a few months before he died. As well as memorabilia and displays about mountaineering, there's a domed digital planetarium (showing four different digital presentations) and a cinema (screening four documentaries, including the *Mt Cook Magic* 3D movie and a fascinating 75-minute film about Sir Ed's conquest of Mt Everest).

🏃 Activities

Tramping & Climbing

Various easy walks from the Hermitage area are outlined in the (multilingual) *Walking & Cycling Tracks* pamphlet available from the visitor centre and online. Longer tramps are only recommended for those with mountaineering experience, as tracks and conditions at higher altitudes become dangerous. Highly changeable weather is typical around here: Aoraki/Mt Cook is only 44km from the coast and weather conditions rolling in from the Tasman Sea can mean sudden storms.

As for climbing, there's unlimited scope for the experienced, but those without experience must go with a guide. Regardless of your skills, take every precaution – more than 200 people have died in climbing accidents in the park. The bleak *In Memoriam* book in the visitor information centre begins with the first death on Aoraki/Mt Cook

Aoraki/Mt Cook National Park

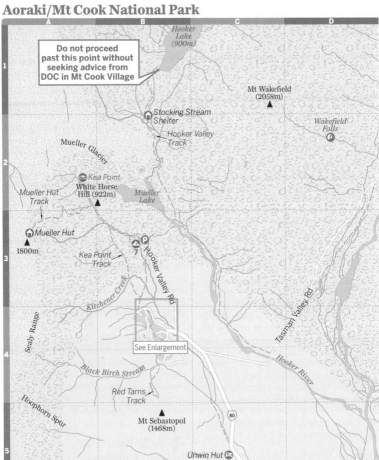

Aoraki/Mt Cook National Park

⊚ Sights

1 Aoraki/Mt Cook National Park Visitor Centre	E4
2 Public Shelter	E5
3 Sir Edmund Hillary Alpine Centre	E4

✪ Activities, Courses & Tours

4 Alpine Guides	E4
Big Sky	(see 8)
Glacier Explorers	(see 8)
Glacier Kayaking	(see 10)
Southern Alps Guiding	(see 10)

⊜ Sleeping

5 Aoraki Court Motel	F5
6 Aoraki/Mt Cook Alpine Lodge	E5
7 DOC White Horse Hill Campground	B3
8 Hermitage	E4
9 Mt Cook YHA	F5

⊗ Eating

10 Old Mountaineers' Cafe	E4

⊕ Drinking & Nightlife

11 Chamois Bar & Grill	F5

village, which has running water, toilets and coin-operated showers. Note that this shelter cannot be used for overnight stays.

★ Sealy Tarns Track   TRAMPING
The walk to Sealy Tarns (three to four hours return) branches off the Kea Point Track and continues up the ridge to Mueller Hut (dorm $36), a comfortable 28-bunk hut with gas, cooking facilities and long-drop toilets.

Hooker Valley Track   TRAMPING
Perhaps the best of the area's day walks, this track (three hours return from Mt Cook Village) heads up the Hooker Valley and crosses three swing bridges to the Stocking Stream and the terminus of the Hooker Glacier. After the second swing bridge, Aoraki/Mt Cook totally dominates the valley, and you may see icebergs floating in Hooker Lake.

Kea Point Track   TRAMPING
The trail to Kea Point (two hours return from Mt Cook Village) is lined with native plants and ends at a platform with excellent views of Aoraki/Mt Cook, the Hooker Valley and the ice faces of Mt Sefton and the Footstool. Despite the name, you're no more likely to see a kea here than in other parts of the park. If you do, don't feed it.

Snow Sports
Southern Alps
Guiding   ROCK CLIMBING, SNOW SPORTS
(☑ 03-435 1890; www.mtcook.com; Old Mountaineers' Cafe, 3 Larch Grove Rd) Offers mountaineering instruction and guiding, plus three-to four-hour helihiking trips on Tasman Glacier year-round ($495). From June to October heliskiers can head up Tasman Glacier for a 10km to 12km downhill run (three runs, from $895). There's also a ski-plane option (two runs, from $895).

Alpine Guides   ROCK CLIMBING
(☑ 03-435 1834; www.alpineguides.co.nz; 98 Bowen Dr, Mt Cook Village) Guided climbs and mountaineering courses, along with ski-touring including heli options. Its Hermitage shop stocks outdoor clothing and mountaineering gear, and rents ice axes, crampons, day-packs and sleeping bags.

Other Activities
Glacier Kayaking   KAYAKING
(☑ 03-435 1890; www.mtcook.com; Old Mountaineers' Cafe, Bowen Dr; per person $155; ☉ Oct-Apr) Suitable for paddlers with just an ounce of experience, these guided trips head out on the terminal lake of the Tasman or Mueller

in 1907; since then more than 80 climbers have died on the peak.

Check with the park rangers before attempting any climb and always heed their advice. If you're climbing, or even going on a longer walk, fill out an intentions card before starting out so rangers can check on you if you're overdue coming back. Sign out again when you return. The visitor centre also hires locator beacons (per three days/week $30/40).

If you intend to stay at any of the park's huts, it's essential to register your intentions at the visitor centre and pay hut fees. Walkers can use the public shelter in Mt Cook

Glaciers. With luck there will be icebergs to negotiate, but regardless this is a cool adventure in a crazy place with a fascinating geology lesson thrown in. Expect to spend about two hours on the water; book at the Old Mountaineers' Cafe (p181).

Big Sky STARGAZING
(☑0800 686 800; www.hermitage.co.nz; The Hermitage, Terrace Rd; adult/child $65/32.50; ⊙9.30pm Oct-Apr, 8.30pm May-Sep) NZ's southern sky is introduced with a 45-minute presentation in the Alpine Centre's digital planetarium. Afterwards participants venture outside to study the real deal with telescopes, binoculars and an astronomy guide.

Glentanner Horse Trekking HORSE RIDING
(☑03-435 1855; www.glentanner.co.nz; Glentanner Park Centre, SH80; 1/2/3hr rides $70/90/150; ⊙Nov-Apr) Leads guided treks on a high-country sheep station with options suited to all levels of experience.

☞ Tours

Mount Cook Ski Planes SCENIC FLIGHTS
(☑03-430 8026; www.mtcookskiplanes.com; Mt Cook Airport) Based at Mt Cook Airport, this outfit offers 45-minute (adult/child $425/310) and 55-minute (adult/child $560/425) flights, both with snow landings. Flight-seeing without a landing is a cheaper option; try the 25-minute Mini Tasman trip (adult/child $245/200) or 45-minute Alpine Wonderland (adult/child $310/250).

Glacier Explorers BOAT TOUR
(☑03-435 1641; www.glacierexplorers.com; The Hermitage, Terrace Rd; adult/child $155/77.50; ⊙Sep-May) Head out on the terminal lake of the Tasman Glacier for this small-boat tour, which gets up close and personal with old icebergs and crazy moraines. Includes a short walk. Book at the activities desk at the Hermitage.

Tasman Valley 4WD & Argo Tours TOUR
(☑0800 686 800; www.mountcooktours.co.nz; adult/child $79/39.50) Offers year-round, 90-minute Argo (8WD all-terrain vehicle) tours checking out the Tasman Glacier and its terminal lake, with alpine flora and an interesting commentary along the way. Book online or at the Hermitage activities desk.

Helicopter Line SCENIC FLIGHTS
(☑03-435 1801; www.helicopter.co.nz; Glentanner Park, Mt Cook Rd) From Glentanner Park, the Helicopter Line offers 20-minute Alpine Vista flights ($235), an exhilarating 35-minute flight over the Ben Ohau Range ($355) and

a 40-minute Mountains High flight over the Tasman Glacier and alongside Aoraki/Mt Cook ($450). All feature snow landings.

🛏 Sleeping

Mt Cook YHA HOSTEL $
(☑03-435 1820; www.yha.co.nz; 4 Bowen Dr; dm/d $38/137; ☜) ☕ Handsomely decked out in pine, this excellent hostel has a free sauna, a drying room, log fires and DVDs. Rooms are clean and warm, although some are a tight squeeze (particularly the twin bunk rooms).

DOC White Horse Hill Campground CAMPGROUND $
(☑03-435 1186; www.doc.govt.nz; Hooker Valley Rd; sites per adult/child $10/5) Located 2km up the Hooker Valley from Mt Cook Village, this self-registration camping ground has a basic shelter with (cold-water) sinks, tables and toilets, along with blissful views and close proximity to various walking tracks.

Glentanner Park Centre HOLIDAY PARK $
(☑03-435 1855; www.glentanner.co.nz; Mt Cook Rd; sites $22-25, dm $32, units with/without bathroom $180/100; @☜) ☕ On the northern shore of Lake Pukaki, 22km south of the Mt Cook Village, this is the nearest fully equipped campground to the national park. Features include cabins and motel units, a bunk room, a cafe and free-roaming rabbits.

★ **Aoraki/Mt Cook Alpine Lodge** LODGE $$
(☑03-435 1860; www.aorakialpinelodge.co.nz; Bowen Dr; d $169-240; ☜) This lovely modern lodge has en suite rooms, including some suitable for families and two with kitchenettes; most have views. The huge lounge and kitchen area also has a superb mountain outlook, as does the barbecue area – a rather inspiring spot to sizzle your dinner.

Hermitage HOTEL $$$
(☑03-435 1809; www.hermitage.co.nz; Terrace Rd; r $215-510; @☜) Completely dominating Mt Cook Village, this famous hotel offers awesome mountain views. While the corridors in some of the older wings can seem a little hospital-like, all of the rooms have been renovated to a reasonable standard. In addition to the on-site shop and Sir Ed Alpine Centre, there are three dining options of low to middling standard.

Aoraki Court Motel MOTEL $$$
(☑03-435 1111; www.aorakicourt.co.nz; 26 Bowen Dr; d $185-265) While it wouldn't command these prices elsewhere, this clump of modern motel units is sharp, with good views.

TASMAN GLACIER

At 29km long and up to 4km wide, the Tasman Glacier (www.doc.govt.nz) is the largest of NZ's glaciers, but it's melting fast, losing hundreds of metres from its length each year. It is also melting from the surface down, shrinking around 150m in depth since it was first surveyed in 1891. In its lower section the melts have exposed rocks, stones and boulders, which form a solid unsightly mass on top of the ice. Despite this considerable shrinkage, at its thickest point the ice is still estimated to be over 600m deep.

Tasman Lake, at the foot of the glacier, started to form only in the early 1970s and now stretches to 4km. The ongoing effects of climate change are expected to extend it to 8km within the next 20 years. The lake is covered by a maze of huge icebergs which are continuously being sheared off the glacier's terminal face. On 22 February 2011 the Christchurch earthquake caused a 1.3km long, 300m high, 30-million-ton chunk of ice to break off, causing 3.5m waves to roll into the tourist boats on the lake at the time (no one was injured). You can kayak on Tasman Lake with Glacier Kayaking (p179).

In the glacier's last major advance (17,000 years ago), the glacier crept south far enough to carve out Lake Pukaki. A later advance did not reach out to the valley sides, so there's a gap between the outer valley walls and the lateral moraines of this later advance. The unsealed Tasman Valley Rd, which branches off Mt Cook Rd 800m south of Mt Cook Village, travels through this gap. From the Blue Lakes shelter, 8km along the road, the Tasman Glacier View Track (30 minutes return) climbs interminable steps to an aptly rewarding viewpoint on the moraine wall, with a side trip to Blue Lakes on the way.

Feature wallpaper sharpens up the decor, and the tiled bathrooms have designery touches. Some units even have spa baths, and there are bikes for hire.

🍴 Eating & Drinking

Old Mountaineers' Cafe   CAFE **$$**
(www.mtcook.com; Bowen Dr; breakfast $10-15, lunch $14-26, dinner $18-35; ☺10am-9pm daily Nov-Apr, Tue-Sun May & Jul-Oct; 🛜) 🌿 Encouraging lingering with books, memorabilia and mountain views through picture windows, the village's best eatery also supports local and organic suppliers through a menu sporting salmon and bacon pies, cooked breakfasts, burgers and pizza.

Chamois Bar & Grill   PUB
(www.mountcookbackpackers.co.nz; Bowen Dr; ☺4pm-late) Upstairs in Mt Cook Backpacker Lodge, this large bar offers pub grub (meals $15 to $30), a pool table, a big-screen TV and the occasional live gig, but the views are its best feature.

ℹ️ Information

The **DOC Visitor Centre** (p177) is the best source of local information. The nearest ATM and supermarket are in Twizel.

ℹ️ Getting There & Away

Mt Cook Village's small airport only serves aerial sightseeing companies. Some of these may be willing to combine transport to the West Coast (ie Franz Josef) with a scenic flight, but flights are heavily dependent on weather.

If you're driving, fill up at Lake Tekapo or Twizel. There is petrol at Mt Cook, but it's expensive and involves summoning an attendant from the Hermitage (for a fee).

Cook Connection (📞0800 266 526; www.cookconnect.co.nz) runs shuttle services to Lake Tekapo ($38, 1½ hours) and Twizel ($27, one hour).

Daily InterCity coaches (see table below stop at the YHA and the Hermitage, both of which handle bookings.

DESTINATION	FARES FROM	DURATION (HR)
Christchurch	$67	5¼
Cromwell	$59	2¾
Geraldine	$38	3
Lake Tekapo	$30	1½
Queenstown	$64	4

Dunedin & Otago

Best Places to Eat

➡ Riverstone Kitchen (p191)

➡ Fleur's Place (p192)

➡ No 7 Balmac (p199)

➡ Bracken (p199)

➡ Otago Farmers Market (p198)

Best Places to Sleep

➡ Pen-y-bryn Lodge (p190)

➡ Oliver's (p211)

➡ Pitches Store (p208)

➡ Old Bones Backpackers (p189)

➡ Kiwi's Nest (p197)

Why Go?

Otago has attractions both urban and rural, ranging from quirky towns to world-class wineries and some of the country's most accessible wildlife. Its historic heart is Dunedin, home to a vibrant student culture and arts scene. From the town's stately Edwardian train station it's possible to catch the famous Taieri Gorge Railway inland, and continue on two wheels along the craggily scenic Otago Central Rail Trail.

Those seeking colonial New Zealand can soak up the frontier atmosphere of gold-rush towns such as Clyde, St Bathans, Naseby and cute-as-a-button Ophir. For wildlife, head to the Otago Peninsula, where penguins, albatross, sea lions and seals are easily sighted. Seaside Oamaru has a wonderful historic precinct, resident penguin colonies and a quirky devotion to steampunk culture.

Unhurried and overflowing with picturesque scenery, Otago is generous to explorers who are after a more leisurely style of holiday.

When to Go

➡ February and March have settled, sunny weather (usually...), and the juicy appeal of fresh apricots, peaches and cherries.

➡ At Easter, hook yourself a 'Southern Man' at the Middlemarch Singles Ball, or drown your sorrows at the Clyde Wine & Food Festival.

➡ Take to two wheels on the Otago Central Rail Trail during the quieter month of September.

➡ In November, watch the pros battle it out on the Highlands Motorsport Park, then ride graciously into the past on a penny farthing bicycle at Oamaru's Victorian Heritage Celebrations.

ⓘ Getting There & Away

Air New Zealand (☑ 0800 737 000; www.
airnewzealand.co.nz) flies from Dunedin to
Christchurch, Wellington and Auckland, and
Jetstar (☑ 0800 800 995; www.jetstar.com)
flies to Wellington and Auckland.

The only train services are **heritage trips**
(p196) from Dunedin to Middlemarch and Dunedin to Palmerston.

The main bus routes follow SH1 or SH8.

WAITAKI DISTRICT

The broad, braided Waitaki River provides
a clear dividing line between Otago and
Canterbury to the region's north. The Waitaki Valley is a direct but less-travelled route
from the Southern Alps to the sea, featuring
freaky limestone formations, Māori rock
paintings and ancient fossils. The area is
also one of NZ's newest winemaking regions,
and a major component of the new Alps 2
Ocean Cycle Trail (p175), which links Aora-
ki/Mt Cook National Park to Oamaru on the
coast. The district's main town, Oamaru, is
a place of penguins and glorious heritage
architecture.

ⓘ Getting There & Away

Buses stop in Oamaru and Moeraki, en route
from Christchurch to Dunedin and Te Anau. Other
services pass through Omarama on their journey
between Queenstown/Wanaka and Christchurch.
No buses traverse the Waitaki Valley.

The only rail service is the Seasider tourist
train that heads between Dunedin and Oamaru.

Omarama

POP 267

At the head of the Waitaki Valley, Omarama
is surrounded by mountain ranges and fabulous landscapes. Busy times in this sleepy
place include the rodeo (28 December) and
the sheepdog trials (March).

⊙ Sights & Activities

Clay Cliffs Paritea   LANDMARK
(Henburn Rd; vehicles $5) This bizarre moon-
scape is the result of two million years of
erosion on layers of silt and gravel that were
exposed along the active Ostler fault line.
The cliffs are on private land; before setting
out, pay the vehicle admission fee at Omarama Hot Tubs. To get to the area, head north
from town for 3km on SH8, turn left onto

Quailburn Rd, and then turn left after 3km
onto unsealed Henburn Rd.

Wrinkly Rams   FARM
(☑ 03-438 9751; www.thewrinklyrams.co.nz; 24-
30 Omarama Ave/SH8; adult/child $20/10) A
regular stop for tour buses, Wrinkly Rams
stages 30-minute shearing and sheepdog
shows, including lamb-feeding in season.
Phone ahead to tag along with a tour group,
or book your own one-off show. Attached is
one of Omarama's better **cafes** (mains $10-25;
⊙ 7am-4.30pm; 🛜).

Omarama Hot Tubs   SPA
(☑ 03-438 9703; www.hottubsomarama.co.nz;
29 Omarama Ave/SH8; per 1/2/3/4-person tub
$52/90/114/136, pod $75/140/180/200; ⊙ 11am-
late) If your legs are weary after mountain
biking or tramping, or you just want to cosy
up with your significant other, these private,
wood-fired hot tubs could be just the ticket. Choose between a 90-minute soak in a
tub (each has its own dressing room) or a
two-hour session in a 'wellness pod', which
includes a sauna.

The chemical-free glacier and snow-melt
water is changed after each booking, and the
used water is recycled for irrigation.

The concept is Japanese, but with the
surrounding mountain ranges, the lakeside
setting and a pristine night sky, you could

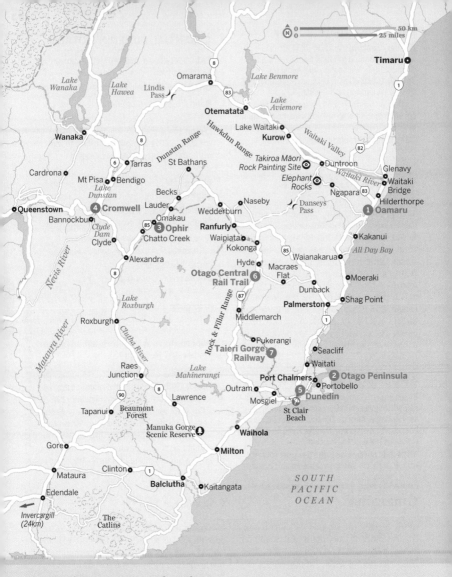

Dunedin & Otago Highlights

1 Oamaru (p186)
Experiencing a heritage past and a possible steampunk future.

2 Otago Peninsula (p202)
Peering at penguins, admiring albatross and staring at seals.

3 Ophir (p208) Exploring New Zealand's gold-mining heritage in a quaint backcountry village.

4 Cromwell (p212) Taste-testing some of the planet's best pinot noir in the wineries scattered around the fruit bowl of the south.

5 Dunedin (p192) Sampling local beers and listening out for local bands in the city's bars and cafes.

6 Otago Central Rail Trail (p210) Cycling through lonely vistas of brown and gold on the route of a defunct train line.

7 Taieri Gorge Railway (p196) Winding through gorges, alongside canyons and across tall viaducts on this snaking railway.

only be on the South Island of NZ. Therapeutic massages (30/60 minutes $60/100) are also available.

Glide Omarama   GLIDING
(☑ 03-438 9555; www.glideomarama.com) The area's westerlies and warm summer thermals allow for world-class gliding over the hills and spectacular Southern Alps, and a national gliding meet is held here in December or January. This crew offers lessons and scenic flights ranging from 30 minutes ($345) to 2½ hours ($745).

🛏 Sleeping & Eating

Buscot Station   FARMSTAY, HOSTEL $
(☑ 027 222 1754; SH8; site/dm/s/d $10/25/40/60) For a completely different and uniquely Kiwi experience, grab a room in the home-style farmhouse attached to a huge sheep and cattle station, or a bed in the large dormitory out the back. The sunset views are terrific and there's plenty of acreage for quiet explorations. Look for it on SH8, 10km north of Omarama.

Omarama Top 10
Holiday Park   HOLIDAY PARK $
(☑ 03-438 9875; www.omaramatop10.co.nz; 1 Omarama Ave (SH8); sites $35-40, units with/ without bathroom $115/58; @ 🛜) 🏊 Facilities are good at this holiday park, squeezed between the highway and a stream. Standard cabins are compact, but larger en suite cabins and self-contained motel units are also available.

Ladybird Hill   MODERN NZ $$
(☑ 03-438 9550; www.ladybirdhill.co.nz; 1 Pinot Noir Ct; mains lunch $16-24, dinner $28-33; ⊙10am-4pm Wed, 10am-10pm Thu-Sun Aug-May) Sure, you can do it the easy way and simply order a leisurely lunch from the menu. Or you can grab a rod, catch a salmon from the well-stocked ponds (around $49) and wait until it's prepared and either smoked or sliced into sashimi ($55, feeding several people). Other attractions include a kids playground and walking tracks through the vineyard.

ℹ Information

Omarama Hot Tubs (p183) doubles as the information office, and can assist with accommodation and transport information. See www.discoveromarama.co.nz for more details.

MĀORI NZ: DUNEDIN & OTAGO

The early Māori history of Otago echoes that of Canterbury (p143), with Ngāi Tahu the dominant tribe at the time the British arrived. One of the first parcels of land that Ngāi Tahu sold was called the Otago block, a 1618-sq-km parcel of land which changed hands in 1844 for £2400. The name Otago reflects the Ngāi Tahu pronunciation of Ōtākou, a small village on the far reaches of the Otago Peninsula, where there's still a *marae* (meeting place).

Dunedin's **Otago Museum** (p193) has the finest Māori exhibition on the South Island, including an ornately carved *waka taua* (war canoe) and finely crafted *pounamu* (greenstone). Māori rock art can still be seen in situ in the Waitaki Valley.

ℹ Getting There & Away

Atomic Shuttles (☑ 03-349 0697; www.atomic travel.co.nz) Services stop in Omarama for a break before continuing on to Christchurch ($35, four hours), Lake Tekapo ($20, one hour), Twizel ($20, 20 minutes), Cromwell ($25, 1½ hours) and Queenstown ($30, 2¼ hours).

InterCity (☑ 03-471 7143; www.intercity.co.nz) Two coaches a day head to/from Christchurch (from $42, 5¾ hours), Twizel (from $13, 19 minutes), Cromwell (from $23, 1½ hours) and Queenstown (from $32, 2½ hours), and one heads to/from Mt Cook Village ($70, 1¼ hours).

Naked Bus (www.nakedbus.com; prices vary) Two daily services to/from Christchurch (5¾ hours), Lake Tekapo (1½ hours) and Cromwell (2½ hours), with one terminating in Queenstown (3¼ hours) and the other in Wanaka (1¾ hours).

Waitaki Valley

Wine, waterskiing and salmon-fishing are just some of the treats on offer along this little-travelled route. Coming from Omarama, SH83 passes an array of arrestingly blue lakes, each abutted by a hydroelectric power station. For a scenic detour along the north bank, leave the highway at Otematata and cross over the huge Benmore Dam, then cross over Aviemore Dam to rejoin the highway.

A succession of sleepy little heartland towns line the highway, peppered with rustic old bank buildings and pubs. One of the most appealing is tiny lost-in-time **Kurow** (population 302), the hometown of World Cup–winning retired All Blacks captain Richie McCaw. From almost-as-cute **Duntroon** (population 90), adventurous (and appropriately insured) drivers can take the unsealed road over Danseys Pass to Naseby.

Although they've got a long way to go to attain the global reputation enjoyed by their colleagues on the other side of the mountains in Central Otago, a few winemaking pioneers in Waitaki Valley are producing wine of which international experts are taking notice.

◉ Sights

◎ Kurow

Kurow Heritage & Information Centre MUSEUM
(☑ 03-436 0950; www.kurow.org.nz; 57 Bledisloe St; ⊙ 9.30am-4pm Mon-Fri) **FREE** While Richie McCaw might get all the attention these days, Kurow's other famous son was Arnold Nordmeyer (1901–89), a Labour Party leader who was one of the key architects of NZ's welfare and public health system. His memory is honoured in this interesting community museum, which jokingly refers to itself as the National Museum of Social Security.

Pasquale Kurow Winery WINERY
(☑ 03-436 0443; www.pasquale.co.nz; 5292 Kurow-Duntroon Rd/SH83; ⊙ 10am-4pm Nov-Mar) The valley's most impressive winery, Pasquale produces killer pinot noir, pinot gris and riesling, as well as less common varietals such as gewürztztraminer, arneis and viognier. Drop in for a wine-tasting session ($10, refundable upon purchase) and an antipasto and cheese platter.

◎ Duntroon & Around

Takiroa Māori Rock Painting Site ARCHAEOLOGICAL SITE
FREE Hidden within the honeycomb cliffs lining the highway, this well-signposted site, 3km west of Duntroon, features centuries-old drawings of mystical creatures, animals and even a sailing ship.

Maerewhenua Māori Rock Painting Site ARCHAEOLOGICAL SITE
(Livingstone-Duntroon Rd) **FREE** Sheltered by an impressive limestone overhang, this site contains charcoal-and-ochre paintings dating to before the arrival of Europeans in NZ. Head east from Duntroon and take the first right after crossing the Maerewhenua River; the site is on the left after about 400m.

Vanished World Centre MUSEUM
(www.vanishedworld.co.nz; 7 Campbell St, Duntroon; adult/child $10/free; ⊙ 10am-4.30pm daily Nov-Mar, 10.30am-4pm Fri-Mon Apr-Oct) Perhaps there wouldn't be quite so many bad dolphin tattoos and dancing penguin films if more people stopped in Duntroon to check out this small but interesting volunteer-run centre. Once you see the 25-million-year-old fossils of shark-toothed dolphins and giant penguins, they suddenly don't seem so cute.

Pick up a copy of the *Vanished World Trail* map ($6.50) outlining 20 different interesting geological locations around the Waitaki Valley and North Otago coast.

⭐ Activities

Awakino Skifield SKIING
(☑ 021 890 584; www.skiawakino.com; Awakino Skifield Rd; daily lift pass adult/child $50/25) Situated high above Kurow, Awakino is a small player on the NZ ski scene, but worth a visit for intermediate skiers who fancy some peace and quiet. Weekend lodge-and-ski packages are available.

Oamaru

POP 12,900
Nothing moves very fast in Oamaru. Tourists saunter, locals linger and penguins waddle. Even its recently resurrected heritage modes of transport – penny farthings and steam trains – reflect an unhurried pace. Most travellers come here for the penguins, but hang around and you'll sense the wellspring of eccentricity bubbling under the surface. Put simply, this is NZ's coolest town.

Down by the water, a neighbourhood of once-neglected Victorian buildings now swarms with oddballs, antiquarians and bohemians of all stripes, who run offbeat galleries, fascinating shops, hip venues and even an 'urban winery'. Most visible are the steampunks, their aesthetic boldly celebrating the past and the future with an ethos of 'tomorrow as it used to be'.

What Oamaru used to be was rich and ambitious. In its 1880s heyday, Oamaru was about the same size as Los Angeles was at the time. Refrigerated meat-shipping had its origins nearby and the town became wealthy enough to erect the imposing buildings that grace Thames St today. However, the town overreached itself and spent the end of the 19th century teetering on the verge of bankruptcy.

Economic decline in the 20th century meant that there wasn't the impetus to swing the wrecking ball with the same reckless abandon that wiped out much of the built heritage of NZ's main centres. It's only in recent decades that canny creative types have cottoned on to the uniqueness of Oamaru's surviving Victorian streetscapes and have started to unlock this otherwise unremarkable town's potential for extreme kookiness.

◎ Sights

★ **Blue Penguin Colony**   BIRD SANCTUARY
(🖉 03-433 1195; www.penguins.co.nz; 2 Waterfront Rd; ◷ 10am until 2hr after sunset) 🖋 Every evening the little tykes from the Oamaru little-penguin colony surf in and wade ashore, heading to their nests in an old stone quarry near the waterfront. Stands are set up on either side of the waddle route. General admission (adult/child $28/14) will give you a good view of the action but the premium stand ($40/20), accessed by a boardwalk through the nesting area, will get you closer.

You'll see the most penguins (up to 250) in November and December. From March to August there may be only 10 to 50 birds. They arrive in clumps called rafts just before dark (around 5.30pm in midwinter and 9.30pm midsummer), and it takes them about an hour to all come ashore; nightly viewing times are posted at the i-SITE. Use of cameras is prohibited and you're advised to dress warmly.

To understand the centre's conservation work and its success in increasing the penguin population, take the daytime, behind-the-scenes tour (adult/child self-guided $10/5 or guided $16/8); packages that combine night viewing and the daytime tour are available.

Do not under any circumstances wander around the rocks beside the sea here at night looking for penguins. It's damaging to their environment and spoils studies into the human effects on the birds.

★ **Victorian Precinct**   NEIGHBOURHOOD
Consisting of only a couple of blocks centred on Harbour and Tyne Sts, this atmospheric enclave has some of NZ's best-preserved Victorian commercial buildings. Descend on a dark and foggy night and it's downright Dickensian. It's also ground zero for all that is hip, cool and freaky in Oamaru, and one of the most fun places to window-shop in the entire South Island.

Wander around during the day and you'll discover antiquarian bookshops, antique stores, galleries, vintage-clothing shops, kooky gift stores, artist studios, old-fashioned lolly shops and craft bookbinders. At night there are some cute little bars, and you might even see a penguin swaggering along the street – we did!

The precinct is at its liveliest on Sundays when the excellent Oamaru farmers market is in full swing. Note that some shops and attractions are closed on Mondays. There's also a brand new heritage centre in the works; enquire about its progress at the i-SITE.

Yellow-Eyed Penguin Colony   BIRD SANCTUARY
(Bushy Beach Rd) FREE Larger and much rarer than their little blue cousins, yellow-eyed penguins waddle ashore at Bushy Beach in the late afternoon to feed their young. In order to protect these endangered birds, the beach is closed to people at 3pm, but there are hides set up on the cliffs (you'll need binoculars for a decent view). The best time to see them is two hours before sunset.

Despite their Māori name, hoiho, meaning 'noisy shouter', they're extremely shy critters; if they see or hear you they'll head back into the water and the chicks will go hungry.

Thames St   AREA
Oamaru's main drag owes its expansive girth to the need to accommodate the minimum turning circle of a bullock cart. Oamaru's grand pretensions reached their peak in a series of gorgeous buildings constructed from the milky local limestone (known as Oamaru stone or whitestone), with their forms reflecting the fashion of the times; there's a particular emphasis on the neoclassical.

Impressive examples include the Forrester Gallery (at No 9, built 1883), the ANZ Bank (No 11, 1871), the Waitaki District Council building (No 20, 1883), the North Otago Museum (No 60, 1882), the Courthouse (No 88, 1883) and the Opera House (No 92, 1907).

Steampunk HQ   GALLERY
(🖉 027 778 6547; www.steampunkoamaru.co.nz; 1 Itchen St; adult/child $10/2; ◷ 10am-5pm)

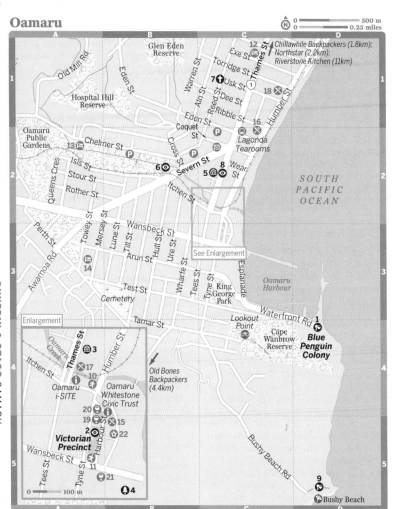

Discover an alternative past – or maybe a quirky version of the future – in this fascinating art project celebrating steampunk culture. Ancient machines wheeze and splutter, and the industrial detritus of the last century or so is repurposed and reimagined to creepy effect. Bring a $2 coin to fire up the sparking, space-age locomotive out the front.

St Patrick's Basilica   CHURCH
(☑ 03-434 8543; www.cdd.org.nz/st-patrick-oamaru; 64 Reed St) If you've ever fantasised about being transported back to Ancient Rome, stroll through the Corinthian col-

umns and into this gorgeous Catholic church (built in 1873). Renowned architect Francis Petre went for the full time warp with this one, right down to a coffered ceiling and a cupola above the altar.

Forrester Gallery   GALLERY
(☑ 03-433 0853; www.culturewaitaki.org.nz; 9 Thames St; ⊙ 10.30am-4.30pm) FREE Housed in a temple-like former bank building, the Forrester Gallery has an excellent collection of regional and NZ art. It's a good place to see works by Colin McCahon, one of NZ's most significant modern artists.

Oamaru

Oamaru Public Gardens GARDENS
(Severn St; ⊙ dawn-dusk) Opened in 1876, these beautiful gardens are a lovely place to chill out on a hot day, with expansive lawns, waterways, bridges and a children's playground.

North Otago Museum MUSEUM
(☎ 03-433 0852; www.culturewaitaki.org.nz; 58-60 Thames St; ⊙ 10.30am-4.30pm Mon-Fri, 1-4.30pm Sat & Sun) FREE Behind its classical facade, the North Otago Museum has exhibits on Māori and Pākehā history, local writer Janet Frame, architecture and geology.

🏃 Activities

Vertical Ventures CYCLING, ROCK CLIMBING
(☎ 03-434 5010; www.alps2oceancycletours.co.nz; 4 Wansbeck St) Rent a mountain bike (from $45 per day), or join guided mountain-biking trips, including the Alps 2 Ocean Cycle Trail (seven days including transport, food and accommodation for $2695) and helibiking day trips (from $415). The 'vertical' part comes in the form of rock climbing (from $140 per person).

Oamaru Steam & Rail TOURIST TRAIN
(www.oamaru-steam.org.nz; adult/child/family one-way $5/2/12, return $8/3/20; ⊙ 11am-4.30pm Sun Oct-Apr, to 3pm Sun May-Sep) On Sundays, take a half-hour ride on a vintage steam train from the Victorian Precinct to the waterfront.

👉 Tours

Penguins Crossing WILDLIFE WATCHING
(☎ 03-477 9083; www.travelheadfirst.com; 4 Wansbeck St; adult/child from $65/25) Door-to-door tour taking in the blue- and yellow-eyed-penguin colonies. Prices include admission to the blue-penguin colony.

★ Festivals & Events

Victorian Heritage Celebrations CULTURAL
(www.vhc.co.nz; ⊙ mid-Nov) Five days of costumed hijinks, culminating in a grand fete.

🛏 Sleeping

★ **Old Bones Backpackers** HOSTEL $
(☎ 03-434 8115; www.oldbones.co.nz; Beach Rd; r $95, campervans per person $20; @ 🛜) About 5km south of Oamaru on the coast road, this top-notch dorm-free hostel has tidy rooms off a huge, sunny, central space. Relax in this isolated setting listening to the surf crashing over the road. Or book one of the hot tubs (from $50) and drift into ecstasy while gazing at the stars.

Chillawhile Backpackers HOSTEL $
(☎ 03-437 0168; www.chillawhile.co.nz; 1 Frome St; dm $28-32, s/d without bathroom $56/72; 🛜) Unleash your creative spirit at this funky and colourful hostel in a two-storey Victorian residence. Guests are encouraged to draw and paint, or create sweet soul music on the hostel's varied instruments.

Oamaru Top 10 Holiday Park HOLIDAY PARK $
(☎ 03-434 7666; www.oamarutop10.co.nz; 30 Chelmer St; sites $36-44, units with/without bathroom from $105/73; @ 🛜) Grassy and well maintained, this Top 10 has trees out the back and the public gardens next door. Standard cabins are basic, but the other units (with varying levels of self-contained comfort) are much nicer.

DUNEDIN & OTAGO OAMARU

Highfield Mews
MOTEL **$$**

(☑03-434 3437; www.highfieldmews.co.nz; 244 Thames St; units from $170; @☎) ✎ Motels have come a long away from the gloomy concrete-block constructions of the 1960s and '70s, as this new build attests. The units are basically smart apartments, with kitchens, desks, stereos, tiled bathrooms and outdoor furniture.

★ Pen-y-bryn Lodge
B&B **$$$**

(☑03-434 7939; www.penybryn.co.nz; 41 Towey St; r $625-750; ☎) Well-travelled foodie owners have thoroughly revitalised this beautiful 1889 residence. There are two rooms in the main house but we prefer the three recently and luxuriously refurbished ones in the rear annexe. Predinner drinks and canapés are served in the antique-studded drawing room, and you can arrange a four-course dinner in the fabulous dining room ($125 per person).

✗ Eating

Steam
CAFE **$**

(www.facebook.com/steamoamaru; 7 Thames St; mains $10-13; ☉7.30am-4.30pm Mon-Fri, 8am-3pm Sat & Sun; ☎) Steam specialises in coffees and fruit juices, and it's a good spot to stock up on freshly ground beans for your own travels. Aside from crêpes, the food is mainly limited to what you see on the counter: freshly baked muffins, croissants and the like.

Whitestone Cheese Factory
DELI, CAFE **$**

(☑03-434 8098; www.whitestonecheese.com; 3 Torridge St; platters $7.50-15; ☉9am-5pm) The home of award-winning artisan cheeses, Whitestone is a local culinary institution and the little factory-door cafe is a fine place to challenge one's arteries. Food is limited to the likes of cheese scones, cheese-only platters and large platters with crackers and quince paste.

Harbour St Bakery
BAKERY **$**

(☑03-434 0444; www.harbourstreetbakery.com; 4 Harbour St; pies $5.50; ☉10am-4pm Tue-Sun) Selling both European-style bread and pastries and Kiwi meat pies, this Dutch bakery covers its bases well. Grab an outdoor seat and watch Oamaru's heritage streetlife scroll past like an old-time movie.

Midori
JAPANESE **$$**

(☑03-434 9045; www.facebook.com/Midori JapaneseSushiBarAndRestaurant; 1 Ribble St; sushi $5-11, mains $13-20; ☉10.30am-8.30pm Mon-Sat, noon-8.30pm Sun) Midori, housed in a heritage stone building, serves sashimi and sushi that makes the most of fresh local seafood. Other carefully prepared dishes include teriyaki salmon and blue cod, udon soup and a variety of bento boxes. If you just want to grab and go, it also runs the Sushi Espresso takeaway next door.

Northstar
MODERN NZ **$$**

(☑03-437 1190; www.northstarmotel.co.nz; 495a Thames Hwy; mains lunch $19-23, dinner $30-34; ☉noon-3pm & 6-9pm) Surprisingly upmarket for a restaurant attached to an SH1 motel, Northstar is the first choice for Oamaruvians with something to celebrate. Expect robust bistro fare with a touch of contemporary flair. The bar is popular, too.

☕ Drinking & Entertainment

Criterion Hotel
PUB

(☑03-434 6247; www.criterionhotel.co.nz; 3 Tyne St; ☉11.30am-late Tue-Sun) The most Victorian of the Victorian Precinct's watering holes, this corner beauty has a good beer selection and plenty of local wines. There's usually live music on Fridays.

Scott's Brewing Co.
BREWERY

(☑03-434 2244; www.scottsbrewing.co.nz; 1 Wansbeck St; ☉11am-7.30pm) Drop into this old waterfront warehouse to sample the output of Oamaru's premier craft brewers. Slouch against the counter for a tasting or head out onto the sunny deck for a pint and a pizza.

★ Penguin Club
LIVE MUSIC

(www.thepenguinclub.co.nz; Emulsion Lane, off Harbour St; admission varies) Tucked down an atmospheric alley off a 19th-century street, the Penguin's unusual location matches its acts: everything from touring Kiwi bands to punky/grungy/rocky/country locals.

ℹ Information

Oamaru i-SITE (☑03-434 1656; www.visit oamaru.co.nz; 1 Thames St; ☉9am-5pm; ☎) Mountains of information including details on local walking trips and wildlife, plus daily penguin-viewing times are posted here. There's also bike hire ($28/40 per half-/full day) and an interesting 10-minute DVD on the history of the town.

Oamaru Whitestone Civic Trust (☑03-434 5385; www.victorianoamaru.co.nz; 2 Harbour St; ☉10am-4pm) Vintage B&W photos of Oamaru's heritage, information and walking-tour brochures covering the historic precinct.

WORTH A TRIP

RIVERSTONE

It's well worth taking the 14km trip from Oamaru to this idiosyncratic complex, hidden along the unassuming short stretch of SH1 between the braided mouth of the Waitaki River and SH83 turn-off.

First and foremost it's the home of **Riverstone Kitchen** (☑ 03-431 3505; www.river stonekitchen.co.nz; 1431 SH1, Waitaki Bridge; breakfast $16-18, lunch $20-32, dinner $32-35; ⊙ 9am-5pm Thu-Mon, 6pm-late Thu-Sun), a sophisticated cafe-restaurant that outshines any in Oamaru itself. A riverstone fireplace and polished concrete floors set the scene for a menu that's modern without being overworked. Much of the produce is from the extensive on-site kitchen gardens (take a look, they're impressive), topped up with locally sourced venison, pork, salmon and beef. It's a smashing brunch option, with excellent coffee and legendary truffled scrambled eggs.

Next door, behind a set of fake heritage shopfronts, **Riverstone Country** (☑ 03-431 3872; 1431 SH1, Waitaki Bridge; ⊙ 9am-5pm) is literally packed to the rafters with gifts, crafts, homewares, fake flowers, garden ornaments and Christmas decorations. Outside, there's an aviary stocked with canaries, lorikeets and guinea pigs.

If this all points to an eccentric mind at the helm, take a look at the moated castle being constructed at the rear of the complex. Once the finishing touches are added to the six towers, moat and drawbridge, that's where the owners will reside.

If you're looking for a good place to stay nearby, **Waitaki Waters** (☑ 03-431 3880; www.campingoamaru.co.nz; 305 Kaik Rd, Waitaki Bridge; sites/cabins from $15/40; 🐾) is a holiday park with sparkling facilities, manicured hedges and an enthusiastic young owner, 3km off SH1. Cabins are simple but well maintained; bring your own bedding.

Post Office (☑ 03-433 1190; www.nzpost. co.nz; 2 Severn St; ⊙ 9am-5pm Mon-Fri, to 1pm Sat)

❶ Getting There & Away

Most buses and shuttles depart from the **Lagonda Tearooms** (☑ 03-434 8716; www.facebook. com/LagondaTeaRooms; 191 Thames St; ⊙ 9am-4.30pm; 🐾). Both the tearooms and the i-SITE take bookings.

Atomic Shuttles (☑ 03-349 0697; www.atomic travel.co.nz) Buses to/from Christchurch ($30, four hours), Timaru ($20,1½ hours) and Dunedin ($20, 1½ hours), twice daily.

Coast Line Tours (☑ 03-434 7744; www. coastline-tours.co.nz; one-way/return $30/55) Shuttles to/from Dunedin; detours to Moeraki and Dunedin Airport can be arranged.

InterCity (☑ 03-471 7143; www.intercity.co.nz) Two daily coaches to/from Christchurch (from $33, four hours), Timaru (from $22, one hour), the Moeraki turn-off (from $17, 28 minutes) and Dunedin (from $22, 1½ hours), and one to Te Anau (from $45, 6½ hours).

Naked Bus (www.nakedbus.com; prices vary) Daily buses head to/from Christchurch (3¾ hours), Timaru (1¼ hours), Moeraki (35 minutes) and Dunedin (1¾ hours).

The Seasider tourist train, operated by **Dunedin Railways** (p196) is a scenic way to travel to Dunedin.

Moeraki

The name Moeraki means 'a place to sleep by day', which should give you some clue as to the pace of life in this little fishing village. You might be surprised to learn that this was one of the first European settlements in NZ, with a whaling station established here in 1836. Since then, Moeraki has nurtured the creation of several national treasures, from Frances Hodgkins' paintings to author Keri Hulme's *The Bone People,* and Fleur Sullivan's cooking.

Apart from Fleur's eponymous restaurant, the main attraction is the collection of large spherical boulders scattered along a beautiful stretch of beach like a giant kid's discarded marbles. The famed **Moeraki Boulders** (Te Kaihinaki) lie just off SH1, a kilometre north of the Moeraki turn-off. Try to time your visit with low tide.

It's a pleasant 45-minute walk along the beach from the village to the boulders. Head in the other direction on the Kaiks Wildlife Trail and you'll reach a cute old wooden lighthouse. You might even spot yellow-eyed penguins and fur seals (be sure to keep your distance).

🛏 Sleeping & Eating

Riverside Haven Lodge
& Holiday Park   HOSTEL **$**
(☑03-439 5830; www.riversidehaven.nz; 2328
Herbert Hampden Rd/SH1, Waianakarua; sites/dm
$12/31, s/d without bathroom $50/75, d with bathroom $85; 🛜) 🛇 Nestled in a loop of the Wa-
ianakarua River, 12km north of the Moeraki
turn-off, this pretty farm offers both bucolic
camping sites and a colourful lodge with a
sunny communal lounge. Kids will love the
playground and highland cattle; parents will
love the spa and peaceful vibe.

Moeraki Beach Motel   MOTEL **$**
(☑03-439 4862; www.moerakibeachmotels.co.nz;
cnr Cleddy & Haven Sts; units from $115; 🛜) The
four split-level units at this wood-lined motel are spacious and comfortable. Each has
two bedrooms, a full kitchen and a balcony.

⭐**Fleur's Place**   SEAFOOD **$$$**
(☑03-439 4480; www.fleursplace.com; Old Jetty,
169 Haven St; mains $35-44; ⊙10.30am-late Wed-
Sun) There's a rumble-tumble look about it,
but this much graffitied timber hut houses
one of the South Island's best seafood res-
taurants. Head for the upstairs deck and
tuck into fresh shellfish, tender muttonbird
and other recently landed ocean bounty.
Bookings are strongly recommended.

ℹ Getting There & Around

All of the buses on the Oamaru–Dunedin run
stop on SH1 by the Moeraki turn-off. From here
it's about a 2km walk to both the centre of the
village and to the boulders.

DUNEDIN

POP 121,000

Two words immediately spring to mind
when Kiwis think of their seventh-largest
city: 'Scotland' and 'students'. The 'Edin-
burgh of the South' is immensely proud of
its Scottish heritage, never missing an op-
portunity to break out the haggis and bag-
pipes on civic occasions.

In fact, the very name Dunedin is derived
from the Scottish Gaelic name for Edin-
burgh: *Dùn Èideann*. The first permanent
European settlers, two shiploads of pious,
hard-working Scots, arrived at Port Chalm-
ers in 1848, including the nephew of Scot-
land's favourite son, Robbie Burns. A statue
of the poet dominates the Octagon, the city's
civic heart, and the city even has its own
tartan.

If there were a tenuous link between the
Scottish and the students that dominate
Dunedin in term time, it would probably be
whisky. The country's oldest university pro-
vides plenty of student energy to sustain the
local bars, and in the 1980s it even spawned
its own internationally influential indie mu-
sic scene, with Flying Nun Records and the
'Dunedin sound'.

Dunedin is an easy place in which to
while away a few days. Weatherboard
houses ranging from stately to ramshackle
pepper its hilly suburbs, and bluestone Vic-
torian buildings punctuate the compact city
centre. It's a great base for exploring the
wildlife-rich Otago Peninsula, which official-
ly lies within the city limits.

⊙ Sights

◉ City Centre

⭐**Toitū Otago Settlers Museum**   MUSEUM
(Map p194; ☑03-477 5052; www.toituosm.com; 31
Queens Gardens; ⊙10am-5pm) **FREE** Storytell-
ing is the focus of this excellent interactive
museum. The engrossing Māori section is
followed by a large gallery where floor-to-
ceiling portraits of Victorian-era settlers
stare out from behind their whiskers and
lace; click on a terminal to learn more about
the individuals that catch your eye. Other
displays include a recreated passenger-ship
cabin, an awesome car collection and a
room devoted to the underground stars of
Flying Nun Records.

Dunedin Railway Station   HISTORIC BUILDING
(Map p194; 22 Anzac Ave) Featuring mosaic-
tile floors and glorious stained-glass win-
dows, Dunedin's striking bluestone railway
station (built between 1903 and 1906) claims
to be NZ's most photographed building.
Head upstairs for the **New Zealand Sports
Hall of Fame** (Map p194; ☑03-477 7775; www.
nzhalloffame.co.nz; Dunedin Railway Station; adult/
child $6/2; ⊙10am-4pm), a small museum
devoted to the nation's obsession, and the
Art Station (Map p194; ☑03-477 9465; www.
otagoartsociety.co.nz; ⊙10am-4pm) **FREE**, the
local Art Society's gallery and shop.

Dunedin Public Art Gallery   GALLERY
(Map p194; ☑03-474 3240; www.dunedin.art.
museum; 30 The Octagon; ⊙10am-5pm) **FREE**
Explore NZ's art scene at this expansive and
airy gallery. Only a fraction of the collection
is displayed at any given time, with most of

the space given over to often-edgy temporary shows.

St Paul's Cathedral
CHURCH

(Map p194; www.stpauls.net.nz; Moray Pl; ☺10am-3pm) Even in Presbyterian Dunedin, the 'established church' (aka the Church of England) gets the prime spot on the Octagon. A Romanesque portal leads into the Gothic interior of this beautiful Anglican cathedral, where soaring white Oamaru-stone pillars spread into a vaulted ceiling. The main part of the church dates from 1919 although the sanctuary was left unfinished until 1971; hence the jarring modern extension. The massive organ (3500 pipes) is said to be one of the finest in the southern hemisphere.

Dunedin Chinese Garden
GARDENS

(Map p194; ☑03-477 3248; www.dunedin chinesegarden.com; cnr Rattray & Cumberland Sts; adult/child $9/free; ☺10am-5pm) Built to recognise the contribution of Chinese people to Dunedin since its earliest days, this walled garden was prefabricated in Shanghai before being dismantled then reassembled here. Its tranquil confines contain all of the elements of a classical Chinese garden, including ponds, pavilions, rockeries, stone bridges and a tea house. There's also a small display on the history of the local Chinese community.

Speight's Brewery
BREWERY

(Map p194; ☑03-477 7697; www.speights.co.nz; 200 Rattray St; adult/child $28/12; ☺tours noon, 2pm, 4pm & 6pm Jun-Sep, plus 5pm & 7pm Oct-May) Speight's has been churning out beer on this site since the late 1800s. The 90-minute tour offers samples of six different brews, and there's an option to combine a tour with a meal at the neighbouring Ale House (lunch/dinner $58/65).

◎ North Dunedin

Otago Museum
MUSEUM

(Map p194; ☑03-474 7474; www.otagomuseum. nz; 419 Great King St; ☺10am-5pm) ✔ FREE
The centrepiece of this august institution is *Southern Land, Southern People,* showcasing Otago's cultural and physical past and present, from geology and dinosaurs to the modern day. The *Tāngata Whenua* Māori gallery houses an impressive *waka taua* (war canoe), wonderfully worn old carvings, and some lovely *pounamu* (greenstone) weapons, tools and jewellery. Other major galleries include *Pacific Cultures, People of the World* (including the requisite mummy), *Nature, Maritime* and the *Animal Attic.*

The hands-on *Discovery World* science centre (adult/child $10/5) is mainly aimed at kids, although the adjoining tropical forest, filled with colourful live butterflies, is an all-ages treat.

Guided highlights tours depart at 2pm daily (gold coin admission).

Knox Church
CHURCH

(Map p194; www.knoxchurch.net; 449 George St) Dunedin's second grand Presbyterian church sprung up in 1876, only three years after the equally imposing First Church, and quickly became an emblem of the city. Built in the Gothic Revival style out of bluestone edged in white Oamaru stone, its most striking feature is its soaring 50m steeple. Inside there's a beautiful wooden ceiling and such good acoustics that the church is regularly used for concerts and other events.

Dunedin Botanic Garden
GARDENS

(Map p204; www.dunedinbotanicgarden.co.nz; cnr Great King St & Opoho Rd; ☺dawn-dusk) FREE
Dating from 1863, these 22 peaceful, grassy and shady hectares include rose gardens, rare natives, a four-hectare rhododendron dell, glasshouses, a playground and a cafe. Kids love tooting about on the Community Express 'train' (adult/child $3/1).

◎ Other Suburbs

★Olveston
HOUSE

(Map p194; ☑03-477 3320; www.olveston.co.nz; 42 Royal Tce, Roslyn; adult/child $20/11; ☺tours 9.30am, 10.45am, noon, 1.30pm, 2.45pm & 4pm) Although it's a youngster by European standards, this spectacular 1906 mansion provides a wonderful window into Dunedin's past. Entry is via fascinating guided tours; it pays to book ahead. There's also a pretty little garden to explore.

Until 1966 Olveston was the family home of the wealthy Theomin family, notable patrons of the arts who were heavily involved with endowing the Public Art Gallery. This artistic bent is evident in Olveston's grand interiors, which include works by Charles Goldie and Frances Hodgkins (a family friend). A particular passion was Japanese art, and the home is liberally peppered with exquisite examples. The family was Jewish, and the grand dining table is set up as if for Shabbat dinner.

Central Dunedin

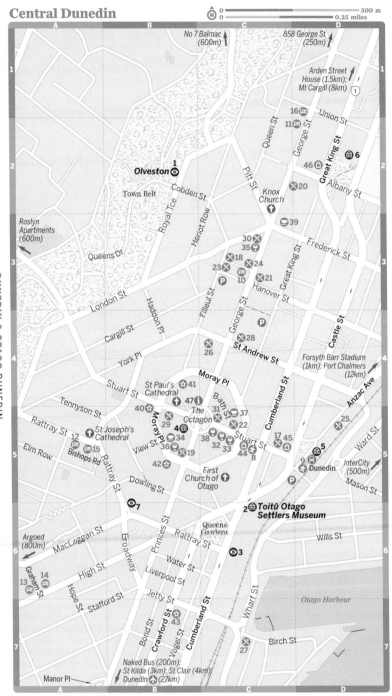

No 7 Balmac (600m)

858 George St (250m)

Arden Street House (1.5km); Mt Cargill (8km)

Olveston 1

Town Belt

Roslyn Apartments (600m)

Queens Dr

Queen St

Union St

George St

Great King St

6

46

Albany St

Knox Church

Cobden St

Royal Tce

Heriot Row

Pitt St

20

39

London St

Frederick St

Great King St

30
35

18
24

23
10
21

Hanover St

Haddon Pl

Filleul St

George St

Cargill St

York Pl

28
26

St Andrew St

Cumberland St

Forsyth Barr Stadium (1km); Port Chalmers (12km)

Castle St

Moray Pl

St Paul's Cathedral

41

47

The Octagon

31
37

Bath St

22

Anzac Ave

Ward St

25

Stuart St

Tennyson St

40

Moray Pl

29
4
34
38
32 33
44
8

17 45

Rattray St

St Joseph's Cathedral

12

15

Bishops Rd

View St

36
19

42

Elm Row

Stuart St

5

9
Dunedin

InterCity (500m)

Mason St

First Church of Otago

Dowling St

7

Queens Garden

2 Toitū Otago Settlers Museum

Argoed (800m)

MacLaggan St

Broadway

Princes St

Rattray St

3

Wills St

High St

Water St

Liverpool St

Graham St

13
14

Hope St

Stafford St

Jetty St

Bond St

Crawford St

43

Yogel St

Cumberland St

Wharf St

Otago Harbour

Birch St

27

Naked Bus (200m); St Kilda (3km); St Clair (4km); Dunedin (27km)

Manor Pl

0   500 m
0   0.25 miles

Central Dunedin

Baldwin St LANDMARK
(Map p204; North East Valley) The world's steepest residential street (or so says the *Guinness Book of World Records*), at its peak Baldwin St has a gradient of 1 in 2.86 (19°). From the city centre, head 2km north up Great King St to where the road branches sharp left to Timaru. Get in the right-hand lane and continue straight ahead. This becomes North Rd, and Baldwin St is on the right after 1km.

🏃 Activities

Swimming & Surfing

St Clair and St Kilda are both popular swimming beaches (though you need to watch for rips at St Clair). Both have consistently good left-hand breaks, and you'll also find good surfing at Blackhead further south, and at Aramoana on Otago Harbour's North Shore.

St Clair Hot Salt Water Pool SWIMMING
(Map p204; www.dunedin.govt.nz; Esplanade, St Clair; adult/child $6.20/3.10; ⊙8.30am-6pm daily Oct-Apr, 9am-5pm Wed-Mon May-Sep) This heated, outdoor pool sits on the western headland of St Clair Beach.

Esplanade Surf School SURFING
(Map p204; ☑0800 484 141; www.espsurfschool. co.nz; 1 Esplanade, St Clair; 90min group lesson $60, private instruction $120) Operating from a van parked at St Clair Beach in summer (call at other times), this experienced crew provides equipment and lessons.

Hiking/Tramping

The Otago Tramping & Mountaineering Club (www.otmc.co.nz) organises day and overnight tramps on weekends, often to the Silver Peaks Reserve north of Dunedin. Non-members are welcome, but must contact trip leaders beforehand.

Tunnel Beach Walkway
WALKING

(Tunnel Beach Rd, Blackhead) This short but extremely steep track (15 minutes down, 30 back up) accesses a dramatic stretch of coast where the wild Pacific has carved sea stacks, arches and unusual formations out of the limestone. Strong currents make swimming here dangerous.

It takes its name from a hand-hewn stone tunnel at the bottom of the track, which civic father John Cargill had built to give his family access to secluded beachside picnics.

The track is 7km southwest of central Dunedin. Head south on Princes St and continue as it crosses under the motorway and then a railway bridge. Turn right at the next traffic lights onto Hillside Rd and follow it until the end, then make a quick left then right onto Easther Cres. Stay on this road for 3.5km (it changes name several times) and then look for Tunnel Beach Rd on the left.

Mt Cargill-Bethunes Gully Walkway
WALKING

(Map p204; Norwood St, Normanby) Yes, it's possible to drive up 676m Mt Cargill, but that's not the point. The track (3½ hours return) starts from Norwood St, which is accessed from North Rd. From Mt Cargill, a trail continues to the 10-million-year-old, lava-formed Organ Pipes and, after another half-hour, to Mt Cargill Rd on the other side of the mountain.

Other Activities

Dunedin Railways
TOURIST TRAIN

(Map p194; 03-477 4449; www.dunedin railways.co.nz; Dunedin Railway Station; office 8am-5pm Mon-Fri, 8.30am-3pm Sat & Sun) Two interesting heritage train journeys start at Dunedin's railway station. The best is the scenic **Taieri Gorge Railway**, with narrow tunnels, deep gorges, winding tracks, rugged canyons and viaduct crossings. The four-hour return trip aboard 1920s heritage coaches travels to Pukerangi (one-way/return $63/91), 58km away. Some trains carry on to Middlemarch ($75/113, six hours return) – handy for the Otago Central Rail Trail.

The **Seasider** heads north, partly along the coast, as far as Oamaru ($72/109, seven hours return), although it's possible to get off the train at Moeraki ($66/99) for a two-hour stop before hopping on the return train. Shorter trips head as far as Palmerston ($59/89, four hours return). Aim for a seat on the right-hand side of the train for better sea views.

Cycle World
BICYCLE RENTAL

(Map p194; 03-477 7473; www.cycleworld. co.nz; 67 Stuart St; per day $40; 8.30am-6pm Mon-Fri, 10am-3pm Sat & Sun) Rents out bikes, performs repairs and has mountain-biking information.

🛏 Sleeping

🛏 City Centre

Hogwartz
HOSTEL $

(Map p194; 03-474 1487; www.hogwartz.co.nz; 277 Rattray St; dm $31, with/without bathroom s $82/65, d $90/74, apt from $106; P@) The Catholic bishop's residence from 1872 to 1999, this beautiful building is now a fascinating warren of comfortable and sunny rooms, many with harbour views. The old coach house and stables have recently been converted into swankier en suite rooms and apartments.

Chalet Backpackers
HOSTEL $

(Map p194; 03-479 2075; www.chaletback packers.co.nz; 296 High St; dm/s/d $31/50/68; P@) The kitchen of this rambling old building is big, sunny and festooned with flowers, and there's also a compact garden, pool table, piano and rumours of a ghost. There are no en suite rooms but some have handbasins.

315 Euro
MOTEL $$

(Map p194; 03-477 9929; www.eurodunedin. co.nz; 315 George St; apt from $175; P) This sleek complex is accessed by an unlikely looking alley off Dunedin's main retail strip. Choose from modern studios or larger one-bedroom apartments with full kitchens and laundries. Double glazing keeps George St's irresistible buzz at bay.

Brothers Boutique Hotel
HOTEL $$$

(Map p194; 03-477 0043; www.brothershotel. co.nz; 295 Rattray St; r $170-395; P) Rooms in this 1920s Christian Brothers residence have been refurbished beyond any monk's dreams, while still retaining many unique features. The chapel room even has its original arched stained-glass windows. There are great views from the rooftop units. Rates include a continental breakfast and an evening drink.

Fletcher Lodge
B&B $$$

(Map p194; 03-477 5552; www.fletcherlodge. co.nz; 276 High St; s/d/apt from $295/355/650; P@) Originally home to one of NZ's wealthiest industrialists, this gorgeous redbrick mansion is just minutes from the city, but the secluded gardens feel wonderfully remote. Rooms are elegantly trimmed with antique furniture and ornate plaster ceilings.

🛏 North Dunedin

★ Kiwi's Nest   HOSTEL $

(Map p194; ☑ 03-471 9540; www.kiwisnest.co.nz; 597 George St; dm $28, with/without bathroom s $68/48, d $88/68, apt $105; P @ 🛜) This wonderfully homely two-storey house has a range of tidy centrally heated rooms, some with en suites, fridges and kettles. Plus it's a flat walk to the Octagon – something few Dunedin hostels can boast.

★ 858 George St   MOTEL $$

(☑ 03-474 0047; www.858georgestreetmotel. co.nz; 858 George St; units from $150; P 🛜) ✦ Cleverly designed to blend harmoniously with the neighbourhood's two-storey Victorian houses, this top-quality motel complex has units ranging in size from studios to two bedrooms. Studios are fitted with microwaves, fridges, toasters and kettles, while the larger units also have stove tops or full ovens.

★ Bluestone on George   APARTMENT $$$

(Map p194; ☑ 03-477 9201; www.bluestone dunedin.co.nz; 571 George St; apt from $225; P @ 🛜) ✦ If you're expecting an imposing old bluestone building, think again: this four-storey block couldn't be more contemporary. The elegant studio units are decked out in muted tones, with kitchenettes, laundry facilities and decks or tiny balconies. There's also a small gym and a guest lounge.

🛏 St Clair

Majestic Mansions   APARTMENT $$

(Map p204; ☑ 03-456 5000; www.st-clair.co.nz; 15 Bedford St; apt from $140; P 🛜) One street back from St Clair beach, this venerable 1920s apartment block has been thoroughly renovated, keeping the layout of the original little flats but sprucing them up with feature wallpaper and smart furnishings. Each has kitchen and laundry facilities.

Hotel St Clair   HOTEL $$$

(Map p204; ☑ 03-456 0555; www.hotelstclair.com; 24 Esplanade; r $205-255, ste $370; P 🛜) Soak up St Clair's surfy vibe from the balcony of your chic room in this contemporary medium-rise hotel. All but the cheapest have ocean views, and the beach is only metres from the front door.

🛏 Other Suburbs

Leith Valley Touring Park   HOLIDAY PARK $

(Map p204; ☑ 03-467 9936; www.leithvalley touringpark.co.nz; 103 Malvern St, Woodhaugh; sites per person $19, units with/without bathroom from $92/59; P @ 🛜) ✦ This holiday park is surrounded by native bush studded with walks, glowworm caves and a creek. Self-contained modern motel units are spacious, and tourist flats are smaller but have a more rustic feel (linen required).

Argoed   B&D $$

(☑ 03-474 1639; www.argoed.co.nz; 504 Queens Dr, Belleknowes; s/d from $150/190; P 🛜) Roses and rhododendrons encircle this gracious two-storey wooden villa, built in the 1880s. Each of the three charmingly old-fashioned bedrooms has its own bathroom but only one is en suite. Guests can relax in the conservatory or tinkle the ivories of the grand piano in the lounge.

Arden Street House   B&B $$

(Map p204; ☑ 03-473 8860; www.ardenstreet house.co.nz; 36 Arden St, North East Valley; s $75, d with/without bathroom $130/120; P @ 🛜) With crazy artworks, an organic garden, charming hosts and a lived-in feeling, this 1930s hill-top house makes a wonderfully eccentric base. Some of the rooms have great views and one, in a converted garage, has a kitchenette. To get here from the city, drive up North Rd, turn right into Glendining Ave and then left into Arden St.

Roslyn Apartments   APARTMENT $$$

(☑ 03-477 6777; www.roslynapartments.co.nz; 23 City Rd, Roslyn; apt from $215; P 🛜) Modern decor and brilliant city and harbour views are on tap at these apartments, just a short walk from Roslyn's eating strip. Each has full kitchen and laundry facilities.

✖ Eating

Cafes and inexpensive Asian restaurants are clustered along George St. Uphill from the Octagon, Roslyn has good restaurants and cafes, and the beachy ambience of St Clair is great for a lazy brunch.

✕ City Centre

★ Otago Farmers Market
MARKET $

(Map p194; www.otagofarmersmarket.org.nz; Dunedin Railway Station; ◷ 8am-12.30pm Sat) This thriving market is all local, all edible (or drinkable) and mostly organic. Grab felafels or an espresso to sustain you while you browse, and stock up on fresh meat, seafood, vegies and cheese for your journey. Sorted.

Good Oil
CAFE $

(Map p194; ☑ 03-479 9900; www.thegoodoilcafe. com; 314 George St; mains $9-18; ◷ 7.30am-4pm) This sleek little cafe is a great spot for coffee and cake or fresh salads. If you're still waking up, kickstart the day with imaginative brunches such as kumara hash with hot smoked salmon.

Modaks Espresso
CAFE $

(Map p194; ☑ 03-477 6563; 337-339 George St; mains $9-17; ◷ 7.30am-3.30pm; ☑) This funky little place with brick walls, mismatched formica tables, plastic animal heads and bean bags for slouching in is popular with students and those who appreciate sweet indie pop while they nurse a pot of tea. Plump, toasted bagels warm the insides in winter.

JUST GIVE ME THE COFFEE & NO ONE WILL GET HURT

Dunedin has some excellent coffee bars in which you can refuel and recharge:

The Fix (Map p194; www.thefixcoffee. co.nz; 15 Frederick St; ◷ 7am-4pm Mon-Fri, 8am-noon Sat) Wage slaves queue at the pavement window every morning, while students and others with time on their hands relax in the courtyard.

Mazagran Espresso Bar (Map p194; 36 Moray Pl; ◷ 8am-6pm Mon-Fri, 10am-2pm Sat) The godfather of Dunedin's coffee scene, this compact wood-and-brick coffee house is the source of the magic bean for many of the city's restaurants and cafes.

Strictly Coffee Company (Map p194; ☑ 03-479 0017; www.strictlycoffee.co.nz; 23 Bath St; ◷ 7.30am-4pm Mon-Fri) This stylish retro coffee bar is hidden down grungy Bath St. Different rooms provide varying views and artworks to enjoy while you sip and sup.

Best Cafe
FISH & CHIPS $

(Map p194; www.facebook.com/bestcafedunedin; 30 Stuart St; takeaways $6-10, mains $10-23; ◷ 11am-2.30pm & 5-8pm Mon-Sat) Serving up fish and chips since 1932, this local stalwart has its winning formula down pat, complete with vinyl tablecloths, hand-cut chips and curls of butter on white bread.

Velvet Burger
BURGERS $

(Map p194; ☑ 03-477 7089; www.velvetburger. co.nz; 150 Stuart St; mains $9-16; ◷ 11.30am-late) Well positioned for the post-beer crowd, Velvet Burger has gourmet offerings that are an excellent alcohol sop, especially the mammoth Goneburger (beef, chicken *and* bacon). There's another branch at **375 George St** (Map p194; ☑ 03-477 0124; mains $9-16; ◷ 11.30am-late).

Miga
KOREAN $$

(Map p194; ☑ 03-477 4770; www.migadunedin. co.nz; 4 Hanover St; mains lunch $9.50-13, dinner $16-39; ◷ 11.30am-2pm & 5-10pm Mon-Sat) Settle into a booth at this attractive brick-lined eatery, and order claypot rice or noodle dishes from the extensive menu. Japanese dishes include tempura, katsu and incredible ramen soups, made with fresh noodles that are specially made for them. Otherwise go for broke and cook a Korean barbecue right at your table.

Etrusco at the Savoy
ITALIAN $$

(Map p194; ☑ 03-477 3737; www.etrusco.co.nz; 8a Moray Pl; mains $17-21; ◷ 5.30pm-late) New Zealand has very few dining rooms to match the Edwardian elegance of the Savoy, with its moulded ceilings, stained-glass crests, brass chandeliers, green Ionian columns and fabulously over-the-top lamps. Pizza and pasta might seem like an odd fit, but Etrusco's deliciously rustic dishes absolutely hold their own.

Paasha
TURKISH $$

(Map p194; ☑ 03-477 7181; www.paasha.co.nz; 31 St Andrew St; mains lunch $12-21, dinner $21-36; ◷ 11.30am-3pm & 5-9pm Mon-Wed, 11.30am-late Thu-Sun; ▦) Authentic Turkish kebabs, dips and salads are faithfully created at this long-running Dunedin favourite. It's a top place for takeaways, and most nights the spacious and warm interior is filled with groups drinking Efes beer and sharing heaving platters of tasty Ottoman goodness.

Saigon Van VIETNAMESE **$$**
(Map p194; ☑03-474 1445; 66a St Andrew St; mains $11-23; ☺11.30am-2pm & 5-9pm Tue-Sun; ✐) The decor looks high-end Asian, but the prices are more moderate than you'd imagine. Try the combination spring rolls and a bottle of Vietnamese beer to recreate lazy nights in Saigon. The bean-sprout-laden *pho* (noodle soup) and salads are also good.

Izakaya Yuki JAPANESE **$$**
(Map p194; ☑03-477 9539; 29 Bath St; dishes $4-12; ☺noon-2pm Mon-Fri, 5pm-late daily; ☜) Cute and cosy, with a huge array of small dishes on which to graze, Yuki is a lovely spot for supper or a relaxed, drawn-out Japanese meal. Make a night of it with sake or Asahi beer, sashimi, teppanyaki and multiple plates of *kushiyaki* (grilled skewers).

★Bracken MODERN NZ **$$$**
(Map p194; ☑03-477 9779; www.bracken restaurant.co.nz; 95 Filleul St; 5/7/9-course menu $79/99/120; ☺5.30-11pm Tue-Sat) Bracken's tasting menus offer a succession of pretty little plates bursting with flavour. While the dishes are intricate, nothing's overly gimmicky, and the setting, in an old wooden house, is classy without being too formal.

Plato MODERN NZ **$$$**
(Map p194; ☑03-477 4235; www.platocafe.co.nz; 2 Birch St; mains lunch $19-24, dinner $34-36; ☺noon-2pm Wed-Sun, 6pm-late daily) The kooky decor (including collections of toys and beer tankards) gives little indication of the seriously good food on offer at this relaxed eatery by the harbour. Fresh fish and shellfish feature prominently in a lengthy menu full of international flavours and subtle smoky elements. Servings are enormous.

Scotia SCOTTISH **$$$**
(Map p194; ☑03-477 7704; www.scotiadunedin. co.nz; 199 Stuart St; mains $32-38; ☺5pm-late Tue-Sat) Occupying a cosy heritage townhouse, Scotia toasts all things Scottish with a wall full of single-malt whisky and hearty fare such as smoked salmon and Otago hare. The two Scottish Robbies – Burns and Coltrane – look down approvingly on a menu that also includes haggis and whisky-laced pâté.

North Dunedin

Everyday Gourmet CAFE, DELI **$**
(Map p194; www.everydaygourmet.net.nz; 466 George St; mains $9-19; ☺8am-4pm Mon-Sat)

Apart from cooked breakfasts and pasta, most of the good stuff beckons from the counter of this excellent bakery-style cafe and deli. It's light, bright and extremely popular, with a good selection of magazines and newspapers.

St Clair

Starfish CAFE **$$**
(Map p204; ☑03-455 5940; www.starfishcafe. co.nz; 7/240 Forbury Rd; mains brunch $14-20, dinner $20-30; ☺7am-5pm Sun-Tue, to late Wed-Sat) Starfish is the coolest creature in the growing restaurant scene at St Clair Beach. Pop out on a weekday to score an outside table, and tuck into gourmet pizza and wine. Evening meals are big and robust (steak, fish and chips, pulled-pork sliders), and there's a good selection of craft beer.

Other Suburbs

★No 7 Balmac CAFE **$$**
(☑03-464 0064; www.no7balmac.co.nz; 7 Balmacewen Rd, Maori Hill; mains brunch $14-25, dinner $29-37; ☺7am-late Mon-Fri, 8.30am-late Sat, 8.30am-5pm Sun; ☜) We wouldn't recommend walking to this sophisticated cafe at the top of Maori Hill, but luckily it's well worth the price of a cab. The fancy cafe fare stretches to the likes of venison loin and dry-aged beef. If you're on a diet, avoid eye contact with the sweets cabinet.

Drinking & Nightlife

★Mou Very BAR
(Map p194; ☑03-477 2180; www.facebook.com/ MouVeryBar; 357 George St; ☺7am-5pm Mon & Tue, 7am-12.30am Wed-Fri, 9am-12.30pm Sat, 9am-5pm Sun) Welcome to one of the world's smallest bars – it's only 1.8m wide, but is still big enough to host regular DJs, live bands and poetry readings. There are just six bar stools, so patrons spill out into an adjacent laneway. By day, it's a handy caffeine-refueling spot.

Carousel COCKTAIL BAR
(Map p194; ☑03-477 4141; www.carouselbar.co.nz; upstairs, 141 Stuart St; ☺5pm-late Tue-Sat) Tartan wallpaper, a roof deck and great cocktails leave the dressed-up clientele looking pleased to be seen somewhere so deadly cool. DJs spin deep house until late from Thursday through to Saturday, and there's live jazz on Friday evenings from 8.30pm.

Inch Bar   BAR

(Map p204; ☑ 03-473 6496; 8 Bank St, North East Valley; ⊘ 3-11.30pm) Make the short trek from town to this cavelike little bar for its selection of Kiwi craft beers and tasty tapas, and the cute little indoor-outdoor beer garden. Despite its diminutive dimensions, it oftens hosts live music.

Albar   BAR

(Map p194; 135 Stuart St; ⊘ 11am-late) This former butcher is now a bohemian little bar attracting maybe the widest age range in Dunedin. Most punters are drawn by the many single-malt whiskies, interesting tap beers and cheap-as-chips bar snacks ($6 to $9).

Pequeno   COCKTAIL BAR

(Map p194; ☑ 03-477 7830; www.pequeno.co.nz; behind 12 Moray Pl; ⊘ 5pm-late Mon-Fri, 7pm-late Sat) Down the alley opposite the Rialto Cinema, Pequeno attracts a sophisticated crowd with leather couches, a cosy fireplace and an excellent wine and tapas menu. Music is generally laid-back, with regular live acts.

Di Lusso   COCKTAIL BAR

(Map p194; ☑ 03-477 3885; www.dilusso.co.nz; 117 Stuart St; ⊘ 3pm-3am Mon-Sat) Upmarket and designery with wood panelling, chandeliers and a backlit drinks display, Di Lusso serves seriously good cocktails. DJs play from Thursday to Saturday.

Stuart St Brew Bar   BAR

(Map p194; ☑ 03-477 3776; www.stuartst.co.nz; 12 The Octagon; ⊘ 11am-late) Nelson's Mac's brewery is making a strike deep into Speight's territory in the form of this funky bar right on the Octagon. It's the sunniest spot for an afternoon drink, and after the sun sets there's often live music or DJs.

Speight's Ale House   PUB

(Map p194; ☑ 03-471 9050; www.thealehouse. co.nz; 200 Rattray St; ⊘ 11.30am-late) Busy even in the non-university months, the Ale House is a favourite of strapping young lads in their cleanest dirty shirts. It's a good spot to watch the rugby on TV and to try the full range of Speight's beers.

☆ Entertainment

Metro Cinema   CINEMA

(Map p194; ☑ 03-471 9635; www.metrocinema. co.nz; Moray Pl) Within the town hall, Metro shows art-house and foreign flicks.

Rialto Cinemas   CINEMA

(Map p194; ☑ 03-474 2200; www.rialto.co.nz; 11 Moray Pl) Blockbusters and art-house flicks. Rates cheaper on Tuesdays.

Fortune Theatre   THEATRE

(Map p194; ☑ 03-477 8323; www.fortunetheatre. co.nz; 231 Stuart St) The world's southernmost professional theatre company has been staging dramas, comedies, pantomimes, classics and contemporary NZ productions for over 40 years. Shows are performed – watched over by the obligatory theatre ghost – in an old Gothic-style Wesleyan church.

Sammy's   LIVE MUSIC

(Map p194; ☑ 03-477 2185; 65 Crawford St) Dunedin's premier live-music venue draws an eclectic mix of genres from noisy-as-hell punk to chilled reggae and gritty dubstep. It's the venue of choice for visiting Kiwi bands and up-and-coming international acts.

🛍 Shopping

Gallery De Novo   ARTS

(Map p194; ☑ 03-474 9200; www.gallerydenovo. co.nz; 101 Stuart St; ⊘ 9.30am-5.30pm Mon-Fri, 10am-3pm Sat & Sun) This interesting, contemporary fine art gallery is worth a look whether you're likely to invest in a substantial piece of Kiwi art or not.

University Book Shop   BOOKS

(Map p194; ☑ 03-477 6976; www.unibooks.co.nz; 378 Great King St, North Dunedin; ⊘ 8.30am-5.30pm Mon-Fri, 11am-3pm Sat & Sun) Dunedin's best bookshop, with lots of Māori, Pacific and NZ titles.

Stuart Street Potters Cooperative   CRAFTS

(Map p194; ☑ 03-471 8484; 14 Stuart St; ⊘ 10am-5pm Mon-Fri, 9am-3pm Sat) Locally designed and made pottery and ceramic art.

ℹ Information

DOC Visitors Centre (Department of Conservation; Map p194; ☑ 03-474 3300; www. doc.govt.nz; 50 The Octagon; ⊘ 8.30am-5pm Mon-Fri) Housed within the Dunedin i-SITE, this office provides information and maps on regional walking tracks, Great Walks bookings and hut tickets. When the DOC desk isn't staffed, the i-SITE workers fill in the gaps.

Dunedin Hospital (☑ 03-474 0999; www. southerndhb.govt.nz; 201 Great King St)

Dunedin i-SITE (Map p194; ☑ 03-474 3300; www.isitedunedin.co.nz; 50 The Octagon; ⊘ 8.30am-5pm) Dunedin's tourist office incorporates the DOC Visitors Centre.

Urgent Doctors (☑ 03-479 2900; www.dunedinurgentdoctors.com; 95 Hanover St; ☺8am-10pm) There's also a late-night pharmacy next door.

❶ Getting There & Away

AIR

Air New Zealand (☑ 0800 737 000; www.airnewzealand.co.nz) Flies to/from Auckland, Wellington and Christchurch.

Jetstar (☑ 0800 800 995; www.jetstar.com) Flies to/from Auckland and Wellington.

Kiwi Regional Airlines (☑ 07-444 5020; www.flykiwiair.co.nz) Flies to Nelson from Dunedin, with connections to Tauranga and Hamilton.

Virgin Australia (☑ 0800 670 000; www.virginaustralia.com) Flies to/from Brisbane.

BUS

Buses and shuttles leave from the Dunedin Railway Station, except where we've noted otherwise.

Alpine Connexions (☑ 03-443 9120; www.alpineconnexions.co.nz) Shuttles head to/from Alexandra ($40, 2½ hours), Clyde ($40, three hours), Cromwell ($45, 3¼ hours), Wanaka ($45, four hours) and Queenstown ($45, 4½ hours), as well as key stops on the Otago Central Rail Trail.

Atomic Shuttles (☑ 03-349 0697; www.atomictravel.co.nz) Buses to/from Christchurch ($35, 5¾ hours), Timaru ($25,1¾ hours) and Oamaru ($20, 1½ hours), twice daily.

Catch-a-Bus (☑ 03-449-2024; www.trailjourneys.co.nz) Bike-friendly shuttles to/from key Rail Trail towns, including Middlemarch ($45, one hour), Ranfurly ($49, two hours), Alexandra ($56, 3¼ hours), Clyde ($56, 3½ hours) and Cromwell ($60, 3¾ hours).

Coast Line Tours (☑ 03-434 7744; www.coastline-tours.co.nz) Shuttles to Oamaru depart from the Octagon; detours to Dunedin Airport and Moeraki can be arranged.

InterCity (Map p204; ☑ 03-471 7143; www.intercity.co.nz; departs 7 Halsey St) Coaches to/from Christchurch (from $40, six hours) and Oamaru (from $22, 1½ hours) twice daily, and Cromwell (from $22, 3¾ hours), Queenstown (from $36, 4¼ hours) and Te Anau (from $37, 4½ hours) daily.

Naked Bus (www.nakedbus.com; departs 630 Princes St; prices vary) Daily buses head to/from Christchurch (six hours), Timaru (3½ hours), Dunedin Airport (45 minutes), Gore (2½ hours) and Invercargill (3¼ hours).

TRAIN

The tourist trains operated by **Dunedin Railways** (p196) can be used as a transport connection. The Taieri Gorge Railway heads to Middlemarch twice a week, while the Seasider is an option for Moeraki and Oamaru.

❶ Getting Around

TO/FROM THE AIRPORT

Dunedin Airport (DUD; ☑ 03-486 2879; www.dnairport.co.nz; 25 Miller Rd, Momona) is 27km southwest of the city. A standard taxi ride between the city and the airport costs around $90. There is no public bus service. For door-to-door shuttles, try **Kiwi Shuttles** (☑ 03-487 9790; www.kiwishuttles.co.nz; per 1/2/3/4 passengers $20/36/48/60) or **Super Shuttle** (☑ 0800 748 885; www.supershuttle.co.nz; per 1/2/3/4 passengers $30/40/50/60).

BUS

Dunedin's **GoBus** (☑ 03-474 0287; www.orc.govt.nz; adult fare $2.20-6.70) network extends across the city. It's particularly handy for getting to St Clair, St Kilda, Port Chalmers and as far afield as Portobello on the Otago Peninsula. Buses run regularly during the week, but services are greatly reduced (or nonexistent) on weekends and holidays.

CAR

The big rental companies all have offices in Dunedin, and inexpensive local outfits include **Mainland Rental Vehicles** (☑ 0800 284 284; www.mainlandcarrentals.co.nz) and **Hanson Rental Vehicles** (☑ 03-453 6576; www.hanson.net.nz).

TAXI

Dunedin Taxis (☑ 03-477 7777; www.dunedintaxis.co.nz)

Southern Taxis (☑ 03-476 6300; www.southerntaxis.co.nz)

AROUND DUNEDIN

Port Chalmers

POP 1370

Little Port Chalmers is only 13km out of central Dunedin but it feels a world away. Somewhere between working class and bohemian, Port Chalmers has a history as a port town but has long attracted Dunedin's arty types. Dunedin's best rock-and-roll pub, **Chick's Hotel** (Map p204; ☑ 022 672 4578; www.facebook.com/ChicksHotel; 2 Mount St; ☺4pm-1am Wed-Sun), is an essential after-dark destination, and daytime attractions include a few raffish cafes, design stores and galleries.

⊙ Sights

Orokonui Ecosanctuary   WILDLIFE RESERVE
(Map p204; ☑ 03-482 1755; www.orokonui.org.nz; 600 Blueskin Rd; adult/child $16/8; ⊙ 9.30am-4.30pm) 🏃 From the impressive visitors centre there are great views over this 307-hectare predator-free nature reserve, which encloses cloud forest on the mountainous ridge above Port Chalmers and stretches to the estuary on the opposite side. Its mission is to provide a mainland refuge for species usually exiled to offshore islands for their own protection. Visiting options include self-guided explorations, hour-long guided tours (adult/child $30/15; 11am and 1.30pm daily) and two-hour guided tours (adult/child $45/22; 11am daily).

Rare bird species finding sanctuary here include kiwi, takahe and kaka, while reptiles include tuatara and Otago skinks.

Orokonui is a well-signposted 6km drive from the main road into Port Chalmers.

🏃 Activities

Traditional rock climbing (nonbolted) is popular at Long Beach and the cliffs at Mihiwaka, both accessed via Blueskin Rd north of Port Chalmers.

Hare Hill   HORSE RIDING
(Map p204; ☑ 03-472 8496; www.horseriding-dunedin.co.nz; 207 Aramoana Rd, Deborah Bay; treks $85-160) Horse treks include thrilling beach rides and farm trips.

🛏 Sleeping

Billy Brown's   HOSTEL $
(Map p204; ☑ 03-472 8323; www.billybrowns.co.nz; 423 Aramoana Rd, Hamilton Bay; dm/d $30/75; ⊙ Sep-May) On a farm 5km further along the road from Port Chalmers, this hostel has magnificent views across the harbour to the peninsula. There's a lovely rustic shared lounge with a cosy wood-burner and plenty of retro vinyl to spin.

If you're not comfortable with big dogs, look elsewhere.

ⓘ Getting There & Away

On weekdays, 17 buses travel between Dunedin and Port Chalmers, with two additional services on Friday nights (adult/child $5.20/3). On Saturdays this reduces to 11, and on Sundays to three.

Otago Peninsula
POP 4220

The Otago Peninsula is home to the South Island's most accessible diversity of wildlife. Albatross, penguins, fur seals and sea lions are some of the highlights, as well as rugged countryside, wild walks, beaches and interesting historical sites. Despite a host of tours exploring the peninsula, it maintains its quiet rural air.

⊙ Sights

**★ Nature's Wonders
Naturally**   WILDLIFE RESERVE
(Map p204; ☑ 03-478 1150; www.natureswonders.co.nz; Taiaroa Head; adult/child $59/45; ⊙ tours from 10.15am) What makes the improbably beautiful beaches of this coastal sheep farm different from other important wildlife habitats is that (apart from pest eradication and the like) they're left completely alone. Many of the multiple private beaches haven't suffered a human footprint in years. The result is that yellow-eyed penguins can often be spotted (through binoculars) at any time of the day, and NZ fur seals laze around rocky swimming holes, blissfully unfazed by tour groups passing by.

Depending on the time of year, you might also see whales and little penguin chicks.

The tour is conducted in 'go-anywhere' Argo vehicles by enthusiastic guides, at least some of whom double as true-blue Kiwi farmers. If you don't believe it, ask about the sheep-shed experience (price on application).

**Royal Albatross Centre
& Fort Taiaroa**   BIRD SANCTUARY
(Map p204; ☑ 03-478 0499; www.albatross.org.nz; Taiaroa Head; ⊙ 11.30am-dusk Oct-Apr, 10.15am-dusk May-Sep) Taiaroa Head, at the peninsula's northern tip, has the world's only mainland royal albatross colony, along with a late 19th-century military fort. The only public access to the area is by guided tour. The hour-long Classic tour (adult/child $50/15) focuses on the albatross, or there's a 30-minute Fort tour ($25/10); the two can be combined on the Unique tour ($55/20). Otherwise you can just call into the centre to look at the displays and have a bite in the cafe.

Albatross are present on Taiaroa Head throughout the year, but the best time to see them is from December to March, when one parent is constantly guarding the young while the other delivers food throughout the day. Sightings are most common in the afternoon when the winds pick up; calm days don't see as many birds in flight.

Little penguins swim ashore at Pilots Beach (just below the car park) around dusk to head to their nests in the dunes. For their protection, the beach is closed to the public every evening, but viewing is possible from a specially constructed wooden platform (adult/child $30/10). Depending on the time of year, 50 to 300 penguins might waddle past.

Fort Taiaroa was built in 1885 in response to a perceived threat of Russian invasion. Its Armstrong Disappearing Gun was designed to be loaded and aimed underground, then popped up like the world's slowest jack-in-the-box to be fired.

Larnach Castle CASTLE
(Map p204; ☑03-476 1616; www.larnachcastle. co.nz; 145 Camp Rd; adult/child castle & grounds $30/10, grounds only $15/4; ☺9am-7pm Oct-Mar, 9am-5pm Apr-Sep) ✐ Standing proudly on top of a hill, this gorgeous Gothic Revival mansion was built in 1871 by Dunedin banker, merchant and Member of Parliament William Larnach to impress his wife, who was descended from French nobility. It's filled with intricate woodwork and exquisite antique furnishings, and the crenellated tower offers expansive views of the peninsula. A self-guided tour brochure is provided with admission, or you can buy an iPhone tour app ($5) that digitally peoples the rooms with costumed actors.

The castle didn't end up bringing Larnach much happiness. After his first two wives died and his third was rumoured to be having an affair with his son, he shot himself in a committee room in Parliament in 1898. His son later followed suit.

After lording it about in the mansion, take a stroll through the pretty gardens or settle in for high tea in the ballroom cafe.

Penguin Place BIRD SANCTUARY
(Map p204; ☑03-478 0286; www.penguinplace. co.nz; 45 Pakihau Rd, Harington Point; adult/child $52/15) On private farmland, this reserve protects nesting sites of the yellow-eyed penguin. The 90-minute tours focus on penguin conservation and close-up viewing from a system of hides. The 2½-hour Ultimate Combo includes the penguins and a guided trek through forest and wetlands. Bookings are essential.

Glenfalloch Woodland Garden GARDENS
(Map p204; ☑03-476 1006; www.glenfalloch.co.nz; 430 Portobello Rd, Macandrew Bay; ☺8am-dusk) **FREE** Expect spectacular harbour views at this 12-hectare garden, filled with flowers, walking tracks and swaying, mature trees, including a 1000-year-old matai. There's also a good restaurant on-site. The Portobello bus stops out the front.

Activities

The peninsula's coastal and farmland walkways offer blissful views and the chance of spotting some wildlife; pick up or download the DOC *Dunedin Walks* brochure. A popular walking destination is beautiful **Sandfly Bay**, reached from Seal Point Rd (moderate, one hour return). You can also follow a trail from the end of Sandymount Rd to the Sandymount summit and on to the impressive Chasm and Lovers Leap (one hour return). Note that this track is closed from September to mid-October for lambing.

Wild Earth Adventures KAYAKING
(☑03-489 1951; www.wildearth.co.nz; trips $115-235) Offers trips in double sea kayaks, with wildlife often sighted en route. Trips take between three hours and a full day, with pickups from the Octagon in Dunedin.

☞ Tours

Back to Nature Tours BUS TOUR
(☑0800 286 000; www.backtonaturetours.co.nz) ✐ The full-day Royal Peninsula tour (adult/child $189/125) heads to points of interest around Dunedin before hitting the Otago Peninsula. Stops include Larnach Castle's gardens (castle entry is extra), Penguin Place and the Royal Albatross Centre. There's also a half-day option that visits various bays and beaches ($79/55) and another tackling the Lovers Leap and Chasm tracks ($89/55).

Elm Wildlife Tours WILDLIFE WATCHING
(☑03-454 4121; www.elmwildlifetours.co.nz; tours from $99) ✐ Well-regarded, small-group, wildlife-focused tours, with options to add the Royal Albatross Centre or a Monarch Cruise. Pick-up and drop-off from Dunedin is included.

Monarch Wildlife Cruises & Tours BOAT TOUR
(Map p204; ☑03-477 4276; www.wildlife.co.nz) ✐ One-hour boat trips from Wellers Rock (adult/child $52/22), and half-day ($90/33) and full-day ($240/124) tours cruising right along the harbour from Dunedin. You may

Dunedin & the Otago Peninsula

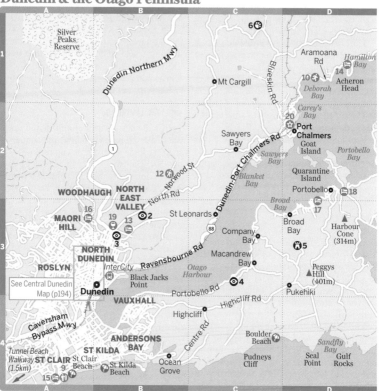

Dunedin & the Otago Peninsula

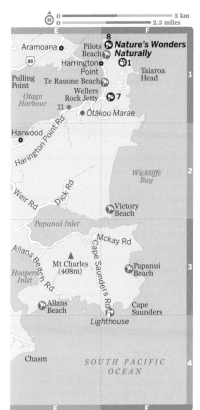

overlooking the bay. Spacious one- and two-bedroom versions are also available, but lack the views.

Larnach Castle
B&B $$$

(Map p204; 03-476 1616; www.larnachcastle. co.nz; 145 Camp Rd; r stable/lodge/estate $160/290/460; @🛜) Pricey Larnach Castle's back-garden lodge has 12 individually whimsically decorated rooms with views. Less frivolous are the atmospheric rooms in the 140-year-old stables (bathrooms are shared). A few hundred metres from the castle, Camp Estate has luxury suites worthy of a romantic splurge. The rates for each option include breakfast and castle entry; dinner in the castle is extra ($70).

1908 Cafe
CAFE, BISTRO $$

(Map p204; 03 478 0801; www.1908cafe.co.nz; 7 Harington Point Rd, Portobello; mains lunch $13-24, dinner $31-34; noon-2pm & 6-10pm, closed Mon & Tue Apr-Oct) Salmon, venison and steak are joined by fresh fish and blackboard specials at this casual, friendly eatery. Cafe fare, such as soup and toasted sandwiches, is served at lunch. The venerable interiors are cheerfully embellished with local art.

Portobello Hotel & Bistro
PUB FOOD $$

(Map p204; www.portobellohotelandbistro.co.nz; 2 Harington Point Rd, Portobello; mains lunch $15-17, dinner $25-29; 11.30am-11.30pm) Refreshing thirsty travellers since 1874, the Portobello pub is still a popular pit stop. Grab a table in the sun and tuck into seafood chowder, a burger or a lamb pie.

ⓘ Getting There & Around

On weekdays, 13 buses (adult/child $6/3.60) travel between Dunedin's Cumberland St and Portobello Village, two of which continue on to Harrington Point at the tip of the peninsula. On Saturdays this reduces to 10, and on Sundays to four. Once on the peninsula, it's tough to get around without your own transport. Most tours will pick you up from your Dunedin accommodation.

There's no petrol available on the peninsula.

CENTRAL OTAGO

Rolling hills that turn from green to gold in the relentless summer sun provide a backdrop to a succession of tiny, charming goldrush towns where rugged, laconic 'Southern Man' types can be seen propping up the bar in lost-in-time pubs. As well as being one of the country's top wine regions, the area

spot sea lions, penguins, albatross and seals. The full-day option includes admission to the Royal Albatross Centre and Penguin Place.

🛏 Sleeping & Eating

McFarmers Backpackers
HOSTEL $

(Map p204; 03-478 0389; mcfarmers@xtra. co.nz; 774 Portobello Rd, Broad Bay; s/d without bathroom $55/66, cottage $120-150) On a working sheep farm with harbour views, the rustic timber lodge and self-contained cottage here are steeped in character and feel instantly like home. The Portobello bus goes past the gate.

★Portobello Motel
MOTEL $$

(Map p204; 03-478 0155; www.portobello motels.com; 10 Harington Point Rd, Portobello; units from $160; 🛜) These sunny, modern, self-contained units are just off the main road in Portobello. Studio units have small decks

provides fantastic opportunities for those on two wheels, whether mountain biking along old gold-mining trails or traversing the district on the Otago Central Rail Trail.

Middlemarch

POP 156

With the Rock & Pillar Range as an impressive backdrop, the small town of Middlemarch is the terminus of both the Taieri Gorge Railway and the Otago Central Rail Trail. It's famous in NZ for the Middlemarch Singles Ball (held across Easter in odd-numbered years), where southern men gather to entice city gals to the country life.

🏃 Activities

Cycle Surgery   BICYCLE RENTAL
(☑ 03-464 3630; www.cyclesurgery.co.nz; Swansea St; rental per day from $35; ⊘ depot mid-Sep–mid-May) Rents bikes and serves coffee to Rail Trailers from its main office in Middlemarch. Also has a drop-off depot at the Clyde trailhead.

Trail Journeys   BICYCLE RENTAL
(☑ 03-464 3213; www.trailjourneys.co.nz; Swansea St; rental per day from $42; ⊘ depot Oct-Apr) Provides bike rental and logistical support to riders on the Otago Central Rail Trail. This includes shuttles, bag transfers and an accommodation booking service. Also has a depot in Clyde, at the other end of the trail.

🛏 Sleeping & Eating

Otago Central Hotel   HOTEL $$
(☑ 03-444 4800; www.hydehotel.co.nz; SH87, Hyde; with/without bathroom s $120/100, d $170/120) Most of the tidy rooms in this cool old hotel, 27km along the trail from Middlemarch, have private bathrooms, but only some are en suite. It's no longer a working pub and the licensed cafe on the sunny terrace shuts at 4pm, leaving the $40 set dinner the only meal option for many miles around.

Kissing Gate Cafe   CAFE $
(☑ 03-464 3224; 2 Swansea St; mains $7-18; ⊘ 8.30am-4pm; 🐕) Sit out under the fruit trees in the pretty garden of this cute little wooden cottage and tuck into a cooked breakfast, fancy meat pie, zingy salad or some home baking. Nana-chic at its best.

❶ Getting There & Away

Both of the main cycle companies offer shuttles to Dunedin, Pukerangi and the Rail Trail towns.

In the warmer months, Trail Journey's **Catch-a-Bus** (☑ 03-449 2150; www.trailjourneys.co.nz) has scheduled daily services to/from Dunedin ($45, one hour), Ranfurly ($27, one hour), Alexandra ($55, two hours), Clyde ($55, 2½ hours) and Cromwell ($59, 2¾ hours).

The scenic **Taieri Gorge Railway** (☑ 03-477 4449; www.dunedinrailways.co.nz; ⊘ Sun May-Sep, Fri & Sun Oct-Apr) has only limited runs between Dunedin and Middlemarch ($75, 2½ hours); most services end at Pukerangi Station, 20km away.

Ranfurly

POP 663

After a series of fires in the 1930s, Ranfurly was rebuilt in the architectural style of the day, and a few attractive art-deco buildings still line its sleepy main drag. The teensy town is trying hard to cash in on this meagre legacy, calling itself the 'South Island's art deco capital'. There's even an Art Deco Museum in the admittedly fabulous Centennial Milk Bar building on the main street.

There are a couple of cafes in town and an old pub which serves meals and rents rooms.

🏃 Activities

Maniototo 4WD Safaris   DRIVING TOUR
(☑ 03-444 9703; www.maniototo4wdsafaris.co.nz; half-/full day $130/190) Explore the rugged terrain made famous by noted Central Otago landscape artist Grahame Sydney.

🛏 Sleeping

Peter's Farm Lodge   LODGE $
(☑ 03-444 9811; www.petersfarm.co.nz; 113 Tregonning Rd, Waipiata; per person $55) Set on a sheep farm 13km south of Ranfurly, this rustic 1882 farmhouse offers comfy beds, hearty barbecue dinners ($25) and free pickups from the Rail Trail. Kayaks, fishing rods and gold pans are all available, so it's worth staying a couple of nights. Further beds are available in neighbouring Tregonnings Cottage (1882).

Hawkdun Lodge   MOTEL $$
(☑ 03-444 9750; www.hawkdunlodge.co.nz; 1 Bute St; s/d from $113/150; 🐕) ✈ This smart boutique motel is the best option in the town centre by far. Each unit has a kitchenette with a microwave, but travelling chefs can flex their skills in the guest kitchen and on the barbecue. Rates include a continental breakfast.

Kokonga Lodge B&B $$$
(📞03-444 9774; www.kokongalodge.co.nz; 33 Kokonga-Waipiata Rd; s/d $235/285; @🐾) Just off SH87 between Ranfurly and Hyde, this upmarket rural property offers six contemporary en suite rooms, one of which was occupied by Sir Peter Jackson when he was filming *The Hobbit* in the area. The Rail Trail passes nearby.

ℹ️ Information

Ranfurly i-SITE (📞03-444 1005; www.centralotagonz.com; 3 Charlemont St; ⊙9am-5pm; 🐾) Located in the old train station. Grab a copy of *Rural Art Deco – Ranfurly Walk* for a self-guided tour.

ℹ️ Getting There & Away

In the warmer months, Trail Journey's **Catch-a-Bus** (📞03-449 2150; www.trailjourneys.co.nz; ⊙Nov-Apr) passes through Ranfurly on its way between Cromwell ($52, 1¾ hours) and Dunedin ($49, two hours).

Naseby

POP 120

Cute as a button, surrounded by forest and dotted with 19th-century stone buildings, Naseby is the kind of small settlement where life moves slowly. That the town is pleasantly obsessed with the fairly insignificant world of NZ curling indicates there's not much else going on. It's that lazy small-town vibe, along with good mountain-biking and walking trails through the surrounding forest, that makes Naseby an interesting place to stay for a couple of days.

🏃 Activities

**Maniototo Curling
International** SNOW SPORTS
(📞03-444 9878; www.curling.co.nz; 1057 Channel Rd; per 90min adult/child $30/12; ⊙10am-5pm May-Oct, 9am-7.30pm Nov-Apr) All year-round you can shimmy after curling stones at the indoor ice rink; tuition is available. In winter there's also an outdoor ice rink to skate around.

🛏️ Sleeping

Royal Hotel PUB $
(📞03-444 9990; www.naseby.co.nz; 1 Earne St; dm $40, r with/without bathroom $110/80; 🐾) The better of the town's historic pubs, the 1863 Royal Hotel sports the royal coat of arms and what just might be NZ's most rustic garden bar. Rooms are simple but spotless.

Naseby Lodge APARTMENT $$
(📞03-444 8222; www.nasebylodge.co.nz; cnr Derwent & Oughter Sts; 1-/2-bedroom apt $170/260) Constructed of environmentally friendly straw-bale walls sheathed in rustic corrugated iron, these free-standing modern apartments are smart and spacious, with fully equipped kitchens and underfloor heating in the bathrooms. There's also a good restaurant on-site.

Old Doctor's Residence B&B $$$
(📞03-444 9775; www.olddoctorsresidence.co.nz; 58 Derwent St; r/ste $295/345; 🐾) 🎗️ Old doctors take note: this is how to reside! Sitting behind a pretty garden, this gorgeous 1870s house offers two luxurious guest rooms and a lounge where wine and nibbles are served of an evening. The suite has a sitting room and an en suite bathroom (with a fabulous make-up desk). The smaller room's bathroom is accessed from the corridor.

ℹ️ Information

Ernslaw One Forestry Office (📞03-444 9995; www.ernslaw.co.nz/naseby-recreational-area; 16 Oughter St; ⊙9am-4pm Mon-Fri) Administers the 500-hectare recreation reserve within the privately owned Naseby Forest. Call in for maps of walking tracks and mountain-bike trails.

Naseby Information Centre (📞03-444 9961; www.nasebyinfo.org.nz; Old Post Office, Derwent St; ⊙9am-1pm Tue-Thu, 10am-4pm Fri-Mon, reduced hours in winter)

ℹ️ Getting There & Away

The Ranfurly–Naseby Rd leaves SH85, 4km north of Ranfurly. There's no public transport and cyclists should factor in a 12km detour from the Rail Trail. From Naseby, you can wind your way on unsealed roads northeast through spectacular scenery to Danseys Pass and through to Duntroon in the Waitaki Valley.

St Bathans

POP 6

A worthwhile 17km detour north from SH85 heads into the foothills of the imposing Dunstan Mountains and on to diminutive St Bathans. This once-thriving gold-mining town of 2000 people is now home to only half a dozen permanent residents living amid a cluster of cutesy 19th-century buildings, almost all of which have 'For Sale' signs in front of them.

The Blue Lake is an accidental attraction: a large hollow filled with blue water that has run off abandoned gold workings. Walk along the sculpted cliffs to the lookout for a better view of the alien landscape (one hour return).

Sleeping

Vulcan Hotel
PUB $$

(☑ 03-447 3629; stbathans.vulcanhotel@xtra. co.nz; Main St; r per person $60) The Vulcan Hotel is an atmospheric (and famously haunted) spot to drink, eat or stay in, even if the reception isn't always entirely welcoming. Considering St Bathans' tiny population, you'll find the bar here pretty busy on a Friday night as thirsty farmers from around the valley descend en masse.

St Bathans Jail
& Constable's Cottage
RENTAL HOUSE $$

(☑ 0800 555 016; www.stbathansnz.co.nz; 1648 Loop Rd; house $145-340) Built in 1884, these neighbouring buildings are an atmospheric option. The cottage has three bedrooms (sleeping six) and is fully self-contained, with a barbecue in the garden. The jail has been converted into a bedroom with an en suite bathroom in the old cell and a kitchen in the entrance lobby.

Lauder, Omakau & Ophir

Separated by 8km of SH85, tiny Lauder (population 12) and larger Omakau (population 250) are good stops if you're a hungry Rail Trailer with a sore bum and in need of a feed and a bed. However, the area's real gem is adorable Ophir (population 58), 2km from Omakau across the Manuherikia River.

Gold was discovered here in 1863 and the town swiftly formed, adopting the name of the biblical place where King Solomon sourced his gold. By 1875, the population hit over 1000 but when the gold disappeared, so did the people. Ophir's fate was sealed when the railway bypassed it in 1904, leaving its main street trapped in time.

The most photogenic of Ophir's many heritage buildings is the still-functioning 1886 post office (www.historic.org.nz; 53 Swindon St; ◷ 9am-noon Mon-Fri). At the far end of the town, the sealed road ends at the 1870s wooden-planked Dan O'Connell Bridge, a bumpy but scenic crossing that continues via a gravel road to SH85.

Ophir lays claim to the country's widest range of temperatures: from -21.6°C to 35°C.

Sleeping & Eating

Muddy Creek Cutting
B&B $$

(☑ 03-447 3682; www.muddycreekcutting.co.nz; SH85, Lauder; per person $80) Art fills the walls of this charmingly restored 1930s mudbrick farmhouse, with five bedrooms that share two bathrooms. Dinners with a local, organic spin are also available ($60 per person).

Chatto Creek Tavern
HERITAGE HOTEL $$

(☑ 03-447 3710; www.chattocreektavern.co.nz; 1544 SH85, Chatto Creek; dm/s/d without bathroom $60/100/130; ☎) Dating from 1886, this attractive stone hotel sits right beside the Rail Trail and highway, 10km southwest of Omakau. Pop in for a whitebait fritter (in season) or lamb shanks, or rest your weary calf muscles in a dorm bed or double room. Rates include breakfast. Free, informal camping is also possible, with a $5 charge for a shower.

★ Pitches Store
B&B $$$

(☑ 03-447 3240; www.pitches-store.co.nz; 45 Swindon St, Ophir; r $280; ◷ restaurant 10am-late daily Nov-Apr, 10am-3pm Mon, Sun & Thu, 10am-late Fri & Sat May & Aug-Oct) Formerly a general store and butcher, this heritage building has been sensitively transformed into six elegant guest rooms and a humdinger of a cafe-restaurant (brunch mains $13 to $19, dinner mains $33 to $37). Exposed stone walls may speak of the past but the menu offers contemporary country cooking.

Muddy Creek Cafe
CAFE $

(2 Harvey St, Omakau; mains $8-16; ◷ 8.30am-7pm Mon-Sat, 10am-7pm Sun) Take a break from the Rail Trail at this friendly spot festooned with old radios. Cafe treats include all-day breakfasts, paninis, pies and ice cream, or you can grab a burger or fish and chips from the takeaway counter.

Stationside Cafe
CAFE $

(Lauder-Matakanui Rd, Lauder; mains $8-18; ◷ 8am-5pm Oct-Apr) Home baking and country cooking are showcased at this great little trailside place with a wonderfully charming hostess. Options include healthy salads, sandwiches, soups and pasta. Sadly, the coffee's not up to much.

Alexandra
POP 4800

Unless you've come especially for the Easter Bunny Hunt or the springtime Blossom Festival and NZ Merino Shearing Championships, the main reason to visit unassum-

ROXBURGH

Heading south from Alexandra, SH8 winds along rugged, rock-strewn hills above the Clutha River as it passes Central Otago's famous orchards. In season, roadside fruit stalls sell just-picked stone fruit, cherries and berries. En route are a scattering of small towns, many dating from gold-rush days.

Thirteen kilometres south of Alexandra, the historic **Speargrass Inn** (☏ 03-449 2192; www.speargrassinn.co.nz; 1300 Fruitlands-Roxburgh Rd/SH8, Fruitlands; r $180; ⊙ cafe 8.30am-4pm Mon-Thu, 8.30am-9pm Fri-Sun, closed Tue & Wed May-Sep; 🐾) has three handsome rooms in a block out the back, set in attractive gardens. The original 1869 building houses a charming cafe (mains $18 to $26). It's a good place to stop for coffee and cake or a more substantial meal.

Further south, the Clutha broadens into **Lake Roxburgh**, with a large hydroelectric power station at its terminus, before rushing past Roxburgh itself (population 522). Call into the friendly **i-SITE** (☏ 03-446 8920; www.centralotagonz.com; 120 Scotland St; ⊙ 9am-5pm daily Nov-Mar, 9am-5pm Mon-Fri Apr-Oct) for information on mountain biking, water sports and seasonal fruit-picking work in the surrounding apple and stone-fruit orchards.

Another source of fruit-picking contacts is **Villa Rose Backpackers** (☏ 03-446 8761; www.villarose.co.nz; 79 Scotland St; dm $35, d with/without bathroom from $120/100; 🐾). This lovely old bungalow has spacious dorm rooms, comfortable self-contained units and a huge modern kitchen.

Before you leave Roxburgh, drop into **Jimmy's Pies** (☏ 03-446 9012; www.jimmyspies. co.nz; 143 Scotland St; pies $4-6.50; ⊙ 7.30am-5pm Mon-Fri), renowned across the South Island since 1959. If you're at a loss as to which meaty pastry to choose, try the apricot chicken – you're in orchard country after all.

Continuing south from Roxburgh, the road passes through Lawrence and the Manuka Gorge Scenic Reserve, a picturesque route through wooded hills and gullies. SH8 joins SH1 near Milton.

ing Alexandra is mountain biking. It's the biggest Central Otago Rail Trail settlement by far, offering more eating and sleeping options than the rest of the one-horse (or fewer) towns on the route. It's also the start of the new Roxburgh Gorge Trail.

Alex, as it's known to the locals, marks the southeastern corner of the acclaimed Central Otago wine region. Of the dozen wineries in the immediate vicinity, only a handful are open for tastings. These are detailed in the *Central Otago Wine Map*, available from the i-SITE (p210).

◉ Sights

Central Stories   MUSEUM
(☏ 03-448 6230; www.centralstories.com; 21 Centennial Ave; admission by donation; ⊙ 10am-4pm) Central Otago's history of gold-mining, winemaking, orcharding and sheep farming is covered in this excellent regional museum and gallery, which shares a building with the i-SITE.

🏃 Activities

Walkers and mountain bikers will love the old gold trails weaving through the hills; collect maps from the i-SITE. The **Alexandra–Clyde**

150th Anniversary Walk (12.8km, three hours one way) is a riverside trail that's fairly flat, with ample resting spots and shade.

Roxburgh Gorge Trail   MOUNTAIN BIKING
(www.cluthagold.co.nz) Opened to considerable fanfare in 2013, this well-constructed cycling and walking track was intended to connect Alexandra to Roxburgh Dam. As access through some of the farmland in the middle section wasn't successfully negotiated, riding the 'full trail' requires prearranging a scenic 13km jet-boat ride (adult/child $95/55) through the local information centres or directly with Clutha River Cruises (p210).

Once you add on the noncompulsory track maintenance donation ($25/50 per adult/family), it's an expensive ride.

An alternative is to make a return trip from each end: Alexandra–Doctors Point (20km return) or Roxburgh Dam–Shingle Creek (22km return).

From Roxburgh Dam you can continue on the Clutha Gold Trail, an easier 73km track that follows the Clutha through Roxburgh to Beaumont and then heads to Lawrence. The same maintenance fee covers both tracks.

Clutha River Cruises BOAT TOUR
(☑0800 258 842; www.clutharivercruises.co.nz; boat ramp, Dunorling St; adult/child $95/45; ☺2pm Oct-May) Explore the scenery and history of the region on a 2½-hour heritage cruise. They also run the jetboat transfer for cyclists on the Roxburgh Gorge Trail.

Altitude Bikes BICYCLE RENTAL
(☑03-448 8917; www.altitudeadventures.co.nz; 88 Centennial Ave; per day from $25; ☺8.30am-5.30pm Mon-Fri, 9am-1pm Sat) Rents bikes in conjunction with Henderson Cycles and organises logistics for riders on the Otago Central, Clutha Gold and Roxburgh Gorge Trails.

🛏 Sleeping & Eating

Marj's Place HOSTEL $
(☑03-448 7098; www.marjsplace.co.nz; 5 Theyers St; dm/s/d without bathroom $30/40/80; ☜) The standard varies widely between the three neighbouring houses that comprise Marj's sprawling 'place'. The 'homestay' has private rooms, a Finnish sauna and a spa bath. It's much nicer than the 'backpackers', which is let mainly to seasonal workers.

★ Courthouse Cafe & Larder CAFE $
(☑03-448 7818; www.packingshedcompany.com; 8 Centennial Ave; mains $10-20; ☺8am-4pm) Floral wallpaper and bright vinyl tablecloths help to dispel any lingering austerity from this stone courthouse building, dating from 1878 and surrounded by lawns. The counter groans under the weight of an extraordinary array of baked goods (macadamia custard croissants, gooey doughnuts, slices, cakes), which compete with a menu full of interesting dishes (beef-cheek burgers, pulled-pork sliders, eggy breakfasts).

ℹ Information

Alexandra i-SITE (☑03-262 7999; www.centralotagonz.com; 21 Centennial Ave; ☺9am-5pm; ☜) Pick up a free map of this very spread-out town.

ℹ Getting There & Away

Atomic Shuttles (☑03-349 0697; www.atomictravel.co.nz) A daily bus heads to/from Dunedin ($30, 2¼ hours), Roxburgh ($15, 30 minutes), Cromwell ($15, 30 minutes) and Wanaka ($25, 1¾ hours).

Catch-a-Bus (☑03-449 2024; www.trail journeys.co.nz) Shuttles to Cromwell ($25, 30 minutes), Clyde ($15, 10 minutes), Ranfurly ($43, one hour), Middlemarch ($55, two hours) and Dunedin ($56, 3¼ hours).

InterCity (☑03-471 7143; www.intercity.co.nz) A daily coach heads to/from Dunedin (from $21, three hours), Roxburgh (from $14, 34 minutes), Clyde (from $10, nine minutes), Cromwell (from $12, 24 minutes) and Queenstown (from $15, 1½ hours).

OTAGO CENTRAL RAIL TRAIL

Stretching from Dunedin to Clyde, the Central Otago rail branch linked small, inland goldfield towns with the big city from the early 20th century through to the 1990s. After the 150km stretch from Middlemarch to Clyde was permanently closed, the rails were ripped up and the trail resurfaced. The result is a year-round mainly gravel trail that takes bikers, walkers and horse riders along a historic route containing old rail bridges, viaducts and tunnels.

With excellent trailside facilities (toilets, shelters and information), few hills, gob-smacking scenery and profound remoteness, the trail attracts well over 25,000 visitors annually. March is the busiest time, when there are so many city slickers on the track that you might have to wait 30 minutes at cafes en route for a panini. Consider September for a quieter ride.

The trail can be followed in either direction. The entire trail takes approximately four to five days to complete by bike (or a week on foot), but you can obviously choose to do as short or as long a stretch as suits your plans. There are also easy detours to towns such as Naseby and St Bathans.

Mountain bikes can be rented in Dunedin, Middlemarch, Alexandra and Clyde. Any of the area's i-SITEs can provide detailed information. See www.otagocentralrailtrail.co.nz and www.otagorailtrail.co.nz for track information, recommended timings, accommodation options and tour companies.

Due to the popularity of the trail, a whole raft of sleeping and eating options have sprung up in remote locales en route, although some stops are still poorly served.

Clyde

POP 1020

Much more charming than his buddy Alex, 8km down the road, Clyde looks more like a 19th-century gold-rush film set than a real town. Set on the banks of the emerald-green Clutha River, Clyde retains a friendly, small-town feel, even when holidaymakers arrive in numbers over summer. It's also at one end of the Otago Central Rail Trail.

◎ Sights

Clyde Historical Museums MUSEUM
(5 Blyth St; admission by donation; ◷3-5pm Tue-Sun Nov-Apr) The main building showcases Māori and Victorian exhibits and provides information about the Clyde Dam. Larger exhibits (machinery, horse-drawn carts etc) are housed in the Herb Factory complex at 12 Fraser St.

🏃 Activities

Pick up a copy of *Walk Around Historic Clyde* from the Alexandra i-SITE (p210). The **Alexandra–Clyde 150th Anniversary Walk** (three hours one way) is a riverside trail that's fairly flat, with ample resting spots and shade.

Trail Journeys BICYCLE RENTAL
(☑03-449 2150; www.trailjourneys.co.nz; 16 Springvale Rd; ◷tours Sep-Apr) 🚲 Right by the Rail Trailhead, Trail Journeys rents bikes (from $42 per day) and arranges cycling tours, baggage transfers and shuttles. It also has a depot in Middlemarch.

🎊 Festivals & Events

Clyde Wine & Food Festival WINE, FOOD
(www.promotedunstan.org.nz; ◷10.30am-4.30pm Easter Sun) Showcases the region's produce and wines.

🛏 Sleeping & Eating

Dunstan House B&B $$
(☑03-449 2295; www.dunstanhouse.co.nz; 29 Sunderland St; s/d without bathroom from $110/130, d/ste with bathroom from $170/240; ◷Oct-Apr; 🛜) This restored late-Victorian balconied inn has lovely bar and lounge areas, and rooms decorated in period style. The less expensive rooms share bathrooms but are just as comfortable and atmospheric.

★ Oliver's B&B $$$
(☑03-449 2600; www.oliverscentralotago.co.nz; Holloway Rd; r/ste from $225/495; 🛜) 🚲 Oliver's

fills an 1860s merchant's house and stone stables with luxurious rooms decked out with old maps, heritage furniture and claw-foot baths. Most of the rooms open onto a secluded garden courtyard.

Bank Cafe CAFE $
(www.bankcafe.co.nz; 31 Sunderland St; mains $10-15; ◷9am-4pm) Grab a table inside or out and tuck into cakes, slices, waffles and delicious burgers. The robust takeaway sandwiches are perfect for lunch on two wheels.

★ Oliver's MODERN NZ $$
(☑03-449 2805; www.oliverscentralotago.co.nz; 34 Sunderland St; mains lunch $18-26, dinner $30-39; ◷11.30am-2.30pm & 5.30-9.30pm) Housed in a gold-rush-era general store, this wonderful complex incorporates a craft brewery (the Victoria Store Brewery), bar and deli-cafe within its venerable stone walls. The restaurant shifts gears from on-trend cafe fare at lunchtime (tuna sliders, pulled pork belly etc) to a bistro showcasing the best local, seasonal produce in the evenings (venison noisette, lamb rump, salmon etc).

🛍 Shopping

Central Gourmet Galleria FOOD
(☑03-449 3331; www.centralgourmetgalleria.co.nz; 27 Sunderland St; ◷10am-4pm Tue-Sun) This former butcher's stocks a selection of award-winning local wines, many of which you won't find anywhere else. There are also plenty of Central Otago foodie treats such as jams and chutneys.

ⓘ Getting There & Away

Alpine Connexions (☑03-443 9120; www.alpineconnexions.co.nz) Shuttles head to/from Dunedin ($40, three hours), Alexandra ($15, 15 minutes), Cromwell ($24, 20 minutes), Queenstown ($35, 1½ hours) and Wanaka ($35, one hour), as well as key stops on the Otago Central Rail Trail.

Catch-a-Bus (☑03-449 2024; www.trailjourneys.co.nz; ◷Nov-Apr) Shuttles to Cromwell ($25, 20 minutes), Alexandra ($15, 10 minutes), Ranfurly ($43, 1½ hours), Middlemarch ($55, 2½ hours) and Dunedin ($56, 3½ hours) during the main cycling season.

InterCity (☑03-471 7143; www.intercity.co.nz) A daily coach heads to/from Dunedin (from $32, 3½ hours), Roxburgh (from $21, 44 minutes), Alexandra (from $10, nine minutes), Cromwell (from $16, 14 minutes) and Queenstown (from $22, 1½ hours).

DUNEDIN & OTAGO CLYDE

Cromwell

POP 4150

Cromwell has a charming lakeside historic precinct, a great weekly farmers market and perhaps the South Island's most over-the-top 'big thing' – a selection of giant fruit by the highway.

It's also at the very heart of the prestigious Central Otago wine region (www.cowa.org.nz), known for its extraordinarily good pinot noir and, to a lesser extent, riesling, pinot gris and chardonnay. The Cromwell Basin – which stretches from Bannockburn, 5km southwest of Cromwell, to north of Lake Dunstan – accounts for over 70% of Central Otago's total wine production. Pick up the *Central Otago Wine Map* for details of upwards of 50 local wineries.

◎ Sights

Cromwell Heritage Precinct HISTORIC BUILDINGS

(www.cromwellheritageprecinct.co.nz; Melmore Tce) When the Clyde Dam was completed in 1992 it flooded Cromwell's historic town centre, 280 homes, six farms and 17 orchards. Many historic buildings were disassembled before the flooding and have since been rebuilt in a pedestrianised precinct beside Lake Dunstan. While some have been set up as period pieces (stables and the like), others house some good cafes, galleries and interesting shops. In summer it plays host to an excellent weekly **farmers market** (◎ 9am-1pm Sun Nov-Feb).

🏃 Activities

Highlands Motorsport Park ADVENTURE SPORTS
(☑ 03-445 4052; www.highlands.co.nz; cnr SH6 & Sandflat Rd; ◎ 10am-5pm) Transformed from a paddock into a top-notch 4km racing circuit in just 18 months, this revheads' paradise hosted its first major event in 2013. The action isn't reserved just for the professionals, with various high-octane experiences on offer, along with an excellent museum.

Budding speed freaks can start out on the **go-karts** ($39 per 10 minutes) before taking a 200km/h ride in the **Highlands Taxi** ($75/120 for two/four people), completing three laps of the circuit as a passenger in a **Porsche GT3** ($295), or having a go at the wheel of a **V8 muscle car** ($395).

If you'd prefer a less racy experience, the **National Motorsport Museum** (adult/child $25/10) showcases racing cars and displays

about Kiwi legends such as Bruce McLaren, Possum Bourne, Emma Gilmour and Scott Dixon. Family groups can opt for the **Jurassic Safari Adventure**, a trip in a safari van through a forest inhabited by dinosaurs ($79 including museum entry). Plus there's free **mini-golf** and, across the car park, the **Nose cafe**, which offers wine tastings.

⭐ Tours

Central Otago Motorcycle Hire TOUR
(☑ 03-445 4487; www.comotorcyclehire.co.nz; 271 Bannockburn Rd; per day from $165) The sinuous and hilly roads of Central Otago are perfect for negotiating on two wheels. This crew hires out bikes and advises on improbably scenic routes. Is also offers guided trail-bike tours (from $195) and extended road tours (from $575).

Goldfields Jet ADVENTURE TOUR
(☑ 03-445 1038; www.goldfieldsjet.co.nz; SH6; adult/child $109/49) Zip through the Kawarau Gorge on a 40-minute jetboat ride.

🎊 Festivals & Events

Highlands 101 SPORTS
(◎ Nov) A three-day motor-racing festival at Highlands Park, including the final round of the Australian GT Championship.

🛏 Sleeping

Cromwell Top 10 Holiday Park HOLIDAY PARK $
(☑ 03-445 0164; www.cromwellholidaypark.co.nz; 1 Alpha St; sites $40-44, units with/without bathroom from $110/75; @ 🛜) The size of a small European nation and packed with cabins and self-contained units of various descriptions, all set in tree-lined grounds.

Carrick Lodge MOTEL $$
(☑ 03-445 4519; www.carricklodge.co.nz; 10 Barry Ave; units $140-180; 🛜) One of Cromwell's more stylish motels, Carrick has spacious, modern units and is just a short stroll from the main shopping complex. Executive units have spa baths and views over the golf course.

⭐ **Burn Cottage Retreat** B&B, COTTAGE $$$
(☑ 03-445 3050; www.burncottageretreat.co.nz; 168 Burn Cottage Rd; r/cottages $200/225; 🛜) Set among walnut trees and gardens 3km northwest of Cromwell, this peaceful retreat has three luxurious, self-contained cottages with classy decor, spacious kitchens and modern bathrooms. B&B accommodation is available in the main house.

✗ Eating

★ Armando's Kitchen   CAFE **$$**
(☑ 03-445 0303; 71 Melmore Tce; mains $10-22; ⊙ 10am-3pm Sat-Thu, to 9pm Fri, extended hours in summer) Cromwell's heritage precinct is best enjoyed from the veranda of Armando's Kitchen, with an espresso or gourmet ice cream in hand. The homemade pasta, pizza and cakes are all excellent, and the breakfasts are legendary. On Friday nights it opens late for pizza and drinks.

Mt Difficulty   MODERN NZ **$$**
(☑ 03-445 3445; www.mtdifficulty.co.nz; 73 Felton Rd, Bannockburn; mains $30-35; ⊙ tastings 10.30am-4.30pm, restaurant noon-4pm) As well as making our favourite NZ pinot noir, Mt Difficulty is a lovely spot for a leisurely lunch looking down over the valley. There are large wine-friendly platters to share, but save room for the decadent desserts. Wines can be tasted for a gold coin donation.

Bannockburn Hotel   PUB FOOD **$$**
(☑ 03-445 0615; www.bannockburnhotel.com; 420 Bannockburn Rd, Bannockburn; mains $24-30; ⊙ 11am-9pm) Head out to the historic Bannockburn watering hole for massive serves of pub grub (ribs, steaks, fish and chips) and even bigger skies from the front terrace. It's 5km out of town, but they operate a free courtesy bus.

① Information

Cromwell i-SITE (☑ 03-445 0212; www.central otagonz.com; 2d The Mall; ⊙ 9am-7pm Jan-Mar, to 5pm Apr-Dec) Stocks the *Walk Cromwell* brochure, covering local mountain-bike and walking trails, including the nearby gold-rush ghost-town of Bendigo.

① Getting There & Away

Alpine Connexions (☑ 03-443 9120; www.alpineconnexions.co.nz) Scheduled shuttles to/from Dunedin ($45, 3¼ hours), Alexandra ($24, 25 minutes), Clyde ($24, 20 minutes), Wanaka ($25, 45 minutes) and Queenstown ($25, one hour).

Atomic Shuttles (☑ 03-349 0697; www.atomictravel.co.nz) Daily buses head to/from Queenstown ($15, 55 minutes), Alexandra ($15, 50 minutes), Roxburgh ($25, 1¼ hours), Dunedin ($30, 3¾ hours) and Christchurch ($40, 5¼ hours).

Catch-a-Bus (☑ 03-449 2024; www.trail journeys.co.nz; ⊙ Nov-Apr) Bike-friendly shuttles to Clyde ($25, 20 minutes), Alexandra ($25, 30 minutes), Ranfurly ($52, 1¾ hours), Middlemarch ($59, 2¾ hours) and Dunedin ($60, 3¾ hours).

InterCity (☑ 03-471 7143; www.intercity.co.nz) There are four daily coaches to Queenstown (from $11, one hour), and one to Fox Glacier (from $44, 6½ hours), Christchurch (from $51, 7¼ hours), Alexandra (from $12, 24 minutes) and Dunedin (from $22, 3¾ hours).

Naked Bus (www.nakedbus.com; prices vary) One bus per day from Queenstown (one hour) and one from Wanaka (55 minutes) stop in Cromwell before continuing on to Omarama (2½ hours), Lake Tekapo (3¾ hours) and Christchurch (8¼ hours).

Queenstown & Wanaka

Best Places to Eat

➡ Blue Kanu (p229)

➡ Chop Shop (p239)

➡ La Rumbla (p239)

➡ Fergbaker (p228)

➡ Saffron (p239)

Best Places to Sleep

➡ Adventure Queenstown (p225)

➡ The Dairy (p227)

➡ Wanaka Bakpaka (p243)

➡ Lakeside (p244)

➡ Criffel Peak View (p244)

Why Go?

With a cinematic background of mountains and lakes, and a 'what can we think of next?' array of adventure activities, it's little wonder Queenstown tops the itineraries of many travellers.

Slow down slightly in Wanaka – Queenstown's less flashy cousin – which also has good restaurants, bars and outdoor adventures on tap. With Mt Aspiring National Park nearby, you're only a short drive from true NZ wilderness.

Slow down even more in Glenorchy, an improbably scenic reminder of what Queenstown and Wanaka were like before the adventure groupies moved in. Negotiate the Greenstone and Routeburn Tracks for extended outdoor thrills, or kayak the upper reaches of Lake Wakatipu.

Across in historic Arrowtown, consider the town's gold-mining past over a chilled wine or dinner in a cosy bistro. The following day there'll be plenty more opportunities to dive back into Queenstown's action-packed whirlwind.

When to Go

➡ The fine and settled summer weather from January to March is the perfect backdrop to Queenstown's active menu of adventure sports and outdoor exploration. March also brings the Gibbston Wine & Food Festival to Queenstown Gardens.

➡ Mid- to late March sees an inundation of mountain bikers for the Queenstown Bike Festival.

➡ In late June the Queenstown Winter Festival celebrates the coming of the ski season. From June to August, the slopes surrounding Queenstown and Wanaka are flush with an international crew of ski and snowboard fans.

➡ The Wanaka Fest heralds the spring thaw in October.

ⓘ Getting There & Away

Domestic flights head to Queenstown from Auckland, Wellington and Christchurch, with smaller planes servicing Dunedin, Nelson and Hamilton. International flights head to Queenstown from Australian destinations including Brisbane, the Gold Coast, Sydney and Melbourne. Queenstown is the main bus hub for the region, with services radiating out to the West Coast (via Wanaka and Haast Pass), Christchurch, Dunedin (via Central Otago), Invercargill and Te Anau. Wanaka also has services to Christchurch and Dunedin.

QUEENSTOWN

POP 12,500

Surrounded by the soaring indigo heights of the Remarkables and framed by the meandering coves of Lake Wakatipu, Queenstown is a right show-off. Looking like a small town, but displaying the energy of a small city, it wears its 'Global Adventure Capital' badge proudly, and most visitors take the time to do crazy things that they've never done before. No-one's ever visited and said, 'I'm bored'.

Then there's the other Queenstown. The one with the cosmopolitan restaurant and arts scene, excellent vineyards and five international-standard golf courses. Go ahead and jump off a bridge or out of a plane, but take time to slow down and experience Queenstown without the adrenaline. At the very least, find a lakeside bench at dusk and immerse yourself in one of NZ's most beautiful views.

Queenstown is well used to visitors with international accents, so expect great tourist facilities but also big crowds, especially in summer and winter. Autumn (March to May) and spring (October to November) are slightly quieter, but Queenstown is a true year-round destination.

The town's bars are regularly packed with a mainly young crowd that really know how to holiday. If you're a more private soul, drop in to see what all the fuss is about, but then get out and explore the sublime wilderness further up the lake at Glenorchy.

History

The region was deserted when the first British people arrived in the mid-1850s, although there is evidence of previous Māori settlement. Sheep farmers came first, but after two shearers discovered gold on the banks of the Shotover River in 1862, a deluge of prospectors followed.

Queenstown & Wanaka Highlights

① **Queenstown** (p215) Doing things you've only dreamed about in the adrenaline-rush capital of NZ.

② **Wanaka** (p240) Soaking up the sophisticated small-town vibe and sublime lake views.

③ **Arrowtown** (p236) Relaxing and dining after a day's mountain biking and gold panning.

④ **Routeburn Track** (p233) Walking this peaceful and diverse alpine trail, arguably the best of NZ's Great Walks.

⑤ **Glenorchy** (p233) Exploring the upper reaches of Lake Wakatipu by horseback, kayak or jetboat.

⑥ **Rob Roy Glacier Track** (p243) Restraining the urge to yodel as you stroll through the sublime Matukituki Valley before climbing to the glacier.

⑦ **Queenstown bar-hopping** (p230) Partying until the early hours among a multitude of accents in cosmopolitan Queenstown.

Within a year Queenstown was a mining town with streets, permanent buildings and a population of several thousand. It was declared 'fit for a queen' by the NZ government, hence Queenstown was born. Lake Wakatipu was the principal means of transport, and at the height of the boom there were four paddle steamers and 30 other craft plying the waters.

By 1900 the gold had petered out and the population was a mere 190. It wasn't until the 1950s that Queenstown became a popular holiday destination.

◉ Sights

Lake Wakatipu LAKE
(Map p220) Shaped like a perfect cartoon thunderbolt, this gorgeous lake has a 212km shoreline and reaches a depth of 379m (the average depth is over 320m). Five rivers flow into it but only one (the Kawarau) flows out, making it prone to sometimes quite dramatic floods.

If the water looks clean, that's because it is. Scientists have rated it as 99.9% pure – making it the second-purest lake water in the world. In fact, you're better off dipping your glass in the lake than buying bottled water. It's also very cold. That beach by Marine Parade may look tempting on a scorching day, but trust us – you won't want to splash about in water that hovers at around 10°C year-round. Because cold water increases the risk of drowning, local bylaws require the wearing of lifejackets in all boats

under 6m, including kayaks, on all of the district's lakes.

Māori tradition sees the lake's shape as the burnt outline of the evil giant Matau sleeping with his knees drawn up. Local lad Matakauri set fire to the bed of bracken on which the giant slept in order to rescue his beloved Manata, a chief's daughter who was kidnapped by the giant. The fat from Matau's body created a fire so intense that it burnt a hole deep into the ground.

Queenstown Gardens PARK
(Map p220; Park St) Set on its own little tongue of land framing Queenstown Bay, this pretty park was laid out in 1876 by those garden-loving Victorians as a place to promenade. The clothes may have changed (they've certainly shrunk), but people still flock to this leafy peninsula to stroll, picnic and laze about. Less genteel types head straight for the frisbee golf course (p222).

Other attractions include an ice-skating rink, skate park, lawn-bowling club, tennis courts, mature exotic trees (including large sequoias and some fab monkey puzzles by the rotunda) and a rose garden. There's also a memorial to Captain Robert Scott (1868–1912), leader of the doomed South Pole expedition, which includes an engraving of his moving final message.

Kiwi Birdlife Park ZOO
(Map p220; ✆03-442 8059; www.kiwibird.co.nz; Brecon St; adult/child $45/23; ⊗9am-5pm, shows 11am & 3pm) These five acres are home to 10,000 native plants, tuatara and scores of birds, including kiwi, kea, moreporks, parakeets and extremely rare black stilts. Stroll around the aviaries, watch the conservation show, and tiptoe quietly into the darkened kiwi houses.

Skyline Gondola CABLE CAR
(Map p220; ✆03-441 0101; www.skyline.co.nz; Brecon St; adult/child return $32/20; ⊗9am-late) 🛈 Hop aboard for fantastic views. At the top there's the inevitable cafe, restaurant, souvenir shop and observation deck, as well as the Queenstown Bike Park (p221), Skyline Luge (p222), **Ledge Bungy** (Map p220; ✆0800 286 4958; www.bungy.co.nz; adult/child $195/145), **Ledge Swing** (Map p220; ✆0800 286 4958; www.bungy.co.nz; adult/child $160/110) and Ziptrek Ecotours (p222). At night there are Māori culture shows from Kiwi Haka (p231) and stargazing tours (including gondola adult/child $85/45).

Walking trails include a loop track through the Douglas firs (30 minutes return). The energetic (or frugal) can forgo the gondola and hike to the top on the **Tiki Trail** (Map p220) and then continue on the **Ben Lomond Track** (Map p220; www.doc.govt.nz).

Underwater Observatory   VIEWPOINT
(Map p226; 03-409 0000; www.kjet.co.nz; main jetty; adult/child $10/5; 9am-7pm Nov-Mar, to 5pm Apr-Oct) Six windows showcase life under the lake in this reverse aquarium (the people are behind glass). Large brown trout abound, and look out for freshwater eels and scaup (diving ducks), which cruise right past the windows – especially when the coin-operated food-release box is triggered.

Activities

A baffling array of activities is offered by a baffling number of shops in the town centre. It's even more confusing due to the fact that some shops change their name from winter to summer, some run multiple activities from the same shop, and some activities are branded differently but are actually the same thing. Several places call themselves information centres, but only the i-SITE (p232) is the true, independent, official information centre.

If you're planning on tackling several activities, various combination tickets are available, including those offered by **Queenstown Combos** (Map p226; 03-442 7318; www.combos.co.nz; The Station, cnr Shotover & Camp Sts).

Hiking/Tramping & Climbing

Pick up the *Wakatipu Walks* brochure ($5) from DOC and the i-SITE for local tramping tracks ranging from easy one-hour strolls to tough eight-hour slogs.

Ultimate Hikes   TRAMPING
(Map p226; 03-450 1940; www.ultimatehikes. co.nz; 9 Duke St; Nov-Apr) Offers day walks on the Routeburn Track (from $179) and the Milford Track (from $299), departing from Queenstown. Or you can do these multiday tracks in their entirety, staying in Ultimate Hike's own staffed lodges rather than DOC huts, where hot meals and en suite bathrooms await. In the winter the office is rebranded as Snowbiz and rents skis and snowboards.

Guided Walks New Zealand WALKING, TRAMPING
(03-442 3000; www.nzwalks.com; adult/child from $107/67) Excellent walks in the Queen-

stown area, ranging from half-day nature walks to the full three-day Hollyford Track. Also offers snowshoeing in winter.

Climbing Queenstown   ROCK CLIMBING
(Map p226; 027 477 9393; www.climbingqueenstown.com; 23 Brecon St; from $149) Rock climbing, via ferrata (climbing with fixed metal rungs, rails, pegs and cables), mountaineering and alpine trekking lead by qualified guides.

Bungy & Swings

Shotover Canyon Swing   ADVENTURE SPORTS
(Map p226; 03-442 6990; www.canyonswing. co.nz; 35 Shotover St; per person $219, additional swings $45) Be released loads of different ways – backwards, in a chair, upside down. From there it's a 60m free fall and a wild swing across the canyon at 150km/h. The price includes the transfer from the Queenstown booking office.

AJ Hackett Bungy   ADVENTURE SPORTS
(Map p226; 03-450 1300; www.bungy.co.nz; The Station, cnr Camp & Shotover Sts) The bungy originators now offer jumps from three sites in the Queenstown area, with giant swings available at two of them. It all started at the historic 1880 **Kawarau Bridge** (Map p218; 0800 286 4958; www.bungy.co.nz; Gibbston Hwy; adult/child $190/145), 23km from Queenstown (transport included). In 1988 it became the world's first commercial bungy site, offering a 43m leap over the river. It's also the only bungy site in the region to offer tandem jumps.

New to the Kawarau Bridge site is the **Kawarau Zipride** (Map p218; 0800 286

Queenstown Region

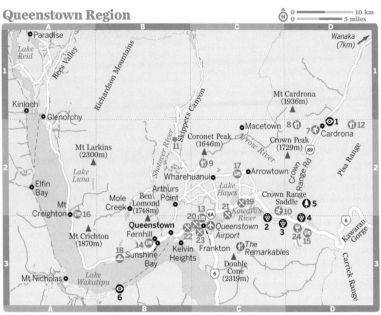

Queenstown Region

4958; www.bungy.co.nz; Gibbston Hwy; adult/child $50/40, 3-/5-ride pack $105/150), three 130m ziplines mainly targeted to kids – but also a thrill for adults not keen to take a giant leap of faith. Multi-ride packs can be split between groups, making it a far cheaper alternative to the bungy.

The closest options to Queenstown are the Ledge Bungy and Ledge Swing (p216) at the top of the Skyline Gondola; the drop is only 47m, but it's 400m above town. In winter you can even leap into the dark.

Last but most pant-wetting is the **Nevis Bungy** (☎0800 286 4958; www.bungy.co.nz; per

QUEENSTOWN IN...

Two Days

Start your day at **Bespoke Kitchen** before either hitting the slopes or heading to Shotover St to book your adrenaline-charged activities. Ride the **Skyline Gondola** to get the lay of the land and have a go on the **luge**. Head out on the **Shotover Jet** and then wind down with a walk through **Queenstown Gardens** to capture dramatic views of the **Remarkables** at dusk. Have a sunset drink at **Atlas Beer Cafe** before dinner at **Rata** and an evening of bar hopping.

The next day fuel up at **Fergbaker** before devoting the morning to snowboarding, bungy jumping, skydiving or white-water rafting. Spend the afternoon on two wheels, either at the **Queenstown Bike Park** or touring around the **Gibbston** wineries. Have dinner at **Blue Kanu** before hitting the bars.

Four Days

Follow the two-day itinerary, then head to **Arrowtown** to wander the **Chinese settlement**, have lunch at **Chop Shop** and browse the stores. The following day, drive along the shores of Lake Wakatipu to tiny **Glenorchy**. Have lunch at the **Glenorchy Cafe** and then drive to the trailhead of the **Routeburn Track** for a short tramp.

---

person $275) – the highest bungy in Australasia. 4WD buses will transport you onto private farmland where you can jump from a specially constructed pod, 134m above the Nevis River. The **Nevis Swing** (☑ 0800 286 4958; www.bungy.co.nz; solo/tandem $195/350) starts 160m above the river and cuts a 300m arc across the canyon on a rope longer than a rugby field – yes, it's the world's biggest swing.

If you're keen to try more than one AJ Hackett experience, enquire about combo tickets.

White-Water Rafting

Queenstown Rafting   RAFTING
(Map p226; ☑ 03-442 9792; www.rafting.co.nz; 35 Shotover St; rafting/helirafting $209/309) 🌊 Rafts year-round on the choppy Shotover River (Grades III to V) and calmer Kawarau River (Grades II to III). Trips take four to five hours with two to three hours on the water. Helirafting trips are an exciting alternative. Participants must be at least 13 years old and weigh more than 40kg.

If you book through other rafting companies such as **Extreme Green** (☑ 03-442 8517; www.extremegreenrafting.co.nz; rafting/helirafting $209/309) and **Challenge** (Map p226; ☑ 03-442 7318, 0800 423 836; www.raft.co.nz; The Station, cnr Shotover & Camp Sts; rafting/helirafting $219/319) you'll end up on the same trips.

It's possible to drive in to the rafting launch sites on the Kawarau River all year, but in winter, access to the Shotover River requires a helicopter.

Family Adventures   RAFTING
(☑ 03-442 8836; www.familyadventures.co.nz; adult/child $179/120; 🛶) Gentler (Grades I to II) trips on the Shotover suitable for children three years and older. Operates in summer only.

Jetboating

Shotover Jet   BOAT TOUR
(☑ 03-442 8570; www.shotoverjet.com; Gorge Rd, Arthurs Point; adult/child $135/75) 🌊 Half-hour jetboat trips through the rocky Shotover Canyon, with lots of thrilling 360-degree spins.

Skippers Canyon Jet   BOAT TOUR
(Map p218; ☑ 03-442 9434; www.skipperscanyonjet.co.nz; Skippers Rd; adult/child $139/79) 🌊 Incorporates a 30-minute blast through the narrow gorges of the remote Skippers Canyon, on the upper reaches of the Shotover River. The three-hour return trips (picking up from Queenstown) also cover the region's gold-mining history.

Hydro Attack   BOAT TOUR
(Map p226; ☑ 0508 493 762; www.hydroattack.co.nz; Lapsley Butson Wharf; 15min $149; ⊙ 9am-6pm Nov-Mar, 10am-4.30pm Apr-Oct) Did you see that 5.5m shark leaping out of the lake? Well jump inside, strap yourself in and take a ride. This 'Seabreacher X Watercraft' can travel at 80km/h on the water, dive 2m underneath and then launch itself nearly 6m into the air. It's almost as much fun to watch as it is to ride.

QUEENSTOWN & WANAKA QUEENSTOWN

Queenstown

QUEENSTOWN & WANAKA QUEENSTOWN

500 m
0.25 miles

Queenstown Hill Recreation Reserve

Villa del Lago (250m)

Frankton Rd

Walking Track to Frankton

Frankton Arm

Belfast Tce

Edinburgh Dr

Panorama Tce

The Terrace

Suburb St

Dublin St

Suburb St

York St

Kent St

Adelaide St

Hobart St

Hallenstein St

Melbourne St

Frankton Rd

Park St

Ballarat St

Sydney St

Stanley St

Coronation Dr

Park St

Anderson Heights

Turner St

Weaver St

Gorge Rd

Robins Rd

Hamilton Rd

Brecon St

Shotover St

See Central Queenstown Map (p226)

Steamer Wharf

Queenstown Bay

Lake St

TSS Earnslaw Route

Queenstown Route

Lake Wakatipu

Bob's Peak

Brunswick St

Lake Esp

St Omer Park

Lomond Ave

Thompson St

Fernhill (1km)

Queenstown

Skydiving, Gliding & Parasailing

NZone　　　　　　　　　　　ADVENTURE SPORTS
(Map p226; ☑03-442 5867; www.nzonesky
dive.co.nz; 35 Shotover St; from $299) ⏹ Jump
out of a perfectly good airplane – with a
tandem-skydiving expert.

GForce Paragliding　　　　　　　　PARAGLIDING
(Map p220; ☑03-441 8581; www.nzgforce.com;
incl gondola $219) Tandem paragliding from
the top of the gondola (9am departures are
$30 cheaper).

Queenstown Paraflights　ADVENTURE SPORTS
(Map p226; ☑0800 225 520; www.paraflights.
co.nz; solo/tandem/triple $159/258/297) Para-
glide 200m above the lake as you're pulled
behind a boat. Departs from the town pier.

Mountain Biking

With the opening of the Queenstown Bike
Park, the region is now firmly established as
an international destination for mountain
bikers. If you're in town for a while, consider
joining the Queenstown Mountain Bike Club
(www.queenstownmtb.co.nz).

The **Queenstown Trail** – more than
100km in total – links five scenic smaller
cycling routes showcasing Queenstown, Arrowtown, Gibbston, Lake Wakatipu, Jack's
Point and Lake Hayes. The trail is suitable
for cyclists of all levels.

Queenstown Bike Park　　　MOUNTAIN BIKING
(Map p220; ☑03-441 0101; www.skyline.co.nz;
Skyline; half/full day incl gondola $60/85;
⊙10am-6pm, extended to 8pm as light permits
Oct-Apr) Over 20 different trails – from easy
(green) to extreme (double black) – traverse

Bob's Peak high above the lake. Once you've
descended on two wheels, simply jump on
the gondola and do it all over again. The
best trail for novice riders is the 6km-long
Hammy's Track, which is studded with lake
views and picnic spots. BYO bike.

Vertigo Bikes　　　　　　　MOUNTAIN BIKING
(Map p226; ☑03-442 8378; www.vertigobikes.
co.nz; 4 Brecon St; rental half-/full day from $39/59)
If you're serious about getting into mountain biking QT-style, Vertigo is an essential
first stop. Options include skills-training
clinics (from $149), guided sessions in the
Queenstown Bike Park (from $159) and Re-
markables helibiking ($399).

Fat Tyre Adventures　　　MOUNTAIN BIKING
(☑0800 328 897; www.fat-tyre.co.nz; from
$209) Tours cater to different abilities with
backcountry day tours, multiday tours,
high-country helibiking and single-track riding. Bike hire and trail snacks are included.

Skiing & Snowboarding

Queenstowners have two excellent ski fields
to chose between in **the Remarkables** (Map
p218; ☑03-442 4615; www.nzski.com; Remarkables Skifield Rd; daily lift pass adult/child $104/59)
and **Coronet Peak** (Map p218; ☑03-442 4620;
www.nzski.com; Coronet Peak Rd; daily lift pass
adult/child $104/59), and when they fancy a
change of scenery, there's always Cardrona Alpine Resort (p247) and **Treble Cone**
(☑03-443 1406, snow-phone 03-443 7444; www.
treblecone.com; daily lift pass adult/child $106/52)
⏹ near Wanaka. Coronet Peak is the only
field to offer night skiing, which on a star-
filled night is an experience not to be missed.

QUEENSTOWN & WANAKA QUEENSTOWN

QUEENSTOWN FOR CHILDREN

While Queenstown is brimming with activities, some of them have age restrictions that may exclude the youngest in your group. Nevertheless, you shouldn't have any trouble keeping the littlies busy.

All-age attractions include the **Kiwi Birdlife Park** (p216), lake cruises on the **TSS Earnslaw** (p223) and 4WD tours of narrow, snaking Skippers Canyon. **Queenstown Gardens** (p216) has a good beachside **playground** (Map p220) near the entrance on Marine Pde. Also in the park, **Queenstown Ice Arena** (Map p220; ☑03-441 8000; www.queenstownicearena.co.nz; 29 Park St; entry incl skate hire adult/child $19/15; ☺10am-5pm Sat-Thu, to 9.30pm Fri Apr-Oct) is great for a rainy day, and there's **Frisbee Golf**. The **Skyline Gondola** (p216) offers a slow-moving activity from dizzying heights. Small children can also ride the **luge** with an adult, but need to be at least six years old and taller than 110cm to go it alone.

For a high that will make sugar rushes seem passé, a surprising number of activities cater to little daredevils. Children as young as two can take a tandem ride with **Queenstown Paraflights** (p221), provided the smallest harness fits them. **Family Adventures** (p219) runs gentler rafting trips suitable for three-year-olds. Under-fives can ride on the **Shotover Jet** (p219) for free, provided they're over a metre tall, and six-year-olds can tackle the ziplines with **Ziptrek Ecotours**. Fearless 10-year-olds can bungy or swing at any of **AJ Hackett's jumps** (p217), except the Nevis Bungy (minimum age 13). Eight- and nine-year-olds can, however, tackle the **Kawarau Zipride** (p217).

Several places in town hire out tandem bicycles and child-sized bikes.

For more ideas and information – including details of local babysitters – visit the **i-SITE** (p232) or www.kidzgo.co.nz.

The ski season generally lasts from around June to September. In winter, the shops are full of ski gear for purchase and hire; **Outside Sports** (Map p226; ☑03-441 0074; www.outsidesports.co.nz; 9 Shotover St; ☺8.30am-8pm) is a reliable option.

Even outside of the main season, heliskiing is an option for cashed-up serious skiers; try Over The Top (p223), **Harris Mountains Heli-Ski** (Map p226; ☑03-442 6722; www.heliski.co.nz; The Station, cnr Shotover & Camp Sts; from $940), **Alpine Heliski** (Map p226; ☑03-441 2300; www.alpineheliski.com; 37 Shotover St; 3-8 runs $875-1275; ☺Jul-Sep) or **Southern Lakes Heliski** (Map p226; ☑03-442 6222; www.heliskinz.com; Torpedo 7 building, 20 Athol St; from $895).

Other Activities

It would be impractical to list absolutely every activity on offer in Queenstown. If you're interested in golf, minigolf, sailing or diving, enquire at the i-SITE (p232).

Frisbee Golf
OUTDOORS

(Map p220; www.queenstowndiscgolf.co.nz; Queenstown Gardens) `FREE` A series of 18 tree-mounted chain baskets set among the trees; local sports stores sell frisbees and scorecards.

Ziptrek Ecotours
ADVENTURE SPORTS

(Map p220; ☑03-441 2102; www.ziptrek.co.nz; Skyline) ✈ Incorporating a series of ziplines (flying foxes), this harness-clad thrill-ride takes you from treetop to treetop high above Queenstown. Ingenious design and eco-friendly values are a bonus. Choose from the two-hour four-line 'Moa' tour (adult/child $135/85) or the gnarlier three-hour six-line 'Kea' option ($185/135).

Skyline Luge
ADVENTURE SPORTS

(Map p220; ☑03-441 0101; www.skyline.co.nz; Skyline; 2/3/4/5 rides incl gondola $45/48/49/55; ☺10am-8pm Oct-Mar, to 5pm Apr-Sep) ✈ Ride the gondola to the top, then hop on a three-wheeled cart to ride the 800m track. Nail the Blue Track once and you're allowed on the more advanced Red Track, with its banked corners and tunnel.

☞ Tours

Lake Cruises

Million Dollar Cruise
BOAT TOUR

(Map p226; ☑03-442 9770; www.milliondollarcruise.co.nz; cruise $35; ☺11am, 2pm & 4pm) Good-value, informative, 90-minute cruises heading up the Frankton end of the lake, past the multi-million-dollar real estate of Kelvin Heights.

TSS Earnslaw   BOAT TOUR
(Map p226; ☑0800 656 501; www.realjourneys.
co.nz; Steamer Wharf, Beach St; adult/child $57/22)
The stately, steam-powered TSS *Earnslaw*
celebrated a centenary of continuous service in 2012. Once the lake's major means
of transport, now its ever-present cloud
of black soot seems a little incongruous in
such a pristine setting. Climb aboard for
the standard 1½-hour Lake Wakatipu tour
or take a 3½-hour excursion to the high-
country **Walter Peak Farm** (Map p218; 1
Mount Nicholas-Beach Bay Rd; sheep show incl
cruise adult/child $77/22) for sheepdog and
shearing demonstrations.

Scenic Flights

Air Milford   SCENIC FLIGHTS
(☑03-442 2351; www.airmilford.co.nz; 1 Tex Smith
Lane, Frankton) Options include a Milford
Sound flyover (adult/child $420/255), a fly-
cruise-fly combo ($499/300), and longer
flights to Doubtful Sound and Aoraki/Mt
Cook.

Glenorchy Air   SCENIC FLIGHTS
(☑03-442 2207; www.glenorchyair.co.nz; Queenstown Airport, Frankton) Scenic trips from
Queenstown or Glenorchy include a Milford Sound fly-cruise-fly option (adult/child
$485/295) and an Aoraki/Mt Cook flyover
(adult/child $645/365).

Over The Top   SCENIC FLIGHTS
(☑03-442 2233; www.flynz.co.nz; Tex Smith
Lane, Frankton) Offers helicopter flights to

the Sounds, secluded fishing spots and a
high-country sheep station. From July to October it offers heliskiing.

Sunrise Balloons   BALLOONING
(☑03-442 0781; www.ballooningnz.com; adult/
child $495/295) One-hour sunrise rides in-
cluding a champagne breakfast; allow four
hours for the entire experience.

Winery Tours

Most tours include wineries in the Gibbston, Bannockburn and Cromwell Basin
subregions.

Appellation Central Wine Tours   TOUR
(☑03-442 0246; www.appellationcentral.co.nz;
tours $185-230) ✎ Tours visit wineries in
Gibbston, Bannockburn and Cromwell,
and include platter lunches at a winery
restaurant.

New Zealand Wine Tours   TOUR
(☑027 305 2004; www.nzwinetours.co.nz; from
$185) Small-group or private winery tours,
including lunch, snacks and an 'aroma
room' experience.

Milford Sound Tours

Day trips from Queenstown to Milford
Sound via Te Anau take 12 to 13 hours, including a two-hour cruise on the sound. Bus-
cruise-flight options are also available, as is
pick-up from the Routeburn Track trailhead.
To save on travel time and cost, consider visiting Milford from Te Anau.

REMEMBER, YOU'RE ON HOLIDAY

Here's our pick of the best experiences to slow down, recharge, and remind your body
that there's more to the travelling life than scaring yourself silly.

➜ **Onsen Hot Pools** (☑03-442 5707; www.onsen.co.nz; 160 Arthurs Point Rd, Arthurs Point;
1/2/3/4 people $46/88/120/140; ⊙11am-10pm) has private Japanese-style hot tubs with
mountain views. Book ahead and one will be warmed up for you.

➜ To reboot your system after a few days of skiing, biking and jetboating, ease into in-
room massage and spa treatments with the **Mobile Massage Company** (Map p226;
☑0800 426 161; www.queenstownmassage.co.nz; 2c Shotover St; 1hr from $120; ⊙9am-9pm).

➜ Slow down even more by checking into **Hush Spa** (Map p226; ☑03-442 9656; www.
hushspa.co.nz; 1st fl, 32 Rees St; 30/60min massage from $70/128; ⊙9am-6pm Fri-Mon, to 9pm
Tue-Thu) for a massage or a pedicure.

➜ For truly world-class spa treatments, make the short trek to Millbrook near
Arrowtown, where the **Spa at Millbrook** (Map p218; ☑03-441 7017; www.millbrook.co.nz;
Malaghans Rd; treatments from $79) has been rated one of NZ's best.

➜ Catch a water taxi across the lake to **Eforea Spa at Hilton** (Map p218; ☑03-450 9416;
www.queenstownhilton.com; 79 Peninsula Rd, Kelvin Heights; treatments from $70; ⊙9am-late).

QUEENSTOWN & WANAKA QUEENSTOWN

BBQ Bus TOUR
(☑ 03-442 1045; www.milford.net.nz; adult/child $199/100) Smaller group tours to Milford Sound (up to 22 people), including a cruise and a barbecue lunch. Te Anau drop offs and pick-ups are $30 cheaper.

Real Journeys TOUR
(Map p226; ☑ 0800 656 501; www.realjourneys. co.nz; Steamer Wharf, Beach St; adult/child from $230/115) ✔ Day or overnight tours to Milford and Doubtful Sounds, along with a host of other experiences.

Other Tours

Off Road Adventures DRIVING TOUR
(Map p226; ☑ 03-442 7858; www.offroad.co.nz; 61a Shotover St) Exciting offroad tours by 4WD (from $109), or you can drive yourself on a quad-bike (from $199), dirt-bike (from $289) or 4WD buggy ($248, seats two).

Nomad Safaris DRIVING TOUR
(Map p226; ☑ 03-442 6699; www.nomadsafaris. co.nz; 37 Shotover St; adult/child from $175/89) ✔ Take in spectacular scenery and hard-to-get-to backcountry vistas around Skippers Canyon and Macetown, or head on a 'Safari of the Scenes' through Middle-earth locations around Glenorchy and the Wakatipu Basin. You can also quad-bike through a sheep station on Queenstown Hill ($245).

⭐ Festivals & Events

Gibbston Wine & Food Festival WINE, FOOD
(www.gibbstonwineandfood.co.nz) Gibbston comes to Queenstown Gardens for a day in mid-March.

Queenstown Bike Festival SPORTS
(www.queenstownbikefestival.co.nz) Ten days of two-wheeled action in mid- to late March.

THE GIBBSTON VALLEY

Gung-ho visitors to Queenstown might be happiest dangling off a giant rubber band, but as they're plunging towards the Kawarau River, they might not realise they're in the heart of Gibbston, one of Central Otago's main wine subregions, accounting for around 20% of plantings.

Almost opposite the Kawarau Bridge, a precipitous 2km gravel road leads to **Chard Farm** (Map p218; ☑ 03-441 8452; www.chardfarm.co.nz; Chard Rd, Gibbston; ☉ 11am-5pm) **FREE**, the most picturesque of the Gibbston wineries. A further 800m along the Gibbston Hwy (SH6) is **Gibbston Valley** (Map p218; ☑ 03-442 6910; www.gibbstonvalley.com; 1820 Gibbston Hwy (SH6), Gibbston; tastings $5-12, tour incl tastings $15; ☉ 10am-5pm), a large complex with a 'cheesery' and a restaurant. Tours of its impressive wine cave leave on the hour from 10am to 4pm.

A further 3km along SH6, **Peregrine** (Map p218; ☑ 03-442 4000; www.peregrinewines. co.nz; 2127 Gibbston Hwy (SH6), Gibbston; ☉ 10am-5pm) is one of Gibbston's top wineries, producing excellent sauvignon blanc, pinot gris, riesling and, of course, pinot noir. Also impressive is the winery's architecture – a bunker-like building with a roof reminiscent of a falcon's wing in flight.

The **Gibbston River Trail** is a scenic walking and mountain-biking track that follows the Kawarau River from the Kawarau Bridge to Peregrine winery (one to two hours, 5km). From Peregrine, walkers (but not cyclists) can continue on the **Wentworth Bridge Loop** (one hour, 2.7km), which crosses over old mining works on various timber and steel bridges.

While you're in the area, be sure to call into the impossibly rustic **Gibbston Tavern** (Map p218; ☑ 03-409 0508; www.gibbstontavern.co.nz; Coal Pit Rd, Gibbston; ☉ 11.30am-7pm Sun-Thu, to 10.30pm Fri & Sat Oct-Apr, closed Mon May-Sep), just off the highway past Peregrine. Ask to try the tavern's own Moonshine Wines, as you won't find them anywhere else.

If you're keen to explore the valley's wines without needing to contemplate a drive afterwards, considering staying among the vines in **Kinross Cottages** (Map p218; ☑ 021 0881 6595; www.kinrosscottages.co.nz; 2300 Gibbston Hwy (SH6), Gibbston; r $225; 🖥). Each heritage-looking but brand-new cottage is split into two luxurious studio rooms. Plus it has its own tasting room, representing several of Gibbston's smaller producers (tastings are $15 for five wines).

Ask at the **Queenstown i-SITE** or **DOC visitor centre** (p232) for maps and information about touring the area.

Queenstown Winter Festival   SPORTS
(www.winterfestival.co.nz) Ten days of wacky ski and snowboard activities, live music, comedy, fireworks, a community carnival, parade, ball and plenty of frigid frivolity in late June and early July.

Gay Ski Week   GAY & LESBIAN
(www.gayskiweekqt.com) The South Island's biggest and best gay-and-lesbian event, held in late August/early September.

🛏 Sleeping

Queenstown has endless accommodation options, but midpriced rooms are hard to come by. The hostels, however, are extremely competitive, offering ever-more extras to win custom – they're worth considering even if it's not usually your thing. Places book out and prices rocket during the peak summer (Christmas to February) and ski (June to September) seasons; book well in advance.

Goodstays (Map p226; 🗷 03-409 0537; www.goodstays.co.nz; 1st fl, 19 Camp St) has a huge variety of holiday homes and apartments on its website, with prices ranging from around $190 to $2000 per night; a minimum stay of between two and five nights usually applies.

Central Queenstown

Haka Lodge   HOSTEL $
(Map p226; 🗷 03-442 4970; www.hakalodge.com; 6 Henry St; dm/r without bathroom from $31/89, apt $180; 🅿🛜) Slap your thighs and kick up your heels, this *haka* is well worth participating in. In response to traveller research, the brightly painted dorms have custom-built bunks including large lockable storage chests, privacy curtains, personal lights and electrical sockets. There's also a two-bedroom apartment attached, with its own kitchen, spacious lounge and laundry facilities.

Butterfli Lodge   HOSTEL $
(Map p220; 🗷 03-442 6367; www.butterfli.co.nz; 62 Thompson St; dm/s/d $30/66/69; 🅿🛜) This little hostel sits on a quiet hillside west of the town centre, ruled over by Jimmy the cat. There are no bunks but no en suite bathrooms either. You won't believe the views from the deck.

Nomads   HOSTEL $
(Map p226; 🗷 03-441 3922; www.nomadsworld.com; 5 Church St; dm with/without bathroom $32/30, r $110-140; @🛜) 🅟 With a prime location in the heart of Queenstown's nightlife, this massive hostel has facilities galore, including its own mini-cinema, en suite rooms, large kitchens, a free sauna and an on-site travel agency. It even sweetens the deal with free breakfast and dinner.

Hippo Lodge   HOSTEL $
(Map p220; 🗷 03-442 5785; www.hippolodge.co.nz; 4 Anderson Heights; site $25, dm $30-36, s $50, d with/without bathroom from $96/76; 🅿@🛜) Homely and slightly shabby but well kept, this relaxed hostel has a student-flat vibe, although it's a lot cleaner than that implies. The terrific views come with a correspondingly high number of stairs.

Flaming Kiwi Backpackers   HOSTEL $
(Map p220; 🗷 03-442 5494; www.flamingkiwi.co.nz; 39 Robins Rd; dm/s/d without bathroom $35/72/82; 🅿@🛜) Close to the town centre but on a quiet and mercifully hill-free street, this friendly hostel offers tidy dorms with a locker for every bed, three kitchens, unlimited wi-fi and a bottle of sunblock at reception. An excellent choice, then.

Bumbles   HOSTEL $
(Map p220; 🗷 03-442 6298; www.bumblesbackpackers.co.nz; cnr Lake Esplanade & Brunswick St; site/dm/r $30/33/72; 🅿@🛜) Enjoying a prime lakeside location, this popular wee hive has colourful decor and a supremely laid-back vibe. All of the rooms share bathrooms and there's limited space for tents out the back.

Sir Cedric's Southern Laughter   HOSTEL $
(Map p226; 🗷 03-441 8828; www.sircedrics.co.nz; 4 Isle St; dm $27-32, r with/without bathroom $85/75; 🅿🛜) Lame jokes cover the walls of this sprawling old-school hostel, but don't let that put you off as it's perfectly pleasant otherwise. The friendly staff, free vegie soup and spa pool should at least put a smile on your face.

YHA Queenstown Lakefront   HOSTEL $
(Map p220; 🗷 03-442 8413; www.yha.co.nz; 88-90 Lake Esplanade; dm/s/d without bathroom from $32/70/89; @) 🅟 This large lakefront hostel has recently been renovated. Queenstown's nightlife is a 10- to 15-minute lakeside stroll away.

Adventure Queenstown   HOSTEL $$
(Map p226; 🗷 03-409 0862; www.aqhostel.co.nz; 36 Camp St; dm with/without $33/31, d/tr $130/150; @🛜) Run by experienced travellers (as evidenced by the photos displayed

Central Queenstown

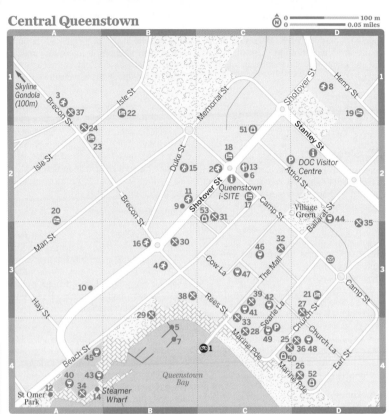

throughout), this central hostel has spotless dorms, a modern kitchen and envy-inducing balconies. Free stuff includes unlimited internet, international calling to 30 countries, bicycles and frisbees. Private rooms have en suite bathrooms, as do some of the dorms.

Creeksyde Queenstown Holiday Park & Motels   HOLIDAY PARK $$
(Map p220; ☑03-442 9447; www.camp.oo.nz; 54 Robins Rd; site $55, d without bathroom $81, unit from $138; P@♠) ⚡ In a garden setting, this pretty and extremely well-kept holiday park has accommodation ranging from small tent sites to fully self-contained motel units. Quirky touches include oddball sculptures and an ablutions block disguised as a medieval oast house (hop kiln).

Coronation Lodge   LODGE $$
(Map p220; ☑03-441 0860; www.coronation lodge.co.nz; 10 Coronation Dr; d $170-210; P♠) Right beside Queenstown Gardens, this tidy

block has basement parking, plush bed linen, wooden floors and Turkish rugs. Larger rooms have kitchenettes. The attractive little wood-lined breakfast room at the front serves both cooked and continental options (costs extra).

Alexis   MOTEL $$
(Map p220; ☑03-409 0052; www.alexis queenstown.co.nz, 69 Frankton Rd; unit from $165; P♠) This modern hillside motel is an easy 10-minute walk from town along the lakefront. The pleasant self-contained units have thoughtful extras such as stereos and robes, along with beaut lake views.

Lomond Lodge   MOTEL $$
(Map p226; ☑03-442 7375; www.lomondlodge. com; 33 Man St; d $145-169; P♠) A makeover has modernised this midrange motel's decor. Share your on-the-road stories with fellow travellers around the garden barbecue or in the guest kitchen, although all rooms also

Central Queenstown

have their own fridges and microwaves. It's worth paying extra for a lake view.

★ **Dairy**   BOUTIQUE HOTEL **$$$**
(Map p226; ☑ 03-442 5164; www.thedairy.co.nz; 10 Isle St; s/d from $435/465; P 🛜) Once a corner store, the Dairy is now a luxury B&B with 13 rooms packed with classy touches such as designer bed linen, silk cushions and luxurious mohair rugs. Rates include cooked breakfasts and freshly baked afternoon teas.

Queenstown Park   BOUTIQUE HOTEL **$$$**
(Map p220; ☑ 03-441 8441; www.queenstown park.co.nz; 21 Robins Rd; r from $360; P 🛜) 🪶 White curtains billow over beds decked out in luxurious linen at this very chic 19-room hotel. The 'Remarkables rooms' have balconies facing over a park to the mountain range (there aren't any lake views). The gondola-facing rooms are smaller but have courtyards or balconies. All have kitchen-

ettes, and guests can avail themselves of free wine and nibbles during 'canapé hour'.

Historic Stone House   APARTMENT **$$$**
(Map p220; ☑ 03-442 9812; www.historicstone house.co.nz; 47 Hallenstein St; apt from $245; P 🛜) Formerly the mayor's digs, this lovely stone building (1874) has been converted into a three-bedroom apartment, with an additional one-bedroom unit in a wooden extension and another in an elevated building behind it. Inside, modern kitchens and bathrooms meld with antique furniture, while outside there are pretty gardens and a spa pool.

Platinum Villas   RENTAL HOUSE **$$$**
(Map p220; ☑ 03-746 7700; www.platinumqueens town.co.nz; 96 Fernhill Rd, Fernhill; house from $383; P 🛜) Nab one of these 32 identical, luxurious, three-bedroom townhouses and make yourself at home. Each has a large

open-plan living area with a big stone fireplace, laundry facilities and a proper garage. The 'lakeside' villas aren't actually on the lake, but they do have unimpeded watery views, while the 'alpine' villas catch silvery glimpses.

Chalet Queenstown B&B $$$
(Map p220; ☑ 03-442 7117; www.chaletqueens town.co.nz; 1 Dublin St; r $245; P 🕏) The seven perfectly appointed rooms at this stylish B&B are decked out with flat-screen TVs, interesting original artworks and quality bed linen. All have bathrooms, although some of them are tiny. Most also have balconies with views; get in early and request one looking over the lake.

🛏 Surrounds

**Queenstown Top 10
Holiday Park** HOLIDAY PARK $
(☑ 03-442 9369; www.qtowntop10.co.nz; 70 Arthurs Point Rd, Arthurs Point; sites $48, units with/ without bathroom from $95/85; P 🕏) ✈ High above the Shotover River, this relatively small, family-friendly park with excellent motel units is 10 minutes' drive from the hustle and bustle of Queenstown. Fall out of your campervan straight onto the famous Shotover Jet.

Twelve Mile Delta Campsite CAMPGROUND $
(Map p218; www.doc.govt.nz; Glenorchy Rd, Mt Creighton; adult/child $10/5) Right by the lake, 12km west of Queenstown, this DOC campsite offers little more than a flat space to pitch a tent or park a campervan, and toilets of the nonflushing variety. The scenery's gorgeous and you can even pan for gold flakes on the lakefront.

Little Paradise Lodge LODGE $$
(Map p218; ☑ 03-442 6196; www.littleparadise. co.nz; Glenorchy-Queenstown Rd, Mt Creighton; dm $45, r with/without bathroom $160/140; P) Wonderfully eclectic, this slice of arty paradise is the singular vision of the Swiss/ Filipina owners. Each rustic room features wooden floors, quirky artwork and handmade furniture. Outside the fun continues with well-crafted walkways through beautiful gardens.

**Asure Queenstown
Gateway Apartments** MOTEL $$
(Map p218; ☑ 03-442 3599; www.gateway.net.nz; 1066 Frankton Rd, Frankton; s/d from $148/175; P 🕏) On the highway near the airport

(and hence cheaper than its equivalents in the town proper), this motel complex has two-bedroom split-level apartments with private courtyards. Request a rear unit for a quieter stay.

Villa del Lago APARTMENT $$$
(☑ 03-442 5727; www.villadellago.co.nz; 249 Frankton Rd, Queenstown East; apt from $360; P 🕏) ✈ Clinging to the cliffs between the highway and the lake, these spacious one- to three-bedroom apartments have lake-facing terraces, incredible views and all the mod-cons including full kitchens, laundries and gas fires. The water taxi stops at the private jetty, or you can walk along the lake to Queenstown in 20 minutes.

Evergreen Lodge B&B $$$
(Map p218; ☑ 03-442 6636; www.evergreenlodge. co.nz; 28 Evergreen Pl, Sunshine Bay; r $695; P @ 🕏) Tucked away above Sunshine Bay, this luxurious American-run B&B offers bigger-than-Texas rooms in a supremely private location with unfettered lake and mountain views. Add complimentary beer and wine, and a sauna and gym, and you've got a very relaxing escape from Queenstown's bustle.

✖ Eating

✖ Central Queenstown

★**Fergbaker** BAKERY $
(Map p226; 42 Shotover St; items $5-9; ⊙ 6.30am-4.30am) Fergburger's sweeter sister bakes all manner of tempting treats – and although most things look tasty with 3am beer goggles on, it withstands the daylight test admirably. Goodies include meat pies, filled rolls, danish pastries and banoffee tarts. If you're after gelato, call into Mrs Ferg next door.

Taco Medic FAST FOOD $
(Map p226; www.tacomedic.co.nz; 11 Brecon St; tacos $7; ⊙ 11am-9pm Nov-Apr, 10am-6.30pm May-Oct) Operating out of a food truck by the bike-hire place on Brecon St, these convivial lads dispense tacos of tasty fish, beef, pork belly and black bean to a devoted group of fans. One's a snack and two's a meal. During the ski season they move to an empty lot on the corner of Gorge Rd and Bowen St.

Empanada Kitchen FAST FOOD $
(Map p226; ☑ 021 0279 2109; www.the empanadakitchen.com; 60 Beach St; empanadas $5.50; ⊙ 10am-5.30pm) This little hole-in-the-

wall kiosk (attached to a public toilet, would you believe) serves only empanadas accompanied by a variety of sauces, and they're absolutely delicious. The flavours change daily and include savoury and sweet options.

Habebe's   MIDDLE EASTERN $
(Map p226; ☑ 03-442 9861; www.habebes.co.nz; Plaza Arcade, 30 Shotover St; meals $8-18; ⊗ 8am-5pm; ☑) Middle Eastern–inspired kebabs, salads and wraps are the go. Soups and yummy pies (try the chicken, kumara and mushroom one) break the mould.

Blue Kanu   MODERN NZ $$
(Map p226; ☑ 03-442 6060; www.bluekanu.co.nz; 16 Church St; mains $27-39; ⊗ 4pm-late) Disproving the rule that all tiki houses are inherently tacky, Blue Kanu somehow manages to be not just tasteful but stylish. The menu meshes robust Māori, Pasifika and Asian flavours with local ingredients to come up with an exotic blend of delicious dishes, designed to be shared. The service is excellent, too.

Public Kitchen & Bar   MODERN NZ $$
(Map p226; ☑ 03-442 5969; www.publickitchen. co.nz; Steamer Wharf, Beach St; dishes $15-45; ⊗ 9am-11pm) The trend towards informal, shared dining has come to Queenstown in the form of this excellent waterfront eatery. Grab a posse and order a selection of plates of varying sizes from the menu; the meaty dishes, in particular, are excellent.

Fergburger   BURGERS $$
(Map p226; ☑ 03-441 1232; www.fergburger.com; 42 Shotover St; burgers $11-19; ⊗ 8.30am-5am) Queenstown's famous Fergburger has now become a tourist attraction in itself, forcing many locals to look elsewhere for their big-as-your-head gourmet burger fix. The burgers are as tasty and satisfying as ever, but is any burger worth a 30-minute wait? You decide.

Vudu Cafe & Larder   CAFE $$
(Map p226; ☑ 03-441 8370; www.vudu.co.nz; 16 Rees St; mains $14-20; ⊗ 7.30am-6pm) Excellent home-style baking combines with great coffee and tasty cooked breakfasts at this cosmopolitan cafe. Admire the huge photo of a much less populated Queenstown from an inside table, or head through to the rear garden for lake and mountain views.

Devil Burger   BURGERS $$
(Map p226; www.devilburger.com; 5-11 Church St; mains $10-20; ⊗ 10am-4am; ☑) Look out Ferg –

you've got competition in the Queenstown burger wars. This diabolical new kid on the block also does tasty wraps. Try the hangover-busting 'Walk of Shame' wrap, stuffed with what's basically a full cooked breakfast.

Eichardt's Bar   TAPAS $$
(Map p226; www.eichardtshotel.co.nz; 1-3 Marine Pde; breakfast $16-18, lunch $25-26, tapas $7.50-12; ⊗ 7.30am-late) Elegant without being stuffy, the small bar attached to Eichardt's Private Hotel is a wonderful refuge from the buzz of the streets. Foodwise, tapas is the main focus – and although the selection isn't particularly Spanish, it is particularly delicious.

Bespoke Kitchen   CAFE $$
(Map p226; ☑ 03-409 0552; www.facebook.com/ Bespokekitchenqueenstown; 9 Isle St; mains $11-19; ⊗ 7.30am-5pm; ☜) Occupying a light-filled corner site between the town centre and the gondola, Bespoke delivers everything you'd expect of a smart Kiwi cafe. There's a good selection of counter food, beautifully presented cooked options, free wi-fi and, of course, great coffee.

Madam Woo   MALAYSIAN $$
(Map p226; ☑ 03-442 9200; www.madamwoo. co.nz; 5 The Mall; mains $16-32; ⊗ noon-late; ☑) Wooing customers with a playful take on Chinese and Malay hawker food, the Madame serves up lots of tasty snacks for sharing (wontons, steamed dumplings, greasy filled-roti rolls), alongside larger dishes (beef rendang, duck salad, sambal prawns). Kids and distracted adults alike can have fun colouring in the menu.

Sasso   ITALIAN $$
(Map p226; ☑ 03-409 0994; www.sasso.co.nz; 14 Church St; mains $26-36; ⊗ 4-11pm) Whether you're snuggled by one of the fireplaces inside the stone cottage (1882) or you've landed a table under the summer stars on the front terrace, this upmarket Italian eatery isn't short on atmosphere. Thankfully the food is also excellent.

Winnie's   PIZZA $$
(Map p226; www.winnies.co.nz; L1, 7 The Mall; mains $18-29; ⊗ noon-late; ☜) Part-bar and part-restaurant, Winnie's always seems busy. Pizzas with a Thai, Mexican or Moroccan accent and massive burgers, pasta and steaks soak up the alcohol and keep energy levels high. On balmy nights the whole roof opens up and the party continues into the wee smalls.

Kappa
JAPANESE $$

(Map p226; ☑ 03-441 1423; L1, 36a The Mall; lunch $11-17, dinner $16-20; ☺ noon-2.30pm & 5.30pm-late Mon-Sat) See if you can grab a spot on the tiny balcony so you can watch the passing parade on the Mall as you down a sake or Japanese beer and graze your way through *izakaya*-style dishes (food to snack on while you're drinking). The menu is short, sharp and very tasty.

Rata
MODERN NZ $$$

(Map p226; ☑ 03-442 9393; www.ratadining.co.nz; 43 Ballarat St; mains $36-42, 2-/3-course lunch $28/38; ☺ noon-11pm) After gaining Michelin stars for restaurants in London, New York and LA, chef-owner Josh Emett has brought his exceptional but surprisingly unflashy cooking back home in the form of this upmarket but informal back-lane eatery. Native bush, edging the windows and in a large-scale photographic mural, sets the scene for a short menu showcasing the best seasonal NZ produce.

Botswana Butchery
MODERN NZ $$$

(Map p226; ☑ 03-442 6994; www.botswana butchery.co.nz; 17 Marine Pde; mains $38-53; ☺ noon-11pm) Lake views and schmick interiors set the scene for a scintillating menu that's predominantly but not exclusively meaty, and a wine list of telephone directory dimensions. The $15 Express Lunch is a great deal.

✕ Surrounds

Boat Shed
CAFE $$

(Map p218; ☑ 03-441 4146; www.boatshed queenstown.com; Sugar Lane, Frankton; mains $12-25; ☺ 8am-5pm) Occupying a historic NZ Railways shipping office right by the lake, this great little cafe serves excellent, artfully arranged breakfasts and the likes of venison-and-bacon burgers for lunch. It's the perfect pit stop if you're cycling or walking the lakeside trail.

Sherwood
MODERN NZ $$

(Map p218; ☑ 03-450 1090; www.sherwood queenstown.nz; 554 Frankton Rd, Queenstown East; brunch $9-16, dinner $20-30; ☺ 7am-late) Despite being located at the heart of a faux-Tudor resort and having a ludicrously complicated wine list, this oasis of cool is well worth the 3km schlep from the town centre. Dishes are relatively simple but beautifully cooked (chicken, salmon, slow-cooked lamb, skirt steak) and are designed to be mixed and matched with vegetable dishes and shared.

Wakatipu Grill
EUROPEAN $$$

(Map p218; ☑ 03-450 9400; www.queenstown hilton.com; Hilton Queenstown, Peninsula Rd, Kelvin Heights; mains $34-40; ☺ 6-11pm) The Hilton sprawls along the lakeside by the Kawarau River outlet, and part of the fun of visiting its signature restaurant is the 8km water-taxi ride. As the name implies, there's always a decent selection of steak on the menu, but much more besides, including locally sourced fish and lamb.

Gantley's
MODERN NZ $$$

(☑ 03-442 8999; www.gantleys.co.nz; 172 Arthurs Point Rd, Arthurs Point; mains $40-44; ☺ 6-10pm) Gantley's French-influenced menu and highly regarded wine list justify the 7km journey from Queenstown. The atmospheric dining experience is showcased in a stone-and-timber building, built in 1863 as a wayside inn. If you feel like splurging, try the six-course degustation ($90).

🍷 Drinking & Nightlife

Queenstown offers a good range of options for after-dark carousing, even on Monday and Tuesday nights. However, in a bid to curb drunkenness and unruly behaviour, many venues enforce a one-way door policy after 2am, meaning you can leave but not enter.

A couple of outfits run organised pub crawls, where a wristband buys you a riotous night of discounted drinks, giveaways and games along the way; look for the ads in hostels and bars around town.

Zephyr
BAR

(Map p226; ☑ 03-409 0852; www.facebook.com/zephyrqt; 1 Searle Lane; ☺ 8pm-4am) Queenstown's coolest indie rock bar is located – as all such places should be – in a grungy basement off a back lane. There's a popular pool table and regular live bands.

Atlas Beer Cafe
BAR

(Map p226; ☑ 03-442 5995; www.atlasbeer cafe.com; Steamer Wharf, Beach St; ☺ 10am-late) Perched at the end of Steamer Wharf, this pint-sized bar specialises in beers from Dunedin's Emerson's Brewery, Queenstown's Altitude and regular guest brews from further afield. It's also one of the best places in Queenstown for a good-value meal, serving excellent cooked breakfasts and simple hearty fare such as steaks, burgers and chicken parmigiana (mains $10 to $20).

Ballarat Trading Company
PUB

(Map p226; ☑ 03-442 4222; www.ballarat.co.nz; 7-9 The Mall; ☺ 11am-4am) Beyond the eclectic decor (stuffed bear, rampant wall-mounted ducks), Ballarat is quite a traditional spot, with gleaming beer taps, cover bands, sports on TV, quiz nights, occasional lapses into 1980s music and robust meals.

Pub on Wharf
PUB

(Map p226; ☑03-441 2155; www.pubonwharf.co.nz; 88 Beach St; ☺10am-late; 🤶) Ubercool interior design combines with handsome woodwork and lighting fit for a hipster hideaway, with fake sheep heads to remind you that you're still in NZ. Mac's beers on tap, scrummy nibbles and a decent wine list make this a great place to settle in for the evening. There's live music nightly and comedy occasionally.

Vinyl Underground
BAR

(Map p226; www.facebook.com/Vinylunder groundqt; 12 Church St; ☺6pm-2am) Enter the underworld, or at least the space under the World Bar, for a devilishly appealing venue lined with band posters, album covers and a large Ron Burgundy (*Anchorman*) portrait. There are live bands on Sundays, open-mic night on Mondays and DJs most other times. Plus it's fun to play 'count the Bowie pictures' – we stopped at five.

Bunker
COCKTAIL BAR

(Map p226; ☑03-441 8030; www.thebunker.co.nz; 14 Cow Lane; ☺5pm-4am) Perversely located upstairs rather than down, this chichi little bar clearly fancies itself the kind of place that Sean Connery's James Bond might frequent, if the photos on the wall are anything to go by. Best of all is the roof terrace, with couches, a big TV screening classic movies, and a fire in winter.

Little Blackwood
COCKTAIL BAR

(Map p226; ☑03-441 8066; www.littleblackwood. com; Steamer Wharf; ☺3pm-1am) With subway tiles on the walls, interesting art and barmen dressed in stripy shirts looking like old-fashioned sailor boys or perhaps extras from '*Allo 'Allo!*, Little Blackwood is an appealingly quirky addition to the Steamer Wharf complex. It's much more stylish than it sounds, and the cocktails are good, too.

Pig & Whistle
PUB

(Map p226; ☑03-442 9055; www.pigandwhistle pub.co.nz; 41 Ballarat St; ☺11am-midnight; 🤶) With 17 beers on tap, eight large TV screens and big sloppy serves of ribs to chew on, this British-style pub is a great place to watch the rugger, catch a covers band or to test your mettle in the highly competitive Tuesday night quiz.

Rhino's Ski Shack
BAR

(Map p226; ☑03-441 3329; www.rhinosskishack. com; 8 Cow Lane; ☺3pm-late Jun-Sep, 5pm-2am Oct-May) Queenstown's number-one spot for hip-hop loving, hipster, ski bunnies, Rhino's is a vibey basement bar serving a scattering of craft beers, $5 Rhino's lager on tap and pizza. Animal pelts and skis line the recycled wood-lined walls, giving it an appropriately rustic après-ski feel.

Bardeaux
WINE BAR

(Map p226; ☑03-442 8284; www.goodgroup.co.nz; Eureka Arcade, Searle Lane; ☺3pm-4am) This small, low-key, cavelike wine bar is all class. Under a low ceiling are plush leather armchairs and a fireplace made from Central Otago schist. The wine list is extraordinary, with the price of several bottles reaching four digits.

☆ Entertainment

Pick up *The Source* (www.facebook.com/ SourceNZ), a free monthly flyer with a gig guide and events listings.

Sherwood
LIVE MUSIC

(Map p218; ☑03-450 1090; www.sherwood queenstown.nz; 554 Frankton Rd, Queenstown East) As well as being a brilliant spot for a meal or a drink, the Sherwood has quickly become Queenstown's go-to spot for visiting musos. Many of NZ's bigger names have performed here; check the website for coming gigs.

Kiwi Haka
TRADITIONAL MUSIC

(Map p220; ☑03-441 0101; www.skyline.co.nz; Skyline; adult/child excl gondola $39/26) For a traditional Māori cultural experience, head to the top of the gondola for one of the 30-minute shows. There are usually three shows per night; bookings are essential.

🔒 Shopping

★Vesta
ARTS, CRAFTS

(Map p226; ☑03-442 5687; www.vestadesign. co.nz; 19 Marine Pde; ☺10am-6pm) Showcasing really cool NZ-made art and craft, Vesta is full of interesting prints, paintings, glass art and gifts. It's housed in Williams Cottage (1864), Queenstown's oldest home. It's worth visiting just to check out the 1930s wallpaper and 1920s garden.

Artbay Gallery
ARTS

(Map p226; ☑03-442 9090; www.artbay.co.nz; 13 Marine Pde; ☺11am-6pm Mon-Wed, to 9pm Thu-Sun) Occupying an attractive 1863-built

Freemason's Hall on the lakefront, Artbay is always an interesting place to peruse, even if you don't have thousands to spend on a delicately carved ram's skull. It showcases the work of contemporary NZ artists, most of whom have a connection to the region.

Walk In Wardrobe CLOTHING
(Map p226; ☑ 03-409 0190; www.thewalkin wardrobe.co.nz; Beech Tree Arcade, 34 Shotover St; ☺10am-6pm Tue & Wed, to 8.30pm Thu-Mon) Benefitting from wealthy travellers lightening their suitcases before jetting out, this 'preloved fashion boutique' is a great place to hunt for bargain designer duds. Womenswear fills most of the racks.

ⓘ Information

DOC Visitor Centre (Map p226; ☑ 03-442 7935; www.doc.govt.nz; 50 Stanley St; ☺8.30am-5pm) Head here to pick up confirmed bookings for the Routeburn Track and backcountry hut passes, and to get the latest weather and track updates. It can also advise on walks to suit your level of ability.

Post Office (Map p226; ☑ 0800 501 501; www. nzpost.co.nz; 13 Camp St; ☺9am-5pm Mon-Fri, 10am-2pm Sat)

Queenstown i-SITE (Map p226; ☑ 03-442 4100; www.queenstowninformation.com; cnr Shotover & Camp Sts; ☺8.30am-7pm) Friendly and informative despite being perpetually frantic, the saintly staff here can help with bookings and information on Queenstown, Gibbston, Lake Hayes, Arrowtown and Glenorchy.

ⓘ Getting There & Away

AIR

Air New Zealand (☑ 0800 737 000; www. airnewzealand.co.nz) flies to Queenstown from Auckland, Wellington and Christchurch. **Jetstar** (☑ 0800 800 995; www.jetstar.com) also flies the Auckland route.

Various airlines offer direct flights to Queenstown from Australian destinations including Brisbane, the Gold Coast, Sydney and Melbourne.

BUS

Alpine Connexions (☑ 03-443 9120; www. alpineconnexions.co.nz) Shuttles head to/from Cardrona ($35, 55 minutes, two daily), Wanaka ($35, 1¼ hours, four daily), Cromwell ($25, one hour, four daily), Alexandra ($35, 1¾ hours, two daily) and Dunedin ($45, 4½ hours, daily).

Atomic Shuttles (☑ 03-349 0697; www.atomic travel.co.nz) Daily bus to and from Cromwell ($15, 55 minutes), Omarama ($30, 2¼ hours), Twizel ($30, 3¼ hours), Lake Tekapo ($30, 3¾ hours) and Christchurch ($50, seven hours).

Catch-a-Bus South (☑ 03-479 9960; www. catchabussouth.co.nz) Runs shuttles from Invercargill ($55, 2¾ hours) and Bluff ($70, 3¼ hours) most days, heading via Gore ($56, 2¾ hours) twice a week.

Connect Wanaka (☑ 0800 405 066; www. connectabus.com) Heads to/from Wanaka twice daily ($35, 1½ hours).

InterCity (☑ 03-442 4922; www.intercity. co.nz) Daily coaches to/from Wanaka (from $17, 1½ hours), Franz Josef (from $62, eight hours), Dunedin (from $24, 4¾ hours) and Invercargill ($48, three hours), and twice daily to Christchurch (from $55, 8½ to 11½ hours).

Naked Bus (www.nakedbus.com; prices vary) Two buses to Wanaka (1¼ hours) daily; one to Cromwell (one hour), Te Anau (2¾ hours), Franz Josef (5½ hours) and Christchurch (nine hours).

HIKERS' & SKIERS' TRANSPORT

Buckley Track Transport (☑ 03-442 8215; www.buckleytracktransport.nz) Transport between Queenstown and the trailheads of the Routeburn and Greenstone tracks.

Info & Track (☑ 03-442 9708; www.infotrack. co.nz; 37 Shotover St; ☺7.30am-9pm) During the Great Walks season, this agency provides transfers to the trailheads of the Routeburn and Greenstone & Caples tracks. In winter it morphs into Info & Snow and heads to the Cardrona and Treble Cone ski fields instead.

NZSki Snowline Express (www.nzski.com; return $20) During the ski season shuttles depart from outside the Snow Centre on Duke St every 20 minutes from 8am until 11.30am, heading to both Coronet Peak and the Remarkables. Buses return as they fill up, from 1.30pm onwards. They also leave on the hour from 4pm to 7pm for night skiing at Coronet Peak, returning on the half-hour from 5.30pm to 9.30pm.

Trackhopper (☑ 021-187 7732; www.trackhopper. co.nz; from $230, plus fuel) Offers a handy car-relocation service from either end of the Routeburn, Greenstone & Caples and Milford tracks.

Tracknet (☑ 03-249 7777; www.tracknet.net) This Te Anau–based outfit offers Queenstown connections to the Routeburn, Greenstone & Caples, Kepler, Hollyford and Milford tracks throughout the Great Walks season.

ⓘ Getting Around

TO/FROM THE AIRPORT

The **Queenstown Airport** (ZQN; Map p218; ☑ 03-450 9031; www.queenstownairport.co.nz; Sir Henry Wrigley Dr, Frankton) is 7km east of the town centre. **Queenstown Taxis** (☑ 03-450 3000; www.queenstown.bluebubbletaxi.co.nz) and **Green Cabs** (☑ 0508 447 336; www.green-cabs.co.nz) charge around $40 to $45 for a trip into town from the airport, but only $35 to $40 for the return leg.

Alpine Connexions (p232) Has scheduled shuttles to/from Queenstown ($5, 15 minutes, four daily), Cromwell ($25, 50 minutes, daily) and Wanaka (from $25, one hour, four daily).

Connectabus (☑ 03-441 4471; www.connectabus.com) Route 11 runs between the airport and Camp St in Queenstown every 15 minutes from 6.50am to 11pm (adult/child $13/8). There's also a twice daily service to Wanaka ($35/20).

Super Shuttle (☑ 0800 748 885; www.supershuttle.co.nz; fare $20) Picks up and drops off in Queenstown.

PUBLIC TRANSPORT

Connectabus has various colour-coded routes, reaching as far as Sunshine Bay, Fernhill, Arthurs Point, Frankton and Arrowtown. A day pass (adult/child $33/17) allows travel on the entire network. Pick up a route map and timetable from the i-SITE. Buses leave from Camp St.

AROUND QUEENSTOWN

Glenorchy & Around

POP 360

Set in achingly beautiful surroundings, postage-stamp-sized Glenorchy is the perfect low-key antidote to Queenstown. An expanding range of adventure operators will get you active on the lake and in nearby mountain valleys by kayak, horse or jetboat, and if you prefer to strike out on two legs, the mountainous region at the northern end of Lake Wakatipu is the setting for some of the South Island's finest tramps.

Those with sturdy wheels can explore the superb valleys north of Glenorchy. **Paradise** lies 15km northwest of town, just before the start of the Dart Track. Keep your expectations low: Paradise is just a paddock, but the gravel road there runs through beautiful farmland fringed by majestic mountains. You might recognise it from *The Lord of the Rings* movies as the approach to both Isengard and Lothlórien.

🏃 Activities

Almost all operators offer shuttles to and from Queenstown for a small surcharge. Other activities on offer include farm tours, fly fishing, guided photography tours and cookery classes; enquire at the Queenstown i-SITE (p232).

Hiking/Tramping

DOC's *Head of Lake Wakatipu* and *Wakatipu Walks* brochures (both $5, or download for free) detail day walks taking in the Routeburn Valley, Lake Sylvan, Dart River and Lake Rere. Two of the best short tracks are the **Routeburn Nature Walk** (one hour), at the trailhead of the Routeburn Track, and the **Lake Sylvan tramp** (one hour 40 minutes).

Another goody is the **Glenorchy Walkway**, which starts in the town centre and loops around Glenorchy lagoon, switching to boardwalks for the swampy bits. It's split into the Southern Circuit (30 minutes) and the Northern Circuit (one hour), and there are plenty of seats along the way, well positioned for views over the water to the mountains.

Before setting out on any of the longer tramps, call into the DOC in Queenstown (p232) or Te Anau (p254) for the latest track conditions and to purchase detailed maps. Another good resource is Lonely Planet's *Hiking & Tramping in New Zealand*.

For track snacks or meals, stock up on groceries in Queenstown. Track transport is at a premium during the Great Walks season (late October to March); try to book in advance. Many of the local accommodation providers offer trailhead transport.

★**Routeburn Track**   TRAMPING
(www.doc.govt.nz) Passing through a huge variety of landscapes with fantastic views all along the way, the 32km-long, two- to four-day Routeburn Track is one of the most popular rainforest/subalpine tracks in NZ. It's one of NZ's nine designated 'Great Walks', and many trampers rate it as the very best of them all.

Along the way you'll encounter mirror-like tarns, gurgling streams, fairy glades lined with plush moss, craggy mountain vistas and gnarled trees with long, straggly, lichen beards.

The track can be started from either end but we think the views are marginally better if you start from the Divide. Not far from the Divide, a highly recommended one-hour detour heads up to the **Key Summit**, where there are panoramic views of the Hollyford Valley and the Eglinton and Greenstone River Valleys. The hardest part of the Routeburn is the climb up to the **Harris Saddle**. From here, if you have any energy left you can expend it on a steep 1½- to two-hour

Routeburn, Greenstone & Caples Tracks

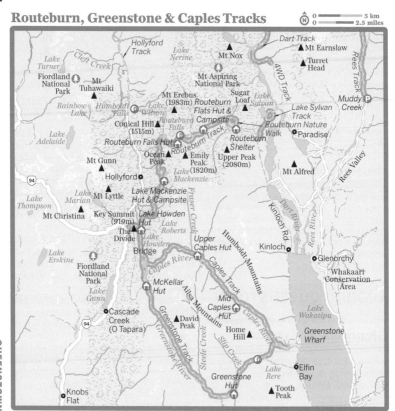

detour up **Conical Hill**. On a clear day you can see waves breaking at Martins Bay, far away on the West Coast, but it's not worth doing on a cloudy or windy day.

Increased pressure on the track has necessitated the introduction of an online booking system in the Great Walks season, which covers all huts and campsites on the route. You'll then need to call into the DOC Visitor Centre in either Queenstown or Te Anau to collect actual tickets, either the day before or on the day of departure. Outside of the season, bookings aren't required but you'll still need to visit one of the DOC centres to purchase your hut and campsite tickets. There are four basic huts along the track: Lake Howden, Lake Mackenzie, Routeburn Falls and Routeburn Flats. Both the Lake Mackenzie and Routeburn Flats huts have campsites nearby. The

other option is to take a guided walk staying at luxury lodges along the way, operated by Ultimate Hikes (p235).

The Routeburn track remains open in winter. However, to traverse the alpine section after the snow falls is not recommended for casual hikers, as winter mountaineering skills are required. There are 32 avalanche paths across the section between the Lake Howden and Routeburn Falls huts, and the avalanche risk continues through to spring. Always check conditions with DOC.

There are car parks at both ends of the track, but they're unattended, so don't leave any valuables in your vehicle. Various track shuttles are available, and many people arrange to get dropped at the Divide to start their walk after a Milford Sound tour, or alternatively they time the end of their walk to catch one of the Milford Sound buses.

ROUTE	ESTIMATED WALKING TIME (HR)
Routeburn Shelter to Flats Hut	1½-2½
Flats Hut to Falls Hut	1-1½
Falls Hut to Lake Mackenzie Hut	4½-6
Lake Mackenzie Hut to Howden Hut	3-4
Howden Hut to the Divide	1-1½

Greenstone & Caples Tracks TRAMPING

(www.doc.govt.nz; Greenstone Station Rd) Following meandering rivers through lush, peaceful valleys, these two tracks form a loop that many trampers stretch out into a moderate four- or five-day tramp. En route are the basic DOC-run Mid Caples Hut, McKellar Hut and Greenstone Hut; backcountry hut passes must be purchased in advance.

The tracks connect to the Routeburn Track; you can either follow the Routeburn's tail end to the Divide or (if you've prebooked) pursue it back towards the Glenorchy side of the mountains. From the McKellar Hut you can tramp two or three hours to the Howden Hut on the Routeburn Track, which is an hour from the Divide.

Access to the Greenstone & Caples Tracks is from Greenstone Wharf; you'll find unattended parking nearby.

ROUTE	ESTIMATED WALKING TIME (HR)
Greenstone Wharf to Mid Caples Hut	2-3
Mid Caples Hut to McKellar Hut	6-7
McKellar Hut to Greenstone Hut	4½-6½
Greenstone Hut to Greenstone Wharf	3-5

Other Activities

Dart Stables HORSE RIDING

(☑ 03-442 5688; www.dartstables.com; Coll St) Guided treks traverse many locations familiar from Sir Peter Jackson's Tolkien adaptations, including a two-hour 'River Wild' ride ($145), a 1½-hour 'Ride of the Rings' ($165) and an hour-long 'Hobbits' Hack' ($85). If you're really keen and a fit, advanced rider, consider the three-hour 'Trilogy Loop' ($185).

Skydive Paradise ADVENTURE SPORTS

(☑ 03-442 8333; www.skydiveparadise.co.nz; Glenorchy Airfield, Glenorchy-Queenstown Rd;

12,000-15,000ft jump $335-409) Tandem sky-diving above some of the planet's most spectacular scenery.

Heli Glenorchy SCENIC FLIGHTS

(☑ 0800 435 449; www.heliglenorchy.co.nz; Mull St) You'd be driving for the best part of a day to get from Glenorchy to Milford Sound, but it's only 15 minutes by helicopter. This crew offers a three-hour Milford Sound heli-cruise-heli package ($795) and a wilderness drop-off so that you can walk the last 11km of the famous Milford Track before being whisked back over the mountains ($850).

☞ Tours

Ultimate Hikes WALKING TOUR

(☑ 03-450 1940; www.ultimatehikes.co.nz; ⊗ Nov-Apr) If you value comfort as much as adventure, Ultimate Hikes offers three-day guided tramps on the Routeburn (from $1325); a six-day Grand Traverse, combining walks on the Routeburn and Greenstone tracks (from $1760); and the Classic, an eight-day tour combining the Routeburn and Milford tracks (from $3355). Prices include transfers from Queenstown, meals and accommodation in Ultimate's own well-appointed lodges.

Also offers a one-day Routeburn Encounter ($179).

Dart River Wilderness Jet BOAT TOUR

(☑ 03-442 9992; www.dartriver.co.nz; 45 Mull St; adult/child $229/129; ⊗ departs 9am & 1pm) Journeys into the heart of spectacular wilderness, including a short walk through beech forest and a backroad excursion. The round trip from Glenorchy takes three hours. Also offers jetboat rides combined with a river descent in an inflatable three-seater 'fun-yak' (departs 8.30am, adult/child $329/229). Prices include Queenstown pick-ups, which depart an hour prior to each trip.

Private Discovery Tours DRIVING TOUR

(☑ 03-442 2299; www.privatediscoverytours.co.nz; half-/full day $185/395) Tours head by 4WD through a high-country sheep station in a remote valley between Mts Earnslaw and Alfred and include Middle-earth movie locations. Prices include pick-up from Queenstown.

🛏 Sleeping & Eating

Kinloch Lodge LODGE **$$**

(☑ 03-442 4900; www.kinlochlodge.co.nz; Kinloch Rd; dm $35, d with/without bathroom from $159/95; @🔋) Across Lake Wakatipu from Glenorchy (26km by road; five minutes by boat), this wonderfully remote 1868 lodge rents mountain bikes, offers guided kayaking and provides transfers to tramping trailheads. The Heritage Rooms are small but stylish, with shared bathrooms. Rooms in the YHA-associated hostel are comfy and colourful, and there's a post-tramp hot tub.

The cafe-bar is open for lunch year-round, for à la carte dinners in summer, and for set dinners in winter.

Glenorchy Lake House   B&B $$$
(☑ 03-442 4900; www.glenorchylakehouse. co.nz; Mull St, Glenorchy; r/house $295/495; 🖝) 🖎 After a day's tramping, recharge in the spa pool of this boutique B&B, attached to the excellent Trading Post cafe. The two guest bedrooms are decked out with Egyptian cotton sheets, flat-screen TVs and nice toiletries. Packages including transfers to the Routeburn and Greenstone Tracks are available.

Glenorchy Cafe   CAFE $$
(GYC; ☑ 03-442 9978; 25-27 Mull St, Glenorchy; mains $10-20, pizza $25; ⊙9am-5pm Sun-Thu, to 9pm Fri & Sat Jan-Apr, 10am-4.30pm Sun-Fri, to 9pm Sat May-Dec) Grab a sunny table out the back of this cute little cottage and tuck into cooked breakfasts, sandwiches and soup. Head inside at night to partake in pizza and beer underneath the oddball light fixtures.

ℹ Information

Glenorchy Information Centre & Store
(☑ 03-409 2049; www.glenorchy-nz.co.nz; 42-50 Mull St, Glenorchy; ⊙8.30am-6pm) Attached to the Glenorchy Hotel, this little shop is a good source of updated weather and track information. Fishing rods and mountain bikes can be hired. Ask about trail maps for walking or mountain biking in the nearby Whakaari Conservation Area.

ℹ Getting There & Away

Glenorchy lies at the head of Lake Wakatipu, a scenic 40-minute (46km) drive northwest from Queenstown. With sweeping vistas and gem-coloured waters, the sealed road is wonderfully scenic, although its constant hills are a killer for cyclists. There are no bus services but there are **trampers' shuttles** (p232) during the Great Walks season (late October to March).

There is a petrol station in Glenorchy, but fill up with cheaper fuel before you leave Queenstown.

Arrowtown
POP 2450

Beloved by day-trippers from Queenstown, exceedingly quaint Arrowtown sprang up in the 1860s following the discovery of gold in the Arrow River. Today its pretty, tree-lined avenues retain more than 60 of their original gold-rush buildings, but the only gold flaunted these days are the credit cards being waved in the expanding array of fashionable shops.

Instead of joining the bonanza of daytime tourists, consider using Arrowtown as a base for exploring Queenstown and the wider region. That way you can enjoy its history, charm and excellent restaurants when the tour buses have decamped back to Queenstown.

Exciting things are afoot in the high country surrounding Arrowtown. Record producer Mutt Lange (famous for his work with AC/DC, the Cars and Shania Twain, to whom he was once married) owns a vast chunk of the land between Arrowtown and Wanaka, having purchased four huge sheep stations covering 555 sq km. In 2014 Lange placed a covenant over the land through the QEII National Trust, protecting it for future generations, and embarked on a massive campaign of pest eradication and environmental restoration. There are moves afoot to build an interpretation centre and to improve public access through the construction of walking tracks – creating something akin to a private national park. Watch this space.

◉ Sights

Lakes District Museum & Gallery   MUSEUM
(www.museumqueenstown.com; 49 Buckingham St; adult/child $10/3; ⊙8.30am-5pm) Exhibits cover the gold-rush era and the early days of Chinese settlement around Arrowtown. Younger travellers will enjoy the Museum Fun Pack ($5), which includes activity sheets, museum treasure hunts, greenstone and a few flecks of gold. You can also rent pans here to try your luck panning for gold on the Arrow River ($3); you're more likely to find some traces if you head away from the town centre.

Chinese Settlement   HISTORIC SITE
(Buckingham St; ⊙24hr) FREE Arrowtown has NZ's best example of an early Chinese settlement. Interpretive signs explain the lives of Chinese diggers during and after the gold rush (the last resident died in 1932), while

Arrowtown

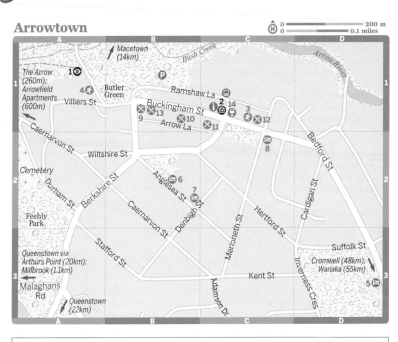

Arrowtown

restored huts and shops make the story more tangible. Subjected to significant racism, the Chinese often had little choice but to rework old tailings rather than seek new claims.

🏃 Activities

The information centre stocks a *Cycling & Walking Trail* brochure ($1) outlining some excellent tracks in the area. One particularly good new cycling route is the **Arrow River Bridges Ride** (12km, 90 minutes each way) from Arrowtown to the Kawarau Bridge, which traverses various new suspension bridges and a tunnel cut under the highway.

Arrowtown Bike Hire   MOUNTAIN BIKING
(☑0800 224 473; www.arrowtownbikehire.co.nz; 59 Buckingham St; half-/full-day rental $38/55) Hires bikes and provides great advice about local trails. If you fancy tackling the Arrow River Bridges Ride and then indulging in tastings at some of the Gibbston wineries, staff will collect you, your mates and your bikes for $60. Multiday rentals are also available.

Queenstown Bike Tours   MOUNTAIN BIKING
(☑03-442 0339; www.queenstownbiketours.co.nz; Dudley's Cottage, 4 Buckingham St; per half-/full day $45/55; ⊙Sep-May) Rents bikes and

LAKE HAYES

Around 14,000 years ago, little Lake Hayes was joined to the Frankton Arm of Lake Wakatipu. Now it sits in quiet isolation, reflecting the neighbouring hills in its placid waters. It's a great place for an unchallenging two-hour walk, as the 8km bike-friendly **Lake Hayes Walkway** loops right around it.

On the lake's eastern flank is **Amisfield** (Map p218; ☑ 03-442 0556; www.amisfield.co.nz; 10 Lake Hayes Rd; mains $38-45; ⊙ tasting 10am-6pm, restaurant 11.30am-8pm) 🍴, a match for any of the wineries in nearby Gibbston. After tasting its acclaimed wines ($10 for five, free if you're dining), grab a spot on the sunny terrace and continue the sensory stimulation with plates of exquisitely presented food from the bistro. If you're feeling adventurous, opt for the 'Trust the Chef' shared dining menu ($70).

Hidden in a natural depression across the highway, south of the lake, is **Lake Hayes Estate**, established in the 1990s as a more affordable, less touristy residential option to Queenstown. It's worth dropping by for a bite at **Graze** (Map p218; ☑ 03-441 4074; www. grazenz.co.nz; 1 Onslow Rd, Lake Hayes Estate; brunch $12-20, dinner $20-25; ⊙ 7.30am-5pm Mon, to 10pm Tue-Sun; 🛜), a stylish cafe-bar delivering substantial serves of good, honest food. It's a popular detour for cyclists tackling the Arrow River Bridges Ride or the Twin Rivers Ride, and it's even got a microbrewery attached.

Lake Hayes is 4km south of Arrowtown, on the road to Frankton.

gets you started on various self-guided adventures, including wine tours ($125). The price includes transfers from Queenstown, a Gibbston pick-up at the end of the day, a cheese board at Gibbston Valley Cheese and, of course, the bike.

Dudley's Cottage
GOLD PANNING

(☑ 03-409 8162; www.dudleyscottagenz.com; 4 Buckingham St; ⊙ 9am-5pm) Call into this historical cottage for a gold-panning lesson ($10, plus an extra $5 if you're keen to rent a pan and give it a go). If you've already got the skills, rent a pan and shovel ($6) or sluice box ($25) and head out on your own. The cottage also houses an interesting gift shop and a cafe.

Tours

Arrowtown Time Walks
WALKING TOUR

(☑ 021 782 278; www.arrowtowntimewalks.com; adult/child $20/12; ⊙ 1.30pm Oct-Apr) Guided walks (90 minutes) depart from the museum daily, tracing a path through the township, pointing out places of interest along the way and delving into Arrowtown's goldrush history.

🛏 Sleeping

Arrowtown Born Of Gold
HOLIDAY PARK $

(☑ 03-442 1876; www.arrowtownholidaypark. co.nz; 12 Centennial Ave; sites/units from $38/130, r without bathroom $75; @ 🛜) Close to the centre, this small holiday park offers a lane of en suite cabins trimmed with roses and a newish amenities block with coin-operated showers for campers. When it's not booked

up by school groups, budget travellers can book a room in Oregon Lodge, each of which has two sets of bunks and shares the communal kitchen and bathrooms.

Arrowtown Lodge
B&B $$

(☑ 03-442 1101; www.arrowtownlodge.co.nz; 7 Anglesea St; r/cottage $195/395; 🛜) From the outside, the guest rooms look like heritage cottages, but inside they're cosy and modern, with en suite bathrooms. Each has a private entrance from the pretty gardens. A continental breakfast is provided.

Old Villa
B&B $$

(☑ 03-442 1682; www.arrowtownoldvilla.co.nz; 13 Anglesea St; s $110, d $140-160; 🛜) Freshly baked bread and homemade preserves welcome visitors to this heritage-style villa with a garden just made for summer barbecues. The two en suite double rooms come trimmed with fresh flowers and antique-style furnishings. One of the rooms has an additional single bed.

Shades of Arrowtown
MOTEL $$

(☑ 03-442 1613; www.shadesofarrowtown.co.nz; cnr Buckingham & Merioneth Sts; unit from $150; 🛜) Tall shady trees and a garden setting give these stylish bungalow-style cottages a relaxed air. Some have full kitchens and spa baths. The two-storey family unit is good value if you're travelling with the whole clan.

Arrow
BOUTIQUE HOTEL $$$

(☑ 03-409 8600; www.thearrow.co.nz; 63 Manse Rd; ste from $385; 🛜) Five understated but luxurious suites feature at this modern property on the outskirts of Arrowtown. Accommodation is chic and contemporary with huge picture windows showcasing the surrounding countryside. Breakfast is included.

Arrowfield Apartments   RENTAL HOUSES **$$$**
(☑ 03-442 0012; www.arrowfield.co.nz; 115 Essex Ave, Butel Park; houses from $250; ☎ ✉) Lining a quiet crescent in a new development on the edge of Arrowtown, these 13 identical spacious townhouses all have internal garages, full kitchens, gas fires and three bedrooms. Bedroom doors can be locked off for a smaller, cheaper rental.

Millbrook   RESORT **$$$**
(Map p218; ☑ 03-441 7000; www.millbrook.co.nz; Malaghans Rd; r from $212; @ ☎ ✉) ✎ Just outside Arrowtown, this enormous resort is a town unto itself. Cosy private villas have every luxury and there's a top-class golf course right at your front door. At the end of the day, take your pick from four restaurants, or relax at the spa (p223).

✖ Eating

Arrowtown Bakery   BAKERY, CAFE **$**
(☑ 03-442 1587; www.arrowtownbakery.co.nz; Buckingham St; mains $6.50-13; ⊙ 8am-5pm) Equal parts bakery and cafe, this little eatery serves a wide selection of gourmet savoury pies, including exotic flavours such as venison and Thai chicken. Also on the menu are cooked breakfasts and fish and chips, or you can just settle in for coffee and a slice.

La Rumbla   TAPAS **$$**
(☑ 03-442 0509; www.facebook.com/larumbla. arrowtown; 54 Buckingham St; tapas $11-22; ⊙ 4pm-midnight Tue-Sun) Tucked behind the post office, this little gem does a brilliant job of bringing the bold flavours and late-dining habits of Spain to sleepy little Arrowtown. Local produce is showcased in tasty bites such as lamb meatballs and Southland suede croquettes. The decor is a little uninspired but there's some serious NZ art on the walls.

Chop Shop   CAFE **$$**
(☑ 03-442 1116; 7 Arrow Lane; mains $18-27; ⊙ 8am-3.30pm) Perhaps the tables are a little tightly packed and the staff a tad too chirpy, but we're splitting hairs. This place is uniformly fabulous – from the internationally inspired menu (pork dumplings, Turkish eggs, smoked pork-hock hash) to the interesting decor (pressed-tin bar, cool wallpaper, bevel-edged mirrors). Great coffee, too.

Provisions   CAFE **$$**
(☑ 03-445 4048; www.provisions.co.nz; 65 Buckingham St; mains $8.50-24; ⊙ 8.30am-5pm; ☎) One of Arrowtown's oldest cottages is now a cute cafe surrounded by fragrant gardens. Pop in for breakfast or a coffee and don't leave town without trying one of its deservedly famous sticky buns. Everything is baked on-site, including bread and bagels.

Saffron   MODERN NZ **$$$**
(☑ 03-442 0131; www.saffronrestaurant.co.nz; 18 Buckingham St; lunch $22-29, dinner $39-40; ⊙ noon-3pm & 6pm-late) Saffron offers hefty and delicious serves of grown-up food in a formal setting. The ever-changing trio of curries effortlessly traverses Asia, while other dishes jet to Europe and back. Fans can purchase *The Taste of Central Otago* cookbook, showcasing the restaurant's best recipes.

🍺 Drinking & Nightlife

Blue Door   BAR
(☑ 03-442 0131; www.saffronrestaurant.co.nz; 18 Buckingham St; ⊙ 5pm-late; ☎) Hidden away behind a tricky-to-find blue door, this cool little bar has a formidable wine list and enough rustic ambience to keep you entertained for the evening. Low ceilings, an open fire and abundant candles create an intimate quaffing location. On Wednesdays there's an open mic jam night.

Fork & Tap   PUB
(☑ 03-442 1860; www.theforkandtap.co.nz; 51 Buckingham St; ⊙ 11am-11pm) Craft beers, great food and a sunny, kid-friendly back garden make this the pick of Arrowtown's pubs. Built in 1870 as a bank, it now hosts Irish bands on Wednesdays and other acts on Sundays in summer. Brew aficionados can sample four 150ml craft beers for $14.

☆ Entertainment

Dorothy Browns   CINEMA
(☑ 03-442 1964; www.dorothybrowns.com; Ballarat Arcade, 18 Buckingham St; adult/child $19/10) This is what a cinema should be like: ultra-comfortable seating with the option to cuddle with your neighbour. Fine wine and cheese boards are available to accompany the mostly art-house films on offer. Most screenings in the main theatre have an intermission – the perfect opportunity to tuck into a tub of gourmet ice cream.

QUEENSTOWN & WANAKA ARROWTOWN

WORTH A TRIP

MACETOWN

Macetown, 14km north of Arrowtown, is a gold-rush ghost town reached via a rugged, flood-prone road (the original miners' wagon track), which crosses the Arrow River more than 25 times.

Don't even think about taking the rental car here. A much more sensible option is the 4WD tour offered by Nomad Safaris (p224), which also includes gold panning. You can also hike there from Arrowtown (16km each way, 7½ hours return), but it's particularly tricky in winter and spring; check with the information centre about conditions before heading out.

ℹ Information

Arrowtown Visitor Information Centre (☑03-442 1824; www.arrowtown.com; 49 Buckingham St; ☺8.30am-5pm) Shares premises with the Lake District Museum & Gallery.

ℹ Getting There & Away

Connectabus (☑03-441 4471; www.connectabus.com) Runs regular services (roughly hourly from 7.45am to 11pm) on its No 10 route from Frankton to Arrowtown. From Queenstown, you'll need to catch a No 11 bus to Frankton and change there.

WANAKA

POP 6480

Which is better, Queenstown or Wanaka? That's the perennial question around these parts and one which doesn't have an easy answer. It's hard to say which is more beautiful – both have blissful lake and mountain settings. Ditto, the jury's out as to which offers better skiing and tramping opportunities.

The main difference is in size, scale and buzz. Unlike its amped up sibling across the Crown Range, Wanaka retains a laid-back, small-town feel. It's definitely not a sleepy hamlet anymore, though, and new restaurants and bars are adding a veneer of sophistication. And while it doesn't have quite the same range of adrenaline-inducing activities on offer, Wanaka is no slacker on the outdoor adventure front. Importantly, it's also cheaper.

◎ Sights

National Transport & Toy Museum MUSEUM
(☑03-443 8765; www.nttmuseumwanaka.co.nz; 891 Wanaka Luggate Hwy/SH6; adult/child $17/5;

☺8.30am-5pm; ⊞) Small armies of Smurfs, Star Wars figurines and Barbie dolls share billing with dozens of classic cars and a mysteriously acquired MiG jet fighter in this vast collection, which fills four giant hangers near the airport. There are around 30,000 items in total, including plenty of toys that you're bound to remember from rainy childhood afternoons.

Puzzling World AMUSEMENT PARK
(☑03-443 7489; www.puzzlingworld.com; 188 Wanaka Luggate Hwy/SH84; adult/child $20/14; ☺8.30am-5.30pm; ⊞) A 3D Great Maze and lots of fascinating brain-bending visual illusions to keep people of all ages bemused, bothered and bewildered. It's en route to Cromwell, 2km from town.

Warbirds & Wheels MUSEUM
(www.warbirdsandwheels.com; Wanaka Airport, 11 Lloyd Dunn Av; adult/child $20/5; ☺9am-4pm) Dedicated to NZ combat pilots, the aircraft they flew and the sacrifices they made, this museum features Hawker Hurricanes, a de Havilland Vampire and lots of shiny, beautifully restored classic cars. There's also an art gallery and retro diner attached.

Rippon WINERY
(☑03-443 8084; www.rippon.co.nz; 246 Mt Aspiring Rd; ☺noon-5pm Jul-Apr) FREE Along with just about the best view of any NZ winery, Rippon has great wine, too. To save fights over who's going to be the designated driver, take a 2km stroll along the lakeside and look out for the track up the hill from the end of Sargood Dr.

Wanaka Beerworks BREWERY
(☑03-443 1865; www.wanakabeerworks.co.nz; 891 Wanaka Luggate Hwy/SH6; tour incl tasting $15; ☺tours 2pm Sun-Thu) Somewhat incongruously attached to the toy museum, this small brewery's main beers (Cardrona Gold lager, Brewski pilsner, Treble Cone wheat beer and Black Peak coffee stout) are complemented by those of its sister label Jabberwocky, along with various seasonal brews.

🏃 Activities

Wanaka is the gateway to Mt Aspiring National Park and to the Treble Cone (p221), Cardrona (p247), Harris Mountains and Pisa Range Ski Areas.

Hiking/Tramping

For walks close to town, including various lakeside walks, pick up the DOC brochure *Wanaka Outdoor Pursuits* ($3.50). The

Wanaka

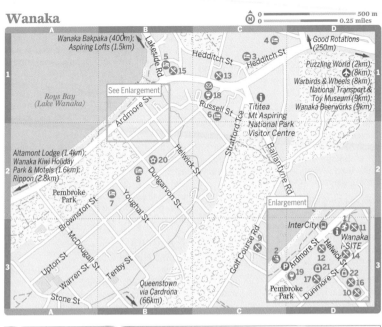

Wanaka

⊕ Activities, Courses & Tours
1 Aspiring Guides	D3
2 Wanaka Kayaks	C3

😴 Sleeping
3 Archway Motels	C1
4 Criffel Peak View	C1
5 Lakeside	B1
6 Mountain View Backpackers	C1
7 Wanaka View Motel	B2
8 YHA Wanaka Purple Cow	B2

✕ Eating
9 Bistro Gentil	C3
10 Federal Diner	D3
11 Francesca's Italian Kitchen	D3
12 Kai Whakapai	D3

13 Red Star	C1
14 Ritual	D3
15 Soulfood	B1
16 Spice Room	D3
17 Yohei	D3

🍷 Drinking & Nightlife
18 Barluga & Woody's	C1
19 Gin & Raspberry	D3
Lalaland	(see 1)

✪ Entertainment
20 Cinema Paradiso	B2

🛍 Shopping
21 Chop Shop	D3
22 Gallery Thirty Three	D3

short climb to the top of **Mt Iron** (527m, 1½ hours return) reveals panoramic views.

To the north of Wanaka, the usually unpeopled **Minaret Burn Track** (six to seven hours) in the Mt Alta Conservation Area is suitable for walking and mountain biking. After about two to three hours, a track heads down to **Colquhouns Beach**, a great swimming spot.

Aspiring Guides   ADVENTURE SPORTS
(☑03-443 9422; www.aspiringguides.com; L1, 99 Ardmore St) This crew offers a multitude

of options, including guided wilderness tramping (from two to eight days); mountaineering and ice-climbing courses; guided ascents of Tititea/Mt Aspiring, Aoraki/Mt Cook, Mt Brewster and Mt Tasman; and off-piste skiing (one- to five-day backcountry expeditions).

Adventure Consultants   ADVENTURE SPORTS
(☑03-443 8711; www.adventureconsultants.com) Offers two-days guided excursions on Brewster Glacier (from $890), three-day trips in the Gillespie Pass ($1250) and four-day

'Alpine Adventures' in Mt Aspiring National Park (from $1390). Also runs mountaineering and ice-climbing courses.

Rock Climbing & Mountaineering

Excellent rock climbing can be found at Hospital Flat – 25km from Wanaka towards Mt Aspiring National Park.

Basecamp Wanaka ROCK CLIMBING
(☑ 03-443 1110; www.basecampwanaka.co.nz; 50 Cardrona Valley Rd; day pass $23-30; ☺ noon-8pm Mon-Fri, 10am-6pm Sat & Sun) Before you hit the mountains, learn the ropes on climbing walls. Even fearless three-year-olds can have a go on the Clip 'n Climb (from $10).

Wanaka Rock Climbing ROCK CLIMBING
(☑ 03-443 6411; www.wanakarock.co.nz) Introductory rock-climbing course (half-/full day $140/210), a half-day abseiling intro ($140), and bouldering and multipitch climbs for the experienced.

Mountain Biking

Hundreds of kilometres of tracks and trails in the region are open to mountain bikers. Pick up the DOC brochure *Wanaka Outdoor Pursuits* ($3.50), describing mountain-bike rides ranging from 2km to 24km, including the **Deans Bank Loop Track** (12km).

One particularly scenic new route is the **Newcastle Track** (12km), which follows the raging blue waters of the Clutha River from the Albert Town Bridge to Red Bridge. You can make it a 30km loop by joining the **Upper Clutha River Track** at Luggate.

Good Rotations BICYCLE RENTAL
(☑ 027 874 7377; www.goodrotations.co; 34 Anderson Rd; half-/full day $59/89) Hires bicycles including electric bikes and all-terrain 'fat bikes' with superwide tyres (great for the pebbles on the lakefront). Drop by the neighbouring coffee-and-food cart for a pre-ride rev-up.

Other Activities

Wanaka Kayaks KAYAKING
(☑ 0800 926 925; www.wanakakayaks.co.nz; Ardmore St; ☺ 9am-6pm Oct-Easter) Rents kayaks ($20 per hour) and stand-up paddle boards ($20 per hour), and offers guided paddle-powered tours of the lake (half-/full day $95/189) and the 'Mighty Clutha' River (half-day $189). You'll find them on the lakefront, opposite the Lake Bar.

Skydive Lake Wanaka ADVENTURE SPORTS
(☑ 03-443 7207; www.skydivewanaka.com; from $329) Jump from 12,000ft, or go the whole hog with a 15,000ft leap and 60 seconds of freefall.

Deep Canyon ADVENTURE SPORTS
(☑ 03-443 7922; www.deepcanyon.co.nz; from $230; ☺ Oct-Apr) Specialises in canyoning expeditions: climbing, walking and waterfall-abseiling through confined, wild gorges.

Wanaka Paragliding PARAGLIDING
(☑ 0800 359 754; www.wanakaparagliding.co.nz; tandem $199) Count on around 20 minutes soaring on the summer thermals around Treble Cone.

Hatch FISHING
(☑ 03-443 8446; www.hatchfishing.co.nz; half-/full day $450/750) Lakes Wanaka and Hawea and the surrounding rivers are excellent for trout fishing. Hatch offers guided fly-fishing, with the option of accessing remote spots by helicopter or jetboat.

🏃 Tours

Scenic Flights

U-Fly SCENIC FLIGHTS
(☑ 03-445 4005; www.u-flywanaka.co.nz; from $199) Scratch 'flying a plane' off the bucket list on a scenic flight over Mt Aspiring National Park. Don't fret, there are dual controls ready for the pilots to take over at a moment's notice – they're not completely insane.

Classic Flights SCENIC FLIGHTS
(☑ 03-443 4043; www.classicflights.co.nz; from $249) Runs sightseeing flights in a vintage Tiger Moth or Waco biplane. 'Biggles' goggles and flowing silk scarf provided.

Wanaka Helicopters SCENIC FLIGHTS
(☑ 03-443 1085; www.wanakahelicopters.co.nz) Options range from 10-minute tasters ($99) to two-hour-plus trips to Milford Sound (from $995).

Wanaka Flightseeing SCENIC FLIGHTS
(☑ 03-443 8787; www.flightseeing.co.nz) Spectacular flyovers of Tititea/Mt Aspiring (adult/child $248/165), Aoraki/Mt Cook ($445/285) and Milford Sound ($498/315).

Other Tours

Wanaka Bike Tours MOUNTAIN BIKING
(☑ 03-443 6363; www.wanakabiketours.co.nz; from $199) Guided trips including helibiking options.

Eco Wanaka Adventures TRAMPING, CRUISE
(☑ 03-443 2869; www.ecowanaka.co.nz) 🪶 Guided tours include a full-day trek to the Rob Roy Glacier ($275), a four-hour cruise and walk on Mou Waho island ($225), and a full-day cruise-4WD combo ($450). Also offers helihikes.

MT ASPIRING NATIONAL PARK

Verdant valleys, alpine meadows, unspoiled rivers, craggy mountains and more than 100 glaciers make Mt Aspiring National Park an outdoor enthusiast's paradise. Protected as a national park in 1964, and later included in the Te Wāhipounamu (Southwest New Zealand) World Heritage Area, the park now blankets 3555 sq km along the Southern Alps, from the Haast River in the north to its border with Fiordland National Park in the south. Lording it over all is colossal Tititea/Mt Aspiring (3033m), the highest peak outside the Aoraki/Mt Cook area.

While the southern end of the national park near Glenorchy includes better known tramps such as the **Routeburn** (p233) and **Greenstone & Caples** (p235) tracks, there are plenty of blissful short walks and more demanding multiday tramps in the Matukituki Valley, close to Wanaka; see the DOC brochure *Matukituki Valley Tracks* ($2).

The dramatic **Rob Roy Glacier Track** (9km, three to four hours return) takes in glaciers, waterfalls and a swing bridge. It's a moderate walk, but some parts are quite steep. The **West Matukituki Valley Track** goes on to the Aspiring Hut (four to five hours return; peak/off-peak $30/25 per night), a scenic walk over mostly grassy flats. For overnight or multiday tramps offering great views of Mt Aspiring, continue up the valley to the Liverpool Hut (at an elevation of 1000m; $15 per night) and French Ridge Hut (at 1465m; $25 per night).

Many of these tramps are prone to snow and avalanches and can be treacherous. It is extremely important to consult with the DOC staff at the **Tititea Mt Aspiring National Park Visitor Centre** (p246) in Wanaka and to purchase hut tickets before heading off. You should also register your intentions on www.adventuresmart.org.nz.

Tracks are reached from Raspberry Creek at the end of Mt Aspiring Rd, 50km from Wanaka. The road is unsealed for 30km and involves nine ford crossings; it's usually fine in a 2WD, except in very wet conditions (check at the visitor centre).

Wanaka River Journeys TOUR
(☑ 03-443 4416; www.wanakariverjourneys.co.nz; adult/child $229/139) 🌊 Combination bush walk (50 minutes) and jetboat ride in the gorgeous Matukituki Valley.

Ridgeline Adventures DRIVING TOUR
(☑ 0800 234 000; www.ridgelinenz.com; from $165) 🌊 Explore the wilderness surrounding Wanaka on a 4WD nature safari.

✪ Festivals & Events

Rippon Festival MUSIC
(www.ripponfestival.co.nz) Big-name Kiwi bands and musicians headline at the lakeside Rippon Vineyard. It's held in even-numbered years on Waitangi weekend (around 6 February).

Warbirds over Wanaka AIR SHOW
(☑ 0800 496 920, 03-443 8619; www.warbirds overwanaka.com; Wanaka Airport; 3-day adult/child $190/25) Held every second Easter (in even-numbered years), this incredibly popular international airshow attracts upwards of 50,000 people. Individual day tickets can be purchased separately.

Wanaka Fest CARNIVAL
(www.wanakafest.co.nz) This mid-October event has the feel of a small-town fair. Street parades, live music, wacky competitions and fine regional produce get the locals saying 'g'day' to the warmth of spring.

🛏 Sleeping

⭐**Wanaka Bakpaka** HOSTEL $
(☑ 03-443 7837; www.wanakabakpaka.co.nz; 117 Lakeside Rd; dm $30-31, d with/without bathroom $92/74; @🛜) An energetic husband-and-wife team run this friendly hostel above the lake with just about the best views in town. Amenities are top-shelf and the onto-it staff consistently offer a red-carpet welcome to weary travellers. It's worth considering paying a bit extra for the en suite double with the gorgeous views.

YHA Wanaka Purple Cow HOSTEL $
(☑ 03-443 1880; www.yha.co.nz; 94 Brownston St; dm $30-35, d with/without bathroom from $100/89; @🛜) 🌊 In the top echelons of NZ YHAs, the Purple Cow offers a range of shared and private rooms, including some with en suites in a newer building out the back. Best of all are the large lounge, with commanding lake and mountain views, and a wood stove.

Altamont Lodge
LODGE **$**

(☑ 03-443 8864; www.altamontlodge.co.nz; 121 Mt Aspiring Rd; s/d $55/89; ☎) At the quiet end of town, Altamont is like a hostel for grown-ups. There are no dorms but the tidy little rooms share bathrooms and a spacious, well-equipped kitchen. Pine-lined walls give it a ski-lodge ambience, while the spa pool and roaring fire in the lounge will warm you up post-slopes.

Wanaka Kiwi Holiday Park & Motels
HOLIDAY PARK **$**

(☑ 03-443 7766; www.wanakakiwiholidaypark. nz; 263 Studholme Rd North; campsites $25-27, unit with/without bathroom from $100/85; @ ☎) Grassy sites for tents and campervans, lots of trees, and pretty views add up to a charming and relaxing campground. Facilities include a barbecue area with gas heaters, and free wi-fi, spa pool and sauna. Older-style motel units have all been renovated, and the newest budget cabins are warm and cosy with wooden floors.

Mountain View Backpackers
HOSTEL **$**

(☑ 03-443 9010; www.wanakabackpackers.co.nz; 7 Russell St; dm $28-29, d without bathroom $68; P @ ☎) This colourful and characterful house features a manicured lawn and warm, comfortable rooms. Fire up the barbecue after a busy day's exploring. Handy features include a drying room and off-street parking.

★ Alpine View Lodge
B&B **$$**

(☑ 03-443 7111; www.alpineviewlodge.co.nz; 23 Studholme Rd South; d from $180, cottage $285; ☎) In a peaceful, rural setting on the edge of town, this excellent lodge has three B&B rooms, one of which has its own, private, bush-lined deck. Little extras include homemade shortbread in the rooms and a hot tub. Alternatively, you can opt for the fully self-contained two-bedroom cottage, which opens onto the garden.

★ Criffel Peak View
B&B **$$**

(☑ 03-443 5511; www.criffelpeakview.co.nz; 98 Hedditch St; s/d/apt from $135/160/270; ☎) Situated in a quiet cul-de-sac, this excellent B&B has three rooms sharing a large lounge with a log fire and a sunny wisteria-draped deck. The charming hostesses live in a separate house behind, which also has a self-contained two-bedroom apartment attached.

Wanaka View Motel
MOTEL **$$**

(☑ 03-443 7480; www.wanakaviewmotel.co.nz; 122 Brownston St; unit $120-195; ☎) The refurbished Wanaka View has five apartments with Sky TV, spa baths and full kitchens. The largest has three bedrooms and most of them have lake views. There's also a comfortable studio unit tucked around the back, which is cheaper but doesn't have a kitchen or view.

Archway Motels
MOTEL **$$**

(☑ 03-443 7698; www.archwaymotels.co.nz; 64 Hedditch St; unit from $125; ☎) This older motel with clean and spacious units and chalets a short uphill walk from the town centre. Cedar hot tubs with mountain views give this place an extra edge. Book directly for good off-peak discounts.

★ Lakeside
APARTMENTS **$$$**

(☑ 03-443 0188; www.lakesidewanaka.co.nz; 7 Lakeside Rd; apt from $295; ☎ ⛷) ✦ Luxuriate in a modern apartment in a prime position overlooking the lake, right by the town centre. All have three bedrooms but can be rented with only one or two bedrooms open. The swimming pool is a rarity in these parts and an appealing alternative to the frigid lake on a sweltering day.

Aspiring Lofts
B&B **$$$**

(☑ 03-443 7856; www.aspiringlofts.co.nz; 42 Manuka Cres; s/d $180/220; ☎) Perched on a ridge overlooking the lake, this modern house has a beautiful garden and two upmarket B&B rooms in the loft above the garage. Each has its own private balcony to make the most of the views.

Riverview Terrace
B&B **$$$**

(☑ 03-443 7377; www.riverviewterrace.co.nz; 31 Matheson Cres, Albert Town; r $350; ☎) ✦ Part of a new development on a hill overlooking the Clutha River, this swish, modern house has three well-appointed guest rooms. Rates include a cooked breakfast, bikes to borrow and a natural-water hot tub under the stars,

✕ Eating

Florence's Foodstore & Cafe
CAFE **$**

(☑ 03-443 7078; www.florencesfoodstore.co.nz; 71 Cardrona Valley Rd; mains $9.50-18; ⊗ 8.30am-3pm) Wood, corrugated iron and jute-cladding create a rustic feel for this edge-of-town gourmet provedore. Call in for the region's prettiest smoked salmon benedict, as well as French-style pastries and delicious filled bagels.

Red Star
BURGERS **$**

(www.facebook.com/redstarwanaka; 26 Ardmore St; burgers $10-17; ⊗ 11.30am-late) Red Star spoils diners with a menu featuring inventive ingredients and 19 different burgers made Kiwi-style, with crunchy toasted buns. Grab a seat on the terrace and sup on a craft beer while you wait.

Soulfood
CAFE $

(☑ 03-443 7885; www.soulfoodwanaka.co.nz; 74 Ardmore St; mains $10-18; ☺ 8am-6pm Mon-Fri, to 4pm Sat & Sun; ☑) 🍃 It's not soul food in the African American sense, rather this little organics store offers a healthy range of id-affirming soups, pizzas, pastas and muffins. Not everything's strictly vegetarian, with wild venison and free-range pork sausages breaking the spell. Juices and smoothies are suitably virtuous, but coffee's limited to the plunger variety.

Yohei
JAPANESE $

(☑ 03-443 4222; Spencer House Mall, 23 Dunmore St; mains $9-14; ☺ 9am-5.30pm; ☎ ☑) Tucked away in a shopping arcade, this relaxed eatery does interesting local spins on sushi (how about venison?), Japanese curries, noodles and superlative juices and smoothies.

★ Francesca's Italian Kitchen
ITALIAN $$

(☑ 03-443 5599; www.fransitalian.co.nz; 93 Ardmore St; mains $20-26; ☺ noon-3pm & 5pm-late) Ebullient expat Francesca has brought the big flavours and easy conviviality of an authentic Italian family trattoria to Wanaka in the form of this stylish and perennially busy eatery. Even simple things such as pizza, pasta and polenta chips are exceptional. She also runs a pizza cart on Brownston St, opposite Cinema Paradiso.

Ritual
CAFE $$

(☑ 03-443 6662; 18 Helwick St; mains $11-20; ☺ 9am-5pm) A classic 21st-century Kiwi cafe, Ritual is smart but not too trendy, gay-friendly but family-friendly, too, and filled to the gills with delicious food. The counter positively groans under the weight of tasty salads, slices and scones.

Spice Room
INDIAN $$

(☑ 03-443 1133; www.spiceroom.co.nz; 43 Helwick St; mains $21-27; ☺ 5-10pm; ☑) The combination of authentic curry, crispy garlic naan and cold beer is a great way to recharge after a day's snowboarding or tramping. Beyond the spot-on renditions of all your subcontinental favourites, the Spice Room springs a few surprises, with starters including a zingy scallop masala salad.

Federal Diner
CAFE $$

(☑ 03-443 5152; www.federaldiner.co.nz; 47 Helwick St; brunch $12-20, mains $18-35; ☺ 7am-4pm Mon & Tue, to 9pm Wed-Sun; ☎) Tucked away in a back lane, this cosmopolitan cafe delivers robust breakfasts, excellent coffee, legendary scones and chunky gourmet sandwiches. In the evenings, the menu shifts to substantial dishes meant for sharing.

Kai Whakapai
CAFE $$

(☑ 03-443 7795; cnr Helwick & Ardmore Sts; brunch $13-19, dinner $19-23; ☺ 7am-11pm; ☑) An absolute Wanaka institution, Kai (the Māori word for 'food') is the place to be for a liquid sundowner accompanied by a massive filled baguette or pizza. Locally brewed craft beers are on tap and there are Central Otago wines as well.

Bistro Gentil
FRENCH $$$

(☑ 03-443 2299; www.bistrogentil.co.nz; 76a Golf Course Rd; mains $38-44; ☺ 11.30am-late) Lake views, fabulous NZ art and delicious modern French cuisine – Gentil ticks plenty of boxes for a memorable night out. There's oodles of wines by the glass, but at these prices we would prefer it was poured for us, rather than having to contend with the gimmicky digital self-pour system. On a balmy night, request an outside table.

🍸 Drinking & Nightlife

Gin & Raspberry
COCKTAIL BAR

(☑ 03-443 4216; www.ginandraspberry.co.nz; L1, 155 Ardmore St; ☺ 3pm-late) If you're in the swing for bling, this lush bar offers gilded mirrors, sparkling chandeliers, a piano and a central fireplace. Classic movies provide a backdrop to classic cocktails (including various martinis), and the occasional live band fires things up.

Lalaland
COCKTAIL BAR

(☑ 03-443 4911; www.lalalandwanaka.co.nz; L1, 99 Ardmore St; ☺ 6pm-2.30am) Keep a watchful eye on the lake or sink into a comfy chair at this little, low-lit, completely over-the-top cocktail palace/bordello. The young barmeister-owner truly knows his stuff, concocting elixirs to suit every mood. Entry is via the rear stairs.

Barluga & Woody's
BAR

(☑ 03-443 5400; Post Office Lane, 33 Ardmore St; ☺ 4pm-2.30am) Sharing both a courtyard and owners, these neighbouring bars operate more or less in tandem, especially when there's a DJ event on. Barluga's leather

QUEENSTOWN & WANAKA WANAKA

armchairs and retro wallpaper bring to mind a refined gentlemen's club. Wicked cocktails and killer back-to-back beats soon smash that illusion. Woody's plays the role of the younger, sportier brother, with pool tables and indie sounds.

☆ Entertainment

Ruby's CINEMA
(☑03-443 6901; www.rubyscinema.co.nz; 50 Cardrona Valley Rd; adult/child $19/15) Channelling a lush New York or Shanghai vibe, this hip-art-house-cinema-meets-chic-cocktail-bar is a real surprise in outdoorsy Wanaka. Luxuriate in the huge cinema seats, or chill out in the red-velvet lounge with craft beers, classic cocktails and sophisticated bar snacks. You'll find Ruby's concealed within the Basecamp Wanaka building on the outskirts of town.

Cinema Paradiso CINEMA
(☑03-443 1505; www.paradiso.net.nz; 72 Brownston St; adult/child $15/9.50) Stretch out on a comfy couch, a dentist's chair or in an old Morris Minor at this Wanaka institution, screening the best of Hollywood and art-house flicks. At intermission the smell of freshly baked cookies and pizza wafts through the theatre, although the homemade ice cream is just as alluring.

🛍 Shopping

Chop Shop CLOTHING
(☑03-443 8297; www.chopshopwanaka.co.nz; 3 Pembroke Mall; ⊙10am-6pm) The best coffee in town and a natty range of locally designed beanies and cool T-shirts for the discerning snowboarder.

Gallery Thirty Three ARTS, CRAFTS
(☑03-443 4330; www.gallery33.co.nz; 33 Helwick St; ⊙10am-5pm) Pottery, glass and jewellery from local artists.

ℹ Information

Post Office (☑03-443 8211; www.nzpost.co.nz; 39 Ardmore St; ⊙9am-5pm Mon-Fri, to noon Sat)
Tititea Mt Aspiring National Park Visitor Centre (☑03-443 7660; www.doc.govt.nz; cnr Ardmore & Ballantyne Sts; ⊙8.30am-5pm daily Nov-Apr, Mon-Sat May-Oct) In an A-framed building on the edge of the town centre, this DOC centre takes hut bookings and offers advice on tracks and conditions. Be sure to call in before undertaking any wilderness tramps. There's also a small display on Wanaka geology, flora and fauna.
Wanaka i-SITE (☑03-443 1233; www.lakewanaka.co.nz; 103 Ardmore St; ⊙8.30am-5.30pm) Extremely helpful but always busy.

Wanaka Medical Centre (☑03-443 0710; www.wanakamedical.co.nz; 23 Cardrona Valley Rd; ⊙9am-5pm Mon-Fri) Patches up adventure-sports mishaps.

ℹ Getting There & Away

Alpine Connexions (☑03-443 9120; www.alpinecoachlines.co.nz) Links Wanaka with Queenstown, Cromwell, Alexandra, Dunedin and the Rail Trail towns of Central Otago. Also have shuttles to Wanaka Airport, the Mt Aspiring trailheads and Lake Hawea in summer, and Cardrona and Treble Cone in winter.
Atomic Shuttles (☑03-349 0697; www.atomictravel.co.nz) Daily bus to/from Dunedin ($35, 4½ hours) via Cromwell ($15, 50 minutes), Alexandra ($25, 1¾ hours) and Roxburgh ($30, 2¼ hours).
Connectabus (☑0800 405 066; www.connectabus.com; one way/return $35/65) Handy twice-daily service linking Wanaka with Queenstown Airport (1¼ hours) and Queenstown (1½ hours). Free pick-up from most accommodation.
InterCity (☑03-442 4922; www.intercity.co.nz) Coaches depart from outside the Log Cabin on the lakefront, with daily services to Cromwell (from $10, 44 minutes), Queenstown (from $17, 1½ hours), Lake Hawea (from $10, 20 minutes), Makarora (from $12, 1¾ hours) and Franz Josef (from $43, 6½ hours).
Naked Bus (www.nakedbus.com; prices vary) Services to Queenstown (1¼ hours), Cromwell (40 minutes), Franz Josef (4¼ hours), Lake Tekapo (three hours) and Christchurch (7¼ hours).

ℹ Getting Around

Adventure Rentals (☑03-443 6050; www.adventurerentals.co.nz; 51 Brownston St) Rents out cars and 4WDs.
Yello (☑03-443 5555; www.yello.co.nz) Operates taxis and shuttles to the ski fields.

AROUND WANAKA

Cardrona

The cute hamlet of Cardrona reached its zenith in the 1870s at the height of the gold rush when its population numbered over a thousand. Now it's a sleepy little place that wakes up with a jolt for the ski season.

With views of foothills and countless snowy peaks, the **Crown Range Road** from Cardrona to Queenstown is one of the South Island's most scenic drives. At 1076m, it's the highest sealed road in NZ. It passes through tall, swaying tussock grass in the **Pisa Conservation Area** (Map p218), which has several short walking trails. There are some great places to stop and drink in the view, particularly at the Queenstown end of the road before you start the switchback down towards Lake Hayes. However, the road is narrow and winding, and needs to be tackled with care in poor weather. In winter it's sometimes closed after heavy snows, and you'll often need snow chains for your wheels.

☉ Sights

Cardrona Distillery & Museum   DISTILLERY
(Map p218; ☏ 03-443 1393; www.cardrona distillery.com; 2125 Cardrona Valley Rd; tours from $45; ⊙ 9.30am-5pm) An interesting diversion for those travelling along the valley, this brand-new distillery produces single-malt whisky, vodka, gin and an orange liqueur. Book ahead for tours, which leave on the hour from 10am to 3pm.

🏃 Activities

Cardrona Alpine Resort   SKIING
(Map p218; ☏ 03-443 8880, snow phone 03-443 7007; www.cardrona.com; Cardrona Skifield Access Rd; day pass adult/child $101/52; ⊙ 9am-4pm Jul-Sep) Well organised and professional, this 345-hectare ski field offers runs to suit all abilities (25% beginners, 50% intermediate, 25% advanced) at elevations ranging from 1670m to 1860m. Cardrona has several high-capacity chairlifts, beginners' tows and extreme snowboard terrain. Buses run from Wanaka and Queenstown during ski season. In summer, the mountain bikers take over.

**Backcountry
Saddle Expeditions**   HORSE RIDING
(Map p218; ☏ 03-443 8151; www.backcountry saddles.co.nz; 2416 Cardrona Valley Rd; adult/child $90/70) Runs horse treks through the Cardrona Valley on Appaloosa horses.

Snow Farm   SKIING
(Map p45; ☏ 03-443 7542; www.snowfarmnz. com; Snow Farm Access Rd; day pass adult/child $40/20; ⛷) In winter this is home to fantastic cross-country skiing and snow-shoeing, with 55km of groomed trails. Lessons and ski hire are available.

🛏 Sleeping

Cardrona Hotel   PUB $$
(☏ 03-443 8153; www.cardronahotel.co.nz; 2310 Cardrona Valley Rd; r $185; 🛜) Such an icon of the region that it was featured in Speight's Brewery's 'Southern Man' beer commercials, this 1863 hotel really comes into its own

après-ski. There's a good restaurant (breakfast $14 to $20, mains $26 to $34) and in summer you can relax in the garden bar at the rear. The lovingly restored rooms have snug, country-style furnishings and patios opening onto the garden (expect some noise on summer nights).

Waiorau Homestead   B&B $$$
(Map p218; ☏ 03-443 2225; www.waiorau homestead.co.nz; 2127 Cardrona Valley Rd; r $270; @ 🛜 ⛷) Tucked away in a private, bucolic nook near the Snow Farm, this lovely stone house has deep verandas and three luxurious guest bedrooms, each with their own bathroom. Rates include a full cooked breakfast and afternoon tea. Enquire about the cheaper 'pool room' ($140); the owners usually rent it on Airbnb.

❶ Getting There & Away

Ski shuttles are offered by Alpine Connexions (p246), Yello (p246) and Ridgeline Adventures (p243) in Wanaka, and Kiwi Discovery (Map p226; ☏ 03-442 7340; www.kiwidiscovery.com; 37 Camp St) in Queenstown.

Lake Hawea

POP 2180

The small town of Lake Hawea, 15km north of Wanaka, sits near the dam at the southern end of its 141-sq-km namesake. Separated from Lake Wanaka by a narrow isthmus called the Neck, blue-grey Lake Hawea is 35km long and 410m deep. It's particularly popular with fisherfolk looking to do battle with its trout and landlocked salmon. The lake was raised 20m in 1958 to facilitate the power stations downriver.

🛏 Sleeping

Lake Hawea Holiday Park   HOLIDAY PARK $
(☏ 03-443 1767; www.haweaholidaypark.co.nz; SH6; sites from $16, unit with/without bathroom $130/60; @ 🛜) On the lakeshore, this spacious and peaceful old-fashioned holiday park is a favourite of fishing and boating enthusiasts. Units range from a block of basic cabins with brightly painted doors to motel units and cottages.

Lake Hawea Hotel   HOTEL $$$
(☏ 03-443 1224; www.lakehawea.co.nz; 1 Capell Ave; r $240; 🛜) The rooms have been refurbished and have unbeatable views across the lake, but they're rather pricey for what's basically an upmarket motel. The complex

includes a large bar and restaurant (mains $18 to $25) with equally stellar vistas.

ⓘ Getting There & Away

InterCity (☑ 03-442 4922; www.intercity. co.nz) Coaches stop at the dam (SH6) daily, heading to/from Queenstown (from $20, two hours), Cromwell (from $14, 1¼ hours), Wanaka (from $10, 20 minutes), Makarora (from $10, 1¼ hours) and Franz Josef (from $40, six hours).

Makarora

POP 40

Remote Makarora is the last frontier before you cross Haast Pass and enter the wild West Coast – and it certainly feels that way. Aside from the tour buses passing through, it feels wonderfully remote.

🏃 Activities

The best short walk in this secluded area is the **Haast Pass Lookout Track** (one hour return, 3.5km), which offers great views from above the bush line. Other options include the **Bridle Track** (1½ hours one way, 3.5km), from the top of Haast Pass to Davis Flat, and the **Blue Pools Walk** (30 minutes return), where you may see huge rainbow and brown trout.

Longer tramps go through magnificent countryside but shouldn't be undertaken lightly. Changeable alpine and river conditions mean you must be well prepared; consult with DOC before heading off. Its *Tramping in the Makarora Region* brochure ($2) is a worthwhile investment. Call in to the Tititea Mt Aspiring National Park Visitor Centre (p246) in Wanaka to check conditions and routes before undertaking any wilderness tramps.

Gillespie Pass   TRAMPING
The three-day Gillespie Pass loop tramp goes via the Young, Siberia and Wilkin Valleys. This is a high pass with avalanche danger in winter and spring. With a jetboat ride down the Wilkin to complete it, this rates as one of NZ's most memorable tramps. Jetboats go to Kerin Forks, and a service goes across the Young River mouth when the Makarora floods.

Wilkin Valley Track   TRAMPING
The Wilkin Valley Track starts from the Makarora River and heads along the Wilkin River to the Kerin Forks Hut (four to five hours, 15km). After another day's walk up the valley you'll reach the Top Forks Huts (six to eight hours, 15km), from which the picturesque Lakes Diana, Lucidus and Castalia (one hour, 1½ hours, and three to four hours respectively) can be reached.

Wilkin River Jets   BOATING
(☑ 03-443 8351; www.wilkinriverjets.co.nz; adult/child $119/69) A superb 50km, one-hour jet-boating trip into Mt Aspiring National Park, following the Makarora and Wilkin Rivers. Trips can be combined with a helicopter ride.

🖝 Tours

Siberia Experience   ADVENTURE TOUR
(☑ 03-443 4385; www.siberiaexperience.co.nz; adult/child $355/287) 🏊 This thrill-seeking extravaganza combines a 25-minute scenic small-plane flight, a three-hour bush walk through a remote mountain valley and a half-hour jetboat trip down the Wilkin and Makarora Rivers in Mt Aspiring National Park.

Southern Alps Air   SCENIC FLIGHTS
(☑ 03-443 4385, 0800 345 666; www.southernalps-air.co.nz) 🏊 Flies to Aoraki/Mt Cook and the glaciers (adult/child $445/285), along with Milford Sound flyovers ($415/265) and Milford fly-cruise combos ($498/315).

ⓘ Information

Makarora Tourist Centre (☑ 03-443 8372; www.makarora.co.nz; 5944 Haast Pass-Makarora Rd/SH6; ⊙ 8am-8pm) A large complex incorporating a cafe, bar, shop, information centre, campground, bunk house and self-contained units.

ⓘ Getting There & Away

InterCity (☑ 03-442 4922; www.intercity. co.nz) Daily coaches to/from Queenstown (from $24, 3½ hours), Cromwell (from $19, 2½ hours), Wanaka (from $12, 1¾ hours), Lake Hawea (from $10, 1¼ hours) and Franz Josef (from $36, 4¾ hours).

Fiordland & Southland

Best Places to Eat

➜ Batch (p267)

➜ Redcliff Cafe (p253)

➜ Louie's (p267)

➜ Elegance at 148 on Elles (p267)

➜ Miles Better Pies (p253)

Best Places to Sleep

➜ Newhaven Holiday Park (p272)

➜ Observation Rock Lodge (p278)

➜ Bushy Point Fernbirds (p266)

➜ Mohua Park (p272)

➜ Slope Point Backpackers (p270)

Why Go?

Welcome to scenery that travellers dream of and cameras fail to do justice to.

To the west is Fiordland National Park, with jagged misty peaks, glistening lakes and fiords, and a remarkable surfeit of stillness. Enter this beautiful isolation via the world-famous Milford Track, just one of many trails that meander through densely forested, glacier-sculptured valleys confined by mighty mountain ranges. Fiordland is also home to Milford and Doubtful Sounds, where verdant cliffs soar almost vertically from deep, indigo waters.

In Southland's east, a sharp turn off the beaten track leads through the peaceful Catlins, where waterfalls cascade through lush forest and diverse wildlife congregates around a rugged and beautiful coastline.

And then there's the end of the line – Stewart Island/Rakiura, an isolated isle home to friendly seafarers and a flock of beautiful rare birds, including New Zealand's beloved icon, the kiwi.

When to Go

➜ Visit from December to April for the best chance of settled weather amid Fiordland's notoriously fickle climate (although chances are, you'll still see rain!).

➜ Late October to late April is the Great Walks season for the Milford, Kepler, Routeburn and Rakiura Tracks, so you'll need to book in advance if you want to hike these popular routes.

➜ Stewart Island/Rakiura's changeable weather can bring four seasons in one day, at any time of year, although the temperature is milder than you'd expect, with winter averaging around 10°C and summer 16.5°C.

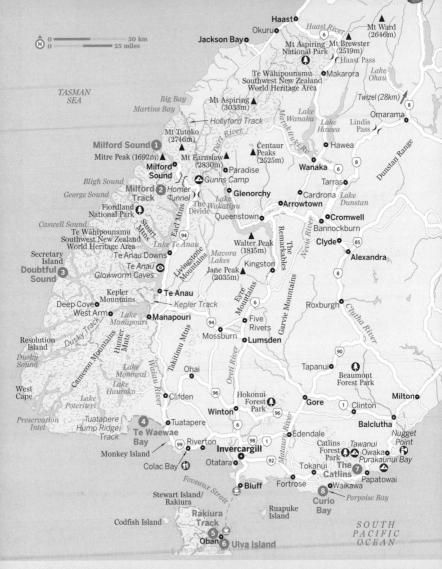

Fiordland & Southland Highlights

① Milford Sound (p259)
Being overwhelmed by your first glimpse of the sheer majesty of Mitre Peak rising from the inky waters of the fiord.

② Milford Track (p256)
Tramping through a World Heritage wilderness.

③ Doubtful Sound (p261)
Soaking up sunset and sunrise in glorious surrounds on an overnight cruise.

④ Te Waewae Bay (p263)
Marvelling at the wild power of nature on this surf-battered stretch of coast.

⑤ Rakiura Track (p276)
Savouring the solitude on NZ's southernmost Great Walk.

⑥ Ulva Island (p275)
Immersing yourself in a bird-filled paradise.

⑦ The Catlins (p269)
Exploring side roads, forest waterfalls and lonely southern beaches in this peaceful, windswept corner of the country.

⑧ Curio Bay (p269)
Spotting rare wildlife such as Hector's dolphins and yellow-eyed penguins.

ℹ Getting There & Away

Invercargill is the main transport hub, welcoming flights from Wellington and Christchurch, and buses from as far afield as Queenstown and Dunedin. Te Anau has direct bus connections with Queenstown, Dunedin and Christchurch.

FIORDLAND

Formidable Fiordland is NZ's largest and most impenetrable wilderness, a jagged, mountainous, densely forested landmass ribbed with deeply recessed sounds (technically fiords) reaching inland like crooked fingers from the Tasman Sea.

Fiordland National Park forms part of the Te Wāhipounamu Southwest New Zealand World Heritage Area, a combination of four national parks in the bottom left corner of NZ (the others being Aoraki/Mt Cook, Westland Tai Poutini and Mt Aspiring). This vast wilderness covers 2.6 million hectares and is recognised internationally for its unique geological features and ecosystems. It's also of great cultural significance to the local Ngāi Tahu people, who revered it as Te Wāhipounamu, 'The Place of Greenstone'.

Popular boat trips head out on the sounds, but it's walkers who can delve the deepest into this remote and magical area, not only on the famous, multiday Milford, Kepler and Hollyford Tracks, but even on short day walks, easily accessible from the highway.

Te Anau

POP 1910

Peaceful, lakeside Te Anau township is the main gateway to Fiordland National Park tramps and the ever-popular Milford Sound, as well as a pleasant place to while away a few days. It's large enough to have a smattering of good eateries and places to stay, but it's much easier on the liver and the wallet than attention-grabbing Queenstown.

To the east are the pastoral areas of central Southland, while west across Lake Te Anau lie the rugged mountains of Fiordland. The lake, NZ's second-largest, was gouged out by a huge glacier and has several arms that extend into the mountainous, forested western shore. Its deepest point is 417m, about twice the depth of Loch Ness.

◉ Sights

Punanga Manu o Te Anau   BIRD SANCTUARY
(www.doc.govt.nz; Te Anau–Manapouri Rd; ☉dawn-dusk) FREE By the lake, this set of

outdoor aviaries offers a chance to see native bird species difficult to spot in the wild, including the precious icon of Fiordland, the extremely rare takahe.

Te Anau Glowworm Caves   CAVE
(☏0800 656 501; www.realjourneys.co.nz; adult/child $79/22) Once present only in Māori legends, these impressive caves were rediscovered in 1948. Accessible only by boat, the 200m-long system of caves is a magical place with sculpted rocks, waterfalls small and large, whirlpools and a glittering glowworm grotto in its inner reaches. Real Journeys runs 2¼-hour guided tours, reaching the heart of the caves via a lake cruise, walkway and a short underground boat ride. Journeys depart from its office on Lakefront Dr.

🏃 Activities

Te Anau's **Lakeside Track** makes for a very pleasant stroll or cycle in either direction – north to the marina and around to the Upukerora River (around an hour return), or south past the Fiordland National Park Visitor Centre and on to the control gates and start of the Kepler Track (50 minutes).

Day tramps in the national park are readily accessible from Te Anau. Kepler Water Taxi (p255) will scoot you over to Brod Bay, from where you can walk to Mt

Te Anau

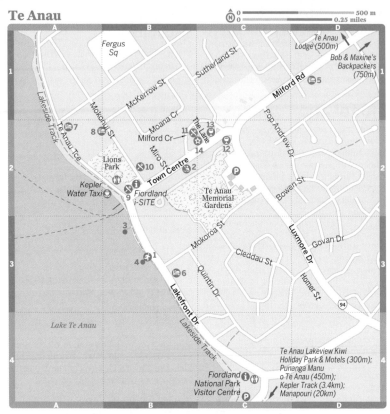

Te Anau

Activities, Courses & Tours
1 Luxmore Jet	B3
2 Rosco's Milford Kayaks	B2
3 Southern Lakes Helicopters	B3
4 Wings & Water	B3

Sleeping
5 Keiko's Cottages	D1
6 Radfords on the Lake	B3
7 Te Anau Top 10	A2
8 Te Anau YHA	A2

Eating
9 Miles Better Pies	B2
10 Redcliff Cafe	B2
11 Sandfly Cafe	B2

Drinking & Nightlife
Black Dog Bar	(see 14)
12 Fat Duck	C2
13 Ranch Bar & Grill	C2

Entertainment
14 Fiordland Cinema	C2

Luxmore (seven to eight hours) or back along the Lakeside Track to Te Anau (two to three hours). During summer, Trips & Tramps (p258) offers small-group, guided day hikes on the Kepler and Routeburn, among other tracks. Real Journeys (p262) runs guided day hikes (adult/child $195/127, November to mid-April) along an 11km stretch of the Milford Track. Various day walks can also be completed by linking with regular bus services run by Tracknet (p254).

For self-guided adventures, pick up DOC's *Fiordland National Park Day Walks* brochure ($2) from the Fiordland i-SITE or Fiordland National Park Visitor Centre, or download it at www.doc.govt.nz.

👉 Tours

Fiordland Tours TOUR
(☑0800 247 249; www.fiordlandtours.co.nz; adult/child from $139/59) Runs small-group bus and Milford Sound cruise tours, departing from Te Anau and stopping at some interesting sights on the way. It also provides track transport and guided day walks on the Kepler Track.

Luxmore Jet JETBOATING
(☑0800 253 826; www.luxmorejet.com; Lakefront Dr; adult/child $99/49) One-hour trips on the Upper Waiau River (aka the River Anduin).

Southern Lakes Helicopters SCENIC FLIGHTS
(☑03-249 7167; www.southernlakeshelicopters.co.nz; Lakefront Dr) Flights over Te Anau for 30 minutes ($240), longer trips over Doubtful, Dusky and Milford Sounds (from $685), and various helihike, helibike and heliski options.

🛏 Sleeping

Te Anau Top 10 HOLIDAY PARK $
(☑0800 249 746, 03-249 7462; www.teanautop10.co.nz; 128 Te Anau Tce; sites from $44, unit from $129, without bathroom from $77; @🖥🕿) Near the town and lake, this excellent, compact holiday park has private sites, a playground, lake-facing hot tubs, bike hire, a barbecue area and modern kitchen facilities. The motels units are very good indeed and there are well-priced cabins for those not bothered by communal bathrooms.

Bob & Maxine's Backpackers HOSTEL $
(☑03-249 7429; www.bbh.co.nz; 20 Paton Pl, off Oraka St; dm $36, s/tw $70/90; 🕿) Only 2.5km out of town, off the Te Anau–Milford Hwy, this relaxed and modern hostel gets rave reviews for the big mountain vistas from the communal lounge. Warm up beside the woodburner, cook up a storm in the well-equipped kitchen, or just chill out in a private en suite room. Free bikes and wi-fi.

Te Anau YHA HOSTEL $
(☑03-249 7847; www.yha.co.nz; 29 Mokonui St; dm $34-39, s without bathroom $80-100, d with/without bathroom $105/96; @🕿) This centrally located, modern hostel has great facilities and comfortable, colourful rooms. Play volleyball in the grassy backyard, crank up the barbecue or get cosy by the fire in the lounge.

Keiko's Cottages B&B $$
(☑03-249 9248; www.keikos.co.nz; 228 Milford Rd; d from $175; ☉closed Jun-Aug; 🕿) Surrounded by Japanese-style gardens, Keiko's self-contained cottages are private, comfortable and quite lovely. Breakfast poses a difficult choice: Kiwi- or Japanese-style? The spa and sauna are worthy extras.

Radfords on the Lake MOTEL $$$
(☑03-249 9186; www.radfordsonthelake.co.nz; 56 Lakefront Dr; units from $285; 🕿) 〽 Radfords isn't your bog-standard motel, as you've probably already guessed by the grand-sounding name and commensurate prices. Set on manicured lawns across from the lake, this angular complex offers 14 luxurious units over two levels, all angled towards the view. They all have kitchens and five of them have spa baths.

Te Anau Lodge B&B $$$
(☑03-249 7477; www.teanaulodge.com; 52 Howden St; s/d from $210/240; 🕿) The former 1930s-built Sisters of Mercy Convent, relocated to just north of town, offers an old-fashioned ambience with decor to match. Sip your complimentary wine in a chesterfield in front of the fire, retire to your spa bath before collapsing on a king-size bed, then awaken to a fresh, delicious breakfast in the old chapel.

🍴 Eating

⭐**Miles Better Pies** FAST FOOD $
(☑03-249 9044; www.milesbetterpies.co.nz; 19 Town Centre; pies $5-6.50; ☉6am-3pm) The bumper selection includes venison, lamb and mint, and fruit pies. There are a few pavement tables, but sitting and munching beside the lake is nicer.

Sandfly Cafe CAFE $
(☑03-249 9529; 9 The Lane; mains $7-20; ☉7am-4.30pm; 🕿) Clocking the most local votes for the town's best espresso, simple but satisfying Sandfly is a top spot to enjoy an all-day breakfast, soup, sandwich or sweet treat, while listening to cruisy music or sunning yourself on the lawn.

⭐**Redcliff Cafe** MODERN NZ $$$
(☑03-249 7431; www.theredcliff.co.nz; 12 Mokonui St; mains $38-42; ☉4-10pm) Housed in a replica settler's cottage, relaxed Redcliff offers generous fine-dining in a convivial atmosphere backed by sharp service. The predominantly locally sourced food is truly terrific: try the wild venison or hare. Kick off or wind it up with a drink in the rustic front bar, which often hosts live music.

🍷 Drinking & Entertainment

Ranch Bar & Grill PUB
(☑03-249 8801; www.theranchbar.co.nz; 111 Town Centre; ☺noon-late) Popular with locals for its generous pub meals, head to the Ranch for a quality Sunday roast dinner ($15), Thursday jam night or a big sports match.

Fat Duck BAR
(☑03-249 8480; 124 Town Centre; ☺noon-late Tue-Sun; 🛜) This corner bar with pavement seating is a sound choice for supping a pint or two of Mac's beer. The kitchen dishes up marginally trendy gastropub and cafe fare, opening for breakfast daily in summer.

Fiordland Cinema CINEMA
(☑03-249 8812; www.fiordlandcinema.co.nz; 7 The Lane; 🛜) In between back-to-back showings of the excellent *Ata Whenua/Fiordland on Film* (adult/child $10/5), essentially a 32-minute advertisement for Fiordland scenery, Fiordland Cinema serves as the local movie house. The **Black Dog Bar** (☑03-249 8844; www.blackdogbar.co.nz; ☺10am-late; 🛜) downstairs is the town's most sophisticated watering hole.

ℹ️ Information

Fiordland i-SITE (☑03-249 8900; www.fiordland.org.nz; 19 Town Centre; ☺8.30am-7pm Dec-Mar, to 5.30pm Apr-Nov) Activity, accommodation and transport bookings.

Fiordland Medical Centre (☑03-249 7007; 25 Luxmore Dr; ☺8am-5.30pm Mon-Fri, 9am-noon Sat)

Fiordland National Park Visitor Centre (DOC; ☑03-249 7924; www.doc.govt.nz; cnr Lakefront Dr & Te Anau–Manapouri Rd; ☺8.30am-4.30pm) Can assist with Great Walks bookings, general hut tickets and information, with the bonus of a natural history display, and a shop stocking tramping supplies and essential topographical maps for backcountry trips.

ℹ️ Getting There & Away

InterCity (☑03-442 4922; www.intercity.co.nz) Twice daily services to Milford Sound (from $28, 1½ hours) and Queenstown (from $28, 3¼ hours), and daily buses to Gore (from $30, 1¾ hours), Dunedin (from $37, 4½ hours) and Christchurch (from $61, 11 hours). Buses depart outside Kiwi Country on Miro St.

Naked Bus (www.nakedbus.com; prices vary) Has a daily bus to Queenstown (2¾ hours) and Milford Sound (2¼ hours).

Topline Tours (☑03-249 8059; www.toplinetours.co.nz) Offers year-round shuttles

between Te Anau and Manapouri ($20), and transfers from Te Anau to the Kepler Track trailheads at the control gates ($5) and the Rainbow Reach swing bridge ($8) from November to March.

Tracknet (☑0800 483 262; www.tracknet.net) From November to April Te Anau–based Tracknet has three scheduled buses to/from Te Anau Downs ($25, 30 minutes), the Divide ($39, 1¼ hours) and Milford Sound ($49, 2¼ hours), and two buses to/from Manapouri ($25, 30 minutes) and Queenstown ($45, 2¾ hours). In winter, services are on demand.

Around Te Anau

Te Anau is the gateway to three Great Walks – the Kepler, Milford and Routeburn – and the less visited but equally worthy Hollyford. Detailed information can be found in Lonely Planet's *Hiking & Tramping New Zealand* guide, and from the helpful folk at the Fiordland National Park Visitor Centre, where you can also register your intentions via the Adventuresmart website (www.adventuresmart.org.nz).

Kepler Track

Opened in 1988 to relieve pressure on the Milford and Routeburn tracks, the Kepler is one of NZ's best-planned tracks and now one of its most popular. The route takes the form of a moderately strenuous 60km loop beginning and ending at the Waiau River control gates at the southern end of Lake Te Anau. It features an all-day tramp across the mountain tops taking in incredible panoramas of the lake, the Jackson Peaks and the Kepler Mountains. Along the way it traverses rocky ridges, tussock lands and peaceful beech forest.

The route can be covered in four days, staying in the three huts, although it is possible to reduce the tramp to three days by continuing past Moturau Hut and leaving the track at the Rainbow Reach swing bridge. However, spending a night at Moturau Hut on the shore of Lake Manapouri is an ideal way to end this tramp. The track can be walked in either direction, although the most popular is Luxmore–Iris Burn–Moturau.

The alpine sections require a good level of fitness and may be impassable in winter, although this is a heavily weather-dependent track at any time of year.

Kepler Track

Estimated walking times:

DAY	ROUTE	TIME
1	Fiordland National Park Visitor Centre to control gates	45min
1	Control gates to Brod Bay	1½hr
1	Brod Bay to Luxmore Hut	3½-4½hr
2	Luxmore Hut to Iris Burn Hut	5-6hr
3	Iris Burn Hut to Moturau Hut	5-6hr
3	Moturau Hut to Rainbow Reach	1½-2hr
4	Rainbow Reach to control gates	2½-3½hr

ℹ Bookings & Transport

The Kepler is officially a Great Walk. Between late October and mid-April you must obtain a Great Walk pass for the **Luxmore Hut, Iris Burn Hut** and **Moturau Hut**. Passes must be obtained in advance, and it pays to book well in advance, either online via DOC's **Great Walks Bookings** (☑ 0800 694 732; www.greatwalks.co.nz) or in person at a DOC visitor centre. In the low season the huts revert to the Serviced category. There are campsites at **Brod Bay** and **Iris Burn**.

The recommended map for this tramp is 1:60,000 *Parkmap 335-09 (Kepler Track).*

Conveniently, the track begins under an hour's walk from the Fiordland National Park Visitor Centre, via the lakeside track alongside the Manapouri–Te Anau Rd (SH95). There's a car park and shelter near the control gates. **Tracknet** (p254) and **Topline Tours** (p254) both run shuttles to and from both the control gates and the Rainbow Reach trailheads.

Kepler Water Taxi (☑ 027 249 8365; www.facebook.com/keplerwatertaxi; each way $25) offers morning boat services across Lake Te Anau to Brod Bay, slicing 1½ hours off the first day's tramp.

Milford Track

The best-known track in NZ and routinely touted as 'the finest walk in the world', the Milford is an absolute stunner, complete with rainforest, deep glaciated valleys, a glorious alpine pass surrounded by towering peaks and powerful waterfalls, including the legendary Sutherland Falls, one of the loftiest in the world. All these account for its popularity: more than 14,000 trampers complete the 54km-long track each year.

During the Great Walks season, the track can only be walked in one direction, starting from Glade Wharf. You must stay at Clinton Hut the first night, despite it being only one hour from the start of the track, and you must complete the trip in the prescribed three nights and four days. This is perfectly acceptable if the weather is kind, but when the weather turns sour you'll still have to push on across the alpine Mackinnon Pass and may miss some rather spectacular views. It's all down to the luck of the draw.

During the Great Walk season, the track is also frequented by guided tramping parties, which stay at cosy, carpeted lodges with hot showers and proper food. If that sounds appealing, contact Ultimate Hikes (☑0800 659 255, 03-450 1940; www.ultimatehikes.co.nz; 5-day tramp incl food dm/s/d $2195/3085/5210; ☉Nov-Apr) 🍂, the only operator permitted to run guided tramps on the Milford.

The track is covered by 1:70,000 *Parkmap 335-01 (Milford Track)*.

Estimated walking times:

DAY	ROUTE	TIME
1	Glade Wharf to Glade House	20min
1	Glade House to Clinton Hut	1hr
2	Clinton Hut to Mintaro Hut	5-6hr
3	Mintaro Hut to Dumpling Hut	6-7hr
3	Side trip to Sutherland Falls	1½hr return
4	Dumpling Hut to Sandfly Point	5½-6hr

❶ Bookings & Transport

The Milford Track is officially a Great Walk. Between late October and mid-April, you need a Great Walk pass ($162) to cover your three nights in the huts: **Clinton Hut**, **Mintaro Hut** and **Dumpling Hut**. Passes must be obtained in advance, either online via DOC's Great Walks Bookings or in person at a DOC visitor centre. Book early to avoid disappointment as the entire season books up very quickly.

In the low season the huts revert to the Serviced category ($15), and the track can be walked in any time frame you like. This makes late April and early May a great time to tramp, weather dependent. The same can't be said of the month prior to the season starting, as there's a very real danger of avalanches in spring.

The track starts at Glade Wharf, at the head of Lake Te Anau, accessible by a 1½-hour boat trip from Te Anau Downs, itself 29km from Te Anau on the road to Milford Sound. The track finishes at Sandfly Point, a 15-minute boat trip from Milford Sound village, from where you can return by road to Te Anau, around two hours away. You will be given options to book this connecting transport online, at the same time as you book your hut tickets.

Tracknet (p254) offers transport from Queenstown and Te Anau to meet the boats at Te Anau Downs and Milford Sound. There are other options for transport to and from the track, including a float-plane hop from Te Anau to Glade Wharf with **Wings & Water** (☑03-249 7405; www.wingsandwater.co.nz; Lakefront Dr). Fiordland i-SITE and the Fiordland National Park Visitor Centre can advise on options to best suit you.

Hollyford Track

The four- to five-day (each way), 58km Hollyford Track is an easy to moderate tramp through the lower Hollyford – the longest valley in Fiordland National Park – to remote Martin's Bay. Track upgrades and improved transport services, combined with the fact that it's a low-level hike achievable year-round, have resulted in more trampers discovering the splendid mountain and lake vistas, beautiful forest, extensive bird life and magical coast that make the Hollyford so special. Even so, the track averages only 4000 trampers a year, making it a good option for those in search of solitude.

The track is basically one way (unless combined with the super-challenging Pyke–Big Bay Route), with the majority of trampers turning tail and retracing their steps, or flying out from the airstrip at Martins Bay. If possible, spend an extra day in the bay, where you can view a seal colony and get a sneaky peak at a penguin, if you're lucky. This will more than make up for the misdeeds of the most demonic sandflies in NZ.

Milford Track

0 — 5 km
0 — 2.5 miles

Transit River

Terror Peak (1786m)

Mt Phillips (1446m)

Milford Sound

Milford Sound

Milford Sound Hwy

Camp Oven Creek

Danger Mountain (1825m)

Devils Armchair (1627m)

Sandfly Point

Milford Sound Lodge

Cleddau River

Sheerdown Peak (1878m)

Shoulder Hill (1129m)

Giant Gate Falls

Sheerdown Hills

Poseidon Creek

Lake Ada

Giant Gate Falls Shelter

Odyssey Peak (1821m)

The Chasm

Mackay Creek

Steep Hill (1631m)

Mt Ada (1881m)

Access Peak (1865m)

Te Anau–Milford Hwy

Mt Isolation (1620m)

North Branch

West Branch

South Branch

Mt Edgar (1673m)

Mackay Falls

Bell Rock

Swing Bridge

Lake Brown

Joes River

1655m

Homer Tunnel

Boatshed Shelter (Private)

Arthur River

Talbot River

Gulliver Peak (1776m)

Dumpling Hill (575m)

Mt Kepka (1781m)

Lloyd Peak (1962m)

Basin Peak (1865m)

Buttercup Lake

Cirque Peak (1902m)

Dumpling Hut

Mt Elliot (1990m)

Surprise Creek

Mt Gendarme (1931m)

Lake Thompson

Sutherland Falls

Jervois Glacier

Mt Wilmur (1710m)

1350m

Wick Mountains

Dudleigh Falls

Robert Allen Shelter

Mt Balloon (1847m)

Mt Hart (1769m)

Mackinnon Pass Shelter

Mackinnon Pass (1069m)

Lake Mintaro

Mintaro Hut

Mirror Lake

Mt Mitchelson (1936m)

Marshall Pass

Lake Iceberg

Clinton Canyon

Epidote Cataract

North Branch

St Quintin Falls

Pompolona Hut (Private)

Swing Bridge

Bus Stop Shelter

Prairie Shelter

Castle Mtn (2122m)

1920m

Milford Track

Mt Fisher (1869m)

Hidden Lake

Mt Anau (1956m)

Castle River

Fiordland National Park

Hirere Falls

Hirere Shelter (MTGW)

Lookout

Neale Burn

Clinton Forks

Lake Ross

Clinton River (West Branch)

Worsley Stream

McQueen Creek

Indecision Creek

1713m

Clinton Hut

Wetland Walk

Clinton River

Glade Burn

Lookout

Glade House (Private)

1483m

Glade Wharf

Te Anau Downs (by launch) (45km)

Lake Te Anau

The best maps for this tramp are *CA09 (Alabaster)* and *CA08 (Milford Sound)*. DOC produces a *Hollyford Track* brochure.

ⓘ Bookings & Transport

Trampers have the use of six DOC huts on the track, ranging from Serviced ($15) to Standard ($5). Camping ($5) is permitted next to the huts, although sandflies will prevent this from being remotely enjoyable. Tickets should be obtained in advance online from DOC Visitor Centres.

Tracknet (p254) and **Trips & Tramps** (☎ 03-249 7081, 0800 305 807; www.tripsandtramps.com) both run shuttles to the Hollyford trailhead. Nine kilometres (two hours' walk) shy of the trailhead is **Gunn's Camp** (www.gunnscamp.org.nz; sites per person $15, dm $25, cabins $65, bed linen extra $5), a good bolthole before or after the feat with car storage available.

Fly Fiordland (☎ 0800 359 346; www.flyfiord land.com; up to 4 people $620) flies between Te Anau and the Martins Bay airstrip, usually as a charter but with a per-person rate of $175 at busy times.

Ngāi Tahu-owned **Hollyford Track** (☎ 03-442 3000; www.hollyfordtrack.com; adult/child from $1795/1395; ☺ late Oct-late Apr) runs excellent three-day guided trips on the Hollyford staying at private lodges. The journey is shortened with a jetboat trip down the river and Lake McKerrow on day two, and ends with a scenic flight to Milford Sound.

Te Anau–Milford Highway

Sometimes the road is the destination in itself and that's certainly true of the superlative 119km stretch from Te Anau to Milford Sound (SH94). It offers the most easily accessible experience of Fiordland in all its diversity, taking in stretches of beautiful beech forest, gentle river valleys, mirror-like lakes, exquisite alpine scenery and ending at arguably NZ's most breathtaking vista.

Head out from Te Anau early (by 8am) or later in the morning (11am) to avoid the tour buses heading for midday sound cruises. Fill up with petrol in Te Anau before setting off, and note that chains must be carried on icy or avalanche-risk days from May to November (there will be signs on the road); these can be hired from most service stations in Te Anau.

The trip takes two to 2½ hours if you drive straight through, but take time to stop and experience the majestic landscape. Pull off the road and explore the many viewpoints and nature walks en route. Pick up DOC'S *Fiordland National Park Day Walks* brochure ($2) from Fiordland i-SITE or

Fiordland National Park Visitor Centre, or download it at www.doc.govt.nz.

The first part of the road meanders through rolling farmland atop the lateral moraine of the glacier that once gouged out Lake Te Anau. At the 29km mark it passes **Te Anau Downs**, where the boats for the Milford Track depart. From here, an easy 45-minute return walk leads through forest to **Lake Mistletoe**, a small glacier-formed lake.

The road then heads into the Eglinton Valley, at first pocketed with sheepy pasture, then reaching deeper wilderness immersion as it crosses the boundary into Fiordland National Park. The knobby peaks, thick beech forest, lupin-lined river banks and grassy meadows are a grand sight indeed.

Just past the **Mackay Creek** campsite (at 51km) are great views to Pyramid Peak (2295m) and Ngatimamoe Peak (2164m) ahead. The boardwalk at **Mirror Lakes** (at 58km) takes you through beech forest and wetlands, and on a calm day the lakes reflect the mountains across the valley.

At the 77km mark is **Cascade Creek** and **Lake Gunn**. This area was known to Māori as O Tapara, and a stopover for parties heading to Anita Bay in search of *pounamu* (greenstone). The **Lake Gunn Nature Walk** (45 minutes return) loops through tall red beech forest ringing with bird calls, with side trails leading to quiet lakeside beaches.

At 84km the vegetation changes as you pass across the **Divide**, the lowest east–west pass in the Southern Alps. The roadside shelter here is used by trampers either finishing or starting the Routeburn or Greenstone and Caples Tracks. From here you can embark on a marvellous two-hour return walk along the the start of the Routeburn, climbing up through beech forest to the alpine tussockland of **Key Summit**. On a good day the views of the Humboldt and Darran Mountains are sure to knock your socks off, and the nature walk around the boggy tops and stunted beech is a great excuse to linger.

From the Divide, the road falls into the beech forest of the **Hollyford Valley** (stop at Pop's View for a great outlook) and there's a worthwhile detour off SH94 down the Lower Hollyford to Gunn's Camp, 8km along the unsealed road leading to the Hollyford Track. The track starts a further 9km away, where you will also find the track to **Humboldt Falls** (30 minutes return).

Back on the main road to Milford, the road climbs through a cascade-tastic valley to the **Homer Tunnel**, 101km from Te Anau and framed by a spectacular, high-walled, ice-carved amphitheatre. Begun as a relief project in the 1930s and finally opened to motor traffic in 1954, the tunnel is one way, with the world's most alpine set of traffic lights to direct vehicle flow. Dark, magnificently rough-hewn and dripping with water, the 1270m-long tunnel emerges at the other end at the head of the spectacular **Cleddau Valley**. Any spare 'wows' might pop out about now. Kea (alpine parrots) hang around the tunnel entrance looking for food from tourists, but don't feed them as it's bad for their health.

About 10km before Milford Sound, the wheelchair- and pram-friendly **Chasm Walk** (20 minutes return) is well worth a stop. The forest-cloaked Cleddau River plunges through scooped-out boulders in a narrow chasm, creating deep falls and a natural rock bridge. From here, watch for glimpses of **Mt Tutoko** (2746m), Fiordland's highest peak, above the beech forest.

🛏 Sleeping

There are nine basic DOC campsites (per adult/child $6/3) along the highway. All are scenic but also popular with sandflies.

Knob's Flat   MOTEL $$
(☑ 03-249 9122; www.knobsflat.co.nz; sites per adult/child $15/8, d $130-150) In the Eglinton Valley, 63km from Te Anau, Knob's Flat has six self-contained units that are perfect for those who appreciate the simple things in life, such as a cosy room with a view. And boy, do these units have views. Unpowered sites cater to those who want back-to-nature camping with the relative luxuries of hot showers ($5) and a kitchen.

ℹ Getting There & Away

Tracknet (☑ 0800 483 262; www.tracknet. net) From November to April, Tracknet has three scheduled buses on the Milford Sound–Te Anau route that stop at the Divide and Te Anau Downs; two continue on to Queenstown ($90, five hours). In winter, services are on demand.

Milford Sound

POP 114

Sydney Opera House, Big Ben, the Eiffel Tower – one's first glimpse of the world's most famous sights can stop you in your tracks and immediately insert a lump in your throat. So it is with Mitre Peak (Rahotu), the spectacular, 1692m-high mountain rising from the

dark waters of Milford Sound (Piopiotahi). This image has dominated NZ tourism brochures since Maui was a lad and is one of very few such vistas that is truly worthy of the word 'iconic'.

From the road's end it sits dead centre of an exceedingly beautiful landscape of sheer rocky cliffs anchored in inky waters. From time to time the precarious forests clinging to the slopes relinquish their hold, causing a 'tree avalanche' into the fiord.

Milford Sound receives about half a million visitors each year, many of them crammed into the peak months (January and February). Some 14,000 arrive by foot, via the Milford Track, which ends at the sound. Some buzz through in helicopters. Many more drive from Te Anau, but most arrive via the multitude of bus tours. But don't worry: out on the water all this humanity seems tiny compared to nature's vastness.

🏃 Activities

The clue is in the name: Milford Sound is all about the water, and the landforms that envelop it. It's enough to make you go misty-eyed, as an average annual rainfall of 7m fuels innumerable cascading waterfalls. The unique ocean environment – caused by freshwater sitting atop warmer seawater – replicates deep-ocean conditions, encouraging the activity of marine life such as dolphins, seals and penguins. Getting out on the water is a must.

Rosco's Milford Kayaks   KAYAKING
(☑ 03-249 8500, 0800 476 726; www.roscosmilfordkayaks.com; 72 Town Centre, Te Anau; trips $99-199; ⊙ Nov-Apr) Guided, tandem-kayak trips including the 'Morning Glory' ($199), a challenging paddle the full length of the fiord to Anita Bay, and the easier 'Stirling Sunriser' ($195), which ventures beneath the 151m-high Stirling Falls. Among many other options are trips 'your grandmother could do', and kayak-walk combos on the Milford Track.

Descend Scubadiving   DIVING
(www.descend.co.nz; 2 dives incl gear $299) Descend runs day trips with four hours of cruising on Milford Sound in a 7m catamaran and two dives along the way. The marine reserve is home to unique marine life, including a multitude of corals. Transport, equipment, hot drinks and snacks are supplied.

👉 Tours

A cruise on Milford Sound is Fiordland's most accessible experience, as evident from the slew of companies located in the flash cruise terminal, which is a 10-minute walk from the main car park.

Each cruise company claims to be quieter, smaller, bigger, cheaper, or in some way preferable to the rest. What really makes a difference is the timing of the cruise. Most bus tours aim for 1pm sailings, so if you avoid that time of day there will be less people on the boat, less boats on the water and less buses on the road. With some companies you get a better price on cruises outside rush hour, too.

If you're particularly keen on wildlife, ask whether there will be a nature guide on board. It's wise to book ahead regardless. You generally need to arrive 20 minutes before departure. Most companies offer coach transfers from Te Anau for an additional cost. Day trips from Queenstown make for a very long 13-hour day.

All the cruises visit the mouth of the sound, just 15km from the wharf, poking their prow into the choppy waves of the Tasman Sea. The shorter cruises visit less of the en route 'highlights', which include Bowen Falls, Mitre Peak, Anita Bay and Stirling Falls.

Only visitable on trips run by Southern Discoveries and Mitre Peak Cruises, **Milford Discovery Centre** (www.southerndiscoveries. co.nz; Harrison Cove; adult/child $36/18; ⊘9am-4pm) is a floating underwater observatory offering a chance to view deep-water corals, tube anemones and bottom-dwelling sea perch from 10m below the waterline.

Cruise Milford   BOAT TOUR
(☑0800 645 367; www.cruisemilfordnz.com; adult/child from $80/18; ⊘10.45am. 12.45pm & 2.45pm) A small boat heads out three times a day on a 1¾-hour cruise.

Go Orange   BOAT TOUR
(☑0800 246 672, 03-249 8585; www.goorange. co.nz; adult/child from $55/15; ⊘9am, 12.30pm & 3pm) Real Journeys' low-cost two-hour cruises along the full length of MIlford Sound, with the added bonus of a complimentary breakfast, lunch or snack.

Real Journeys   BOAT TOUR
(☑0800 656 501, 03-249 7416; www.realjourneys. co.nz) ⬤ Milford's biggest operator runs various trips, including the popular 1¾-hour scenic cruise (adult/child from $76/22). The 2½-hour nature cruise (adult/child from $88/22) hones in on wildlife with a specialist nature guide providing commen-

tary. Overnight cruises are also available, on which you can kayak and take nature tours in small boats en route.

Overnight trips depart from the cruise terminal in the mid-afternoon and return around 9.30am the following day. The *Milford Wanderer,* modelled on an old trading scow, accommodates 36 passengers in two- and four-bunk cabins with shared bathrooms (dorm/single/double $305/621/710). The *Milford Mariner* sleeps 60 in more-up-market single ($744) or double ($850) en suite cabins. Cheaper prices apply from April through to September; coach transport from Te Anau is extra.

🛏 Sleeping

Milford Sound Lodge   LODGE $$$
(☑03-249 8071; www.milfordlodge.com; SH94; sites from $25, dm/d without bathroom $35/99, chalets $345-395; 🛜) Alongside the Cleddau River, 1.5km from the Milford hub, this simple but comfortable lodge has a down-to-earth, active vibe. Travellers and trampers commune in the lounge or on-site Pio Pio Cafe, which provides meals, wine and espresso. Luxurious chalets enjoy an absolute riverside location. Booking ahead is strongly recommended.

ℹ Information

Discover Milford Sound Information Centre
(☑03-249 7931; www.southerndiscoveries. co.nz; ⊘8am-4pm) Although it's run by Southern Discoveries, this centre near the main car park sells tickets for most of the tour and cruise companies, as well as for scenic flights and InterCity buses. There's also a cafe attached.

ℹ Getting There & Away

BUS
InterCity (☑03-442 4922; www.intercity. co.nz) Runs twice daily bus services to Milford Sound from Te Anau (from $28, 1½ hours) and Queenstown (from $47, 4¼ hours), on to which you can add a cruise or scenic flight when you book.

Naked Bus (www.nakedbus.com; prices vary) Daily buses between Te Anau and Milford Sound (2¼ hours).

Tracknet (☑03-249 7777; www.tracknet.net) From November to April Tracknet has three scheduled buses to/from the Divide ($35, 45 minutes), Te Anau Downs ($47, 1¾ hours) and Te Anau ($49, 2¼ hours), and two buses to/from Queenstown ($90, five hours). In winter, services are on demand.

CAR

Fill up with petrol in Te Anau before setting off. Snow chains must be carried on ice- and avalanche-risk days from May to November (there will be signs on the road), and can be hired from service stations in Te Anau.

Manapouri

POP 228

Manapouri is the jumping-off point for cruises to Doubtful Sound, with most visitors heading straight to the boat harbour for the ferry to West Arm. This leaves it sleepy and somewhat underrated, for not only is Lake Manapouri one of NZ's most beautiful towns, with a backdrop bettering Te Anau, there are ample interesting things to do and local people to do them with.

In 1969 Manapouri was the site of NZ's first major environmental campaign. The original plan for the West Arm hydroelectric power station, built to supply electricity for the aluminium smelter near Invercargill, required raising the level of the lake by 30m. A petition gathered a staggering 265,000 signatures (17% of voting-age New Zealanders at the time) and the issue contributed to the downfall of the government at the following election. The win proved big for environmentalists, for not only was the power station built without the lake levels being changed, it also spawned more nationwide environmental action through the 1970s and '80s.

Activities

By crossing the Waiau River at Pearl Harbour you can embark on day walks as detailed in DOC's *Fiordland National Park Day Walks* brochure. The classic outing is the **Circle Track** (three hours return), which can be extended to **Hope Arm** (five to six hours return). You can cross the river aboard a hired rowboat or water taxi from **Adventure Manapouri** (☑ 03-249 8070; www.adventuremanapouri.co.nz; rowboat hire per day $40, water taxi return $20), which also offers guided walks and fishing tours.

Running between the northern entrance to Manapouri township and Pearl Harbour, the one-hour **Frasers Beach** walk offers picnic and swimming spots as well as fantastic views across the lake.

The Kepler Track (p254) is accessible from the northern end of Lake Manapouri at Rainbow Reach, 10km north of town.

Manapouri is also a staging point for the remote **Dusky Track**, a highly challenging 84km tramp taking eight to 10 days. For more information contact DOC.

Sleeping

Manapouri Motels & Holiday Park HOLIDAY PARK $
(☑ 03-249 6624; www.manapourimotels.co.nz; 86 Cathedral Dr; sites from $36, units from $95, without bathroom from $60; ☎) This eccentric but ultimately charming old-style camping ground features inexpensive cabins (from mock-Swiss Alpine to sweet little weatherboard), quiet campsites, and a homey amenities block. But wait, there's more...including a fleet of old Morris Minors and a collection of vintage pinball machines.

Freestone Backpackers HOSTEL $
(☑ 03-249 6893; www.freestone.co.nz; 270 Hillside Rd; dm $22-33, d $86, without bathroom $66; ☎) These rustic cabins nestle on a hillside about 3km east of town, each with a gas hob, potbelly stove and veranda. Bathrooms are basic and communal. A converted family home offers another eight beds for singles, doubles and twins, with communal facilities including a full kitchen. Ask about boat cruises.

Getting There & Away

Topline Tours (p254) Offers year-round shuttles between Te Anau and Manapouri ($20).

Tracknet (☑ 03-249 7777; www.tracknet.net; adult/child $25/18) Runs between Te Anau and Manapouri twice daily from November to April, and on demand at other times of the year.

Doubtful Sound

Magnificent Doubtful Sound is a wilderness area of fractured and gouged mountains, dense forest and thundering waterfalls. Technically a fiord, having being carved by glaciers, Doubtful is one of NZ's largest sounds – three times the length and 10 times the area of Milford. It is also much, *much* less visited. If you have the time and the money and the weather's behaving, it's an essential experience.

Until relatively recently, only the most intrepid tramper or sailor ever explored Doubtful Sound. Even Captain Cook only observed it from off the coast in 1770, because he was 'doubtful' whether the winds in the sound would be sufficient to blow the ship back out to sea. The sound became more accessible when the road over Wilmot Pass opened in 1959 to facilitate construction of the West Arm power station.

☞ Tours

Your major considerations here are overnight (pricey but preferable) or day trip, and size of boat. Another consideration is whether you want to tour the power station. Overnight cruises include meals plus the option of fishing and kayaking.

Real Journeys   BOAT TOUR
(☑ 0800 656 501; www.realjourneys.co.nz) 🌐
The day-long 'wilderness cruise' (adult/child from $250/65) includes a three-hour journey aboard a modern catamaran with a specialist nature guide. The overnight cruise, which runs from September to May, is aboard the *Fiordland Navigator*, which sleeps 70 in en suite cabins (quad-share per adult/child $385/193, single/double $1076/1230). Some trips include a visit to the West Arm power station.

Adventure Kayak & Cruise   KAYAKING
(☑ 0800 324 966; www.fiordlandadventure.co.nz; day/overnight tour $249/295; ☉ Oct-Apr) Runs day trips to Doubtful Sound, or two-day trips with a night camping on a beach.

Fiordland Cruises   BOAT TOUR
(☑ 0800 368 283; www.fiordlandcruises.co.nz; tour from $1650; ☉ Oct-May) Overnight cruise on the *Southern Secret* (maximum 12 passengers); cabins are en suite doubles.

Go Orange Kayaks   KAYAKING
(☑ 03-249 8585; www.goorangekayaks.co.nz; 1/2/3/5 days $245/399/550/775; ☉ Oct-Apr) Two- to five-day kayaking and camping trips around Doubtful Sound, or single day 'tasters'. The price includes transfers from Te Anau and hot drinks, but not food.

❶ Getting There & Away

Getting to Doubtful Sound involves boarding a boat at Pearl Harbour in Manapouri for a one-hour trip to West Arm power station, followed by a 22km (40-minute) drive over Wilmot Pass to Deep Cove (permanent population: two), where you hop aboard a boat for your cruise on the sound. Manapouri is the easiest place to base yourself, although Te Anau and Queenstown pick-ups are readily organised through the cruise-boat operators.

CENTRAL SOUTHLAND

New Zealand's 'deep south' is a starkly contrasting mix of raw coastlines, untouched wilderness and great swaths of farmland. Laid-back and lightly populated, it's a region where getting off the beaten path goes with the territory.

Tuatapere

POP 558

Formerly a timber-milling town, sleepy Tuatapere is now largely a farming centre that for no easily explainable reason likes to refer to itself as the 'sausage capital of the world'. Those early woodcutters were very efficient, so only a remnant of a once-large tract of native podocarp (conifer) forest remains.

Wilderness, however, is not far away. Tuatapere is the base for the **Hump Ridge Track**, conceived and built by the local community, and opened in 2001. The three-day, 58km track makes relatively easy work of a tramp across craggy heights. Rich in natural and cultural history – from spectacular coastal and alpine scenery to the intriguing relics of a historic timber town – there's bird life aplenty, and the chance to see Hector's dolphins on the lonely windswept coast. En route the path crosses a number of towering historic wooden viaducts, including NZ's highest.

To hike the track you need to book through the Tuatapere Hump Ridge Track Information Centre (p263). Packages include transport to the trailhead (at Rarakau, 19km from Tuatapere) and comfortable lodge accommodation. The tramp is possible year-round and operates in three seasonal bands, priced accordingly (from $175), with guided tramps also available. Advance bookings are essential.

Another outstanding slice of wilderness surrounds **Lake Hauroko**, west of Tuatapere, reached by a mostly unsealed 32km road. Lined with dark, brooding, steeply forested slopes, it's the deepest lake in NZ, reaching a depth of 462m. The **Dusky Track** ends (or begins) on its northern shores; book a boat with Tuatapere-based **Lake Hauroko Tours** (☑ 03-225 5677; www.duskytrack.co.nz; track transport $99) 🌐 to access the trailhead.

Lake Hauroko drains into the Tasman Sea from its southern end via the Wairaurahiri River. Two local jetboat operators – **W-Jet** (☑ 0800 376 174; www.wjet.co.nz; tour from $225) 🌐 and **Hump Ridge**

Jet (☑0800 270 556; www.wildernessjet.co.nz; day tour $225) – offer thrill-seeking rides along the forest-shrouded river.

◎ Sights

Clifden Suspension Bridge   BRIDGE
Spanning the Waiau River about 12km north of Tuatapere, this elegant wooden suspension bridge is the longest of its kind in NZ. Information panels, a picnic table and toilets encourage a pit stop.

✖ Eating

Yesteryears Museum Cafe   CAFE $
(☑03-226 6682; 3a Orawia Rd; light meals $5-10; ☺8am-5pm, reduced hours in winter) Rip into Aunt Daisy's sugar buns and a quintessentially Kiwi milkshake, and buy homemade jams for on-the-road breakfasts. There's an interesting jumble of quirky household items from a bygone era to peruse while you're at it.

ⓘ Information

Tuatapere Hump Ridge Track Information Centre (☑03-226 6739, 0800 486 774; www.humpridgetrack.co.nz; 31 Orawia Rd; ☺7.30am-5pm, limited hours in winter) Assists with local information, Hump Ridge hut passes and transport.

ⓘ Getting There & Away

Trips and Tramps (☑03-249 7081, 0800 305 807; www.tripsandtramps.co.nz) Offers transport from Te Anau to the launching point of the boats to the Dusky Track trailhead.

Te Waewae & Colac Bays

Te Waewae – why wouldn't you! Arguably the most dramatically beautiful spot on the entire Scenic Southern Route, this long, moody, windswept stretch of beach sets a steely glare towards Antarctica. It's particularly impressive if you're travelling from the east, as it provides a first glimpse of the snowcapped Southern Alps descending into the sea, framing the western end of the bay.

Stop at the spectacular lookout at **McCracken's Rest** and keep an eye out for the Hector's dolphins and southern right whales that are occasionally sighted here. Just past Orepuki is the turn-off for **Monkey Island**, a grassy islet just metres off shore and accessible at low tide. Linger at the beach until dusk to watch the sun sink below the distant snowy peaks.

Colac Bay, 15km to the east, is a popular holiday place and a good surfing spot. Southerlies provide the best swells here, but it's pretty consistent year-round and never crowded. **Colac Bay Tavern** (☑03-234 8399; jilly.wazza@xtra.co.nz; 15 Colac Bay Rd; sites from $15, cabins s/d $30/65; ☺11am-9.30pm; 🐾) is a welcoming spot for a meal of wood-fired pizza or fish and chips, with the convenience of a camping ground with basic rooms out the back.

Riverton

POP 1430
Quiet little Riverton (in Māori, Aparima), only 38km short of Invercargill, is worth a lunch stop. If near-Antarctic swimming takes your fancy, the long, broad sands of **Taramea Bay** are good for a dip.

◎ Sights

Te Hikoi Southern Journey   MUSEUM
(☑03-234 8260; www.tehikoi.co.nz; 172 Palmerston St; adult/child $6/free; ☺10am-4pm) This cracker little museum relates local stories in clever and inspiring ways, starting off with an interesting 16-minute film. Oh, that all small-town museums could be this good! Inside you will also find the Riverton Visitor Information Centre, which can assist with maps and heritage trail brochures, as well as accommodation.

✖ Eating

Mrs Clark's Cafe   CAFE $$
(☑03-234 8600; 108 Palmerston St; meals $12-24; ☺8am-3pm Sun-Thu, to 8pm Fri & Sat; 🐾) Housed in an insanely turquoise building that has been various forms of eatery since 1891, Mrs Clark's serves thoroughly contemporary and delicious day-time food (beaut baking!), ace espresso, craft beer, and pizza on Friday and Saturday evenings.

Invercargill

POP 51,700

This flat and somewhat featureless town tends to inspire ambivalence in its visitors (except for Keith Richards, who famously dubbed it the 'arsehole of the world' during the Rolling Stones' 1965 visit), yet it satisfies all key requirements as a pit-stop between the Catlins, Stewart Island/Rakiura and Fiordland. Moreover, it sports some handsome buildings, a notable craft brewery, a handful of good eateries, beautiful parks and significant sites of interest for the devoted rev-head.

◉ Sights

The streets of Invercargill boast a slew of historic buildings and other features that can be discovered with the *Invercargill Heritage Trail* brochure. The *Short Walks* brochure details various walks in and around the town, including several around **Sandy Point** butting out on to the Oreti River. **Oreti Beach**, 10km to the southwest of town, is a nice spot for a walk or swim.

Southland Museum & Art Gallery MUSEUM
(☑ 03-219 9069; www.southlandmuseum.com; Queens Park, 108 Gala St; ⊙ 9am-5pm Mon-Fri, 10am-5pm Sat & Sun) FREE Housed in a big white pyramid (a low-rent Louvre?), Invercargill's cultural hub has permanent displays on Southland's natural and human history, recounting plenty of fascinating tales around maritime exploits, in particular. The museum's rock stars are undoubtedly the tuatara, NZ's unique lizard-like reptiles, unchanged for 220 million years. If the slow-moving 115-years-old-and-counting patriarch Henry is any example, they're not planning to do much for the next 220 million years either. Feeding time is 4pm on Fridays.

Outside of opening hours the tuatara can be viewed through windows at the rear of the pyramid.

Queens Park PARK
(Gala St) Half-wild, half-tamed Queens Park encompasses a whopping 80 hectares of trees, plant collections, playing fields, ponds, playgrounds, farm animals, aviaries and even a Wonderland castle.

E Hayes & Sons MUSEUM
(☑ 03-218 2059; www.ehayes.co.nz; 168 Dee St; ⊙ 7.30am-5.30pm Mon-Fri, 10am-4pm Sat & Sun) FREE We can't think of another hardware shop to have made it into a Lonely Planet guidebook, but in among the aisles of bolts, barbecues and brooms in this classic art-deco building are over 100 items of motoring memorabilia, including the actual motorbike on which the late Burt Munro broke the world speed record (as immortalised in the 2005 film *The World's Fastest Indian*, starring Sir Anthony Hopkins). There's also a replica of Burt's Indian, which you can be photographed in.

Other highlights include a 1910 Buick 8, a Ford Thunderbolt and some shiny Chevies. Admission is free, but you're invited to leave a donation for the local hospice – that is unless you're just calling by to stock up on nails and turpentine.

Anderson Park PARK
(☑ 03-215 7432; www.andersonparkgallery.co.nz; 91 McIvor Rd, Waikiwi; ⊙ gardens 8am-dusk) Stretching over 24 hectares, this beautiful park includes landscaped gardens surrounding an elegant 1925 Georgian-style mansion, fringed with an expanse of native bush. The children's playground is extremely popular with local families and there's also an interesting carved *wharepuni* (traditional Māori sleeping house) to discover.

Sadly the house itself is off limits at present due to a potential earthquake risk. When (and if) a solution is found, you'll be able to visit the excellent gallery within, which features works from many prominent NZ artists.

Bill Richardson Transport World MUSEUM
(☑ 03-217 1600; www.transportworld.co.nz; 26 Dart St, Hawthorndale) At the time of writing, the doors were soon expected to be flung open to this vast private museum, housing what is reputed to be the world's biggest collection of vintage trucks (over 300, including a significant number of rare Fords) and petrol bowsers (over 150). If for any reason it hasn't opened, enquire directly about a private viewing.

Invercargill Brewery BREWERY
(☑ 03-214 5070; www.invercargillbrewery.co.nz; 72 Leet St; tour $25; ⊙ 10am-6pm Mon-Sat) New Zealand's great southern brewery has 20 taps for flagon-fills plus a bottled section of its own brews and guests. Pop in for a tasting, or the 45-minute daily tour at 1pm. Our favourites are the crisp B.man Pilsner and the chocolatey Pitch Black stout.

Invercargill

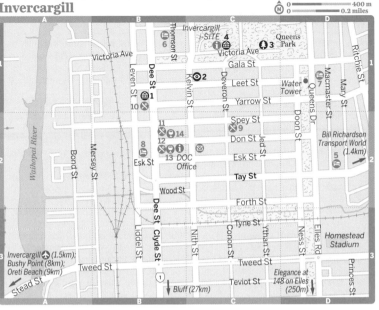

Invercargill

🛏 Sleeping

Many places will store luggage for guests heading to Stewart Island/Rakiura. Motels cluster along Hwy 1 East (Tay St) and Hwy 6 North (North Rd).

Southern Comfort Backpackers   HOSTEL **$**
(☑ 03-218 3838; www.southerncomfortbackpackers.com; 30 Thomson St. Avenal; dm/s/d from $30/54/68; 🛜) This large, lovely Victorian house offers a well-equipped kitchen and a TV-free lounge (hooray!) as well as colourful rooms, including spacious doubles. Pick herbs from the peaceful gardens; you'd hardly know you were five minutes' walk from town.

Lorneville Lodge   HOLIDAY PARK **$**
(☑ 0800 234 600, 03-235 8031; www.lornevillelodge.nz; 352 Lorne-Dacre Rd, Lorneville; sites per person $19, units $120, without bathroom $60; 🛜 🐾) Plenty of personality is packed into this well-set-out holiday park surrounded by farmland. Homey units feature lovingly preserved and enhanced retro style. Rural relaxation, grassy sites, a playground and friendly animals – what a charmer. It's located around 10km north of central Invercargill, east of the Lorneville roundabout.

Invercargill Top 10   HOLIDAY PARK **$**
(☑ 0800 486 873, 03-218 9032; www.invercargilltop10.co.nz; 77 McIvor Rd, Waikiwi; sites from $40, unit $102, without bathroom $80; 🛜 🐾) A particularly attractive option for motel- and

WORTH A TRIP

GORE

Around 66km northeast of Invercargill, Gore (pop 9910) is the proud 'home of country music' in NZ, with the annual **Gold Guitar Week** (www.goldguitars.co.nz; late May-early Jun) in late May and early June ensuring the town's accommodation is booked out for at least 10 days per year. For the other 355 days, good reasons to stop include a notable art gallery, a neat little museum, and the chance to fly in vintage aeroplanes.

The **Hokonui Heritage Centre** (03-208 7032; 16 Hokonui Dr; 8.30am-5pm Mon-Sat, 1-4pm Sun) FREE incorporates the Gore Visitor Centre, the Gore Historical Museum and the **Hokonui Moonshine Museum** (03-208 9907; www.hokonuiwhiskey.com; 16 Hokonui Dr; adult/child $5/free; 8.30am-5pm Mon-Sat, 1-4pm Sun). Together they celebrate the town's proud history of fishing, farming and illegal distilleries. Admission to the Moonshine Museum includes a wee dram of the local liquid gold.

The outstanding **Eastern Southland Gallery** (03-208 9907; www.esgallery.co.nz; 14 Hokonui Dr; 10am-4.30pm Mon-Fri, 1-4pm Sat & Sun) FREE – aka the 'Goreggenheim' – in Gore's century-old former public library houses a hefty collection of NZ art, including a large Ralph Hotere collection. The amazing John Money Collection combines indigenous folk art from West Africa and Australia with works by esteemed NZ artist Rita Angus.

Croydon Aircraft Company (03-208 9755; www.croydonaircraft.com; 1558 Waimea Hwy, SH94; 10/30min flight $95/220; 9.30am-4.30pm Mon-Fri Nov-Mar, 11am-3pm Mon-Fri Apr-Oct), 16km along SH94 towards Queenstown, restores vintage aircraft. Inside a viewing hangar (admission $10) several gems can be seen, including a rare Dragonfly. Flights are offered in a 1930s Tiger Moth biplane and other wee aircraft. Adjacent, the **Moth** (03-208 9662; www.themoth.co.nz; 1558 Waimea Hwy, SH94; lunch $12-26, dinner $27-34; 10am-late Wed-Sun year-round, plus 10am-4pm Mon & Tue Dec-Feb) is a bright and breezy place for a meal.

cabin-dwellers, this leafy park 6.5km north of town also has pleasant tent and campervan sites and smart communal facilities.

★ Bushy Point Fernbirds
B&B $$

(03-213 1302; www.fernbirds.co.nz; 197 Grant Rd, Otatara; s/d $150/170) Two friendly corgis are among the hosts at this eco-aware homestay set on the edge of 4.5 hectares of private forest reserve and wetlands. Fernbirds is very popular with birding types, so booking ahead is essential. It's five minutes' drive from central Invercargill, and rates include a guided walk in the reserve.

Bella Vista
MOTEL $$

(03-217 9799; www.bellavista.co.nz; 240 Tay St, unit from $120;) Friendly hosts, reasonable prices and tidy, well-equipped units put this modern, two-level place near the top of Invercargill's competitive motel pack. Units range from cosy studios with tea- and toast-making facilities, to proper apartments with full kitchens.

Tower Lodge Motel
MOTEL $$

(03-217 6729; www.towerlodgemotel.co.nz; 119 Queens Dr; unit from $130;) Right opposite Invercargill's oddly ornate Victorian wa-

ter tower, this older motel has been made over with new carpets, fresh decor and a mushroom colour scheme. Even the studio units are spacious and some of the one-bedrooms have spa baths.

Victoria Railway Hotel
HOTEL $$

(03-218 1281, 0800 777 557; www.hotel invercargill.com; cnr Leven & Esk Sts; s/d from $130/145;) For a hit of 19th-century heritage, this grand old refurbished hotel fits the bill – although the dated, generic decor doesn't really live up to its potential. Partake of breakfast or dinner in the dining room, or a locally brewed ale in the cosy house bar.

✗ Eating

Three Bean Café
CAFE $

(03-214 1914; 73 Dee St; meals $11-18; 7am-4pm Mon-Fri, 8am-2.30pm Sat;) This borderline old-fashioned main-street cafe prides itself on good coffee then matches the promise with carefully prepared snacks, such as savoury pies and delightful lemon cake, and more substantial meals such as soup, salad and burgers. Helpful staff get our thumbs up, too.

★ **Batch** CAFE $$
(☑ 03-214 6357; 173 Spey St; meals $13-20; ☺ 7am-4.30pm; ☜) Large, shared tables, a relaxed beachy ambience, and top-notch coffee and smoothies add up to this cafe being widely regarded as Southland's best. Delicious counter food includes bagels, sumptuously filled rolls, banoffee brioches, brownies and cakes that are little works of art. A smallish wine and beer list partners healthy lunch options. In summer, it stays open until 8pm on Fridays.

★ **Louie's** TAPAS $$
(☑ 03-214 2913; 142 Dee St; tapas $13-16, mains $29-32; ☺ 5pm-late Wed-Sat) Proving that cool Invercargill isn't quite an oxymoron, this cosy tapas bar is a great place to while away an evening, snuggled into a sofa or a fireside nook. The menu veers from creative tapas (venison tacos, muttonbird, mussels with lime and chilli) to more substantial mains. You really can't go wrong with the locally sourced blue cod.

Rocks CAFE $$
(☑ 03-218 7597; www.shop5rocks.com; Courtville Pl, 101 Dee St; lunch $18-23, dinner $28-41; ☺ 10am-2pm & 5pm-late Tue-Sat) Tucked away in a shopping arcade, this family-style eatery offers a relaxed and fairly unchallenging dining experience. Lunch highlights include pork-belly open sandwiches, pastas and salads, while stars of the extended evening menu are venison in blueberry sauce and a particularly delicious Sicilian fish bowl.

★ **Elegance at**
148 on Elles FRENCH, BRITISH $$$
(☑ 03-216 1000; 148 Elles Rd, Georgetown; mains $26-38; ☺ 6-11pm Mon-Sat) Welcome to 1984, and we mean that in a completely affectionate way. Elegance is the sort of old-fashioned, upmarket, regional restaurant where the menu is vaguely French, vaguely British, and you can be guaranteed of a perfectly cooked piece of venison served on a bed of creamy mash. And there's an awful lot to be said for that.

🍸 Drinking & Nightlife

Tillermans Music Lounge BAR, CLUB
(☑ 03-218 9240; 16 Don St; ☺ 11pm-3.30am Fri & Sat) The saviour of Southland's live-music scene, Mr Tillerman's venue hosts everything from thrash to flash, with a battered old dance floor to show for it. Visit the fun downstairs Vinyl Bar, which is open from 8pm, to find out what's coming up and to put in your request for whichever battered old LP takes your fancy.

Kiln BAR
(☑ 03-218 2258; www.thekiln.co.nz; 7 Don St; ☺ 11am-late; ☜) Invercargill's best gastropub is also its most appealing, with trendy wallpaper and muted lighting from oversized lampshades. Food comes in epic portions (mains $31 to $37) and runs a well-honed gamut between mussels and Caesar salad, to fish and chips, to a joint of meat to share between friends. There's live music on Fridays and Saturdays.

ℹ️ Information

DOC Office (☑ 03-211 2400; www.doc.govt.nz; 7th fl, 33 Don St; ☺ 8.30am-4.30pm Mon-Fri) An office rather than a visitor centre, you're best to make the i-SITE your first port of call. However, it can sort you out with maps and advice if you draw a blank elsewhere.

Invercargill i-SITE (☑ 03-211 0895; www.invercargillnz.com; Queens Park, 108 Gala St; ☺ 8am-5pm) Sharing the Southland Museum pyramid, the i-SITE can help with general enquiries and is a godsend if you're stuck for Stewart Island/Rakiura or Catlins accommodation options .

Post Office (☑ 03-214 7700; www.nzpost.co.nz; 51 Don St; ☺ 9am-5.30pm Mon-Fri, to 1pm Sat)

ℹ️ Getting There & Away

AIR

Air New Zealand (☑ 0800 737 000; www.airnz.co.nz) Flights link Invercargill to Christchurch and Wellington.

Stewart Island Flights (☑ 03-218 9129; www.stewartislandflights.com) Regular connections to Stewart Island/Rakiura.

BUS

Catch-a-Bus South (☑ 03-479 9960; www.catchabussouth.co.nz) Offers scheduled shuttle services at least daily to Bluff ($22, 30 minutes), Queenstown Airport ($55, three hours), Queenstown ($55, 3¼ hours), Gore ($27, 1½ hours) and Dunedin ($55, 3½ hours).

InterCity (☑ 03-471 7143; www.intercity.co.nz) Direct coaches to/from Gore (from $12, one hour, two daily), Queenstown Airport ($48, 3½ hours, daily) and Queenstown ($48, 3¾ hours, daily).

Naked Bus (www.nakedbus.com) Daily buses to and from Gore (50 minutes), Dunedin (3½ hours) and Queenstown (3¾ hours).

ⓘ Getting Around

Invercargill Airport (☑ 03-218 6367; www.invercargillairport.co.nz; 106 Airport Ave) is 3km west of central Invercargill. The door-to-door **Airport Shuttle** (☑ 03-214 3434; exec.car. service@xtra.co.nz) costs around $14 from the city centre; more for residential pick-up. By taxi it's around $20; try **Blue Star Taxis** (☑ 03-217 7777; www.bluestartaxis.co.nz).

Bluff

POP 1800

Windswept and more than a little bleak, Bluff is Invercargill's port, located at the end of a protruding strip of land, 27km south of the city. It's also home to NZ's only aluminium smelter.

The main reason folk come here is to catch the ferry to Stewart Island/Rakiura or to pose for photos beside the **Stirling Point signpost**, which signifies that you've reached the furthest southern reaches of NZ. Sorry to disappoint you, but you haven't. Despite the oft-quoted phrase 'from Cape Reinga to Bluff' and the fact that SH1 terminates at Stirling Point, the South Island's southernmost point is Slope Point in the Catlins, with Stewart Island/Rakiura and remote dots of rock lying even further south. But let's not let the facts get in the way of a good story...

Mention Bluff to any New Zealander and what's the bet that they'll be thinking of oysters. Bluff's bulging bivalves are in huge demand from the minute they come into season (late March to late August). Top restaurants from as far away as Auckland compete to be the first to add them to their menus. As oysters go, they're whoppers. Don't expect to be able to slurp one down in a dainty gulp – these beasts take some chewing. If you want to know what all the fuss is about, you can buy fresh Bluff oysters when they're in season from Fowlers Oysters on the way into town on the left. Otherwise, time your visit for the annual Bluff Oyster & Food Festival in May.

⊙ Sights

Bluff Hill   HILL
(Flagstaff Rd) A steep sealed road leads up to the top of 265m Bluff Hill (Motupōhue), where a path spirals up to a lookout. If the wind isn't threatening to sweep you off your feet, stop to read the information panels

along the way. Various walking tracks head up here, including the Foveaux Walkway to Stirling Point and Ocean Beach.

Bluff Maritime Museum   MUSEUM
(☑ 03-212 7534; 241 Foreshore Rd; adult/child $3/1; ⊙ 10am-4.30pm Mon-Fri year-round, 12.30-4.30pm Sat & Sun Oct-Apr) Salty tales abound round these parts, and many are preserved in this small museum, alongside a century-old oyster boat and a big old steam engine. It also houses interesting displays on Bluff history and on the annual muttonbird (tītī) harvest, an important tradition for local Māori.

★ Festivals & Events

Bluff Oyster & Food Festival   FOOD
(www.bluffoysterfest.co.nz; ⊙ May) Celebrate Bluff's most famous export.

✗ Eating

Oyster Cove   SEAFOOD $$
(☑ 03-212 8855; www.oystercove.co.nz; 8 Ward Pde; mains $18-33; ⊙ 11am-4pm Mon-Thu, to 7pm Fri-Sun; 🐾) Right by the famous signpost at Stirling Point, this restaurant gazes out to sea through large curvy glass windows. In reality the view trumps the food, but it's not a bad place to try local delicacies such as muttonbird, paua, Stewart Island mussels, blue cod and, of course, the renowned oysters.

ⓐ Shopping

Fowlers Oysters   FOOD
(☑ 03-212 8792; Ocean Beach Rd; ⊙ 9am-5pm Mar-Aug) To buy fresh Bluff oysters, visit Fowlers Oysters on the way into town on the left.

ⓘ Getting There & Away

Catch-a-Bus South (☑ 03-479 9960; www.catchabussouth.co.nz) Offers scheduled shuttle services at least daily to Invercargill ($22, 30 minutes), Queenstown Airport ($70, 3½ hours), Queenstown ($70, 3¾ hours), Gore ($40, two hours) and Dunedin ($70, four hours).

Stewart Island Experience (☑ 03-212 7660; www.stewartislandexperience.co.nz) Runs a shuttle between Bluff and Invercargill connecting with its Stewart Island ferry. It also offers secure vehicle storage by the ferry terminal ($8 per day). Transfers from Te Anau and Queenstown to Bluff are available from late October to late April.

THE CATLINS

Bypassed entirely by SH1, the often-overlooked Catlins coast is tucked away at the southeastern corner of the South Island, straddling Southland and Otago. Named after a 19th-century whaling captain, it's an enchanting region, combining fecund farmland, native forest, lonely lighthouses, empty beaches, bushwalks and wildlife-spotting opportunities. On a clear summer's day it is a beauty to behold. In the face of an Antarctic southerly it's an entirely different kettle of fish. Good luck.

The only way to properly explore the area is with your own wheels. It's a slow-going route, with plenty of winding bits, narrows, gravel sections and optional detours, but this is *all* about the journey, rather than the destination.

From Invercargill, the Southern Scenic Route (p263) cuts an arc through the Catlins. However we suggest you leave it at Fortrose in order to visit Waipapa Point, Slope Point, Curio Bay and Waikawa before rejoining it north of Niagara. Note, the section between Haldane and Curio Bay involves 9km of unsealed road.

Flora & Fauna

The Catlins is a wonderful place for independent wildlife-watching. Fur seals and sea lions laze along the coast, while in spring migratory southern right whales are occasionally spotted. Dolphins are also frequent visitors.

Unlike much of Southland, tall kahikatea, totara and rimu forests still exist in the Catlins. Prolific bird life includes tui, bellbird, kereru (wood pigeon), the endangered yellow-eyed penguin and the rare mohua (yellowhead).

ℹ Information

The i-SITEs in Invercargill and Balclutha have lots of Catlins information. On the road, you'll pass two information centres: the small **Owaka Museum & Catlins Information Centre** (p272) and the even smaller **Waikawa Museum & Information Centre** (p270). For further information, see www.catlins.org.nz and www.catlins-nz.com.

The Catlins has no banks and limited options for eating out and grocery shopping. There's an ATM at the Four Square supermarket in Owaka, and petrol stations (hours can be irregular) in Fortrose, Papatowai and Owaka.

ℹ Getting There & Away

There is no public transport in the Catlins area.

Curio Bay & Around

The beachy settlement of Curio Bay attracts a deluge of sunseekers in the summer months but it's a sleepy hamlet at other times. Most of the holiday houses are lined up along Porpoise Bay, a glorious long stretch of sand that's arguably the best swimming beach in the Catlins. Blue penguins nest in the dunes and in summer Hector's dolphins come here to rear their young. Whales are occasional visitors, and fur seals and sea lions may also be spotted.

Curio Bay itself lies just around the southern headland on a much less inviting stretch of coast. It's famous for its fossilised Jurassic-age trees, which are visible for four hours either side of low tide. Yellow-eyed penguins waddle ashore here an hour or so before sunset. Do the right thing and keep your distance.

◉ Sights & Activities

Waipapā Lighthouse   LIGHTHOUSE
(Waipapa Lighthouse Rd) Standing on a desolate but beautiful point surrounded by farmland, this lighthouse dates from 1884, three years after 131 people lost their lives in the wreck of SS *Tararua*. Information panels recount the terrible tale. Tip-toe through the sea lions to survey the beach. The turn-off to Waipapa Point is at Otara, 12km southeast of Fortrose.

Slope Point   LANDMARK
(Slope Point Rd) A 20-minute walk across farmland leads to a signpost designating the South Island's true southerly point in underwhelming fashion. The views more than make up for it, not only of the ocean but of the chunky rocks tumbling down to meet it. The track is closed in September and October for lambing. To get here, follow the signs from Haldane.

Catlins Surf   SURFING
(☏ 03-246 8552; www.catlins-surf.co.nz; 601 Curio Bay Rd; 2hr lesson $60, hire per 3hr/day $50/65) Based at the Curio Bay Holiday Park, this surf school offers lessons on Porpoise Bay, much to the amusement of any passing dolphins. If you're already confident on the waves, you can hire a board, wetsuit (very necessary) and flippers. Owner Nick also offers stand-up paddleboarding tuition ($75, 2½ hours).

The Catlins

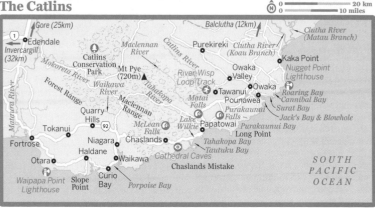

Sleeping

Lazy Dolphin Lodge
HOSTEL $

(☎03-246 8579; www.lazydolphinlodge.co.nz; 529 Curio Bay Rd; dm/r without bathroom $38/80; @🖥) This perfect hybrid of seaside holiday home and hostel has light-filled bedrooms sporting cheerful linen. There are two kitchens and lounges, but you'll want to hang out upstairs on the deck overlooking Porpoise Bay. A path at the rear of the property leads directly to the beach.

Slope Point Backpackers
HOSTEL $

(☎03-246 8420; www.slopepoint.co.nz; 164 Slope Point Rd; sites from $15, dm $25-30, d with/without bathroom $90/50; 🖥) This rural property has modern dorms and rooms, along with a great-value self-contained unit and a whole three-bedroom house a little further up the road. There are grassy tent pitches and gravel sites for campervans, and the owners' children are always keen to show off the working farm. Board games, puzzles and loads of magazines take the place of TV.

Curio Bay Boutique Studios
APARTMENT $$

(☎03-246 8797; www.curiobay.co.nz; 521a Curio Bay Rd; apt from $180) Three plush units are on offer here – one apartment attached to the hosts' house, and two similar units down the road. All are self-contained, decorated in rustic, beachy style, with big windows and sun-drenched decks right next to the beach. There's also an old-fashioned Kiwi bach, sleeping up to six people.

Waikawa & Around

Waikawa occupies a pretty spot on an estuary, 5km north of Curio Bay. It was once a major timber port but now it's most famous for its fish-and-chip truck, which does a roaring trade in summer.

Sights

Waikawa Museum & Information Centre
MUSEUM

(☎03-246 8464; waikawamuseum@hyper.net. nz; 604 Niagara–Waikawa Rd; gold coin donation; ⊙10am-5pm) Something of a one-stop shop in a one-horse town, this little museum features the usual array of dusty agricultural artefacts and photographs of mainly local interest. However, it also incorporates the information centre, acts as the reception for some local holiday rentals, and sells important stuff like newspapers and stamps.

Sleeping & Eating

Penguin Paradise Holiday Lodge
HOSTEL $

(☎03-246 8552; www.catlins-surf.co.nz; 612 Niagara–Waikawa Rd; dm/r without bathroom $30/68) This laid-back backpackers occupies a heritage cottage in the heart of Waikawa village, near the estuary. Special deals combine one night's accommodation and a 90-minute surf lesson ($85).

Waikava Harbour View
RENTAL HOUSE $$

(☎03-246 8866; www.southcatlins.co.nz; 14 Larne St; house from $120) Right on the estuary, Harbour View is a modern four-bedroom house that's an excellent option for families or a group; up to 12 people can be accommodated. The newer one-bedroom Harakeke and Toi Tois units are also good value, sleeping up to four.

Niagara Falls CAFE $$
(☑ 03-246 8577; www.niagarafallscafe.co.nz; 256 Niagara–Waikawa Rd, Niagara; mains $14-22; ☺ 11am-late Dec-Mar, 11am-4pm Thu-Mon Apr-Nov; ☎) Located in a Victorian schoolhouse, this is a decent spot to linger over coffee and a scone, or to tuck into homemade meals. Tasty lamb burgers are sandwiched into freshly baked bread, and there's blue cod, chowder and decadent chocolate brownies. Relax in the grassy garden with a local craft beer or a glass of wine.

Papatowai & Around

Nestled near the mouth of the Tahakopa River, the leafy village of Papatowai has perhaps a few dozen regular inhabitants but swells with holidaymakers in summer, mainly drawn by the languid vibe and the potential for some good bushwalks. There are a couple of short walks in the immediate vicinity, as well as a picnic spot at the river mouth, but further places of interest are spread along the highway in both directions.

Twelve kilometres to the west is the turn-off to **McLean Falls**. The car park is 4km off the highway, with the falls themselves a 40-minute return walk through tree ferns and rimu. Around 5km west of Papatowai, an easy forest walk leads to the dark peaty waters of **Lake Wilkie** (20 minutes return). Bellbirds may ring. Another 1km east of here, a short gravel road leads to sweeping **Tautuku Bay**, which can also be viewed from on high at the **Florence Hill Lookout** just before the descent into Papatowai.

Heading north you can follow the highway to **Matai Falls** (a 30-minute return walk) on the Maclennan River, then head southeast on the signposted road to the tiered **Purakaunui Falls** (20 minutes return). Both falls are reached via cool, dark forest walks through totara and tree fern.

Continue along the gravel road from Purakaunui through Tarara, Ratanui and Hinahina to Jacks Bay, where a track leads through farmland to the 55m-deep **Jack's Blowhole**. In the middle of a paddock 200m from the sea but connected by a subterranean cavern, this huge cauldron was named after Chief Tuhawaiki, nicknamed Bloody Jack for his cussin'. It's a fairly brisk 30-minute walk each way.

◉ Sights & Activities

Lost Gypsy Gallery GALLERY
(☑ 03-415 8908; www.thelostgypsy.com; 2532 Papatowai Hwy; admission $5; ☺ 10am-5pm Thu-Tue, closed May-Sep) Fashioned from remaindered bits and bobs, artist Blair Sommerville's intricately crafted automata are wonderfully irreverent. The bamboozling collection in the bus (free entry) is a teaser for the carnival of creations through the gate (young children not allowed, sorry...). The buzz, bong and bright lights of the organ are bound to tickle your ribs. Espresso caravan and wi-fi on-site.

Cathedral Caves CAVE
(www.cathedralcaves.co.nz; 1069 Chaslands Hwy; adult/child $5/1; ☺ Nov-May) Cutting back into cliffs right on the beach, the huge, arched Cathedral Caves are only accessible for two hours either side of low tide (tide timetables are posted on the website, at the highway turn-off and at visitor information centres) – and even then they can be closed at short notice if the conditions are deemed too dangerous. If you're happy to wade, you can walk in one entrance and out the other.

From SH92 it's 2km to the car park, then a peaceful 15-minute forest walk down to the beach and a further 25 minutes to the caves.

Catlins Wildlife Trackers WILDLIFE
(☑ 03-415 8613, 0800 228 5467; www.catlinsecotours.co.nz) ✔ Running since 1990, Catlins Wildlife Trackers offers customised guided walks and tours with a focus on ecology. If you want to see the beloved mohua, penguins, sea lions or other wildlife, Mary and Fergus will track them down for you. The fully guided three-night/two-day package costs $1200, including all food, accommodation and transport.

🛏 Sleeping & Eating

Hilltop LODGE $
(☑ 03-415 8028; www.hilltopcatlins.co.nz; 77 Tahakopa Valley Rd; dm $38, d $110, withouth bathroom $100) High on a hill 1.5km out of town, with native forest at the back door and surrounded by a sheep farm, these two

ship-shape cottages command spectacular views of the Tahakopa Valley and coast. Rent by the room or the whole house; the en suite double is the pick of a very nice bunch.

Catlins Kiwi Holiday Park　HOLIDAY PARK $
(☑ 03-415 8338; www.catlinskiwiholidaypark.com; 9 Rewcastle Rd, Chaslands; sites from $46, units from $145, without bathroom from $189; @ 🖙) This modern holiday park offers personality-packed accommodation ranging from cute cabins to smart family motels. Tenters share good communal amenities with the cute 'Kiwiana' cabins. Hop along to the on-site Whistling Frog Cafe for the Catlins' best food.

★ Mohua Park　COTTAGE $$
(☑ 03-415 8613; www.catlinsmohuapark.co.nz; 744 Catlins Valley Rd; cottage $190) 🏖 Situated on the edge of a peaceful 14-hectare nature reserve (7km off the highway), these four spacious self-contained cottages offer peace, quiet and privacy with an interesting mixed forest on the doorstep and a Disney movie worth of feathery companions. The owners also have beachfront accommodation at Papatowai.

Whistling Frog Cafe & Bar　CAFE $$
(☑ 03-415 8338; www.whistlingfrogcafe.com; 9 Rewcastle Rd, Chaslands; mains $18-23; ⊙ 8.30am-9.30pm Nov-Mar, 9.30am-6.30pm Apr-Oct; 🖙) Colourful and fun, the Frog is the best dining option in the Catlins, offering craft beer on tap and a crowd-pleasing menu. We're talking seafood chowder, gourmet burgers and a seriously rich steak, lager and aged-cheddar pie. Ribbit! It's located at the Catlins Kiwi Holiday Park, near McLean Falls.

Owaka & Around

Owaka is the Catlins' main town (population a hefty 303), and it's well worth calling in to visit the excellent museum and to stock up on petrol and groceries before continuing on.

Pounawea, a beautiful hamlet on the edge of the Catlins River Estuary, 4km to the east, is a much more appealing place to put down roots. Just across the inlet is **Surat Bay**, notable for the sea lions that lie around the beach between here and **Cannibal Bay**, an hour's beach-walk away.

◉ Sights & Activities

Owaka Museum & Catlins Information Centre　MUSEUM
(☑ 03-415 8323; www.owakamuseum.org.nz; 10 Campbell St, Owaka; adult/child $5/free; ⊙ 10am-4pm) More interesting than most local history museums, this whizz-bang modern establishment supports Māori and settler stories with an interesting array of artefacts. The Catlins' reputation as a shipwreck coast is explained in short video presentations. It also doubles as the main information centre for the Catlins.

Catlins River–Wisp Loop Track　TRAMPING
(www.doc.govt.nz) This 24km loop comprises two 12km sections: the low-level, well-formed Catlins River Walk (five to six hours), and the Wisp Loop Walk (four to five hours), a higher-altitude tramp with a side trip to Rocky Knoll boasting great views and sub-alpine vegetation.

The routes can be walked in either direction as one long day, divided over two days, or split into shorter sections accessed via various entry/exit points. The main access is via Catlins Valley Road, south of Owaka.

Catlins Horse Riding　HORSE RIDING
(☑ 03-415 8368; www.catlinshorseriding.co.nz; 41 Newhaven Rd, Owaka; 1/2/3hr rides $60/105/145) Explore the idiosyncratic coastline and landscapes on four legs. Both learners' treks and the full gallop available.

🛏 Sleeping & Eating

★ Newhaven Holiday Park　HOLIDAY PARK $
(☑ 03-415 8834; www.newhavenholiday.com; 324 Newhaven Rd, Owaka; sites from $32, units from $100, without bathroom from $66; 🖙) Sitting on the estuary edge at the gateway to the Surat Bay beach walk, this excellent little holiday park has good communal facilities, cheerful cabins and three self-contained units. When we last sneaked around, not only were we serenaded by a bellbird but we swear the toilets smelt of cinnamon.

Split Level　HOSTEL $
(☑ 03-415 8868; www.thesplitlevel.co.nz; 9 Waikawa Rd, Owaka; dm $33, r from $82, without bathroom from $74; 🖙) Very much like staying at a mate's house, this tidy two-level home has a comfortable lounge with a large TV and leather couches, and a very well-equipped kitchen. Upstairs rooms open onto decks, while downstairs there's a little en suite unit with its own fridge and microwave.

Pounaewa Grove Motel　MOTEL $$
(☎ 03-415 8339; www.pounaweagrove.co.nz; 5 Ocean Grove; r $140; ☎) If you're looking for modern units with big, comfy beds, plush textiles, art on the walls, flat-screen TVs and sharp bathrooms, this four-unit studio complex will tick all the boxes.

Catlins Cafe　CAFE $$
(☎ 03-415 8040; www.catlinscafe.co.nz; 3 Main Rd, Owaka; brunch $15-22, dinner $23-30; ☺ 9am-8.30pm; ☎) The best of the Owaka bunch starts the day with cooked breakfasts and continues into the evening with fish and chips, burgers, a roast-of-the-day and, in season, whitebait fritters served with a truck-load of salad.

Kaka Point & Around

With a permanent population nudging just over the 200 mark, Kaka Point is a lethargic coastal community set back from a surfy swimming beach.

The biggest attraction in the vicinity is **Nugget Point** (Tokatā), 8km further down the coast. This is the king of the Catlins viewpoints, made all the more interesting by the wave-thrashed cliffs and the toothy islets known as the Nuggets protruding from the surf. Seals and sea lions can often be spotted lolling about below and there's also plenty of bird life, such as soaring shearwaters and spoonbills huddling in the lee of the breeze. A 900m walk leads from the car park to the lighthouse on the point itself.

Just shy of the Nugget Point car park is the car park for **Roaring Bay**, where a well-placed hide allows you to see yellow-eyed penguins (hōiho) coming ashore (best two hours before sunset). Obey all signs: as you can see, this is a pretty precarious existence.

⛺ Sleeping

Kaka Point Camping Ground　HOLIDAY PARK $
(☎ 03-412 8801; www.kakapointcamping.co.nz; 39 Tarata St, Kaka Point; sites unpowered/powered from $129/32, cabins s/d $30/56; ☎) Cabins are basic but functional, and there are grassy, hedged areas for campers. Bushwalks delve into the surrounding forest, and it's a short, though steep, stroll downhill to the beach and village.

Nugget Lodge　RENTAL HOUSE $$
(☎ 03-412 8783; www.nuggetlodge.co.nz; 367 The Nuggets Rd, Kaka Point; unit $190; ☎) Sitting on a seaside knoll on the road to the lighthouse are two modern bach-style self-contained units – one with balcony, one with private garden. It's worth opting for the huge continental breakfast ($15 per person) with freshly baked bread and homemade muesli. If you're lucky, you might spy a couple of resident sea lions lolling on the beach below you.

🍸 Drinking & Nightlife

Point Cafe & Bar　PUB
(☎ 03-412 8800; 58 Esplanade, Kaka Point; ☺ 8.30am-7.30pm) Prop yourself at the driftwood bar for a cool beer, hit the pool table or grab a window seat for a sea view. Takeaways and ice creams are available at the attached store, or you can tuck into blue cod and chips or a seafood chowder in the cafe (mains $26 to $29).

STEWART ISLAND

POP 378

If you make the short but extremely rewarding trip to Stewart Island/Rakiura you'll have one up on most New Zealanders, many of whom maintain an active curiosity about the country's 'third island' without ever actually going there.

Travellers who make the effort are rewarded with a warm welcome from both the local kiwi and the local Kiwis. This is arguably the best place to spy the country's shy, feathered icon in the wild, and the close-knit community of Stewart Islanders are relaxed hosts. If you're staying on the island for just a few days, don't be too surprised if most people quickly know who you are and where you came from – especially if you mix and mingle over a beer at NZ's southernmost pub in Oban, the island's only settlement.

Stewart Island offers plenty of active adventure opportunities including kayaking, and tramping the Great Walk or other tracks in Rakiura National Park, which makes up 85% of the land area. As well as beautiful coastal and inland scenery, a major impetus for such excursions is bird life. Stewart Island/Rakiura is a bird sanctuary of international repute, and even the most amateur of spotters are likely to be distracted by the constant – and utterly glorious – squawking, singing and flitting of feathery flocks.

History

Stewart Island's Māori name is Rakiura (Glowing Skies), and you only need to catch a glimpse of a spectacular blood-red sunset or the aurora australis to see why. According

Stewart Island (North)

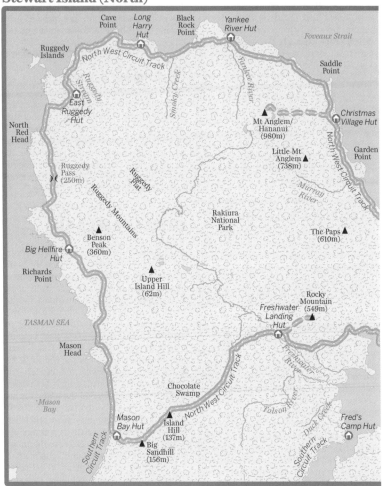

to myth, New Zealand was hauled up from the ocean by Māui, who said, 'Let us go out of sight of land, far out in the open sea, and when we have quite lost sight of land, then let the anchor be dropped'. The North Island was the fish that Māui caught, the South Island his canoe and Rakiura was the anchor – Te Punga o te Waka o Māui.

There is evidence that parts of Rakiura were occupied by moa hunters as early as the 13th century. The tīti (muttonbird or sooty shearwater) on adjacent islands were an important seasonal food source for the southern Māori.

The first European visitor was Captain Cook. Sailing around the eastern, southern and western coasts in 1770 he mistook it for the bottom end of the South Island and promptly named it South Cape. In 1809 the sealing vessel *Pegasus* circumnavigated Rakiura and named it after its first officer, William Stewart.

In June 1864 Stewart and the adjacent islets were bought from local Māori for £6000. Early industries were sealing, timber-milling, fish-curing and shipbuilding, with a short-lived gold rush towards the end of the 19th century. Today the island's economy is dependent on tourism and fishing.

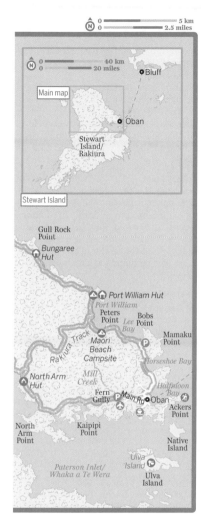

Flora & Fauna

With an absence of mustelids (ferrets, stoats and weasels) and large areas of intact forest, Stewart Island/Rakiura has one of the largest and most diverse bird populations of anywhere in NZ. Even in the streets of Oban the air resonates with birds such as tui, bellbirds and kaka, which share their island home with weka, kakariki, fernbirds, robins and Rakiura tokoeka/kiwi. There are also plenty of shore- and seabirds, including dotterels, shags, mollymawks, prions, petrels and albatross, as well as the sooty shearwater, which is seen in large numbers during breeding season. Ask locals about the evening parade of penguins on cliffs near the wharf; and *please* – don't feed the birds. It's bad for them.

Exotic animals include two species of deer, the red and the Virginia (whitetail), introduced in the early 20th century, as were brush-tailed possums, which are now numerous throughout the island and destructive to the native bush. Stewart Island/Rakiura also has NZ fur seals, NZ sea lions, elephant seals and occasionally leopard seals that visit the beaches and rocky shores.

Beech, the tree that dominates much of NZ, is absent from Stewart Island/Rakiura. The predominant lowland bush is podocarp forest, with exceptionally tall rimu, miro and totara forming the canopy. Because of mild winters, frequent rainfall and porous soil, most of the island is a lush forest, thick with vines and carpeted in deep green ferns and mosses.

⊙ Sights

★ Ulva Island
BIRD SANCTUARY

(Map p274) A tiny paradise covering only 250 hectares, Ulva Island/Te Wharawhara is a great place to see lots of native NZ birds. Established as a bird sanctuary in 1922, it remains one of Stewart Island/Rakiura's wildest corners – 'a rare taste of how NZ once was and perhaps could be again', according to DOC. The island was declared rat-free in 1997 and three years later was chosen as the site to release endangered South Island saddlebacks.

Today the air is bristling with birdsong, which can be appreciated on walking tracks in the island's northwest as detailed in *Ulva: Self-Guided Tour* ($2), available from the Rakiura National Park Visitor Centre. Many paths intersect amid beautiful stands of rimu, miro, totara and rata. Any water-taxi company will run you to the island from Golden Bay wharf, with scheduled services offered by **Ulva Island Ferry** (Map p274; ☑ 03-219 1013; return adult/child $20/10; ⊙ departs 9am, noon, 4pm, returns noon, 4pm, 6pm). To get the most out of Ulva Island, go on a tour with Ulva's Guided Walks (p277).

Rakiura Museum
MUSEUM

(Map p277; ☑ 03-219 1221; www.rakiuramuseum. co.nz; 9 Ayr St, Halfmoon Bay; adult/child $2/50c; ⊙ 10am-1.30pm Mon-Sat, noon-2pm Sun Oct-Apr, 10am-noon Mon-Fri, 10am-1.30pm Sat, noon-2pm Sun May-Sep) Historic photographs are stars of this small museum focused on local natural and human history, and featuring Māori artefacts, whaling gear and household items.

🏃 Activities

Rakiura National Park protects 85% of the island, making it a mecca for trampers and birdwatchers. There are plenty of tracks on which to explore the wilderness, ranging from short, easy trails, readily accessible on foot from Oban, to the epic North West Circuit, one of NZ's most isolated backcountry tramps.

Numerous operators offer guided tours: walking, driving, boating and by air, most focusing on wildlife with history slotted in. Independent walkers have plenty to choose from; visit Rakiura National Park Visitor Centre for details on local tramps, long and short, and huts along the way. The trails in DOC's *Stewart Island/Rakiura Short Walks* pamphlet ($2) would keep you busy for several days, and a bit less if you hire a bike from the Red Shed to fast-track the road sections. Longer tramps can also be shortened and indeed enhanced via an air hop with Stewart Island Flights (p280), which works with Seaview Water Taxis to offer the fulfilling day-long **Coast to Coast** cross-island hike.

If you haven't ever sea-fished, or just fancy it, this is the place for NZ boasts no better fishermen. Oh, and the answer to the question of swimming is definitely 'yes': yes, it is possible, and yes, you will probably freeze solid.

Short Walks

Observation Rock   WALKING
(Map p277) This short but quite sharp 15-minute climb through Oban's back streets reaches the Observation Rock lookout where there are panoramic views of Paterson Inlet, Mt Anglem and Rakeahua. The trail is clearly marked from the end of Leonard Rd, off Ayr St.

Ackers Point   WALKING
(Map p274) This three-hour return walk features an amble around the bay to a bushy track passing the historic 1835 **Stone House** at **Harrald Bay** before reaching **Ackers Point Lighthouse**, where there are wide views of Foveaux Strait and the chance to see blue penguins and a muttonbird (titi) colony.

Overnight Hikes

⭐**Rakiura Track**   TRAMPING
(www.doc.govt.nz) One of NZ's nine Great Walks, the 39km, three-day Rakiura Track is a peaceful and leisurely loop that sidles around beautiful beaches before climbing over a 250m-high forested ridge and traversing the sheltered shores of Paterson Inlet/Whaka ā Te Wera. It passes sites of historical interest and introduces many of the common sea and forest birds of the island.

SPOTTING A KIWI

Stewart Island/Rakiura is one of the few places on earth where you can spot a kiwi in the wild – and certainly the only place you're likely to see them in daylight. The bird has been around for 70 million years and is related to the now-extinct moa. Brown feathers camouflage the kiwi against its bush surroundings and a largely nocturnal lifestyle means spying one in the wild is a challenge.

As big as a barnyard chicken and estimated to number around 15,000 birds, the Stewart Island/Rakiura brown kiwi (*Apteryx australis lawryi*, also known as the tokoeka) is larger in size, longer in the beak and thicker in the legs than its northern cousins. They are also the only kiwi active during daylight hours, and birds may be seen around sunrise and sunset foraging for food in grassed areas and on beaches, where they mine sandhoppers under washed-up kelp. If you spot one, keep silent, and stay still and well away. The birds' poor eyesight and single-mindedness in searching for food will often lead them to bump right into you.

Organised tours are your best bet for a sighting. Given the island's fickle weather – with tours sometimes cancelled – allow a few nights on the island if you're desperate for an encounter. Otherwise, it's sometimes possible to spot the birds in and around Oban itself. Head to the bushy fringes of the rugby field after sundown and you might get lucky. And let's face it, it's the most perfectly apposite place for such an occurrence.

Oban

Rakiura Track is actually only 32km long, but adding in the road sections at either end bumps it up to 39km, conveniently forming a circuit from Oban. It's a well-defined loop requiring a moderate level of fitness, suitable for tramping year-round. Being a Great Walk, it has been gravelled to eliminate most of the mud for which the island is infamous.

There are two Great Walk huts ($22) en route, which need to be booked in advance, either via the DOC website or in person at the Rakiura National Park Visitor Centre. There is a limit of two consecutive nights in any one hut. Camping ($6) is permitted at the Standard campsites near the huts, and also at Māori Beach.

North West Circuit Track   TRAMPING
(www.doc.govt.nz) The North West Circuit Track is Stewart Island/Rakiura's legendary tramp, a demanding coastal epic around a remote and natural coastline featuring isolated beaches, sand dunes, birds galore and miles of mud. It's 125km, and takes nine to 11 days, although there are several options for shortening it involving boats and planes.

The track begins and ends in Oban. There are well-spaced huts along the way, all of which are Standard ($5) except for two Great Walk Huts ($22), which must be booked in advance. A North West Circuit Pass ($35) provides for a night in each of the Standard huts.

Locator beacons are advised and be sure to call into DOC for up-to-date information and to purchase the essential topographical maps. You should also register your intentions at Adventuresmart (www.adventuresmart.org.nz) as this is no easy walk in the park.

🐾 Tours

Ulva's Guided Walks   WALKING TOUR
(📞 03-219 1216; www.ulva.co.nz) Focused firmly on birding and guided by expert naturalists, these excellent half-day tours ($125; transport included) explore Ulva Island. Book at the **Stewart Island Gift Shop** (Map p277;

03-219 1453; www.stewartislandgiftshop.co.nz; 20 Main Rd, Oban; ☺10.30am-5pm, reduced hours in winter). If you're a mad-keen twitcher, look for the Birding Bonanza trip ($395) on Ulva's website.

Bravo Adventure Cruises   BIRDWATCHING
(☑03-219 1144; www.kiwispotting.co.nz) Departing around sunset, Bravo runs small-group kiwi-spotting tours ($140) on a scenic reserve reached by a 30-minute boat trip and involving gentle walking through forest and on a beach.

Rakiura Charters & Water Taxi   BOAT TOUR
(Map p277; ☑0800 725 487, 03-219 1487; www.rakiuracharters.co.nz; 10 Main Rd, Oban; adult/child from $100/70) The most popular outing on the *Rakiura Suzy* is the half-day fishing cruise that stops in at the historic Whalers' Base. Trips can be tailored to suit timing and interests, such as wildlife-spotting and tramping.

Ruggedy Range Wilderness Experience   ECOTOUR
(Map p277; ☑0274 784 433, 03-219 1066; www.ruggedyrange.com; 14 Main Rd, Oban) Nature-guide Furhana runs small-group guided walks, including 'bird and forest' trips to Ulva Island (half-/full day $135/205); overnight trips to see kiwi in the wild (from $680); and a three-day guided wilderness walk where your packs are ferried to huts along the route ($970).

Lo-Loma Fishing Charters   FISHING
(☑03-219 1141, 027 393 8362; www.loloma.co.nz) Join Squizzy Squires on the *Lo-Loma* for a fun, hand-lining fishing trip.

Phil's Sea Kayak   KAYAKING
(☑027 444 2323; www.observationrocklodge.co.nz; trips from $90) Stewart Island/Rakiura's only kayaking guide, Phil runs trips on Paterson Inlet tailored for all abilities, with sightings of wildlife along the way.

Stewart Island Experience   TOUR
(Map p277; ☑0800 000 511, 03-219 0056; www.stewartislandexperience.co.nz; 12 Elgin Tce) Runs 2½-hour Paterson Inlet cruises (adult/child $95/22), including an hour's guided walk on Ulva Island; and 1½-hour minibus tours of Oban and the surrounding bays ($45/22).

🛏 Sleeping

Finding accommodation can be difficult, especially in the low season when many places shut down. Booking ahead is highly recommended. The island has many holiday homes, which are often good value and offer the benefit of self-catering, which is especially handy if you do a spot of fishing (although many impose a two-night minimum stay or charge a surcharge for one night). Invercargill i-SITE (p267) and the Red Shed Oban Visitor Centre (p279) can help you book such rentals. See also www.stewartisland.co.nz.

Jo & Andy's B&B   B&B $
(Map p277; ☑03-219 1230; jariksem@clear.net.nz; 22 Main Rd, Oban; s $60, d & tw $90; @ 🛜) A great option for budget travellers, this cosy blue home squeezes in twin, double and single rooms that share bathroom facilities. A big breakfast of muesli, fruit and homemade bread prepares you for the most active of days. Jo is splendid company and there's hundreds of books if the weather packs up.

Bunkers Backpackers   HOSTEL $
(Map p277; ☑027 738 1796; www.bunkersbackpackers.co.nz; 15 Argyle St, Oban; dm/s/d $34/56/80; ☺closed mid-Apr–mid-Oct; 🛜) A converted wooden villa houses Stewart Island/Rakiura's best hostel option, which is somewhat squeezed but offers the benefits of a cosy lounge, sunny garden, inner village location and friendly vibe.

Bay Motel   MOTEL $$
(Map p277; ☑03-219 1119; www.baymotel.co.nz; 9 Dundee St, Oban; unit from $175; 🛜) This hillside motel offers spacious, comfortable units with lots of light and views over the harbour. Some rooms have spa baths, all have kitchens and two are wheelchair-accessible. When you've exhausted the island's bustling after-dark scene, Sky TV's on hand for on-tap entertainment.

★ Observation Rock Lodge   B&B $$$
(Map p277; ☑03-219 1444; www.observationrocklodge.co.nz; 7 Leonard St, Oban; r $395; 🛜) Secluded in bird-filled bush and angled for sea, sunset and aurora views, Annett and Phil's lodge has three stylish, luxurious rooms with private decks and a shared lounge. Guided activities, a sauna, a hot tub and Annett's gourmet dinners are included in the

deluxe package ($780) or by arrangement as additions to the standard B&B rate.

Port of Call B&B   B&B $$$
(☑03-219 1394, 027 2244 4722; www.portofcall. co.nz; Leask Bay Rd; s/d incl breakfast $320/385, cottages $175-250) Take in ocean views, relax before an open fire, or explore an isolated beach. Two cosy self-contained options are also available – The Bach, near the B&B (which is 2km southwest of Oban, near Acker's Point), and Turner Cottage in Oban. All have a two-night minimum stay, and guided walks and water-taxi trips can be arranged.

✖ Eating & Drinking

**Stewart Island Smoked
Salmon**   SEAFOOD $
(Map p277; ☑03-219 1323; www.siss.co.nz, 11 Miro Cres, Oban; 200g salmon $15) If you're a fan of freshly smoked salmon, pop up to the smokehouse to see if anyone's in. This sweet, hot-smoked fish is a tasty treat for a picnic or pasta.

**Church Hill
Restaurant & Oyster Bar**   MODERN NZ $$$
(Map p277; ☑03-219 1123; www.churchhill.co.nz; 36 Kamahi Rd, Oban; lunch $14-28, dinner $37-39; ☺noon-2.30pm Sun, 5.30pm-late daily) During summer this heritage villa's sunny deck provides hilltop views, and in cooler months you can get cosy inside beside the open fire. Big on local seafood, highlights include oysters, crayfish and salmon, prepared in refined modern style, followed by excellent desserts. Dinner bookings advisable.

South Sea Hotel   PUB
(Map p277; ☑03-219 1059; www.stewart-island. co.nz; 26 Elgin Tce, Oban; ☺7am-9pm; ☏) Welcome to one of NZ's classic pubs, complete with stellar cod and chips, beer by the quart, a reliable cafe (mains $15 to $33) and plenty of friendly banter in the public bar. Great at any time of day (or night), try to wash up for the Sunday night quiz – an unforgettable slice of island life. Basic rooms are available, too.

☆ Entertainment

Bunkhouse Theatre   CINEMA
(Map p277; ☑027 867 9381; www.bunkhousetheatre.co.nz; 10 Main Rd, Oban; tickets $10; ☺screenings 11am, 2pm & 4pm) Oban's comfy little theatre screens the quirky, cute 40-minute film *A*

Local's Tail, which provides an entertaining overview of Stewart Island/Rakiura history and culture. Jaffas and DIY popcorn.

🛍 Shopping

Glowing Sky   CLOTHING
(Map p277; ☑03-219 1518; www.glowingsky.co.nz; Elgin Tce, Oban; ☺10.30am-3.30pm Mon-Thu, 10am-5pm Fri-Sun) Founded on the island but now produced on the mainland, Glowing Sky sells T-shirts with Māori designs and merino clothing.

ℹ Information

The best place for information is the **Invercargill i-SITE** (p267) back on the mainland.

Rakiura National Park Visitor Centre (Map p277; ☑03-219 0009; www.doc.govt. nz; 15 Main Rd, Oban; ☺8am-5pm Dec-Apr, 8.30am-4.30pm Mon-Fri, 10am-3pm Sat & Sun May-Nov) Stop in to obtain information on walking tracks, as well as hut bookings and passes, topographical maps, locator beacons, books and a few tramping essentials, such as insect repellent and wool socks. Information displays introduce Stewart Island/Rakiura's flora and fauna, while a video library provides entertainment and education (a good rainy day Plan B). Register your intentions here via Adventuresmart (www.adventuresmart. org.nz).

Red Shed Oban Visitor Centre (Map p277; ☑0800 000 511, 03-219 0056; www.stewart islandexperience.co.nz; 12 Elgin Tce, Oban; ☺7.30am-6.30pm Oct-Apr, 8am-5pm May-Sep) Conveniently located next to the wharf, this Stewart Island Experience booking office can hook you up with nearly everything on and around the island, including accommodation, guided tours, boat trips, bikes, scooters and rental cars.

Stewart Island/Rakiura has no banks. In the Four Square supermarket there's an ATM, which has a mind of its own; credit cards are accepted for most activities.

ℹ Getting There & Away

Stewart Island Experience (Map p277; ☑0800 000 511, 03-212 7660; www.stewart islandexperience.co.nz; Main Wharf, Oban; adult/child one way $175/38, return $130/65) The passenger-only ferry runs between Bluff and Oban up to four times daily (reduced in winter). Book a few days ahead in summer. The crossing takes one hour and can be a rough ride. The company also runs a shuttle between Bluff and Invercargill (adult/child $24/12) with pick-ups and drop-offs in Invercargill at the i-SITE, Tuatara Backpackers and Invercargill Airport.

Vehicles can be stored in a secure car park at Bluff for an additional cost.

Stewart Island Flights (☎ 03-218 9129; www. stewartislandflights.com; Elgin Tce, Oban; adult/child one way $123/80, return $213/128) Flies between the island and Invercargill three times daily, with good standby and over-60s discounts. The price includes transfers between the island airport and its office on the Oban waterfront.

ℹ Getting Around

Roads on the island are limited to Oban and the bays surrounding it. Stewart Island Experience rents cars and scooters from the **Red Shed** (p279).

Water taxis offer pick-ups and drop-offs to Ulva Island and to remote parts of the main island – a handy service for trampers. Operators include **Aihe Eco Charters & Water Taxi** (☎ 03-219 1066; www.aihe.co.nz), **Rakiura Charters & Water Taxi** (p278) and **Stewart Island Water Taxi & Eco Guiding** (☎ 0800 469 283, 03-219 1394; www.stewartislandwatertaxi.co.nz).

Understand the South Island

New Zealand Today

New Zealand has had a bad run on the disaster front in recent years, with devastating earthquakes and mining and helicopter tragedies rattling the national psyche. But things are looking up: tourism is booming, the arts and local craft-beer scenes are effervescing, and the Kiwi rugby and cricket teams are in awesome form – there's plenty to put a smile on the country's collective dial.

Best on Film

Lord of the Rings trilogy (Sir Peter Jackson; 2001–03) Hobbits, dragons and magical rings – Tolkien's vision comes to life.

The Hobbit trilogy (Sir Peter Jackson; 2012–14) Hairy feet on the move – more eye-popping Tolkienism.

The Piano (Jane Campion; 1993) A piano and its owners arrive on a mid-19th century West Coast beach.

Whale Rider (Niki Caro; 2002) Magical tale of family and heritage on the East Coast.

Once Were Warriors (Lee Tamahori; 1994) Brutal relationship dysfunction in South Auckland.

Best in Print

The Luminaries (Eleanor Catton; 2013) Man Booker Prize winner: crime and intrigue on the West Coast goldfields.

Mister Pip (Lloyd Jones; 2007) Tumult on Bougainville, mirroring Dickens' *Great Expectations*.

Live Bodies (Maurice Gee; 1998) Post-WWII loss and redemption in New Zealand.

The 10pm Question (Kate de Goldi; 2009) Twelve-year-old Frankie grapples with life's big anxieties.

The Collected Stories of Katherine Mansfield (2006) Kathy's greatest hits.

Reasons to be Cheerful

Christchurch's recovery from the 2010 and 2011 earthquakes is ongoing, producing as much good news and bad. On one hand it is testing relationships between the citizens and government agencies, as tough decisions are made about fix-ups and pay-outs. On the other, Christchurch's recovery reinforces Kiwis' perceptions of themselves as 'battlers' with strong communities and civic pride.

Speaking of pride, New Zealanders have been flush with it of late. Following the All Blacks' success at the 2011 Rugby World Cup at home, the beloved national team beat arch-rivals Australia 34-17 in the 2015 final in London. In doing so, NZ became the first country ever to win back-to-back Rugby World Cups, capping off a remarkable four-year period in which the All Blacks lost just three (and drew one) of their 53 matches between World Cup wins.

But the depth of Kiwi sporting talent ranges beyond the rugby pitch. In 2015 the national men's cricket team, the Black Caps, made the final of the Cricket World Cup for the first time, stringing together an impressive series of test cricket results both before and afterwards. Other Kiwi sporting stars making their mark include golfing sensation Lydia Ko, who became world No 1 in 2015, aged just 17; NBA seven-footer Steven Adams (from Rotorua), currently playing with the Oklahoma City Thunder; quadruple US IndyCar champion Scott Dixon; and Valerie Adams, the greatest female shot-putter the world has ever seen (also from Rotorua – something in the water?).

On the arts front, Canadian director James Cameron has set up a rural home base near Wellington, and will create three *Avatar* sequels in the capital from 2016, bringing substantial investment and cementing NZ's reputation as a world-class film-making destination.

And at the end of a long day, Kiwi craft beer is consolidating itself at the top of the global scene. You can't go anywhere in NZ these days without stumbling across these microbrewed delights: local, flavoursome, potent and passionately marketed. The NZ wine industry is looking nervously over its shoulder, wondering where all its sav blanc drinkers have gone.

A New Flag?

At the time of writing, New Zealanders were in the throes of deciding whether or not to adopt a new national flag. What was wrong with the old one? Nothing, really, it was just fine. Except that it had a big British Union Jack in the corner, harking back to the days when NZ was a British colony.

In a post-colonial age – and in keeping with NZ's progressive way of viewing itself and its place on the planet – the suggestion was that perhaps the time had come to cut this last remaining tie with Mother England and unite, free and independent, beneath a new national flag. Of course, NZ has been united, free and independent for many decades, but changing the flag seemed to be the last symbolic gesture. Canada pulled off this manoeuvre with aplomb back in 1965 – why not New Zealand?

A public referendum to decide which of five proposed designs Kiwis preferred happened in late 2015. The winner was the 'Silver Fern Flag', replacing the Union Jack with a black-backed silver fern. Yet the second referendum, held in 2016, determined that New Zealanders preferred the old flag to the challenger. Was it a waste of time and taxpayers' money, or an important step in furthering New Zealand's independence? Time will tell.

The Trans-Pacific Partnership

In October 2015 after seven long years of negotiations, the Trans-Pacific Partnership was ratified by 12 nations with Pacific interests – Australia, Brunei, Canada, Chile, Japan, Malaysia, Mexico, New Zealand, Peru, Singapore, the United States and Vietnam – bringing into effect a broad raft of initiatives aimed at boosting relationships and economies within the region. For New Zealand, the new agreement will cut taxes and tariffs on NZ exports, which it's hoped will have a beneficial effect on exports, particularly in the dairy sector.

Critics of the TPP suggest that it will lead to increased costs of basic medicines in NZ, and that it grants too much freedom to large corporations to sidestep international and internal labour, environmental, health, financial and food-safety laws, angling for profit rather than social benefit. It remains to be seen whether the TPP will sink or swim – watch this space.

POPULATION: **4.64 MILLION**

AREA: **268,021 SQ KM**

GDP GROWTH: **2.4% (2015)**

INFLATION: **0.4% (2015)**

UNEMPLOYMENT: **6% (2015)**

if New Zealand were 100 people

65 would be European
15 would be Māori
12 would be Asian
7 would be Pacific Islanders
1 would be Other

where they live
(% of New Zealanders)

North Island — 63
South Island — 20

Australia — 10
Rest of the World — 5
Travelling — 2

population per sq km

NEW ZEALAND · AUSTRALIA · USA

≈ 3 people

History

by James Belich

New Zealand's history is not long, but it is fast. In less than a thousand years these islands have produced two new peoples: the Polynesian Māori and European New Zealanders. The latter are often known by their Māori name, 'Pākehā' (though not all like the term). NZ shares some of its history with the rest of Polynesia, and with other European settler societies, but has unique features as well. It is the similarities that make the differences so interesting, and vice versa.

Making Māori

One of New Zealand's foremost modern historians, James Belich has written a number of books on NZ history and hosted the TV documentary series *The New Zealand Wars*.

Despite persistent myths, there is no doubt that the first settlers of NZ were the Polynesian forebears of today's Māori. Beyond that, there are a lot of question marks. Exactly where in east Polynesia did they come from – the Cook Islands, Tahiti...maybe the Marquesas? When did they arrive? Did the first settlers come in one group or several? Some evidence, such as the diverse DNA of the Polynesian rats that accompanied the first settlers, suggests multiple founding voyages. On the other hand, only rats and dogs brought by the founders have survived, not the more valuable pigs and chickens. The survival of these cherished animals would have had high priority, and their failure to be successfully introduced suggests fewer voyages.

For a thorough overview of NZ history from Gondwanaland to today, visit www.history-nz.org.

NZ seems small compared with Australia, but it is bigger than Britain, and very much bigger than other Polynesian islands. Its regions vary wildly in environment and climate. Prime sites for first settlement were warm coastal gardens for the food plants brought from Polynesia (kumara or sweet potato, gourd, yam and taro); sources of workable stone for knives and adzes; and areas with abundant big game. NZ has no native land mammals apart from a few species of bat, but 'big game' is no exaggeration: the islands were home to a dozen species of moa (a large flightless bird), the largest of which weighed up to 240kg, about twice the size of an ostrich. There were also other species of flightless birds and large sea mammals such as fur seals, all unaccustomed to being hunted. For people from small Pacific islands, this was like hitting the jackpot. The

TIMELINE	AD 1000–1200	1642	1769
	Possible date of the arrival of Māori in NZ. Solid archaeological evidence points to about AD 1200, but much earlier dates have been suggested for the first human impact on the environment.	First European contact: Abel Tasman arrives on an expedition from the Dutch East Indies (Indonesia) to find the 'Great South Land'. His party leaves without landing, after a sea skirmish with Māori.	European contact recommences with visits by James Cook and Jean de Surville. Despite some violence, both manage to communicate with Māori. This time NZ's link with the outside world proves permanent.

THE MYTHICAL MORIORI

One of NZ's most persistent legends is that Māori found mainland NZ already occupied by a more peaceful and racially distinct Melanesian people, known as the Moriori, whom they exterminated. This myth has been regularly debunked by scholars since the 1920s, but somehow hangs on.

To complicate matters, there were real 'Moriori', and Māori did treat them badly. The real Moriori were the people of the Chatham Islands, a windswept group about 900km east of the mainland. They were, however, fully Polynesian, and descended from Māori – 'Moriori' was their version of the same word. Mainland Māori arrived in the Chathams in 1835, as a spin-off of the Musket Wars, killing some Moriori and enslaving the rest, but they did not exterminate them.

first settlers spread far and fast, from the top of the North Island to the bottom of the South Island within the first 100 years. High-protein diets are likely to have boosted population growth.

By about 1400, however, with big-game supply dwindling, Māori economics turned from big game to small game – forest birds and rats – and from hunting to gardening and fishing. A good living could still be made, but it required detailed local knowledge, steady effort and complex communal organisation, hence the rise of the Māori tribes. Competition for resources increased, conflict did likewise, and this led to the building of increasingly sophisticated fortifications, known as *pa*. Vestiges of *pa* earthworks can still be seen around the country (on the hilltops of Auckland, for example).

Māori had no metals and no written language (and no alcoholic drinks or drugs). But their culture and spiritual life was rich and distinctive. Below Ranginui (sky father) and Papatuanuku (earth mother) were various gods of land, forest and sea, joined by deified ancestors over time. The mischievous demigod Māui was particularly important. In legend, he vanquished the sun and fished up the North Island before meeting his death between the thighs of the goddess Hine-nui-te-pō in an attempt to conquer the human mortality embodied in her. Traditional Māori performance art, the group singing and dancing known as *kapa haka,* has mesmerising power, even for modern audiences. Visual art, notably woodcarving, is something special – 'like nothing but itself', in the words of 18th-century explorer-scientist, Sir Joseph Banks.

Rumours of late survivals of the giant moa bird abound, but none have been authenticated. So if you see a moa on your travels, photograph it – you have just made the greatest zoological discovery of the last 100 years.

Enter Europe

NZ became an official British colony in 1840, but the first authenticated contact between Māori and the outside world took place almost two centuries earlier in 1642, in Golden Bay at the top of the South Island.

1772	1790s	1818–36	1837
Marion du Fresne's French expedition arrives; it stays for some weeks at the Bay of Islands. Relations with Māori start well, but a breach of Māori *tapu* (sacred law) leads to violence.	Whaling ships and sealing gangs arrive in the country. Relations are established with Māori, with Europeans depending on the contact for essentials such as food, water and protection.	Intertribal Māori 'Musket Wars' take place: tribes acquire muskets and win bloody victories against tribes without them. The war tapers off in 1836, probably due to the equal distribution of weapons.	Possums are introduced to NZ from Australia. Brilliant.

CAPTAIN JAMES COOK

If aliens ever visit earth, they may wonder what to make of the countless obelisks, faded plaques and graffiti-covered statues of a stiff, wigged figure gazing out to sea from Alaska to Australia, from NZ to North Yorkshire, from Siberia to the South Pacific. James Cook (1728–79) explored more of the Earth's surface than anyone in history, and it's impossible to travel the Pacific without encountering the captain's image and his controversial legacy in the lands he opened to the West.

For a man who travelled so widely, and rose to such fame, Cook came from an extremely pinched and provincial background. The son of a day labourer in rural Yorkshire, he was born in a mud cottage, had little schooling, and seemed destined for farm work – and for his family's grave plot in a village churchyard. Instead, Cook went to sea as a teenager, worked his way up from coal-ship servant to naval officer, and attracted notice for his exceptional charts of Canada. But Cook remained a little-known second lieutenant until, in 1768, the Royal Navy chose him to command a daring voyage to the South Seas.

In a converted coal ship called *Endeavour*, Cook sailed to Tahiti, and then became the first European to land in New Zealand and the east coast of Australia. Though the ship almost sank after striking the Great Barrier Reef, and 40% of the crew died from disease and accidents, the *Endeavour* limped home in 1771. On a return voyage (1772–75), Cook became the first navigator to pierce the Antarctic Circle and circled the globe near its southernmost latitude, demolishing the ancient myth that a vast, populous and fertile continent surrounded the South Pole. Cook also criss-crossed the Pacific from Easter Island to Melanesia, charting dozens of islands between. Though islanders killed and cooked 10 of his sailors, the captain remained strikingly sympathetic to islanders. 'Notwithstanding they are cannibals,' he wrote, 'they are naturally of a good disposition.'

On Cook's final voyage (1776–79), in search of a northwest passage between the Atlantic and Pacific, he became the first European to visit Hawaii, and coasted America from Oregon to Alaska. Forced back by Arctic pack ice, Cook returned to Hawaii, where he was killed during a skirmish with islanders who had initially greeted him as a Polynesian god. In a single decade of discovery, Cook had filled in the map of the Pacific and, as one French navigator put it, 'left his successors with little to do but admire his exploits'.

But Cook's travels also spurred colonisation of the Pacific, and within a few decades of his death, missionaries, whalers, traders and settlers began transforming (and often devastating) island cultures. As a result, many indigenous people now revile Cook as an imperialist villain who introduced disease, dispossession and other ills to the region (hence the frequent vandalising of Cook monuments). However, as islanders revive traditional crafts and practices, from tattooing to *tapa* (traditional barkcloth), they have turned to the art and writing of Cook and his men as a resource for cultural renewal. For good and ill, a Yorkshire farm boy remains the single most significant figure in the shaping of the modern Pacific.

Tony Horwitz is a Pulitzer-winning reporter and nonfiction author. In researching Blue Latitudes *(or* Into the Blue*), Tony travelled the Pacific – 'boldly going where Captain Cook has gone before'.*

1840	1844	1858	1860–69
Starting at Waitangi in the Bay of Islands on 6 February, around 500 chiefs countrywide sign the Treaty of Waitangi to 'settle' sovereignty once and for all. NZ becomes a nominal British colony.	Young Ngāpuhi chief Hone Heke challenges British sovereignty, first by cutting down the British flag at Kororareka (now Russell), then by sacking the town itself. The ensuing Northland war continues until 1846.	The Waikato chief Te Wherowhero is installed as the first Māori King.	First and Second Taranaki wars, starting with the controversial swindling of Māori land by the government at Waitara, and continuing with outrage over the confiscation of more land as a result.

Two Dutch ships sailed from Indonesia, to search for southern land and anything valuable it might contain. The commander, Abel Tasman, was instructed to pretend to any natives he might meet 'that you are by no means eager for precious metals, so as to leave them ignorant of the value of the same'.

When Tasman's ships anchored in the bay, local Māori came out in their canoes to make the traditional challenge: friends or foes? Misunderstanding this, the Dutch challenged back, by blowing trumpets. When a boat was lowered to take a party between the two ships, it was attacked. Four crewmen were killed. Tasman sailed away and did not come back; nor did any other European for 127 years. But the Dutch did leave a name: initially 'Statenland', which was then changed to 'Nieuw Zeeland' or 'New Sealand'.

Contact between Māori and Europeans was renewed in 1769, when English and French explorers arrived, under James Cook and Jean de Surville. Relations were more sympathetic, and exploration continued, motivated by science, profit and political rivalry. Cook made two more visits between 1773 and 1777, and there were further French expeditions.

Unofficial visits, by whaling ships in the north and sealing gangs in the south, began in the 1790s. The first mission station was founded in 1814, in the Bay of Islands, and was followed by dozens of others: Anglican, Methodist and Catholic. Trade in flax and timber generated small European–Māori settlements by the 1820s. Surprisingly, the most numerous category of European visitor was probably American. New England whaling ships favoured the Bay of Islands for rest and recreation; 271 called there between 1833 and 1839 alone. To whalers, 'rest and recreation' meant sex and drink. Their favourite haunt, the little town of Kororareka (now Russell), was known to the missionaries as 'the hellhole of the Pacific'. New England visitors today might well have distant relatives among the local Māori.

One or two dozen bloody clashes dot the history of Māori–European contact before 1840 but, given the number of visits, inter-racial conflict was modest. Europeans needed Māori protection, food and labour, and Māori came to need European articles, especially muskets. Whaling stations and mission stations were linked to local Māori groups by intermarriage, which helped keep the peace. Most warfare was between Māori and Māori: the terrible intertribal 'Musket Wars' of 1818–36. Because Northland had the majority of early contact with Europe, its Ngāpuhi tribe acquired muskets first. Under their great general Hongi Hika, Ngāpuhi then raided south, winning bloody victories against tribes without muskets. Once they acquired muskets, these tribes then saw off Ngāpuhi, but also raided further south in their turn. The domino effect continued to the far south of the South Island in 1836. The missionaries

Abel Tasman named NZ 'Statenland', assuming it was connected to Staten Island near Argentina. It was subsequently named after the province of Zeeland in Tasman's native Holland.

Similarities in language between Māori and Tahitian indicate close contact in historical times. Māori is about as similar to Tahitian as Spanish is to French, despite the 4294km separating these island groups.

1861	1863–64	1868–72	1886–87
Gold discovered in Otago by Gabriel Read, an Australian prospector. As a result, the population of Otago climbs from less than 13,000 to over 30,000 in six months.	Waikato Land War. Up to 5000 Māori resist an invasion mounted by 20,000 imperial, colonial and 'friendly' Māori troops. Despite surprising successes, Māori are defeated and much land is confiscated.	East Coast war. Te Kooti, having led an escape from his prison on the Chatham Islands, leads a holy guerrilla war in the Urewera region. He finally retreats to establish the Ringatu Church.	Tuwharetoa tribe gifts the mountains of Ruapehu, Ngauruhoe and Tongariro to the government to establish what is only the world's fourth national park.

claimed that the Musket Wars then tapered off through their influence, but the restoration of the balance of power through the equal distribution of muskets was probably more important.

Europe brought such things as pigs (at last) and potatoes, which benefited Māori, while muskets and diseases had the opposite effect. The negative effects have been exaggerated, however. Europeans expected peoples like the Māori to simply fade away at contact, and some early estimates of Māori population were overly high – up to one million. Current estimates are between 85,000 and 110,000 for 1769. The Musket Wars killed perhaps 20,000, and new diseases did considerable damage, too (although NZ had the natural quarantine of distance: infected Europeans usually recovered or died during the long voyage, and smallpox, for example, which devastated indigenous North Americans, did not make it here). By 1840, Māori had been reduced to about 70,000, a decline of at least 20%. Māori bent under the weight of European contact, but they certainly did not break.

The Waitangi Treaty Grounds, where the Treaty of Waitangi was first signed in 1840, is now a tourist attraction for Kiwis and non-Kiwis alike. Each year on 6 February, Waitangi hosts treaty commemorations and protests.

Making Pākehā

By 1840, Māori tribes described local Europeans as 'their Pākehā', and valued the profit and prestige they brought. Māori wanted more of both, and concluded that accepting nominal British authority was the way to get them. At the same time, the British government was overcoming its reluctance to undertake potentially expensive intervention in NZ. It too was influenced by profit and prestige, but also by humanitarian considerations. It believed, wrongly but sincerely, that Māori could not handle the increasing scale of unofficial European contact. In 1840, the two peoples struck a deal, symbolised by the treaty first signed at Waitangi on 6 February that year. The Treaty of Waitangi now has a standing not dissimilar to that of the Constitution in the US, but is even more contested. The original problem was a discrepancy between British and Māori understandings of it. The English version promised Māori full equality as British subjects in return for complete rights of government. The Māori version also promised that Māori would retain their chieftainship, which implied local rights of government. The problem was not great at first, because the Māori version applied outside the small European settlements. But as those settlements grew, conflict brewed.

'Kaore e mau te rongo – ake, ake!' (Peace never shall be made – never, never!) War chief Rewi Maniapoto in response to government troops at the battle of Orakau, 1864

In 1840 there were only about 2000 Europeans in NZ, with the shanty town of Kororareka as the capital and biggest settlement. By 1850 six new settlements had been formed with 22,000 settlers between them. About half of these had arrived under the auspices of the New Zealand Company and its associates. The company was the brainchild of Edward Gibbon Wakefield, who also influenced the settlement of South Australia. Wakefield hoped to short-circuit the barbarous frontier phase of set-

1893	1901	1908	1914–18
NZ becomes the first country in the world to grant the vote to women, following a campaign led by Kate Sheppard, who petitioned the government for years.	New Zealand politely declines the invitation to join the new Commonwealth of Australia, but thanks for asking.	NZ physicist Ernest Rutherford is awarded the Nobel Prize in chemistry for 'splitting the atom', investigating the disintegration of elements and the chemistry of radioactive substances.	NZ's contribution to WWI is staggering: for a country of just over one million people, about 100,000 NZ men serve overseas. Some 60,000 become casualties, mostly on the Western Front in France.

tlement with 'instant civilisation', but his success was limited. From the 1850s his settlers, who included a high proportion of upper-middle-class gentlefolk, were swamped by succeeding waves of immigrants that continued to wash in until the 1880s. These people were part of the great British and Irish diaspora that also populated Australia and much of North America, but the NZ mix was distinctive. Lowland Scots settlers were more prominent in NZ than elsewhere, for example, with the possible exception of parts of Canada. NZ's Irish, even the Catholics, tended to come from the north of Ireland. NZ's English tended to come from the counties close to London. Small groups of Germans, Scandinavians and Chinese made their way in, though the last faced increasing racial prejudice from the 1880s, when the Pākehā population reached half a million.

The Ministry for Culture & Heritage's history website (www. nzhistory.net.nz) is an excellent source of info on NZ history.

LAND WARS

Five separate major conflicts made up what are now collectively known as the New Zealand Wars (also referred to as the Land Wars or Māori Wars). Starting in Northland and moving throughout the North Island, the wars had many complex causes, but *whenua* (land) was the one common factor. In all five wars, Māori fought both for and against the NZ government, on whose side stood the Imperial British Army, Australians and NZ's own Armed Constabulary. Land confiscations imposed on the Māori as punishment for involvement in these wars are still the source of conflict today, with the government struggling to finance compensation for what are now acknowledged to have been illegal seizures.

Northland War (1844–46) 'Hone Heke's War' began with the famous chopping of the flagpole at Kororareka (now Russell) and 'ended' at Ruapekapeka (south of Kawakawa). In many ways, this was almost a civil war between rival Ngāpuhi factions, with the government taking one side against the other.

First Taranaki War (1860–61) Starting in Waitara, the first Taranaki War inflamed the passions of Māori across the North Island.

Waikato War (1863–64) The largest of the five wars. Predominantly involving Kingitanga, the Waikato War was caused in part by what the government saw as a challenge to sovereignty. However, it was land, again, that was the real reason for friction. Following defeats such as Rangiriri, the Waikato people were pushed entirely from their own lands, south into what became known as the King Country.

Second Taranaki War (1865–69) Caused by Māori resistance to land confiscations stemming from the first Taranaki War, this was perhaps the war in which the Māori came closest to victory, under the brilliant, one-eyed prophet-general Titokowaru. However, once he lost the respect of his warriors (probably through an indiscretion with the wife of one of his warriors), the war, too, was lost.

East Coast War (1868–72) Te Kooti's holy guerrilla war.

1931	1935–49	1936	1939–45
A massive earthquake in Napier and Hastings kills 131 people.	First Labour government in power, under Michael Savage. This government creates NZ's pioneering version of the welfare state, and also takes some independent initiatives in foreign policy.	NZ aviatrix Jean Batten becomes the first aviator to fly solo from Britain to NZ.	NZ troops back Britain and the Allied war effort during WWII; from 1942 around 100,000 Americans arrive to protect NZ from the Japanese.

'I believe we were all glad to leave New Zealand. It is not a pleasant place. Amongst the natives there is absent that charming simplicity...and the greater part of the English are the very refuse of society.' Charles Darwin, referring to Kororareka (Russell), in 1860.

Maurice Shadbolt's *Season of the Jew* (1987) is a semifictionalised story of bloody campaigns led by warrior Te Kooti against the British in Poverty Bay in the 1860s. Te Kooti and his followers compared themselves to the Israelites cast out of Egypt. To find out more about the New Zealand Wars, visit www.newzealandwars.co.nz.

Much of the mass immigration from the 1850s to the 1870s was assisted by the provincial and central governments, which also mounted large-scale public works schemes, especially in the 1870s under Julius Vogel. In 1876 Vogel abolished the provinces on the grounds that they were hampering his development efforts. The last imperial governor with substantial power was the talented but Machiavellian George Grey, who ended his second governorship in 1868. Thereafter, the governors (governors-general from 1917) were largely just nominal heads of state; the head of government, the premier or prime minister, had more power. The central government, originally weaker than the provincial governments, the imperial governor and the Māori tribes, eventually exceeded the power of all three.

The Māori tribes did not go down without a fight, however. Indeed, their resistance was one of the most formidable ever mounted against European expansion, comparable to that of the Sioux and Seminole in the US. The first clash took place in 1843 in the Wairau Valley, now a wine-growing district. A posse of settlers set out to enforce the myth of British control, but encountered the reality of Māori control. Twenty-two settlers were killed, including Wakefield's brother, Arthur, along with about six Māori. In 1845 more serious fighting broke out in the Bay of Islands, when Hone Heke sacked a British settlement. Heke and his ally Kawiti baffled three British punitive expeditions, using a modern variant of the traditional *pa* fortification. Vestiges of these innovative earthworks can still be seen at Ruapekapeka (south of Kawakawa). Governor Grey claimed victory in the north, but few were convinced at the time. Grey had more success in the south, where he arrested the formidable Ngāti Toa chief Te Rauparaha, who until then wielded great influence on both sides of Cook Strait. Pākehā were able to swamp the few Māori living in the South Island, but the fighting of the 1840s confirmed that the North Island at that time comprised a European fringe around an independent Māori heartland.

In the 1850s settler population and aspirations grew, and fighting broke out again in 1860. The wars burned on sporadically until 1872 over much of the North Island. In the early years a Māori nationalist organisation, the King Movement, was the backbone of resistance. In later years some remarkable prophet-generals, notably Titokowaru and Te Kooti, took over. Most wars were small-scale, but the Waikato war of 1863–64 was not. This conflict, fought at the same time as the American Civil War, involved armoured steamships, ultramodern heavy artillery, telegraph and 10 proud British regular regiments. Despite the odds, Māori forces won several battles, such as that at Gate Pa, near Tauranga, in 1864. But in the end they were ground down by European numbers and resources. Māori political, though not cultural, independence ebbed away in the last decades of the 19th century. It finally expired when police invaded its last sanctuary, the Urewera Mountains, in 1916.

1948	1953	1973	1974
Maurice Scheslinger invents the Buzzy Bee, NZ's most famous children's toy.	New Zealander Edmund Hillary, with Tenzing Norgay, 'knocks the bastard off'; the pair become the first men to reach the summit of Mt Everest.	Fledgling Kiwi prog-rockers Split Enz enter a TV talent quest...finishing second to last.	Pacific Island migrants who have outstayed visas are subjected to Dawn Raids (crackdowns by immigration police) under Robert Muldoon and the National government. These raids continue until the early 1980s.

Welfare & Warfare

From the 1850s to the 1880s, despite conflict with Māori, the Pākehā economy boomed on the back of wool exports, gold rushes and massive overseas borrowing for development. The crash came in the 1880s, when NZ experienced its Long Depression. In 1890 the Liberals came to power, and stayed there until 1912, helped by a recovering economy. The Liberals were NZ's first organised political party, and the first of several governments to give NZ a reputation as 'the world's social laboratory'. NZ became the first country in the world to give women the vote in 1893, and introduced old-age pensions in 1898. The Liberals also introduced a long-lasting system of industrial arbitration, but this was not enough to prevent bitter industrial unrest in 1912-13. This happened under the conservative 'Reform' government, which had replaced the Liberals in 1912. Reform remained in power until 1928, and later transformed itself into the National Party. Renewed depression struck in 1929, and the NZ experience of it was as grim as any. The derelict little farmhouses still seen in rural areas often date from this era.

In 1935 a second reforming government took office: the First Labour government, led by Michael Joseph Savage, easily NZ's favourite Australian. For a time the Labour government was considered the most socialist government outside Soviet Russia. But, when the chips were down in Europe in 1939, Labour had little hesitation in backing Britain.

NZ had also backed Britain in the Boer War (1899–1902) and WWI (1914–18), with dramatic losses in WWI in particular. You can count the cost in almost any little NZ town: a central square or park will contain a memorial lined with names – more for WWI than WWII. Even in WWII, however, NZ did its share of fighting: 100,000 or so New Zealanders fought in Europe and the Middle East. New Zealand, a peaceful-seeming country, has spent much of its history at war. In the 19th century it fought at home; in the 20th, overseas.

Better Britons?

British visitors have long found NZ hauntingly familiar. This is not simply a matter of the British and Irish origin of most Pākehā. It also stems from the tightening of NZ links with Britain from 1882, when refrigerated cargoes of food were first shipped to London. By the 1930s, giant ships carried frozen meat, cheese and butter, as well as wool, on regular voyages taking about five weeks one way. The NZ economy adapted to the feeding of London, and cultural links were also enhanced. NZ children studied British history and literature, not their own. NZ's leading scientists and writers, such as Ernest Rutherford and Katherine Mansfield, gravitated to Britain. This tight relationship has been described as

'God's own country, but the devil's own mess.' NZ Prime Minister (1893–1906) Richard 'King Dick' Seddon, explaining the source of the country's self-proclaimed nickname 'Godzone'.

Wellington-born Nancy Wake (codenamed 'The White Mouse') led a guerrilla attack against the Nazis with a 7000-strong army. She had the multiple honours of being the Gestapo's most wanted person and the most decorated Allied servicewoman of WWII.

HISTORY WELFARE & WARFARE

1981	1985	1992	1995
Springbok rugby tour divides the nation. Many New Zealanders show a strong anti-apartheid stance by protesting the games. Other Kiwis feel that sport and politics should not mix, and support the South African tour going ahead.	*Rainbow Warrior* sunk in Auckland Harbour by French government agents to prevent the Greenpeace protest ship from making its intended voyage to Moruroa, where the French government is conducting a nuclear-testing program.	Government begins reparations for land confiscated in the Land Wars, and confirms Māori fishing rights in the 'Sealord deal'. Major settlements follow, including, in 1995, reparations for the Waikato land confiscations.	Peter Blake and Russell Coutts win the Americas Cup for NZ, sailing *Black Magic*; red socks become a matter of national pride.

'recolonial', but it is a mistake to see NZ as an exploited colony. Average living standards in NZ were normally better than in Britain, as were the welfare and lower-level education systems. New Zealanders had access to British markets and culture, and they contributed their share to the latter as equals. The list of 'British' writers, academics, scientists, military leaders, publishers and the like who were actually New Zealanders is long. Indeed, New Zealanders, especially in war and sport, sometimes saw themselves as a superior version of the British – the Better Britons of the south. The NZ–London relationship was rather like that of the American Midwest and New York.

'Recolonial' NZ prided itself, with some justice, on its affluence, equality and social harmony. But it was also conformist, even puritanical. Until the 1950s it was technically illegal for farmers to allow their cattle to mate in fields fronting public roads, for moral reasons. The 1953 Marlon Brando movie, *The Wild One,* was banned until 1977. Sunday newspapers were illegal until 1969, and full Sunday trading was not allowed until 1989. Licensed restaurants hardly existed in 1960, nor did supermarkets or TV. Notoriously, from 1917 to 1967, pubs were obliged to shut at 6pm. Yet the puritanical society of Better Britons was never the whole story. Opposition to Sunday trading stemmed, not so much from belief in the sanctity of the Sabbath, but from the belief that workers should have weekends, too. Six o'clock closing was a standing joke in rural areas, notably the marvellously idiosyncratic region of the South Island's West Coast. There was always something of a Kiwi counterculture, even before imported countercultures took root from the 1960s onward.

There were also developments in cultural nationalism, beginning in the 1930s but really flowering in the 1970s. Writers, artists and film-makers were by no means the only people who 'came out' in that era.

Coming In, Coming Out

The 'recolonial' system was shaken several times after 1935, but managed to survive until 1973, when Mother England ran off and joined the Franco–German commune now known as the EU. NZ was beginning to develop alternative markets to Britain, and alternative exports to wool, meat and dairy products. Wide-bodied jet aircraft were allowing the world and NZ to visit each other on an increasing scale. NZ had only 36,000 tourists in 1960, compared with more than two million a year now. Women were beginning to penetrate first the upper reaches of the workforce and then the political sphere. Gay people came out of the closet, despite vigorous efforts by moral conservatives to push them back in. University-educated youths were becoming more numerous and more assertive.

Scottish influence can still be felt in NZ, particularly in the south of the South Island. NZ has more Scottish pipe bands per capita than Scotland itself.

The Six o'clock Swill referred to the frantic after-work drinking at pubs when men tried to drink as much as possible from 5.05pm until the 6pm strict closing time.

2004	**2010**	**2011**	**2011**
Māori TV begins broadcasting – for the first time a channel committed to NZ content and the revitalisation of Māori language and culture hits the small screen.	A cave-in at Pike River coalmine on the South Island's West Coast kills 29 miners.	A severe earthquake strikes Christchurch, killing 185 people and badly damaging the central business district.	NZ hosts and wins the Rugby World Cup for just the second time; brave France succumbs 8-7 in the final.

From 1945, Māori experienced both a population explosion and massive urbanisation. In 1936, Māori were 17% urban and 83% rural. Fifty years later, these proportions had reversed. The immigration gates, which until 1960 were pretty much labelled 'whites only', widened, first to allow in Pacific Islanders for their labour, and then to allow in (East) Asians for their money. These transitions would have generated major socioeconomic change whatever happened in politics. But most New Zealanders associate the country's recent 'Big Shift' with the politics of 1984.

That year, NZ's third great reforming government was elected – the Fourth Labour government, led nominally by David Lange, and in fact by Roger Douglas, the Minister of Finance. This government adopted an antinuclear foreign policy, delighting the left, and a more-market economic policy, delighting the right. NZ's numerous economic controls were dismantled with breakneck speed. Middle NZ was uneasy about the antinuclear policy, which threatened NZ's ANZUS alliance with Australia and the US. But in 1985 French spies sank the antinuclear protest ship *Rainbow Warrior* in Auckland Harbour, killing one crewman. The lukewarm American condemnation of the French act brought middle NZ in behind the antinuclear policy, which became associated with national independence. Other New Zealanders were uneasy about the more-market economic policy, but failed to come up with a convincing alternative. Revelling in their new freedom, NZ investors engaged in a frenzy of speculation, and suffered even more than the rest of the world from the economic crash of 1987.

New Zealand's staunch anti-nuclear stance earned it the nickname 'The Mouse that Roared'.

The early 21st century is an interesting time for NZ. Like NZ food and wine, film and literature are flowering as never before, and the new ethnic mix is creating something very special in popular music. There are continuities, however – the pub, the sportsground, the quarter-acre section, the bush, the beach and the bach – and they too are part of the reason people like to come here. Understanding that New Zealand has a rich culture and an intriguing history, as well as a superb natural environment, will double the bang for your buck.

2013	2013	2015	2015
New Zealand becomes one of just 15 countries in the world to legally recognise same-sex marriage.	Auckland teenager Ella Yelich-O'Connor, aka Lorde, hits No 1 on the US music charts with her mesmeric, chant-like tune 'Royals'.	New Zealand's beloved All Blacks win back-to-back Rugby World Cups in England, defeating arch-rivals Australia 34-17 in the final.	Having watched NZ win its third Rugby World Cup, legendary former All Black Jonah Lomu dies aged 40 after a long battle with kidney disease.

Environment

by Vaughan Yarwood

New Zealand is a young country – its present shape is less than 10,000 years old. Having broken away from the supercontinent of Gondwanaland (which included Africa, Australia, Antarctica and South America) in a stately geological dance some 85 million years ago, it endured continual uplift and erosion, buckling and tearing, and the slow fall and rise of the sea as ice ages came and went.

The Land

Straddling the boundary of two great colliding slabs of the earth's crust – the Pacific plate and the Indian/Australian plate – to this day NZ remains the plaything of nature's strongest forces.

Vaughan Yarwood is a historian and travel writer who is widely published in New Zealand and internationally. Get a hold of his book *The History Makers: Adventures in New Zealand Biography*.

The result is one of the most varied and spectacular landscapes in the world, ranging from snow-dusted mountains and drowned glacial valleys to rainforests, dunelands and an otherworldly volcanic plateau. It is a diversity of landforms you would expect to find across an entire continent rather than a small archipelago in the South Pacific.

Evidence of NZ's tumultuous past is everywhere. The South Island's mountainous spine – the 650km-long ranges of the Southern Alps – is a product of the clash of the two plates; the result of a process of rapid lifting that, if anything, is accelerating today. Despite NZ's highest peak, Aoraki/Mt Cook, losing 10m from its summit overnight in a 1991 landslide, the Alps are on an express elevator that, without erosion and landslides, would see them reach 10 times their present height within a few million years.

On the North Island, the most impressive changes have been wrought by volcanoes. Auckland is built on an isthmus peppered by scoria cones, on many of which you can still see the earthworks of *pa* (fortified villages) built by early Māori. The city's biggest and most recent volcano, 600-year-old Rangitoto Island, is just a short ferry ride from the downtown wharves. Some 300km further south, the classically shaped cone of snowcapped Mt Taranaki overlooks tranquil dairy pastures.

But the real volcanic heartland runs through the centre of the North Island, from the restless bulk of Mt Ruapehu in Tongariro National Park, northeast through the Rotorua lake district out to NZ's most active volcano, White Island, in the Bay of Plenty. Called the Taupo Volcanic Zone, this great 250km-long rift valley – part of a volcano chain known as the 'Pacific Ring of Fire' – has been the seat of massive eruptions that have left their mark on the country physically and culturally.

Most spectacular were the eruptions from the volcano that created Lake Taupo. Considered the world's most productive volcano in terms of the amount of material ejected, Taupo last erupted 1800 years ago in a display that was the most violent anywhere on the planet within the past 5000 years.

You can experience the aftermath of volcanic destruction on a smaller scale at Te Wairoa (the Buried Village), near Rotorua on the shores of Lake Tarawera. Here, partly excavated and open to the public, lie the remains of a 19th-century Māori village overwhelmed when nearby Mt Tarawera erupted without warning. The famous Pink and White Terraces (one of several claimants to the popular title 'eighth wonder of the world') were destroyed overnight by the same upheaval.

But when nature sweeps the board clean with one hand she often rebuilds with the other: Rotorua's Waimangu Volcanic Valley, born of all that geothermal violence, is the place to go to experience the hot earth up close and personal amid geysers, silica pans, bubbling mud pools, and the world's biggest hot spring; or you can wander around Rotorua's Whakarewarewa Village, where descendants of Māori displaced by the eruption live in the middle of steaming vents and prepare food for visitors in boiling pools.

A second by-product of movement along the tectonic plate boundary is seismic activity – earthquakes. Not for nothing has New Zealand been called 'the Shaky Isles'. Most quakes only rattle the glassware, but one was indirectly responsible for creating an internationally celebrated tourist attraction: in 1931, an earthquake measuring 7.9 on the Richter scale levelled the Hawke's Bay city of Napier, causing huge damage and loss of life. Napier was rebuilt almost entirely in the then-fashionable art-deco architectural style, and walking its streets today you can relive its brash exuberance in this mecca for lovers of art deco.

However, the North Island doesn't have a monopoly on earthquakes. In September 2010 Christchurch was rocked by a magnitude 7.1 earthquake. Less than six months later, in February 2011, a magnitude 6.3 quake destroyed much of the city's historic heart and claimed 185 lives, making it the country's second-deadliest natural disaster. NZ's second city continues to be jostled by aftershocks as it builds anew.

The South Island can also see some evidence of volcanism – if the remains of the old volcanoes of Banks Peninsula weren't there to repel the sea, the vast Canterbury Plains, built from alpine sediment washed down the rivers from the Alps, would have eroded long ago.

But in the south it is the Southern Alps themselves that dominate, dictating settlement patterns, throwing down engineering challenges and offering outstanding recreational opportunities. The island's mountainous backbone also helps shape the weather, as it stands in the path of the prevailing westerly winds that roll in, moisture-laden, from the Tasman Sea. As a result, bush-clad lower slopes of the western Southern Alps are among the wettest places on earth, with an annual precipitation of some 15,000mm. Having lost its moisture, the wind then blows dry across the eastern plains towards the Pacific coast.

The North Island has a more even rainfall and is spared the temperature extremes of the South, which can plunge when a wind blows in from Antarctica. The important thing to remember, especially if you are tramping at high altitude, is that NZ has a maritime climate. This means weather can change with lightning speed, catching out the unprepared.

Native Fauna

New Zealand may be relatively young, geologically speaking, but its plants and animals go back a long way. The tuatara, for instance, an ancient reptile unique to these islands, is a Gondwanaland survivor closely related to the dinosaurs, while many of the distinctive flightless birds here (ratites) have distant African and South American cousins.

Due to its long isolation, the country became a veritable warehouse of unique and varied plants, most of which are found nowhere else. And with separation of the landmass occurring before mammals appeared on the scene, birds and insects have evolved in spectacular ways to fill the gaps.

ENVIRONMENT NATIVE FAUNA

NZ is one of the most spectacular places in the world to see geysers. Rotorua's short-lived Waimangu geyser, formed after the Mt Tarawera eruption, was once the world's largest, often gushing to a dizzying height of 400m.

Nature Guide to the New Zealand Forest by J Dawson and R Lucas is a beautifully photographed foray into the world of NZ's forests. These lush treasure houses are home to ancient species dating from the time of the dinosaurs.

The now-extinct flightless moa, the largest of which grew to 3.5m tall and weighed over 200kg, browsed open grasslands much as cattle do today (skeletons can be seen at Auckland Museum), while the smaller kiwi still ekes out a nocturnal living rummaging among forest leaf litter for insects and worms, much as small mammals do elsewhere. One of the country's most ferocious-looking insects, the mouse-sized giant weta, meanwhile, has taken on a scavenging role elsewhere filled by rodents.

As one of the last places on Earth to be colonised by humans, NZ was for millennia a safe laboratory for such risky evolutionary strategies, but with the arrival of Māori, and Europeans soon after, things went downhill fast.

ENVIRONMENTAL ISSUES IN NEW ZEALAND

Employing images of untouched landscapes, Tourism New Zealand's 100% Pure marketing campaign has been critically acclaimed, and is the envy of tourism organisations worldwide. Such portrayals of a pristine environment have, however, been repeatedly rumbled in recent years as environmentalists – and the media – place NZ's 'clean green' credentials under the microscope. Mining, offshore oil and gas exploration, pollution, biodiversity loss, conservation funding cuts, and questionable urban planning – there have been endless hooks for bad-news stories, and numerous reasons to protest.

A 2013 university study found that New Zealanders rate water quality as the country's most serious environmental issue. Their concern is well founded, with one-third of the country's 425 lakes, rivers and beaches deemed unsafe for swimming; research from diverse quarters confirms that the health of NZ's waterways is in serious decline. The primary culprit is 'dirty dairying' – cow effluent leaching into freshwater ecosystems, carrying with it high levels of nitrates, as well as bacteria and parasites such as E. coli and giardia.

The dairy industry is NZ's biggest export earner, and it continues to boom with more land being converted to dairy farming, despite clear evidence of its detrimental effects, which include the generation of half of NZ's greenhouse gas emissions. Present Parliamentary Commissioner for the Environment, Jan Wright, has referred to the matter as a 'classic economy versus environment dilemma'. NZ's dominant dairy cooperative – Fonterra – has expressed a commitment to upping its game to ensure farm management practices 'preserve New Zealand's clean green image'; some farmers are indeed cleaning up their act.

There are many other threats to water and land ecosystems, including proliferation of invasive weeds and pests, with biodiversity loss continuing in parallel. The worst offenders are possums, stoats and rats, which chomp through swaths of forest and kill wildlife, particularly birds. Controversy rages at the Department of Conservation (DOC) use of 1080 poison (sodium fluoroacetate) to control these pests, despite it being sanctioned by prominent environmental groups such as Forest & Bird and the Parliamentary Commissioner for the Environment. Vehement opposition to 1080 is expressed by such diverse camps as hunters and animal-rights activists, who cite detriments such as by-kill and the poison's transmittal into waterways.

This is just one of DOC's increasing range of duties, which includes processing applications for mining within the conservation estate. Public feeling runs high on this issue, too, as demonstrated by recent ructions over opencast coalmining on the West Coast's Denniston Plateau. DOC has increasingly found itself in the thick of it; at the same time, budget cuts and major internal restructuring have left it appearing thinner on the ground.

Meanwhile, the principle legislation governing the NZ environment – the 1991 Resource Management Act – has been undergoing controversial reforms suspected of opening the door to further exploitation of the environment. NGOs and community groups – ever-vigilant and already making major contributions to the welfare of NZ's environment – will find plenty to keep them occupied in the years to come.

Sarah Bennett & Lee Slater

Many endemic creatures, including moa and the huia, an exquisite songbird, were driven to extinction, and the vast forests were cleared for their timber and to make way for agriculture. Destruction of habitat and the introduction of exotic animals and plants have taken a terrible environmental toll and New Zealanders are now fighting a rearguard battle to save what remains.

Bird-Watching

The first Polynesian settlers found little in the way of land mammals – just two species of bat – but forests, plains and coasts alive with birds. Largely lacking the bright plumage found elsewhere, NZ's birds – like its endemic plants – have an understated beauty that does not shout for attention.

Among the most musical is the bellbird, common in both native and exotic forests everywhere except Northland, though like many birds it is more likely to be heard than seen. Its call is a series of liquid bell notes, most often sounded at dawn or dusk.

The tui, another nectar eater and the country's most beautiful songbird, is a great mimic, with an inventive repertoire that includes clicks, grunts and chuckles. Notable for the white throat feathers that stand out against its dark plumage, the tui often feeds on flax flowers in suburban gardens but is most at home in densely tangled forest ('bush' to New Zealanders).

Fantails are commonly encountered on forest trails, swooping and jinking to catch insects stirred up by passing hikers; while pukeko, elegant swamp-hens with blue plumage and bright-red beaks, are readily seen along wetland margins and even on the sides of roads nearby – be warned, they have little road sense.

If you spend any time in the South Island high country, you are likely to come up against the fearless and inquisitive kea – an uncharacteristically drab green parrot with bright-red underwings. Kea are common in the car parks of the Fox and Franz Josef Glaciers, where they hang out for food scraps or tear rubber from car windscreens.

Then there is the takahe, a rare flightless bird thought extinct until a small colony was discovered in 1948; and the equally flightless kiwi, NZ's national emblem and the nickname for New Zealanders themselves. The kiwi has a round body covered in coarse feathers, strong legs and a long, distinctive bill with nostrils at the tip for sniffing out food. It is not easy to find them in the wild, but they can be seen in simulated environments.

To get a feel for what the bush used to be like, take a trip to Tiritiri Matangi Island just north of Auckland. This regenerating island is an open sanctuary and one of the country's most successful exercises in community-assisted conservation.

Marine Mammal–Watching

Kaikoura, on the northeast coast of the South Island, is NZ's nexus of marine mammal–watching. The main attraction here is whale-watching. The sperm whale, the largest toothed whale, is pretty much a year-round resident here, and depending on the season you may also see migrating humpback whales, pilot whales, blue whales and southern right whales. Other mammals – including fur seals and dusky dolphins – are seen year-round.

Kaikoura is also a hot-spot for swimming with dolphins, with pods of up to 500 dusky dolphins commonly seen. Dolphin swimming is common elsewhere in NZ, with the animals gathering off the North Island near Whakatane, Paihia, Tauranga and in the Hauraki Gulf, and off Akaroa on the South Island's Banks Peninsula. Seal swimming also happens in Kaikoura and in Abel Tasman National Park.

B Heather and H Robertson's *Field Guide to the Birds of New Zealand* is a comprehensive guide for bird-watchers and a model of helpfulness for anyone even casually interested in the country's remarkable bird life. Another good guide is *Birds of New Zealand: Locality Guide* by Stuart Chambers.

Travellers seeking sustainable tourism operators should look for businesses accredited with Qualmark Green (www.qualmark. co.nz) or those listed at Organic Explorer (www. organicexplorer. co.nz).

But these kinds of wildlife encounters are controversial. Whale populations around the world have declined rapidly over the past 200 years: the same predictable migration habits that once made the giants easy prey for whalers nowadays make them easy targets for whale-watchers. As NZ's whale-watching industry has grown, so has concern over its impact. At the centre of the debate is the practice of swimming with whales and dolphins. While it's undoubtedly one of the more unusual experienc-

National Parks & Forest Parks

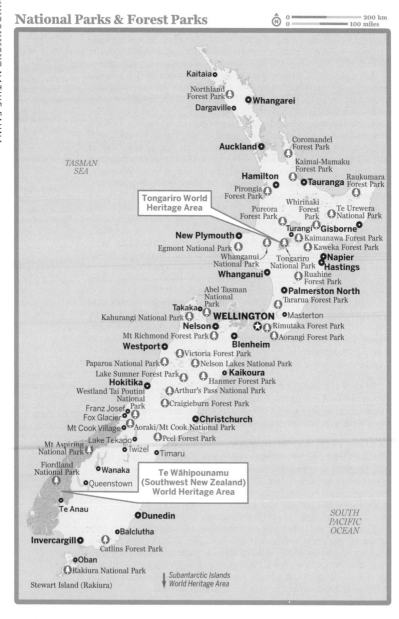

es you can have on the planet, some suggest that human interaction with these marine mammals – especially with mothers and calves, when they are at their most vulnerable – has a disruptive effect on behaviours and breeding patterns. Taking a longer view, others say that given humanity's historic propensity for slaughtering whales by the tens of thousands, it's time we gave them a little peace and quiet.

That said, if whale-watching is a bucket-list essential for you, there are few better places to do it than New Zealand. The Department of Conservation's strict guidelines and protocols ensure that all operators are licensed and monitored. Still – give yourself a few days to do it so that there is no pressure on the operator to 'chase' whales in order to keep you happy. And if you feel your whale-, dolphin- or seal-swim operator has breached the boundaries and 'hassled' the animals in any way, report them to DOC immediately.

National Parks

A third of the country – more than 50,000 sq km – is protected in environmentally important parks and reserves that embrace almost every conceivable landscape: from mangrove-fringed inlets in the north to the snow-topped volcanoes of the Central Plateau, and from the forested fastness of the Ureweras in the east to the Southern Alps' majestic mountains, glaciers and fiords. The 14 national parks and more than 25 marine reserves and parks, along with numerous forest parks, offer huge scope for wilderness experiences, ranging from climbing, snow skiing and mountain biking to tramping, kayaking and trout fishing.

Three places are World Heritage Areas: NZ's Subantarctic Islands, Tongariro National Park, and Te Wāhipounamu (Southwest New Zealand), an amalgam of several national parks in southwest NZ that boast the world's finest surviving Gondwanaland plants and animals in their natural habitats.

Access to the country's wild places is relatively straightforward, though huts on walking tracks require passes and may need to be booked in advance. In practical terms, there is little difference for travellers between a national park and a forest park, though dogs are not allowed in national parks without a permit. Camping is possible in all parks, but may be restricted to dedicated camping grounds – check with DOC first.

The Department of Conservation website (www. doc.govt.nz) has useful information on the country's national parks, tracks and walkways. It also lists backcountry huts and campsites.

Māori Culture

by John Huria

'Māori' once just meant 'common' or 'everyday', but now it means...let's just begin by saying that there is a lot of 'then' and a lot of 'now' in the Māori world. Sometimes the cultural present follows on from the past quite seamlessly; sometimes things have changed hugely; sometimes we just want to look to the future.

John Huria (Ngāi Tahu, Muaūpoko) has an editorial, research and writing background with a focus on Māori writing and culture. He was senior editor for Māori publishing company Huia (NZ) and now runs an editorial and publishing services company, Ahi Text Solutions Ltd (www.ahitext solutions.co.nz).

Māori today are a diverse people. Some are engaged with traditional cultural networks and pursuits; others are occupied with adapting tradition and placing it into a dialogue with globalising culture. The Māori concept of *whanaungatanga* – family relationships – is central to the culture: families spread out from the *whānau* (extended family) to the *hapū* (subtribe) and *iwi* (tribe) and even, in a sense, beyond the human world and into the natural and spiritual worlds.

Māori are New Zealand's *tangata whenua* (people of the land), and the Māori relationship with the land has developed over hundreds of years of occupation. Once a predominantly rural people, many Māori now live in urban centres, away from their traditional home base. But it's still common practice in formal settings to introduce oneself by referring to home: an ancestral mountain, river, sea or lake, or an ancestor. There's no place like home, but it's good to be away as well.

If you're looking for a Māori experience in NZ you'll find it – in performance, in conversation, in an art gallery, on a tour...

Māori Then

Some three millennia ago people began moving eastward into the Pacific, sailing against the prevailing winds and currents (hard to go out, easier to return safely). Some stopped at Tonga and Samoa, and others settled the small central East Polynesian tropical islands.

Kupe's passage is marked around NZ: he left his sails (Nga Ra o Kupe) near Cape Palliser as triangular landforms; he named the two islands in Wellington Harbour Matiu and Makoro after his daughters; his blood stains the red rocks of Wellington's south coast.

The Māori colonisation of Aotearoa began from an original homeland known to Māori as Hawaiki. Skilled navigators and sailors travelled across the Pacific, using many navigational tools – currents, winds, stars, birds and wave patterns – to guide their large, double-hulled ocean-going craft to a new land. The first of many was the great navigator Kupe, who arrived, the story goes, chasing an octopus named Muturangi. But the distinction of giving NZ its well-known Māori name – Aotearoa – goes to his wife, Kuramarotini, who cried out, '*He ao, he ao tea, he ao tea roa!*' (A cloud, a white cloud, a long white cloud!).

Kupe and his crew journeyed around the land, and many places around Cook Strait (between the North and South Islands) and the Hokianga in Northland still bear the names that the crew gave them and the marks of their passage. Kupe returned to Hawaiki, leaving from (and naming) Northland's Hokianga. He gave other seafarers valuable navigational information. And then the great *waka* (ocean-going craft) began to arrive.

HOW THE WORLD BEGAN

In the Māori story of creation, first there was the void, then the night, then Ranginui (sky father) and Papatuanuku (earth mother) came into being, embracing with their children nurtured between them. But nurturing became something else. Their children were stifled in the darkness of their embrace. Unable to stretch out to their full dimensions and struggling to see clearly in the darkness, their children tried to separate them. Tāwhirimātea, the god of winds, raged against them; Tūmatauenga, the god of war, assaulted them. Each god child in turn tried to separate them, but still Rangi and Papa pressed against each other. And then Tāne Mahuta, god of the great forests and of humanity, placed his feet against his father and his back against his mother and slowly, inexorably, began to move them apart. Then came the world of light, of demigods and humanity.

In this world of light Māui, the demigod ancestor, was cast out to sea at birth and was found floating in his mother's topknot. He was a shape-shifter, becoming a pigeon or a dog or an eel if it suited his purposes. He stole fire from the gods. Using his grandmother's jawbone, he bashed the sun so that it could only limp slowly across the sky, so that people would have enough time during the day to get things done (if only he would do it again!). Using the South Island as a canoe, he used the jawbone as a hook to fish up Te Ika-a-Māui (the fish of Māui) – the North Island. And, finally, he met his end trying to defeat death itself. The goddess of death, Hine-nui-te-pō, had obsidian teeth in her vagina (obsidian is a volcanic glass that takes a razor edge when chipped). Māui attempted to reverse birth (and hence defeat death) by crawling into her birth canal to reach her heart as she slept. A small bird – a fantail – laughed at the absurd sight. Hine-nui-te-pō awoke, and crushed Māui between her thighs. Death one, humanity nil.

The *waka* that the first settlers arrived on, and their landing places, are immortalised in tribal histories. Well-known *waka* include *Tākitimu, Kurahaupō, Te Arawa, Mataatua, Tainui, Aotea* and *Tokomaru*. There are many others. Māori trace their genealogies back to those who arrived on the *waka* (and further back as well).

What would it have been like making the transition from small tropical islands to a much larger, cooler land mass? Goodbye breadfruit, coconuts, paper mulberry; hello moa, fernroot, flax – and immense space (relatively speaking). NZ has over 15,000km of coastline. Rarotonga, by way of contrast, has a little over 30km. There was land, lots of it, and a flora and fauna that had developed more or less separately from the rest of the world for 80 million years. There was an untouched, massive fishery. There were great seaside mammalian convenience stores – seals and sea lions – as well as a fabulous array of birds.

The early settlers went on the move, pulled by love, by trade opportunities and greater resources; pushed by disputes and threats to security. When they settled, Māori established *mana whenua* (regional authority), whether by military campaigns, or by the peaceful methods of intermarriage and diplomacy. Looking over tribal history it's possible to see the many alliances, absorptions and extinctions that went on.

Histories were carried by the voice, in stories, songs and chants. Great stress was placed on accurate learning – after all, in an oral culture where people are the libraries, the past is always a generation or two away from oblivion.

Māori lived in *kainga* (small villages), which often had associated gardens. Housing was quite cosy by modern standards – often it was

Māori legends are all around you as you tour NZ: Maui's *waka* became today's Southern Alps; a *taniwha* formed Lake Waikaremoana in its death throes; and a rejected Mt Taranaki walked into exile from the central North Island mountain group, carving the Whanganui River.

hard to stand upright while inside. From time to time people would leave their home base and go to harvest seasonal foods. When peaceful life was interrupted by conflict, the people would withdraw to *pa* (fortified dwelling places).

And then Europeans began to arrive.

Māori Today

Today's culture is marked by new developments in the arts, business, sport and politics. Many historical grievances still stand, but some *iwi* (Ngāi Tahu and Tainui, for example) have settled historical grievances and are major forces in the NZ economy. Māori have also addressed the decline in Māori language use by establishing *kohanga reo, kura kau-papa Māori* and *wananga* (Māori-medium preschools, schools and universities). There is now a generation of people who speak Māori as a first language. There is a network of Māori radio stations, and Māori TV attracts a committed viewership. A recently revived Māori event is becoming more and more prominent – Matariki, or Māori New Year. The constellation Matariki is also known as the Pleiades. It begins to rise above the horizon in late May or early June and its appearance traditionally signals a time for learning, planning and preparing as well as singing, dancing and celebrating. Watch out for talks and lectures, concerts, dinners, and even formal balls.

The best way to learn about the relationship between the land and the *tangata whenua* (people of the land) is to get out there and start talking with Māori.

Religion

Christian churches and denominations are important in the Māori world: televangelists, mainstream churches for regular and occasional worship, and two major Māori churches (Ringatu and Ratana) – we've got it all.

But in the (non-Judeo-Christian) beginning there were the *atua Māori,* the Māori gods, and for many Māori the gods are a vital and relevant force still. It is common to greet the earth mother and sky father when speaking formally at a *marae* (meeting-house complex). The gods are represented in art and carving, sung of in *waiata* (songs), invoked through *karakia* (prayer and incantation) when a meeting house is opened, when a *waka* is launched, even (more simply) when a meal is served. They are spoken of on the *marae* and in wider Māori contexts. The traditional Māori creation story is well known and widely celebrated.

The Arts

There are many collections of Māori *taonga* (treasures) around the country. Some of the largest and most comprehensive are at Wellington's Te Papa Museum and the Auckland Museum. Canterbury Museum (p137) in Christchurch also has a good collection, and Hokitika Museum (p116) has an exhibition showing the story of *pounamu* (nephrite jade, or greenstone).

You can check out a map that shows *iwi* distribution and a good list of *iwi* websites on Wikipedia (www.wikipedia.org/wiki/list_of_iwi).

You can stay up to date with what's happening in the Māori arts by reading *Mana* magazine (available from most newsagents), listening to *iwi* stations (www.irirangi.net) or weekly podcasts from Radio New Zealand (www.radionz.co.nz). Māori TV also has regular features on the Māori arts – check out www.maoritelevision.com.

Māori TV went to air in 2004, an emotional time for many Māori who could at last see their culture, their concerns and their language in a mass medium. Over 90% of content is NZ made, and programs are in both Māori and English: they're subtitled and accessible to everyone. If you want to really get a feel for the rhythm and meter of spoken Māori from the comfort of your own chair, switch to Te Reo (www.maori television.com/tv/te-reo-channel), a Māori-language-only channel.

Ta Moko

Ta Moko is the Māori art of tattoo, traditionally worn by men on their faces, thighs and buttocks, and by women on their chins and lips. *Moko* were permanent grooves tapped into the skin using pigment (made from burnt caterpillar or kauri gum soot) and bone chisels (fine, sharp combs for broad work, and straight blades for detailed work). Museums in the major centres – Auckland Museum, Te Papa (Wellington) and Canterbury Museum (p137) in Christchurch – all display traditional implements for *ta moko*.

The modern tattooist's gun is common now, but bone chisels are coming back into use for Māori who want to reconnect with tradition. Since the general renaissance in Māori culture in the 1960s, many artists have taken up *ta moko* and now many Māori wear *moko* with quiet pride and humility.

Can visitors get involved, or even get some work done? The term *kirituhi* (skin inscriptions) has arisen to describe Māori-motif-inspired modern tattoos that non-Māori can wear.

See Ngahuia Te Awekotuku's book *Mau Moko: The World of Maori Tattoo* (2007) for the big picture, with powerful, beautiful images and an incisive commentary.

Carving

Traditional Māori carving, with its intricate detailing and curved lines, can transport the viewer. It's quite amazing to consider that it was done with stone tools, themselves painstakingly made, until the advent of iron (nails suddenly became very popular).

Some major traditional forms are *waka* (canoes), *pataka* (storage buildings), and *wharenui* (meeting houses). You can see sublime examples of traditional carving at Te Papa in Wellington, and at the following:

Auckland Museum Māori Court

Hells Gate Carver in action every day; near Rotorua

Otago Museum (p193) Nice old *waka* and *whare runanga* (meeting house) carvings; Dunedin

Putiki Church Interior covered in carvings and *tukutuku* (wall panels); Whanganui

Taupo Museum Carved meeting house

Te Manawa Museum with a Māori focus; Palmerston North

Waikato Museum Beautifully carved *waka taua* (war canoe); Hamilton

Wairakei Terraces Carved meeting house; Taupo

Waitangi Treaty Grounds *Whare runanga* and *waka taua*

Whakarewarewa Thermal Village The 'living village' – carving, other arts, meeting house and performance; Rotorua

Whanganui Regional Museum Wonderful carved *waka*

The apex of carving today is the *whare whakairo* (carved meeting house). A commissioning group relates its history and ancestral stories to a carver, who then draws (sometimes quite loosely) on traditional motifs to interpret or embody the stories and ancestors in wood or composite fibreboard.

Rongomaraeroa Marae by artist Cliff Whiting, at Te Papa in Wellington, is a colourful example of a contemporary re-imagining of a traditional art form. The biggest change in carving (as with most traditional arts) has been in the use of new mediums and tools. Rangi Kipa uses a

VISITING MARAE

As you travel around NZ, you will see many *marae* complexes. Often *marae* are owned by a descent group. They are also owned by urban Māori groups, schools, universities and church groups, and they should only be visited by arrangement with the owners. Some *marae* that may be visited include: **Huria Marae** (📞07-578 7838; www.ngaitamarawaho. co.nz/marae; Te Kaponga St, Judea) **FREE** in Tauranga; **Koriniti Marae** (📞06-345 0303, 021 0292 4785; Koriniti Pa Rd; ⊙9am-5pm) **FREE** on the Whanganui River Rd; **Te Manuka Tutahi Marae** in Whakatane; and the *marae* at **Te Papa museum** in Wellington.

Marae complexes include a *wharenui* (meeting house), which often embodies an ancestor. Its ridge is the backbone, the rafters are ribs, and it shelters the descendants. There is a clear space in front of the *wharenui* (ie the *marae atea*). Sometimes there are other buildings: a *wharekai* (dining hall); a toilet and shower block; perhaps even classrooms, play equipment and the like.

Hui (gatherings) are held at *marae*. Issues are discussed, classes conducted, milestones celebrated and the dead farewelled. Te reo Māori (the Māori language) is prominent, and sometimes the only language used.

Visitors sleep in the meeting house if a *hui* goes on for longer than a day. Mattresses are placed on the floor, someone may bring a guitar, and stories and jokes always go down well as the evening stretches out...

The Powhiri

If you visit a *marae* as part of an organised group, you'll be welcomed in a *powhiri*. The more common ones are outlined here.

There may be a *wero* (challenge). Using *taiaha* (quarter-staff) moves a warrior will approach the visitors and place a baton on the ground for a visitor to pick up.

There is a *karanga* (ceremonial call). A woman from the host group calls to the visitors and a woman from the visitors responds. Their long, high, falling calls begin to overlap and interweave and the visiting group walks on to the *marae atea*. It is then time for *whaikōrero* (speechmaking). The hosts welcome the visitors, the visitors respond. Speeches are capped off by a *waiata* (song), and the visitors' speaker places a *koha* (gift, usually an envelope of cash) on the *marae*. The hosts then invite the visitors to *hariru* (shake hands) and *hongi*. Visitors and hosts are now united and will share light refreshments or a meal.

The Hongi

Press forehead and nose together firmly, shake hands, and perhaps offer a greeting such as *'Kia ora'* or *'Tēnā koe'*. Some prefer one press (for two or three seconds, or longer), others prefer two shorter (press, release, press). Men and women sometimes kiss on one cheek. Some people mistakenly think the *hongi* is a pressing of noses only (awkward to aim!) or the rubbing of noses (even more awkward).

Tapu

Tapu (spiritual restrictions) and *mana* (power and prestige) are taken seriously in the Māori world. Sit on chairs or seating provided (never on tables), and walk around people, not over them. The *powhiri* is *tapu,* and mixing food and *tapu* is right up there on the offence-o-meter. Do eat and drink when invited to do so by your hosts. You needn't worry about starvation: an important Māori value is *manaakitanga* (kindness).

Depending on area, the *powhiri* has gender roles: women *karanga* (call), men *whaikōrero* (orate); women lead the way on to the *marae,* men sit on the *paepae* (the speakers' bench at the front). In a modern context, the debate around these roles continues.

synthetic polymer called Corian to make his *hei tiki,* the same stuff that is used to make kitchen benchtops. You can check out his gallery at www. rangikipa.com.

Weaving

Weaving was an essential art that provided clothing, nets and cordage, footwear for rough country travel, mats to cover earthen floors, and *kete* (bags) to carry stuff in. Many woven items are beautiful as well as practical. Some were major works – *korowai* (cloaks) could take years to finish. Woven predominantly with flax and bird feathers, they are worn now on ceremonial occasions – a stunning sight.

Working with natural materials for the greater good of the people involved getting things right by maintaining the supply of raw material and ensuring that it worked as it was meant to. Protocols were necessary, and women were dedicated to weaving under the aegis of the gods. Today, tradition is greatly respected, but not all traditions are necessarily followed.

Flax was (and still is) the preferred medium for weaving. To get a strong fibre from flax leaves, weavers scraped away the leaves' flesh with a mussel shell, then pounded until it was soft, dyed it, then dried it. But contemporary weavers are using everything in their work: raffia, copper wire, rubber – even polar fleece and garden hoses!

The best way to experience weaving is to contact one of the many weavers running workshops. By learning the art, you'll appreciate the examples of weaving in museums even more. And if you want your own? Woven *kete* and backpacks have become fashion accessories and are on sale in most cities. Weaving is also found in dealer art galleries around the country.

Read Hirini Moko Mead's *Tikanga Māori,* Pat and Hiwi Tauroa's *Visiting a Marae,* and Anne Salmond's *Hui* for detailed information on Māori customs.

Haka

Experiencing *haka* can get the adrenaline flowing, as it did for one Pākehā observer in 1929 who thought of dark Satanic mills: 'They looked like fiends from hell wound up by machinery'. *Haka* can be awe-inspiring; they can also be uplifting. The *haka* is not only a war dance – it is used to welcome visitors, honour achievement, express identity or to put forth very strong opinions.

Haka involve chanted words, vigorous body movements, and *pukana* (when performers distort their faces, eyes bulging with the whites showing, perhaps with tongue extended).

The well-known *haka* 'Ka Mate', performed by the All Blacks before rugby test matches, is credited to the cunning fighting chief Te Rauparaha. It celebrates his escape from death. Chased by enemies, he hid himself in a food pit. After they had left, a friendly chief named Te Whareangi (the 'hairy man' referred to in the *haka*), let him out; he climbed out into the sunshine and performed 'Ka Mate'.

You can experience *haka* at various cultural performances, including at Mitai Māori Village, Tamaki Māori Village, Te Puia and Whakarewarewa Thermal Village in Rotorua; Ko Tane (p143) at Willowbank in Christchurch; and Māori Tours (p73) in Kaikoura.

But the best displays of *haka* are at the national Te Matatini National Kapa Haka Festival (www.tematatini.co.nz), when NZ's top groups compete. It's held every two years (in odd-numbered years).

Contemporary Theatre

The 1970s saw the emergence of many Māori playwrights and plays, and theatre is a strong area of the Māori arts today. Māori theatre drew heavily on the traditions of the *marae*. Instead of dimming the lights and immediately beginning the performance, many Māori theatre groups began with a stylised *powhiri*, had space for audience members to respond to the play, and ended with a *karakia* or a farewell.

Taki Rua is an independent producer of Māori work for both children and adults and has been in existence for over 25 years. As well as staging its shows in the major centres, it tours most of its work – check out its website (www.takirua.co.nz) for the current offerings. Māori drama is also often showcased at the professional theatres in the main centres as well as the biennial New Zealand Festival. Hone Kouka and Briar Grace-Smith (both have published playscripts available) have toured their works around NZ and to festivals in the UK.

For information on Māori arts today, check out Toi Māori at www.maoriart.org.nz.

Contemporary Dance

Contemporary Māori dance often takes its inspiration from *kapa haka* (cultural dance) and traditional Māori imagery. The exploration of pre-European life also provides inspiration. For example, a Māori choreographer, Moss Patterson, used *kokowai* (a body-adorning paste made from reddish clay and shark oil) as the basis of his most recent piece of the same name.

NZ's leading specifically Māori dance company is the Atamira Dance Collective (www.atamiradance.co.nz), which has been producing critically acclaimed, beautiful and challenging work since 2000. If that sounds too earnest, another choreographer to watch out for is Mika Torotoro, who happily blends *kapa haka*, drag, opera, ballet and disco. You can check out clips of his work at www.mika.co.nz.

Māori Film-Making

Although there had already been successful Māori documentaries (*Patu!* and the *Tangata Whenua* series are brilliant, and available from some urban video stores), it wasn't until 1987 that NZ had its first fictional feature-length movie by a Māori director, with Barry Barclay's *Ngati*. Mereta Mita was the first Māori woman to direct a fiction feature, with *Mauri* (1988). Both Mita and Barclay had highly political aims and ways of working, which involved a lengthy pre-production phase, during which they would consult with and seek direction from their *kaumātua* (elders). Films with significant Māori participation or control include the harrowing *Once Were Warriors* and the uplifting *Whale Rider*. Oscar-shortlisted Taika Waititi, of Te Whanau-a-Apanui descent, wrote and directed *Eagle vs Shark* and *Boy*.

The New Zealand Film Archive (www.filmarchive.org.nz) is a great place to experience Māori film, with most showings being either free or relatively inexpensive. It has offices in Auckland and Wellington.

Māori Writing

There are many novels and collections of short stories by Māori writers, and personal taste will govern your choices. How about approaching Māori writing regionally? Read Patricia Grace (*Potiki, Cousins, Dogside Story, Tu*) around Wellington, and maybe Witi Ihimaera (*Pounamu, Pounamu; The Matriarch; Bulibasha; The Whale Rider*) on the North Island's East Coast. Keri Hulme (*The Bone People, Stonefish*) and the South Island go together like a mass of whitebait bound in a frying pan by a single egg (ie very well). Read Alan Duff *(Once Were Warriors)* anywhere, but only if you want to be saddened, even shocked. Definitely take James George *(Hummingbird, Ocean Roads)* with you to Auckland's West Coast beaches and Northland's Ninety Mile Beach. Paula Morris *(Queen of Beauty, Hibiscus Coast, Trendy but Casual)* and Kelly Ana Morey *(Bloom, Grace Is Gone)* – hmm, Auckland and beyond? If poetry appeals you can't go past the giant of Māori poetry in English, the late, lamented Hone Tuwhare *(Deep River Talk: Collected Poems)*. Famously sounding like he's at church and in the pub at the same time, you *can* take him anywhere.

Arts & Music

It took a hundred years for post-colonial New Zealand to develop its own distinctive artistic identity. In the first half of the 20th century it was writers and visual artists who led the charge. By the 1970s NZ pub rockers had conquered Australia, while in the 1980s, indie-music obsessives the world over hooked into Dunedin's weird and wonderful alternative scene. However, it took the success of the film industry in the 1990s to catapult the nation's creativity into the global consciousness.

Literature

In 2013 New Zealanders rejoiced to hear that 28-year-old Eleanor Catton had become only the second NZ writer to ever win the Man Booker Prize, arguably the world's most prestigious award for literature. Lloyd Jones had come close in 2007 when his novel *Mister Pip* was shortlisted, but it had been a long wait between drinks since Keri Hulme took the prize in 1985. Interestingly, both Catton's epic historical novel *The Luminaries* and Hulme's haunting *The Bone People* were set on the numinous West Coast of the South Island – both books capturing something of the raw and mysterious essence of the landscape.

Catton and Hulme continue in a proud line of NZ women writers, starting in the early 20th century with Katherine Mansfield. Mansfield's work began a Kiwi tradition in short fiction, and for years the standard was carried by novelist Janet Frame, whose dramatic life was depicted in Jane Campion's film of her autobiography, *An Angel at My Table*. Frame's novel *The Carpathians* won the Commonwealth Writers' Prize in 1989.

Less recognised internationally, Maurice Gee has gained the nation's annual top fiction gong six times, most recently with *Blindsight* (2005). His much-loved children's novel *Under the Mountain* (1979) was made into a seminal NZ TV series in 1981, and then a major motion picture in 2009. In 2004 the adaptation of another of his novels, *In My Father's Den* (1972), won major awards at international film festivals and is one of the country's highest-grossing films.

Maurice is an auspicious name for NZ writers, with the late Maurice Shadbolt achieving much acclaim for his many novels, particularly those set during the NZ Wars Try *Season of the Jew* (1987) or *The House of Strife* (1993).

MĀORI VOICES IN PRINT

Some of the most interesting and enjoyable NZ fiction voices belong to Māori writers, with Booker winner Keri Hulme leading the way. Witi Ihimaera's novels give a wonderful insight into small-town Māori life on the East Coast – especially *Bulibasha* (1994) and *The Whale Rider* (1987), which was made into an acclaimed film. Patricia Grace's work is similarly filled with exquisitely told stories of rural *marae*-centred life: try *Mutuwhenua* (1978), *Potiki* (1986), *Dogside Story* (2001) or *Tu* (2004). *Chappy* (2015) is Grace's expansive tale of a prodigal son returning to NZ to untangle his cross-cultural heritage.

MIDDLE-EARTH TOURISM

If you are one of those travellers inspired to come to Aotearoa by the scenery of the *Lord of the Rings (LOTR)* movies, you won't be disappointed. Jackson's decision to film in NZ wasn't mere patriotism. Nowhere else on earth will you find such wildly varied, unspoiled landscapes – not to mention poorly paid actors.

You will doubtless recognise some places from the films: for example, Hobbiton (near Matamata), Mt Doom (instantly recognisable as towering Ngauruhoe) and the Misty Mountains (the South Island's Southern Alps). The visitor information centres in Wellington, Twizel or Queenstown should be able to direct you to local *LOTR* sites of interest. If you're serious about finding the exact spots where scenes were filmed, buy a copy of Ian Brodie's nerdtastic *The Lord of the Rings: Location Guidebook,* which includes instructions, and even GPS coordinates, for finding all the important places.

Cinema & TV

If you first got interested in New Zealand by watching it on the silver screen, you're in good company. Sir Peter Jackson's NZ-made *The Lord of the Rings* and *The Hobbit* trilogies were the best thing to happen to NZ tourism since Captain Cook.

Yet NZ cinema is hardly ever easygoing. In his BBC-funded documentary, *Cinema of Unease,* NZ actor Sam Neill described the country's film industry as producing bleak, haunted work. One need only watch Lee Tamahori's harrowing *Once Were Warriors* (1994) to see what he means.

The Listener's former film critic, Philip Matthews, made a slightly more upbeat observation: 'Between (Niki Caro's) *Whale Rider,* (Christine Jeffs') *Rain* and *The Lord of the Rings,* you can extract the qualities that our best films possess. Beyond slick technical accomplishment, all share a kind of land-mysticism, an innately supernatural sensibility'.

You could add to this list Jane Campion's *The Piano* (1993) and *Top of the Lake* (2013), Brad McGann's *In My Father's Den* (2004) and Jackson's *Heavenly Creatures* (1994) – all of which use magically lush scenery to couch disturbing violence. It's a land-mysticism constantly bordering on the creepy.

Even when Kiwis do humour it's as resolutely black as their rugby jerseys; check out Jackson's early splatter-fests and Taika Waititi's *Boy* (2010). Exporting NZ comedy hasn't been easy, yet the HBO-produced TV musical parody *Flight of the Conchords* – featuring a mumbling, bumbling Kiwi folk-singing duo trying to get a break in New York – found surprising international success.

It's the Polynesian giggle-factor that seems likeliest to break down the bleak house of NZ cinema, with feel-good-through-and-through *Sione's Wedding* (2006) netting the second-biggest local takings of any NZ film.

New Zealanders have gone from never seeing themselves in international cinema to having whole cloned armies of Temuera Morrisons invading the universe in *Star Wars.* Familiar faces such as Cliff Curtis and Karl Urban seem to constantly pop up playing Mexican or Russian gangsters in action movies. Many of them got their start in long-running soap opera *Shortland St* (7pm weekdays, TV2).

Visual Arts

The NZ 'can do' attitude extends to the visual arts. If you're visiting a local's home don't be surprised to find one of the owner's paintings on the wall or one of their mate's sculptures in the back garden, pieced together out of bits of shell, driftwood and a length of the magical 'number 8 wire'.

This is symptomatic of a flourishing local art and crafts scene cultivated by lively tertiary courses churning out traditional carvers and

Other than 2003's winner *The Return of the King, The Piano* is the only NZ movie to be nominated for a Best Picture Oscar. Jane Campion was the first Kiwi nominated as Best Director and Peter Jackson the first to win it.

The only Kiwi actors to have won an Oscar are Anna Paquin (for *The Piano*) and Russell Crowe (for *Gladiator*). Paquin was born in Canada but moved to NZ when she was four, while Crowe moved from NZ to Australia at the same age.

weavers, jewellery-makers, multimedia boffins, and moulders of metal and glass. The larger cities have excellent dealer galleries representing interesting local artists working across all media.

Not all the best galleries are in Auckland or Wellington. The amazing new Len Lye Centre – home to the legacy of sculptor and film-maker Len Lye – is worth a visit to New Plymouth in itself, and Gore's Eastern Southland Gallery (p266) has an important and growing collection.

Traditional Māori art has a distinctive visual style with well-developed motifs that have been embraced by NZ artists of every race. In the painting medium, these include the cool modernism of the work of Gordon Walters and the more controversial pop-art approach of Dick Frizzell's *Tiki* series. Likewise, Pacific Island themes are common, particularly in Auckland. An example is the work of Niuean-born, Auckland-raised John Pule.

It should not be surprising that in a nation so defined by its natural environment, landscape painting constituted the first post-European body of art. John Gully and Petrus van der Velden were among those to arrive and paint memorable (if sometimes overdramatised) depictions of the land.

A little later, Charles Frederick Goldie painted a series of compelling, realist portraits of Māori, who were feared to be a dying race. Debate over the political propriety of Goldie's work raged for years, but its value is widely accepted now: not least because Māori themselves generally acknowledge and value them as ancestral representations.

From the 1930s NZ art took a more modern direction and produced some of the country's most celebrated artists, including Rita Angus, Toss Woollaston and Colin McCahon. McCahon is widely regarded to have been the country's most important artist. His paintings might seem inscrutable, even forbidding, but even where McCahon lurched into Catholic mysticism or quoted screeds from the Bible, his spirituality was rooted in geography. His bleak, brooding landscapes evoke the sheer power of New Zealand's terrain.

Music

NZ music began with the *waiata* (singing) developed by Māori following their arrival in the country. The main musical instruments were wind instruments made of bone or wood, the most well known of which is the *nguru* (also known as the 'nose flute'), while percussion was provided by chest- and thigh-slapping. These days, the liveliest place to see Māori music being performed is at *kapa haka* competitions in which groups compete with their own routines of traditional song and dance: track down the Te Matatini National Kapa Haka Festival, which happens in March in odd-numbered years at different venues (it's at Kahungunu in Hawke's Bay in 2017). In a similar vein, Auckland's Pasifika Festival represents each of the Pacific Islands. It's a great place to see both traditional and modern forms of Polynesian music: modern hip-hop, throbbing Cook Island drums, or island-style guitar, ukulele and slide guitar.

Classical & Opera

Early European immigrants brought their own styles of music and gave birth to local variants during the early 1900s. In the 1950s Douglas Lilburn became one of the first internationally recognised NZ classical composers. More recently the country has produced a number of world-renowned musicians in this field, including opera singer Dame Kiri Te Kanawa, million-selling pop diva Hayley Westenra, composer John Psathas (who created music for the 2004 Olympic Games) and composer/percussionist Gareth Farr (who also performs in drag under the name Lilith).

Gareth Shute wrote the Music section. He is the author of four books, including *Hip Hop Music in Aotearoa* and *NZ Rock 1987–2007.* He is also a musician and has toured the UK, Europe and Australia as a member of the Ruby Suns and the Brunettes. He now plays in garage rock group, The Conjurors.

For indie-rock fans, a great source of local info is www.cheeseontoast.co.nz, which lists gigs and has band interviews and photos. For more on local hip-hop, pop and rock, check out www.thecorner.co.nz and the long-running www.muzic.net.nz.

An up-to-date list of gigs in the main centres is listed at www.ripitup.co.nz. Tickets for most events can be bought at www.ticketek.co.nz, www.ticketmaster.co.nz, or, for smaller gigs, www.undertheradar.co.nz.

Rock

New Zealand has a strong rock scene, its most acclaimed exports being the revered indie label Flying Nun and the music of the Finn Brothers.

In 1981 Flying Nun was started by Christchurch record-store owner Roger Shepherd. Many of the early groups came from Dunedin, where local musicians took the DIY attitude of punk but used it to produce a lo-fi indie-pop that received rave reviews from the likes of *NME* in the UK and *Rolling Stone* in the US. *Billboard* even claimed in 1989: 'There doesn't seem to be anything on Flying Nun Records that is less than excellent.'

Many of the musicians from the Flying Nun scene still perform live to this day, including David Kilgour (from the Clean) and Shayne Carter (from the Straitjacket Fits, and subsequently Dimmer and the Adults). The Bats are still releasing albums, and Martin Phillipps' band the Chills released a comeback album *Silver Bullets* in 2015.

Reggae, Hip-Hop & Dance

The genres of music that have been adopted most enthusiastically by Māori and Polynesian New Zealanders have been reggae (in the 1970s) and hip-hop (in the 1980s), which has led to distinct local forms. In Wellington, a thriving jazz scene took on a reggae influence to create a host of groups that blended dub, roots, and funky jazz – most notably Fat Freddy's Drop. The national public holiday, Waitangi Day, on 6 February, also happens to fall on the birthday of Bob Marley, and annual reggae concerts are held on this day in Auckland and Wellington.

The local hip-hop scene has its heart in the suburbs of South Auckland, which have a high concentration of Māori and Pacific Island residents. This area is home to one of New Zealand's foremost hip-hop labels, Dawn Raid, which takes its name from the infamous 1970s early-morning house raids that police performed on Pacific Islanders suspected of outstaying their visas. Dawn Raid's most successful artist

THE BROTHERS FINN

There are certain tunes that all Kiwis can sing along to, given a beer and the opportunity. A surprising proportion of these were written by Tim and Neil Finn, many of which have been international hits. Tim and Neil were both born in the small town of Te Awamutu: the local museum has a collection documenting their work.

Tim Finn first came to prominence in the 1970s group Split Enz. When the original guitarist quit, Neil flew over to join the band in the UK, despite being only 15 at the time. Split Enz amassed a solid following in Australia, NZ and Canada before disbanding in 1985.

Neil then formed Crowded House with two Australian musicians (Paul Hester and Nick Seymour) and one of their early singles, 'Don't Dream It's Over', hit number two on the US charts. Tim later did a brief spell in the band, during which the brothers wrote 'Weather With You' – a song that reached number seven on the UK charts, pushing their album *Woodface* to gold sales. The original line-up of Crowded House played their final show in 1996 in front of 100,000 people on the steps of the Sydney Opera House (though Finn and Seymour reformed the group in 2007 and continue to tour and record occasionally). Tim and Neil have both released a number of solo albums, as well as releasing material together as the Finn Brothers.

More recently, Neil has also remained busy, organising a set of shows/releases under the name 7 Worlds Collide – a collaboration with well-known overseas musicians including Jeff Tweedy (Wilco), Johnny Marr (The Smiths) and members of Radiohead. His latest band is the Pajama Club, a collaboration with wife Sharon and Auckland musicians Sean Donnelly and Alana Skyring.

Neil's son Liam also has a burgeoning solo career, touring the US with Eddie Vedder and the Black Keys and appearing on the *Late Show with David Letterman*.

GOOD LORDE!

Of course, the big news in Kiwi music recently has been the success of Lorde, a singer-songwriter from Devonport on Auckland's North Shore. Known less regally to her friends as Ella Yelich-O'Connor, Lorde was 16 years old when she cracked the number-one spot on the US Billboard charts in 2013 with her magical, schoolyard-chant-evoking hit 'Royals' – the first NZ solo artist to top the American charts. 'Royals' then went on to win the Song of the Year Grammy in 2014. Her debut album *Pure Heroine* has spawned a string of hits and is selling millions of copies worldwide.

is Savage, who sold a million copies of his single 'Swing' after it was featured in the movie *Knocked Up*. Within New Zealand, the most well-known hip-hop acts are Scribe, Che Fu, and Smashproof (whose song 'Brother' held number one on the NZ singles charts longer than any other local act).

Dance music gained a foothold in Christchurch in the 1990s, spawning dub/electronica outfit Salmonella Dub and its offshoot act, Tiki Taane. Drum 'n' bass remains popular locally and has spawned internationally renowned acts such as Concord Dawn and Shapeshifter.

A wide range of cultural events are listed on www.eventfinda.co.nz. This is a good place to find out about concerts, classical music recitals and *kapa haka* performances. For more specific information on the NZ classical music scene, see www.sounz.org.nz.

New Music

Since 2000, the NZ music scene has developed new vitality after the government convinced commercial radio stations to adopt a voluntary quota of 20% local music. This enabled commercially oriented musicians to develop solid careers. Rock groups such as Shihad, the Feelers and Op-shop have thrived in this environment, as have a set of soulful female solo artists (who all happen to have Māori heritage): Bic Runga, Anika Moa, and Brooke Fraser (daughter of All Black Bernie Fraser). NZ also produced two internationally acclaimed garage rock acts over this time: the Datsuns and the D4.

Current Kiwis garnering international recognition include the incredibly gifted songstress Kimbra (who sang on Gotye's global smash 'Somebody That I Used To Know'); indie anthem alt-rockers the Naked & Famous; multitalented singer-songwriter Ladyhawke; the arty Lawrence Arabia; and the semi-psychedelic Unknown Mortal Orchestra. Aaradhna is a much-touted R&B singer who made a splash with her album *Treble & Reverb,* which won Album of the Year at the 2013 New Zealand Music Awards. The 2015 awards were dominated by Broods, a brother-sister alt-pop duo from Nelson, and Marlon Williams, a Christchurch singer with Jeff Buckley–like gravitas.

Survival Guide

Directory A–Z

Accommodation

Book your accommodation well in advance during peak tourist times: summer holidays from Christmas to late January, at Easter, and during winter in snowy resort towns like Queenstown and Wanaka.

B&Bs

Bed and breakfast (B&B) accommodation in NZ pops up in the middle of cities, in rural hamlets and on stretches of isolated coastline, with rooms on offer in everything from suburban bungalows to stately manors.

Breakfast may be 'continental' (cereal, toast and tea or coffee), 'hearty continental' (add yoghurt, fruit, home-baked bread or muffins) or a stomach-loading cooked meal (eggs, bacon, sausages...). Some B&B hosts may also cook dinner for guests and advertise dinner, bed and breakfast (DB&B) packages.

B&B tariffs are typically in the $120 to $200 bracket (per double), though some places cost upwards of $300 per double. Some hosts cheekily charge hefty prices for what is, in essence, a bedroom in their home. Off-street parking is often a bonus in the big cities.

Resources include:

New Zealand Bed & Breakfast www.bnb.co.nz

Bed and Breakfast New Zealand www.bed-and-breakfast. co.nz

Booking Services

Local visitor information centres around NZ provide reams of local accommodation information, sometimes in the form of folders detailing facilities and up-to-date prices; many can also make bookings on your behalf.

Online, check out the following:

Lonely Planet (www.lonely planet.com/new-zealand/hotels) The full range of NZ accommodation, from hostels to hotels.

Automobile Association (www. aa.co.nz) Online accommodation bookings (especially good for motels, B&Bs and holiday parks).

Jasons (www.jasons.com) Long-running travel service with myriad online booking options.

New Zealand Bed & Breakfast (www.bnb.co.nz) The name says it all.

Bed & Breakfast New Zealand (www.bed-and-breakfast.co.nz) B&B and self-contained accommodation listings.

Farm Helpers in NZ (www.fhinz. co.nz) Produces a booklet ($25) that lists around 350 NZ farms providing lodging in exchange for four to six hours' work per day.

Rural Holidays NZ (www. ruralholidays.co.nz) Farm and homestay listings across NZ.

Book a Bach (www.booka bach.co.nz) Apartment and holiday-house bookings (and maybe even a bach or two!).

Holiday Houses (www.holiday houses.co.nz) Holiday-house rentals NZ-wide.

New Zealand Apartments (www.nzapartments.co.nz) Rental listings for upmarket apartments of all sizes.

Camping & Holiday Parks

Campers and campervan drivers alike converge upon NZ's hugely popular 'holiday parks' to slumber peacefully in powered and unpowered sites, cheap bunk rooms (dorm rooms), cabins and self-contained units (often called motels or tourist flats). Well-equipped communal kitchens, dining areas, and games and TV rooms often feature. In cities, holiday parks are usually a fair way from the action, but in smaller towns they can be impressively central or near lakes, beaches, rivers and forests.

BOOK YOUR STAY ONLINE

For more accommodation reviews by Lonely Planet authors, check out http://lonelyplanet.com/hotels. You'll find independent reviews, as well as recommendations on the best places to stay. Best of all, you can book online.

The nightly cost of holiday-park camping is usually between $15 and $20 per adult, with children charged half-price; powered sites are a couple of dollars more. Cabin/unit accommodation normally ranges from $70 to $120 per double. Unless noted otherwise, Lonely Planet lists campsite, campervan site, hut and cabin prices for two people.

DOC & FREEDOM CAMPING

A fantastic option for those in campervans is the 250-plus vehicle-accessible NZ 'Conservation Campsites' run by the Department of Conservation (www.doc.govt.nz), with fees ranging from free (basic toilets and fresh water) to $15 per adult (flush toilets and showers). DOC publishes free brochures with detailed descriptions and instructions to find every campsite (even GPS coordinates). Pick up copies from DOC offices before you hit the road, or visit the website.

DOC also looks after hundreds of Backcountry Huts and Backcountry Campsites, which can only be reached on foot. See the website for details. Great Walk huts and campsites are also managed by DOC. See p33 for more.

The South Island is so photogenic, it's tempting to just pull off the road at a gorgeous viewpoint and camp for the night. But never just assume it's OK to camp somewhere: always ask a local or check with the local i-SITE, DOC office or commercial campground. If you are freedom camping, treat the area with respect. Note that if your chosen campsite doesn't have toilet facilities and neither does your campervan, it's illegal for you to sleep there (your campervan must also have an on-board grey-water storage system). Legislation allows for $200 instant fines for camping in prohibited areas or improper disposal of waste (in cases where dumping waste could damage the environment,

fees are up to $10,000). See www.camping.org.nz for more freedom-camping tips.

Farmstays

Farmstays open the door to the agricultural side of NZ life, with visitors encouraged to get some dirt beneath their fingernails at orchards, and dairy, sheep and cattle farms. Costs can vary widely, with bed and breakfast generally ranging from $80 to $140. Some farms have separate cottages where you can fix your own food; others offer low-cost, shared, backpacker-style accommodation.

Farm Helpers in NZ (www.fhinz. co.nz) Produces a booklet ($25) that lists around 350 NZ farms providing lodging in exchange for four to six hours' work per day.

Rural Holidays NZ (www.rural holidays.co.nz) Lists farmstays and homestays throughout the country.

Hostels

NZ's South Island is packed to the rafters with back-packer hostels – both independent and part of large chains – ranging from small, homestay-style affairs with a handful of beds, to refurbished hotels and towering modern structures in the big cities. Hostel bed prices listed by Lonely Planet are nonmember rates – usually

between $25 and $35 per night.

HOSTEL ORGANISATIONS

Budget Backpacker Hostels (www.bbh.co.nz) NZ's biggest hostel group with around 220 hostels. Membership costs $45 for 12 months and entitles you to stay at member hostels at rates listed in the annual (free) BBH Backpacker Accommodation booklet. Nonmembers pay an extra $3 per night. Pick up a membership card from any member hostel or order one online ($50); see the website for details.

YHA New Zealand (www.yha. co.nz) Around 40 hostels in prime NZ locations. The YHA is part of the Hostelling International network (www.hihostels. com), so if you're already an HI member in your own country, membership entitles you to use NZ hostels. If you don't already have a home membership, you can join at major NZ YHA hostels or online for $25, valid for 12 months. Nonmembers pay an extra $3 per night.

Base Backpackers (www.stayat base.com) Chain with 10 hostels around NZ, including Wanaka, Queenstown, Nelson, Dunedin and Christchurch on the South Island. Expect clean dorms, girls-only areas and party opportunities aplenty. Offers a 10-night 'Base Jumping' accommodation card for $259, bookable online.

WWOOFING

If you don't mind getting your hands dirty, an economical way of travelling around NZ involves doing some voluntary work as a member of the international **Willing Workers On Organic Farms** (WWOOF; ☑03-544 9890; www.wwoof.co.nz) scheme. Down on the farm, in exchange for a hard day's work, owners provide food, accommodation and some hands-on organic farming experience. Contact farm owners a week or two beforehand to arrange your stay, as you would for a hotel or hostel – don't turn up unannounced!

A one-year online membership costs $40. A farm-listing book, which is mailed to you, costs an extra $10 to $30, depending on where in the world your mailbox is. You should have a Working Holiday Visa when you visit NZ, as the immigration department considers WWOOF-ers to be working.

VIP Backpackers (www.vip backpackers.com) International organisation affiliated with around 20 NZ hostels (not BBH or YHA), mainly in the cities and tourist hot spots. For around $61 (including postage) you'll receive a 12-month membership entitling you to a $1 discount off nightly accommodation. Join online or at VIP hostels.

Nomads Backpackers (www. nomadsworld.com) Aussie outfit with seven franchises in NZ, plus affiliations with Base Backpackers. South Island locations include Abel Tasman National Park, Wanaka, Dunedin and Queenstown. Membership costs A$19.50 for 12 months and offers a 5% discount on the cost of nightly accommodation. Join at participating hostels or online.

Haka Lodge (www.hakalodge. com) A local chain on the way up, with snazzy South Island hostels in Queenstown and Christchurch. Rates are comparable to other hostels around NZ, and quality is high. Tours are also available.

Pubs, Hotels & Motels

The least expensive form of NZ hotel accommodation is the humble pub. Some are full of character (and characters); others are grotty, ramshackle places that are best avoided (especially by women travelling solo). Check whether there's a band playing the night you're staying – you could be in for a sleepless night. In the cheapest pubs, singles/ doubles might cost as little as $30/60 (with a shared

bathroom down the hall); $50/80 is more common.

At the top end of the hotel scale are five-star international chains, resort complexes and architecturally splendorous boutique hotels, all of which charge a hefty premium for their mod cons, snappy service and/or historic opulence. We quote 'rack rates' (official advertised rates) for such places, but discounts and special deals often apply.

NZ's towns have a glut of nondescript, low-rise motels and 'motor lodges', charging between $80 and $180 for double rooms. These tend to be squat structures skulking by highways on the edges of towns. Most are modernish (though decor is often mired in the early 2000s) and have similar facilities, namely tea- and coffee-making equipment, fridge and TV. Prices vary with standard.

Rental Accommodation

The basic Kiwi holiday home is called a 'bach' (short for 'bachelor', as they were historically used by single men as hunting and fishing hideouts); in Otago and Southland they're known as 'cribs'. These are simple self-contained cottages that can be rented in rural and coastal areas, often in isolated locations. Prices are typically $80 to $150 per night, which isn't bad for a whole house or self-contained bungalow. For more upmarket holiday houses, expect to pay any-

thing from $150 to $400 per double.

Online resources:

➡ www.holidayhomes.co.nz

➡ www.bookabach.co.nz

➡ www.holidayhouses.co.nz

➡ www.nzapartments.co.nz

Customs Regulations

For the low-down on what you can and can't bring into NZ, see the New Zealand Customs Service website (www. customs.govt.nz). Per-person duty-free allowances:

➡ Three 1125mL (max) bottles of spirits or liqueur

➡ 4.5L of wine or beer

➡ 50 cigarettes, or 50g of tobacco or cigars

➡ dutiable goods up to the value of $700

It's a good idea to declare any unusual medicines. Tramping gear (boots, tents etc) will be checked and may need to be cleaned before being allowed in. You must declare any plant or animal products (including anything made of wood), and food of any kind. Weapons and firearms are either prohibited or require a permit and safety testing. Don't take these rules lightly – non-compliance penalties will really hurt your hip pocket.

Discount Cards

The internationally recognised **International Student Identity Card** is produced by the ISIC Association (www. isic.org), and issued to full-time students aged 12 and over. It provides discounts on accommodation, transport and admission to attractions. The same folks also produce the **International Youth Travel Card**, available to travellers under 30 who are not full-time students, with equivalent benefits to the

ISIC. Also similar is the **International Teacher Identity Card**, available to teaching professionals. All three cards ($30 each) are available online at www.isiccard.co.nz, or from student travel companies such as STA Travel.

The **New Zealand Card** (www.newzealandcard.com) is a $35 discount pass that'll score you between 5% and 50% off a range of accommodation, tours, sights and activities.

Travellers over 60 with some form of identification (eg an official seniors card from your home country) are often eligible for concession prices.

Electricity

To plug yourself into the electricity supply (230V AC, 50Hz), use a three-pin adaptor (the same as in Australia; different to British three-pin adaptors).

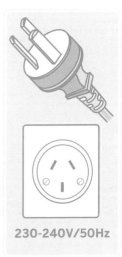

230-240V/50Hz

Embassies & Consulates

Most principal diplomatic representations to NZ are on the North island, mostly

Climate

Christchurch

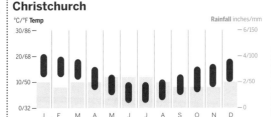

Nelson

Queenstown

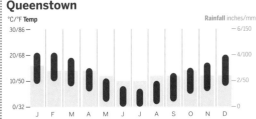

in Wellington with a few in Auckland.

Australian High Commission (04-473 6411; www.new zealand.highcommission.gov. au; 72-76 Hobson St, Thorndon, Wellington; 9am-4pm Mon-Fri)

Canadian High Commission (04-473 9577; www.canada international.gc.ca; L11, 125 The Terrace, Wellington ; 8.30am-noon Mon-Fri)

Chinese Embassy (04-473 3514; www.chinaembassy.org. nz; 4 Halswell St, Thorndon, Wellington; 9-11.30am Mon-Fri, 2-4pm Mon, Wed & Fri)

Fijian High Commission (04-473 5401; www.fiji.org.nz; 31 Pipitea St, Thorndon, Wellington; 9am-5pm Mon-Fri)

French Embassy (04-384 2555; www.ambafrance-nz.org; 34-42 Manners St, Wellington;

9am-noon & 2-5pm Mon-Thu, 9am-noon & 2-4pm Fri)

German Embassy (04-473 6063; www.wellington.diplo.de; 90-92 Hobson St, Thorndon, Wellington; 10.45am-noon Mon-Fri)

Irish Consulate (09-977 2252; www.ireland.co.nz; L3, Tower 1, 205 Queen St, Auckland)

Israeli Embassy (04-439 9500; www.embassies.gov. il/wellington; Lvl 13, Bayleys Building, 36 Brandon St, Wellington; by appointment 9.30am-12.30pm Mon-Fri)

Japanese Embassy (04-473 1540; www.nz.emb-japan.go.jp; Lvl 18, The Majestic Centre, 100 Willis St, Wellington; 9am-5pm Mon-Fri)

Netherlands Embassy (0800 388 243, 04-471 6395; newzea-land.nlembassy.org; Lvl 10,

Cooperative Bank Building, cnr Featherstone & Ballance Sts; ⊙by appointment 9.30am-12.30pm & 1-3.30pm Mon-Fri)

UK High Commission (☑04-924 2888; www.gov.uk; 44 Hill St, Thorndon, Wellington; ⊙9am-5pm Mon-Fri)

US Embassy (☑04-462 6000; http://nz.usembassy.gov; 29 Fitzherbert Tce, Thorndon, Wellington; ⊙9am-5pm Mon-Fri)

Food & Drink

The South Island is a mighty fine place to wine and dine. For the low-down, see Food & Drink (p47).

GLBTI Travellers

The gay tourism industry in NZ isn't as high-profile as it is in other developed nations, but NZ has progressive laws protecting human rights: same-sex marriage was legalised here in 2013, while the legal minimum age for sex between consenting persons is 16. Generally speaking, Kiwis are fairly relaxed and accepting about gender fluidity, but that's not to say that homophobia doesn't exist. Rural communities tend to be more conservative; here public displays of affection should probably be avoided.

Resources & Events

There are loads of websites dedicated to gay and lesbian travel in NZ. Gay Tourism New Zealand (www.gay tourismnewzealand.com) is

EATING PRICE RANGES

The following price ranges refer to the average price of a main course:

$ Less than $15

$$ $15–32

$$$ More than $32

a good starting point, with links to various sites. Other worthwhile websites include the following:

➡ www.gaynz.com

➡ www.gaynz.net.nz

➡ www.lesbian.net.nz

➡ www.gaystay.co.nz

Check out the nationwide monthly magazine *Express* (www.gayexpress.co.nz) for the latest happenings, reviews and listings on the NZ gay scene.

On the South Island festival front, Gay Ski Week (www.gayskiweekqt.com) is an annual Queenstown snow-fest held in August/September.

Health

New Zealand is one of the healthiest countries in the world in which to travel. Diseases such as malaria and typhoid are unheard of, and the absence of poisonous snakes or other dangerous animals makes outdoor adventures here less risky than in neighbouring Australia.

Before You Go
HEALTH INSURANCE

Health insurance is essential for all travellers. While health care in NZ is of a high quality and not overly expensive by international standards, considerable costs can be built up and repatriation can be pricey.

If your current health insurance doesn't cover you for medical expenses incurred overseas, consider extra insurance – see www.lonelyplanet.com/travel-insurance for more information. Find out in advance if your insurance plan will make payments directly to providers or reimburse you later for overseas health expenditures.

MEDICATIONS

Bring any prescribed medications for your trip in their original, clearly labelled con-

tainers. A signed and dated letter from your physician describing your medical conditions and medications (including generic names) and any requisite syringes or needles is also wise.

VACCINATIONS

NZ has no vaccination requirements for any traveller, but the World Health Organization recommends that all travellers should be covered for diphtheria, tetanus, measles, mumps, rubella, chickenpox and polio, as well as hepatitis B, regardless of their destination. Ask your doctor for an *International Certificate of Vaccination* (or 'the yellow booklet') in which they will list all the vaccinations you've received.

On the South Island
AVAILABILITY & COST OF HEALTH CARE

NZ's public hospitals offer a high standard of care (free for residents). All travellers are covered for medical care resulting from accidents that occur while in NZ (eg motor-vehicle and adventure-activity accidents) by the Accident Compensation Corporation (www.acc.co.nz). Costs incurred due to treatment of a medical illness that occurs while in NZ will only be covered by travel insurance. For more details, see www.health.govt.nz.

The 24-hour, free-call **Healthline** (☑0800 611 116) offers health advice throughout NZ.

ENVIRONMENTAL HAZARDS

There's very little that can bite, sting or eat you in NZ, but hypothermia and drowning are genuine threats.

Hypothermia

A significant risk, especially during winter and year-round at altitude. Mountain ranges and/or strong winds produce a high chill factor, which can cause hypothermia even in moderate temperatures. Early signs include the inability to perform fine movements (such as doing up buttons), shivering and a bad case of the 'umbles' (fumbles, mumbles, grumbles, stumbles).

To treat, minimise heat loss: remove wet clothing, add dry clothes with wind- and waterproof layers, and consume water and carbohydrates to allow shivering to build the internal temperature. In severe hypothermia cases, shivering actually stops; this is a medical emergency requiring rapid evacuation in addition to the above measures.

Surf Beaches

The South Island has some wild surf beaches. The power of the surf can fluctuate as a result of the varying slope of the seabed: rips and undertows are common, and drownings do happen. Check with local surf-lifesaving organisations before jumping in the sea and be aware of your own limitations and expertise.

INFECTIOUS DISEASES

Aside from the usual sexually transferred discomforts (take normal precautions), giardiasis does occur in NZ. The giardia parasite is widespread in NZ waterways: drinking untreated water from streams and lakes is not recommended. Using water filters and boiling or treating water with iodine are effective ways of preventing the disease. Symptoms consist of intermittent diarrhoea, abdominal bloating and wind. Effective treatment is available (tinidazole or metronidazole).

PHARMACEUTICALS

Over-the-counter medications are widely available in NZ through private chemists (pharmacies). These include painkillers, antihistamines, skin-care products and sunscreen. Some medications, such as antibiotics and the contraceptive pill, are only available via a prescription

---

PRACTICALITIES

Newspapers Check out Auckland's *New Zealand Herald* (www.nzherald.co.nz), Wellington's *Dominion Post* (www.stuff.co.nz/dominion-post) or Christchurch's *The Press* (www.stuff.co.nz/the-press).

TV Watch one of the national government-owned TV stations – including TV One, TV2, Māori TV or the 100% Māori-language Te Reo – or subscriber-only Sky TV (www.skytv.co.nz).

Radio Tune in to Radio New Zealand (www.radionz.co.nz) for news, current affairs, classical and jazz. Radio Hauraki (www.hauraki.co.nz) cranks out the rock.

DVDs Kiwi DVDs are encoded for Region 4, which includes Australia, the Pacific, Mexico, Central America, the Carribean and South America.

Weights & Measures NZ uses the metric system.

---

obtained from a general practitioner. If you take regular medications, bring an adequate supply and details of the generic name, as brand names differ country-to-country.

TAP WATER

Tap water throughout New Zealand is generally safe to drink. NZ has strict standards about drinking water, applicable across the country.

Insurance

➡ A watertight travel-insurance policy covering theft, loss and medical problems is essential. Some policies specifically exclude designated 'dangerous activities' such as scuba diving, bungy jumping, white-water rafting, skiing and even tramping. If you plan on doing any of these things (a distinct possibility on the South Island!), make sure your policy covers you fully.

➡ It's worth mentioning that under NZ law, you cannot sue for personal injury (other than exemplary damages). Instead, the country's Accident Compensation Corporation (www.acc.co.nz) administers an accident compensation scheme

that provides accident insurance for NZ residents and visitors to the country, regardless of fault. This scheme, however, does not negate the necessity for your own comprehensive travel-insurance policy, as it doesn't cover you for such things as income loss, treatment at home or ongoing illness.

➡ Consider a policy that pays doctors or hospitals directly, rather than you paying on the spot and claiming later. If you have to claim later, keep all documentation. Some policies ask you to call (reverse charges) to a centre in your home country where an immediate assessment of your problem is made. Check that the policy covers ambulances and emergency medical evacuations by air.

➡ Worldwide travel insurance is available at www.lonelyplanet.com/travel-insurance. You can buy, extend and claim online anytime – even if you're already on the road.

Internet Access

Getting online on the South Island is easy in all but the most remote locales. In Lonely Planet's NZ reviews, we use the wi-fi and internet icons to indicate the availability of wireless access or actual computers on which you can get online.

Wi-fi & Internet Service Providers

Wi-fi You'll be able to find wi-fi access around the country, from hotel rooms to pub beer gardens and hostel dorms. Usually you have to be a guest or customer to log on; you'll be issued with an access code. Sometimes it's free, sometimes there's a charge.

Hot spots The country's main telecommunications company is Spark New Zealand (www.spark.co.nz), which has wireless hot-spots around the country where you can purchase prepaid access cards. Alternatively, purchase a prepaid number from the login page at any wireless hot spot using your credit card. See Spark's website for hot spot listings.

Equipment & ISPs If you've brought your palmtop or laptop, consider buying a prepay USB modem (aka a 'dongle') with a local SIM card: both Spark and Vodafone (www.vodafone.co.nz) sell these from around $100. If you want to get connected via a local internet service provider (ISP), options include the following:

Clearnet (☑0508 888 800; www.clearnet.co.nz) Affiliated with Vodafone.

Earthlight (☑03-479 0303; www.earthlight.co.nz)

Slingshot (☑0800 892 000; www.slingshot.co.nz)

Internet Cafes

There are fewer internet cafes around these days than there were five years ago, but you'll still find them in the bigger cities. Access costs anywhere from $4 to $6 per hour.

Similarly, most youth hostels have done away with actual computers in favour of wi-fi. Most hotels, motels, B&Bs and holiday parks also offer wi-fi, sometimes for free, but usually for a small charge.

Legal Matters

Marijuana is widely indulged in but illegal: anyone caught carrying this or other illicit drugs will have the book thrown at them.

Drink-driving is a serious offence and remains a significant problem in NZ. The legal blood alcohol limit is 0.05% for drivers over 20, and zero for those under 20.

If you are arrested, it's your right to consult a lawyer before any formal questioning begins.

Maps

New Zealand's **Automobile Association** (AA; ☑0800 500 444; www.aa.co.nz/travel) produces excellent city, town, regional, island and highway maps, available from its local offices. The AA also produces a detailed *New Zealand Road Atlas*. Other reliable countrywide atlases, available from visitor information centres and bookshops, are published by Hema, KiwiMaps and Wises.

Land Information New Zealand (www.linz.govt.nz) publishes several exhaustive map series, including street, country and holiday maps, national park and forest park maps, and topographical trampers' maps. Scan the larger bookshops, or try the nearest DOC office or visitor information centre for topo maps.

Online, log onto AA Maps (www.aamaps.co.nz) or Wises (www.wises.co.nz) to pinpoint exact NZ addresses.

Money

ATMs & Eftpos

Branches of the country's major banks across the South Islandshave ATMs, but you won't find them everywhere (eg not in small towns).

Many NZ businesses use Eftpos (electronic funds

transfer at point of sale), allowing you to use your bank card (credit or debit) to make direct purchases and often withdraw cash as well. Eftpos is available practically everywhere: just like an ATM, you'll need a personal identification number (PIN).

Bank Accounts

We've heard mixed reports on the subject of travellers opening bank accounts in NZ, and bank websites are vague. Some sources say opening an account is as simple as flashing a few pieces of ID; others say banks won't allow visitors to open an account unless the application is accompanied by proof of employment. Either way, you'll need to open account if you want to work in NZ in any capacity (incudling working holiday scenarios). Do your homework before you arrive.

Credit & Debit Cards

CREDIT CARDS

Credit cards (Visa and MasterCard) are widely accepted for everything from a hostel bed to a bungy jump, and are pretty much essential for car hire. They can also be used for over-the-counter cash advances at banks and from ATMs, but be aware that such transactions incur charges. Diners Club and American Express cards are not as widely accepted.

DEBIT CARDS

Debit cards enable you to draw money directly from your home bank account using ATMs, banks or Eftpos facilities. Any card connected to the international banking network (Cirrus, Maestro, Visa Plus and Eurocard) should work with your PIN. Fees will vary depending on your home bank; check before you leave. Alternatively, companies such as Travelex offer debit cards with set withdrawal fees and a balance you can top up from your personal bank account while on the road.

Currency

NZ's currency is the NZ dollar, comprising 100 cents. There are 10c, 20c, 50c, $1 and $2 coins, and $5, $10, $20, $50 and $100 notes. Prices are often still marked in single cents and then rounded to the nearest 10c when you hand over your money.

Moneychangers

Changing foreign currency (and to a lesser extent old-fashioned travellers cheques) is usually no problem at South Island banks or at licensed money changers (eg Travelex) in major tourist areas, cities and airports.

Taxes & Refunds

The Goods and Services Tax (GST) is a flat 15% tax on all domestic goods and services. NZ prices listed by Lonely Planet include GST. There's no GST refund available when you leave NZ.

Tipping

Tipping is completely optional in NZ – the total at the bottom of a restaurant bill is all you need to pay (note that sometimes there's an additional service charge). That said, it's totally acceptable to reward good service – between 5% and 10% of the bill is fine.

Travellers Cheques

Amex, Travelex and other international brands of travellers cheques are a bit old-hat these days, but they're still easily exchanged at banks and money changers. Present your passport for identification when cashing them; shop around for the best rates.

Opening Hours

Opening hours vary seasonally (eg Dunedin is quiet during winter), but use the following as a general guide.

Note that most places close on Christmas Day and Good Friday.

Banks 9.30am–4.30pm Monday to Friday; some also 9am–noon Saturday

Cafes 7am–4pm

Post offices 8.30am–5pm Monday to Friday; larger branches also 9.30am–1pm Saturday

Pubs & bars noon–late ('late' varies by region and day)

Restaurants noon–2.30pm and 6.30–9pm

Shops & businesses 9am–5.30pm Monday to Friday and 9am to noon or 5pm Saturday

Supermarkets 8am–7pm; often 9pm or later in cities.

Post

The services offered by **New Zealand Post** (☑0800 501 501; www.nzpost.co.nz) are reliable and reasonably inexpensive. See the website for info on national and international zones and rates, plus post office locations.

Public Holidays

NZ's main public holidays are as follows:

New Year 1 and 2 January

Waitangi Day 6 February

Easter Good Friday and Easter Monday; March/April

Anzac Day 25 April

Queen's Birthday First Monday in June

Labour Day Fourth Monday in October

Christmas Day 25 December

Boxing Day 26 December

In addition, each NZ province has its own anniversary-day holiday. The dates of these provincial holidays vary: when they fall on Friday to Sunday, they're usually observed the following Monday; if they fall on Tuesday to Thursday, they're held on the preceding Monday.

Provincial South Island anniversary holidays:

Southland 17 January

Nelson 1 February

Otago 23 March

South Canterbury 25 September

Marlborough 1 November

Chatham Islands 30 November

Westland 1 December

Canterbury 16 December

School Holidays

The Christmas holiday season, from mid-December to late January, is part of the summer school vacation: expect transport and accommodation to book out in advance, and queues at tourist attractions. There are three shorter school-holiday periods during the year: from mid- to late April, early to mid-July, and mid-September to early October. For exact dates see the Ministry of Education website (www.education.govt.nz).

Safe Travel

It's no more dangerous than any other developed country, but violent crime does happen in NZ. Play it safe on the streets after dark and in remote areas.

➡ Avoid leaving valuables in vehicles: theft from cars is a problem.

➡ NZ's climate is unpredictable: hypothermia is a risk in high-altitude areas.

➡ At the beach, beware of rips and undertows, which can drag swimmers out to sea.

➡ Kiwi roads are often made hazardous by map-distracted tourists, wide-cornering campervans and traffic-ignorant sheep.

➡ In the annoyances category, NZ's sandflies are a royal (and intensely itchy) pain. Lather yourself with insect repellent in coastal areas.

Telephone

Spark New Zealand (www.spark.co.nz) is the country's key domestic telephone service provider, also with a stake in the local mobile (cell) market.

Key mobile service providers include the following:

Skinny Mobile (www.skinny.co.nz)

Vodafone (www.vodafone.co.nz)

2 Degrees (www.2degreesmobile.co.nz)

Mobile Phones

Most NZ mobile (cell) phone numbers are preceded by the prefix ⌨021, ⌨022 or ⌨027. Mobile phone coverage is good in cities and towns on the South Island, but can be a bit patchy away from urban centres.

If you want to bring your own phone and use a prepaid service with a local SIM card (rather than pay for expensive global roaming on your home network), Vodafone (www.vodafone.co.nz) is a practical option. Any Vodafone shop (in most major towns) will set you up with a NZ Travel SIM and a phone number (from around $30; valid for 30, 60 or 90 days). Top-ups can be purchased at newsagencies, post offices and petrol stations all over the country.

Alternatively, you can rent a phone from Vodafone, with South Island pick-up and drop-off outlets at Christchurch and Queenstown international airports. Phone Hire New Zealand (www.phonehirenz.com) also rents out mobiles, SIM cards, modems and GPS systems.

Local Calls

Local calls from private phones are free! Local calls from payphones cost $1 for the first 15 minutes, and $0.20 per minute thereafter, though coin-operated payphones are scarce (and if you do find one, chances are the coin slot will be gummed up; you'll generally need a phonecard). Calls to mobile phones attract higher rates.

International Calls

To make international calls from NZ (which is possible on payphones), you need to dial the international access code ⌨00, then the country code and the area code (without the initial '0'). So for a London number, for example, you'd dial ⌨00-44-20, then the number.

If dialling NZ from overseas, the country code is ⌨64, followed by the appropriate area code minus the initial '0'.

Long Distance Calls & Area Codes

NZ uses regional two-digit area codes for long-distance calls, which can be made from any payphone. If you're making a local call (ie to someone else in the same town), you don't need to dial the area code. But if you're dialling within a region (even if it's to a nearby town with the same area code), you do have to dial the area code.

Information & Toll-Free Calls

Numbers starting with ⌨0900 are usually recorded information services, charging upwards of $1 per minute (more from mobiles). These numbers cannot be dialled from payphones, and sometimes not from prepay mobile phones.

Toll-free numbers in NZ have the prefix ⌨0800 or ⌨0508 and can be called from anywhere in the country, though they may not be accessible from certain areas or from mobile phones. Numbers beginning with ⌨0508, ⌨0800 or ⌨0900 cannot be dialled from outside NZ.

Phonecards

NZ has a wide range of phonecards available, which can be bought at hostels, newsagencies and post offices for a fixed-dollar value (usually $5, $10, $20 and $50). These can be used with any public or private phone by dialling a toll-free access number and then the PIN number on the card. Shop around – rates vary from company to company.

GOVERNMENT TRAVEL ADVICE

The following government websites offer travel advisories and information on current hot-spots:

Australian Department of Foreign Affairs & Trade (www.smarttraveller.gov.au)

British Foreign & Commonwealth Office (www.gov.uk/fco)

Foreign Affairs, Trade & Development Canada (www.international.gc.ca)

Dutch Ministry of Foreign Affairs (www.government.nl/ministries/ministry-of-foreign-affairs)

German Federal Foreign Office (www.auswaertiges-amt.de)

Japanese Ministry of Foreign Affairs (www.mofa.go.jp)

US Department of State (www.travel.state.gov)

Time

NZ is 12 hours ahead of GMT/UTC and two hours ahead of Australian Eastern Standard Time. The Chathams are 45 minutes ahead of NZ's main islands.

In summer, NZ observes daylight saving time, where clocks are wound forward by one hour on the last Sunday in September; clocks are wound back on the first Sunday of the following April.

Toilets

Toilets in NZ are sit-down Western style. Public toilets are plentiful, and are usually reasonably clean with working locks and plenty of toilet paper.

See www.toiletmap.co.nz for public toilet locations around the country.

Tourist Information

The website for the official national tourism body, Tourism New Zealand (www. newzealand.com), is the best place for pretrip research. Emblazoned with the hugely successful 100% Pure New Zealand branding, the site has information in several languages, including German, Spanish, French, Chinese and Japanese.

Local Tourist Offices

Almost every South Island city or town seems to have a visitor information centre. The bigger centres stand united within the outstanding i-SITE network (www. newzealand.com/travel/ i-sites) – around 80 info centres affiliated with Tourism New Zealand. i-SITEs have trained staff, information on local activities and attractions, and free brochures and maps. Staff can also book activities, transport and accommodation.

Bear in mind that some information centres only promote accommodation and tour operators who are paying members of the local tourist association, and that sometimes staff aren't supposed to recommend one activity or accommodation provider over another.

There's also a network of Department of Conservation (DOC; www.doc. govt.nz) visitor centres to help you plan activities and make bookings. DOC visitor centres – in national parks, regional centres and major cities – usually also have displays on local lore, flora, fauna and biodiversity.

Travellers with Disabilities

South Island accommodation generally caters fairly well for travellers with disabilities, with many hostels, hotels, motels and B&Bs equipped with wheelchair-accessible rooms. Many tourist attractions similarly provide wheelchair access, with wheelchairs often available.

Tour operators with accessible vehicles operate from most major centres. Key cities are also serviced by 'kneeling' buses (buses that hydraulically stoop down to kerb level to allow easy access), and taxi companies offer wheelchair-accessible vans. Large car-hire firms (Avis, Hertz etc) provide cars with hand controls at no extra charge (but advance notice is required). Air New Zealand is also very well equipped to accommodate travellers in wheelchairs.

Activities

Out and about, the Department of Conservation maintains plenty of tracks that are wheelchair accessible, categorised as 'easy access short walks': the Milford Foreshore Walk is a prime example.

If cold-weather activity is more your thing, see the Disabled Snowsports NZ

website (www.disabledsnow sports.org.nz).

Resources

Weka (www.weka.net.nz) Good general information, with categories including Transport and Travel.

Blind Foundation (www.blind foundation.org.nz)

National Foundation for the Deaf (www.nfd.org.nz)

Mobility Parking (www.mobility parking.org.nz) Info on mobility parking permits and online applications.

Visas

Visa application forms are available from NZ diplomatic missions overseas, travel agents and **Immigration New Zealand** (☑0508 558 855, 09-914 4100; www.immi gration.govt.nz). Immigration New Zealand has over a dozen offices overseas; consult the website.

Visitor Visa

Citizens of Australia don't need a visa to visit NZ and can stay indefinitely (provided they have no criminal convictions). UK citizens don't need a visa either and can stay in the country for up to six months.

Citizens of another 58 countries that have visa-waiver agreements with NZ don't need a visa for stays of up to three months per visit, for no more than six months within any 12-month period, provided they have an onward ticket and sufficient funds to support their stay: see the website for details. Nations in this group include Canada, France, Germany, Ireland, Japan, the Netherlands, South Africa and the USA.

Citizens of other countries must obtain a visa before entering NZ. Visitor visas allow stays of up to nine months within an 18-month period, and cost between NZ$170 and $220, depending on where in the world the application is processed.

A visitor visa can be extended from nine to 12 months, but if you get this extension you'll have to leave NZ after your 12-month stay has expired and wait another 12 months before you can come back. Applications are assessed on a case-by-case basis; you may need to provide proof of adequate funds to sustain you during your visit (NZ$1000 per month) plus an onward ticket establishing your intent to leave. Apply for extensions at any Immigration New Zealand office – see the website for locations.

Work Visa

It's illegal for foreign nationals to work in NZ on a visitor visa, except for Australians who can legally gain work without a visa or permit. If you're visiting NZ to find work, or you already have an employment offer, you'll need to apply for a work visa, which can be valid for up to three years, depending on your circumstance. You can apply for a work permit after you're in NZ, but its validity will be backdated to when you entered the country. The fee for a work visa can be anything upwards of NZ$190, depending on where and how it's processed (paper or online) and the type of application.

Working Holiday Scheme

Eligible travellers who are only interested in short-term employment to supplement their travels can take part in one of NZ's working holiday schemes (WHS). Under these schemes citizens aged 18 to 30 years from 42 countries – including Canada, France, Germany, Ireland, Japan, Malaysia, the Netherlands, Scandinavian countries, the UK and the USA – can apply for a visa. For most nationalities the visa is valid for 12 months. It's only issued to those seeking a genuine working holiday, not per-

manent work, so you're not supposed to work for one employer for more than three months.

WHS-eligible nationals must apply online for this visa from within their own country. Applicants must have an onward ticket, a passport valid for at least three months from the date they will leave NZ and evidence of at least NZ$4200 in accessible funds. The application fee is NZ$165 regardless of where you apply, and isn't refunded if your application is declined.

The rules vary for different nationalities, so make sure you read up on the specifics of your country's agreement with NZ at www.immigration. govt.nz/migrant/stream/ work/workingholiday.

Volunteering

NZ presents a swath of active, outdoorsy volunteer opportunities for travellers to get some dirt under their fingernails and participate in conservation programs. Programs can include anything from tree planting and weed removal to track construction, habitat conservation and fencing. Ask about local opportunities at any regional i-SITE visitor information centre, join one of the programs run by the DOC (www. doc.govt.nz/getting-involved) or check out these online resources:

➡ www.conservation volunteers.org.nz

➡ www.helpx.net

➡ www.nature.org.nz

➡ www.volunteeringnz. org.nz

➡ www.wwf.org.nz

Women Travellers

NZ is generally a very safe place for female travellers, although the usual sensible precautions apply (for both sexes): avoid walking alone at

night; never hitchhike alone; and if you're out on the town have a plan on how to get back to your accommodation safely. Sexual harassment is not a widely reported problem in NZ, but of course that doesn't mean it doesn't happen. See www.womentravel. co.nz for tours aimed at solo women.

Work

If you arrive in NZ on a visitor visa, you're not allowed to work for pay. If you're caught breaching this (or any other) visa condition, you could be booted back to where you came from.

If you have been approved for a working holiday scheme (WHS) visa, there are a number of possibilities for temporary employment in NZ. Pay rates are around $14 to $20 an hour (ie not very high). There's plenty of casual work around, mainly in agriculture (fruit picking, farming, wineries), in hospitality (bar work, waiting tables) or at ski resorts. Office-based work can be found in IT, banking, finance and telemarketing. Register with a local office-work agency to get started.

Seasonal fruit picking, pruning and harvesting is prime short-term work for visitors. More than 30,000 hectares of apples, kiwifruit and other fruit and veg are harvested from December to May. It is physically taxing toil, working in the dirt under the hot sun – turnover of workers is high. You're usually paid by how much you pick (per bin, bucket or kilogram): if you stick with it for a while, you'll get faster and fitter and can actually make some reasonable cash. On the South Island try Nelson (Tapawera and Golden Bay), Marlborough (around Blenheim) and Central Otago (Alexandra and Roxburgh).

Winter work at ski resorts and their service towns includes bartending, waiting, cleaning, ski-tow operation and, if you're properly qualified, ski or snowboard instructing.

Resources

Backpacker publications, hostel managers and other travellers are the best sources of info on local work possibilities. Base Backpackers (www.stayatbase.com/work) runs an employment service via its website, while the Notice Boards page on the Budget Backpacker Hostels website (www.bbh.co.nz) lists job vacancies in BBH hostels and a few other possibilities.

Kiwi Careers (www.careers.govt.nz) lists professional opportunities in various fields (agriculture, creative, health, teaching, volunteer work and recruitment), while Seek (www.seek.co.nz) is one of the biggest NZ job-search networks, with thousands of jobs listed.

Check ski-resort websites for work opportunities in the snow. In the fruit-picking/horticultural realm, try the following websites:

➡ www.seasonalwork.co.nz

➡ www.seasonaljobs.co.nz

➡ www.picknz.co.nz

➡ www.pickingjobs.com

Income Tax

Death and taxes – no escape! For most travellers, Kiwi dollars earned in NZ will be subject to income tax, deducted from payments by employers – a process called Pay As You Earn (PAYE).

PAYE income tax rates are 11.95% for annual salaries up to $14,000, then 18.95% up to $48,000, 31.45% up to $70,000, then 34.45% for higher incomes. An NZ Accident Compensation Corporation (ACC) scheme levy (around 1.5%) will also be deducted from your pay packet. Note that these rates tend to change slightly year-to-year.

If you visit NZ and work for a short time (eg on a working holiday scheme), you may qualify for a tax refund when you leave. Lodging a tax return before you leave NZ is the best way of securing a refund. For more info, see the Inland Revenue Department website (www.ird.govt.nz) or call ☏03-951 2020.

IRD Number

Travellers undertaking paid work in NZ (including working holiday scenarios) must first open a New Zealand bank account, then obtain an IRD (Inland Revenue Department) number. Download the 'IRD number application – non-resident/offshore individual IR742' form from the Inland Revenue Department website (www.ird.govt.nz). IRD numbers normally take eight to 10 working days to be issued.

Transport

GETTING THERE & AWAY

The South Island of New Zealand is a long way from almost everywhere – most travellers jet in from afar to Auckland Airport on the North Island then take a domestic flight south. Flights, cars and tours can be booked online at lonelyplanet.com/bookings.

Entering the Country

Disembarkation in New Zealand is generally a straightforward affair, with only the usual customs declarations and the luggage-carousel scramble to endure. Under the the Orwellian title of 'Advance Passenger Screening', documents that used to be checked after you touched down in NZ (passport, visa etc) are now checked before you board your flight – make sure all your documenta-tion is in order so that your check-in is stress-free.

Passports

There are no restrictions when it comes to foreign citizens entering NZ. If you have a current passport and visa (or don't require one), you should be fine.

Air

The South Island's abundance of year-round activities means that airports here are busy most of the time: if you want to fly at a particularly popular time of year (eg over the Christmas period), book well in advance.

The high season for flights into the region is summer (December to February), with slightly less of a premium on fares over the shoulder months (October/November and March/April). The low season generally tallies with the winter months (June to August), though this is still a busy time for airlines ferry-ing ski bunnies and powder hounds.

Airports & Airlines

INTERNATIONAL AIRPORTS

While Auckland airport is New Zealand's main air hub, a number of South Island airports handle international flights, mostly from Australia and Asia:

Christchurch Airport (CHC; ☑03-358 5029; www.christchurchairport.co.nz; 30 Durey Rd)

Dunedin Airport (DUD; ☑03-486 2879; www.dnairport.co.nz; 25 Miller Rd, Momona)

Queenstown Airport (ZQN; ☑03-450 9031; www.queenstownairport.co.nz; Sir Henry Wrigley Dr, Frankton)

AIRLINES FLYING TO & FROM NEW ZEALAND

New Zealand's international carrier is Air New Zealand (www.airnewzealand.co.nz), which flies to runways across Europe, North America, east-

---

CLIMATE CHANGE & TRAVEL

Every form of transport that relies on carbon-based fuel generates CO_2, the main cause of human-induced climate change. Modern travel is dependent on aeroplanes, which might use less fuel per kilometre per person than most cars but travel much greater distances. The altitude at which aircraft emit gases (including CO_2) and particles also contributes to their climate change impact. Many websites offer 'carbon calculators' that allow people to estimate the carbon emissions generated by their journey and, for those who wish to do so, to offset the impact of the greenhouse gases emitted with contributions to portfolios of climate-friendly initiatives throughout the world. Lonely Planet offsets the carbon footprint of all staff and author travel.

ern Asia, Australia and the Pacific, and has an extensive network across NZ.

Winging in from Australia, Virgin Australia (www. virginaustralia.com), Qantas (www.qantas.com.au), Jetstar (www.jetstar.com) and Air New Zealand are the key players. Air New Zealand also flies in from North America. Other operators from North America include Air Canada (www.aircanada.com) and American Airlines (www. aa.com).

From Europe, the options are a little broader, with British Airways (www.britishairways.com), Lufthansa (www. lufthansa.com) and Virgin Atlantic (www.virginatlantic. com) entering the fray, and plenty of others stopping in NZ on broader round-the-world routes.

From Asia and the Pacific there are myriad options, with direct flights from China, Japan, Singapore, Malaysia, Thailand and Pacific Island nations.

Sea

Yacht It is possible (though by no means straightforward) to make your way between the South Island, Australia and the Pacific islands by crewing on a yacht. Try asking around at harbours, marinas, and yacht and sailing clubs. March and April are the best months to look for boats heading to Australia. From Fiji, October to November is a peak departure season to beat the cyclones that soon follow in that neck of the woods.

Cruise Ship If you're looking for something with a slower pace, plenty of passenger cruise liners stop in NZ on the South Pacific legs of their respective schedules: try P&O Cruises (www. pocruises.com.au) for starters.

Cargo Ship Alternatively, a berth on a cargo ship or freighter to/from New Zealand is a quirky way to go: check out websites such as www.freightercruises. com and www.freighterexpeditions.com.au for more info.

GETTING AROUND

Air

Those who have limited time to get between the South Island's attractions can make the most of a widespread (and very reliable and safe) network of domestic flights.

Airlines in the South Island

The country's major domestic carrier, Air New Zealand, has an aerial network covering most of the country, often operating under the Air New Zealand Link moniker on less popular routes. Australia-based Jetstar also flies between main urban areas. Between them, these two airlines carry the vast majority of domestic passengers in NZ. Beyond this, several small-scale regional operators provide essential transport services to outlying islands such as Stewart Island and the Chathams. There are also plenty of scenic- and charter-flight operators around NZ, which are not listed here. Operators include the following:

Air Chathams (☑03-305 0209; www.airchathams.co.nz) Services to the remote Chatham Islands from Wellington, Christchurch and Auckland. Auckland–Whakatane flights also available.

Air New Zealand (☑0800 737 000; www.airnewzealand.co.nz) Offers flights between 20-plus domestic destinations, plus myriad overseas hubs.

Air2there.com (☑0800 777 000; www.air2there.com) Connects destinations across

Cook Strait, including including Paraparaumu, Wellington, Nelson and Blenheim.

Golden Bay Air (☑0800 588 885; www.goldenbayair.co.nz) Flies regularly between Wellington and Takaka in Golden Bay. Also connects to Karamea for Heaphy Track trampers.

Jetstar (☑0800 800 995; www. jetstar.com) Joins the dots between key tourism centres: Auckland, Wellington, Christchurch, Dunedin, Queenstown, Nelson, Napier, New Plymouth and Palmerston North.

Kiwi Regional Airlines (☑07-444 5020; www.flykiwiair.co.nz) New operator with services linking Nelson with Dunedin, Hamilton and Tauranga.

Soundsair (☑0800 505 005; www.soundsair.co.nz) Numerous flights each day between Picton and Wellington, plus flights from Wellington to Blenheim, Nelson, Westport and Taupo. Also flies Blenheim to Paraparaumu and Napier, and Nelson to Paraparaumu.

Stewart Island Flights (☑03-218 9129; www.stewartisland flights.com) Flies between Invercargill and Stewart Island.

Air Passes

Available exclusively to travellers from the USA or Canada who have bought an Air New Zealand fare to NZ from the USA or Canada, Australia or the Pacific Islands, Air New Zealand offers the good-value New Zealand Explorer Pass (www.airnewzealand.com/explorer-pass). The pass lets you fly between up to 27 destinations in New Zealand, Australia and the South Pacific islands (including Norfolk Island, Tonga, New Caledonia, Samoa, Vanuatu,

---

DEPARTURE TAX

An international 'passenger service charge' of up to NZ$25 applies when leaving New Zealand's various international airports, which is built into your ticket price. Other charges also apply ($1.50 civil aviation fee, $12 aviation security service fee, $6 departure fee, $16 arrival fee), which are also added to your ticket price.

Tahiti, Fiji, Niue and the Cook Islands). Fares are broken down into four discounted, distance-based zones: zone one flights start at US$99 (eg Auckland to Christchurch); zone two from US$129 (eg Auckland to Queenstown); zone three from US$214 (eg Wellington to Sydney); and zone four from US$295 (eg Tahiti to Auckland). You can buy the pass before you travel, or after you arrive in NZ.

Bicycle

Touring cyclists proliferate on the South Island, particularly over summer. The country is clean, green and relatively uncrowded, and there's lots of cheap accommodation (including camping) and abundant fresh water. The roads are generally in good nick, and the climate is usually not too hot or cold. Road traffic is the biggest danger: trucks overtaking too close to cyclists are a particular threat. Bikes and cycling gear are readily available to rent or buy in the main centres, and bicycle-repair shops are common.

By law all cyclists must wear an approved safety helmet (or risk a fine); it's also vital to have good reflective safety clothing. Cyclists who use public transport will find that major bus lines and trains only take bicycles on a 'space available' basis and charge up to $10. Some of the smaller shuttle bus companies, on the other hand, make sure they have storage space for bikes, which they carry for a surcharge.

If importing your own bike or transporting it by plane within NZ, check with the relevant airline for costs and the degree of dismantling and packing required.

See www.nzta.govt.nz/traffic/ways/bike for more bike safety and legal tips, and the New Zealand Cycle Trail (Nga Haerenga; p42) – a network of 23 Great Rides across NZ.

Hire

Rates offered by most outfits for renting road or mountain bikes are usually around $20 per hour to $60 per day. Longer-term rentals may be available by negotiation. You can often hire bikes from your accommodation (hostels, holiday parks etc) or rent more reputable machines from bike shops in the larger towns.

Buying a Bike

Bicycles can be readily bought in NZ's larger cities, but prices for newer models are high. For a decent hybrid bike or rigid mountain bike you'll pay anywhere from $800 to $1800, though you can get a cheap one for around $500 (but you still then need to buy panniers, helmet, lock etc, and the cost quickly climbs). Other options include the post-Christmas sales and midyear stocktakes, when newish cycles can be heavily discounted.

Boat

NZ may be an island nation but there's virtually no long-distance water transport around the country. On the South Island the obvious exceptions include the interisland ferries that cross the Cook Strait between Picton and Wellington and the passenger ferry that negotiates Foveaux Strait between Bluff and the town of Oban on Stewart Island.

If you're cashed-up, consider the cruise liners that chug around the NZ coastline as part of broader South Pacific itineraries: P&O Cruises (www.pocruises.com.au) is a major player.

Bus

Bus travel on the South Island is easygoing and well organised, with services transporting you to the far reaches of both islands (including the start/end of various walking track) but it can be expensive, tedious and time-consuming.

NZ's main bus company is **InterCity** (www.intercity.co.nz), which can drive you to just about anywhere on the North and South Islands. **Naked Bus** (www.nakedbus.com) has similar routes and remains the main competition. Both bus lines offer fares as low as $1!

InterCity also has a South Island sightseeing arm called **Newmans Coach Lines** (www.newmanscoach.co.nz), travelling between Queenstown, Christchurch and the West Coast glaciers.

Seat Classes & Smoking

There are no allocated economy or luxury classes on NZ buses (very democratic), and smoking on the bus is a definite no-no.

Reservations

Over summer, school holidays and public holidays, book well in advance on popular routes (a week or two if possible). At other times a day or two ahead is usually fine. The best prices are generally available online, booked a few weeks in advance.

Bus Passes

If you're covering a lot of ground, both InterCity and Naked Bus offer bus passes that can be cheaper than paying as you go, but they do of course lock you into using their respective networks. Passes are usually valid for 12 months.

On fares other than bus passes, InterCity offers a discount of around 10% for YHA, ISIC, Nomads, BBH or VIP backpacker card holders.

SOUTH ISLAND PASSES

On the South Island, InterCity offers six hop-on/hop-off, fixed-itinerary passes, ranging from $119 runs along the West Coast between

Picton and Queenstown, to a $509 loop around the whole island. See www.intercity.co.nz/bus-pass/travelpass for details.

NATIONWIDE PASSES

Flexipass A hop-on/hop-off InterCity pass, allowing travel to pretty much anywhere in NZ, in any direction, including the Interislander ferry across Cook Strait. The pass is purchased in blocks of travel time: minimum 15 hours ($119) to maximum 60 hours ($449). The average cost of each block becomes cheaper the more hours you buy. You can top up the pass if you need more time.

Aotearoa Explorer, Tiki Tour & Island Loop Hop-on/hop-off, fixed-itinerary nationwide passes offered by InterCity. These passes link up tourist hot spots and range in price from $738 to $995. See www.intercity.co.nz/bus-pass/travelpass for details.

Naked Passport (www.nakedpassport.com) A Naked Bus pass that allows you to buy trips in blocks of five, which you can add to any time, and book each trip as needed. Five/15/30 trips cost $151/318/491. An unlimited pass costs $597 – great value if you're travelling NZ for many moons.

Shuttle Buses

As well as InterCity and Naked Bus, regional shuttle buses fill in the gaps between the smaller towns. South Island operators include the following (see www.tourism.net.nz/transport/bus-and-coach-services for a complete list), offering regular scheduled services and/or bus tours and charters:

Abel Tasman Travel (www.abeltasmantravel.co.nz) Traverses the roads between Nelson, Motueka, Golden Bay and Abel Tasman National Park.

Atomic Shuttles (www.atomictravel.co.nz) Has services throughout the South Island, including to Christchurch, Dunedin, Invercargill, Picton, Nelson, Greymouth, Hokitika, Queenstown and Wanaka.

Catch-a-Bus South (www.catchabussouth.co.nz) Invercargill and Bluff to Dunedin and Queenstown.

Cook Connection (www.cookconnect.co.nz) Triangulates between Mt Cook, Twizel and Lake Tekapo.

East West Coaches (www.eastwestcoaches.co.nz) Offers a service between Christchurch and Westport via Lewis Pass.

Hanmer Connection (www.hanmerconnection.co.nz) Daily services between Hanmer Springs and Christchurch.

Tracknet (www.tracknet.net) Summer track transport (Milford, Routeburn, Kepler) with Queenstown, Te Anau and Invercargill connections.

Trek Express (www.trekexpress.co.nz) Shuttle services to all tramping tracks in the top half of the South Island.

West Coast Shuttle (www.westcoastshuttle.co.nz) Daily bus from Greymouth to Christchurch and back.

Backpacker Buses

If you feel like clocking up some kilometres (and often some hangovers) with like-minded fellow travellers, the following operators run fixed-itinerary bus tours, nationwide or on the North or South Islands. Accommodation, meals and hop-on/hop-off flexibility are often included.

Adventure Tours New Zealand (www.adventuretours.com.au) Five 11- to 22-day NZ tours, either South Island, North Island or both.

Bottom Bus (www.travel-headfirst.com/local-legends/bottom-bus) South Island nether-region tours ex-Dunedin, Invercargill and Queenstown.

Flying Kiwi (www.flyingkiwi.com) Good-fun, activity-based trips around NZ (four to 28 days) with camping and cabin accommodation.

Haka Tours (www.hakatours.com) Three- to 16-day tours with adventure, snow or mountain-biking themes.

Kiwi Experience (www.kiwiexperience.com) The major hop-on/hop-off player, with myriad tours available.

Stray Travel (www.straytravel.com) A wide range of flexible hop-on/hop-off passes and tours.

Car & Motorcycle

The best way to explore the South Island in depth is to have your own wheels. It's easy to hire cars and campervans at good rates. Alternatively, if you're here for a few months you might consider buying your own vehicle.

Automobile Association

NZ's **Automobile Association** (AA; ☎0800 500 444; www.aa.co.nz/travel) provides emergency breakdown services, maps and accommodation guides (from holiday parks to motels and B&Bs).

Members of overseas automobile associations should bring their membership cards – many of these bodies have reciprocal agreements with the AA.

Driving Licences

International visitors to NZ can use their home country driving licence – if your licence isn't in English, it's a good idea to carry a certified translation with you. Alternatively, use an International Driving Permit (IDP), which will usually be issued on the spot (valid for 12 months) by your home country's automobile association.

Fuel

Fuel (petrol, aka gasoline) is available from service stations across NZ: unless you're cruising around in something from the '70s, you'll be filling up with 'unleaded', or LPG (gas). LPG is not always stocked by rural suppliers; if you're on gas, it's safer to have dual-fuel capability. Aside from remote locations like Milford Sound and Mt Cook, petrol prices don't vary much from place to place: per-litre costs at the time of research were around $2.

Hire
CAMPERVAN

Check your rear-view mirror on any far-flung NZ road and you'll probably see a shiny white campervan (aka mobile home, motor home or RV) packed with liberated travellers, mountain bikes and portable barbecues cruising along behind you.

Most towns of any size have a campground or holiday park with powered sites (where you can plug your vehicle in) for around $35 per night. There are also 250-plus vehicle-accessible Department of Conservation (www.doc.govt.nz) camp-sites around NZ, ranging in price from free to $15 per adult: check the website for info. Also see p314 for more.

You can hire campervans from dozens of companies. Prices vary with season, vehicle size and length of rental.

A small van for two people typically has a minikitchen and fold-out dining table, the latter transforming into a double bed when dinner is done and dusted. Larger 'superior' two-berth vans include shower and toilet. Four- to six-berth camper-vans are the size of trucks (and similarly sluggish) and, besides the extra space, usually contain a toilet and shower.

Over summer, rates offered by the main rental firms for two-/four-/six-berth vans booked six months in advance start at around $110/150/210 per day for a month-long rental, dropping to as low as $50/70/100 per day during winter.

Major operators include the following:

Apollo (☑09-889 2976, 0800 113 131; www.apollocamper.co.nz)

Britz (☑09-255 3910, 08 00 081 032; www.britz.co.nz)

Also does 'Britz Bikes' (add a mountain or city bike from $12 per day).

Kea (☑09-448 8800, 0800 464 613; www.keacampers.com)

Maui (☑09-255 3910, 0800 688 558; www.maui.co.nz)

Wilderness Motorhomes (☑09-282 3606; www.wilder-ness.co.nz)

BACKPACKER VAN

Budget players in the campervan industry offer slick deals and funky (often gregariously spray-painted), well-kitted-out vehicles for backpackers. Rates are competitive (from $25/50 per day for a two-/four-berth van from May to September; from $90/150 per day from December to February). Op-erators include the following:

Backpacker Sleeper Vans (☑0800 321 939, 03-359 4731; www.sleepervans.co.nz)

Escape Campervans (☑0800 216 171; www.escaperentals.co.nz)

Hippie Camper (☑0800 113 131; www.hippiecamper.co.nz)

Jucy (☑09-929 2462, 0800 399 736; www.jucy.co.nz)

Mighty Cars & Campers (☑0800 422 505; www.mightycampers.co.nz)

Spaceships (☑0800 772 237, 09-526 2130; www.spaceships-rentals.co.nz)

CAR

Competition between car-rental companies on the South Island is torrid, par-ticularly in the big cities and Picton. Remember that if you want to travel far, you need unlimited kilometres. Some (but not all) companies re-quire drivers to be at least 21 years old – ask around.

Most car-hire firms sug-gest (or insist) that you don't take their vehicles between islands on the Cook Strait ferries. Instead, you leave your car at either Wellington or Picton terminal and pick up another car once you've crossed the strait. This saves

you paying to transport a vehicle on the ferries, and is a pain-free exercise.

INTERNATIONAL RENTAL COMPANIES

The big multinational com-panies have offices in most major cities, towns and airports. Firms sometimes offer one-way rentals (eg collect a car in Queenstown and leave it in Christchurch), but there are often re-strictions and fees. On the other hand, an operator in Invercargill may need to get a vehicle back to Blenheim and will offer an amazing one-way car relocation deal (sometimes free!).

The major companies offer a choice of either un-limited kilometres, or 100km (or so) per day free, plus so many cents per subsequent kilometre. Daily rates in main cities typically start at around $40 per day for a compact, late-model Japa-nese car, and around $75 for medium-sized cars (includ-ing GST, unlimited kilometres and insurance).

Avis (☑09-526 2847, 0800 655 111; www.avis.co.nz)

Budget (☑09-529 7784, 0800 283 438; www.budget.co.nz)

Europcar (☑0800 800 115; www.europcar.co.nz)

Hertz (☑03-358 6789, 0800 654 321; www.hertz.co.nz)

Thrifty (☑03-359 2720, 0800 737 070; www.thrifty.co.nz)

LOCAL RENTAL COMPANIES

Local rental firms prolif-erate. These are almost always cheaper than the big boys – sometimes half the price – but the cheap rates may come with serious restrictions: vehicles are often older, depots might be further away from airports/city centres, and with less formality sometimes comes a less protective legal struc-ture for renters.

Rentals from local firms start at around $30 per day for the smallest option. It's

ROAD DISTANCES (KM)

	Aoraki/Mt Cook	Arthur's Pass	Blenheim	Christchurch	Dunedin	Franz Josef Glacier	Greymouth	Hanmer Springs	Hokitika	Invercargill	Kaikoura	Milford Sound	Nelson	Oamaru	Picton	Queenstown	Te Anau	Timaru	Wanaka
Arthur's Pass	410																		
Blenheim	635	420																	
Christchurch	330	150	310																
Dunedin	325	455	665	360															
Franz Josef Glacier	485	230	500	390	560														
Greymouth	510	95	330	250	550	180													
Hanmer Springs	460	265	260	140	490	395	215												
Hokitika	510	100	370	250	550	135	40	255											
Invercargill	440	660	870	570	210	530	710	700	665										
Kaikoura	505	290	130	185	535	540	330	135	390	745									
Milford Sound	540	840	1060	760	410	630	805	890	770	275	930								
Nelson	745	370	115	425	775	470	290	310	335	990	245	1100							
Oamaru	210	340	550	250	115	510	430	375	435	325	420	525	660						
Picton	660	450	30	340	690	530	355	290	400	900	160	1090	120	580					
Queenstown	260	565	785	480	285	355	530	610	490	190	660	290	820	290	815				
Te Anau	420	725	945	640	295	515	690	770	650	160	815	120	980	410	975	170			
Timaru	210	260	465	165	200	490	350	295	360	410	340	605	580	85	495	330	490		
Wanaka	210	510	730	430	280	285	465	555	420	245	600	345	755	230	760	70	230	275	
Westport	610	195	260	340	650	280	100	220	145	810	330	905	230	535	290	630	790	455	565

obviously cheaper if you rent for a week or more, and there are often low-season and weekend discounts.

Affordable, independent operators with national networks include the following:

a2b Car Rentals (☏09-254 4397, 0800 545 000; www.a2b-car-rental.co.nz)

Ace Rental Cars (☏09-303 3112, 0800 502 277; www.acerentalcars.co.nz)

Apex Rentals (☏03-363 3000, 0800 500 660; www.apexrentals.co.nz)

Ezi Car Rental (☏09-254 4397, 0800 545 000; www.ezicarrental.co.nz)

Go Rentals (☏09-974 1598, 0800 467 368; www.gorentals.co.nz)

Omega Rental Cars (☏09-377 5573, 0800 525 210; www.omegarentalcars.com)

Pegasus Rental Cars (☏09-275 3222, 0800 803 580; www.rentalcars.co.nz)

Transfercar (☏09-630 7533; www.transfercar.co.nz) One-way relocation specialists.

MOTORCYCLE

Born to be wild? The South Island has great terrain for motorcycle touring, despite the fickle weather in some regions. Most of the island's motorcycle-hire shops are in Christchurch, where you can hire anything from a little 50cc moped (aka nifty-fifty) to a throbbing 750cc touring motorcycle and beyond. Recommended operators (who also run guided tours)

offer rates of anywhere from $50 per day:

New Zealand Motorcycle Rentals & Tours (☏09-486 2472; www.nzbike.com)

Te Waipounamu Motorcycle Tours (☏03-372-3537; www.motorcycle-hire.co.nz)

Insurance

Rather than risk paying out wads of cash if you have an accident, you can take out your own comprehensive insurance policy, or (the usual option) pay an additional fee per day to the rental company to reduce your excess. This brings the amount you must pay in the event of an accident down from around $1500 or $2000 to around $200 or $300. Smaller operators offering cheap rates often have a compulsory insurance excess, taken as a credit-card bond, of around $900.

Most insurance agreements won't cover the cost of damage to glass (including the windscreen) or tyres, and insurance coverage is often invalidated on beaches and certain rough (4WD) unsealed roads – read the fine print.

See www.acc.co.nz for info on NZ's Accident Compensation Corporation insurance scheme (fault-free personal injury insurance).

Purchase

Buying a car then selling it at the end of your travels can be one of the cheapest and best ways to see NZ. On the South Island, Christchurch is the easiest place to buy a car. Turners Auctions (www.turners.co.nz) is NZ's biggest car-auction operator, with 10 locations around the country.

LEGALITIES

Make sure your prospective vehicle has a Warrant of Fitness (WoF) and registration valid for a reasonable period: see the New Zealand Transport Agency website (www.nzta.govt.nz) for details.

Buyers should also take out third-party insurance, covering the cost of repairs to another vehicle in an accident that is your fault: try the **Automobile Association** (AA; ☎0800 500 444; www.aa.co.nz/travel). NZ's no-fault Accident Compensation Corporation (www.acc.co.nz) scheme covers personal injury, but make sure you have travel insurance, too.

If you're considering buying a car and want someone to check it out for you, various car-inspection companies inspect cars for around $150; find them at car auctions, or they will come to you. Try **Vehicle Inspection New Zealand** (VINZ; ☎09-

573 3230, 0800 468 469; www.vinz.co.nz) or the AA.

Before you buy it's wise to confirm ownership of the vehicle, and find out if there's anything dodgy about the car (eg stolen, or outstanding debts). The AA's **LemonCheck** (☎09-420 3090, 0800 536 662; www.lemoncheck.co.nz) offers this service.

BUY-BACK DEALS

You can avoid the hassle of buying/selling a vehicle privately by entering into a buy-back arrangement with a dealer. Predictably, dealers often find sneaky ways of knocking down the return-sale price, which may be 50% less than what you paid, so hiring or buying and selling a vehicle yourself (if you have the time) is usually a better bet.

Road Hazards

There's an unusually high percentage of international drivers involved in road accidents in NZ – something like 30% of accidents involve a non-local driver. South Island traffic is usually pretty light, but it's easy to get stuck behind a slow-moving truck or campervan – pack plenty of patience, and know your road rules before you get behind the wheel. There are also lots of slow wiggly roads, one-way bridges and plenty of gravel roads, all of which require a more cautious driving approach. And watch out for sheep!

To check road conditions call ☎0800 444 449 or see www.nzta.govt.nz/traffic.

Road Rules

Kiwis drive on the left-hand side of the road; cars are right-hand drive. Give way to the right at intersections.

At single-lane bridges (of which there are a surprisingly large number), a smaller red arrow pointing in your direction of travel means that *you* give way.

Speed limits on the open road are generally 100km/h; in built-up areas the limit is usually 50km/h. Speed cameras and radars are used extensively.

All vehicle occupants must wear a seatbelt or risk a fine. Small children must be belted into approved safety seats. Always carry your licence when driving. Drink-driving is a serious offence and remains a significant problem in NZ, despite widespread campaigns and severe penalties. The legal blood alcohol limit is 0.05% for drivers over 20, and zero for those under 20.

Hitching & Ride-Sharing

Hitching is never entirely safe, and we don't recommend it. Travellers who hitch should understand that they are taking a small but potentially serious risk. That said, it's not unusual to see hitchhikers along NZ country roads.

Alternatively, check hostel noticeboards for ride-share opportunities.

Local Transport

Bus, Train & Tram

The South Island's larger cities have extensive bus services but, with a few honourable exceptions, they are mainly daytime, weekday operations; weekend services can be infrequent or nonexistent. Negotiating inner-city Christchurch is made easier by a free city-shuttle service and the historic tramway.

There are no local train services on the South Island.

Taxi

The main cities have plenty of taxis and even small towns may have a local service. Taxis are metred, and generally reliable and trustworthy.

Train

NZ train travel is all about the journey, not about getting anywhere in a hurry. **KiwiRail Scenic Journeys** (☏0800 872 467, 04-495 0775; www. kiwirailscenic.co.nz) operates four routes, including two on the South Island, listed below. Reservations can be made through KiwiRail Scenic Journeys directly, or at most train stations, travel agents and visitor information centres. All services are for day travel (no sleeper services).

TranzAlpine Over the Southern Alps between Christchurch and Greymouth – one of the world's most famous train rides.

Coastal Pacific Between Christchurch and Picton along the South Island's east coast.

Train Passes

A KiwiRail Scenic Journeys Scenic Journey Rail Pass (www.kiwirailscenic.co.nz/scenic-rail-pass) allows unlimited travel on all of its rail services, including passage on the Picton–Wellington Interislander ferry. There are two types of pass, both requiring you to book your seats a minimum of 24 hours before you want to travel:

Fixed Pass Limited duration fares for one/two/three weeks, costing $599/699/799 per adult (a little bit less for kids).

Freedom Pass Affords you travel on a certain number of days over a 12-month period; a three-/seven-/10-day pass costs $417/903/1290.

Language

New Zealand has three official languages: English, Maori and NZ sign language. Although English is what you'll usually hear, Maori has been making a comeback. You can use English to speak to anyone in New Zealand, but there are some occasions when knowing a small amount of Maori is useful, such as when visiting a *marae,* where often only Maori is spoken. Some knowledge of Maori will also help you interpret the many Maori place names you'll come across.

KIWI ENGLISH

Like the people of other English-speaking countries in the world, New Zealanders have their own, unique way of speaking the language. The flattening of vowels is the most distinctive feature of Kiwi pronunciation. For example, in Kiwi English, 'fish and chips' sounds more like 'fush and chups'. On the North Island sentences often have 'eh!' attached to the end. In the far south a rolled 'r' is common, which is a holdover from that region's Scottish heritage – it's especially noticeable in Southland.

MAORI

The Maori have a vividly chronicled history, recorded in songs and chants that dramatically recall the migration to New Zealand from Polynesia as well as other important events. Early missionaries were the first to record the language in a written form using only 15 letters of the English alphabet.

Maori is closely related to other Polynesian languages such as Hawaiian, Tahitian and Cook Islands Maori. In fact, New Zealand Maori and Hawaiian are quite similar, even though more than 7000km separates Honolulu and Auckland.

The Maori language was never dead – it was always used in Maori ceremonies – but over time familiarity with it was definitely on the decline. Fortunately, recent years have

seen a revival of interest in it, and this forms an integral part of the renaissance of *Maoritanga* (Maori culture). Many Maori people who had heard the language spoken on the *marae* for years but had not used it in their day-to-day lives, are now studying it and speaking it fluently. Maori is taught in schools throughout New Zealand, some TV programs and news reports are broadcast in it, and many English place names are being renamed in Maori. Even government departments have been given Maori names: for example, the Inland Revenue Department is also known as Te Tari Taake (the last word is actually *take,* which means 'levy', but the department has chosen to stress the long 'a' by spelling it 'aa').

In many places, Maori have come together to provide instruction in their language and culture to young children; the idea is for them to grow up speaking both Maori and English, and to develop a familiarity with Maori tradition. It's a matter of some pride to have fluency in the language. On some *marae* only Maori can be spoken.

Pronunciation

Maori is a fluid, poetic language and surprisingly easy to pronounce once you remember to split each word (some can be amazingly long) into separate syllables. Each syllable ends in a vowel. There are no 'silent' letters.

Most consonants in Maori – *h, k, m, n, p, t* and *w* – are pronounced much the same as in English. The Maori *r* is a flapped sound (not rolled) with the tongue near the front of the mouth. It's closer to the English 'l' in pronunciation.

The *ng* is pronounced as in the English words 'singing' or 'running', and can be used at the beginning of words as well as at the end. To practise, just say 'ing' over and over, then isolate the 'ng' part of it.

The letters *wh,* when occuring together, are generally pronounced as a soft English 'f'. This pronunciation is used in many place names in New Zealand, such as Whakatane, Whangaroa and Whakapapa (all pronounced as if they begin with a soft 'f'). There is some local variation: in the region around the Whanganui River, for example, *wh* is pronounced as in the English word 'when'.

The correct pronunciation of the vowels is very important. The examples below are a rough guideline – it helps to listen carefully to someone who speaks the language well. Each vowel has both a long and a short sound, with long vowels often denoted by a line over the letter or a double vowel. We have not indicated long and short vowel forms in this book.

Vowels

a	as in 'large', with no 'r' sound
e	as in 'get'
i	as in 'marine'
o	as in 'pork'
u	as the 'oo' in 'moon'

Vowel Combinations

ae, ai	as the 'y' in 'sky'
ao, au	as the 'ow' in 'how'
ea	as in 'bear'
ei	as in 'vein'
eo	as 'eh-oh'
eu	as 'eh-oo'
ia	as in the name 'Ian'
ie	as the 'ye' in 'yet'
io	as the 'ye o' in 'ye old'
iu	as the 'ue' in 'cue'
oa	as in 'roar'
oe	as in 'toe'
oi	as in 'toil'
ou	as the 'ow' in 'how'
ua	as the 'ewe' in 'fewer'

Greetings & Small Talk

Maori greetings are becoming increasingly popular – don't be surprised if you're greeted with *Kia ora*.

Welcome!	*Haere mai!*
Hello./Good luck./ Good health.	*Kia ora.*
Hello. (to one person)	*Tena koe.*
Hello. (to two people)	*Tena korua.*
Hello. (to three or more people)	*Tena koutou.*
Goodbye. (to person staying)	*E noho ra.*

Goodbye. (to person leaving)	*Haere ra.*
How are you? (to one person)	*Kei te pehea koe?*
How are you? (to two people)	*Kei te pehea korua?*
How are you? (to three or more people)	*Kei te pehea koutou?*
Very well, thanks./ That's fine.	*Kei te pai.*

Maori Geographical Terms

The following words form part of many Maori place names in New Zealand, and help you understand the meaning of these place names. For example: Waikaremoana is the Sea (*moana*) of Rippling (*kare*) Waters (*wai*), and Rotorua means the Second (*rua*) Lake (*roto*).

a – of
ana – cave
ara – way, path or road
awa – river or valley
heke – descend
hiku – end; tail
hine – girl; daughter
ika – fish
iti – small
kahurangi – treasured possession; special greenstone
kai – food
kainga – village
kaka – parrot
kare – rippling
kati – shut or close
koura – crayfish
makariri – cold
manga – stream or tributary
manu – bird
maunga – mountain
moana – sea or lake
moko – tattoo
motu – island
mutu – finished; ended; over
nga – the (plural)
noa – ordinary; not *tapu*
nui – big or great
nuku – distance
o – of, place of...
one – beach, sand or mud
pa – fortified village
papa – large blue-grey mudstone
pipi – common edible bivalve
pohatu – stone
poto – short

pouri – sad; dark; gloomy
puke – hill
puna – spring; hole; fountain
rangi – sky; heavens
raro – north
rei – cherished possession
roa – long
roto – lake
rua – hole in the ground; two
runga – above
tahuna – beach; sandbank
tane – man
tangata – people
tapu – sacred, forbidden or taboo
tata – close to; dash against; twin islands
tawaha – entrance or opening
tawahi – the other side (of a river or lake)
te – the (singular)
tonga – south
ure – male genitals
uru – west
waha – broken
wahine – woman
wai – water
waingaro – lost; waters that disappear in certain seasons

waka – canoe
wera – burnt or warm; floating
wero – challenge
whaka... – to act as ...
whanau – family
whanga – harbour, bay or inlet
where – house
whenua – land or country
whiti – east

Here are some more place names composed of words in the list:

Aramoana – Sea (*moana*) Path (*ara*)
Awaroa – Long (*roa*) River (*awa*)
Kaitangata – Eat (*kai*) People (*tangata*)
Maunganui – Great (*nui*) Mountain (*maunga*)
Opouri – Place of (*o*) Sadness (*pouri*)
Te Araroa – The (*te*) Long (*roa*) Path (*ara*)
Te Puke – The (*te*) Hill (*puke*)
Urewera – Burnt (*wera*) Penis (*ure*)
Waimakariri – Cold (*makariri*) Water (*wai*)
Wainui – Great (*nui*) Waters (*wai*)
Whakatane – To Act (*whaka*) as a Man (*tane*)
Whangarei – Cherished (*rei*) Harbour (*whanga*)

GLOSSARY

Following is a list of abbreviations, 'Kiwi English', Maori and slang terms used in this book and which you may hear in New Zealand.

All Blacks – NZ's revered national rugby union team
ANZAC – Australia and New Zealand Army Corps
Aoraki – *Maori* name for Mt Cook, meaning 'Cloud Piercer'
Aotearoa – *Maori* name for NZ, most often translated as 'Land of the Long White Cloud'
aroha – love

B&B – 'bed and breakfast' accommodation
bach – holiday home (pronounced 'batch'); see also crib
black-water rafting – rafting or tubing underground in a cave
boozer – public bar
bro – literally 'brother'; usually meaning mate

BYO – 'bring your own' (usually applies to alcohol at a restaurant or cafe)

choice/chur – fantastic; great
crib – the name for a bach in Otago and Southland

DB&B – 'dinner, bed and breakfast' accommodation
DOC – Department of Conservation (or Te Papa Atawhai); government department that administers national parks, tracks and huts

eh? – roughly translates as 'don't you agree?'

farmstay – accommodation on a Kiwi farm
football – rugby, either union or league; occasionally soccer

Great Walks – set of nine popular tramping tracks within NZ
greenstone – jade; *pounamu*
gumboots – rubber boots or Wellingtons; originated from diggers on the gum-fields

haka – any dance, but usually a war dance
hangi – oven whereby food is steamed in baskets over embers in a hole; a *Maori* feast
hapu – subtribe or smaller tribal grouping
Hawaiki – original homeland of the *Maori*
hei tiki – carved, stylised human figure worn around the neck; also called a *tiki*
homestay – accommodation in a family house
hongi – *Maori* greeting; the pressing of foreheads and noses, and sharing of life breath

hui – gathering; meeting

i-SITE – information centre

iwi – large tribal grouping with common lineage back to the original migration from *Hawaiki*; people; tribe

jandals – contraction of 'Japanese sandals'; flip-flops; thongs; usually rubber footwear

jersey – jumper, usually woollen; the shirt worn by rugby players

kauri – native pine

kia ora – hello

Kiwi – New Zealander; an adjective to mean anything relating to NZ

kiwi – flightless, nocturnal brown bird with a long beak

Kiwiana – things uniquely connected to NZ life and culture, especially from bygone years

kiwifruit – small, succulent fruit with fuzzy brown skin and juicy green flesh; aka Chinese gooseberry or zespri

kumara – Polynesian sweet potato, a *Maori* staple food

Kupe – early Polynesian navigator from *Hawaiki*, credited with the discovery of the islands that are now NZ

mana – spiritual quality of a person or object; authority or prestige

Maori – indigenous people of NZ

Maoritanga – things *Maori*, ie *Maori* culture

marae – sacred ground in front of the *Maori* meeting house; more commonly used to refer to the entire complex of buildings

Maui – figure in *Maori* (Polynesian) mythology

mauri – life force/principle

moa – large, extinct flightless bird

moko – tattoo; usually refers to facial tattoos

nga – the (plural); see also *te*

ngai/ngati – literally, 'the people of' or 'the descendants of'; tribe (pronounced 'kai' on the South Island)

NZ – universal term for New Zealand; pronounced 'en zed'

pa – fortified *Maori* village, usually on a hilltop

Pacific Rim – modern NZ cuisine; local produce cooked with imported styles

Pakeha – *Maori* for a white or European person

Pasifika – Pacific Island culture

paua – abalone; iridescent paua shell is often used in jewellery

pavlova – meringue cake topped with cream and kiwifruit

PI – Pacific Islander

poi – ball of woven flax

pounamu – *Maori* name for *greenstone*

powhiri – traditional *Maori* welcome onto a marae

rip – dangerously strong current running away from the shore at a beach

Roaring Forties – the ocean between 40° and 50° south, known for very strong winds

silver fern – symbol worn by the *All Blacks* and other national sportsfolk on their jerseys; the national netball team is called the Silver Ferns

sweet, sweet as – all-purpose term like choice; fantastic, great

tapu – strong force in *Maori* life, with numerous meanings; in its simplest form it means sacred, forbidden, taboo

te – the (singular); see also *nga*

te reo – literally 'the language'; the *Maori* language

tiki – short for *hei tiki*

tiki tour – scenic tour

tramp – bushwalk; trek; hike

tuatara – prehistoric reptile dating back to the age of dinosaurs

tui – native parson bird

wahine – woman

wai – water

wairua – spirit

Waitangi – short way of referring to the Treaty of Waitangi

waka – canoe

Warriors – NZ's popular rugby league club, affiliated with Australia's NRL

Wellywood – Wellington, because of its thriving film industry

zorbing – rolling down a hill inside an inflatable plastic ball

Behind the Scenes

SEND US YOUR FEEDBACK

We love to hear from travellers – your comments keep us on our toes and help make our books better. Our well-travelled team reads every word on what you loved or loathed about this book. Although we cannot reply individually to your submissions, we always guarantee that your feedback goes straight to the appropriate authors, in time for the next edition. Each person who sends us information is thanked in the next edition – the most useful submissions are rewarded with a selection of digital PDF chapters.

Visit **lonelyplanet.com/contact** to submit your updates and suggestions or to ask for help. Our award-winning website also features inspirational travel stories, news and discussions.

Note: We may edit, reproduce and incorporate your comments in Lonely Planet products such as guidebooks, websites and digital products, so let us know if you don't want your comments reproduced or your name acknowledged. For a copy of our privacy policy visit lonelyplanet.com/privacy.

AUTHOR THANKS

Charles Rawlings-Way

Thanks to the many generous, knowledgeable and quietly self-assured Kiwis I met on the road. Huge thanks to Tasmin Waby for signing me up, and the in-house LP content deities who electrified this CMS Frankenstein. Humongous gratitude to my tireless, witty and professional co-authors – Lee, Sarah and Peter – who always bring the humour and the class. Most of all, thanks to Meg, Ione and Remy for holding the fort while I was away.

Sarah Bennett & Lee Slater

Thanks to everyone who helped us on the road, including tourism organisations, DOC and visitor centre staff, business operators and travellers. Thanks also to friends and family who provided a park for the campervan, a fridge for the flagon, and company on vital research missions. Finally, thanks to our fellow NZ authors for the camaraderie, as always, and Tasmin Waby for leading the team.

Peter Dragicevich

I owe a great deal of thanks to Hamish, Jill and John Blennerhassett in Wanaka, Scott and Sophie Kennedy in Queenstown and Michael Wilson in Invercargill. Special thanks to Michael Woodhouse for his comradeship on the road in Otago. And to all of my Auckland friends and family who enthusiastically supped and gorged with me in the city's bars and restaurants, good work!

ACKNOWLEDGEMENTS

Climate map data adapted from Peel MC, Finlayson BL & McMahon TA (2007) 'Updated World Map of the Köppen-Geiger Climate Classification', Hydrology and Earth System Sciences, 11, 163344.

Cover photograph: Fiordland National Park, Robert Harding World Imagery / Alamy ©

THIS BOOK

This 5th edition of Lonely Planet's *New Zealand's South Island* guidebook was researched and written by Charles Rawlings-Way, Sarah Bennett, Peter Dragicevich and Lee Slater. The previous two editions were written by Brett Atkinson, Sarah Bennett, Peter Dragicevich, Charles Rawlings-Way and Lee Slater. This guidebook was produced by the following:

Destination Editor
Tasmin Waby
Product Editors
Kate Kiely, Tracy Whitmey
Senior Cartographers
Diana Von Holdt, Julie Sheridan
Book Designers
Cam Ashley, Wendy Wright
Assisting Editors Imogen Bannister, Michelle Bennett, Nigel Chin, Pete Cruttenden, Andrea Dobbin, Paul Harding, Gabrielle Innes, Elizabeth Jones, Jodie Martire, Kristin Odijk, Susan Paterson, Gabrielle Stefanos, Saralinda Turner
Assisting Cartographers
Hunor Csutoros, Corey Hutchison, Rachel Imeson
Cover Researcher
Naomi Parker
Thanks to David Carroll, Daniel Corbett, Jennifer Carey, Jessica Fredericks, Andi Jones, Lauren Keith, Karyn Noble, Kirsten Rawlings, Diana Saengkham, Eleanor Simpson, Angela Tinson, Anna Tyler, Dora Whitaker

Index

NOTES

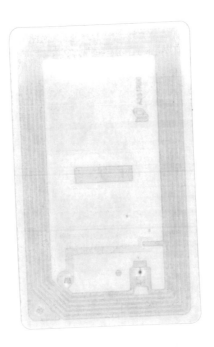

ANNA HARRIS

LONELY PLANET IN THE WILD

Map Legend

Sights
- Beach
- Bird Sanctuary
- Buddhist
- Castle/Palace
- Christian
- Confucian
- Hindu
- Islamic
- Jain
- Jewish
- Monument
- Museum/Gallery/Historic Building
- Ruin
- Shinto
- Sikh
- Taoist
- Winery/Vineyard
- Zoo/Wildlife Sanctuary
- Other Sight

Activities, Courses & Tours
- Bodysurfing
- Diving
- Canoeing/Kayaking
- Course/Tour
- Sento Hot Baths/Onsen
- Skiing
- Snorkelling
- Surfing
- Swimming/Pool
- Walking
- Windsurfing
- Other Activity

Sleeping
- Sleeping
- Camping

Eating
- Eating

Drinking & Nightlife
- Drinking & Nightlife
- Cafe

Entertainment
- Entertainment

Shopping
- Shopping

Information
- Bank
- Embassy/Consulate
- Hospital/Medical
- Internet
- Police
- Post Office
- Telephone
- Toilet
- Tourist Information
- Other Information

Geographic
- Beach
- Gate
- Hut/Shelter
- Lighthouse
- Lookout
- Mountain/Volcano
- Oasis
- Park
- Pass
- Picnic Area
- Waterfall

Population
- Capital (National)
- Capital (State/Province)
- City/Large Town
- Town/Village

Transport
- Airport
- Border crossing
- Bus
- Cable car/Funicular
- Cycling
- Ferry
- Metro station
- Monorail
- Parking
- Petrol station
- Subway station
- Taxi
- Train station/Railway
- Tram
- Underground station
- Other Transport

Note: Not all symbols displayed above appear on the maps in this book

Routes
- Tollway
- Freeway
- Primary
- Secondary
- Tertiary
- Lane
- Unsealed road
- Road under construction
- Plaza/Mall
- Steps
- Tunnel
- Pedestrian overpass
- Walking Tour
- Walking Tour detour
- Path/Walking Trail

Boundaries
- International
- State/Province
- Disputed
- Regional/Suburb
- Marine Park
- Cliff
- Wall

Hydrography
- River, Creek
- Intermittent River
- Canal
- Water
- Dry/Salt/Intermittent Lake
- Reef

Areas
- Airport/Runway
- Beach/Desert
- Cemetery (Christian)
- Cemetery (Other)
- Glacier
- Mudflat
- Park/Forest
- Sight (Building)
- Sportsground
- Swamp/Mangrove

Contributing Writers

Professor James Belich wrote the History chapter. James is one of NZ's pre-eminent historians and the award-winning author of *The New Zealand Wars*, *Making Peoples* and *Paradise Reforged*. He has also worked in TV – *New Zealand Wars* was screened in NZ in 1998.

Tony Horwitz wrote the Captain James Cook boxed text in the History chapter. Tony is a Pulitzer winning reporter and nonfiction author. His fascination with James Cook, and with travel, took him around NZ, Australia and the Pacific while researching *Blue Latitudes* (alternatively titled *Into the Blue*), part biography of Cook and part travelogue.

John Huria (Ngai Tahu, Muaupoko) wrote the Māori Culture chapter. John has an editorial, research and writing background with a focus on Māori writing and culture. He was senior editor for Māori publishing company Huia and now runs an editorial and publishing services company, Ahi Text Solutions Ltd (www.ahitextsolutions.co.nz).

Josh Kronfeld wrote the Surfing the South Island boxed text in the Extreme Sports on the South Island chapter. Josh is an ex–All Black flanker, whose passion for surfing NZ's beaches is legendary and who found travelling for rugby a way to surf other great breaks around the world.

Gareth Shute wrote the Music section in the Arts & Music chapter. Gareth is the author of four books, including *Hip Hop Music in Aotearoa* and *NZ Rock 1987–2007*. He is also a musician and has toured the UK, Europe and Australia as a member of the Ruby Suns and the Brunettes. He now plays in indie soul group The Cosbys.

Vaughan Yarwood wrote the Environment chapter. Vaughan is an Auckland-based writer whose books include *The History Makers: Adventures in New Zealand Biography*, *The Best of New Zealand: A Collection of Essays on NZ Life and Culture by Prominent Kiwis*, which he edited, and the regional history *Between Coasts: From Kaipara to Kawau*. He has written widely for NZ and international publications and is the former associate editor of *New Zealand Geographic*, for which he has also written for many years.

OUR STORY

A beat-up old car, a few dollars in the pocket and a sense of adventure. In 1972 that's all Tony and Maureen Wheeler needed for the trip of a lifetime – across Europe and Asia overland to Australia. It took several months, and at the end – broke but inspired – they sat at their kitchen table writing and stapling together their first travel guide, *Across Asia on the Cheap*. Within a week they'd sold 1500 copies. Lonely Planet was born.

Today, Lonely Planet has offices in Franklin, London, Melbourne, Oakland, Beijing and Delhi, with more than 600 staff and writers. We share Tony's belief that 'a great guidebook should do three things: inform, educate and amuse'.

OUR WRITERS

Charles Rawlings-Way

English by birth, Australian by chance, All Blacks fan by choice: Charles's early understanding of Aotearoa was less than comprehensive (sheep, mountains, sheep on mountains...). He realised there was more to it when a wandering uncle returned with a faux-jade tiki in 1981. He wore it with pride until he saw the NZ cricket team's beige uniforms in 1982... Mt Taranaki's snowy summit, Napier's art-deco deliverance and Whanganui's raffish charm have helped him forgive: he's once again smitten with the country's phantasmal landscapes, disarming locals and its determination to sculpt its own political and indigenous destiny. Charles wrote the Planning chapters (with the exception of Hiking on the South Island, Skiing & Snowboarding on the South Island and Extreme Sports on the South Island), NZ Today, Arts & Music and Survival Guide chapters.

Sarah Bennett & Lee Slater

Marlborough & Nelson, West Coast, Christchurch & Canterbury Sarah and Lee specialise in NZ travel, with a particular focus on outdoor adventure including hiking, mountain biking and camping. In addition to five editions of the *New Zealand* guidebook, they are also co-authors of Lonely Planet's *Hiking & Tramping in New Zealand* and *New Zealand's Best Trips*. Read more at www.bennettandslater.co.nz. Sarah and Lee also wrote Hiking on the South Island, Skiing & Snowboarding on the South Island and Extreme Sports on the South Island.

Peter Dragicevich

Dunedin & Otago, Queenstown & Wanaka, Fiordland & Southland After nearly a decade working for off-shore publishing companies, Peter has come full circle, returning to his home city of Auckland. As managing editor of *Express* newspaper he spent much of the '90s writing about the local arts, club and bar scenes. Peter has contributed to several editions of the *New Zealand* guidebook and, after dozens of Lonely Planet assignments, it remains his favourite gig.

**OVER MORE
PAGE WRITERS**

Published by Lonely Planet Global Limited
CRN 554153
5th edition – September 2016
ISBN 978 1 78657 027 7
© Lonely Planet 2016   Photographs © as indicated 2016
10 9 8 7 6 5 4 3 2 1
Printed in China

Although the authors and Lonely Planet have taken all reasonable care in preparing this book, we make no warranty about the accuracy or completeness of its content and, to the maximum extent permitted, disclaim all liability arising from its use.